GENERAL MOTORS LUMINA/SILHOUETTE/TRANS SPORT/VENTURE 1990-99 REPAIR MANUAL

Cl
Preside
Vice President–Finan
Vice President–Sal

Executive Edit

Manager–Consumer Automoti
Manager–Professional Automoti
Manager–Marine/Recreati
Manager–Electronic Fulfillme

Production Speciali
Project Manage

Schematics Edit

Edit

Chilton is a registered trademark of Cahners Business Information, a division of Reed Elsevier, Inc., and has been licensed to W. G. Nichols, Inc.

www.chiltononline.com

Contents

Contents

SAFETY NOTICE

Proper service and repair procedures are vital to the safe, reliable operation of all motor vehicles, as well as the personal safety of those performing repairs. This manual outlines procedures for servicing and repairing vehicles using safe, effective methods. The procedures contain many NOTES, CAUTIONS and WARNINGS which should be followed, along with standard procedures to eliminate the possibility of personal injury or improper service which could damage the vehicle or compromise its safety.

It is important to note that repair procedures and techniques, tools and parts for servicing motor vehicles, as well as the skill and experience of the individual performing the work vary widely. It is not possible to anticipate all of the conceivable ways or conditions under which vehicles may be serviced, or to provide cautions as to all possible hazards that may result. Standard and accepted safety precautions and equipment should be used when handling toxic or flammable fluids, and safety goggles or other protection should be used during cutting, grinding, chiseling, prying, or any other process that can cause material removal or projectiles.

Some procedures require the use of tools specially designed for a specific purpose. Before substituting another tool or procedure, you must be completely satisfied that neither your personal safety, nor the performance of the vehicle will be endangered.

Although information in this manual is based on industry sources and is complete as possible at the time of publication, the possibility exists that some car manufacturers made later changes which could not be included here. While striving for total accuracy, Nichols Publishing cannot assume responsibility for any errors, changes or omissions that may occur in the compilation of this data.

PART NUMBERS

Part numbers listed in this reference are not recommendations by Nichols Publishing for any product brand name. They are references that can be used with interchange manuals and aftermarket supplier catalogs to locate each brand supplier's discrete part number.

SPECIAL TOOLS

Special tools are recommended by the vehicle manufacturer to perform their specific job. Use has been kept to a minimum, but where absolutely necessary, they are referred to in the text by the part number of the tool manufacturer. These tools can be purchased, under the appropriate part number, from your local dealer or regional distributor, or an equivalent tool can be purchased locally from a tool supplier or parts outlet. Before substituting any tool for the one recommended, read the SAFETY NOTICE at the top of this page.

ACKNOWLEDGMENTS

Portions of materials contained herein have been reprinted with the permission of General Motors Corporation, Service Technology Group.

Nichols Publishing would like to express thanks to all of the fine companies who participate in the production of our books. Hand tools supplied by Craftsman are used during all phases of our vehicle teardown and photography. Many of the fine specialty tools used in our procedures were provided courtesy of Lisle Corporation. Lincoln Automotive Products (1 Lincoln Way, St. Louis, MO 63120) has provided their industrial shop equipment, including jacks (engine, transmission and floor), engine stands, fluid and lubrication tools, as well as shop presses. Rotary Lifts, the largest automobile lift manufacturer in the world, offering the biggest variety of surface and in-ground lifts available (Rotary 1-800-640-5438), has fulfilled our shop's lift needs. Much of our shop's electronic testing equipment was supplied by Universal Enterprises Inc. (UEI).

1

GENERAL INFORMATION AND MAINTENANCE

HOW TO USE THIS BOOK

Chilton's Total Car Care Manual for 1990–97 Chevrolet Lumina APV, 1990–99 Oldsmobile Silhouette, 1990–98 Pontiac Trans Sport, 1999 Montana, and the 1997–99 Chevrolet Venture is intended to help you learn more about the inner workings of your vehicle while saving you money on its upkeep and operation.

The beginning of the book will likely be referred to the most, since that is where you will find information for maintenance and tune-up. The other sections deal with the more complex systems of your vehicle. Operating systems from engine through brakes are covered to the extent that the average do-it-yourselfer becomes mechanically involved. This book will not explain such things as rebuilding a differential for the simple reason that the expertise required and the investment in special tools make this task uneconomical. It will, however, give you detailed instructions to help you change your own brake pads and shoes, replace spark plugs, and perform many more jobs that can save you money, give you personal satisfaction and help you avoid expensive problems.

A secondary purpose of this book is a reference guide for owners who want a better understanding of their vehicles and/or their mechanics. In this case, no tools at all are required.

Where to Begin

Before removing any bolts, read through the entire procedure outlined in the appropriate chapter. This will give you the overall view of what tools and supplies will be required. So read and plan ahead. Each operation should be approached logically and all procedures thoroughly understood before attempting any work.

All sections contain adjustments, maintenance, removal and installation procedures, and in some cases, repair or overhaul procedures. When overhaul is not considered practical, we tell you how to remove the failed part and then how to install the new or rebuilt replacement. In this way, at least you save the labor costs. Backyard repair of some components is just not practical.

Avoiding Trouble

Many procedures in this book require you to "label and disconnect . . ." a group of lines, hoses or wires. Don't think you can remember where everything goes—you won't. If you hook up vacuum or fuel lines incorrectly, the vehicle may run poorly, if at all. If you hook up electrical wiring incorrectly, you may instantly learn a very expensive lesson.

You don't need to know the official or engineering name for each hose or line. A piece of masking tape on the hose and a piece on its fitting will allow you to assign your own label such as the letter A or a short name. As long as you remember your own code, the lines can be reconnected by matching similar letters or names. Do remember that tape will dissolve in gasoline or other fluids; if a component is to be washed or cleaned, use another method of identification. A permanent felt-tipped marker or a metal scribe can be very handy for marking metal parts. Remove any tape or paper labels after assembly.

Maintenance or Repair?

It's necessary to mention the difference between maintenance and repair. Maintenance includes routine inspections, adjustments, and replacement of parts that show signs of normal wear. Maintenance compensates for wear or deterioration. Repair implies that something has broken or is not working. A need for repair is often caused by lack of maintenance. Example: draining and refilling the automatic transmission fluid is maintenance recommended by the manufacturer at specific mileage intervals. Failure to do this can shorten the life of the transmission/transaxle, requiring very expensive repairs. While no maintenance program can prevent items from breaking or wearing out, a general rule can be stated; MAINTENANCE IS CHEAPER THAN REPAIR.

Two basic mechanic's rules should be mentioned here. First, whenever the LEFT side of the vehicle or engine is referred to, it is meant to specify the DRIVER'S side. Conversely, the RIGHT side means the PASSENGER'S side. Second, all screws and bolts are removed by turning counterclockwise and tightened by turning clockwise, unless otherwise noted.

Safety is always the most important rule. Constantly be aware of the dangers involved in working on or around an automobile and take proper precautions to avoid the risk of personal injury or damage to the vehicle. Please refer to the information in this section regarding SERVICING YOUR VEHICLE SAFELY and the SAFETY NOTICE on the acknowledgment page before attempting any service procedures.

Avoiding the Most Common Mistakes

Pay attention to the instructions provided. There are 3 common mistakes in mechanical work:

1. Incorrect order of assembly, disassembly or adjustment. When taking something apart or putting it together, doing things in the wrong order usually just costs you extra time; however it CAN break something. Read the entire procedure before beginning disassembly. Perform everything in the order in which the instructions say you should, even if you can't immediately see a reason for it. When you're taking apart something that is very intricate, you might want to draw a picture of how it looks when partially disassembled in order to make sure you get everything back in its proper position. We will supply exploded views whenever possible. When making adjustments, perform them in order. One adjustment often affects another.

2. Overtorquing (or undertorquing) nuts and bolts. While it is more common for overtorquing to cause damage, undertorquing can cause a fastener to vibrate loose and cause serious damage, especially when dealing with aluminum parts. Pay attention to torque specifications and utilize a torque wrench in assembly. If a torque figure is not available remember that, if you are using the right tool to do the job, you will probably not have to strain yourself to get a fastener tight enough. The pitch of most threads is so slight that the tension you put on the wrench will be multiplied many times in actual force on what you are tightening.

A good example of how critical torque is can be seen in the case of spark plug installation, especially when you are putting the plug into an aluminum cylinder head. Too little torque can fail to crush the gasket, causing leakage of combustion gases and consequent overheating of the plug and engine parts. Too much torque can damage the threads or distort the plug, changing the spark gap.

There are many commercial chemical products available for ensuring that fasteners won't come loose, even if they are not torqued just right (a very common brand is Locktite®). If you're worried about getting something together tight enough to hold, but loose enough to avoid mechanical damage during assembly, one of these products might offer substantial insurance. Read the label on the package and make sure the product is compatible with the materials, fluids, etc. involved.

3. Crossthreading. This occurs when a part such as a bolt is screwed into a nut or casting at the wrong angle and forced, causing the threads to become damaged. Crossthreading is more likely to occur if access is difficult. It helps to clean and lubricate fasteners, and to start threading with the part to be installed going straight in, using your fingers. If you encounter resistance, unscrew the part and start over again at a different angle until it can be inserted and turned several times without much effort. Keep in mind that many parts, especially spark plugs, use tapered threads so that gentle turning will automatically bring the part you're threading to the proper angle if you don't force it or resist a change in angle. Don't put a wrench on the part until it's been turned in a couple of times by hand. If you suddenly encounter resistance and the part has not seated fully, don't force it. Pull it back out and make sure it's clean and threading properly.

Be sure to take your time and be patient, always plan ahead. Allow yourself ample time to perform repairs and maintenance. You may find maintaining your vehicle a satisfying and enjoyable experience.

TOOLS AND EQUIPMENT

♦ **See Figures 1 thru 15**

Naturally, without the proper tools and equipment it is impossible to properly service your vehicle. It would also be virtually impossible to catalog each tool that you would need to perform all of the operations in this book. It would be unwise for the amateur to rush out and buy an expensive set of tools on the theory that he may need one or more of them at some time.

The best approach is to proceed slowly, gathering a good quality set of those tools that are used most frequently. Don't be misled by the low cost of bargain tools. It is far better to spend a little more for better quality. Forged wrenches, 6- or 12- point sockets and fine tooth ratchets are by far preferable to their less expensive counterparts. As any good mechanic can tell you, there are few worse experiences than trying to work on a vehicle with bad tools. Your monetary savings will be far outweighed by frustration and mangled knuckles.

Begin accumulating those tools that are used most frequently; those associated with routine maintenance and tune-up. In addition to the normal assortment of screwdrivers and pliers you should have the following tools:

• Wrenches, sockets and combination open end/box end wrenches in sizes from ⅛ in. or 3mm —19mm (depending on whether your vehicle uses standard or metric fasteners), and a spark plug socket to fit your vehicle.

➡ **If possible, buy various length socket drive extensions. Universal joint and wobble extensions can be extremely useful, but be careful when using them, as they can change the amount of torque applied to the socket.**

• Jackstands for support
• Oil filter wrench
• Spout or funnel for pouring fluids.

TCCS1200

Fig. 1 All but the most basic procedures will require an assortment of ratchets and sockets

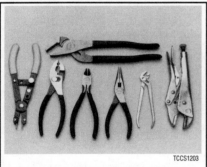

TCCS1201

Fig. 2 In addition to ratchets, a good set of wrenches and hex keys will be necessary

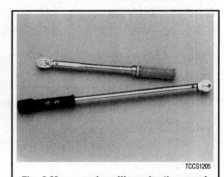

TCCS1202

Fig. 3 A hydraulic floor jack and a set of jackstands are essential for lifting and supporting the vehicle

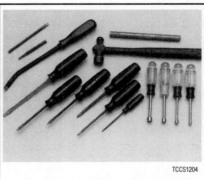

TCCS1203

Fig. 4 An assortment of pliers, grippers and cutters will be handy for old rusted parts and stripped bolt heads

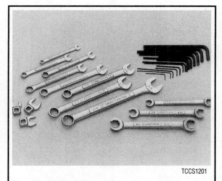

TCCS1204

Fig. 5 Various drivers, chisels and prybars are great tools to have in your toolbox

TCCS1205

Fig. 6 Many repairs will require the use of a torque wrench to assure the components are properly fastened

TCCS1209

Fig. 7 Although not always necessary, using specialized brake tools will save time

TCCS1210

Fig. 8 A few inexpensive lubrication tools will make maintenance easier

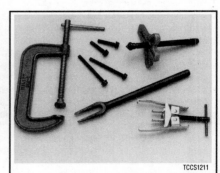

TCCS1211

Fig. 9 Various pullers, clamps and separator tools are needed for many larger, more complicated repairs

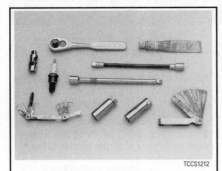

Fig. 10 A variety of tools and gauges should be used for spark plug gapping and installation

TCCS1212

TCCX1P01

Fig. 11 Inductive type timing light

TCCX1P02

Fig. 12 A screw-in type compression gauge is recommended for compression testing

TCCX1P03

Fig. 13 A vacuum/pressure tester is necessary for many testing procedures

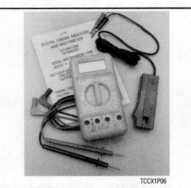

TCCX1P06

Fig. 14 Most modern automotive multimeters incorporate many helpful features

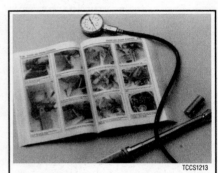

TCCS1213

Fig. 15 Proper information is vital, so always have a Chilton Total Car Care manual handy

• Grease gun for lubrication (unless your vehicle is not equipped with any grease fittings—for details, please refer to information on Fluids and Lubricants, later in this section).

• Hydrometer for checking the battery (unless equipped with a sealed, maintenance free battery).

• A container for draining oil and other fluids.

• Rags for wiping up the inevitable mess.

In addition to the above items there are several others that are not absolutely necessary, but handy to have around. These include Oil Dry® (or an equivalent oil absorbent gravel—such as cat litter) and the usual supply of lubricants, antifreeze and fluids, although these can be purchased as needed. This is a basic list for routine maintenance, but only your personal needs and desire can accurately determine your list of tools.

After performing a few projects on the vehicle, you'll be amazed at the other tools and non-tools on your workbench. Some useful household items are: a large turkey baster or siphon, empty coffee cans and ice trays (to store parts), ball of twine, electrical tape for wiring, small rolls of colored tape for tagging lines or hoses, markers and pens, a note pad, golf tees (for plugging vacuum lines), metal coat hangers, a roll of mechanic's wire (to hold things out of the way), dental pick or scribe or similar long, pointed probe, a strong magnet and a small mirror (to see into the recesses and under manifolds).

A more advanced set of tools suitable for tune-up work, can be drawn up easily. While the tools are slightly more sophisticated, they need not be outrageously expensive. There are several inexpensive tach/dwell meters on the market that are every bit as good for the average mechanic as a professional model. Just be sure that it goes to at least 1200–1500 rpm on the tach scale and that it works on 4, 6, and 8-cylinder engines. However, a special tachometer is required for diesel applications since they don't use spark plug ignition systems. The key to these purchases is to make them with an eye towards adaptability and wide range. A basic list of tune-up tools could include:

• Tach/dwell meter
• Spark plug wrench and gapping tool
• Feeler gauges for valve or point adjustment. (Even if your vehicle does not

use points or require valve adjustment, a feeler gauge is helpful for many repair/overhaul procedures.)

A tachometer/dwell meter will ensure accurate tune-up work on vehicles without electronic ignition. The choice of timing lights should be made carefully. A light which works on the DC current supplied by the vehicle's battery is the best choice. It should have a xenon tube for brightness. On any vehicle with an electronic ignition system, a timing light with an inductive pick-up that clamps around the No. 1 spark plug cable is preferred.

In addition to these basic tools, there are several other tools and gauges you may find useful.

• Compression gauge. The screw-in type is slower to use but it eliminates the possibility of a faulty reading due to escaping pressure.

• A manifold vacuum gauge.

• 12V test light

• A droplight, to light up the work area (make sure yours is UL approved, and has a shielded bulb).

• A volt/ohm meter (multi-tester).

• Induction Ammeter. This is used to determine whether or not there is current in a wire. These are handy for use if a wire is broken somewhere in a wiring harness.

As a final note, you will probably find a torque wrench necessary for all but the most basic work. The beam type models are perfectly adequate, although the newer click (breakaway) type are more precise, and you don't have to crane your neck to see a torque reading in awkward situations. The breakaway torque wrenches are more expensive and should be recalibrated periodically.

Special Tools

Normally, the use of special factory tools is avoided for repair procedures, since these are not readily available for the do-it-yourself mechanic. When it is possible to perform the job with more commonly available tools, it will be pointed out, but occasionally, a special tool was designed to perform a specific function and should be used. Before substituting another tool, you should be convinced that neither your safety nor the performance of the vehicle would be compromised.

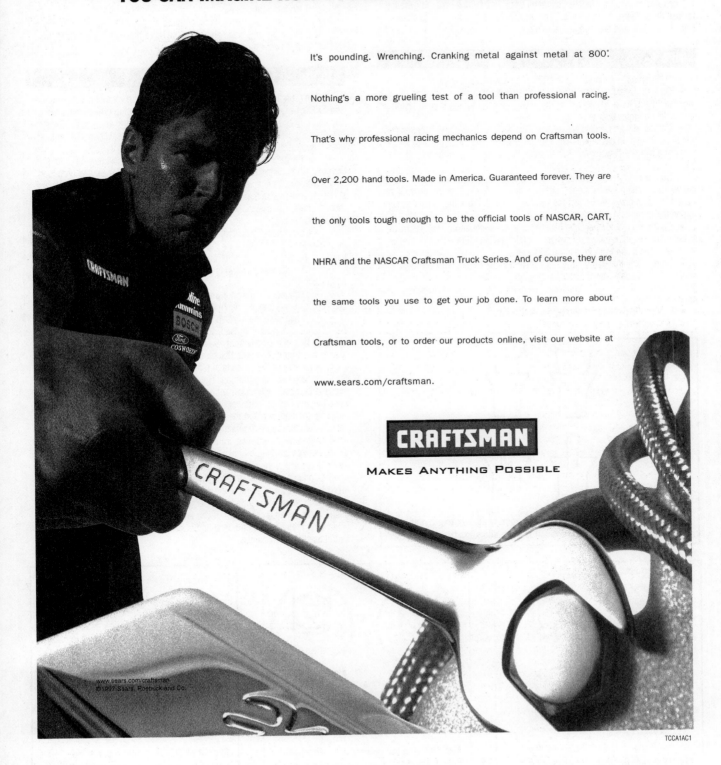

SERVICING YOUR VEHICLE SAFELY

♦ See Figures 16, 17, 18 and 19

It is virtually impossible to anticipate all of the hazards involved with automotive maintenance and service but care and common sense will prevent most accidents.

The rules of safety for mechanics range from "don't smoke around gasoline," to "use the proper tool for the job." The trick to avoiding injuries is to develop safe work habits and take every possible precaution.

Do's

- Do keep a fire extinguisher and first aid kit within easy reach.
- Do wear safety glasses or goggles when cutting, drilling, grinding or prying, even if you have 20–20 vision. If you wear glasses for the sake of vision wear safety goggles over your regular glasses.
- Do shield your eyes whenever you work around the battery. Batteries contain sulfuric acid. In case of contact with the eyes or skin, flush the area with water or a mixture of water and baking soda then seek immediate medical attention.
- Do use safety stands for any under the vehicle service. Jacks are for raising vehicles; safety stands are for making sure the vehicle stays raised until you want it to come down. Whenever the vehicle is raised, block the wheels remaining on the ground and set the parking brake.
- Do disconnect the negative battery cable when working on the electrical system. The secondary ignition system contains EXTREMELY HIGH VOLTAGE. In some cases it can even exceed 50,000 volts.
- Do properly maintain your tools. Loose hammerheads, mushroomed punches and chisels, frayed or poorly grounded electrical cords, excessively worn screwdrivers, spread wrenches (open end), cracked sockets, slipping ratchets, or faulty droplight sockets can cause accidents and injuries.
- Do use the proper size and type of tool for the job being done.

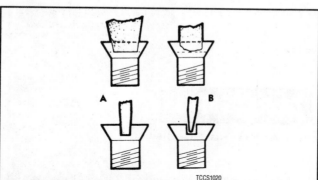

Fig. 16 Screwdrivers should be kept in good condition to prevent injury or damage which could result if the blade slips from the screw

- Do, when possible, pull on a wrench handle rather than push on it, and adjust your stance to prevent a fall.
- Do be sure that adjustable wrenches are tightly adjusted on the nut or bolt and pulled so that the face is on the side of the fixed jaw.
- Do select a wrench or socket that fits the nut or bolt. The wrench or socket should sit straight, not cocked.
- Do strike squarely with a hammer-avoid glancing blows.
- Do set the parking brake and block the drive wheels if the work requires that the engine be running.

Don'ts

- Don't run an engine in a garage or anywhere else without proper ventilation-EVER! Carbon monoxide is poisonous. It takes a long time to leave the human body and you can build up a deadly supply of it in your system by simply breathing in a little every day. Always use power vents, windows, and fans or open the garage doors.
- Don't work around moving parts while wearing a necktie or other loose clothing. Short sleeves are much safer than long, loose sleeves and hard toed shoes with neoprene soles protect your toes and give a better grip on slippery surfaces. Jewelry, such as watches, fancy belt buckles, beads or body adornment of any is not safe working around a vehicle. Long hair should be hidden under a hat or cap.
- Don't use pockets for toolboxes. A fall or bump can drive a screwdriver deep into your body. Even a wiping cloth hanging from the back pocket can wrap around a spinning shaft or fan.
- Don't smoke when working around gasoline, cleaning solvent or other flammable material.
- Don't smoke when working around the battery. When the battery is being charged, it gives off explosive hydrogen gas.
- Don't use gasoline to wash your hands. There are excellent soaps available. Gasoline may contain lead, and lead can enter the body through a cut, accumulating in the body until you are very ill. Gasoline also removes all the natural oils from the skin so that bone dry hands will absorb oil and grease.
- Don't service the air conditioning system unless you are equipped with the necessary tools and training. The refrigerant, is extremely cold and when exposed to the air, will instantly freeze any surface it comes in contact with, including your eyes. Although the refrigerant is normally non-toxic, it becomes a deadly poisonous gas in the presence of an open flame. One good whiff of the vapors from burning refrigerant can be fatal.
- Don't use screwdrivers for anything other than driving screws! A screwdriver used as a prying tool can snap when you least expect it, causing injuries. At the very least, you will ruin a good screwdriver.
- Don't use a bumper or emergency jack (that little ratchet, scissors, or pantograph jack supplied with the vehicle) for anything other than changing a flat! These jacks are only intended for emergency use out on the road; they are not designed as a maintenance tool. If you are serious about maintaining your vehicle yourself, invest in a hydraulic floor jack of at least a 1½ ton capacity, and at least two jackstands.

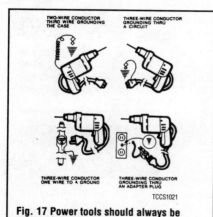

Fig. 17 Power tools should always be properly grounded

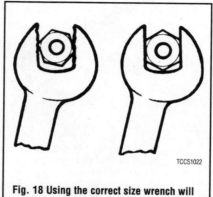

Fig. 18 Using the correct size wrench will help prevent the possibility of rounding off a nut

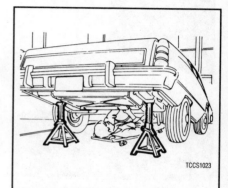

Fig. 19 NEVER work under a vehicle unless it is supported using safety stands (jackstands)

FASTENERS, MEASUREMENTS AND CONVERSIONS

Bolts, Nuts, and Other Threaded Retainers

♦ **See Figures 20, 21, 22 and 23**

Although there are a great variety of fasteners found in the modern car or truck, the most commonly used retainer is the threaded fastener (nuts, bolts, screws, studs, etc.). Most threaded retainers may be reused, provided that they are not damaged in use or during the repair. Some retainers (such as stretch bolts or torque prevailing nuts) are designed to deform when tightened or in use and should not be reinstalled.

Whenever possible, we will note any special retainers which should be replaced during a procedure. But you should always inspect the condition of a retainer when it is removed and replace any that show signs of damage. Check all threads for rust or corrosion that can increase the torque necessary to achieve the desired clamp load for which that fastener was originally selected. Additionally, be sure that rounding or other damage has not compromised the driver surface of the fastener. In some cases a driver surface may become only partially rounded, allowing the driver to catch in only one direction. In many of these occurrences, a fastener may be installed and tightened, but the driver would not be able to grip and loosen the fastener again. (This could lead to frustration down the line should that component ever need to be disassembled again).

If you must replace a fastener, whether due to design or damage, you must ALWAYS be sure to use the proper replacement. In all cases, a retainer of the

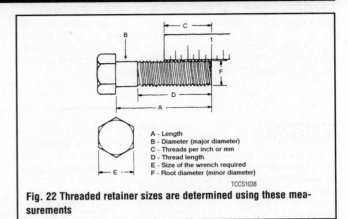

Fig. 22 Threaded retainer sizes are determined using these measurements

A - Length
B - Diameter (major diameter)
C - Threads per inch or mm
D - Thread length
E - Size of the wrench required
F - Root diameter (minor diameter)

TCCS1038

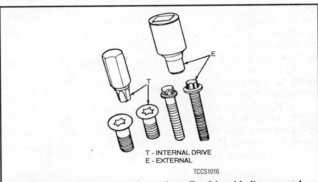

T - INTERNAL DRIVE
E - EXTERNAL

TCCS1016

Fig. 23 Special fasteners such ass these Torx® head bolts are used by manufacturers to discourage people from working on vehicles

same design, material and strength should be used. Markings on the heads of most bolts will help determine the proper strength of the fastener. The same material, thread and pitch must be selected to assure proper installation and safe operation of the vehicle afterwards.

Thread gauges are available to help measure a bolt or stud's thread. Most automotive and hardware stores keep gauges available to help you select the proper size. In a pinch, you can use another nut which threads properly onto the damaged bolt, then use that nut to help select the replacement bolt. If, however, the bolt you are replacing is so badly damaged (broken or drilled out) that its threads cannot be used as a gauge, you might start by looking for another bolt (from the same assembly or a similar location on your vehicle) which will thread into the damaged bolt's mounting. If so, the other bolt can be used to select a nut; the nut can then be used t select the replacement bolt.

In all cases, be absolutely sure you have selected the proper replacement. Don't be shy, you can always ask the store clerk for help.

❊❊ WARNING

Be aware that when you find a bolt with damaged threads, you may also find the nut or drilled hole it was threaded into has also been damaged. If this is the case, you may have to drill and tap the hole, replace the nut or otherwise repair the threads. NEVER try to force a replacement bolt to fit into the damaged threads.

Torque

Torque is defined as the measurement of resistance to turning or rotating. It tends to twist a body about an axis of rotation. A common example of this would be tightening a threaded retainer such as a nut, bolt or screw. Measuring torque is one of the most common ways to help assure that a threaded retainer has been properly fastened.

When tightening a threaded fastener, torque is applied in three distinct areas,

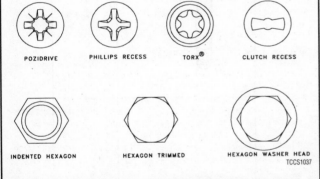

POZIDRIVE   PHILLIPS RECESS   TORX®   CLUTCH RECESS

INDENTED HEXAGON   HEXAGON TRIMMED   HEXAGON WASHER HEAD

TCCS1037

Fig. 20 Here are a few of the most common screw/bolt driver styles

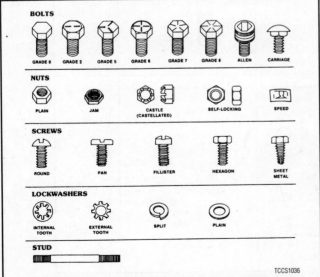

BOLTS
GRADE 0   GRADE 2   GRADE 5   GRADE 6   GRADE 7   GRADE 8   ALLEN   CARRIAGE

NUTS
PLAIN   JAM   CASTLE (CASTELLATED)   SELF-LOCKING   SPEED

SCREWS
ROUND   PAN   FILLISTER   HEXAGON   SHEET METAL

LOCKWASHERS
INTERNAL TOOTH   EXTERNAL TOOTH   SPLIT   PLAIN

STUD

TCCS1036

Fig. 21 There are many different types of threaded retainers found on vehicles

the head, the bearing surface and the clamp load. About 50 percent of the measured torque is used in overcoming bearing friction. This is the friction between the bearing surface of the bolt head, screw head or nut face and the base material or washer (the surface on which the fastener is rotating). Approximately 40 percent of the applied torque is used in overcoming thread friction. This leaves only about 10 percent of the applied torque to develop a useful clamp load (the force that holds a joint together). This means that friction can account for as much as 90 percent of the applied torque on a fastener.

TORQUE WRENCHES

♦ **See Figures 24, 25 and 26**

In most applications, a torque wrench can be used to assure proper installation of a fastener. Torque wrenches come in various designs and most automotive supply stores will carry a variety to suit your needs. A torque wrench should be used any time we supply a specific torque value for a fastener. A torque

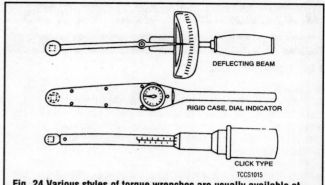

TCCS1015

Fig. 24 Various styles of torque wrenches are usually available at your local automotive supply store

	Mark	Class		Mark	Class
Hexagon head bolt	 Bolt head No. 4 — 4 5 — 6 — 7 — 8 — 9 — 10 — 11 —	4T 5T 6T 7T 8T 9T 10T 11T	Stud bolt	 No mark	4T
	 No mark	4T		Grooved	6T
Hexagon flange bolt w/ washer hexagon bolt	 No mark	4T			
Hexagon head bolt	 Two protruding lines	5T			
Hexagon flange bolt w/ washer hexagon bolt	 Two protruding lines	6T	Welded bolt	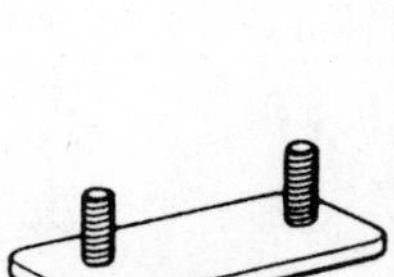	4T
Hexagon head bolt	 Three protruding lines	7T			
Hexagon head bolt	 Four protruding lines	8T			

TCCS1240

Fig. 25 Determining bolt strength of metric fasteners—NOTE: this is a typical bolt marking system, but there is not a worldwide standard

Class	Diameter mm	Pitch mm	Specified torque					
			Hexagon head bolt			Hexagon flange bolt		
			N·m	kgf·cm	ft·lbf	N·m	kgf·cm	ft·lbf
4T	6	1	5	55	48 in.·lbf	6	60	52 in.·lbf
	8	1.25	12.5	130	9	14	145	10
	10	1.25	26	260	19	29	290	21
	12	1.25	47	480	35	53	540	39
	14	1.5	74	760	55	84	850	61
	16	1.5	115	1,150	83	—	—	—
5T	6	1	6.5	65	56 in.·lbf	7.5	75	65 in.·lbf
	8	1.25	15.5	160	12	17.5	175	13
	10	1.25	32	330	24	36	360	26
	12	1.25	59	600	43	65	670	48
	14	1.5	91	930	67	100	1,050	76
	16	1.5	140	1,400	101	—	—	—
6T	6	1	8	80	69 in.·lbf	9	90	78 in.·lbf
	8	1.25	19	195	14	21	210	15
	10	1.25	39	400	29	44	440	32
	12	1.25	71	730	53	80	810	59
	14	1.5	110	1,100	80	125	1,250	90
	16	1.5	170	1,750	127	—	—	—
7T	6	1	10.5	110	8	12	120	9
	8	1.25	25	260	19	28	290	21
	10	1.25	52	530	38	58	590	43
	12	1.25	95	970	70	105	1,050	76
	14	1.5	145	1,500	108	165	1,700	123
	16	1.5	230	2,300	166	—	—	—
8T	8	1.25	29	300	22	33	330	24
	10	1.25	61	620	45	68	690	50
	12	1.25	110	1,100	80	120	1,250	90
9T	8	1.25	34	340	25	37	380	27
	10	1.25	70	710	51	78	790	57
	12	1.25	125	1,300	94	140	1,450	105
10T	8	1.25	38	390	28	42	430	31
	10	1.25	78	800	58	88	890	64
	12	1.25	140	1,450	105	155	1,600	116
11T	8	1.25	42	430	31	47	480	35
	10	1.25	87	890	64	97	990	72
	12	1.25	155	1,600	116	175	1,800	130

TCCS1241

Fig. 26 Typical bolt torques for metric fasteners—WARNING: use only as a guide

wrench can also be used if you are following the general guidelines in the accompanying charts. Keep in mind that because there is no worldwide stan-dardization of fasteners, the charts are a general guideline and should be used with caution. Again, the general rule of "if you are using the right tool for the job, you should not have to strain to tighten a fastener" applies here.

Beam Type

▶ **See Figure 27**

The beam type torque wrench is one of the most popular types. It consists of a pointer attached to the head that runs the length of the flexible beam (shaft) to a scale located near the handle. As the wrench is pulled, the beam bends and the pointer indicates the torque using the scale.

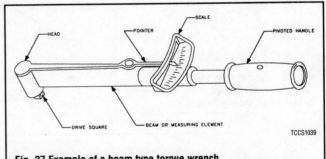

TCCS1039

Fig. 27 Example of a beam type torque wrench

Click (Breakaway) Type

▶ See Figure 28

Another popular design of torque wrench is the click type. To use the click type wrench you pre-adjust it to a torque setting. Once the torque is reached, the wrench has a reflex signaling feature that causes a momentary breakaway of the torque wrench body, sending an impulse to the operator's hand.

Pivot Head Type

▶ See Figures 28 and 29

Some torque wrenches (usually of the click type) may be equipped with a pivot head that can allow it to be used in areas of limited access. BUT, it must be used properly. To hold a pivot head wrench, grasp the handle lightly, and as you pull on the handle, it should be floated on the pivot point. If the handle comes in contact with the yoke extension during the process of pulling, there is a very good chance the torque readings will be inaccurate because this could alter the wrench loading point. The design of the handle is usually such as to make it inconvenient to deliberately misuse the wrench.

➡ **It should be mentioned that the use of any U-joint, wobble or extension would have an effect on the torque readings, no matter what type of wrench you are using. For the most accurate readings, install the socket directly on the wrench driver. If necessary, straight extensions (which hold a socket directly under the wrench driver) will have the least effect on the torque reading. Avoid any extension that alters the length of the wrench from the handle to the head/driving point (such as a crow's foot). U-joint or wobble extensions can greatly affect the readings; avoid their use at all times.**

Rigid Case (Direct Reading)

▶ See Figure 30

A rigid case or direct reading torque wrench is equipped with a dial indicator to show torque values. One advantage of these wrenches is that they can be held at any position on the wrench without affecting accuracy. These wrenches are often preferred because they tend to be compact, easy to read and have a great degree of accuracy.

TORQUE ANGLE METERS

▶ See Figure 31

Because the frictional characteristics of each fastener or threaded hole will vary, clamp loads that are based strictly on torque will vary as well. In most applications, this variance is not significant enough to cause worry. But, in certain applications, a manufacturer's engineers may determine that more precise clamp loads are necessary (such is the case with many aluminum cylinder heads). In these cases, a torque angle method of installation would be specified. When installing fasteners that are torque angle tightened, a predetermined seating torque and standard torque wrench are usually used first to remove any compliance from the joint. The fastener is then tightened the specified additional portion of a turn measured in degrees. A torque angle gauge (mechanical protractor) is used for these applications.

Standard and Metric Measurements

▶ See Figure 32

Throughout this manual, specifications are given to help you determine the condition of various components on your vehicle, or to assist you in their installation. Some of the most common measurements include length (in. or cm/mm), torque (ft. lbs., inch lbs. or Nm) and pressure (psi, in. Hg, kPa or mm Hg). In most cases, we strive to provide the proper measurement as determined by the manufacturer's engineers.

Though, in some cases, that value may not be conveniently measured with what is available in your toolbox. Luckily, many of the measuring devices which are available today will have two scales so the Standard or Metric measurements may easily be taken. If any of the various measuring tools, which are available to you, do not contain the same scale as listed in the specifications, use the accompanying conversion factors to determine the proper value.

The conversion factor chart is used by taking the given specification and multiplying it by the necessary conversion factor. For instance, looking at the first line, if you have a measurement in inches such as "free-play should be 2 in." but your ruler reads only in millimeters, multiply 2 in. by the conversion factor of 25.4 to get the metric equivalent of 50.8mm. Likewise, if the specification was given only in a Metric measurement, for example in Newton Meters (Nm), then look at the center column first. If the measurement is 100 Nm, multiply it by the conversion factor of 0.738 to get 73.8 ft. lbs.

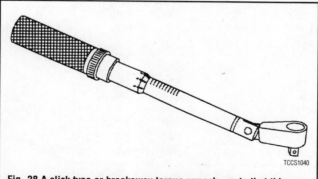

Fig. 28 A click type or breakaway torque wrench—note that this one has a pivoting head

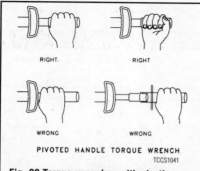

Fig. 29 Torque wrenches with pivoting heads must be grasped and used properly to prevent an incorrect reading

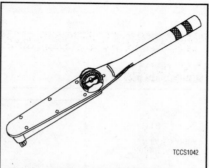

Fig. 30 The rigid case (direct reading) torque wrench uses a dial indicator to show torque

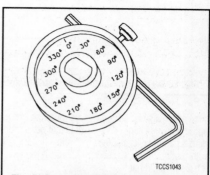

Fig. 31 Some specifications require the use of a torque angle meter (mechanical protractor)

CONVERSION FACTORS

LENGTH–DISTANCE

Inches (in.)	x 25.4	= Millimeters (mm)	x .0394	= Inches
Feet (ft.)	x .305	= Meters (m)	x 3.281	= Feet
Miles	x 1.609	= Kilometers (km)	x .0621	= Miles

VOLUME

Cubic Inches (in3)	x 16.387	= Cubic Centimeters	x .061	= in3
IMP Pints (IMP pt.)	x .568	= Liters (L)	x 1.76	= IMP pt.
IMP Quarts (IMP qt.)	x 1.137	= Liters (L)	x .88	= IMP qt.
IMP Gallons (IMP gal.)	x 4.546	= Liters (L)	x .22	= IMP gal.
IMP Quarts (IMP qt.)	x 1.201	= US Quarts (US qt.)	x .833	= IMP qt.
IMP Gallons (IMP gal.)	x 1.201	= US Gallons (US gal.)	x .833	= IMP gal.
Fl. Ounces	x 29.573	= Milliliters	x .034	= Ounces
US Pints (US pt.)	x .473	= Liters (L)	x 2.113	= Pints
US Quarts (US qt.)	x .946	= Liters (L)	x 1.057	= Quarts
US Gallons (US gal.)	x 3.785	= Liters (L)	x .264	= Gallons

MASS–WEIGHT

Ounces (oz.)	x 28.35	= Grams (g)	x .035	= Ounces
Pounds (lb.)	x .454	= Kilograms (kg)	x 2.205	= Pounds

PRESSURE

Pounds Per Sq. In. (psi)	x 6.895	= Kilopascals (kPa)	x .145	= psi
Inches of Mercury (Hg)	x .4912	= psi	x 2.036	= Hg
Inches of Mercury (Hg)	x 3.377	= Kilopascals (kPa)	x .2961	= Hg
Inches of Water (H_2O)	x .07355	= Inches of Mercury	x 13.783	= H_2O
Inches of Water (H_2O)	x .03613	= psi	x 27.684	= H_2O
Inches of Water (H_2O)	x .248	= Kilopascals (kPa)	x 4.026	= H_2O

TORQUE

Pounds–Force Inches (in–lb)	x .113	= Newton Meters (N·m)	x 8.85	= in–lb
Pounds–Force Feet (ft–lb)	x 1.356	= Newton Meters (N·m)	x .738	= ft–lb

VELOCITY

Miles Per Hour (MPH)	x 1.609	= Kilometers Per Hour (KPH)	x .621	= MPH

POWER

Horsepower (Hp)	x .745	= Kilowatts	x 1.34	= Horsepower

FUEL CONSUMPTION*

Miles Per Gallon IMP (MPG)	x .354	= Kilometers Per Liter (Km/L)		
Kilometers Per Liter (Km/L)	x 2.352	= IMP MPG		
Miles Per Gallon US (MPG)	x .425	= Kilometers Per Liter (Km/L)		
Kilometers Per Liter (Km/L)	x 2.352	= US MPG		

*It is common to covert from miles per gallon (mpg) to liters/100 kilometers (1/100 km), where mpg (IMP) x 1/100 km = 282 and mpg (US) x 1/100 km = 235.

TEMPERATURE

Degree Fahrenheit (°F)	= (°C x 1.8) + 32
Degree Celsius (°C)	= (°F – 32) x .56

TCCS1044

Fig. 32 Standard and metric conversion factors chart

SERIAL NUMBER IDENTIFICATION

Vehicle Identification Plate

▶ See Figures 33 and 34

The Vehicle Identification Number (VIN) is embossed on a plate, which is attached to the top left corner of the instrument panel. The number is visible through the windshield from the outside of the vehicle. The eighth digit of the number, indicates the engine model and the tenth digit represents the model year.

Engine Number

▶ See Figures 35, 36 and 37

All engines and transaxles are stamped with a partial VIN. The stamping contains nine positions.

• Position one is the GM vehicle division identifier: 1 for Chevrolet, 2 for Pontiac, 3 for Oldsmobile

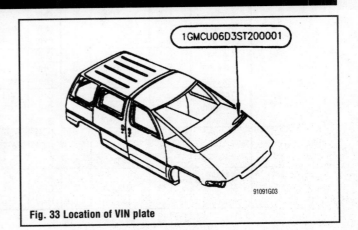

1GMCU06D3ST200001

91091G03

Fig. 33 Location of VIN plate

VEHICLE IDENTIFICATION CHART

		Engine Code					Model Year	
Code	Liters	Cu. In. (cc)	Cyl.	Fuel Sys.	Eng. Mfg.		Code	Year
D	3.1	191 3130	6	TBI	CPC		L	1990
E	3.4	209 3350	6	SFI	CPC		M	1991
L	3.8	231 3785	6	MFI	CPC		N	1992
							P	1993
							R	1994
							S	1995
							T	1996
							V	1997
							W	1998
							X	1999
							Y	2000

CPC - Chevrolet/Pontiac/Canada
SFI - Sequential Fuel Injection
MFI - Multi-port Fuel Injection
TBI - Throttle body Fuel Injection

91091C01

ENGINE IDENTIFICATION AND SPECIFICATIONS

Year	Model	Engine ID/VIN	Engine Displacement Liters (cc)	No. of Cyl.	Engine Type	Fuel System Type	Net Horsepower @ rpm	Net Torque @ rpm (ft. lbs.)	Bore x Stroke (in.)	Compression Ratio	Oil Pressure @ rpm
1990	Lumina	D	3.1 (3130)	6	OHV	TBI	120@4400	175@2200	3.50X3.31	8.5:1	15@1100
	Transport	D	3.1 (3130)	6	OHV	TBI	120@4400	175@2200	3.50X3.31	8.5:1	15@1100
	Silhouette	D	3.1 (3130)	6	OHV	TBI	120@4400	175@2200	3.50X3.31	8.5:1	15@1100
1991	Lumina	D	3.1 (3130)	6	OHV	TBI	120@4400	175@2200	3.50X3.31	8.5:1	15@1100
	Transport	D	3.1 (3130)	6	OHV	TBI	120@4400	175@2200	3.50X3.31	8.5:1	15@1100
	Silhouette	D	3.1 (3130)	6	OHV	TBI	120@4400	175@2200	3.50X3.31	8.5:1	15@1100
1992	Lumina	D	3.1 (3130)	6	OHV	TBI	120@4400	175@2200	3.50X3.31	8.5:1	15@1100
	Transport	D	3.1 (3130)	6	OHV	TBI	120@4400	175@2200	3.50X3.31	8.5:1	15@1100
	Silhouette	D	3.1 (3130)	6	OHV	TBI	120@4400	175@2200	3.50X3.31	8.5:1	15@1100
	Lumina	L	3.8 (3785)	6	OHV	MFI	165@4300	220@3200	3.80X3.40	8.5:1	60@1850
	Transport	L	3.8 (3785)	6	OHV	MFI	165@4300	220@3200	3.80X3.40	8.5:1	60@1850
	Silhouette	L	3.8 (3785)	6	OHV	MFI	165@4300	220@3200	3.80X3.40	8.5:1	60@1850
1993	Lumina	D	3.1 (3130)	6	OHV	TBI	120@4400	175@2200	3.50X3.31	8.5:1	15@1100
	Transport	D	3.1 (3130)	6	OHV	TBI	120@4400	175@2200	3.50X3.31	8.5:1	15@1100
	Silhouette	D	3.1 (3130)	6	OHV	TBI	120@4400	175@2200	3.50X3.31	8.5:1	15@1100
	Lumina	L	3.8 (3785)	6	OHV	MFI	165@4300	220@3200	3.80X3.40	8.5:1	60@1850
	Transport	L	3.8 (3785)	6	OHV	MFI	165@4300	220@3200	3.80X3.40	8.5:1	60@1850
	Silhouette	L	3.8 (3785)	6	OHV	MFI	165@4300	220@3200	3.80X3.40	8.5:1	60@1850
1994	Lumina	D	3.1 (3130)	6	OHV	TBI	120@4400	175@2200	3.50X3.31	8.5:1	15@1100
	Transport	D	3.1 (3130)	6	OHV	TBI	120@4400	175@2200	3.50X3.31	8.5:1	15@1100
	Silhouette	D	3.1 (3130)	6	OHV	TBI	120@4400	175@2200	3.50X3.31	8.5:1	15@1100
	Lumina	L	3.8 (3785)	6	OHV	MFI	165@4300	220@3200	3.80X3.40	8.5:1	60@1850
	Transport	L	3.8 (3785)	6	OHV	MFI	165@4300	220@3200	3.80X3.40	8.5:1	60@1850
	Silhouette	L	3.8 (3785)	6	OHV	MFI	165@4300	220@3200	3.80X3.40	8.5:1	60@1850
1995	Lumina	D	3.1 (3130)	6	OHV	TBI	120@4400	175@2200	3.50X3.31	8.5:1	15@1100
	Transport	D	3.1 (3130)	6	OHV	TBI	120@4400	175@2200	3.50X3.31	8.5:1	15@1100
	Silhouette	D	3.1 (3130)	6	OHV	TBI	120@4400	175@2200	3.50X3.31	8.5:1	15@1100
	Lumina	L	3.8 (3785)	6	OHV	MFI	170@4300	225@3200	3.80X3.40	9.0:1	60@1850
	Transport	L	3.8 (3785)	6	OHV	MFI	170@4300	225@3200	3.80X3.40	9.0:1	60@1850
	Silhouette	L	3.8 (3785)	6	OHV	MFI	170@4300	225@3200	3.80X3.40	9.0:1	60@1850
1996	Lumina	E	3.4 (3350)	6	OHV	MFI	180@5200	205@4000	3.62X3.31	9.5:1	56@3000
	Transport	E	3.4 (3350)	6	OHV	MFI	180@5200	205@4000	3.62X3.31	9.5:1	56@3000
	Silhouette	E	3.4 (3350)	6	OHV	MFI	180@5200	205@4000	3.62X3.31	9.5:1	56@3000
1997	Venture	E	3.4 (3350)	6	OHV	MFI	180@5200	205@4000	3.62X3.31	9.5:1	56@3000
	Transport	E	3.4 (3350)	6	OHV	MFI	180@5200	205@4000	3.62X3.31	9.5:1	56@3000
	Silhouette	E	3.4 (3350)	6	OHV	MFI	180@5200	205@4000	3.62X3.31	9.5:1	56@3000
1998	Venture	E	3.4 (3350)	6	OHV	SFI	180@5200	205@4000	3.62X3.31	9.5:1	56@3000
	Transport	E	3.4 (3350)	6	OHV	SFI	180@5200	205@4000	3.62X3.31	9.5:1	56@3000
	Silhouette	E	3.4 (3350)	6	OHV	SFI	180@5200	205@4000	3.62X3.31	9.5:1	56@3000
1999	Venture	E	3.4 (3350)	6	OHV	SFI	180@5200	205@4000	3.62X3.31	9.5:1	56@3000
	Montana	E	3.4 (3350)	6	OHV	SFI	180@5200	205@4000	3.62X3.31	9.5:1	56@3000
	Silhouette	E	3.4 (3350)	6	OHV	SFI	180@5200	205@4000	3.62X3.31	9.5:1	56@3000

91091C02

Fig. 34 The VIN plate is visible through the windshield

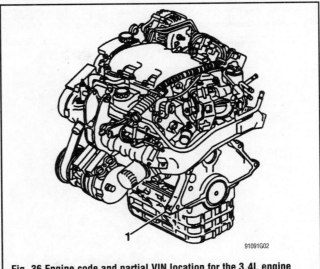

Fig. 36 Engine code and partial VIN location for the 3.4L engine

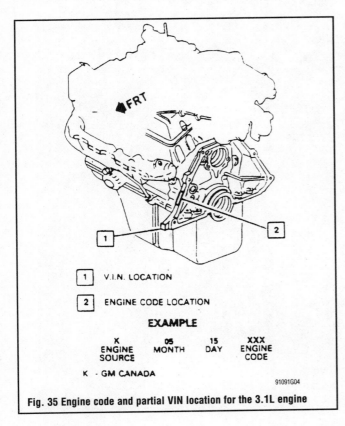

1 V.I.N. LOCATION

2 ENGINE CODE LOCATION

EXAMPLE

K	05	15	XXX
ENGINE SOURCE	MONTH	DAY	ENGINE CODE

K - GM CANADA

Fig. 35 Engine code and partial VIN location for the 3.1L engine

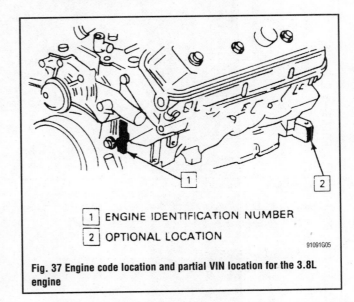

1 ENGINE IDENTIFICATION NUMBER

2 OPTIONAL LOCATION

Fig. 37 Engine code location and partial VIN location for the 3.8L engine

- Position two is the model year
- Position three is the vehicle assembly plant code
- positions four through nine are the assembly plant sequential number of the vehicle

Transaxle Number

▶ See Figure 38

Transaxle identification number is stamped into the horizontal cast rib on right rear of the transaxle housing. The transaxle also contains a partial VIN number.

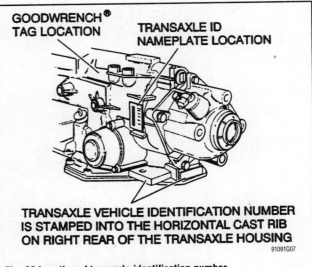

GOODWRENCH® TAG LOCATION

TRANSAXLE ID NAMEPLATE LOCATION

TRANSAXLE VEHICLE IDENTIFICATION NUMBER IS STAMPED INTO THE HORIZONTAL CAST RIB ON RIGHT REAR OF THE TRANSAXLE HOUSING

Fig. 38 Location of transaxle identification number

ROUTINE MAINTENANCE

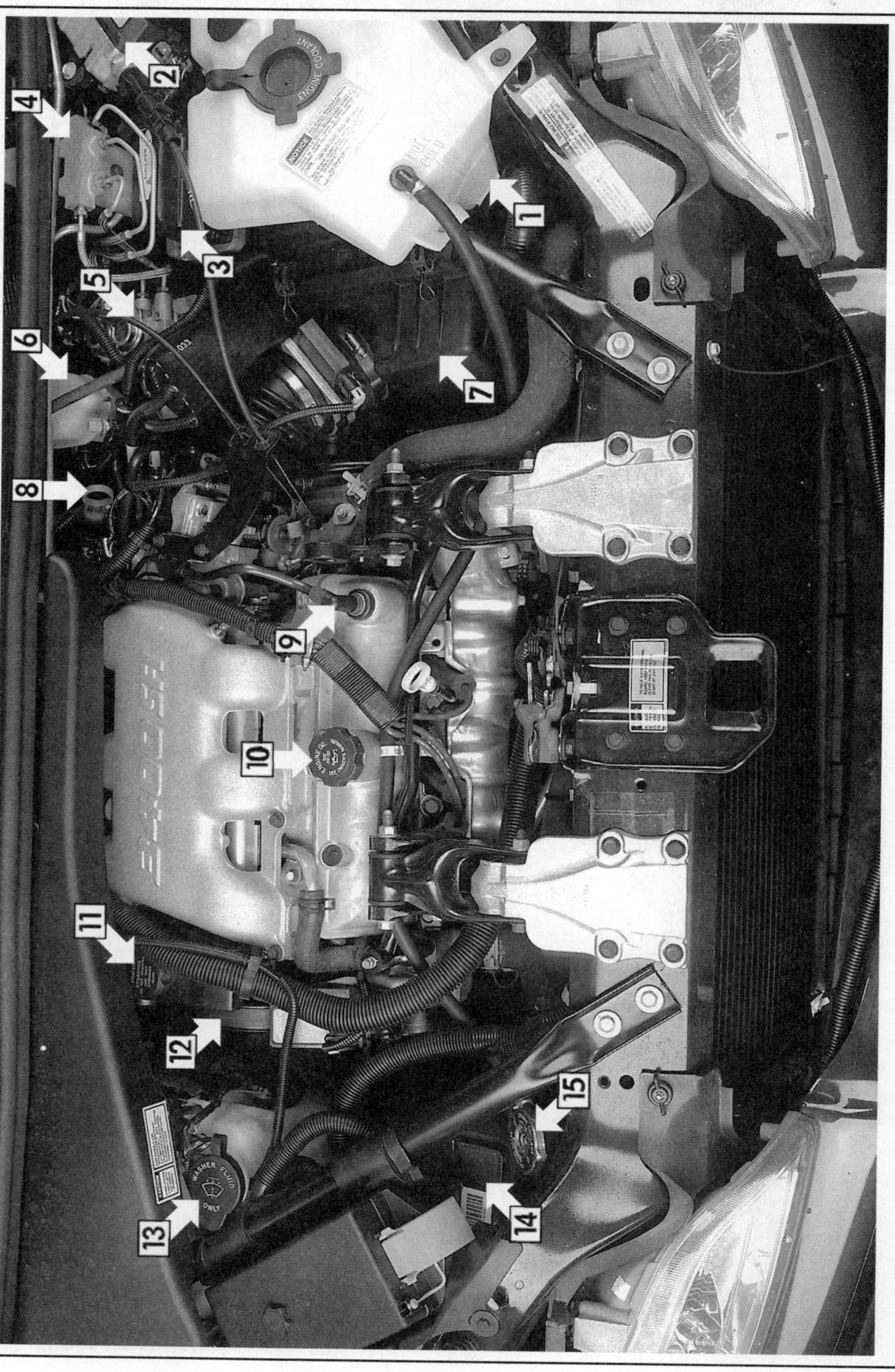

MAINTENANCE COMPONENT LOCATIONS—3.4L ENGINE

1. Engine coolant reservoir
2. Cruise control
3. ABS module
4. Brake distribution block
5. Master cylinder
6. Brake fluid reservoir
7. Air filter box
8. Transaxle dipstick
9. PCV valve
10. Oil fill cap
11. Power steering fill cap
12. Serpentine belt
13. Washer fluid reservoir
14. Battery
15. Radiator fill cap

91091PE4

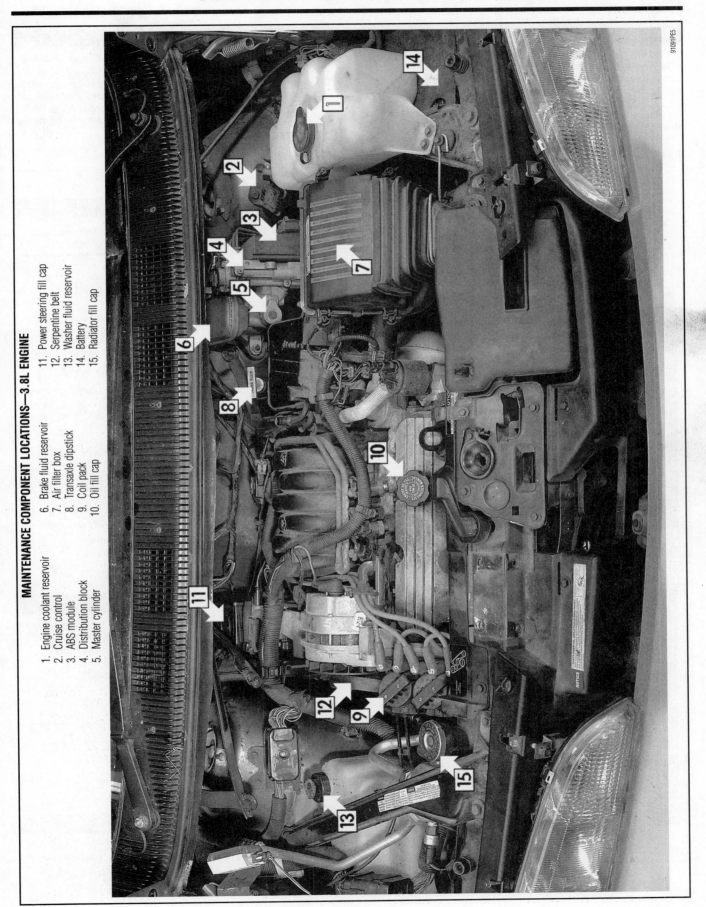

MAINTENANCE COMPONENT LOCATIONS—3.8L ENGINE

1. Engine coolant reservoir
2. Cruise control
3. ABS module
4. Distribution block
5. Master cylinder
6. Brake fluid reservoir
7. Air filter box
8. Transaxle dipstick
9. Coil pack
10. Oil fill cap
11. Power steering fill cap
12. Serpentine belt
13. Washer fluid reservoir
14. Battery
15. Radiator fill cap

Air Cleaner

The air cleaner has a dual purpose. It not only filters the inducted air going to the engine, but also acts as a flame arrester if the engine should backfire. If an engine maintenance procedure requires the temporary removal of the air cleaner, remove it; otherwise, never run the engine without it. The air filter should be replaced every 30,000 miles (50,000 km).

REMOVAL & INSTALLATION

◆ See Figures 39 and 40

1. Disengage the fasteners securing the top of the air cleaner.
2. Carefully pull the air filter cover back to expose the element.
3. Remove the air filter element.
4. Wipe out the housing with a clean rag.

To install:

5. Position the air filter element in the housing, make sure it seats properly.
6. Install the air cleaner cover.
7. Install the air cleaner fasteners, and tighten as necessary.

Fig. 39 Loosen the attaching screws . . .

Fig. 40 . . . and pull back the cover to remove the filter

Fuel Filter

➡The inline fuel filter is located in the fuel feed pipe ahead of the fuel injection system. Quick-connect type fittings are used on both ends of the filter. The in-tank fuel filter is located on the lower end of the fuel pickup tube in the fuel tank. The filter is made of woven plastic and prevents dirt from entering the fuel line and also stops water unless the filter becomes completely submerged in water. This filter is self-cleaning and normally requires no maintenance.

REMOVAL & INSTALLATION

◆ See Figures 41, 42, 43, 44 and 45

✷✷ CAUTION

Never smoke when working around gasoline! Avoid all sources of sparks or ignition. Gasoline vapors are EXTREMELY volatile!

1. Disconnect the negative battery cable.
2. Depressurize the fuel system. Refer to Section 5.
3. Remove the filter bracket retainer.
4. For plastic type fittings:
   a. Grasp the filter and one fuel line fitting. Twist the quick connect fitting ¼ turn in each direction to loosen any dirt within the fitting. Repeat for the other fuel line fitting.
   b. Squeeze the plastic retainer release tabs and pull the connection apart. Repeat for the other fitting.
5. For metal type fittings:
   a. Use a fuel pipe quick-connect separator. This is available from your local parts store.
   b. Insert the tool into the female side of the connector, then push inward to release locking tabs. Pull the connection apart.

To install:

6. Remove the protective caps from the new filter and apply a few drops of clean engine oil to both tube ends of the filter and O-rings. Install the fuel filter so that the flow arrow follows the direction of fuel flow.
7. Install the new plastic connector retainers on the filter inlet and outlet tubes (plastic collar type fittings).
8. Push the connectors together to cause the retaining tabs to snap into place. Once installed pull on both ends of each connection to make sure they are secure.
9. Install the fuel filter and bracket on the frame.
10. Connect the negative battery cable.
11. Start the engine and check for leaks.

PCV Valve

The Positive Crankcase Ventilation (PCV) system must be operating correctly to provide complete scavenging of the crankcase vapors. Fresh air is supplied to the crankcase from the air filter, mixed with the internal exhaust gases, passed through the PCV valve and into the intake manifold.

The PCV system should be checked at every oil change and serviced every 30,000 miles.

REMOVAL & INSTALLATION

◆ See Figures 46 and 47

1. Pull the PCV valve from the rocker arm cover grommet.
2. Remove the hose(s) from the PCV valve.
3. Shake the valve to make sure that it is not plugged.
4. Installation is the reverse of removal.

Evaporative Canister

To limit gasoline vapor discharge into the air when the vehicle is not operating. This system transfers fuel vapors from the fuel tank to a charcoal canister

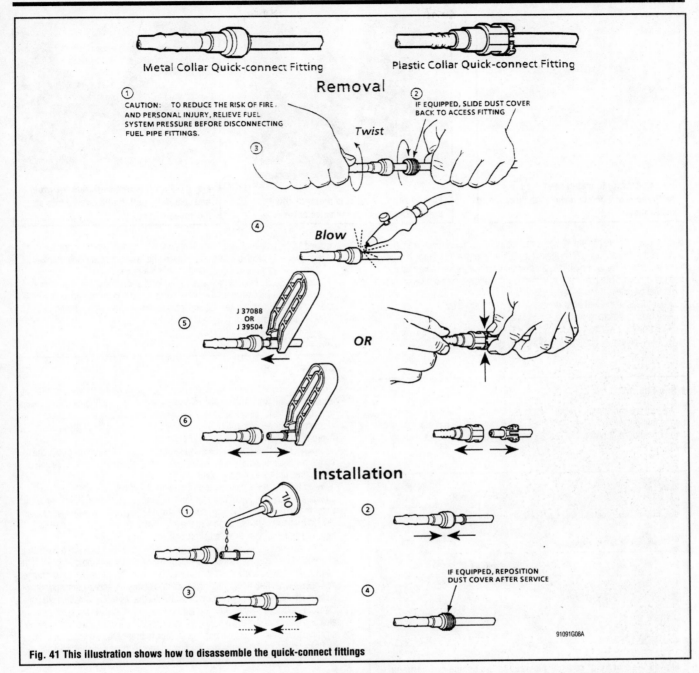

Metal Collar Quick-connect Fitting

Plastic Collar Quick-connect Fitting

Removal

① CAUTION: TO REDUCE THE RISK OF FIRE, AND PERSONAL INJURY, RELIEVE FUEL SYSTEM PRESSURE BEFORE DISCONNECTING FUEL PIPE FITTINGS.

② IF EQUIPPED, SLIDE DUST COVER BACK TO ACCESS FITTING

③ Twist

④ Blow

⑤ J 37088 OR J 39504

OR

⑥

Installation

① OIL

② IF EQUIPPED, REPOSITION DUST COVER AFTER SERVICE

③

④

91091G08A

Fig. 41 This illustration shows how to disassemble the quick-connect fittings

91091PC3

Fig. 42 The inline filter is located along the frame rail

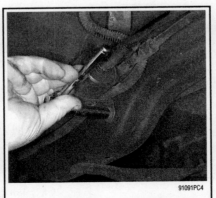

91091PC4

Fig. 43 Remove the bolt securing the filter

91091PC6

Fig. 44 Disengage the locking clips and lower the filter

Fig. 45 Be sure to install the filter properly. The arrow points toward the direction of fuel flow

Fig. 46 The PCV valve is normally fitted to a rubber grommet in the valve cover

Fig. 47 Once it is removed from the grommet, carefully pull the PCV valve free of the vacuum hose

storage device. This canister absorbs fuel vapors and stores them until they can be burned in the engine. When the engine is running, the fuel vapor is purged from the carbon element by intake air flow and consumed in the normal combustion process. The EVAP purge solenoid valve allows manifold vacuum to purge the canister.

Poor idle, stalling and poor driveability can be caused by:

- Hoses split, cracked and/or not connected properly
- Damaged canister
- Malfunctioning purge solenoid

SERVICING

▶ **See Figure 48**

Inspect the canister for cracks or damage and for fuel leaks. If either condition is found it will be necessary to replace the canister. Also check the condition of the hoses. If necessary, replace them. Be sure to use hoses marked EVAP.

Fig. 48 View of EVAP canister mounted in the engine compartment

Battery

PRECAUTIONS

Always use caution when working on or near the battery. Never allow a tool to bridge the gap between the negative and positive battery terminals. Also, be careful not to allow a tool to provide a ground between the positive cable/terminal and any metal component on the vehicle. Either of these conditions will cause a short circuit, leading to sparks and possible personal injury.

Do not smoke, have an open flame or create sparks near a battery; the gases contained in the battery are very explosive and, if ignited, could cause severe injury or death.

A battery hold-down device should carefully secure all batteries, regardless of type. If this is not done, the battery terminals or casing may crack from stress

applied to the battery during vehicle operation. A battery which is not secured may allow acid to leak out, making it discharge faster; such leaking corrosive acid can also eat away at components under the hood.

Always visually inspect the battery case for cracks, leakage and corrosion. A white corrosive substance on the battery case or on nearby components would indicate a leaking or cracked battery. If the battery is cracked, it should be replaced immediately.

GENERAL MAINTENANCE

▶ **See Figure 49**

A battery that is not sealed must be checked periodically for electrolyte level. You cannot add water to a sealed maintenance-free battery (though not all maintenance-free batteries are sealed); however, a sealed battery must also be checked for proper electrolyte level, as indicated by the color of the built-in hydrometer "eye."

Always keep the battery cables and terminals free of corrosion. Check these components about once a year. Refer to the removal, installation and cleaning procedures outlined in this section.

Keep the top of the battery clean, as a film of dirt can help completely discharge a battery that is not used for long periods. A solution of baking soda and water may be used for cleaning, but be careful to flush this off with clear water. DO NOT let any of the solution into the filler holes. Baking soda neutralizes battery acid and will de-activate a battery cell.

Batteries in vehicles which are not operated on a regular basis can fall victim to parasitic loads (small current drains which are constantly drawing current from the battery). Normal parasitic loads may drain a battery on a vehicle that is in storage and not used for 6–8 weeks. Vehicles that have additional accessories such as a cellular phone, an alarm system or other devices that increase parasitic load may discharge a battery sooner. If the vehicle is to be stored for 6–8 weeks in a secure area and the alarm system, if present, is not necessary, the negative battery cable should be disconnected at the onset of storage to protect the battery charge.

Remember that constantly discharging and recharging will shorten battery life. Take care not to allow a battery to be needlessly discharged.

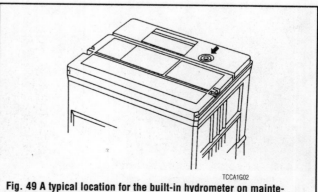

Fig. 49 A typical location for the built-in hydrometer on maintenance-free batteries

BATTERY FLUID

Check the battery electrolyte level at least once a month, or more often in hot weather or during periods of extended vehicle operation. On non-sealed batteries, the level can be checked either through the case on translucent batteries or by removing the cell caps on opaque-cased types. The electrolyte level in each cell should be kept filled to the split ring inside each cell, or the line marked on the outside of the case.

If the level is low, add only distilled water through the opening until the level is correct. Each cell is separate from the others, so each must be checked and filled individually. Distilled water should be used, because the chemicals and minerals found in most drinking water are harmful to the battery and could significantly shorten its life.

If water is added in freezing weather, the vehicle should be driven several miles to allow the water to mix with the electrolyte. Otherwise, the battery could freeze.

Although some maintenance-free batteries have removable cell caps for access to the electrolyte, the electrolyte condition and level on all sealed maintenance-free batteries must be checked using the built-in hydrometer "eye." The exact type of eye varies between battery manufacturers, but most apply a sticker to the battery itself explaining the possible readings. When in doubt, refer to the battery manufacturer's instructions to interpret battery condition using the built-in hydrometer.

➡**Although the readings from built-in hydrometers found in sealed batteries may vary, a green eye usually indicates a properly charged battery with sufficient fluid level. A dark eye is normally an indicator of a battery with sufficient fluid, but one, which may be low in charge. And a light or yellow eye is usually an indication that electrolyte supply has dropped below the necessary level for battery (and hydrometer) operation. In this last case, sealed batteries with an insufficient electrolyte level must usually be discarded.**

Checking the Specific Gravity

▶ **See Figures 50, 51 and 52**

A hydrometer is required to check the specific gravity on all batteries that are not maintenance-free. On batteries that are maintenance-free, observing the built-in hydrometer "eye" on the top of the battery case checks the specific gravity. Check with your battery's manufacturer for proper interpretation of its built-in hydrometer readings.

❊❊ CAUTION

Battery electrolyte contains sulfuric acid. If you should splash any on your skin or in your eyes, flush the affected area with plenty of clear water. If it gets in your eyes, or is ingested, get medical help immediately.

The fluid (sulfuric acid solution) contained in the battery cells will tell you many things about the condition of the battery. Because the cell plates must be kept submerged below the fluid level in order to operate, maintaining the fluid level is extremely important. And, because the specific gravity of the acid is an indication of electrical charge, testing the fluid can be an aid in determining if the battery must be replaced. A battery in a vehicle with a properly operating charging system should require little maintenance, but careful, periodic inspection should reveal problems before they leave you stranded.

As stated earlier, the specific gravity of a battery's electrolyte level can be used as an indication of battery charge. At least once a year, check the specific gravity of the battery. It should be between 1.20 and 1.26 on the gravity scale. Most auto supply stores carry a variety of inexpensive battery testing hydrometers. These can be used on any non-sealed battery to test the specific gravity in each cell.

The battery testing hydrometer has a squeeze bulb at one end and a nozzle at the other. Battery electrolyte is sucked into the hydrometer until the float is lifted from its seat. The specific gravity is then read by noting the position of the float. If gravity is low in one or more cells, the battery should be slowly charged and checked again to see if the gravity has come up. Generally, if after charging, the specific gravity between any two cells varies more than 50 points (0.50), the battery should be replaced, as it can no longer produce sufficient voltage to guarantee proper operation.

CABLES

▶ **See Figures 53 thru 58**

Once a year (or as necessary), the battery terminals and the cable clamps should be cleaned. Loosen the clamps and remove the cables, negative cable first. On batteries with posts on top, the use of a puller specially made for this purpose is recommended. These are inexpensive and available in most auto parts stores. Side terminal battery cables are secured with a small bolt.

Clean the cable clamps and the battery terminal with a wire brush, until all corrosion, grease, etc., is removed and the metal is shiny. It is especially important to clean the inside of the clamp thoroughly (an old knife is useful here), since a small deposit of foreign material or oxidation there will prevent a sound electrical connection and inhibit either starting or charging. Special tools are available for cleaning these parts, one type for conventional top post batteries and another type for side terminal batteries. It is also a good idea to apply some dielectric grease to the terminal, as this will aid in the prevention of corrosion.

After the clamps and terminals are clean, reinstall the cables, negative cable lasts; DO NOT hammer the clamps onto battery posts. Tighten the clamps securely, but do not distort them. Give the clamps and terminals a thin external coating of grease after installation, to retard corrosion.

Check the cables at the same time that the terminals are cleaned. If the cable insulation is cracked or broken, or if the ends are frayed, the cable should be replaced with a new cable of the same length and gauge.

CHARGING

❊❊ CAUTION

The chemical reaction that takes place in all batteries generates explosive hydrogen gas. A spark can cause the battery to explode and splash acid. To avoid serious personal injury, be sure there is proper ventilation and take appropriate fire safety precautions when connecting, disconnecting, or charging a battery and when using jumper cables.

Fig. 50 On non-maintenance-free batteries, the fluid level can be checked through the case on translucent models; the cell caps must be removed on other models

TCCA1P07

Fig. 51 If the fluid level is low, add only distilled water through the opening until the level is correct

TCCA1P08

TCCA1P09

Fig. 52 Check the specific gravity of the battery's electrolyte with a hydrometer

Fig. 53 Loosen the battery cable retaining nut . . .

Fig. 54 . . . then disconnect the cable from the battery

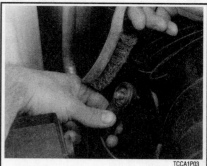

Fig. 55 A wire brush may be used to clean any corrosion or foreign material from the cable

Fig. 56 The wire brush can also be used to remove any corrosion or dirt from the battery terminal

Fig. 57 The battery terminal can also be cleaned using a solution of baking soda and water

Fig. 58 Before connecting the cables, it's a good idea to coat the terminals with a small amount of dielectric grease

A battery should be charged at a slow rate to keep the plates inside from getting too hot. However, if some maintenance-free batteries are allowed to discharge until they are almost "dead," they may have to be charged at a high rate to bring them back to "life." Always follow the charger manufacturer's instructions on charging the battery.

➡Always turn the ignition "OFF" when connecting or disconnecting battery cables, battery chargers or jumper cables. Failure to do so may damage the Powertrain Control Module (PCM) or other electronic components.

REPLACEMENT

When it becomes necessary to replace the battery, select one with amperage rating equal to or greater than the battery originally installed. Deterioration and just plain aging of the battery cables, starter motor, and associated wires makes the battery's job harder in successive years. The slow increase in electrical resistance over time makes it prudent to install a new battery with a greater capacity than the old.

Belts

INSPECTION

The belts, which drive the engine accessories such as the alternator, the air pump, power steering pump, air conditioning compressor and water pump, are of serpentine belt design. Older style belts show wear and damage readily, since their basic design was a belt with a rubber casing. As the casing wore, cracks and fibers were readily apparent. Newer design, caseless belts do not show wear as readily, and many untrained people cannot distinguish between a good, serviceable belt and one that is worn to the point of failure. It is a good idea, therefore, to visually inspect the belt regularly and replace it, routinely, every two to three years.

ADJUSTING

A single belt is used to drive all of the engine accessories formerly driven by multiple drive belts. The single belt is referred to a serpentine belt. All the belt driven accessories are rigidly mounted with belt tension maintained by a spring-loaded tensioner. Because of the belt tensioner, no adjustment is necessary.

REMOVAL & INSTALLATION

◗ **See Figures 59 thru 64**

1. Many applications will have a belt shield for protection. This will have to be removed first to access the serpentine belt.
2. To remove the drive belt on a 3.1 L, or a 3.4L engine, use a ⅜ in. ratchet or breaker bar to unload the tensioner and remove the belt. On the 3.8L engine use an 18mm wrench is used to unload the tension.

❈❈ WARNING

Take care as not to bend the tensioner when applying torque. Damage to the tensioner may occur. Maximum torque to load belt should not exceed 30 ft. lbs.

3. Installation is the reverse of removal. Be sure to install the belt using the proper routing.

Hoses

INSPECTION

◗ **See Figures 65, 66, 67 and 68**

Upper and lower radiator hoses, along with the heater hoses, should be checked for deterioration, leaks and loose hose clamps at least every 15,000

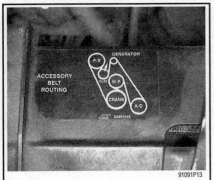

Fig. 59 An underhood decal can usually be found indicating belt routing

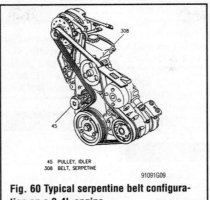

45 PULLEY, IDLER
308 BELT, SERPETINE

Fig. 60 Typical serpentine belt configuration on a 3.4L engine

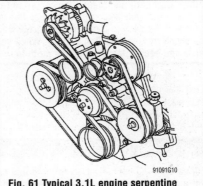

Fig. 61 Typical 3.1L engine serpentine belt configuration

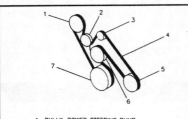
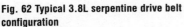

1 PULLY, POWER STEERING PUMP
2 TENSIONER, BELT
3 PULLEY, GENERATOR
4 BELT, SERPENTINE DRIVE
5 PULLEY, AIR CONDITIONING COMPRESSOR
6 PULLEY, ENGINE COOLANT PUMP
7 DAMPER, CRANKSHAFT TORSIONAL

Fig. 62 Typical 3.8L serpentine drive belt configuration

Fig. 63 Use a wrench to disengage the tensioner. The longer the wrench the better leverage you will have

Fig. 64 The belt is easily removed after the tension is released.

Fig. 65 The cracks developing along this hose are a result of age-related hardening

miles (24,000 km). It is also wise to check the hoses periodically in early spring and at the beginning of the fall or winter when you are performing other maintenance. A quick visual inspection could discover a weakened hose, which might leave you, stranded if it remains faulty.

Whenever you are checking the hoses, make sure the engine and cooling system are cold. Visually inspect for cracking, rotting or collapsed hoses, and replace as necessary. Run your hand along the length of the hose. If a weak or swollen spot is noted when squeezing the hose wall, the hose should be replaced.

REMOVAL & INSTALLATION

1. Remove the radiator pressure cap.

⁂ CAUTION

Never remove the pressure cap while the engine is running, or personal injury from scalding hot coolant or steam may result. If pos-

Fig. 66 A hose clamp that is too tight can cause older hoses to separate and tear on either side of the clamp

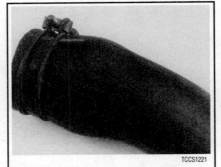

Fig. 67 A soft spongy hose (identifiable by the swollen section) will eventually burst and should be replaced

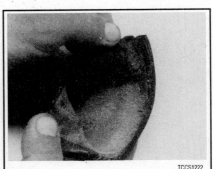

Fig. 68 Hoses are likely to deteriorate from the inside if the cooling system is not periodically flushed

sible, wait until the engine has cooled to remove the pressure cap. If this is not possible, wrap a thick cloth around the pressure cap and turn it slowly to the stop. Step back while the pressure is released from the cooling system. When you are sure all the pressure has been released, use the cloth to turn and remove the cap.

2. Position a clean container under the radiator and/or engine draincock or plug, then open the drain and allow the cooling system to drain to an appropriate level. For some upper hoses, only a little coolant must be drained. To remove hoses positioned lower on the engine, such as a lower radiator hose, the entire cooling system must be emptied.

❄ CAUTION

When draining coolant, keep in mind that cats and dogs are attracted by ethylene glycol antifreeze, and are quite likely to drink any that is left in an uncovered container or in puddles on the ground. This will prove fatal in sufficient quantity. Always drain coolant into a sealable container. Coolant may be reused unless it is contaminated or several years old.

3. Loosen the hose clamps at each end of the hose requiring replacement. Clamps are usually either of the spring tension type (which require pliers to squeeze the tabs and loosen) or of the screw tension type (which require screw or hex drivers to loosen). Pull the clamps back on the hose away from the connection.

4. Twist, pull and slide the hose off the fitting, taking care not to damage the neck of the component from which the hose is being removed.

→If the hose is stuck at the connection, do not try to insert a screwdriver or other sharp tool under the hose end in an effort to free it, as the connection and/or hose may become damaged. Heater connections especially may be easily damaged by such a procedure. If the hose is to be replaced, use a single-edged razor blade or suitable cutting edge, to make a slice along the portion of the hose that is stuck on the connection, perpendicular to the end of the hose. Do not cut too deep so as to prevent damaging the connection. The hose can then be peeled from the connection and discarded.

5. Clean both hose mounting connections. Inspect the condition of the hose clamps and replace them, if necessary.

To install:

6. Dip the ends of the new hose into clean engine coolant to ease installation.

7. Slide the clamps over the replacement hose, then slide the hose ends over the connections into position.

8. Position and secure the clamps at least ¼ in. (6.35mm) from the ends of the hose. Make sure they are located beyond the raised bead of the connector.

9. Close the radiator or engine drains and properly refill the cooling system with the clean drained engine coolant or a suitable mixture of ethylene glycol coolant and water. Be sure to maintain a ⁵⁰/₅₀ mix as a minimum in the system.

10. If available, install a pressure tester and check for leaks. If a pressure tester is not available, run the engine until normal operating temperature is reached (allowing the system to naturally pressurize), then check for leaks.

❄ CAUTION

If you are checking for leaks with the system at normal operating temperature, BE EXTREMELY CAREFUL not to touch any moving or hot engine parts. Once temperature has been reached, shut the engine OFF, and check for leaks around the hose fittings and connections that were removed earlier.

CV-Boots

INSPECTION

♦ See Figures 69 and 70

The CV (Constant Velocity) boots should be checked for damage each time the oil is changed and any other time the vehicle is raised for service. These boots keep water, grime, dirt and other damaging matter from entering the CV-joints. Any of these could cause early CV-joint failure that can be expensive to repair. Heavy grease thrown around the inside of the front wheel(s) and on the brake caliper/drum can be an indication of a torn boot. Thoroughly check the boots for missing clamps and tears. If the boot is damaged, it should be replaced immediately. Please refer to Section 7 for procedures.

Spark Plugs

♦ See Figure 71

Resistor type, tapered seat spark plugs are used on all engines. No gasket is used on these tapered seat plugs.

Normal service is assumed to be a mixture of idling, slow speed, and high speed driving. Occasional intermittent high-speed driving is needed for good spark plug performance. It gives increased combustion heat, burning away carbon or oxides that have built up from frequent idling, or continual stop-and-go driving.

Worn or dirty spark plugs may give satisfactory operation at idling speed, but at higher RPM they frequently fail. Faulty plugs are indicated in a number of ways: poor fuel economy, power loss, loss of speed, hard starting and generally poor engine performance.

Excessive gap wear, on plugs of low mileage, usually indicates the engine is operating at high speeds, or loads that are consistently greater than normal, or that a plug which is too hot is being used. Electrode wear may also be the result of plug overheating, caused by combustion gases leaking past the threads due to insufficient torquing of the spark plug. Excessively lean fuel mixture will also result in accelerated electrode wear.

A typical spark plug consists of a metal shell surrounding a ceramic insulator. A metal electrode extends downward through the center of the insulator and protrudes a small distance. Located at the end of the plug and attached to the side of the outer metal shell is the side electrode. The side electrode bends in at a 90° angle so that its tip is just past and parallel to the tip of the center electrode. The distance between these two electrodes (measured in thousandths of an inch or hundredths of a millimeter) is called the spark plug gap.

The spark plug does not produce a spark, but instead provides a gap across

Fig. 69 CV-boots must be inspected periodically for damage

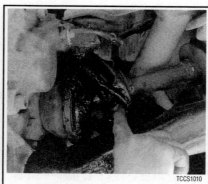

Fig. 70 A torn boot should be replaced immediately

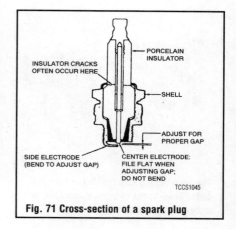

Fig. 71 Cross-section of a spark plug

which the current can arc. The coil produces anywhere from 20,000 to 50,000 volts (depending on the type and application) which travels through the wires to the spark plugs. The current passes along the center electrode and jumps the gap to the side electrode, and in doing so, ignites the air/fuel mixture in the combustion chamber.

SPARK PLUG HEAT RANGE

▶ **See Figure 72**

Spark plug heat range is the ability of the plug to dissipate heat. The longer the insulator (or the farther it extends into the engine), the hotter the plug will operate; the shorter the insulator (the closer the electrode is to the block's cooling passages) the cooler it will operate. A plug that absorbs little heat and remains too cool will quickly accumulate deposits of oil and carbon since it is not hot enough to burn them off. This leads to plug fouling and consequently to misfiring. A plug that absorbs too much heat will have no deposits but, due to the excessive heat, the electrodes will burn away quickly and might possibly lead to preignition or other ignition problems. Preignition takes place when plug tips get so hot that they glow sufficiently to ignite the air/fuel mixture before the actual spark occurs. This early ignition will usually cause a pinging during low speeds and heavy loads.

The general rule of thumb for choosing the correct heat range when picking a spark plug is: if most of your driving is long distance, high speed travel, use a colder plug; if most of your driving is stop and go, use a hotter plug. Original equipment plugs are generally a good compromise between the 2 styles and most people never have the need to change their plugs from the factory-recommended heat range.

REMOVAL & INSTALLATION

▶ **See Figures 73, 74 and 75**

A set of standard spark plugs usually requires replacement after about 20,000–30,000 miles (32,000–48,000 km), depending on your style of driving. In normal operation plug gap increases about 0.001 in. (0.025mm) for every

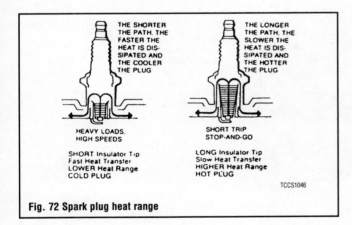

HEAVY LOADS, HIGH SPEEDS

SHORT Insulator Tip
Fast Heat Transfer
LOWER Heat Range
COLD PLUG

SHORT TRIP
STOP-AND-GO

LONG Insulator Tip
Slow Heat Transfer
HIGHER Heat Range
HOT PLUG

TCCS1046

Fig. 72 Spark plug heat range

2500 miles (4000 km). As the gap increases, the plug's voltage requirement also increases. It requires a greater voltage to jump the wider gap and about two to three times as much voltage to fire the plug at high speeds than at idle. The improved air/fuel ratio control of modern fuel injection combined with the higher voltage output of modern ignition systems will often allow an engine to run significantly longer on a set of standard spark plugs, but keep in mind that efficiency will drop as the gap widens (along with fuel economy and power).

When you're removing spark plugs, work on one at a time. Don't start by removing the plug wires all at once, because, unless you number them, they may become mixed up. Take a minute before you begin and number the wires with tape.

1. Disconnect the negative battery cable, and if the vehicle has been run recently, allow the engine to thoroughly cool.

2. On some applications it may be necessary to remove the air cleaner assembly.

3. Carefully twist the spark plug wire boot ½ turn to loosen it, then pull upward and remove the boot from the plug. Be sure to pull on the boot and not on the wire, otherwise the connector located inside the boot may become separated.

4. Using compressed air, blow any water or debris from the spark plug well to assure that no harmful contaminants are allowed to enter the combustion chamber when the spark plug is removed. If compressed air is not available, use a rag or a brush to clean the area.

➡**Remove the spark plugs when the engine is cold, if possible, to prevent damage to the threads. If removal of the plugs is difficult, apply a few drops of penetrating oil or silicone spray to the area around the base of the plug, and allow it a few minutes to work.**

5. Using a spark plug socket that is equipped with a rubber insert to properly hold the plug, turn the spark plug counterclockwise to loosen and remove the spark plug from the bore.

To install:

6. Inspect the spark plug boot for tears or damage. If a damaged boot is found, the spark plug wire must be replaced.

7. Using a wire feeler gauge, check and adjust the spark plug gap. When using a gauge, the proper size should pass between the electrodes with a slight drag. The next larger size should not be able to pass while the next smaller size should pass freely.

8. Carefully thread the plug into the bore by hand. If resistance is felt before the plug is almost completely threaded, back the plug out and begin threading again. In small, hard to reach areas, an old spark plug wire and boot could be used as a threading tool. The boot will hold the plug while you twist the end of the wire and the wire is supple enough to twist before it would allow the plug to crossthread.

✱✱ WARNING

Do not use the spark plug socket to thread the plugs. Always carefully thread the plug by hand or using an old plug wire to prevent the possibility of crossthreading and damaging the cylinder head bore.

9. Carefully tighten the spark plug. These engine applications use a tapered seat plug, tighten the plug to 15 lb.ft. (20N.m) .

10. Apply a small amount of silicone dielectric compound to the end of the

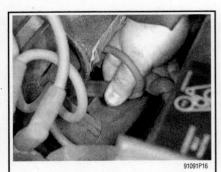

91091P16

Fig. 73 Twist the spark plug boot ½ turn then disconnect the wire from the plug by pulling on the boot

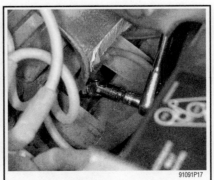

91091P17

Fig. 74 Use a ratchet and plug socket to loosen . . .

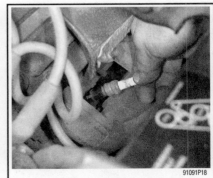

91091P18

Fig. 75 . . . and remove the plug from the cylinder head

spark plug. This assures no water will enter and no corrosion will develop. It will also aid in removal of the boot when the time comes.

Use special care when reinstalling spark plug boots, to assure that the metal terminal within the boot is fully seated on the spark plug terminal and that the boot has not moved on the wire. If boot to wire movement has occurred, the boot will give a false visual impression of being fully seated. A good check to assure that boots have been properly assembled is to push sideways on the installed boots. If they have been correctly installed, a stiff boot, with only slight looseness, will be noted. If the terminal has not been properly seated on the sparkplug, only the resistance of the rubber boot will be felt when pushing sideways.

INSPECTION & GAPPING

♦ **See Figures 76, 77, 78, 79 and 80**

Check the plugs for deposits and wear. If they are not going to be replaced, clean the plugs thoroughly. Remember that any kind of deposit will decrease the efficiency of the plug. Plugs can be cleaned on a spark plug cleaning machine, which can sometimes be found in service stations, or you can do an acceptable job of cleaning with a stiff brush. If the plugs are cleaned, the electrodes must be filed flat. Use an ignition points file, not an emery board or the like, which will leave deposits. The electrodes must be filed perfectly flat with sharp edges; rounded edges reduce the spark plug voltage by as much as 50%.

Check spark plug gap before installation. The ground electrode (the L-shaped one connected to the body of the plug) must be parallel to the center electrode and the specified size wire gauge (please refer to the Specifications chart under the hood for details) must pass between the electrodes with a slight drag.

➡**NEVER adjust the gap on a used platinum type spark plug**

Always check the gap on new plugs as they may have changed during handling. Do not use a flat feeler gauge when measuring the gap on a used plug, because the reading may be inaccurate. A round-wire type gapping tool is the best way to check the gap. The correct gauge should pass through the electrode

A **normally worn** spark plug should have light tan or gray deposits on the firing tip.

A **carbon fouled** plug, identified by soft, sooty, black deposits, may indicate an improperly tuned vehicle. Check the air cleaner, ignition components and engine control system.

This spark plug has been **left in the engine too long,** as evidenced by the extreme gap. Plugs with such an extreme gap can cause misfiring and stumbling accompanied by a noticeable lack of power.

An **oil fouled** spark plug indicates an engine with worn poston rings and/or bad valve seals allowing excessive oil to enter the chamber.

A **physically damaged** spark plug may be evidence of severe detonation in that cylinder. Watch that cylinder carefully between services, as a continued detonation will not only damage the plug, but could also damage the engine.

A **bridged or almost bridged** spark plug, identified by a build-up between the electrodes caused by excessive carbon or oil build-up on the plug.

TCCA1P40

Fig. 76 Inspect the spark plug to determine engine running conditions

Fig. 77 A variety of tools and gauges are needed for spark plug service

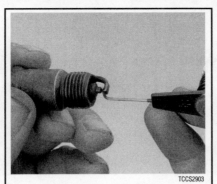

Fig. 78 Checking the spark plug gap with a feeler gauge

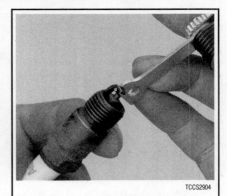

Fig. 79 Adjusting the spark plug gap

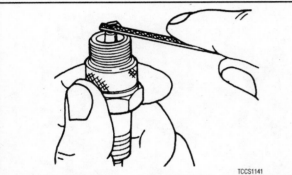

Fig. 80 If the standard plug is in good condition, the electrode may be filed flat—WARNING: do not file platinum plugs

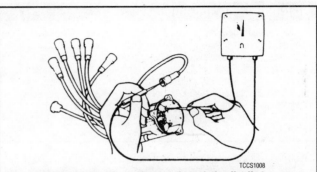

Fig. 81 Checking plug wire resistance through the distributor cap with an ohmmeter

gap with a slight drag. If you're in doubt, try one size smaller and one larger. The smaller gauge should go through easily, while the larger one shouldn't go through at all. Wire gapping tools usually have a bending tool attached. Use that to adjust the side electrode until the proper distance is obtained. Absolutely never attempt to bend the center electrode. Also, be careful not to bend the side electrode too far or too often as it may weaken and break off within the engine, requiring removal of the cylinder head to retrieve it.

Spark Plug Wires

The spark plug wiring used with electronic ignition systems is a carbon impregnated cord conductor, incased in 8 mm diameter silicone rubber insulation. The silicone jacket withstands very high temperatures and also provides an excellent insulator for the higher voltage of the electronic ignition system. Silicone spark plug boots form a tight seal on the plug.

TESTING

♦ See Figure 81

At every tune-up/inspection, visually check the spark plug cables for burns cuts, or breaks in the insulation. Check the boots and the nipples on the distributor cap and/or coil. Replace any damaged wiring. Every 50,000 miles (80,000 Km) or 60 months, the resistance of the wires should be checked with an ohmmeter. Wires with excessive resistance will cause misfiring, and may make the engine difficult to start in damp weather.

1. To check resistance, disconnect plug wires (do only one at a time) from the spark plug and distributor cap or coil pack.
2. Connect one lead of an ohmmeter to the spark plug side of the wire (make sure to contact the metal clip inside the boot).
3. Attach the other lead of the ohmmeter to the distributor (coil pack) side of the wire. Again make sure you contact the metal clip. Spark plug wire resistance is a function of length, the longer the wire the greater the resistance. Generally speaking, you should replace any wire with a resistance over 7,000 ohms per foot.

➡Spraying the secondary ignition wires with a light mist of water while the engine is running may help locate an intermittent problem. Ignition components will arc to ground when a secondary component is faulty.

REMOVAL & INSTALLATION

♦ See Figures 82, 83 and 84

When it becomes necessary to replace spark plug wires, because of age or breakage, it is recommended that you purchase a wire set for your specific engine model. These wire sets are precut to the proper length, and already have the boots installed.

Use care when removing spark plug wire boots from spark plugs. Twist the boot ½- turn before trying to pull the boot off. Pull only on the boot, pulling on the wire could cause separation or breakage.

Make sure, when replacing plug wires, that you route the wires correctly and through the proper retainers. Failure to route the wires properly can lead to radio ignition noise and crossfiring of the plugs, or shorting of the leads to ground.

1. Remove the air cleaner assembly.
2. Remove the spark plug wire retainers.
3. Replace one wire at a time. Match the length of the old wires to new, to ease installation.

➡Make a note of the wire placement to the cap (or coil pack) and routing to the engine so as to maintain correct firing order and proper clearances to engine parts that could cause damage to the wiring.

4. Remove heat shields from the spark plug boots.
To install:
5. Install heat shields onto new plug wires.
6. Coat the spark plug terminal end (or inside of the plug boot) with dielectric compound, install the boot onto the spark plug. Make sure it "clicks" on.
7. Route the wires along the engine, keeping the proper clearances.
8. Install the wires onto the distributor cap (coil pack), keeping the proper firing order
9. Install spark plug wire retainers.
10. Install air cleaner assembly.

Fig. 82 Number the plug wires before removing them. Note that the coil terminals are marked according to cylinder number

Fig. 83 If necessary, detach the loom assembly from the valve cover

Fig. 84 Replace and inspect wires one at a time to avoid confuision

Distributor Cap and Rotor

Ignition systems have changed dramatically since these vehicles were first introduced. Most vehicles today use coil packs instead of distributors. They have no need of distributor caps or rotors. Camshaft and crankshaft sensors have replaced these items. For the most part, timing is no longer adjustable, but is being controlled by the PCM (Powertrain Control Model). However, in the interest of those vehicles that operate with a distributor cap and rotor, some basic information will be given.

INSPECTION

A physical inspection of the distributor cap and rotor should be done at the same time as the plug wires are being checked. When inspecting the distributor cap, check for obvious signs of damage, such as a broken tower, crack in the body of the cap, or external carbon tracks . When checking on the inside of the cap, use a bright light to illuminate the inner surface. Check for charred or eroded terminals, inspect for carbon tracks that go from terminal to terminal or run to the bottom of the cap. Look for a worn or damaged rotor button (center electrode). Also take a close look at the inside terminals for metal to metal contact. Damaged or cut terminals could mean a rotor or cap that was not properly installed; or it could mean that the distributor housing has worn beyond its limits and the shaft is wobbling when it rotates, or that the distributor shaft is bent.

REMOVAL & INSTALLATION

▶ See Figure 85

1. Remove the secondary wiring (spark plug wires) if a new cap is being installed

➡Record wire placement at each wire location in order to maintain the correct firing order.

2. Simultaneously depress and rotate the two retaining screws counterclockwise, in the cap, 180° to disengage from the distributor housing.
3. Remove the cap, this exposes the ignition rotor.
4. Remove the two hold down screws retaining the rotor to the distributor shaft. Note the position of the rotor.

To install:

5. To install the rotor, align it to the distributor shaft. Do not put the square peg into the round hole!

➡The rotor can be mounted incorrectly. If this occurs the engine timing will be off by 180°. Be careful to align the rotor properly, it should seat snugly and level on the distributor shaft.

6. Seat the distributor cap onto the distributor housing, making sure to align the cap properly.
7. Simultaneously depress and rotate the cap screws clockwise 180° to hold the cap in place.

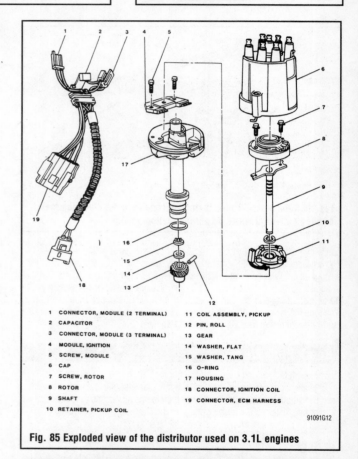

1	CONNECTOR, MODULE (2 TERMINAL)	11 COIL ASSEMBLY, PICKUP
2	CAPACITOR	12 PIN, ROLL
3	CONNECTOR, MODULE (3 TERMINAL)	13 GEAR
4	MODULE, IGNITION	14 WASHER, FLAT
5	SCREW, MODULE	15 WASHER, TANG
6	CAP	16 O-RING
7	SCREW, ROTOR	17 HOUSING
8	ROTOR	18 CONNECTOR, IGNITION COIL
9	SHAFT	19 CONNECTOR, ECM HARNESS
10	RETAINER, PICKUP COIL	

Fig. 85 Exploded view of the distributor used on 3.1L engines

Ignition Timing

ADJUSTMENT

➡This applies to the 3.1L engine only.

The Vehicle Emission Control Information label is attached to the front, right-hand shock tower in the engine compartment. Follow all instructions on the label. However, if the label is missing or defaced making it unreadable, use the following procedures:

➡Make timing adjustment with engine at normal operating temperature and the air conditioning system, if so equipped, turned off.

1. Set the parking brake and block the drive wheels. The vehicle should be in Neutral or Park. Check the Service Engine Soon light. It should not be lit. Set the IC (Ignition Control) in the bypass mode by grounding the bypass circuit.

➡ **The IC bypass circuit is a single tan wire with a black stripe and connector that breaks out from the engine harness located adjacent to the right hand shock tower.**

2. With the ignition off, connect an inductive type timing light to the number one spark plug lead. Find the timing marks on the indicator plate on the front of the engine just above and slightly to the side of the crankshaft pulley. Make sure this is clean and readable. If necessary, mark the timing mark at 10° BTDC with a dot of white paint or White Out®. There is a slot cut on the crankshaft pulley that should be dabbed with a spot of paint to ease in setting the timing.

3. Start the engine and aim the timing light at the timing mark. The line of the balancer or pulley will line up at the timing mark. If a change is necessary, loosen the distributor hold-down clamp bolt at the base of the distributor slightly. While observing the mark with the timing light, slightly rotate the distributor until the line indicates the correct timing. Tighten the hold-down bolt to 25 ft. lbs. (34Nm).

4. Turn off the engine and remove the timing light. Disconnect the Ignition Control (IC) bypass wire from ground and clear any trouble codes from the Electronic Control Module. Refer to section 4 for a further explanation of codes.

Valve Lash

The lifters used in the 3.1L, the 3.4L and the 3.8L engines are all hydraulic and do not require any adjustment as part of a maintenance program.

Idle Speed and Mixture Adjustments

The Powertrain Control Module (PCM) controls engine idle speed by adjusting the position of the Idle Air Control (IAC) motor pintle. The IAC is a bi-directional motor driven by two coils. The PCM pulses current to the IAC coils in steps (counts) to extend the IAC pintle into a passage in the throttle body to decrease air flow. The PCM reverses the current pulses to retract the pintle, increasing air flow. This method allows highly accurate control of idle speed and quick response to changes in engine load. There are no external mechanical adjustments to be made.

Air Conditioning System

SYSTEM SERVICE & REPAIR

➡ **It is recommended that an EPA Section 609 certified automotive technician utilizing a refrigerant recovery/recycling machine service the A/C system.**

The do-it-yourselfer should not service his/her own vehicle's A/C system for many reasons, including legal concerns, personal injury, environmental damages and cost. The following are some of the reasons why you may decide not to service your own vehicle's A/C system.

According to the U.S. Clean Air Act, it is a federal crime to service or repair (involving the refrigerant) a Motor Vehicle Air Conditioning (MVAC) system for money without being EPA certified. It is also illegal to vent R-12 and R-134a refrigerants into the atmosphere. Selling or distributing A/C system refrigerant (in a container that contains less than 20 pounds of refrigerant) to any person whom is not EPA 609 certified is also not allowed by law.

State and/or local laws may be stricter than the federal regulations, so be sure to check with your state and/or local authorities for further information. For further federal information on the legality of servicing your A/C system, call the EPA Stratospheric Ozone Hotline.

➡ **Federal law dictates that a fine of up to $25,000 may be levied on people convicted of venting refrigerant into the atmosphere. Additionally, the EPA may pay up to $10,000 for information or services leading to a criminal conviction of the violation of these laws.**

When servicing an A/C system you run the risk of handling or coming in contact with refrigerant, which may result in skin or eye irritation or frostbite. Although low in toxicity (due to chemical stability), inhalation of concentrated refrigerant fumes is dangerous and can result in death; cases of fatal cardiac arrhythmia have been reported in people accidentally subjected to high levels of refrigerant. Some early symptoms include loss of concentration and drowsiness.

➡ **Generally, the limit for exposure is lower for R-134a than it is for R-12. Exceptional care must be practiced when handling R-134a.**

GASOLINE ENGINE TUNE-UP SPECIFICATIONS

Year	Engine ID/VIN	Engine Displacement Liters (cc)	Spark Plugs Gap (in.)	Ignition Timing (deg.) MT	AT	Fuel Pump (psi)	Idle Speed (rpm) MT	AT	Valve Clearance In.	Ex.
1990	D	3.1 3130	0.045	—	①	9 to 13	—	①	HYD	HYD
1991	D	3.1 3130	0.045	—	①	9 to 13	—	①	HYD	HYD
1992	D	3.1 3130	0.045	—	①	9 to 13	—	①	HYD	HYD
	L	3.8 3785	0.06	—	①	41-47	—	①	HYD	HYD
1993	D	3.1 3130	0.045	—	①	9 to 13	—	①	HYD	HYD
	L	3.8 3785	0.06	—	①	41-47	—	①	HYD	HYD
1994	D	3.1 3130	0.045	—	①	9 to 13	—	①	HYD	HYD
	L	3.8 3785	0.06	—	①	41-47	—	①	HYD	HYD
1995	D	3.1 3130	0.045	—	①	9 to 13	—	①	HYD	HYD
	L	3.8 3785	0.06	—	①	41-47	—	①	HYD	HYD
1996	E	3.4 3350	0.06	—	①	41-47	—	①	HYD	HYD
1997	E	3.4 3350	0.06	—	①	41-47	—	①	HYD	HYD
1998	E	3.4 3350	0.06	—	①	41-47	—	①	HYD	HYD
1999	E	3.4 3350	0.060	—	①	41-47	—	①	HYD	HYD

NOTE: The Vehicle Emission Control Information (VECI) label often reflects specification changes made during production. If the information on the label differs from what is given, use the information from the label.

HYD: Hydraulic

① Idle speed and ignition timing are not adjustable and controlled by the Powertrain Control Module (PCM)

Also, refrigerants can decompose at high temperatures (near gas heaters or open flame), that may result in hydrofluoric acid, hydrochloric acid and phosgene (a fatal nerve gas).

R-12 refrigerant can damage the environment because it is a Chlorofluorocarbon (CFC), which has been proven to add to ozone layer depletion, leading to increasing levels of UV radiation. UV radiation has been linked with an increase in skin cancer, suppression of the human immune system, an increase in cataracts, damage to crops, damage to aquatic organisms, an increase in ground-level ozone, and increased global warming.

R-134a refrigerant is a greenhouse gas which, if allowed to vent into the atmosphere, will contribute to global warming (the Greenhouse Effect).

It is usually more economically feasible to have a certified MVAC automotive technician perform A/C system service on your vehicle. Some possible reasons for this are as follows:

• While it is illegal to service an A/C system without the proper equipment, the home mechanic would have to purchase an expensive refrigerant recovery/recycling machine to service his/her own vehicle.

• Since only a certified person may purchase refrigerant—according to the Clean Air Act, there are specific restrictions on selling or distributing A/C system refrigerant—it is legally impossible (unless certified) for the home mechanic to service his/her own vehicle. Procuring refrigerant in an illegal fashion exposes one to the risk of paying a $25,000 fine to the EPA.

R-12 Refrigerant Conversion

If your vehicle still uses R-12 refrigerant, one way to save A/C system costs down the road is to investigate the possibility of having your system converted to R-134a. The older R-12 systems can be easily converted to R-134a refrigerant by a certified automotive technician by installing a few new components and changing the system oil.

The cost of R-12 is steadily rising and will continue to increase, because it is no longer imported or manufactured in the United States. Therefore, it is often possible to have an R-12 system converted to R-134a and recharged for less than it would cost to just charge the system with R-12.

If you are interested in having your system converted, contact local automotive service stations for more details and information.

PREVENTIVE MAINTENANCE

▶ See Figures 86 and 87

• The easiest and most important preventive maintenance for your A/C system is to be sure that it is used on a regular basis. Running the system for five minutes each month (no matter what the season) will help ensure that the seals and all internal components remain lubricated.

➡Some newer vehicles automatically operate the A/C system compressor whenever the windshield defroster is activated. When running, the compressor lubricates the A/C system components; therefore, the A/C system would not need to be operated each month.

• In order to prevent heater core freeze-up during A/C operation, it is necessary to maintain proper antifreeze protection. Use a hand-held coolant tester (hydrometer) to periodically check the condition of the antifreeze in your engine's cooling system.

➡Antifreeze should not be used longer than the manufacturer specifies.

• For efficient operation of an air conditioned vehicle's cooling system, the radiator cap should have a holding pressure that meets manufacturer's specifications. A cap that fails to hold these pressures should be replaced.

• Any obstruction of or damage to the condenser configuration will restrict air flow that is essential to its efficient operation. It is, therefore, a good rule to keep this unit clean and in proper physical shape.

➡Bug screens that are mounted in front of the condenser (unless original equipment) are regarded as obstructions.

• The condensation drain tube expels any water that accumulates on the bottom of the evaporator housing into the engine compartment. If this tube is obstructed, the air conditioning performance can be restricted and condensation buildup can spill over onto the vehicle's floor.

SYSTEM INSPECTION

▶ See Figure 88

Although the A/C system should not be serviced by the do-it-yourselfer, preventive maintenance can be practiced and A/C system inspections can be performed to help maintain the efficiency of the vehicle's A/C system. For A/C system inspection, perform the following:

The easiest and often most important check for the air conditioning system consists of a visual inspection of the system components. Visually inspect the air conditioning system for refrigerant leaks, damaged compressor clutch, abnormal compressor drive belt tension and/or condition, plugged evaporator drain tube, blocked condenser fins, disconnected or broken wires, blown fuses, corroded connections and poor insulation.

A refrigerant leak will usually appear as an oily residue at the leakage point in the system. The oily residue soon picks up dust or dirt particles from the surrounding air and appears greasy. Through time, this will build up and appear to be a heavy dirt impregnated grease.

For a thorough visual and operational inspection, check the following:

• Check the surface of the radiator and condenser for dirt, leaves or other material that might block air flow.

• Check for kinks in hoses and lines. Check the system for leaks.

• Make sure the drive belt is properly tensioned. When the air conditioning is operating, make sure the drive belt is free of noise or slippage.

• Make sure the blower motor operates at all appropriate positions, then check for distribution of the air from all outlets with the blower on **HIGH** or **MAX**.

➡Keep in mind that under conditions of high humidity, air discharged from the A/C vents may not feel as cold as expected, even if the system is working properly. This is because vaporized moisture in humid air retains heat more effectively than dry air, thereby making humid air more difficult to cool.

• Make sure the air passage selection lever is operating correctly. Start the engine and warm it to normal operating temperature, then make sure the temperature selection lever is operating correctly.

TCCS1233

Fig. 86 A coolant tester can be used to determine the freezing and boiling levels of the coolant in your vehicle

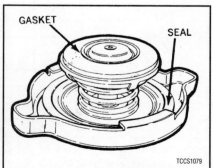

GASKET   SEAL

TCCS1079

Fig. 87 To ensure efficient cooling system operation, inspect the radiator cap gasket and seal

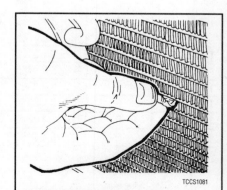

TCCS1081

Fig. 88 Periodically remove any debris from the condenser and radiator fins

Windshield Wipers

ELEMENT (REFILL) CARE & REPLACEMENT

▶ **See Figures 89 thru 98**

For maximum effectiveness and longest element life, the windshield and wiper blades should be kept clean. Dirt, tree sap, road tar and so on will cause streaking, smearing and blade deterioration if left on the glass. It is advisable to wash the windshield carefully with a commercial glass cleaner at least once a month. Wipe off the rubber blades with the wet rag afterwards. Do not attempt to move wipers across the windshield by hand; damage to the motor and drive mechanism will result.

To inspect and/or replace the wiper blade elements, place the wiper switch in the **LOW** speed position and the ignition switch in the **ACC** position. When the wiper blades are approximately vertical on the windshield, turn the ignition switch to **OFF**.

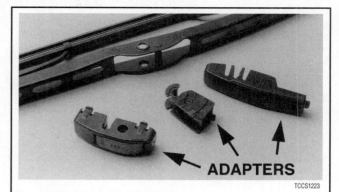

TCCS1223

Fig. 89 Bosch® wiper blade and fit kit

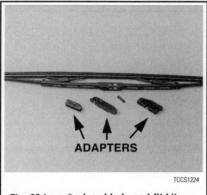

TCCS1224

Fig. 90 Lexor® wiper blade and fit kit

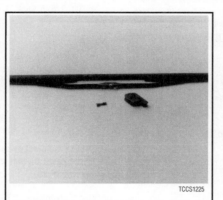

TCCS1225

Fig. 91 Pylon® wiper blade and adapter

TCCS1226

Fig. 92 Trico® wiper blade and fit kit

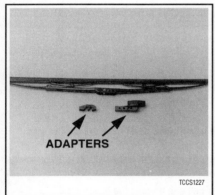

TCCS1227

Fig. 93 Tripledge® wiper blade and fit kit

TCCS1228

Fig. 94 To remove and install a Lexor® wiper blade refill, slip out the old insert and slide in a new one

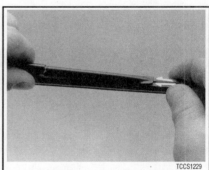

TCCS1229

Fig. 95 On Pylon® inserts, the clip at the end has to be removed prior to sliding the insert off

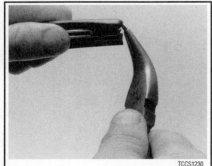

TCCS1230

Fig. 96 On Trico® wiper blades, the tab at the end of the blade must be turned up . . .

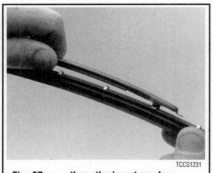

TCCS1231

Fig. 97 . . . then, the insert can be removed. After installing the replacement insert, bend the tab back

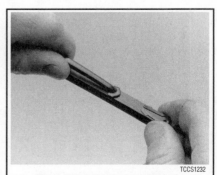

TCCS1232

Fig. 98 The Tripledge® wiper blade insert is removed and installed using a securing clip

Examine the wiper blade elements. If they cracked, broken or torn, they should be replaced immediately. Replacement intervals will vary with usage, although ozone deterioration usually limits element life to about one year. If the wiper pattern is smeared or streaked, or if the blade chatters across the glass, the elements should be replaced. It is easiest and most sensible to replace the elements in pairs.

If your vehicle is equipped with aftermarket blades, there are several different types of refills and your vehicle might have any kind. Aftermarket blades and arms rarely use the exact same type blade or refill as the original equipment. Here are some typical aftermarket wiper blades; not all may be available for your vehicle:

The Anco® type uses a release button that is pushed down to allow the refill to slide out of the yoke jaws. The new refill slides back into the frame and locks in place.

Some Trico® refills are removed by locating where the metal backing strip or the refill is wider. Insert a small screwdriver blade between the frame and metal backing strip. Press down to release the refill from the retaining tab.

Other types of Trico® refills have two metal tabs that are unlocked by squeezing them together. The rubber filler can then be withdrawn from the frame jaws. A new refill is installed by inserting the refill into the front frame jaws and sliding it rearward to engage the remaining frame jaws. There are usually four jaws; be certain when installing that the refill is engaged in all of them. At the end of its travel, the tabs will lock into place on the front jaws of the wiper blade frame.

Another type of refill is made from polycarbonate. The refill has a simple locking device at one end which flexes downward out of the groove into which the jaws of the holder fit, allowing easy release. By sliding the new refill through all the jaws and pushing through the slight resistance when it reaches the end of its travel, the refill will lock into position.

To replace the Tridon® refill, it is necessary to remove the wiper blade. This refill has a plastic backing strip with a notch about 1 in. (25mm) from the end. Hold the blade (frame) on a hard surface so that the frame is tightly bowed. Grip the tip of the backing strip and pull up while twisting counterclockwise. The backing strip will snap out of the retaining tab. Do this for the remaining tabs until the refill is free of the blade. The length of these refills is molded into the end and they should be replaced with identical types.

Regardless of the type of refill used, be sure to follow the part manufacturer's instructions closely. Make sure that all of the frame jaws are engaged as the refill is pushed into place and locked. If the metal blade holder and frame are allowed to touch the glass during wiper operation, the glass will be scratched.

Tires and Wheels

Common sense and good driving habits will afford maximum tire life. Fast starts, sudden stops and hard cornering are hard on tires and will shorten their useful life span. Make sure that you don't overload the vehicle or run with incorrect pressure in the tires. Both of these practices will increase tread wear.

➡ **For optimum tire life, keep the tires properly inflated, rotate them often and have the wheel alignment checked periodically.**

Inspect your tires frequently. Be especially careful to watch for bubbles in the tread or sidewall, deep cuts or underinflation. Replace any tires with bubbles in the sidewall. If cuts are so deep that they penetrate to the cords, discard the tire. Any cut in the sidewall of a radial tire renders it unsafe. Also look for uneven

tread wear patterns that may indicate the front end is out of alignment or that the tires are out of balance.

Most tires today have a service description branded on the side wall after the tire size. This service description consists of two parts: the load index and the speed symbol. The load index is a number usually between 75 and 115, which defines the tire's load capacity at maximum inflation. Higher numbers mean greater load capacity. The speed symbol is a letter usually between P and Z, which defines the speed capability of the tire. In the past, this letter might have been part of the tire size.

TIRE ROTATION

▶ **See Figures 99 and 100**

Tires must be rotated periodically to equalize wear patterns that vary with a tire's position on the vehicle. Tires will also wear in an uneven way as the front steering/suspension system wears to the point where the alignment should be reset.

Rotating the tires will ensure maximum life for the tires as a set, so you will not have to discard a tire early due to wear on only part of the tread. Regular rotation is required to equalize wear.

When rotating "unidirectional tires," make sure that they always roll in the same direction. This means that a tire used on the left side of the vehicle must not be switched to the right side and vice-versa. Such tires should only be rotated front-to-rear or rear-to-front, while always remaining on the same side of the vehicle. These tires are marked on the sidewall as to the direction of rotation; observe the marks when reinstalling the tire(s).

Some styled or "mag" wheels may have different offsets front to rear. In these cases, the rear wheels must not be used up front and vice-versa. Furthermore, if these wheels are equipped with unidirectional tires, they cannot be rotated unless the tire is remounted for the proper direction of rotation.

➡ **The compact or space-saver spare is strictly for emergency use. It must never be included in the tire rotation or placed on the vehicle for everyday use.**

TIRE DESIGN

▶ **See Figure 101**

For maximum satisfaction, tires should be used in sets of four. Mixing of different types (radial, bias-belted, fiberglass belted) must be avoided. In most cases, the vehicle manufacturer has designated a type of tire on which the vehicle will perform best. Your first choice when replacing tires should be to use the same type of tire that the manufacturer recommends.

When radial tires are used, tire sizes and wheel diameters should be selected to maintain ground clearance and tire load capacity equivalent to the original specified tire. Radial tires should always be used in sets of four.

➡ **Changing the tire size or wheel diameter from the original factory installed component could cause speedometer error and driveability concerns.**

✳✳ CAUTION

Radial tires should never be used on only the front axle.

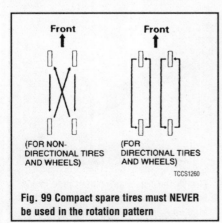

Fig. 99 Compact spare tires must NEVER be used in the rotation pattern

Fig. 100 Unidirectional tires are identifiable by sidewall arrows and/or the word "rotation"

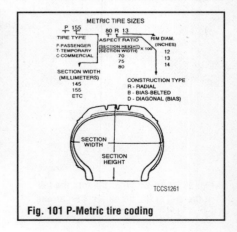

Fig. 101 P-Metric tire coding

When selecting tires, pay attention to the original size as marked on the tire. Most tires are described using an industry size code sometimes referred to as P-Metric. This allows the exact identification of the tire specifications, regardless of the manufacturer. If selecting a different tire size or brand, remember to check the installed tire for any sign of interference with the body or suspension while the vehicle is stopping, turning sharply or heavily loaded.

Snow Tires

Good radial tires can produce a big advantage in slippery weather, but in snow, a street radial tire does not have sufficient tread to provide traction and control. The small grooves of a street tire quickly pack with snow and the tire behaves like a billiard ball on a marble floor. The more open, chunky tread of a snow tire will self-clean as the tire turns, providing much better grip on snowy surfaces.

To satisfy municipalities requiring snow tires during weather emergencies, most snow tires carry either an M + S designation after the tire size stamped on the sidewall, or the designation "all-season." In general, no change in tire size is necessary when buying snow tires.

Most manufacturers strongly recommend the use of 4 snow tires on their vehicles for reasons of stability. If snow tires are fitted only to the drive wheels, the opposite end of the vehicle may become very unstable when braking or turning on slippery surfaces. This instability can lead to unpleasant endings if the driver can't counteract the slide in time.

Note that snow tires, whether 2 or 4, will affect vehicle handling in all non-snow situations. The stiffer, heavier snow tires will noticeably change the turning and braking characteristics of the vehicle. Once the snow tires are installed, you must re-learn the behavior of the vehicle and drive accordingly.

➡**Consider buying extra wheels on which to mount the snow tires. Once done, the "snow wheels" can be installed and removed as needed. This eliminates the potential damage to tires or wheels from seasonal removal and installation. Even if your vehicle has styled wheels, see if inexpensive steel wheels are available. Although the look of the vehicle will change, the expensive wheels will be protected from salt, curb hits and pothole damage.**

TIRE STORAGE

If they are mounted on wheels, store the tires at proper inflation pressure. All tires should be kept in a cool, dry place. If they are stored in the garage or basement, do not let them stand on a concrete floor; set them on strips of wood, a mat or a large stack of newspaper. Keeping them away from direct moisture is of paramount importance. Tires should not be stored upright, but in a flat position.

INFLATION & INSPECTION

▶ See Figures 102 thru 109

The importance of proper tire inflation cannot be overemphasized. A tire employs air as part of its structure. It is designed around the supporting strength of the air at a specified pressure. For this reason, improper inflation drastically reduces the tire's ability to perform as intended. A tire will lose some air in day-to-day use; having to add a few pounds of air periodically is not necessarily a sign of a leaking tire.

Two items should be a permanent fixture in every glove compartment: an

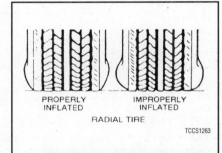

TCCS1097

Fig. 102 Tires should be checked frequently for any sign of puncture or damage

TCCS1095

Fig. 103 Tires with deep cuts, or cuts which bulge, should be replaced immediately

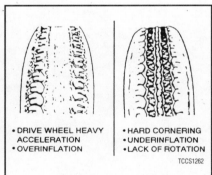

• DRIVE WHEEL HEAVY ACCELERATION
• OVERINFLATION

• HARD CORNERING
• UNDERINFLATION
• LACK OF ROTATION

TCCS1262

Fig. 104 Examples of inflation-related tire wear patterns

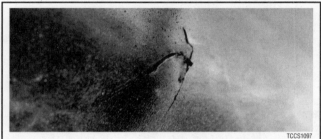

PROPERLY INFLATED   IMPROPERLY INFLATED

RADIAL TIRE

TCCS1263

Fig. 105 Radial tires have a characteristic sidewall bulge; don't try to measure pressure by looking at the tire. Use a quality air pressure gauge

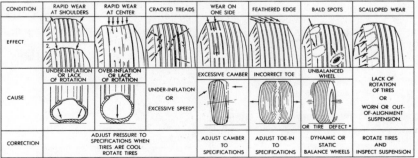

CONDITION	RAPID WEAR AT SHOULDERS	RAPID WEAR AT CENTER	CRACKED TREADS	WEAR ON ONE SIDE	FEATHERED EDGE	BALD SPOTS	SCALLOPED WEAR
EFFECT							
CAUSE	UNDER-INFLATION OR LACK OF ROTATION	OVER-INFLATION OR LACK OF ROTATION	UNDER-INFLATION OR EXCESSIVE SPEED*	EXCESSIVE CAMBER	INCORRECT TOE	UNBALANCED WHEEL OR TIRE DEFECT*	LACK OF ROTATION OF TIRES OR WORN OR OUT-OF-ALIGNMENT SUSPENSION.
CORRECTION	ADJUST PRESSURE TO SPECIFICATIONS WHEN TIRES ARE COOL ROTATE TIRES			ADJUST CAMBER TO SPECIFICATIONS	ADJUST TOE-IN TO SPECIFICATIONS	DYNAMIC OR STATIC BALANCE WHEELS	ROTATE TIRES AND INSPECT SUSPENSION

*HAVE TIRE INSPECTED FOR FURTHER USE.

TCCS1267

Fig. 106 Common tire wear patterns and causes

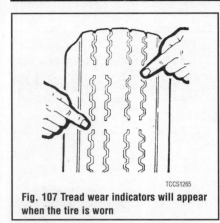

Fig. 107 Tread wear indicators will appear when the tire is worn

TCCS1265

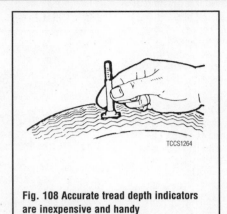

Fig. 108 Accurate tread depth indicators are inexpensive and handy

TCCS1264

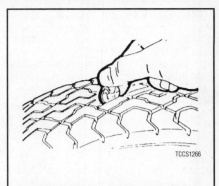

Fig. 109 A penny works well for a quick check of tread depth

TCCS1266

accurate tire pressure gauge and a tread depth gauge. Check the tire pressure (including the spare) regularly with a pocket type gauge. Too often, the gauge on the end of the air hose at your corner garage is not accurate because it suffers too much abuse. Always check tire pressure when the tires are cold, as pressure increases with temperature. If you must move the vehicle to check the tire inflation, do not drive more than a mile before checking. A cold tire is generally one that has not been driven for more than three hours.

A plate or sticker is normally provided somewhere in the vehicle (door post, hood, tailgate or trunk lid)

This shows the proper pressure for the tires. Never counteract excessive pressure build-up by bleeding off air pressure (letting some air out). This will cause the tire to run hotter and wear quicker.

❊❊ CAUTION

Never exceed the maximum tire pressure embossed on the tire! This is the pressure to be used when the tire is at maximum loading, but it is rarely the correct pressure for everyday driving. Consult the owner's manual or the tire pressure sticker for the correct tire pressure.

Once you've maintained the correct tire pressures for several weeks, you'll be familiar with the vehicle's braking and handling personality. Slight adjustments in tire pressures can fine-tune these characteristics, but never change the cold pressure specification by more than 2 psi. A slightly softer tire pressure will give a softer ride but also yield lower fuel mileage. A slightly harder tire will give crisper dry road handling but can cause skidding on wet surfaces. Unless you're fully attuned to the vehicle, stick to the recommended inflation pressures.

All tires made since 1968 have built-in tread wear indicator bars that show up as ½ in. (13mm) wide smooth bands across the tire when ¹⁄₁₆ in. (1.5mm) of tread remains. The appearance of tread wear indicators means that the tires should be replaced. In fact, many states have laws prohibiting the use of tires with less than this amount of tread.

When replacing tires, only the size, load range and construction as were originally installed on the vehicle are recommended.

You can check your own tread depth with an inexpensive gauge or by using a Lincoln head penny. Slip the Lincoln penny (with Lincoln's head upside-down) into several treads grooves. If you can see the top of Lincoln's head in 2 adjacent grooves, the tire has less than ¹⁄₁₆ in. (1.5mm) tread left and should be replaced. You can measure snow tires in the same manner by using the "tails" side of the Lincoln penny. If you can see the top of the Lincoln memorial, it's time to replace the snow tire(s).

CARE OF SPECIAL WHEELS

If you have invested money in magnesium, aluminum alloy or sport wheels, special precautions should be taken to make sure your investment is not wasted and that your special wheels look good for the life of the vehicle.

Special wheels are easily damaged and/or scratched. Occasionally check the rims for cracking, impact damage or air leaks. If any of these are found, replace the wheel. But in order to prevent this type of damage and the costly replacement of a special wheel, observe the following precautions:

• Use extra care not to damage the wheels during removal, installation, balancing, etc. After removal of the wheels from the vehicle, place them on a mat or other protective surface. If they are to be stored for any length of time, support them on strips of wood. Never store tires and wheels upright; the tread may develop flat spots.

• When driving, watch for hazards; it doesn't take much to crack a wheel.

• When washing, use a mild soap or non-abrasive dish detergent (keeping in mind that detergent tends to remove wax). Avoid cleansers with abrasives or the use of hard brushes. There are many cleaners and polishes for special wheels.

• If possible, remove the wheels during the winter. Salt and sand used for snow removal can severely damage the finish of a wheel.

FLUIDS AND LUBRICANTS

Fluid Disposal

Used fluids such as engine oil, transmission fluid, antifreeze and brake fluid are hazardous wastes and must be disposed of properly. Before draining any fluids, consult with your local authorities; in many areas, waste oil, antifreeze, etc. is being accepted as a part of recycling programs. A number of service stations and auto parts stores are also accepting waste fluids for recycling.

Be sure of the recycling center's policies before draining any fluids, as many will not accept different fluids that have been mixed together.

Fuel and Oil Recommendations

FUEL

The engine is designed to operate on unleaded gasoline ONLY and is essential for the proper operation of the emission control system. The use of

unleaded fuel will reduce spark plug fouling, exhaust system corrosion and engine oil deterioration.

In most parts of the United States, fuel with an octane rating of 87 should be used; in high altitude areas, fuel with an octane rating as low as 85 may be used. Using fuels with a lower octane may decrease engine performance, increase emissions and engine wear.

In some areas, fuel consisting of a blend of alcohol may be used; this blend of gasoline and alcohol is known as gasohol. When using gasohol, never use blends exceeding 10% ethanol or 5% methanol.

➡**The use of fuel with excessive amounts of alcohol may jeopardize the new car warranties.**

OIL

♦ See Figures 110 and 111

Use only oil that has the API (American Petroleum Institute) designation SG or later.

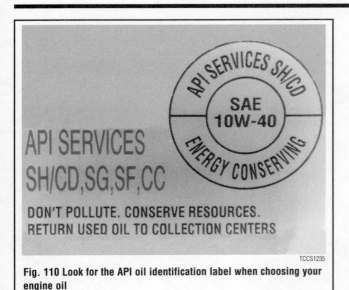

Fig. 110 Look for the API oil identification label when choosing your engine oil

Fig. 111 Recommended SAE engine oil viscosity grades for gasoline driven engines

Since the viscosity (thickness) of the engine oil affects fuel economy, it is recommended to select oil with reference to the outside temperature. For satisfactory lubrication, use lower viscosity oil for colder temperatures and higher viscosity oil for warmer temperatures.

Engine

OIL LEVEL CHECK

▶ See Figures 112, 113 and 114

1. Make sure the vehicle is parked on level ground.
2. When checking the oil level it is best for the engine to be at normal operating temperature, although checking the oil immediately after stopping will lead to a false reading. Wait a few minutes after turning off the engine to allow the oil to drain back into the crankcase.
3. Open the hood and locate the dipstick that will be on either the right or left side depending upon your particular engine. Pull the dipstick from its tube, wipe it clean and then reinsert it.
4. Pull the dipstick out again and, holding it horizontally, read the oil level. The oil should be between the "FULL" and "ADD" marks on the dipstick. If the oil is below the "ADD" mark, add oil of the proper viscosity through the capped opening in the top of the cylinder head cover.
5. Insert the dipstick and check the oil level again after adding any oil. Be careful not to overfill the crankcase. Approximately 1 quart of oil will raise the level from the "ADD" mark to the "FULL" mark. Excess oil will generally be consumed at an accelerated rate.

CHANGING OIL & FILTER

▶ See Figures 115 thru 123

The oil is to be changed every 7,500 miles (12,500 km) or 12 months, whichever occurs first. Under normal conditions, change the filter at first oil change and then at every other oil change, unless 12 months pass between changes. We recommend that the oil filter be changed every time the oil is changed. About a quart of dirty oil remains in the old filter. For a few dollars, it is a small expense for extended engine Life.

If driving under such conditions, such as: dusty areas, trailer towing, idling for long periods of time, low speed operation, or when operating with temperatures below freezing or driving short distances (under 4 miles), change the oil and filter every 3,000 miles (5,000 km) or 3 months.

1. Bring the engine to normal operating temperature, driving a short distance to the parts store to pick up the oil and filter is best way. Turn the engine off. Draining hot oil from the engine removes more acids and contaminants.
2. Raise the vehicle and support it on jack stands.
3. Obtain a drain pan with at least 6qts. capacity. Place the drain pan under the drain plug, in a position to catch the hot oil as it drains out. Loosen the drain plug using a socket and ratchet, or a box end wrench. The drain plug is the bolt inserted at an angle into the lowest point of the oil pan. Turn the drain plug out by hand, using a rag to shield your fingers from the hot oil. By keeping an inward pressure on the plug as you unscrew it, oil won't escape past the

Fig. 112 Pull out the oil level dipstick

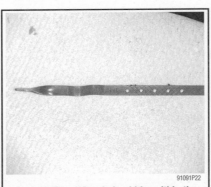

Fig. 113 The oil level should be within the crosshatched area on the dipstick

Fig. 114 Use a funnel when adding oil to avoid spilling it

threads and you can remove it without being burned by hot oil. Quickly remove the oil pan plug and move your hands out of the way. Drain the hot, dirty oil into a catch pan. Allow a few minutes to drain the oil completely. Check the drain plug carefully. Look closely at the threads, make sure the are not crossed, or worn beyond re-use. Check the condition of the plastic drain plug gasket. If it is cracked or distorted in any way, replace it. Reinstall the drain plug and gasket.

4. The oil filter is just about impossible to reach, or even see, from above, and almost as inaccessible from below. It may be easiest to remove the right front wheel to allow more access room on some models.

5. Place the drain pan under the oil filter.

6. Using an oil filter wrench (strap or cap type), loosen the oil filter. Use caution because the filter is very hot.

➡ Regardless of which type wrench you decide to use, be sure to obtain the correct size; filter wrenches come in different sizes (as do oil filters), and one size does not fit all.

7. If the oil filter is on so tightly that it collapses under pressure from the strap wrench, move the wrench as close as possible to the engine. If the filter hasn't torn, but can't turn, it maybe to your advantage to take the vehicle to a shop before a leak develops. It is next to impossible to cut these filters off without special tools. Make sure you are turning it counterclockwise.

8. Unscrew the filter and place it in the oil catch pan. Using a clean rag, wipe the filter-mounting surface.

To Install:

9. When ready to install the oil filter, spread a small amount of clean oil on the sealing gasket. Screw the filter on by hand until the gasket makes contact. Then tighten it by hand an additional ¾ of a turn. Do not overtighten. Install the oil pan plug and torque to no more than 20 ft. lbs. (27 Nm).

10. Using a funnel, add oil through the valve cover cap. Approximate oil capacity with a new filter, is 4.5qts. (4.3liters). Lower the vehicle, start the engine and inspect for oil leaks.

Fig. 115 Use a box wrench to break loose the drain plug

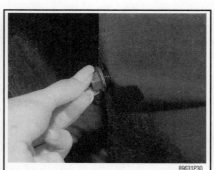

Fig. 116 Keeping pressure against the plug while unscrewing, helps avoid hot oil spilling on your hands.

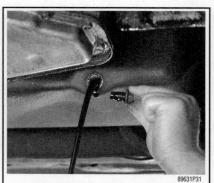

Fig. 117 With the plug out, allow the oil to drain completely

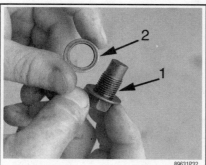

Fig. 118 Clean and inspect the oil drain plug (1) and washer (2), and replace if necessary.

Fig. 119 A special type oil filter wrench may be necessary, because of clearance.

Fig. 120 Removing the oil filter will cause oil to drip out

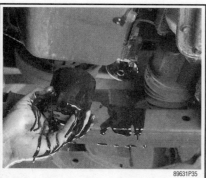

Fig. 121 You may want to wear protective gloves when changing the filter

Fig. 122 Clean the mounting boss with a clean, lint free rag before installing a new filter

Fig. 123 Before installing a new oil filter, lightly coat the rubber gasket with clean oil

✴✴ CAUTION

Do not run the engine above an idle until the engine has built up oil pressure, as indicated by the oil light going out.

11. Turn the engine off, and allow the oil to drain back into the crankcase for a minute, then recheck the oil level. Check for any leaks and correct as necessary.

When you have finished this job, you will notice that you now possess four or five quarts of dirty oil. Pour the dirty oil into some type of plastic jug, an old milk carton, or even an old antifreeze container, will suffice. Now you can dispose of it by taking it to a recycling center.

➥**Improperly disposing of used motor oil, not only pollutes the environment, it violates Federal law. Dispose of waste oil properly.**

Transaxle

FLUID LEVEL CHECK

♦ **See Figures 124 and 125**

Check the automatic transaxle fluid level at least every 15,000 miles or 12 months. The dipstick can be found on the left (driver) side of the engine compartment. The fluid level should be checked only when the transaxle is hot (normal operating temperature). The transaxle is considered hot after about 20 miles of highway driving.

1. Park the van on a level surface with the engine idling. Shift the transaxle into Neutral and set the parking brake.
2. Remove the dipstick, wipe it clean and then reinsert it firmly. Be sure that it has been pushed all the way in. Remove the dipstick again and check the fluid level while holding it horizontally. With the engine running, the fluid level should be between the second notch and the "FULL HOT" line. If the fluid must be checked when it is cool, the level should be between the first and second notches.

3. If the fluid level is below the second notch (engine hot) or the first notch (engine cold), add DEXRON® III automatic transaxle fluid through the dipstick tube. This is easily done with the aid of a funnel. Check the level often as you are filling the transaxle. Be extremely careful not to overfill it. Overfilling will cause slippage, seal damage and overheating. Approximately 1 pint of ATF will raise the fluid level from one notch/line to the other.

➥**Use only DEXRON® III ATF. The use of any other fluid will cause severe damage to the transaxle.**

The fluid on the dipstick should always be a bright red color. If it is discolored (brown or black), or smells burnt, serious transaxle troubles, probably due to overheating, should be suspected. A qualified technician to locate the cause of the burnt fluid should inspect the transaxle.

DRAIN & REFILL

♦ **See Figures 126, 127 and 128**

1. Raise and support the vehicle on jack stands. Place an oil catch pan under the transaxle.
2. Remove the oil pan bolts from the front and side only.
3. Loosen the rear oil pan bolts approximately 4 turns.
4. Using a rubber mallet, lightly tap the oil pan and allow the fluid to drain.
5. Remove the remaining oil pan bolts and remove the pan and gasket. Remove the filter and the O-ring.
6. Clean the old gasket from the oil pan and transaxle surfaces with a scraper. Wash the mating surfaces with solvent to remove the oil film.
   To install:
7. Install the new filter and O-ring (coat the O-ring with petroleum jelly).
8. Raise the oil pan into position with the new gasket and install the bolts. Torque the bolts to 15 ft. lbs. (20.3 Nm) and lower the vehicle.
9. Add new transaxle fluid through the dipstick tube. Approximate fluid replacement after pan removal is 6 qts. (5.7 liters). Operate the engine and transaxle and check for leaks.

Fig. 124 After wiping the transaxle dipstick clean, reinsert it fully into the tube

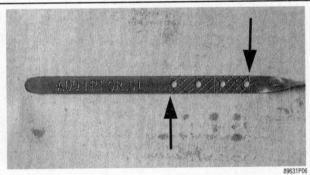

Fig. 125 Do NOT add fluid if the level is anywhere within the cross-hatched area on the dipstick

Fig. 126 Allow the fluid to drain . . .

Fig. 127 . . . then remove the pan from the transaxle

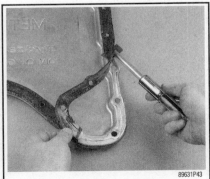

Fig. 128 Removing the gasket from the transaxle oil pan

Cooling System

FLUID RECOMMENDATION

The cooling system was designed to maintain engine temperature at an efficient level during all engine operating conditions. Some GM vehicles came equipped with a new silicate free anti freeze. This is called DEX-COOL®. There will be a label under the hood, in the area of the coolant bottle advising of this. DEX-COOL® was developed to last for 150,000 miles (240,000km) or 5 years, whichever occurs first. Make sure only GM Goodwrench DEX-COOL® or equivalent is used when coolant is added or changed.

A ⁵⁰⁄₅₀ mixture of coolant will provide the following protection:
- Freezing protection down to -37°C (-34°F)
- Boiling protection up to 129°C (265°F), with an operating pressure cap
- Help keep the proper engine operating temperature
- Help protect against rust and corrosion
- Allow the sensors and switches to operate as designed

➡DO not use a solution stronger than 70% antifreeze. Pure antifreeze will freeze at -22°C (-8°F).

LEVEL CHECK

▶ See Figures 129, 130 and 131

Check the coolant level in the recovery bottle or surge tank. The fluid level may be checked by observing the fluid level marks of the recovery tank. With the engine cold, the level should be at the FULL COLD or between the FULL HOT and ADD level. When the engine is at normal operating temperatures, the coolant level should be at the FULL HOT or HOT level. Only add coolant to bring the system to the proper level.

DRAIN, FLUSH & REFILL

▶ See Figures 132, 133, 134, 135 and 136

1. Remove the radiator and recovery tank caps. Run the engine until the upper radiator hose gets hot. This means that the thermostat is open and the coolant is flowing through the system.
2. Turn the engine off and place a large container under the radiator. Open the drain valve at the bottom of the radiator. Open the block drain plugs to speed up the draining process, if so equipped.

Fig. 129 If necessary, add coolant through the expansion tank

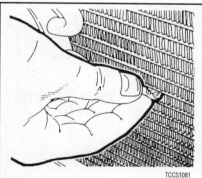

Fig. 130 Periodically remove all debris from the radiator fins

Fig. 131 Cooling systems should be pressure tested for leaks periodically

Fig. 132 If equipped, remove the splash shield to access the drain plug

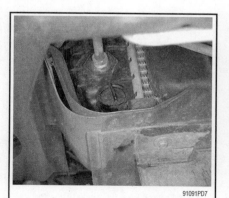

Fig. 133 Loosen the drain plug . . .

Fig. 134 . . . and drain the coolant into a container

Fig. 135 Remove the cap to fill the radiator with coolant

Fig. 136 When installing the cap, make sure the arrows align with the overflow hose

3. Close the drain valves and add water until the system is full. Repeat the draining and filling process several times, until the liquid is nearly colorless.

4. After the last draining, fill the system with the proper mixture of coolant and water. Run the engine until the system is hot and add coolant, if necessary.

Master Cylinder

FLUID RECOMMENDATION

When adding or replacing the brake fluid, always use a top quality fluid, such as Delco Supreme II or DOT-3. DO NOT allow the brake fluid container or master cylinder reservoir to remain open for long periods of time; brake fluid absorbs moisture from the air, reducing its effectiveness and causing corrosion in the lines. General Motors recommends that silicone brake fluid (DOT 5) should NOT be used in the brake system. Damage to the rubber parts may result.

Fig. 137 Use a cloth to clean the dirt and debris from the cover

Fig. 139 Use only the proper fluid

FLUID LEVEL CHECK

▶ See Figures 137 and 138

The master cylinder (located in the left rear section of the engine compartment) consists of an aluminum body and a translucent nylon reservoir with minimum fill indicators. The fluid level of the reservoirs should be kept near the top of the observation windows.

✳ WARNING

Avoid spilling brake fluid on any of the vehicles painted surfaces, wiring cables or electrical connectors. Brake fluid will damage paint and electrical connections. If any fluid is spilled on the vehicle, flush the area with water to lessen the damage.

Any sudden decrease in the fluid level indicates a possible leak in the system and should be checked out immediately.

Power Steering Pump

FLUID RECOMMENDATION

▶ See Figure 139

When filling or replacing the fluid of the power steering pump reservoir, use GM part #1050017 (or equivalent) power steering fluid only. Automatic transmission fluid may cause damage to the internal power steering components.

LEVEL CHECK

▶ See Figures 140 and 141

Power steering fluid level should be checked at least once every 12 months or 7,500 miles. To prevent possible overfilling, check the fluid level only when

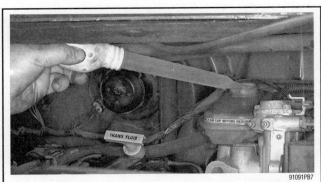

Fig. 138 Add brake fluid until the proper level is reached, according to the marks on the side of the reservoir. A turkey baster is helpful here

Fig. 140 Remove the cap from the reservoir

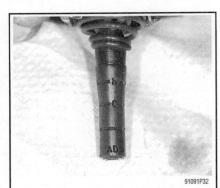

Fig. 141 The levels are clearly marked on the dipstick

the fluid has warmed to operating temperatures and the wheels are turned straight ahead. If the level is low, fill the pump reservoir until the fluid level measures "full" on the reservoir dipstick. Low fluid level usually produces a moaning sound as the wheels are turned (especially when standing still or parking) and increases steering wheel effort.

Chassis Greasing

Chassis greasing can be performed with a pressurized grease gun or by using a hand-operated grease gun. Wipe the grease fittings clean before greasing in order to prevent the possibility of forcing any dirt into the component. Do not over grease the components; because damage may occur to the grease seals.

Body Lubrication

HOOD LATCH AND HINGES

Clean the latch surfaces and apply clean engine oil or all-purpose lithium grease to the latch pilot bolts, spring anchor and hood hinges as well. Use chassis grease to lubricate all the pivot points in the latch release mechanism.

DOOR HINGES

The gas tank filler door, front door hinges, rear tailgate hinges, and sliding door rollers should be wiped clean and lubricated with clean engine oil, Silicone spray also works well on these parts, but must be applied more often. Use engine oil to lubricate the tailgate lock mechanism and the lock bolt and striker. The door lock cylinders can be lubricated easily with a silicone spray or one of the many dry penetrating lubricants commercially available.

The door weatherstrips may be lubricated using silicone type grease. Apply a thin film using a clean cloth.

PARKING BRAKE LINKAGE

Use chassis grease on the parking brake cable where it contacts the guides, links, levers, and pulleys.

Do not lubricate the parking brake cables. Lubrication destroys the plastic coating on the cables.

JUMP STARTING

▶ See Figure 142

Whenever a vehicle is jump started, precautions must be followed in order to prevent the possibility of personal injury. Remember that batteries contain a small amount of explosive hydrogen gas which is a by product of battery charging. Sparks should always be avoided when working around batteries, especially when attaching jumper cables. To minimize the possibility of accidental sparks, follow the procedure carefully.

✳✳ WARNING

NEVER hook up the batteries in a series circuit or the entire electrical system will go up in smoke,, including the starter!

Vehicles equipped with a diesel engine may use two 12 volt batteries. If so, the batteries are connected in a parallel circuit (positive terminal to positive terminal, negative terminal to negative terminal). Hooking the batteries up in parallel circuit increases battery cranking power without increasing total battery voltage output. Out put remains at 12 volts. On the other hand, hooking two 12 volt batteries up in a series circuit (positive terminal to negative terminal, positive terminal to negative terminal) increases total battery output to 24 volts (12 volts plus 12 volts).

Precautions

1. Be sure both batteries are of the same voltage.
2. Be sure both batteries are of the same polarity (have the same grounded terminal).
3. Be sure the vehicles are not touching.
4. Be sure the vent cap holes are not obstructed.
5. Do not smoke or allow sparks around the battery.
6. In cold weather, check for frozen electrolyte in the battery. Do not jump start a frozen battery.
7. Do not allow electrolyte on your skin or clothing.
8. Be sure the electrolyte is not frozen.

✳✳ CAUTION

Make certain that the ignition key, in the vehicle with the dead battery, is in the OFF position. Connecting cables to vehicles with onboard computers will result in computer destruction if the key is not in the OFF position.

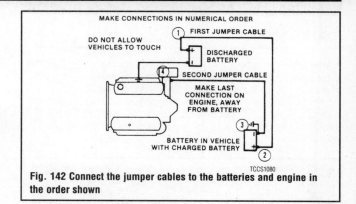

Fig. 142 Connect the jumper cables to the batteries and engine in the order shown

Jump Starting Procedure

1. Determine voltages of the two batteries; they must be the same.
2. Bring the starting vehicle close (they must not touch) so that the batteries can be reached easily.
3. Turn off all accessories and both engines. Put both vehicles in Neutral or Park and set the parking brake.
4. Cover the cell caps with a rag—do not cover terminals.
5. If the terminals on the run-down battery are heavily corroded, clean them.
6. Identify the positive and negative posts on both batteries and connect the cables in the order shown.
7. Start the engine of the starting vehicle and run it at a moderate speed for a few minutes to allow the dead battery to receive an initial charge. On the dead car, switch on the blower motor to high speed, this should absorb any electrical spike created by the initial, sudden draw of the starter.
8. Try to start the car with the dead battery. Crank it for no more than 10 seconds at a time and let it cool for 20 seconds in between tries.
9. If it doesn't start in 3 tries, there is something else wrong.
10. Disconnect the cables in the reverse order.
11. Replace the cell covers and dispose of the rags.

✳✳ CAUTION

Br very careful to keep the jumper cables away from moving parts (cooling fan, belts, etc.) on both engines.

JACKING

▶ **See Figures 143, 144, 145 and 146**

The standard jack utilizes slots in the rocker panels to raise and lower the vehicle. Do not attempt to use the jack on any portion of the vehicle other than specified by the vehicle manufacturer. The jack supplied with the car should never be used for any service operation other than tire changing. Never go under a car that is supported by a jack only. Always block the wheels when changing tires.

The service operations in this book often require that one end or the other, or both, of the car be raised and safely supported. The ideal method, of course, would be a hydraulic hoist. Since this is beyond the resource and requirement of the do-it-yourselfer, a garage or floorjack will suffice for the procedures in this guide.

Two sturdy jackstands should be acquired if you intend to work under the car at any time. An alternate method of raising the car would be drive-on ramps. These are available commercially or can be fabricated from heavy boards or steel. Be sure to block the wheels when using ramps. Never use concrete blocks to support the car. They may break if the load is not evenly distributed.

Regardless of the method of jacking or hoisting the car, there are only certain areas of the undercarriage and suspension you can safely use to support it. See the illustration and make sure that only the frame areas are used. In addition, be especially careful that you do not damage the catalytic converter. Remember that various cross braces and supports on a lift can sometimes-contact low hanging parts of a car.

Jacking Precautions

The following safety points cannot be overemphasized:
- Always block the opposite wheels or wheels to keep the vehicle from rolling off the jack.
- When raising the front of the vehicle, firmly apply the parking brake.
- When the drive wheels are to remain on the ground, leave the vehicle in park to help prevent it from rolling.
- Always use jackstands to support the vehicle when you are working underneath . Place the stands beneath the vehicle's jacking brackets. Before climbing underneath, rock the vehicle a bit to make sure it is firmly supported.
- Never place the jack under the radiator, engine or transmission components, severe and extensive damage will result when he jack is raised• Additionally, never jack under the floorpan or bodywork.

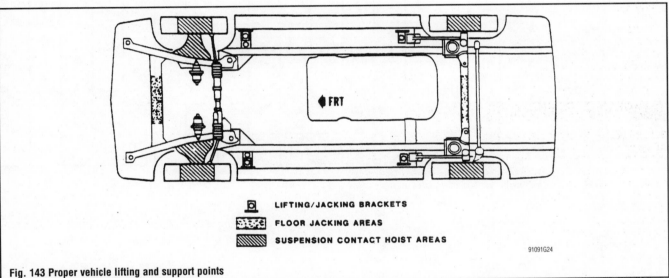

LIFTING/JACKING BRACKETS
FLOOR JACKING AREAS
SUSPENSION CONTACT HOIST AREAS

91091G24

Fig. 143 Proper vehicle lifting and support points

Fig. 144 Raise the front of the vehicle from the crossmember

Fig. 145 Raise the rear of the vehicle from the axle

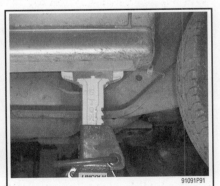

Fig. 146 Properly position the jackstands in the indicated locations

MANUFACTURER RECOMMENDED NORMAL MAINTENANCE INTERVALS

VEHICLE MAINTENANCE INTERVAL

Component		Miles (x1000) 7.5	15	22.5	30	37.5	45	52.5	60	67.5	75	82.5	90	97.5	105	112.5	120
		km (x1000) 12.5	25	37.5	50	62.5	75	87.5	100	112.5	125	137.5	150	162.5	175	187.5	200
Engine oil and filter	Replace	✓	✓	✓	✓	✓	✓	✓	✓	✓	✓	✓	✓	✓	✓	✓	✓
Chassis	Lubricate	✓	✓	✓	✓	✓	✓	✓	✓	✓	✓	✓	✓	✓	✓	✓	✓
Tires	Rotate	✓		✓		✓		✓		✓		✓		✓		✓	
Air cleaner	Replace				✓				✓				✓				✓
Spark plugs ①	Replace														✓		
Drive belts	Inspect				✓				✓				✓				✓
Cooling system	Inspect													✓			
Coolant	Replace													✓			
PCV valve	Replace				✓				✓				✓				✓
Automatic transaxle fluid	Replace							✓							✓		
EGR system	Inspect								✓								✓
Brake linings and drums	Inspect	✓		✓		✓		✓		✓		✓		✓		✓	
Brake pads and rotors	Inspect	✓		✓		✓		✓		✓		✓		✓		✓	
Spark plug wires	Inspect													✓			
CV joint boots	Inspect		✓		✓		✓		✓		✓		✓		✓		✓
Brake line hoses and connections	Inspect	✓		✓		✓		✓		✓		✓		✓		✓	
Front ball joints	Inspect				✓				✓				✓				✓
Fuel tank, cap, and lines	Inspect				✓				✓				✓				✓
Steering linkage operation	Inspect				✓				✓				✓				✓

NOTE: Perform maintenace at the same intervals for mileage beyond that on this chart

① Spark plug replacement is at 100,000 miles (160,900 km)

91091C04

MANUFACTURER RECOMMENDED SEVERE MAINTENANCE INTERVALS

VEHICLE MAINTENANCE INTERVAL

Component	Service	Miles (x1000) 3	6	9	12	15	18	21	24	27	30	33	36	39	42	45	48	51	54	57	60
		km (x1000) 5	10	15	20	25	30	35	40	45	50	55	60	65	70	75	80	85	90	95	100
Engine oil and filter	Replace	✓	✓	✓	✓	✓	✓	✓	✓	✓	✓	✓	✓	✓	✓	✓	✓	✓	✓	✓	✓
Chassis	Lubricate		✓		✓		✓		✓		✓		✓		✓		✓		✓		✓
Tires	Rotate		✓				✓				✓				✓				✓		
Air cleaner	Replace					✓					✓					✓					✓
Spark plugs ①	Replace																				
Drive belts	Inspect										✓										✓
Cooling system	Inspect										✓										✓
Coolant	Replace																				✓
PCV valve	Replace										✓										✓
Automatic transaxle fluid	Replace										✓										✓
EGR system	Inspect										✓										✓
Brake linings and drums	Inspect		✓				✓				✓				✓				✓		
Brake pads and rotors	Inspect		✓				✓				✓				✓				✓		
Spark plug wires	Inspect										✓										✓
CV joint boots	Inspect		✓		✓		✓		✓		✓		✓		✓		✓		✓		✓
Brake line hoses and connections	Inspect		✓				✓				✓				✓				✓		
Front ball joints	Inspect		✓		✓		✓		✓		✓		✓		✓		✓		✓		✓
Fuel tank, cap, and lines	Inspect										✓										✓
Steering linkage operation	Inspect		✓		✓		✓		✓		✓		✓		✓		✓		✓		✓

NOTE: Perform maintenace at the same intervals for mileage beyond that on this chart
① Spark plug replacement is at 100,000 miles (160,900 km)

91091C05

CAPACITIES

Year	Model	Engine ID/VIN	Engine Displacement Liters (cc)	Engine Oil with Filter (qts.)	Transmission (qts.) 4-Spd	5-Spd	Auto.		Transfer Case (pts.)	Drive Axle Front (pts.)	Rear (pts.)	Standrd Fuel Tank (gal.)	Cooling System (qts.)
1990	Lumina	D	3.1 (3130)	4.5	—	—	7.0	①	—	—	—	20.0	12.4
	Transport	D	3.1 (3130)	4.5	—	—	7.0	①	—	—	—	20.0	12.4
	Silhouette	D	3.1 (3130)	4.5	—	—	7.0	①	—	—	—	20.0	12.4
1991	Lumina	D	3.1 (3130)	4.5	—	—	7.0	①	—	—	—	20.0	12.4
	Transport	D	3.1 (3130)	4.5	—	—	7.0	①	—	—	—	20.0	12.4
	Silhouette	D	3.1 (3130)	4.5	—	—	7.0	①	—	—	—	20.0	12.4
1992	Lumina	D	3.1 (3130)	4.5	—	—	7.0	①	—	—	—	20.0	12.4
	Transport	D	3.1 (3130)	4.5	—	—	7.0	①	—	—	—	20.0	12.4
	Silhouette	D	3.1 (3130)	4.5	—	—	7.0	①	—	—	—	20.0	12.4
	Lumina	L	3.8 (3785)	4.5	—	—	8.0	①	—	—	—	20.0	12.4
	Transport	L	3.8 (3785)	4.5	—	—	8.0	①	—	—	—	20.0	12.4
	Silhouette	L	3.8 (3785)	4.5	—	—	8.0	①	—	—	—	20.0	12.4
1993	Lumina	D	3.1 (3130)	4.5	—	—	7.0	①	—	—	—	20.0	12.4
	Transport	D	3.1 (3130)	4.5	—	—	7.0	①	—	—	—	20.0	12.4
	Silhouette	D	3.1 (3130)	4.5	—	—	7.0	①	—	—	—	20.0	12.4
	Lumina	L	3.8 (3785)	4.5	—	—	8.0	①	—	—	—	20.0	12.4
	Transport	L	3.8 (3785)	4.5	—	—	8.0	①	—	—	—	20.0	12.4
	Silhouette	L	3.8 (3785)	4.5	—	—	8.0	①	—	—	—	20.0	12.4
1994	Lumina	D	3.1 (3130)	4.5	—	—	7.0	①	—	—	—	20.0	12.5
	Transport	D	3.1 (3130)	4.5	—	—	7.0	①	—	—	—	20.0	12.5
	Silhouette	D	3.1 (3130)	4.5	—	—	7.0	①	—	—	—	20.0	12.5
	Lumina	L	3.8 (3785)	4.5	—	—	8.0	①	—	—	—	20.0	12.5
	Transport	L	3.8 (3785)	4.5	—	—	8.0	①	—	—	—	20.0	12.5
	Silhouette	L	3.8 (3785)	4.5	—	—	8.0	①	—	—	—	20.0	12.5
1995	Lumina	D	3.1 (3130)	4.5	—	—	7.0	①	—	—	—	20.0	13.4
	Transport	D	3.1 (3130)	4.5	—	—	7.0	①	—	—	—	20.0	13.4
	Silhouette	D	3.1 (3130)	4.5	—	—	7.0	①	—	—	—	20.0	13.4
	Lumina	L	3.8 (3785)	4.5	—	—	8.0	①	—	—	—	20.0	11.4
	Transport	L	3.8 (3785)	4.5	—	—	8.0	①	—	—	—	20.0	11.4
	Silhouette	L	3.8 (3785)	4.5	—	—	8.0	①	—	—	—	20.0	11.4
1996	Lumina	E	3.4 (3350)	4.5	—	—	8.0	①	—	—	—	20.0	②
	Transport	E	3.4 (3350)	4.5	—	—	8.0	①	—	—	—	20.0	②
	Silhouette	E	3.4 (3350)	4.5	—	—	8.0	①	—	—	—	20.0	②
1997	Venture	E	3.4 (3350)	4.5	—	—	8.0	①	—	—	—	20.0	②
	Transport	E	3.4 (3350)	4.5	—	—	8.0	①	—	—	—	20.0	②
	Silhouette	E	3.4 (3350)	4.5	—	—	8.0	①	—	—	—	20.0	②
1998	Venture	E	3.4 (3350)	4.5	—	—	8.0	①	—	—	—	20.0	②
	Transport	E	3.4 (3350)	4.5	—	—	8.0	①	—	—	—	20.0	②
	Silhouette	E	3.4 (3350)	4.5	—	—	8.0	①	—	—	—	20.0	②
1999	Venture	E	3.4 (3350)	4.5	—	—	8.0	①	—	—	—	20.0	②
	Transport	E	3.4 (3350)	4.5	—	—	8.0	①	—	—	—	20.0	②
	Silhouette	E	3.4 (3350)	4.5	—	—	8.0	①	—	—	—	20.0	②

NOTE: All capacities are approximate. Add fluid gradually and ensure a proper fluid level is obtained.

① Includes the differential

② With rear heater: 13.5 qts.
Without rear heater: 11.8 qts.

91091C06

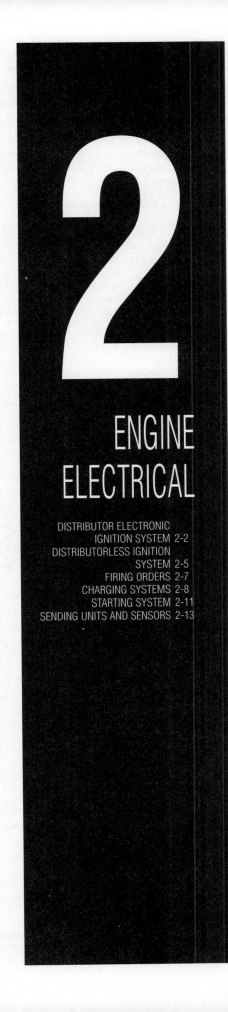

2

ENGINE ELECTRICAL

DISTRIBUTOR ELECTRONIC IGNITION SYSTEM

➡For information on understanding electricity and troubleshooting electrical circuits, please refer to Section 6 of this manual.

General Information

♦ See Figure 1

➡This ignition system is used on the 3.1L engine only.

The Ignition Coil (IC) distributor has an internal magnetic pick-up assembly that contains a permanent magnet, a pole piece with internal teeth and a pick-up coil. When the teeth of the timer core, rotating inside the pole piece, line up with the pole piece, an induced voltage in the pick-up coil signals the electronic module to trigger the coil primary circuit. The primary current decreases and a high voltage is induced in the ignition coil secondary winding. This voltage is directed through the distributor rotor and secondary leads to fire the spark plugs. This system is the only one that has a mechanical adjustment for base timing.

All spark timing changes in the EST distributor are done electronically by the Electronic Control Module (ECM), which monitors information from various engine sensors, computes the desired spark timing and signals the distributor to change the timing accordingly. A back-up spark advance system is incorporated to signal the ignition module n case of (ECM) failure. No vacuum or mechanical advance is used.

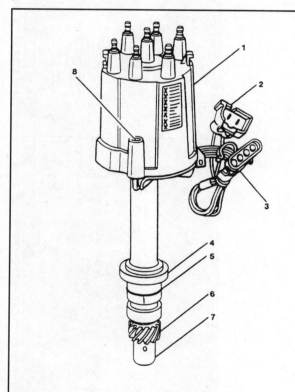

1	CAP
2	CONNECTOR, IGNITION COIL
3	CONNECTOR, ECM HARNESS
4	HOUSING
5	O-RING
6	GEAR
7	SHAFT
8	SCREW

91092G01

Fig. 1 Distributor assembly found on the 3.1L engine

Diagnosis and Testing

SERVICE PRECAUTIONS

The HEI coil secondary voltage output capabilities can exceed 40,000 volts. Avoid body contact with the HEI high voltage secondary components when the engine is running, or personal injury may result.

➡To avoid damage to the ECM or other ignition system components, do not use electrical test equipment such as battery or AC powered voltmeter, ohmmeter, etc. or any type of tester other than specified.

- When making compression checks, disconnect the ignition switch feed wire at the distributor.
- Never allow the tachometer terminal to touch ground, as damage to the module and/or ignition coil can result.
- To prevent Electrostatic Discharge damage, when working with the ECM, do not touch the connector pins or soldered components on the circuit board.
- When handling a PROM, CAL-PAK or MEM-CAL, do not touch the component leads. Also, do not remove the integrated circuit from the carrier.
- Never allow welding cables to lie on, near or across any vehicle electrical wiring.
- Leave new components and modules in the shipping package until ready to install them.
- When performing electrical tests on the system, use a high impedance multimeter, digital voltmeter.
- Never pierce a high tension lead or boot for any testing purpose; otherwise, future problems are guaranteed.

SECONDARY SPARK TEST

It is imperative to check the secondary ignition circuit first. If the secondary circuit checks out properly, then the engine condition is probably not the fault of the ignition system. To check the secondary ignition system, perform a simple spark test.

1. Remove one of the plug wires and insert some sort of extension in the plug socket. An old spark plug with the ground electrode removed makes a good extension.
2. Hold the wire and extension about ⁴in. (0.25mm) away from the block and crank the engine.
3. If a normal spark occurs, then the problem is most likely not in the ignition system. Check for fuel system problems, or fouled spark plugs.
4. If, however, there is no spark or a weak spark, then test the ignition coil and the camshaft and crankshaft position sensors. For testing the camshaft and crankshaft position sensors, refer to Section 4.

IGNITION SYSTEM CHECK

Engine Cranks But Will Not Run

1. Check that the fuel quantity is OK.
2. Turn the ignition switch ON. Verify that the SERVICE ENGINE SOON light is ON.
3. Install the scan tool and check the following:
   - Throttle Position Sensor (TPS): if over 2.5 volts, at closed throttle, check TPS for intermittent, open or short to ground, or faulty TPS.
   - Coolant: if less than 86°F (30°C), check Coolant Temperature Sensor (CTS) for intermittent, open or short to ground, or faulty CTS.
4. Connect spark checker, J 26792 or equivalent, and check for spark while cranking. Check at least 2 wires.
   a. If spark occurs, reconnect the spark plug wires and check for fuel spray at the injector(s) while cranking. If no spark is visible, inspect the system for a trouble code. Refer to Section 4.
   b. If no spark occurs, check for battery voltage to the ignition system. If OK, use the ignition diagnosis chart.

Electronic Spark Timing (EST) Circuit

1. Clear any codes which are present.
2. Idle the engine for approximately 1 minute or until Code 42 sets. If Code 42 does not set, Code 42 is intermittent.
3. If Code 42 sets, turn the ignition **OFF** , then disengage the ECM connectors.
   a. Turn the ignition switch **ON**.
   b. Using an ohmmeter to ground, probe the ECM harness connector, at the EST circuit. Place the ohmmeter selector switch in the 1000–2000 ohms range. The meter should read less than 1000 ohms.
4. If not, check for a faulty connection, open circuit or faulty ignition module.
5. If OK, probe the bypass circuit with a test light to battery voltage.
6. If the test light is ON, disconnect the ignition 4-way connector and observe the test light.
   a. If the test light goes OFF, the problem is a faulty ignition module.
   b. If the test light stays ON, the bypass circuit is shorted to ground.
7. If the test light remains OFF, from Step 5, again probe the bypass circuit with the test light connected to battery voltage, and the ohmmeter still connected to the EST circuit and ground. As the test light contacts the bypass circuit, resistance should switch from under 1000 to over 2000 ohms.
   a. If it does, reconnect the ECM and idle the engine for approximately 1 minute or until Code 42 sets. If Code 42 sets, it is a faulty ECM.
   b. If not, Code 42 is intermittent.
8. If the results are not as indicated in Step 7, disconnect the distributor 4-way connector. With the ohmmeter still connected to the bypass circuit, resistance should have gone high (open circuit).
9. If not, the EST circuit is shorted to ground.
10. If OK, the bypass circuit is open, faulty connections or faulty ignition module.

➡ **When the problem has been corrected, clear codes and confirm Closed Loop operation and no SERVICE ENGINE SOON light.**

Ignition Coil

TESTING

◢ **See Figure 2**

1. Disconnect the negative battery cable.
2. Unplug the two electrical connectors from the coil

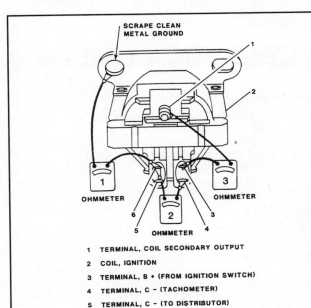

1. TERMINAL, COIL SECONDARY OUTPUT
2. COIL, IGNITION
3. TERMINAL, B + (FROM IGNITION SWITCH)
4. TERMINAL, C – (TACHOMETER)
5. TERMINAL, C – (TO DISTRIBUTOR)
6. TERMINAL, B + (TO DISTRIBUTOR)

91092G03

Fig. 2 To test the coil, connect the ohmmeter as shown

3. Using an ohmmeter, check the ignition coil as follows:
   Step 1
   • Test for short to ground between B+ (to distributor) terminal and ground.
   • Use the high scale on the meter, should read infinity (open circuit).
   • Any reading other than infinity means the coil is bad and needs replacing
   Step 2
   • Test for open circuits between C-(tach) terminal and C-(to distributor) terminals.
   • This test is for continuity. Reading should usually be less than 5 ohms (on the low scale). If not replace the coil.
   Step 3
   • Test for an open between B+ (from the ignition switch) terminal and secondary output terminal (coil wire terminal).
   • Read the high scale on the meter. Should have some resistance, (about 7K ohms) should not read infinity; if it does, install a new coil.
4. Reconnect the two electrical connectors onto the coil.
5. Connect the negative battery cable.

REMOVAL & INSTALLATION

◢ **See Figure 3**

1. Disconnect the secondary lead (coil wire). Twist the boot ¼ turn each way, while tugging on the boot. Do not pull on the wire.
2. Disconnect the primary electrical connectors (do not pry on latch/lock with a screwdriver, as it may break).
3. Remove the ignition coil mounting screw and nuts.
4. Remove the ignition coil.
   To install:
5. Install the screws and nuts to secure the coil.
6. Reconnect the primary electrical connectors. Assure that they are fully seated and latched.
7. Install the secondary lead (coil wire). Make sure it is fully seated and secured on the coil tower.

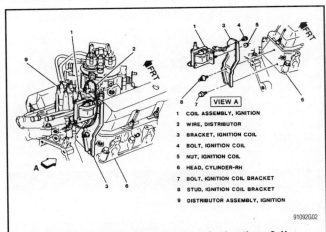

1. COIL ASSEMBLY, IGNITION
2. WIRE, DISTRIBUTOR
3. BRACKET, IGNITION COIL
4. BOLT, IGNITION COIL
5. NUT, IGNITION COIL
6. HEAD, CYLINDER-RH
7. BOLT, IGNITION COIL BRACKET
8. STUD, IGNITION COIL BRACKET
9. DISTRIBUTOR ASSEMBLY, IGNITION

91092G02

Fig. 3 Diagram shows ignition coil and bracket location—3.1L Engine

Ignition Module

REMOVAL & INSTALLATION

◢ **See Figure 4**

1. Remove the negative battery cable
2. Remove the air cleaner assembly
3. Remove the distributor cap by simultaneously depressing and rotating screws counterclockwise 180°. Lift the cap and wire assembly to disengage it from the housing, and move it aside.

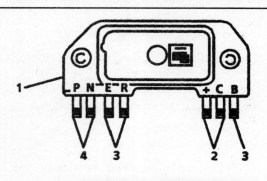

1 **DISTRIBUTOR IGNITION MODULE**

2 **IGNITION COIL TERMINALS**

3 **IC TERMINALS**

4 **PICK-UP COIL TERMINALS**

91092G12

Fig. 4 Distributor ignition module

4. Carefully remove the screws retaining the rotor to the shaft. Be sure to note the rotor position for reinstallation.

5. Remove the electrical connectors from the module, being careful not to break any connector locks.

6. Remove the two screws holding the module to the distributor base, and lift the module from the distributor housing.

➥Do not wipe the grease from the backside of the module or the distributor base, if the same module is going to be reinstalled. If a new module is going to be installed, a package of silicone grease will be included with it. Spread the grease on the metal face of the module and on the distributor base where the module seats. This grease is used for module cooling. The grease used is the same dielectric compound used on spark plug boots.

To install:

7. Apply a thin film of dielectric compound to the base of the module (metal back).

8. Attach the module to the distributor housing using the two attaching screws.

9. Attach the electrical connectors to the module.

10. Seat the rotor on the shaft and secure it with two screws.

11. Replace the distributor cap by simultaneously depressing and rotating the screws 180° clockwise.

12. Install the air cleaner assembly

13. Connect the negative battery cable.

Distributor

REMOVAL

➥If it becomes necessary to replace the distributor, it is critical to maintain proper engine timing. Do not crank the engine after removing the distributor. To facilitate ease of installation: Bring #1 cylinder to TDC on the compression stroke. The timing marks on the damper and indicator block will be aligned. Make sure the rotor is pointing to the #1 spark tower in the cap.

1. Disconnect the negative battery cable.

2. Remove the air cleaner assembly.

3. Unplug the electrical connectors from the ignition coil and ECM harness. (DO NOT use a screwdriver or hammer to release the locking tabs.)

4. Remove the distributor cap by simultaneously pushing down and turning the two screws counterclockwise 180°. Move the cap out of the way.

5. If necessary, remove secondary wires from cap. Note the position of each wire for proper installation.

6. Remove the distributor clamp bolt and hold-down.

a. Scribe an alignment mark on the distributor housing and a corre-

sponding mark on the engine to denote distributor placement, when installed.

b. Mark the position of the rotor, then pull the distributor up gently, until the rotor just stops turning counterclockwise, mark the new position of the rotor against the housing. Remove the distributor.

INSTALLATION

Engine Not Disturbed

1. Align the rotor with the last mark made on distributor housing.

2. Install distributor housing into the engine being careful to keep the scribe mark on housing and on block aligned.

3. As distributor is installed into the block, the rotor will turn clockwise to the first mark and stop as the distributor seats.

➥At this point, the rotor should be aligned with the first mark, and the mark scribed on the distributor housing should be aligned with the mark on the block.

4. Reconnect the electrical connectors

5. Install the distributor cap by seating the cap onto the distributor housing, then simultaneously push down and turn the mounting screws 180°

6. Install the air cleaner assembly

7. Connect the negative battery cable

8. Start engine and check the timing.

Engine Disturbed

➥If the engine was accidentally cranked after the distributor was removed, the following procedure can be used for installing the distributor:

1. Remove No. 1 spark plug.

2. Place a finger over the No. 1 spark plug and crank the engine slowly until compression is felt.

3. Align the timing mark on the crankshaft pulley to the "0" on the engine timing indicator block. It may be necessary to use a breaker bar and socket on the crankshaft bolt to turn the engine.

4. Turn the rotor to point between the #1 and #6 spark plug towers on the distributor cap.

5. Reconnect the electrical connectors

6. Install the distributor cap by seating the cap onto the distributor housing, then simultaneously push down and turn the mounting screws 180°.

7. Install the air cleaner assembly

8. Connect the negative battery cable.

9. Start engine and check the timing.

Pick Up Coil

TESTING

1. Remove the rotor and pickup coil leads from the module.

2. Using an ohmmeter, test as follows:

a. Connect 1 lead of the ohmmeter between the distributor housing and 1 of the pickup coil lead. Meter should read infinity. Flex the leads by hand while observing the ohmmeter, to check for intermittent opens.

b. Connect the ohmmeter between leads between both of the pickup coil leads. Meter should read a steady value between 500–1500 ohms.

REMOVAL & INSTALLATION

If it becomes necessary to replace the pick-up coil, thoroughly inspect the distributor once it is removed from the engine. If the shaft seems to bind or does not spin freely; if there is a great deal of sludge build up on the shaft, if any of the teeth on the distributor gear are chipped, if there is any reason to question the distributor in addition to replacing the pick-up coil; then replace the distributor.

1. Remove the distributor from the engine.

2. Once removed, mark the shaft and the driven gear for proper alignment during installation.

3. Drive the roll pin from the shaft, using a pin punch.

4. Press the driven gear from the shaft. Note the position of the gear for reassembly.

5. Remove the washers from the shaft, noting their order of assembly.

6. Slide the shaft from the housing; clean the shaft if necessary using solvent and/or emery paper.

7. Disconnect the pick-up coil electrical connector from the module .

8. Remove the "C" retainer that holds the pick-up in the distributor housing.

9. Remove the pick-up from the distributor housing .

To install:

10. Install the pick-up coil into the housing and secure it with the "C" clip retainer

11. Connect the pick-up coil electrical connector to the module , slide the shaft into the housing.

12. Slide the washers, in their proper order, back onto the bottom of the shaft

13. Align the marks on the driven gear, housing and shaft assembly and drive or press the gear onto the shaft

14. Install the roll pin into the shaft. Make sure it is centered, and not sticking out on either side.

15. Install the rotor onto the shaft, and install the distributor into the engine following the procedure given in this section.

16. Install the distributor cap and wires (if removed).

17. Reset the timing.

DISTRIBUTORLESS IGNITION SYSTEM

General Information

The electronic ignition system controls fuel combustion by providing a spark to ignite the compressed air/fuel mixture at the correct time. To provide optimum engine performance, fuel economy, and control of exhaust emissions, the PCM controls the spark advance of the ignition system. Electronic ignition has the following advantages over a mechanical distributor system:

- No moving parts.
- Less maintenance.
- Remote mounting capability.
- No mechanical load on the engine.
- More coil cool down time between firing events.
- Elimination of mechanical timing adjustments.
- Increased available ignition coil saturation time.

The electronic ignition system does not use the conventional distributor and coil. The ignition system consists of three ignition coils, an ignition control module, a dual Hall-effect crankshaft position sensor, an engine crankshaft balancer with interrupter rings attached to the rear, related connecting wires, and the Ignition control (IC) and fuel metering portion of the PCM.

There are a number of circuits that affect ignition control. The PCM reads the information supplied by these circuits to properly control ignition timing. The PCM receives the following information:

- Engine load (manifold pressure or vacuum)
- Atmospheric (barometric) pressure
- Engine temperature
- Intake air temperature
- Crankshaft position
- Engine speed (RPM)

Conventional coils have one end of the secondary winding connected to the engine ground. In this ignition system, neither end of the secondary winding is grounded. Instead, each end of a coils secondary winding is attached to a spark plug. Each cylinder is paired with its opposing cylinder in the firing order (1/4,2/5,3/6).These plugs are on companion cylinders. That means that while one cylinder is at TDC on the compression stroke, the companion cylinder is at TDC on the exhaust stroke. When the coil discharges, both plugs, on the same circuit, fire at the same time. The cylinder on compression is the event cylinder; the cylinder on exhaust is the waste cylinder. The cylinder on the compression stroke requires more voltage to fire than does the cylinder on the exhaust stroke. This method is called a "waste" spark ignition system.

The ignition coil design is improved, with saturation time and primary current flow increased. This redesign of the system allows higher secondary voltage to be available from the ignition coils—greater than 40kv. (40,000 volts) at any engine RPM. Secondary voltage requirements are very high with an open spark plug or spark plug wire. The ignition coil has enough reserve energy to fire the plug that is still connected, at idle, but the coil may not fire the spark plug under high engine load. A more noticeable misfire may be evident under load, both spark plugs may then be misfiring. Running for an extended period like this, will burn out the coil.

The system on the 3400 engine uses a coil pack with one ignition coil for each two cylinders in the engine. Mounted under the ignition coils on each system is an ignition control module (ICM) that performs ignition coil switching functions and interacts with the Powertrain Control module (PCM) to optimize ignition system operation.

Three twin-tower ignition coils are individually mounted to the ignition con-trol module. Each coil provides spark for two plugs simultaneously (waste spark distribution). Each coil is serviced separately. Two terminals connect each coil pack to the module. Each coil is provided a fused ignition feed. The other terminal at each coil is individually connected to the module, which will energize one coil at a time by completing and interrupting the primary circuit ground path to each coil at the proper time.

The ignition control module determines the correct ignition coil firing sequence, based on 7X pulses. This coil sequencing occurs at start-up. After the engine is running, the module determines the sequence, and continues triggering the ignition coils in proper sequence. It sends the 3X-crankshaft reference (fuel control) signal to the PCM. The PCM determines engine RPM from this signal. This signal is also used by the PCM to determine crankshaft speed for Ignition Control (IC) spark advance calculations. The 3X-reference signal sent to the PCM by the ignition control module is an on-off pulse occurring 3 times per crankshaft revolution.

Diagnosis and Testing

SECONDARY SPARK TEST

It is imperative to check the secondary ignition circuit first. If the secondary circuit checks out properly, then the engine condition is probably not the fault of the ignition system. To check the secondary ignition system, perform a simple spark test.

1. Remove one of the plug wires and insert some sort of extension in the plug socket. An old spark plug with the ground electrode removed makes a good extension.

2. Hold the wire and extension about ¼ in. (0.25mm) away from the block and crank the engine.

3. If a normal spark occurs, then the problem is most likely not in the ignition system. Check for fuel system problems, or fouled spark plugs.

4. If, however, there is no spark or a weak spark, then test the ignition coil and the camshaft and crankshaft position sensors. For testing the camshaft and crankshaft position sensors, refer to Section 4.

Ignition Coil Pack

TESTING

1. Remove the ignition coil(s).

2. Using an ohmmeter, check the resistance between the primary terminals on the underside of the coil. The resistance should be 0.50–0.90 ohms.

3. Check the resistance between the secondary terminals. It should be 5,000–8,000 ohms.

4. If the coil failed either test, replace the coil.

REMOVAL & INSTALLATION

▶ **See Figures 5, 6 and 7**

1. Tag and disconnect the spark plug wires.

2. Remove the 2 screws securing the coil to the ignition control module.

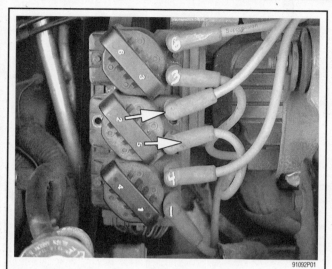

Fig. 5 Number the plug wires before removing them

Fig. 6 Remove the retainers securing the coil . . .

Fig. 7 . . . then pull the coil from the ignition module assembly

3. Remove the coil assembly by pulling straight up on the coil.

To install:

4. Install the coil assembly.

5. Install the two screws securing the coil to the ignition control module. Do not overtighten.

6. Connect the spark plug wires.

Ignition Module

REMOVAL & INSTALLATION

▶ **See Figures 8, 9, 10, 11 and 12**

1. Note the position of the spark plug wires. Remove the plug wires from the ignition coils.

2. Remove the screws securing the coil assemblies to the ignition control module.

3. Remove the coils from the ignition control module.

4. Unplug the electrical connector and remove the module assembly from the engine.

To install:

5. Reconnect the electrical connectors to the ignition control module.

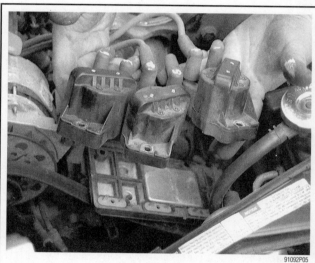

Fig. 8 Remove the coil packs from the module

Fig. 9 Separate the module from the mounting boss

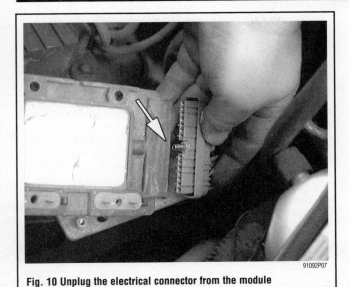

Fig. 10 Unplug the electrical connector from the module

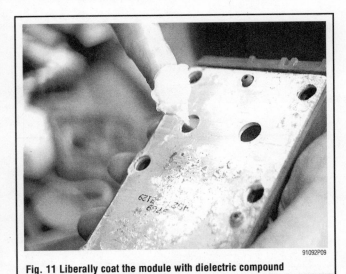

Fig. 11 Liberally coat the module with dielectric compound

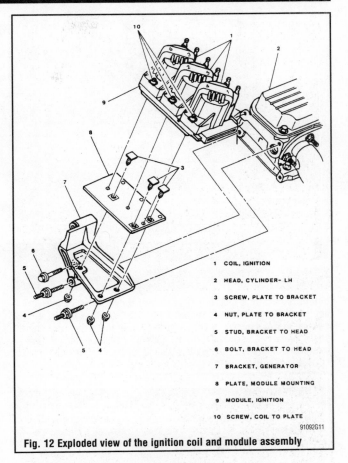

1 COIL, IGNITION

2 HEAD, CYLINDER- LH

3 SCREW, PLATE TO BRACKET

4 NUT, PLATE TO BRACKET

5 STUD, BRACKET TO HEAD

6 BOLT, BRACKET TO HEAD

7 BRACKET, GENERATOR

8 PLATE, MODULE MOUNTING

9 MODULE, IGNITION

10 SCREW, COIL TO PLATE

Fig. 12 Exploded view of the ignition coil and module assembly

6. Liberally coat the module with dielectric compound
7. Position the module assembly and coils on the engine. Tighten the mounting screws.
8. Install the spark plug wires in their proper sequence as noted in the removal procedure.

Crankshaft and Camshaft Position Sensors

Please refer to Section 4 for information on these sensors.

FIRING ORDERS

▶ See Figures 13, 14 and 15

➡ To avoid confusion, remove and tag the spark plug wires one at a time, for replacement.

If a distributor is not keyed for installation with only one orientation, it could have been removed previously and rewired. The resultant wiring would hold the correct firing order, but could change the relative placement of the plug towers in relation to the engine. For this reason, it is imperative that you label all wires before disconnecting any of them. Also, before removal, compare the current wiring with the accompanying illustrations. If the current wiring does not match, make notes in your book to reflect how your engine is wired.

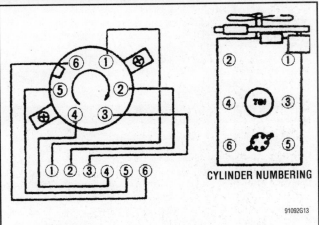

CYLINDER NUMBERING

Fig. 13 3.1L Engine
Firing Order: 1-2-3-4-5-6
Distributor Rotation: Clockwise

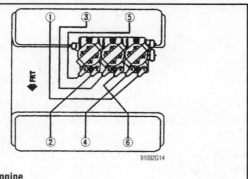

Fig. 14 3.4L Engine
Firing Order: 1-2-3-4-5-6
Distributorless Ignition

91092G14

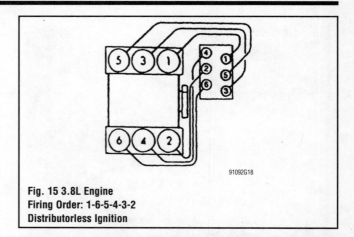

Fig. 15 3.8L Engine
Firing Order: 1-6-5-4-3-2
Distributorless Ignition

91092G18

CHARGING SYSTEMS

✱✱ CAUTION

Before removing or installing any electrical unit, or when a tool or equipment could come in contact with "live" exposed electrical terminals, disconnect the battery negative cable to help prevent personal injury and/or damage to the vehicle or components. Unless instructed otherwise, the ignition switch must be in the "OFF" or "LOCK" position.

General Information

The automotive charging system provides electrical power for operation of the vehicle's ignition and starting systems and all the electrical accessories. The battery serves as an electrical surge or storage tank, storing (in chemical form) the energy originally produced by the engine driven alternator. The system also provides a means of regulating alternator output to protect the battery from being overcharged and to avoid excessive voltage to the accessories.

There are a number of alternators offered for each application depending on the electrical load built into the vehicle. These alternators have several characteristics in common. Most of them use at least two wire connections and a ground path through the mounting bracket for operation. The battery positive "BAT" terminal MUST be connected to a battery during operation. The second required connections through the indicator lamp or voltage regulator. Both connections are necessary to turn the unit on at start-up. Three other regulator terminals are available for optional use in vehicle systems. The "P" terminal is connected to the stator and may be connected to a tachometer or other device. The "I/F" terminal provides an alternate method for turning on the alternator without going through the indicator light or external resistor, and is often used in parallel with the "L" terminal connection. The "S" terminal may be used to sense electrical system voltage somewhere else on the vehicle for voltage control. If the "S" terminal is not used, the regulator uses an internal voltage sense for control.

The alternator does NOT require periodic lubrication. The rotor shaft is mounted on ball bearings at the drive end and at the slip ring end. Each contains a permanent grease supply.

Alternator Precautions

To prevent damage to the alternator and regulator, the following precautionary measures must be taken when working with the electrical system.

- Never reverse the battery connections. Always check the battery polarity visually. This is to be done before any connections are made to ensure that all of the connections correspond to the battery ground polarity of the vehicle.
- Booster batteries must be connected properly. Make sure the positive cable of the booster battery is connected to the positive terminal of the battery that is getting the boost.
- Disconnect the battery cables before using a fast charger; the charger has a tendency to force current though the diodes in the opposite direction for which they were designed.
- Make sure the ignition switch is "OFF" when connecting or disconnecting

any electrical component, especially when equipped with an on-board computer control system.
- NEVER attempt to polarize an alternator.
- Never disconnect the voltage regulator while the engine is running, unless directed to do so for testing purposes.
- Disconnect the battery if any welding is to be done on the vehicle.
- Do not short one terminal to another or short any terminal to ground from the alternator.

Alternator

TESTING

1. Check the condition of the serpentine belt and tensioner. Replace or repair as required.
2. Check the charging system wiring for any breaks where insulation may have rubbed through, and is causing a short to ground (this may be intermittent). Also, turn the key on, engine off, the charging system indicator on the dash should light. This is the bulb check.
3. Make sure the battery is the proper one for the application, tests good and is fully charged.
4. Clean the battery cables connections at the battery. Make sure the connections between the battery cables and battery clamps are good. Reconnect the negative terminal and proceed to the next step.
5. With all electrical loads shut down, including the electric clock (if applicable), and the key off; install a test light between the positive terminal of the battery and the positive cable. If the test light lights, there is a short in the electrical system. This must be repaired before proceeding. If the light does not come on, you can proceed with the test. Install the positive battery cable.

➡ **If the vehicle is equipped with remote door locks, has an alarm system, or lights that operate in a delay mode, and the test light lights in the above test, touch the cable end to the battery post for about 10 seconds and then remove it without disconnecting the test light. If the light is now off , proceed with the test. If the light is dimmer than when first checked, repeat the procedure until the light goes out.**

6. If a battery "load" tester (adjustable carbon pile is best) is available, connect it following the instructions supplied with the tool. Install a digital multimeter to check voltage between alternator output terminal and battery negative terminal (read on a 20 volt scale). Also, install an inductive ammeter on the alternator output wire.
7. Start the vehicle, hold the engine speed to 2500 RPM, and note the voltage reading. If voltage reads no higher than battery voltage— replace the alternator. Begin the load test by turning on the "load" (adjust the carbon pile). Watch the ammeter gauge, it should go up, also watch the voltage reading, it will go down. Do not increase the load to drive the voltage reading below battery voltage. If alternator is not up to spec—replace it.
8. If a load tester is unavailable, you can still test the output of the system. Install the meters as directed and start the vehicle. Now, to increase the load on

the charging system, begin turning accessories on. Use headlights (high beams), rear defroster, air conditioner/blower on high, etc. Watch for the same type reaction on the meters. If the alternator reads weak, replace it.

9.   Test readings should be 70% of rated output.

REMOVAL & INSTALLATION

3.1L Engine

▶ **See Figure 16**

1.   Disconnect the negative battery cable.
2.   Remove the serpentine belt from the alternator pulley
3.   Remove the air cleaner assembly
4.   Disconnect the positive lead at the alternator by removing the nut
5.   Disconnect the electrical connector (PLIS) plug
6.   Remove the bolt (#1) connecting the rear brace to the generator
7.   LOOSEN the bolt (#7)retaining the rear brace to the exhaust manifold, (it is not necessary to remove it) move the brace aside.
8.   Remove the remaining alternator mounting bolts and remove the alternator.
   To install:

➡**For 3.1L (LG6) engine, where a rear brace is used, bolt installation sequence and tightening sequence are important. Use the diagram as a guide.**

9.   Position the alternator and install the pivot (long) mounting bolt (#2). Do not tighten.
10.   Install the other bracket bolt (#4), but do not tighten.
11.   Reposition the rear brace and install the bolt (#1) into the rear of alternator (do not tighten)
12.   Tighten bolt #4 to 18 ft. lbs. (25 Nm). Tighten the pivot bolt to 35 ft. lbs. (47 Nm).
13.   Tighten bolt #7 to 35 ft. lbs. (47 Nm), making sure brace is properly aligned. Tighten bolt # 1 to 18 ft. lbs. (25 Nm).
14.   Assure that tightening brace bolts does not place alternator in a bind. The pulley must spin freely.
15.   Reconnect the electrical connector— (PLIS) plug
16.   Install the battery positive lead to the output (BAT) terminal on the alternator and tighten the nut.
17.   Install the serpentine belt
18.   Install the air cleaner
19.   Connect the negative battery cable.

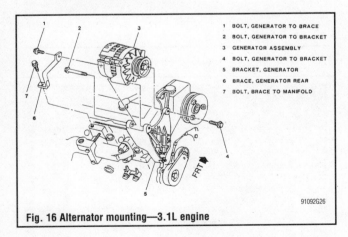

1	BOLT, GENERATOR TO BRACE
2	BOLT, GENERATOR TO BRACKET
3	GENERATOR ASSEMBLY
4	BOLT, GENERATOR TO BRACKET
5	BRACKET, GENERATOR
6	BRACE, GENERATOR REAR
7	BOLT, BRACE TO MANIFOLD

91092G26

Fig. 16 Alternator mounting—3.1L engine

3.4L Engine

➡**There are two different alternators used on the 3.4L engine. Domestic vehicles with rear air conditioning require the larger output Delphi CS144 (140AMP) KG9 alternator. Without rear air conditioning, they come equipped with the Valeo A13VI+ (K68) 105 AMP alternator.**

DELPHI CS 144 (KG9)

▶ **See Figure 17**

1.   Disconnect the negative battery cable.
2.   Remove the serpentine belt from the alternator pulley
3.   Remove the windshield wiper system module cover.
4.   Disconnect the windshield wiper motor crank arm link from the wiper motor and move it aside
5.   Bring the wiper arms to a vertical position on the windshield for access.
6.   Remove the engine mount strut bracket bolts and rotate the engine forward.
7.   Disconnect the electrical connections (PLIS plug) from the alternator and remove the nut and the positive lead from the output terminal (BAT) of the alternator.
8.   Remove the front brace on the alternator.
9.   Remove the alternator's rear brace.
10.   Remove the pivot bolt and nut from the alternator.

➡**Make sure to observe the necessary safety precautions for the next step.**

11.   Install a floor jack at the center front of the frame. Remove the front frame bolts, lower the frame 3 inches.

➡**Ensure that lowering the frame does not interfere with the bumper fascia or subsequent fascia damage may result.**

12.   Remove the alternator.
   To install:
13.   Locate the alternator in its appropriate place on the engine.
14.   Using the floor jack, raise the frame and install new front frame bolts. When secured, remove the floor jack.
15.   Install the pivot bolt and nut and torque to 37 ft. lbs. (50 Nm).
16.   Install the rear brace onto the alternator.
17.   Install the alternator's front brace.
18.   Reconnect the battery positive lead to the alternator output (BAT) terminal and tighten the nut.
19.   Plug in the electrical connections (PLIS plug) to the alternator.
20.   Rotate the engine rearward and allow it to settle into its proper position. Install the engine mount strut bracket bolts.
21.   Move the windshield wipers to the "park" position, and secure the wiper motor crank arm link to the wiper motor.
22.   Install the wiper system module cover.
23.   Install the serpentine belt.
24.   Connect the negative battery cable.

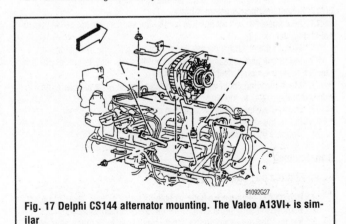

91092G27

Fig. 17 Delphi CS144 alternator mounting. The Valeo A13VI+ is similar

VALEO A13V+ (K68)

▶ **See Figures 17 and 18**

1.   Disconnect the negative battery cable.
2.   Remove the serpentine belt from the alternator pulley.

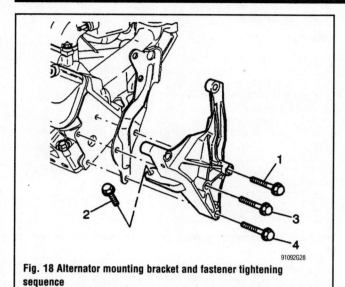

Fig. 18 Alternator mounting bracket and fastener tightening sequence

91092G28

Fig. 19 Loosen the mounting bolt . . .

91092P39

3. Remove the windshield wiper system module cover.

4. Disconnect the windshield wiper motor crank arm link from the wiper motor and move it aside.

5. Bring the wiper arms to a vertical position on the windshield for access.

6. Remove the engine mount strut bracket bolts and rotate the engine forward.

7. Disconnect the electrical connections at the alternator.

8. Remove the nut and battery positive lead to the alternator output "BAT" terminal.

9. Remove the alternator's rear brace.

10. Remove the front brace from the alternator.

11. Remove the mounting bolts from the alternator.

12. Remove the pivot bolt and nut from the alternator and set the alternator aside.

13. Remove the alternator mounting bracket from the engine and remove the alternator. See the diagram

To install:

14. Place the alternator on the engine and install the mounting bracket to the engine.

15. Install the pivot bolt and nut and torque to 37 ft. lbs. (50 Nm).

16. Install the rear brace onto the alternator.

17. Install the alternator's front brace.

18. Reconnect the battery positive lead to the alternator output (BAT) terminal and tighten the nut.

19. Plug in the electrical connections (PLIS plug) to the alternator.

20. Rotate the engine rearward and allow it to settle into its proper position. Install the engine mount strut bracket bolts.

21. Move the windshield wipers to the "park" position, and secure the wiper motor crank arm link to the wiper motor.

22. Install the wiper system module cover.

23. Install the serpentine belt.

24. Connect the negative battery cable.

3.8L Engine

▶ **See Figures 19, 20, 21, 22 and 23**

1. Disconnect the negative battery cable.

2. Remove the serpentine drive belt from the alternator pulley.

3. Remove the nut retaining the battery positive lead from the alternator.

4. Unplug the electrical connector.

5. Remove the mounting bolts, nut, and the bracket for the wiring harness.

6. Remove the alternator.

To install:

7. Install the wiring harness bracket, the mounting nut, and bolts.

8. Reconnect the electrical connector.

9. Install the battery positive lead on the output terminal at the alternator and tighten the nut.

10. Replace the serpentine belt.

11. Connect the negative battery cable.

Fig. 20 . . . then remove it

91092P40

Fig. 21 Remove the bracket-attaching bolt

91092P38

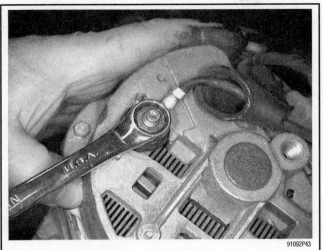

Fig. 22 Remove the retaining nut for the battery feed wire and unplug the connector

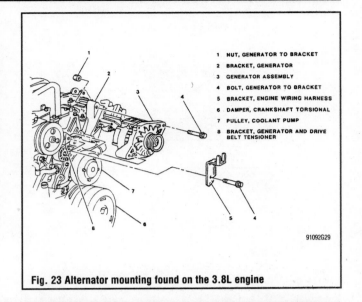

1 NUT, GENERATOR TO BRACKET
2 BRACKET, GENERATOR
3 GENERATOR ASSEMBLY
4 BOLT, GENERATOR TO BRACKET
5 BRACKET, ENGINE WIRING HARNESS
6 DAMPER, CRANKSHAFT TORSIONAL
7 PULLEY, COOLANT PUMP
8 BRACKET, GENERATOR AND DRIVE BELT TENSIONER

91092G29

Fig. 23 Alternator mounting found on the 3.8L engine

STARTING SYSTEM

Starter

TESTING

◆ See Figures 24, 25 and 26

❈❈ CAUTION

Never operate the starter motor more than 30 seconds at a time. Allow it to cool at least two minutes before cranking again. Excessive cranking can cause serious damage due to overheating.

➡Before diagnosing starter problems, make sure the battery is good and fully charged, inspect the wiring for damage. Inspect all connections to the starter motor, solenoid, ignition switch, and all ground connections. Clean and tighten connections as required.

The most common scenario that occurs with starting problems is an audible clicking sound or a slow crank where the engine may or may not start. In either case, a fast test of the starter system is possible with a DVOM (digital volt ohm meter).

1. Make sure the battery is good and fully charged.
2. Disable the fuel delivery system if possible (pull the fuel pump fuse, disconnect the relay) OR
3. Disable the ignition system— disconnect the positive lead into the coil pack
4. Hook up the DVOM across the battery and set the meter to a 20 volt scale

5. While cranking the engine, read the meter. If the meter drops below 9.6 volts (10.5 volts is a good reading) on a nice day (70°F), then the starter draw is too high.

❈❈ WARNING

Do not crank excessively if you could not disable the fuel system. Fuel is delivered to the cylinders each time the engine is cranked.

STARTER MOTOR NOISE DIAGNOSIS TABLE	
SYMPTOM	**CAUSE**
High-pitched whine during cranking (before engine fires), but engine cranks and fires OK.	Distance too great between starter pinion and flywheel.
High-pitched whine after engine fires, as key is being released. Engine cranks and fires OK. This intermittent complaint is often diagnosed as starter "hang-in" or "weak solenoid".	Distance too small between starter pinion and flywheel, flywheel runout contributes to the intermittent nature.
A loud "whoop" after the engine fires but while the starter is still held engaged sounds like a siren if the engine is revved while starter is engaged.	Starter drive problem. A new starter drive will often correct this problem.
A "rumble, growl" or in severe cases a "knock" as the starter is coasting down to a stop after starting the engine.	Bent or unbalanced starter armature. A new armature will often correct this problem.

91092G31

Fig. 24 Starter motor noise diagnosis

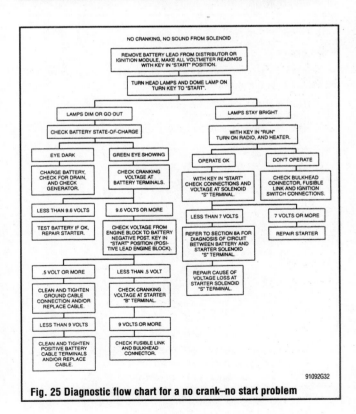

NO CRANKING, NO SOUND FROM SOLENOID

REMOVE BATTERY LEAD FROM DISTRIBUTOR OR IGNITION MODULE, MAKE ALL VOLTMETER READINGS WITH KEY IN "START" POSITION.

TURN HEAD LAMPS AND DOME LAMP ON TURN KEY TO "START".

LAMPS DIM OR GO OUT

CHECK BATTERY STATE-OF-CHARGE

EYE DARK — CHARGE BATTERY, CHECK FOR DRAIN, AND CHECK GENERATOR. — LESS THAN 9.6 VOLTS — TEST BATTERY IF OK, REPAIR STARTER.

GREEN EYE SHOWING — CHECK CRANKING VOLTAGE AT BATTERY TERMINALS. — 9.6 VOLTS OR MORE — CHECK VOLTAGE FROM ENGINE BLOCK TO BATTERY NEGATIVE POST. KEY IN "START" POSITION (POSITIVE LEAD ENGINE BLOCK).

.5 VOLT OR MORE — CLEAN AND TIGHTEN GROUND CABLE CONNECTION AND/OR REPLACE CABLE.

LESS THAN .5 VOLT — CHECK CRANKING VOLTAGE AT STARTER "B" TERMINAL.

LESS THAN 9 VOLTS — CLEAN AND TIGHTEN POSITIVE BATTERY CABLE TERMINALS AND/OR REPLACE CABLE.

9 VOLTS OR MORE — CHECK FUSIBLE LINK AND BULKHEAD CONNECTOR.

LAMPS STAY BRIGHT

WITH KEY IN "RUN" TURN ON RADIO, AND HEATER.

OPERATE OK — WITH KEY IN "START" CHECK CONNECTIONS AND VOLTAGE AT SOLENOID "S" TERMINAL.

LESS THAN 7 VOLTS — REFER TO SECTION 8A FOR DIAGNOSIS OF CIRCUIT BETWEEN BATTERY AND STARTER SOLENOID "S" TERMINAL.

REPAIR CAUSE OF VOLTAGE LOSS AT STARTER SOLENOID "S" TERMINAL.

DON'T OPERATE — CHECK BULKHEAD CONNECTOR, FUSIBLE LINK AND IGNITION SWITCH CONNECTIONS.

7 VOLTS OR MORE — REPAIR STARTER.

91092G32

Fig. 25 Diagnostic flow chart for a no crank—no start problem

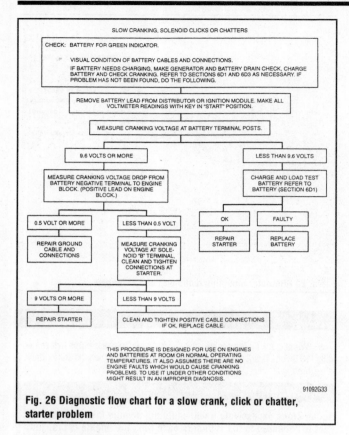

SLOW CRANKING, SOLENOID CLICKS OR CHATTERS

CHECK: BATTERY FOR GREEN INDICATOR.

VISUAL CONDITION OF BATTERY CABLES AND CONNECTIONS.
IF BATTERY NEEDS CHARGING, MAKE GENERATOR AND BATTERY DRAIN CHECK, CHARGE BATTERY AND CHECK CRANKING. REFER TO SECTIONS 6D1 AND 6D3 AS NECESSARY. IF PROBLEM HAS NOT BEEN FOUND, DO THE FOLLOWING.

REMOVE BATTERY LEAD FROM DISTRIBUTOR OR IGNITION MODULE. MAKE ALL VOLTMETER READINGS WITH KEY IN "START" POSITION.

MEASURE CRANKING VOLTAGE AT BATTERY TERMINAL POSTS.

9.6 VOLTS OR MORE

LESS THAN 9.6 VOLTS

MEASURE CRANKING VOLTAGE DROP FROM BATTERY NEGATIVE TERMINAL TO ENGINE BLOCK. (POSITIVE LEAD ON ENGINE BLOCK.)

CHARGE AND LOAD TEST BATTERY REFER TO BATTERY (SECTION 6D1)

0.5 VOLT OR MORE

LESS THAN 0.5 VOLT

OK

FAULTY

REPAIR GROUND CABLE AND CONNECTIONS

MEASURE CRANKING VOLTAGE AT SOLENOID "B" TERMINAL, CLEAN AND TIGHTEN CONNECTIONS AT STARTER.

REPAIR STARTER

REPLACE BATTERY

9 VOLTS OR MORE

LESS THAN 9 VOLTS

REPAIR STARTER

CLEAN AND TIGHTEN POSITIVE CABLE CONNECTIONS IF OK, REPLACE CABLE.

THIS PROCEDURE IS DESIGNED FOR USE ON ENGINES AND BATTERIES AT ROOM OR NORMAL OPERATING TEMPERATURES. IT ALSO ASSUMES THERE ARE NO ENGINE FAULTS WHICH WOULD CAUSE CRANKING PROBLEMS. TO USE IT UNDER OTHER CONDITIONS MIGHT RESULT IN AN IMPROPER DIAGNOSIS.

91092G33

Fig. 26 Diagnostic flow chart for a slow crank, click or chatter, starter problem

REMOVAL & INSTALLATION

3.1L Engine

▶ See Figure 27

➡ Besides regular hand tools, a special oil pressure sensor socket will be necessary to complete this operation.

1. Disconnect the negative battery cable.
2. Raise and support the vehicle safely.
3. Remove the A/C compressor brace (if equipped).

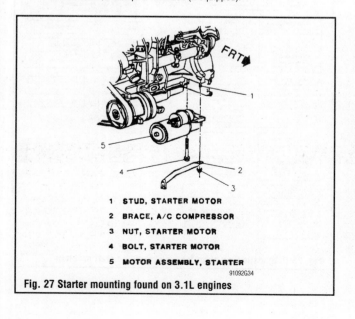

1 STUD, STARTER MOTOR
2 BRACE, A/C COMPRESSOR
3 NUT, STARTER MOTOR
4 BOLT, STARTER MOTOR
5 MOTOR ASSEMBLY, STARTER

91092G34

Fig. 27 Starter mounting found on 3.1L engines

4. Extract the wiring harness from the retainer and position it out of the way.
5. Remove the cover from the starter wiring.
6. Remove the outer nut and disengage the wiring from the starter solenoid.
7. Disconnect the electrical connector from the oil pressure gauge sensor.
8. Using the special socket, remove the oil pressure gauge sensor.
9. Unbolt the starter from the engine. Retain any shims.

To install:

10. Install the starter to the engine, reuse any shims that were removed. Tighten to 32 ft. lbs. (43 Nm).
11. Connect the wiring to the solenoid and install the outer nut.
12. Place the cover over the starter wiring.
13. Replace the oil pressure gauge sensor using the special socket.
14. Plug the electrical connector onto the sensor.
15. Mount the harness to the retainer.
16. Install the A/C compressor brace (if equipped).
17. Lower the vehicle.
18. Connect the negative battery cable.

3.4L Engine

➡ This starter is serviced only as a complete unit.

1. Disconnect the negative battery cable.
2. Raise and support the vehicle safely.
3. Disconnect the electrical connectors at the starter.
4. Remove the converter cover.
5. Remove the starter motor mounting bolts, and remove the starter.

To install:

6. Install the starter motor to the engine using the mounting bolts. Torque the bolts to 35 ft. lbs. (47 Nm).
7. Install the converter cover.
8. Reconnect the electrical connections to the starter.
9. Lower the vehicle.
10. Connect the negative battery cable.

3.8L Engine

▶ See Figures 28 thru 33

1. Disconnect the negative battery cable.
2. Raise and support the vehicle safely.
3. Remove the cover from the starter wiring.
4. Remove the outer nut and wiring from the starter solenoid.
5. Remove the screws retaining the wiring harness clips and position the harness out of the way.

91092P28

Fig. 28 Loosen (do not remove) the starter bolt on the right side of the engine

Fig. 29 Remove the starter bolt on the left side of the engine—slide any starter shims out and save them

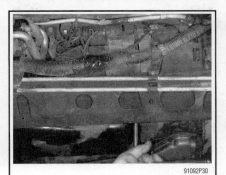

Fig. 30 Now, remove the right side starter bolt. Don't let the starter drop

Fig. 31 It's easier to disconnect the wire leads to the solenoid once the mounting bolts have been removed, and the starter is partially lowered

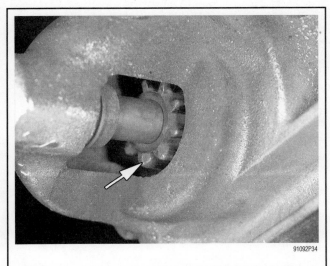

Fig. 32 Inspect the teeth of the starter drive for chipping and wear

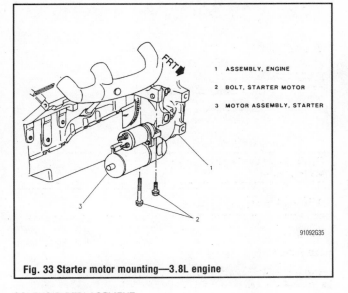

1 ASSEMBLY, ENGINE

2 BOLT, STARTER MOTOR

3 MOTOR ASSEMBLY, STARTER

Fig. 33 Starter motor mounting—3.8L engine

6. Take out the screw that retains the plastic flywheel cover and remove the cover from the vehicle.

7. Remove the bolts retaining the starter to the engine block, and remove the starter from the vehicle.

To install:

8. Install the starter and tighten the bolts to 32 ft. lbs. (43 Nm).

9. Install the plastic flywheel cover and screw

10. Reposition the wiring harness, and screw in the retaining harness clips.

➡**Check the inner nut on the solenoid for tightness.**

11. Reconnect the wiring to the solenoid and install the outer nut.

12. Replace the cover over the starter wiring.

13. Lower the vehicle.

14. Connect the negative battery cable.

SOLENOID REPLACEMENT

If a starter motor condition of no crank and no sound exist, it may pay to check the solenoid before dismantling. The solenoid can be checked for proper operation without removal of the starter. Use the following procedure to remove the solenoid from the starter.

1. Remove the field lead attaching screw from the solenoid terminal.

2. Remove the solenoid attaching screws.

3. Remove the solenoid from the drive end housing of the starter.

To install:

4. Install the solenoid to the drive end of the starter.

5. Install the solenoid attaching screws.

6. Attach the field lead attaching screw to solenoid terminal

SENDING UNITS AND SENSORS

➡**This section describes the operating principles of sending units, warning lights and gauges. Sensors that provide information to the Electronic Control Module (ECM) are covered in Section 4 of this manual.**

Instrument panels contain a number of indicating devices (gauges and warning lights). These devices are composed of two separate components. One is the sending unit, mounted on the engine or other remote part of the vehicle, and the other is the actual gauge or light in the instrument panel.

Several types of sending units exist, however most can be characterized as being either a pressure type or a resistance type. Pressure type sending units convert liquid pressure into an electrical signal that is sent to the gauge. Resistance type sending units are most often used to measure temperature and use variable resistance to control the current flow back to the indicating device. Both types of sending units are connected in series by a wire to the battery (through the ignition switch). When the ignition is turned **ON**, current flows from the battery through the indicating device and on to the sending unit.

Coolant Temperature Sender/Switch

OPERATION

▶ **See Figure 34**

This switch activates a warning lamp in the instrument cluster if the engine overheats. With optional instrumentation, a temperature gauge replaces the warning lamp and the temperature switch is replaced with a sending unit. It does this by changing resistance as coolant temperature increases or decreases.

The engine coolant temperature switch will close the circuit to the temperature indicator, when the coolant reaches the temperature range indicated on the sending switch. The engine coolant temperature switch is not serviceable. If it is malfunctioning, it should be replaced.

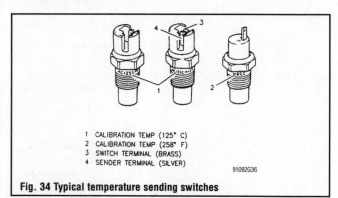

1 CALIBRATION TEMP (125° C)
2 CALIBRATION TEMP (258° F)
3 SWITCH TERMINAL (BRASS)
4 SENDER TERMINAL (SILVER)

91092G36

Fig. 34 Typical temperature sending switches

TESTING

1. Remove the temperature sender from the engine.
2. Position the water temperature sending unit in such a way that the metal shaft (opposite end from the electrical connectors) is situated in a pot of water. Make sure that the electrical connector is not submerged and that only the tip of the sending unit's body is in the water.
3. Heat the pot of water at a medium rate. While the water is warming, continue to measure the resistance of the terminal and the metal body of the sending unit:
    a. As the water warms up, the resistance exhibited by the ohmmeter goes down in a steady manner: the sending unit is good.
    b. As the water warms up, the resistance does not change or changes in erratic jumps: the sender is bad, replace it with a new one.
4. Install the good or new sending unit into the engine, then connect the negative battery cable.

Oil Pressure Sensor

OPERATION

The oil pressure sender/switch relays the engine oil pressure to the dash gauge.

TESTING

If low oil pressure is suspected, because the dash light is on or the indicator gauge on the dash reads low the oil pressure can be checked on the vehicle using the following procedure; however, it will require the use of a special tool.
1. Check the oil level, bring it to the full mark.
2. Remove the oil filter. Expect to lose some oil, as it will drip from the oil filter and filter mounting pad.
3. Assemble the plunger in the large hole of the tester base and the hose in the small hole of the tester base. Connect the gauge to the end of the hose.
4. Insert the flat side of the rubber plug, for ease of installation, in the by-pass valve itself.
5. Install the tester on the filter mounting pad.

6. Start the engine to check the overall pressure, sender switch, or noisy lifters. Engine should be at operating temperature before taking an oil pressure reading. Look for a pressure reading of about 60 psi (414kPa) @ 1850 RPM, if the engine has 10W-30 oil in it.
7. If adequate oil pressure is indicated, replace the pressure sending switch.
8. If a low reading is indicated, depress the valve on the tester base to isolate the oil pump and/or its components from the lubricating system. An adequate reading at this time would indicate a good pump and the previous low pressure was due to worn bearings, etc. A low reading while depressing the valve would indicate a faulty pump.

Electric Fan Switch

OPERATION

▶ **See Figure 35**

The Powertrain control module (PCM) controls the operation of the cooling fans. This is accomplished by providing a ground path for the cooling fan relay coils within the PCM. The relay contacts will close and complete the circuit between the Maxifuse® in the underhood electrical center and the fan motors. Whenever there is a fan "on" request, both fans will be running. A coolant temperature switch activates the fan motors. A transducer can also activate the circuit, depending upon A/C request or A/C compressor head pressure to the condenser.

TESTING

For electric cooling fan testing procedures, please refer to Section 3 of this manual.

REMOVAL & INSTALLATION

1. Disconnect the negative battery cable.
2. Disconnect the sensor electrical lead and unscrew the sensor. The sensor can be found on the right side of the engine.
To install:
3. Install the sensor or relay and connect the electrical lead.
4. Connect the battery cable.

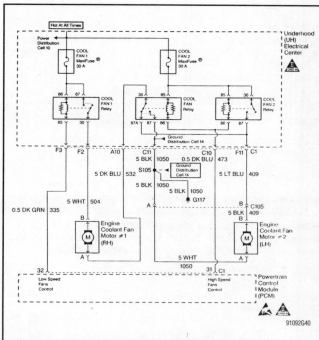

91092G40

Fig. 35 Wiring Schematic of cooling fans, relays, and ground

Troubleshooting Basic Starting System Problems

Problem	Cause	Solution
Starter motor rotates engine slowly	• Battery charge low or battery defective	• Charge or replace battery
	• Defective circuit between battery and starter motor	• Clean and tighten, or replace cables
	• Low load current	• Bench-test starter motor. Inspect for worn brushes and weak brush springs.
	• High load current	• Bench-test starter motor. Check engine for friction, drag or coolant in cylinders. Check ring gear-to-pinion gear clearance.
Starter motor will not rotate engine	• Battery charge low or battery defective	• Charge or replace battery
	• Faulty solenoid	• Check solenoid ground. Repair or replace as necessary.
	• Damaged drive pinion gear or ring gear	• Replace damaged gear(s)
	• Starter motor engagement weak	• Bench-test starter motor
	• Starter motor rotates slowly with high load current	• Inspect drive yoke pull-down and point gap, check for worn end bushings, check ring gear clearance
	• Engine seized	• Repair engine
Starter motor drive will not engage (solenoid known to be good)	• Defective contact point assembly	• Repair or replace contact point assembly
	• Inadequate contact point assembly ground	• Repair connection at ground screw
	• Defective hold-in coil	• Replace field winding assembly
Starter motor drive will not disengage	• Starter motor loose on flywheel housing	• Tighten mounting bolts
	• Worn drive end busing	• Replace bushing
	• Damaged ring gear teeth	• Replace ring gear or driveplate
	• Drive yoke return spring broken or missing	• Replace spring
Starter motor drive disengages prematurely	• Weak drive assembly thrust spring	• Replace drive mechanism
	• Hold-in coil defective	• Replace field winding assembly
Low load current	• Worn brushes	• Replace brushes
	• Weak brush springs	• Replace springs

TCCS2C01

Troubleshooting Basic Charging System Problems

Problem	Cause	Solution
Noisy alternator	• Loose mountings • Loose drive pulley • Worn bearings • Brush noise • Internal circuits shorted (High pitched whine)	• Tighten mounting bolts • Tighten pulley • Replace alternator • Replace alternator • Replace alternator
Squeal when starting engine or accelerating	• Glazed or loose belt	• Replace or adjust belt
Indicator light remains on or ammeter indicates discharge (engine running)	• Broken belt • Broken or disconnected wires • Internal alternator problems • Defective voltage regulator	• Install belt • Repair or connect wiring • Replace alternator • Replace voltage regulator/alternator
Car light bulbs continually burn out—battery needs water continually	• Alternator/regulator overcharging	• Replace voltage regulator/alternator
Car lights flare on acceleration	• Battery low • Internal alternator/regulator problems	• Charge or replace battery • Replace alternator/regulator
Low voltage output (alternator light flickers continually or ammeter needle wanders)	• Loose or worn belt • Dirty or corroded connections • Internal alternator/regulator problems	• Replace or adjust belt • Clean or replace connections • Replace alternator/regulator

TCCS2C02

3

ENGINE AND ENGINE OVERHAUL

ENGINE MECHANICAL

✳✳ CAUTION

Some models covered by this manual may be equipped with a Supplemental Restraint System (SRS), which uses an air bag. Whenever working near any of the SRS components, such as the impact sensors, the air bag module, the steering column or the instrument panel, disable the SRS, as described in Section 6.

An automobile engine is a combination of many machined, honed, polished and lapped surfaces with tolerances that are measured in ten-thousandths of an inch. When any internal engine parts are serviced, care and cleanliness are important. A liberal coating of engine oil should be applied to friction areas during assembly, to protect and lubricate the surfaces on initial operation. Throughout this section, it should be understood that proper cleaning and protection of machined surfaces and friction areas is part of the repair procedure. This is considered standard shop practice even if not specifically stated.

When valve train components are removed for service, they should be kept in order. They should be installed in the same locations, and with the same mating surfaces, as when removed.

Battery cables should be disconnected before any major work is performed on the engine. Failure to disconnect cables may result in damage to wire harnesses or other electrical parts.

Anytime the air cleaner is removed; the intake opening should be covered. This will protect against accidental entrance of foreign material, which could follow the intake passage into the cylinder and cause extensive damage when the engine is started.

Engine

REMOVAL & INSTALLATION

▶ **See Figures 1 and 2**

In the process of removing the engine, you will come across a number of steps which call for the removal of a separate component or system, such as "disconnect the exhaust system" or "remove the radiator." In most instances, a detailed removal procedure can be found elsewhere in this manual.

➡**Removing the engine on these vehicles require the use of a suitable engine/transaxle support table.**

It is virtually impossible to list each individual wire and hose which must be disconnected, simply because so many different model and engine combinations have been manufactured. Careful observation and common sense are the best possible approaches to any repair procedure.

Removal and installation of the engine can be made easier if you follow these basic points:
- If you have to drain any of the fluids, use a suitable container.
- Always tag any wires or hoses and mark the components they came from before disconnecting them.
- Because there are so many bolts and fasteners involved, store and label the retainers from components separately in muffin pans, jars or coffee cans. This will prevent confusion during installation.
- After unbolting the transmission or transaxle, always make sure it is properly supported.
- If it is necessary to disconnect the air conditioning system, have this service performed by a qualified technician using a recovery/recycling station. If the system does not have to be disconnected, unbolt the compressor and set it aside.

➡**If your vehicle is equipped with air conditioning, refer to Section 1 for information regarding the implications of servicing your A/C system yourself. Only an MVAC-trained, EPA-certified, automotive technician should service the A/C system or its components.**

✳✳ CAUTION

Observe all applicable safety precautions when working around fuel. Whenever servicing the fuel system, always work in a well-ventilated area. Do not allow fuel spray or vapors to be exposed to a spark or open flame. Keep a dry chemical fire extinguisher near the work area. Always keep fuel in a container specifically designed for fuel storage; also, always properly seal fuel containers to avoid the possibility of fire or explosion.

- When unbolting the engine mounts, always make sure the engine is properly supported. When removing the engine, make sure that any lifting devices are properly attached to the engine. It is recommended that if your engine is supplied with lifting hooks, your lifting apparatus be attached to them.
- Drop the engine from its compartment slowly, checking that no hoses, wires or other components are still connected.
- After the engine is clear of the compartment, place it on an engine stand or workbench.
- After the engine has been removed, you can perform a partial or full teardown of the engine using the procedures outlined in this manual.

The engine replacement procedure given here is considered typical for this line of vehicles. Because of variations from year to year, or line to line, no exact bolt by bolt process for replacement can be given. These directions are complete for the applications, however, because of production changes or trim level, your vehicle may be different.

Read these instructions completely before beginning to do the work. Be sure you understand each step of the directions before you begin doing it.

Most of the new design front-wheel drive vans extract their engines from underneath the vehicle. These vehicles fall into that category. You will need a suitable lift to complete this procedure. Unless provisions are made to safely raise the body enough to allow the engine to be removed from the bottom, this procedure should not be attempted.

1. If equipped with A/C, take your vehicle to a reputable repair shop to have the A/C system discharged and recovered.
2. Disconnect the negative battery cable.
3. Drain and recycle the engine coolant.
4. Properly relieve the fuel system pressure, as outlined in Section 5 of this manual.
5. Remove the air cleaner assembly.
6. Detach the engine electrical connector, LH side of the engine.
7. Unplug the electrical connector from the cruise control servo.
8. Detach the electrical connector at the emergency jumper block.
9. Disconnect the wiring harness retainer at the RH side of the engine.
10. Detach the electrical connector at the engine-cooling fan.
11. Disconnect the shift cable, heat shield and bracket at the transaxle.
12. Remove the battery cable ground connection from the engine.
13. Detach the engine electrical block connector at the RH side of the engine.
14. Remove the retaining screws from the multi-use relay bracket at the tie bar.

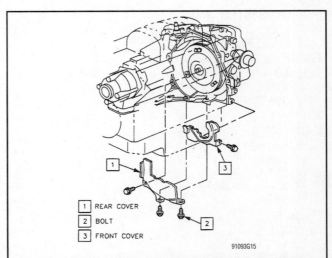

1	REAR COVER
2	BOLT
3	FRONT COVER

91093G15

Fig. 1 View of the front and rear converter covers and the location of the three flywheel to converter bolts

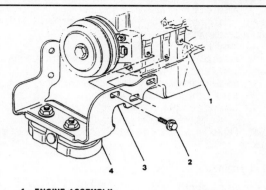

1 ENGINE ASSEMBLY
2 BOLT
3 ENGINE MOUNT BRACKET
4 ENGINE MOUNT BRACKET TO FRAME

91093G70

Fig. 2 Exploded view of the front engine mount and attaching hardware

15. Unplug the electrical connector from the A/C compressor and accumulator.
16. Remove the engine fuel vapor harness from the engine.
17. Disconnect the accelerator and cruise cables and bracket from the throttle body.
18. Disconnect the brake vacuum hose at the engine port.
19. Remove the engine mount strut bolts and nuts from the engine.
20. Disconnect the radiator and heater hoses from the engine.
21. Disconnect the A/C manifold from the compressor.
22. Disconnect the fuel feed hoses at the fuel rail.
23. Raise and suitably support the vehicle.
24. Drain the engine oil into a suitable container.
25. Remove the front wheels.
26. Disconnect the engine wiring harness at the front of the frame.
27. Disconnect the electrical wiring at the starter assembly.
28. Remove the flywheel covers from the transaxle.
29. Remove the starter assembly.
30. Matchmark the relationship of the flywheel to the converter, then remove the attaching bolts.
31. Remove the steering shaft pinch bolt from the steering column.
32. Disconnect both outer tie rod ends.
33. Disconnect both lower ball joints from the steering knuckle.
34. Pull both drive axles from the transaxle and wire them up to the body for support. Do not allow the drive axles to hang unsupported.
35. Disconnect the exhaust pipe from the manifold, by removing the manifold bolts and springs.
36. Disconnect the transaxle cooler lines from the transaxle. Plug the lines to avoid getting debris in them.
37. Remove the engine front mount-to-frame retaining nuts.
38. Position a suitable engine/transaxle support table below the assembly, allowing it to rest on the table.
39. Separate the engine/transaxle frame from the vehicle by lowering the table, or by raising the vehicle.
40. Secure the engine/transaxle assembly to the support table, then remove the retaining bolts from the frame assembly.
41. Remove the serpentine belt.
42. Unbolt power steering pump assembly and set it aside. Do not disconnect the fluid lines.
43. Remove the transaxle indicator tube assembly .
44. Remove the engine-to-transaxle brace assembly, the bolts and the stud.
45. Separate the engine from the transaxle/frame and remove it from the table.
To install:
46. Attach the engine to the transaxle/frame assembly, and tighten the bolts and stud to 55 ft. lbs. (75 Nm).
47. Install the engine-to-transaxle brace and secure with the retaining bolts. Tighten the engine side bolts to 70 ft. lbs. (95 Nm).Tighten the transaxle side bolts to 47 ft. lbs. (63 Nm).
48. Install the transaxle indicator tube assembly and bolt and tighten the lower and upper bolts.

49. Move the power steering pump into position, then securing with the mounting bolts.
50. Install the serpentine belt.
51. Position the engine/transaxle/frame assembly under the vehicle.
52. Lower the vehicle to the assembly and install new frame retaining bolts. Tighten the bolts to 103 ft. lbs. (140 Nm).
53. Raise and suitably support the vehicle.
54. Unplug and attach the transaxle cooler lines to the transaxle.
55. Install the front exhaust pipe to exhaust manifold, and secure with the retainers.
56. Install the LH and RH axles into the transaxle.
57. Connect both lower ball joints into the steering knuckles, then tighten the retaining bolts to 56 ft. lbs. (76 Nm).
58. Install the LH and RH tie rod ends to the steering knuckles, tighten the nuts, and install new cotter pins.
59. Install the intermediate steering shaft to the rack assembly. Insert the pinch bolt and tighten to 35 ft. lbs. (47 Nm).
60. Replace the torque converter-to-flywheel bolts and tighten to 46 ft. lbs. (62 Nm).
61. Install the starter motor. Install the flywheel covers to the transaxle and engine.
62. Attach the electrical wiring to the starter.
63. Connect the engine wiring harness and retainers to the frame.
64. Install the front wheels and tighten the lug nuts.
65. Carefully lower the vehicle.
66. Attach the A/C manifold to the compressor.
67. Reattach the fuel lines to the fuel rail.
68. Reconnect the heater and radiator hoses to the engine.
69. Secure the engine to the front mount.
70. Connect the vacuum lines, and brake booster hose to the engine.
71. Install the accelerator and cruise control cables and bracket to the transaxle. Attach the accelerator and cruise control cable bracket at the throttle body.
72. Connect the fuel vapor harness at the engine.
73. Attach the electrical connections to the engine, as tagged during removal, then secure the battery ground at the engine block.
74. Install a new oil filter, then fill the engine with the proper type and amount of oil.
75. Fill the cooling system and check for proper level and/or leaks.
76. Connect the negative battery cable.
77. Take the vehicle to a reputable repair shop to have the A/C system recharged.

Rocker Arm (Valve) Cover

REMOVAL & INSTALLATION

3.1L Engine

LEFT SIDE—FRONT COVER

♦ See Figure 3

1. Disconnect the negative battery cable.
2. Remove the air cleaner assembly.
3. Drain and recycle the engine coolant.
4. Detach the engine harness from the EVRV and the engine strut mount.
5. Disconnect the coolant tube hose at the water pump.
6. Remove the coolant tube bolt from the thermostat housing.
7. Remove the tube bracket nut and tube.
8. Remove the spark plug wire guide bracket.
9. Disconnect the fuel inlet and return lines from the TBI unit.
10. Remove the Idle Air Control (IAC) motor.
11. Remove the Throttle Position (TP) sensor.
12. Pull the PCV valve out of the rocker arm cover.
13. Remove the nuts and reinforcements, then pull the rocker arm cover off of the cylinder head.

➡If the rocker cover sticks to cylinder head, remove it by bumping the end of the rocker arm cover with the palm of your hand or a soft rubber mallet.

14. Clean the sealing surface on the cylinder head and rocker arm cover with a suitable degreaser.

To install:

15. Install the new gasket, making sure it is properly seated in rocker cover groove.

16. Apply RTV sealer in the notch.

17. Position the rocker arm cover over the gasket and RTV. Install the retainers and tighten to 89 inch lbs. (10 Nm).

18. Install the PCV valve into the grommet on the rocker cover gasket.

19. Install the Throttle Position (TP) sensor and the Idle Air Control (IAC) motor.

20. Attach the fuel inlet and return lines to the TBI assembly.

21. Connect the coolant tube bracket nut and tube.

22. Replace the spark plug wire guide bracket.

23. Install the coolant tube bolt at the thermostat housing.

24. Connect the coolant tube hose to the water pump.

25. Attach the engine harness at the EVRV and to the engine strut mount

26. Install the air cleaner assembly.

27. Fill the cooling system to the proper level.

28. Connect the negative battery cable.

29. Inspect for oil leaks at the sealing surfaces, and check for any coolant leaks.

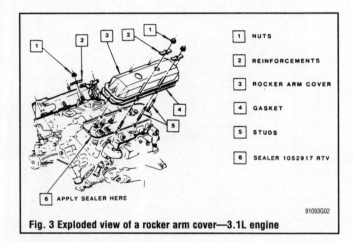

Fig. 3 Exploded view of a rocker arm cover—3.1L engine

1	NUTS
2	REINFORCEMENTS
3	ROCKER ARM COVER
4	GASKET
5	STUDS
6	SEALER 1052917 RTV

6 APPLY SEALER HERE

91093G02

RIGHT SIDE—REAR COVER

▶ See Figure 3

1. Disconnect the negative battery cable.
2. Remove the air cleaner assembly.
3. Drain the coolant into an approved container.
4. Remove the throttle and TV bracket FROM the TBI assembly. Be careful not to change the TV adjustment.
5. Tag and disconnect any wire assemblies and/or vacuum lines that interfere with the cover removal.
6. Remove the serpentine belt.
7. Remove the alternator as outlined in Section 2 of this manual, including the mounting brackets and rear brace.
8. Disconnect the coolant hose from the manifold.
9. Remove the nuts and other retainers, then pull the cover off of the cylinder head.

➡️If the rocker cover sticks to the cylinder head, remove it by bumping the end of the cover with the palm of your hand or soft rubber mallet.

10. Clean the gasket mating surfaces on the cylinder head and rocker arm cover with a suitable degreaser.

To install:

11. Install the new gasket, making sure it is properly seated in rocker cover groove.

12. Apply RTV sealer in the notch.

13. Position the rocker arm cover over the gasket and RTV. Install the retainers and tighten to 89 inch lbs. (10 Nm).

14. Attach the coolant hose to the manifold.

15. Install the alternator bracket, alternator, and rear alternator brace. For details, see the procedure located in Section 2 of this manual.

16. Install the serpentine belt.

17. Attach all wire assemblies and vacuum lines that were disconnected, as tagged during removal.

18. Install the throttle and TV cable bracket assembly.

19. Install the air cleaner assembly.

20. Connect the negative battery cable.

21. Fill the cooling system to the proper level.

22. Inspect for oil leaks at the sealing surfaces, and check for any coolant leaks.

3.4L Engine

LEFT SIDE—FRONT COVER

▶ See Figure 4

1. Disconnect the negative battery cable.
2. Remove the acoustic engine cover.
3. Remove the engine mount strut.
4. Remove the PCV valve from the rocker arm (valve) cover.
5. Tag, then disconnect the spark plug wires from front spark plugs.
6. Unfasten the retaining bolts, then remove the rocker arm (valve) cover.

➡️If the rocker cover sticks to the cylinder head, remove it by bumping the end of the cover with the palm of your hand or soft rubber mallet.

7. Clean the gasket mating surfaces on the cylinder head and rocker arm cover with a suitable degreaser.

To install:

8. Install the new gasket, making sure it is properly seated in rocker cover groove.

9. Apply RTV sealer in the notch.

➡️Install the valve rocker cover bolts finger tight before tightening bolts to specification or damage to the valve rocker cover may occur.

10. Position the rocker arm cover over the gasket and RTV. Install the retainers finger-tight, then tighten to 89 inch lbs. (10 Nm).

11. Reinstall the plug wires onto the front plugs, as tagged during removal.

12. Push the PCV valve back into the grommet on the cover.

13. Install the engine mount strut.

14. Install the acoustic engine cover.

15. Connect the negative battery cable.

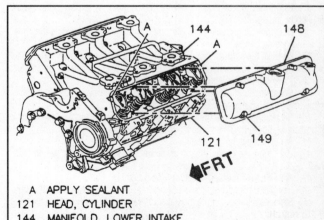

A	APPLY SEALANT
121	HEAD, CYLINDER
144	MANIFOLD, LOWER INTAKE
148	COVER, ROCKER ARM
149	BOLT, ROCKER ARM COVER

91093G01

Fig. 4 Exploded view of the rocker arm (valve) cover—3.4L engine

RIGHT SIDE—REAR COVER

♦ See Figure 4

1. Disconnect the negative battery cable.
2. Remove the acoustic engine cover.
3. Remove the serpentine belt.
4. Remove the alternator, bracket, and braces as outlined in Section 2.
5. Tag and disconnect the spark plug wires from the ignition module/coil assembly.
6. Remove the ignition coil mounting bracket with the coils, purge solenoid and vacuum canister solenoid still attached.
7. Tag and disconnect the vacuum lines from the valve cover.
8. Unfasten the retaining bolts, then remove the rocker arm (valve) cover.

➡If the rocker cover sticks to the cylinder head, remove it by bumping the end of the cover with the palm of your hand or soft rubber mallet.

9. Clean the gasket mating surfaces on the cylinder head and rocker arm cover with a suitable degreaser.

To install:
10. Install the new gasket, making sure it is properly seated in rocker cover groove.
11. Apply RTV sealer in the notch.

➡Install the valve rocker cover bolts finger tight before tightening bolts to specification or damage to the valve rocker cover may occur.

12. Position the rocker arm cover over the gasket and RTV. Install the retainers finger-tight, then tighten to 89 inch lbs. (10 Nm).
13. Reattach the vacuum lines to the valve cover, as tagged during removal.
14. Install the ignition coil bracket with the other parts still attached.
15. Connect the plug wires to the ignition module/coil assembly, being careful to keep them in the proper order.
16. Install the alternator, bracket, and braces as outlined in Section 2.
17. Install the serpentine belt.
18. Install the acoustic engine cover.

19. Connect the negative battery cable.
20. Inspect the work for any oil leaks, make sure of the proper fluid levels.

3.8L Engine

LEFT SIDE—FRONT COVER

♦ See Figures 5 thru 11

1. If necessary for access, unfasten the retaining bolts, then remove the bracket and motor mount for access to the rocker arm (valve) cover.
2. Remove the accessory drive belt (serpentine belt).
3. Unfasten the alternator brace bolt, then remove the brace.
4. Tag and disconnect the wires from the front bank of spark plugs, then position the harness aside.
5. Loosen the six rocker arm cover bolts completely, then remove the bolts. Pull the rocker arm cover off of the cylinder head.

➡If cover sticks to the cylinder head, remove it by bumping the end of the cover with the palm of your hand or a soft rubber mallet.

To install:
6. Position a new gasket, then place the cover onto the gasket.
7. Install the cover retaining bolts and tighten the bolts to 89 inch lbs. (10 Nm).
8. Reconnect the spark plug wires, as attached during removal.
9. Install the alternator brace and secure with the retaining bolt.
10. Install the accessory drive belt (serpentine belt).
11. Check for any fluid leaks.

RIGHT SIDE—REAR COVER

♦ See Figure 11

1. Remove the accessory drive belt (serpentine belt).
2. Loosen the power steering pump bolts, then slide the pump forward to gain the necessary clearance. Do not disconnect the fluid lines.

Fig. 5 Unfastening the two bracket retaining bolts . . .

Fig. 6 . . . and the front motor mount, provides more access for removal of the valve cover

Fig. 7 Tag and disconnect the plug wires, and move the harness aside

Fig. 8 Completely loosen the six attaching bolts without removing them

Fig. 9 Remove the rocker arm cover; the studs and grommets can be removed at the workbench

Fig. 10 If the gasket stuck to the cylinder head mating surface, it must be removed before assembly

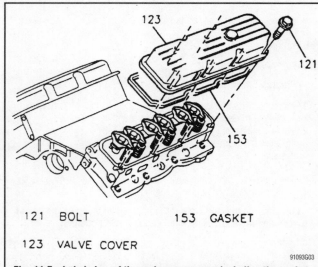

121 BOLT   153 GASKET

123 VALVE COVER

91093G03

Fig. 11 Exploded view of the rocker arm cover, including the gasket

3. Remove the power steering pump braces, as necessary, to gain access.

4. Tag and disconnect the spark plug wires, from the rear bank of spark plugs.

5. Remove the retaining bolts, then pull the cover off of the cylinder head.

➡ **If the rocker cover sticks to the cylinder head, remove it by bumping the end of the cover with the palm of your hand or soft rubber mallet.**

6. Clean the gasket mating surfaces on the cylinder head and rocker arm cover with a suitable degreaser.

To install:

7. Install the new gasket, making sure it is properly seated in rocker cover groove.

8. Apply RTV sealer in the notch.

9. Position the rocker arm cover over the gasket and RTV. Install the retainers and tighten to 89 inch lbs. (10 Nm).

10. Reconnect the spark plug wires, as tagged during removal.

11. Install and tighten the power steering pump braces.

12. Slide the power steering pump back to its proper position and tighten the mounting bolts.

13. Install the accessory drive belt (serpentine belt).

14. Check for any fluid leaks.

Rocker Arms/Shafts

REMOVAL & INSTALLATION

3.1L Engine

A very simple ball pivot-type rocker train is used. Motion is transmitted from the camshaft through the hydraulic lifter and push rod to the rocker arm. The rocker arm pivots on its ball and transmits the camshaft motion to the valve. The rocker arm ball locates on a stud, threaded into the head, and is retained by a nut. The push rod is located by a guide plate held under the rocker arm stud, assuring that the rocker arm operates in the plane of the valve.

1. Disconnect the negative battery cable.

2. Remove the rocker arm (valve) covers, as outlined in this section.

3. Unfasten the rocker arm bolts, then remove the rocker arms by lifting them straight out as an assembly.

4. Remove the pushrods.

➡ **Make sure to keep all components in order for reassembly!**

5. Place rocker arms, bolts and pushrods in a rack so they can be reinstalled in the same locations from which they were removed. Inspect the rocker arms, and pushrods for abnormal/excessive wear, replace as necessary.

To install:

➡ **Before installing the rocker arms, bolts, and pushrods, coat their bearing surface with a suitable prelube. Make sure to install these components in the exact locations from which they were removed.**

6. Install the pushrods, making sure they seat properly in the lifter.

7. Install the rocker arms and bolts.

8. With all the rocker arms attached and the lower ends of the pushrods in the lifter seats, bring #1 cylinder to TDC (Top Dead Center) compression stroke. The rotor would be pointing at the #1 spark plug wire in the distributor cap.

9. Adjust the intake valves on cylinders #1, #5, #6. Adjustment is 1½ turns past zero lash.

10. Adjust the exhaust valves on cylinders #1, #2, #3. Adjustment is 1½ turns past zero lash.

11. Next, bring #4 cylinder to TDC (Top dead Center) compression stroke. The rotor would point to the #4 spark plug wire at the distributor cap.

12. Adjust the intake valves on cylinders #2, #3, #4. Adjustment is 1½ turns past zero lash.

13. Adjust the exhaust valves on cylinders #4, #5, #6. Adjustment is 1½ turns past zero lash.

14. Install the rocker arm (valve) cover(s), as outlined in this section.

15. Connect the negative battery cable.

3.4L Engine

◗ See Figure 12

On these engine, a roller rocker type valve train is used. Motion is transmitted from the camshaft through the hydraulic roller lifter and pushrod to the roller rocker arm. The rocker arm pivots on needle roller bearings and transmits the camshaft motion to the valve. The rocker arm pedestal locates in a slot in the cylinder head and the rocker arm is retained in the cylinder head by a bolt. The pushrod is located by the rocker arm.

1. Disconnect the negative battery cable.

2. Remove the rocker arm (valve) covers as outlined in this section.

3. Unfasten the rocker arm bolts, then remove the rocker arms from the cylinder head.

4. Remove the pushrods, being careful that they do not fall down into the lifter valley. Note that the intake and exhaust pushrods are different lengths, with the exhaust pushrod being the longer of the two. The intake pushrods are 5.68 in. (144.18 mm) long and the exhaust pushrods are 6.0 in. (152.51 mm) long.

5. Place rocker arms, bolts and pushrods in a rack so they can be reinstalled in the same locations from which they were removed. Inspect the rocker arms, and pushrods for abnormal/excessive wear, replace as necessary.

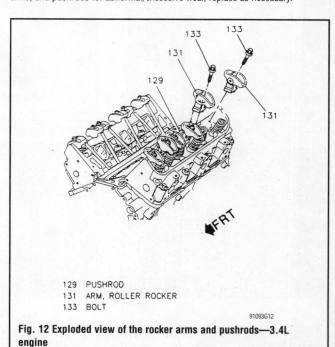

129 PUSHROD
131 ARM, ROLLER ROCKER
133 BOLT

91093G12

Fig. 12 Exploded view of the rocker arms and pushrods—3.4L engine

To install:

➡ **Before installing the rocker arms, bolts, and pushrods, coat their bearing surface with a suitable prelube. Make sure to install these components in the exact locations from which they were removed.**

6. Install the pushrods, making sure they seat properly in the lifter.
7. Install the rocker arms and bolts. Tighten the bolts to 89 inch lbs. (10 Nm), plus an additional 30° turn.
8. Install the rocker arm (valve) cover, as outlined in this section.
9. Connect the negative battery cable, then inspect for proper fluid levels and for oil leaks.

3.8L Engine

▶ **See Figures 13, 14 and 15**

The rocker arms for each bank of cylinders pivot on pedestals which are bolted to the cylinder head. Hydraulic roller valve lifters and tubular pushrods are used to operate the overhead rocker arms and valves of both banks of cylinders from a single camshaft. This system requires no lash adjustment at time of assembly or in service. The operation of hydraulic valve lifters is described below.

In addition to its normal function of a cam follower, each hydraulic valve lifter

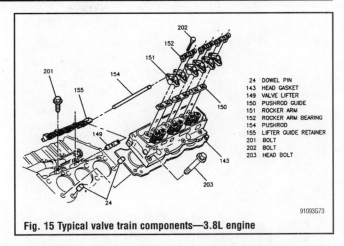

Fig. 15 Typical valve train components—3.8L engine

24	DOWEL PIN
143	HEAD GASKET
149	VALVE LIFTER
150	PUSHROD GUIDE
151	ROCKER ARM
152	ROCKER ARM BEARING
154	PUSHROD
155	LIFTER GUIDE RETAINER
201	BOLT
202	BOLT
203	HEAD BOLT

also serves as an automatic adjuster that maintains zero lash in the valve train under all operating conditions. By eliminating all lash in the valve train and providing a cushion of oil to absorb operating shocks, the hydraulic valve lifter promotes quiet valve operation. It also eliminates the need for periodic valve adjustment to compensate for wear of parts.

Each rocker arm and valve is supplied with oil through the tubular pushrod. This oil comes from the inside of the lifter, passing around the metering valve and through a hole in the lifter pushrod seat. Oil from the pushrod passes through a hole in the rocker arm pushrod seat, and emerges on top of the pushrod seat boss.

1. Disconnect the negative battery cable.
2. Remove the rocker arm (valve) covers, as outlined in this section.
3. Unfasten the rocker arm bolts, then remove the rocker arms by lifting them straight out as an assembly.
4. Remove the pushrods.

➡ **Make sure to keep all components in order for reassembly!**

5. Place rocker arms, bolts and pushrods in a rack so they can be reinstalled in the same locations from which they were removed. Inspect the rocker arms, and pushrods for abnormal/excessive wear, replace as necessary.

To install:

➡ **Before installing the rocker arms, bolts, and pushrods, coat their bearing surface with a suitable prelube. Make sure to install these components in the exact locations from which they were removed.**

6. Install the pushrods, making sure they seat properly in the lifter.
7. Install the rocker arm assemblies and secure with the retaining bolts. Tighten the bolts to 11 ft. lbs. (15 Nm), plus an additional 90° rotation.
8. Install the rocker arm (valve) cover, as outlined in this section.
9. Inspect for proper fluid levels and for oil leaks.

Thermostat

▶ **See Figure 16**

A pellet-type thermostat is used in the coolant outlet passage to control the flow of engine coolant, to provide fast engine warm-up and to regulate coolant temperatures. A wax pellet element in the thermostat expands when heated and contracts when cooled. The pellet element is connected through a piston to a valve. When the pellet element is heated, pressure is exerted against a rubber diaphragm, which forces the valve to open. As the pellet element is cooled, the contraction allows a spring to close the valve. Thus, the valve remains closed while the coolant is cold, preventing circulation of coolant through the radiator. At this point, coolant is allowed to circulate only throughout the engine to warm it quickly and evenly.

As the engine warms, the pellet element expands and the thermostat valve opens, permitting coolant to flow through the radiator, where heat is dissipated through the radiator walls. This opening and closing of the thermostat permits enough coolant to enter the radiator to keep the engine within operating limits.

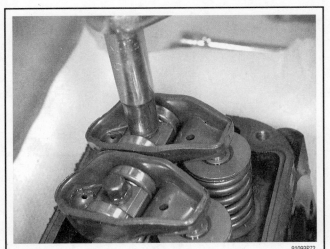

Fig. 13 Removing the rocker arm hold-down bolt

Fig. 14 Removing the rocker arm from the head

Fig. 16 View of the pellet that sits in the engine. This is a 195° thermostat; note the designation on the thermostat

REMOVAL & INSTALLATION

3.1L Engine

▶ **See Figure 17**

1. Disconnect the negative battery cable.
2. Partially drain the cooling system into a suitable container, to a level below the thermostat.
3. Disconnect the radiator hose from the thermostat housing.
4. Unfasten the thermostat housing bolts.
5. Remove the housing. Note the installed position of the thermostat, then remove the thermostat and gasket.
6. Thoroughly clean the gasket mating surfaces.

To install:

7. Position the new thermostat in the manifold.

➡**The pellet MUST go towards the engine.**

8. Install a new gasket, using sealer as necessary.
9. Install the housing and secure with the retaining bolts. Tighten the bolts to 25 Nm (18 ft. lbs.)
10. Reconnect the radiator hose to the housing.
11. Replace the coolant. Check for leaks.
12. Connect the negative battery cable.

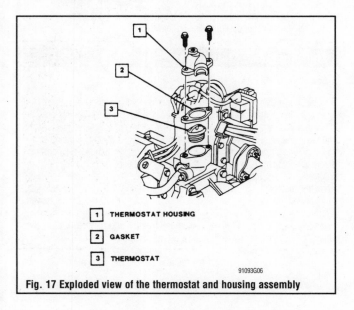

1	THERMOSTAT HOUSING
2	GASKET
3	THERMOSTAT

Fig. 17 Exploded view of the thermostat and housing assembly

3.4L Engine

▶ **See Figures 18, 19 and 20**

1. Disconnect the negative battery cable.
2. Remove the air cleaner and duct assembly.
3. Partially drain the cooling system into a suitable container, to a level below the thermostat.
4. Disconnect the radiator hose from the coolant outlet.
5. Unfasten the coolant outlet retaining bolts.
6. Remove the outlet, then remove the thermostat.
7. Thoroughly clean the gasket mating surfaces.

To install:

8. Install the new thermostat with the pellet towards the engine.
9. Install the outlet to the intake manifold. Apply RTV sealant to the housing bolts and tighten to 18 ft. lbs. (25 Nm)

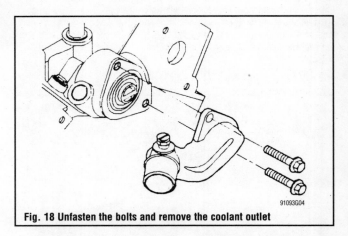

Fig. 18 Unfasten the bolts and remove the coolant outlet

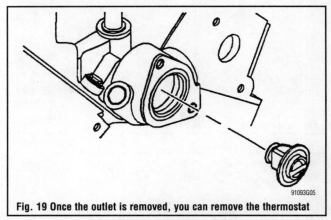

Fig. 19 Once the outlet is removed, you can remove the thermostat

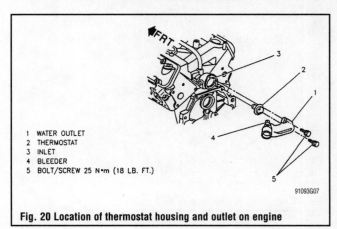

1	WATER OUTLET
2	THERMOSTAT
3	INLET
4	BLEEDER
5	BOLT/SCREW 25 N·m (18 LB. FT.)

Fig. 20 Location of thermostat housing and outlet on engine

10. Reconnect the radiator hose to the thermostat coolant outlet.
11. Install the air cleaner and duct assembly.
12. Refill the coolant and check for leaks.

➡**When adding coolant, it is important that you use DEX-COOL® (orange colored, silicate-free) coolant. If silicate coolant is added to the system, premature engine, heater core or radiator corrosion may result. In addition, the engine coolant will require change sooner.**

13. Connect the negative battery cable.

3.8L Engine

▶ **See Figures 21 thru 26**

1. Disconnect the negative battery cable.
2. Partially drain the cooling system into a suitable container, to a level below the thermostat.
3. Disconnect the radiator hose from the thermostat housing.
4. Unfasten the water outlet bolts, then remove the water outlet and thermostat
5. Thoroughly clean the gasket mating surfaces.

To install:

➡**To perform properly, the thermostat must be installed with the pellet towards the engine.**

6. Install the thermostat into the housing.
7. Position a new gasket on the manifold, using sealer as necessary.
8. Place the water outlet in position. Coat the retaining bolts with RTV, then install and tighten to 20 ft. lbs. (27 Nm).
9. Connect the radiator hose to the water outlet.
10. Refill the coolant and check for leaks.
11. Connect the negative battery cable.

Intake Manifold

REMOVAL & INSTALLATION

3.1L Engine

▶ **See Figure 27**

The intake manifold is a one-piece cast aluminum unit. It centrally supports a TBI unit.

1. Disconnect the negative battery cable.
2. Drain and recycle the engine coolant.
3. Remove the rocker arm covers, as outlined in this section.
4. Remove the TBI unit, as follows:
    a. Relieve the fuel system pressure, as outlined in Section 5.
    b. Remove the air cleaner assembly.
    c. Tag and detach the electrical connectors from the IAC motor, TP sensor and the fuel injectors.
    d. Remove the injector wiring harness.
    e. Disconnect the throttle cable, transmission control cable, and cruise control cable (where applicable).
    f. Unfasten the cable support bracket attaching screws, then remove the bracket.
    g. Tag and disconnect the vacuum hoses that interfere with the TBI assembly, and set them aside.
    h. Using a back-up wrench on the line nuts, remove the fuel feed and return lines. Pull the fuel line O-rings off and discard them, after matching them up with new ones.
    i. Unfasten the TBI attaching nuts/bolts, then remove the TBI unit and flange gasket.

91093P13

Fig. 21 View of the thermostat seated in the engine with the water outlet removed

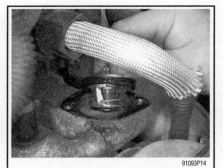
91093P14

Fig. 22 While pulling the thermostat out of the engine, notice how the pellet sits in the engine

91093P15

Fig. 23 If damaged, remove the rubber seal from around the thermostat

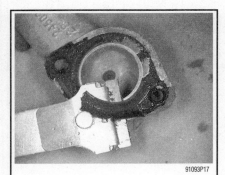
91093P17

Fig. 24 Carefully scrape the old gasket material from the thermostat water outlet

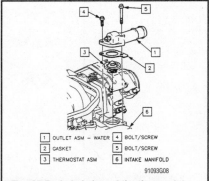

1	OUTLET ASM – WATER	4	BOLT/SCREW
2	GASKET	5	BOLT/SCREW
3	THERMOSTAT ASM	6	INTAKE MANIFOLD

91093G08

Fig. 25 Exploded view of the thermostat and water outlet assembly—3.8L engine

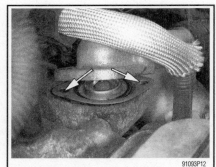
91093P12

Fig. 26 Position a new gasket, then install the water outlet and secure with the retaining bolts

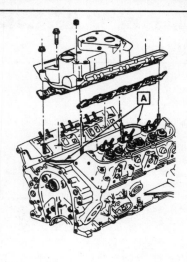

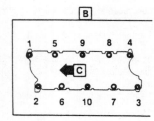

A	SEALER 1052917

B	TIGHTEN IN PROPER SEQUENCE TO
	18 N·m (13 lb.ft.) THEN RETIGHTEN
	TO 26 N·m (19 lb.ft.)

C	FRONT

91093G09

Fig. 27 Exploded view of the intake manifold, including the tightening sequence—3.1L engine

5. Unbolt the power steering pump and lay it aside. Do not disconnect the fluid lines.

6. Remove the distributor, as outlined in Section 2 of this manual.

7. Remove the retaining nuts and bolts, then lift off the intake manifold. Place a clean shop towel in the lifter valley to catch any gasket material.

8. Thoroughly clean the gasket material from the sealing surfaces, and the old RTV from the ridges. Wipe the sealing surfaces clean with degreaser. REMOVE THE SHOP TOWEL from the lifter valley.

To install:

9. Apply a ³⁄₁₆ in. (5 mm) bead of RTV sealer on each ridge. Install a new intake gasket.

10. Apply sealer to the threads of the intake manifold retaining studs.

11. Carefully seat the intake manifold without disturbing the intake gaskets, and to get the best seal from the RTV.

12. Install the intake manifold retainers. Refer to the accompanying diagram for the tightening sequence and specifications.

13. Install the rocker arm covers, as outlined in this section.

14. Position the TBI unit flange gasket, then install the TBI unit and tighten the bolts/nuts to 18 ft. lbs. (25 Nm).

15. Install new O-rings on the fuel lines, then connect the lines. Use a backup wrench to tighten the nuts to 20 ft. lbs. (27 Nm).

16. Tighten the cable support bracket attaching screws and reconnect the throttle cable, transmission control cable, and cruise control cable (where applicable). Make sure the throttle and cruise control cables do not hold the throttle open.

17. Attach the injector wiring harness and the electrical connectors, as tagged during removal. Make sure the connectors are fully seated and their latches locked, if applicable.

18. Connect the negative battery cable. Cycle the ignition key **ON** and **OFF** (do not start the engine) a couple of times and check for fuel leaks.

19. With the engine **OFF**, depress the pedal to the floor and release, to check to see that the accelerator pedal is free.

20. Install the air cleaner assembly.

21. Reset the IAC valve pintle position as follows:

a. Depress the accelerator pedal slightly.

b. Start and run the engine for three seconds—turn ignition off for ten seconds.

c. Restart engine and check for proper idle operation.

3.4L Engine

→This engine uses a sequential multiport fuel injection system. During installation, you must attach the injector electrical connectors to their appropriate fuel injector, or exhaust emissions and engine performance may be seriously affected.

UPPER MANIFOLD

♦ See Figure 28

1. Disconnect the negative battery cable.
2. Drain and recycle the engine coolant.
3. Properly relieve the fuel system pressure, as outlined in Section 5.
4. Remove the fuel injector sight shield.
5. Remove the air cleaner duct.
6. Remove the accelerator control and cruise control cables, with the bracket, from the throttle body.
7. Tag and detach the wiring harness connectors from the throttle body. Lay the harness aside.
8. Remove the thermostat bypass pipe coolant hoses from the throttle body.

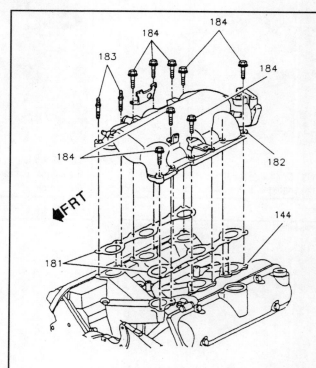

144	MANIFOLD, LOWER INTAKE
181	GASKET, UPPER INTAKE MANIFOLD
182	MANIFOLD, UPPER INTAKE
183	STUD, UPPER INTAKE MANIFOLD
184	BOLT, UPPER INTAKE MANIFOLD

91093G10

Fig. 28 Exploded view of the upper intake manifold assembly—3.4L engine

9. Label the vacuum lines and disconnect them from the connections at the throttle body.

10. Tag and disconnect the left side (front) spark plug wires, and set them aside.

11. Remove the ignition coil bracket with the coils, the purge solenoid and the vacuum canister solenoid.

12. Remove the Manifold Absolute Pressure (MAP) sensor and bracket.

13. Tag and disconnect the vacuum hose connections from the upper intake manifold.

14. Remove the rear alternator brace.

15. Remove the Exhaust Gas Recirculation (EGR) valve.

16. Unfasten the upper intake manifold nuts and bolts, then remove the upper intake manifold.

17. Remove the upper intake gasket, be careful not to mar or scratch the sealing surfaces while cleaning them with degreaser.

➡ **On some applications, you may want to remove the throttle body.**

18. Installation is the reverse of the removal procedure. Make sure to tighten all retainers evenly and securely. Attach all electrical connections and vacuum lines as tagged during removal. Fill all fluids to their proper levels, and check for leaks.

LOWER MANIFOLD

♦ **See Figure 29**

1. Disconnect the negative battery cable.
2. Drain and recycle the engine coolant.
3. Properly relieve the fuel system pressure, as outlined in Section 5 of this manual..
4. Remove the upper intake manifold, as outlined in this section.
5. Remove the left (front) and right (rear) rocker arm covers. Refer to the procedure given in this section.

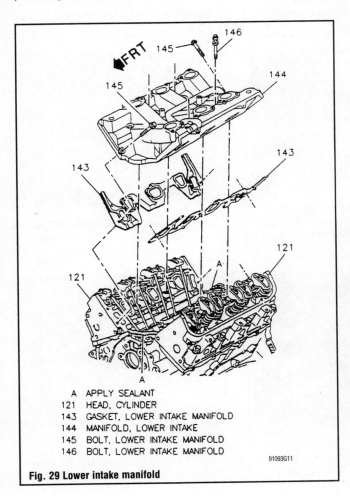

A	APPLY SEALANT
121	HEAD, CYLINDER
143	GASKET, LOWER INTAKE MANIFOLD
144	MANIFOLD, LOWER INTAKE
145	BOLT, LOWER INTAKE MANIFOLD
146	BOLT, LOWER INTAKE MANIFOLD

91093G11

Fig. 29 Lower intake manifold

6. Use a backup wrench to disconnect the fuel feed and return pipe from the fuel injector rail.

7. Remove the fuel rail assembly. For more details, refer to Section 5 of this manual.

8. Unbolt the power steering pump from the front engine cover and reposition it to one side. Do not disconnect the fluid lines.

9. Disconnect the heater inlet pipe from the lower intake manifold and the upper radiator hose from the engine.

10. Unfasten the lower intake manifold bolts, then lift the lower intake manifold off of the engine.

11. Remove the lower intake manifold gasket and the RTV sealer. Thoroughly clean the gasket mating surfaces with a suitable degreaser.

To install:

12. Apply a bead of RTV sealer on each ridge where front and rear of the lower intake manifold contact the engine block. Install the lower intake manifold gaskets.

✳✳ WARNING

An oil leak may result if the vertical attaching bolts are not tightened before the diagonal attaching bolts.

13. Position the lower intake manifold onto the block. Align the bolt holes. Apply sealer to the manifold bolts and install hand tight into the manifold. Tighten the vertical attaching bolts first, to 115 inch lbs. (13 Nm), then the diagonal bolts to 115 inch lbs. (13 Nm).

14. Connect the upper radiator hose to the engine .

15. Connect the heater inlet pipe to the lower intake manifold.

16. Install the power steering pump to the front engine cover.

17. Install the fuel rail, as outlined in Section 5 of this manual.

18. Use back-up wrench to connect the fuel feed and return pipe to the fuel rail.

19. Install the right (rear) and left (front) valve rocker cover. Refer to the procedure in this section.

20. Install the upper intake manifold, as outlined earlier. Make sure to follow the proper torque sequence.

21. Fill the coolant system.

22. Connect the negative battery cable and check for leaks.

3.8L Engine

♦ **See Figures 30 thru 48**

1. Disconnect the negative battery cable.
2. Drain and recycle the engine coolant.
3. Properly relieve the fuel system pressure, as outlined in Section 5 of this manual.
4. Remove the air cleaner intake duct and box assembly.
5. Tag and disconnect the spark plug wires from the right side of the engine, then set them aside.

91091PD0

Fig. 30 Remove the air filter box and duct as an assembly

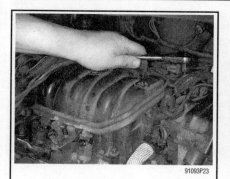

Fig. 31 Unfasten the fuel rail mounting bolts

Fig. 32 Make sure to remove all of the bolts that secure the fuel rail to the manifold

Fig. 33 The fuel delivery system can be lifted to gain access to the manifold without total disassembly

Fig. 34 Remove the throttle body bracket. Note the location of the MAF sensor (A) TP sensor (B) and IAC valve (C), mounted on the throttle body

Fig. 35 The by-pass hose and heater pipe will have to be disconnected to remove the lower intake manifold

Fig. 36 Loosen the clamp retaining screw . . .

Fig. 37 . . then slide the hose off the nipple

Fig. 38 Remove the bolt holding the heater pipe into the manifold: The O-ring (arrow) should be replaced before re-assembly

Fig. 39 If necessary separate the throttle body from the intake manifold. There are usually three mounting studs

Fig. 40 Removing the upper intake manifold, without total disassembly of the fuel system

Fig. 41 Looking into the throat of the upper intake manifold; Note the gasket

Fig. 42 View of the underside of the upper intake manifold

Fig. 43 View of the lower intake manifold installed on the engine

Fig. 44 Unfasten the lower intake manifold bolts

Fig. 45 Unplug the sensor electrical connector; it is not necessary to remove it for manifold removal

Fig. 46 After removing all of the retainers, lift the intake manifold from the engine. Note that the upper hose was disconnected from the radiator

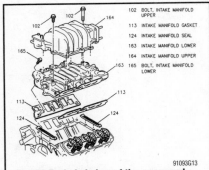

102	BOLT, INTAKE MANIFOLD UPPER
113	INTAKE MANIFOLD GASKET
124	INTAKE MANIFOLD SEAL
163	INTAKE MANIFOLD LOWER
164	INTAKE MANIFOLD UPPER
165	BOLT, INTAKE MANIFOLD LOWER

Fig. 47 Exploded view of the upper and lower intake manifolds and gaskets—3.8L engine

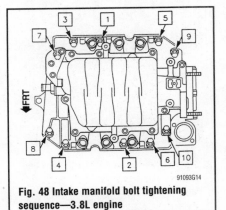

Fig. 48 Intake manifold bolt tightening sequence—3.8L engine

6. Remove the fuel rail, as outlined in Section 5 of this manual.
7. Remove the exhaust crossover heat shield.
8. Remove the cable bracket to cylinder head mounting bolt.
9. Remove the serpentine belt.
10. Remove the power steering pump support bracket.
11. Loosen the alternator mounts and slide it to gain access.
12. Remove the alternator mounting bracket.
13. Remove the heater pipes.
14. Disconnect the by-pass hose.
15. Remove the EGR valve outlet pipe.
16. Unfasten the retaining bolts, then remove the intake manifold from the engine.
17. Clean the cylinder block, heads, and intake manifold sealing surface of all oil with a suitable solvent.

To install:
18. Apply a suitable RTV sealant to the ends of the manifold seals.
19. Clean the intake manifold bolts and bolt holes of old adhesive compound.
20. Position a new intake gasket, then install intake manifold. Tighten the mounting bolts, in two passes, to 11 ft. lbs. (15 Nm) following the sequence given in the accompanying figure.
21. Install the EGR valve outlet pipe.
22. Reconnect the by-pass hose.
23. Install the alternator bracket, position the alternator and tighten the bolts.
24. Install the serpentine belt.
25. Install the power steering pump support bracket.
26. Install the cable bracket to cylinder head mounting bolt.
27. Replace the exhaust crossover heat shield.
28. Install the fuel rail, as outlined in Section 5 of this manual.
29. Replace the plug wires in their respective positions on the right side of the engine.
30. Install the air duct.
31. Fill the coolant system.
32. Connect the negative battery cable.
33. Check for leaks.

Exhaust Manifold

REMOVAL & INSTALLATION

3.1L Engine

LEFT SIDE (FRONT)

♦ See Figure 49

1. Take the vehicle to a reputable repair shop to have the A/C discharge and recovered.

➡If your vehicle is equipped with air conditioning, refer to Section 1 for information regarding the implications of servicing your A/C system yourself. Only an MVAC-trained, EPA-certified, automotive technician should service the A/C system or its components.

2. Disconnect the negative battery cable.
3. Remove the serpentine belt.
4. Remove the A/C compressor and lay it aside.
5. Remove the engine strut, and the engine strut bracket.
6. Disconnect the crossover pipe connection.
7. Unfasten the retainer, then remove the exhaust manifold.
8. Clean the mating surfaces at the cylinder head and manifold.

To install:
9. Install the exhaust manifold.

➡Liberally coat the manifold fasteners, with a suitable anti-seize compound.

10. Reconnect the crossover pipe. Tighten the manifold bolts to 26 ft. lbs. (35 Nm).
11. Install the engine strut bracket and the engine strut.
12. Install the A/C compressor.
13. Install the serpentine belt.

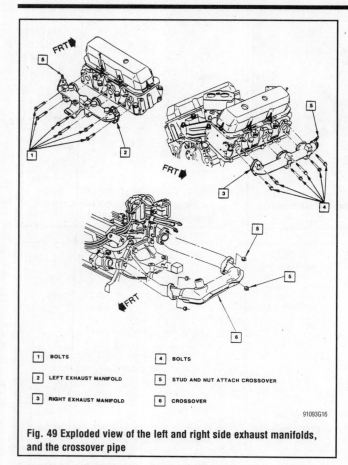

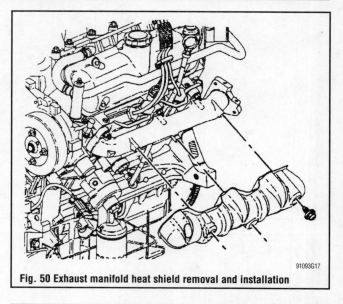

Fig. 50 Exhaust manifold heat shield removal and installation

1	BOLTS	4	BOLTS
2	LEFT EXHAUST MANIFOLD	5	STUD AND NUT ATTACH CROSSOVER
3	RIGHT EXHAUST MANIFOLD	6	CROSSOVER

91093G16

Fig. 49 Exploded view of the left and right side exhaust manifolds, and the crossover pipe

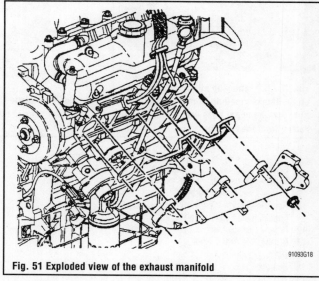

Fig. 51 Exploded view of the exhaust manifold

14. Connect the negative battery cable.

15. Take the vehicle to a reputable repair shop to have the A/C system recharged.

RIGHT SIDE (REAR)

♦ See Figure 49

1. Disconnect the negative battery cable.
2. Remove the oxygen (O2) sensor.
3. Disconnect the crossover pipe connection.
4. Raise and suitably support the vehicle.
5. Disconnect the exhaust pipe.
6. Support the frame at the rear center.
7. Disconnect the rear frame mount bolts. Carefully lower the frame about 10 inches (25.4cm). Remove the exhaust manifold.
8. Clean the mating surfaces at the cylinder head and manifold.

To install:

9. Install the exhaust manifold. Liberally coat the fasteners for the manifold, with an anti-seize compound. Install the manifold bolts, and tighten to 26 ft. lbs. (35 Nm).

10. Raise the engine frame to the mounts, and install the rear frame mount bolts.

11. Install the exhaust pipe.
12. Carefully lower the vehicle.
13. Reconnect the crossover pipe. Install the oxygen (O2) sensor.
14. Connect the negative battery cable.
15. Check for exhaust leaks.

3.4L Engine

LEFT SIDE (FRONT)

♦ See Figures 50 and 51

1. Disconnect the negative battery cable.
2. Drain and recycle the engine coolant.

3. Remove the air cleaner duct.
4. Remove the right engine mount strut bracket.
5. Disconnect the upper radiator hose from the engine.
6. Remove the automatic transaxle vacuum modulator pipe.
7. Remove the thermostat bypass pipe.
8. Remove the exhaust crossover pipe heat shield, and remove the exhaust crossover pipe bolts to the left exhaust manifold.
9. Unfasten the left exhaust manifold heat shield bolts, then remove the heat shield.
10. Remove the left exhaust manifold nuts, then remove the left exhaust manifold and gasket.
11. Clean the mating surfaces with a suitable solvent.

To install:

12. Install the exhaust manifold gasket, the exhaust manifold, and the manifold nuts.

13. Liberally coat the fasteners for the manifold with a suitable anti-seize compound. Tighten the nuts to 12 ft. lbs. (16 Nm).

14. The remainder of installation is the reverse of the removal procedure.

RIGHT SIDE (REAR)

♦ See Figures 52, 53 and 54

1. Disconnect the negative battery cable.
2. Remove the air cleaner duct.

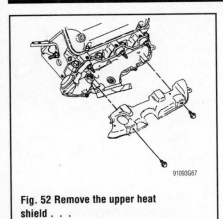

Fig. 52 Remove the upper heat shield . . .

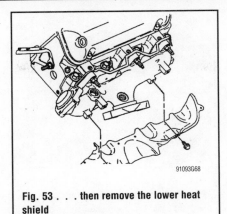

Fig. 53 . . . then remove the lower heat shield

Fig. 54 After the heat shields are removed, unfasten the retainers and remove the exhaust manifold

3. Drain and recycle the engine coolant.
4. Disconnect the upper radiator hose from the engine
5. Remove the automatic transaxle vacuum modulator pipe, then pull the dipstick out.
6. Remove the thermostat bypass pipe.
7. Remove the exhaust crossover pipe heat shield, and then the bolts from the right (rear) exhaust manifold.
8. Detach the oxygen sensor electrical connector.
9. Raise and safely support the vehicle securely on jackstands.
10. Remove the three-way catalytic converter pipe from the right (rear) exhaust manifold.
11. Remove the automatic transaxle fluid filler tube. Move the filler tube aside.
12. Remove the EGR tube and the oxygen sensor from the exhaust manifold.
13. Unfasten the heat shield bolts, then remove the upper and lower heat shields.
14. Remove the exhaust manifold nuts, then remove the manifold and gasket.

To install:

➡**Before installation, liberally coat the fasteners for the manifold, with a suitable anti-seize compound.**

15. Install the exhaust manifold gasket, the exhaust manifold, and the manifold nuts.
16. Tighten the exhaust manifold nuts to 12 ft. lbs. (16 Nm).
17. Install the heat shields. Tighten the upper and lower heat shield nuts to 89 inch lbs. (10 Nm)
18. The remainder of installation is the reverse of the removal procedure.

3.8L Engine

LEFT SIDE (FRONT)

♦ **See Figures 55 thru 62**

1. Disconnect the negative battery cable.
2. Tag and disconnect the spark plug wires from the spark plugs, and put them aside.

3. Remove the EGR tube.
4. Unfasten the two bolts attaching the exhaust crossover pipe to the manifold.
5. Remove the oil level indicator tube and indicator.
6. Unfasten the exhaust manifold retaining nuts, then remove the manifold. Remove and discard the gasket, if equipped. If replacing the manifold, transfer the oxygen sensor to the new manifold.
7. Clean the gasket mating surfaces with a suitable solvent.

To install:

8. Position a new gasket, if equipped, then install the exhaust manifold.
9. Liberally coat the manifold fasteners, with a suitable anti-seize compound, then install them and tighten securely/
10. The remainder of installation is the reverse of the removal procedure.

RIGHT SIDE (REAR)

♦ **See Figure 63**

1. Disconnect the negative battery cable.
2. Tag and disconnect the spark plug wires from the spark plugs, then place them aside.
3. Remove the throttle cable bracket.
4. Remove the crossover pipe heat shield.
5. Remove the transaxle oil level indicator and indicator tube.
6. Disconnect the oxygen sensor lead.
7. Unfasten the two bolts attaching the exhaust crossover pipe to the manifold.
8. Remove the plastic tank mounted on the cowl.
9. Raise and suitably support the vehicle.
10. Remove the catalytic converter heat shield and pipe hanger.
11. Remove the front exhaust pipe from the exhaust manifold.
12. Lower the vehicle and remove the engine lift bracket.
13. Unfasten the exhaust manifold retaining nuts, then remove the manifold. Remove and discard the gasket, if equipped. If replacing the manifold, transfer the oxygen sensor to the new manifold.
14. Clean the gasket mating surfaces with a suitable solvent.

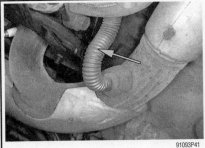

Fig. 55 The EGR valve has a pipe (arrow) that recirculates hot exhaust gas through the intake manifold. This pipe must be removed

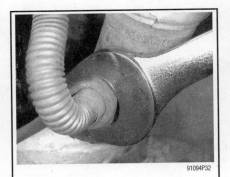

Fig. 56 Unscrew the nut attaching the EGR tube to the exhaust pipe

Fig. 57 View of the exhaust crossover pipe

Fig. 58 This pipe is secured with 2 bolts, one on each side

Fig. 59 The bolts are easily accessible with a socket and long extension

Fig. 60 Remove the retaining nut holding the dipstick tube to the manifold

Fig. 61 Unfasten the nuts from the exhaust manifold studs to remove the exhaust manifold

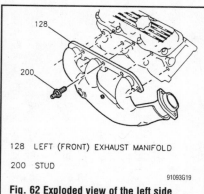

128 LEFT (FRONT) EXHAUST MANIFOLD
200 STUD

Fig. 62 Exploded view of the left side (front) exhaust manifold—3.8L engine

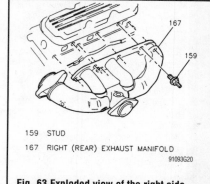

159 STUD
167 RIGHT (REAR) EXHAUST MANIFOLD

Fig. 63 Exploded view of the right side (rear) exhaust manifold—3.8L engine

To install:
15. Install the exhaust manifold and secure with the retaining nuts.
16. Install the engine lift bracket.
17. Raise and suitably support the vehicle.
18. Attach the front exhaust pipe to the exhaust manifold with the nuts previously removed.
19. Install the catalytic converter heat shield and pipe hanger.
20. Lower the vehicle, then attach the plastic vacuum tank onto the cowl.
21. Install the two bolts attaching the exhaust crossover pipe to the manifold.
22. Reconnect the oxygen sensor lead.
23. Install the transaxle oil lever indicator and indicator tube.
24. Replace the crossover pipe heat shield.
25. Install the throttle cable bracket.
26. Attach the spark plug wires to the spark plugs, as tagged during removal.
27. Connect the negative battery cable.

Radiator

♦ **See Figures 64 and 65**

The cooling system includes a radiator and recovery sub-system, cooling fan, thermostat and housing, water pump, and serpentine belt.

The operation of the cooling system requires proper functioning off all components. Coolant is drawn from the radiator by the water pump, circulated through coolant jackets in the engine block, intake manifold, and cylinder heads, and then directed back to the radiator where it is cooled. Coolant should be kept at a 50% solution to maintain an effective level of anti-rust and anti-corrosive properties, as well as protection against freezing and overheating.

A cross-flow aluminum radiator is used. Tanks in this type radiator are located to the right and left of the core instead of above and below. The radiator also has an oil cooler with inlet and outlet fittings for transaxle fluid circulation.

The core is made of aluminum and uses large tubes that resist plugging. The tanks are made of plastic and are attached to the core by the use of clinched tabs, The clinched tabs can be bent if the tank needs to be removed from the core.

A high temperature rubber gasket is used to seal the mating surface between the core and the tanks. The gasket MUST be replaced with the removal of the tanks.

The aluminum radiator uses a two piece drain cock and rubber seal. The drain cock is serviceable.

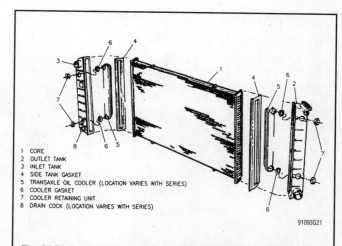

1 CORE
2 OUTLET TANK
3 INLET TANK
4 SIDE TANK GASKET
5 TRANSAXLE OIL COOLER (LOCATION VARIES WITH SERIES)
6 COOLER GASKET
7 COOLER RETAINING UNIT
8 DRAIN COCK (LOCATION VARIES WITH SERIES)

Fig. 64 Exploded view of a typical aluminum radiator, including the coolers and tanks

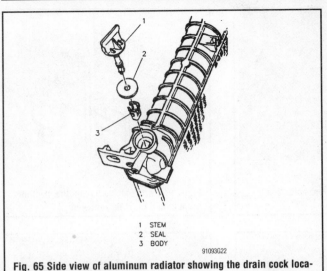

1 STEM
2 SEAL
3 BODY

91093G22

Fig. 65 Side view of aluminum radiator showing the drain cock location at the bottom of the tank

REMOVAL & INSTALLATION

▶ **See Figures 66 thru 79**

1. Disconnect the negative battery cable.
2. Drain and recycle the engine coolant into a suitable container.

✳✳ CAUTION

Never open, service or drain the radiator or cooling system when hot; serious burns can occur from the steam and hot coolant. Also, when draining engine coolant, keep in mind that cats and dogs are attracted to ethylene glycol antifreeze and could drink any that is left in an uncovered container or in puddles on the ground. This will prove fatal in sufficient quantities. Always drain coolant into a sealable container. Coolant should be reused unless it is contaminated or is several years old.

3. Remove the engine forward strut bracket at the radiator, then swing the strut rearward. Make sure to loosen the bolt before swinging the strut, to prevent ripping the rubber bushing.
4. Disconnect the forward lamp harness from the fan frame and unplug the fan connector. Remove the fan and frame assembly by removing the fan attach-

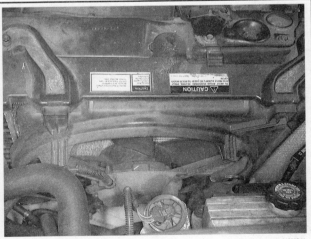

91096P11

Fig. 66 Top engine view of radiator; the fan assembly will have to be removed to remove the radiator

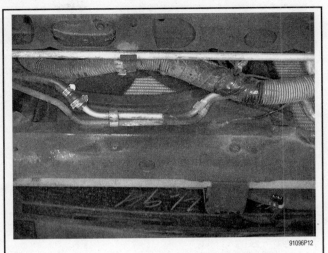

91096P12

Fig. 67 Under vehicle view of the radiator. Note the trans cooler lines and flex connections; they will have to be disconnected to remove the radiator

ing bolts. On some applications, a Low Coolant Module needs to be unplugged and removed also.

5. Scribe the hood latch installed location for reinstallation, then remove the hood latch from the radiator support.
6. Disconnect the coolant hoses from the radiator and coolant recovery tank hose from the radiator neck.
7. Disconnect and plug the transaxle cooler lines.
8. Remove the radiator-to-radiator support attaching bolts and clamps.
9. Lift the radiator out of the vehicle. If the lower mounting pads stick to the radiator during removal, the pads must be placed back in the lower radiator frame for installation of a new radiator.

➡ **If the old radiator is being replaced with a new one, transfer the fittings from the old to the new radiator.**

To install:

10. Place the radiator in the vehicle, locating the bottom of the radiator into the lower mounting pads.

➡ **Try to maintain the location of the air baffles and seals; they help direct the airflow through the radiator.**

11. Install the radiator-to-radiator support attaching clamp and bolts. Tighten to 89 inch lbs. (10 Nm).
12. Unplug and connect the cooler lines for the transaxle, be sure to check the fluid level upon completion.

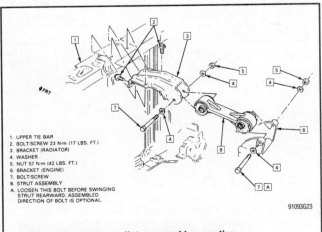

1. UPPER TIE BAR
2. BOLT/SCREW 23 N·m (17 LBS. FT.)
3. BRACKET (RADIATOR)
4. WASHER
5. NUT 57 N·m (42 LBS. FT.)
6. BRACKET (ENGINE)
7. BOLT/SCREW
8. STRUT ASSEMBLY
A. LOOSEN THIS BOLT BEFORE SWINGING STRUT REARWARD. ASSEMBLED DIRECTION OF BOLT IS OPTIONAL.

91093G23

Fig. 68 Engine strut-to-radiator assembly mounting

Fig. 69 This left side bolt holds the cooling fan in place; the left and right side bottom bolts will have to be removed to remove the fan

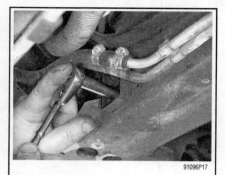

Fig. 70 Unfasten the bottom bolts that secure the fan

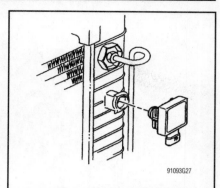

Fig. 71 Some vehicles have a low coolant module that must be removed

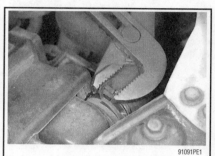

Fig. 72 Use a pair of slip joint pliers to release and move the hose clamp. There are special pliers made for this purpose, for applications that are more difficult

Fig. 73 Slide the clamp back, away from the neck of the radiator

Fig. 74 Disconnect the upper hose from the radiator neck

Fig. 75 Unfasten the retainers, then remove the top radiator cover

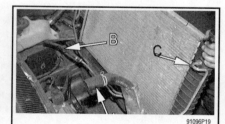

Fig. 76 Lift the radiator up and out of the vehicle. The bottom hose (A) is disconnected from the engine; trans cooler line (B) is disconnected at the rubber hose; and trans cooler line (C) is left connected at radiator

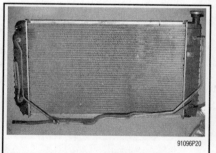

Fig. 77 Radiator removed from vehicle; note the trans cooler lines and lower hose are still attached to radiator. Where clearance allows, this is an easier removal

Fig. 78 These radiator fins are clogged by debris; this can cause over-heating and coolant loss. Check and clean the radiator as part of a regular maintenance schedule

13. Install the coolant hoses to the radiator and the recovery hose to the neck.

14. Replace the hood latch, aligning it to the scribed mark on the radiator frame. Tighten the bolts to 18 ft. lbs. (25 Nm).

15. Install the fan and frame assembly, tighten the radiator attaching bolts, route the forward lamp harness to the fan frame and plug in the fan connector.

16. If equipped, install and reconnect the Low Coolant Module sensor.

17. Swing the engine front strut and brace forward, until brace the contacts the radiator support. Install the brace-to-radiator support attaching bolts and tighten to 37 ft. lbs. (50 Nm).

18. Refill the engine cooling system.

19. Connect the negative battery cable and check for leaks.

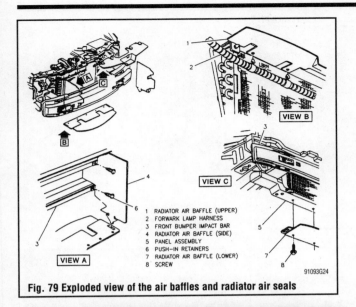

1 RADIATOR AIR BAFFLE (UPPER)
2 FORWARK LAMP HARNESS
3 FRONT BUMPER IMPACT BAR
4 RADIATOR AIR BAFFLE (SIDE)
5 PANEL ASSEMBLY
6 PUSH–IN RETAINERS
7 RADIATOR AIR BAFFLE (LOWER)
8 SCREW

91093G24

Fig. 79 Exploded view of the air baffles and radiator air seals

Engine Fan

♦ See Figures 80 and 81

✳✳ CAUTION

An electric fan under the hood can start up even when the engine is not running and can injure you. Keep hands, clothing and tools away from any underhood electric fan.

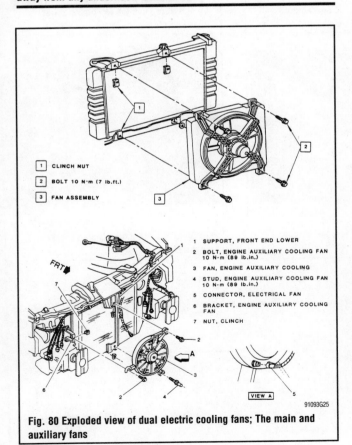

1 CLINCH NUT

2 BOLT 10 N·m (7 lb.ft.)

3 FAN ASSEMBLY

1 SUPPORT, FRONT END LOWER
2 BOLT, ENGINE AUXILIARY COOLING FAN 10 N·m (89 lb.in.)
3 FAN, ENGINE AUXILIARY COOLING
4 STUD, ENGINE AUXILIARY COOLING FAN 10 N·m (89 lb.in.)
5 CONNECTOR, ELECTRICAL FAN
6 BRACKET, ENGINE AUXILIARY COOLING FAN
7 NUT, CLINCH

FRT

VIEW A

91093G25

Fig. 80 Exploded view of dual electric cooling fans; The main and auxiliary fans

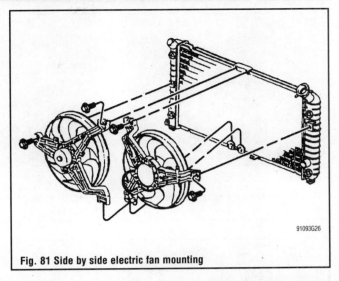

91093G26

Fig. 81 Side by side electric fan mounting

Early models use one large cooling fan with five blades to aid airflow through the radiator/condenser. They are driven by an electric motor mounted to the radiator support. The ECM and a relay activate the fan motor. If the vehicle is equipped with A/C, a second switch can activate the circuit, depending upon A/C compressor head pressure to the condenser.

Later models use two cooling fans; a main cooling fan, and auxiliary fan to aid airflow through the condenser. A coolant temperature switch activates the fans. A transducer can also activate the circuit, depending upon A/C compressor head pressure to the condenser.

REMOVAL & INSTALLATION

Single or Main Fan

♦ See Figures 82, 83 and 84

1. Disconnect the negative battery cable.
2. Remove the air cleaner and duct assembly.
3. Disconnect the wiring harness from the fan motor.
4. Remove the fan mounting bolts.
5. Remove the fan assembly.
6. Installation is the reverse of the removal procedure.

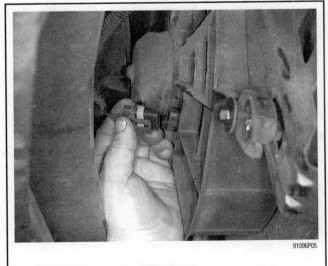

91096P05

Fig. 82 Unplug the fan electrical connector

Fig. 83 Removing the upper fan mounting bolt

Fig. 84 Pulling the engine cooling fan out the top

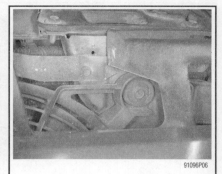

Fig. 85 View of the upper mounting bolt for the condenser fan

Fig. 86 Remove the fan upper mounting bolts

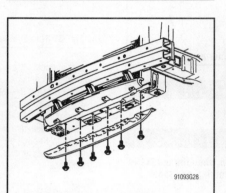

Fig. 87 Exploded view of the radiator lower air deflector

Fig. 88 Insert a small flat-bladed tool, into the slot to release the tab on the lower splash shield . . .

Fig. 89 . . . then lower the front splash shield for access to the fan retainers

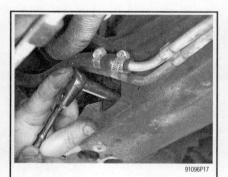

Fig. 90 Remove the lower fan mounting bolt(s)

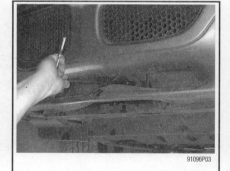

Fig. 91 Use of a long extension makes reaching . . .

Auxiliary Fan

▶ See Figures 85 thru 95

1. Disconnect the negative battery cable.
2. Remove the upper fan mounting bolt.
3. Raise and suitably support the vehicle.
4. Remove the lower air baffle. This may also be called a deflector, or splash shield and may be secured with screws, bolts or retaining clips.
5. Disconnect the wiring harness to fan motor.
6. Remove the lower mounting bolts and/or nuts, then remove the auxiliary (condenser) fan.

To install:

7. Install the auxiliary fan and tighten the mounting bolts to 89 inch lbs. (10 Nm)

8. Connect the wiring harness to the fan motor.
9. Install the lower air baffle.
10. Lower the vehicle and install the upper mounting bolt.
11. Connect the negative battery cable.

TESTING

Electric cooling fans operate when engine coolant temperature exceeds a certain value, or the A/C is engaged. The PCM completes the ground paths for the windings of the cooling fan relays. The relay contacts then close and complete the circuit between the fusible link and the fan motor. When the engine cools down, or the A/C is turned off, the PCM removes the ground for the fan relays and the fans stop.

Diagnosis of the system is done through the PCM and the use of a scan tool.

Fig. 92 . . . this lower retaining nut much easier

Fig. 93 There is more room than appears to access this fan lower mounting bolt

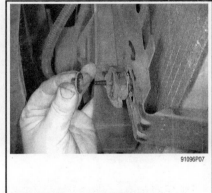

Fig. 94 Remove the retaining nut . . .

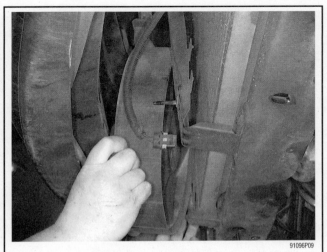

Fig. 95 . . . then slide the condenser fan off the stud, down, and out of the vehicle

It is possible to check the basic condition of the circuits and components to determine their condition.

An intermittent problem may be caused by a poor connection, rubbed through wire insulation, or a wire broken inside the insulation. Inspect the hard-shell connectors for backed out terminals. Check for improper mating, broken locks, improperly formed or damaged terminals, and poor terminal to wire connection.

If connections and harness check OK, connect a digital voltmeter from the affected terminal to ground while moving related connectors and harnesses; if the failure is induced, the voltage reading will change.

3.1L Engine

▶ See Figures 96 and 97

The electric cooling fan is controlled by the PCM, based on inputs from the ECT sensor, A/C request, and the A/C refrigerant fan request switch and vehicle speed. The PCM controls the fans by grounding the circuits that energize the fan control relays. Battery voltage is then supplied to the fan motors.

The PCM grounds the circuit for the cooling fan (puller fan relay terminal '86'), when coolant temperature is approximately 106°C (223°F); or when A/C has been requested, and the A/C refrigerant fan request switch opens with high A/C pressure, about 200 psi (1380 kPa).

The pusher fan relay is grounded by the PCM when coolant temperature is approximately 110°C (217°F), and/or the puller fan is "ON" for A/C pressure.

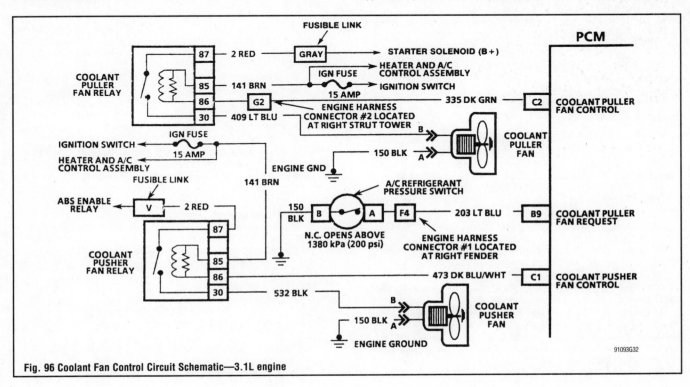

Fig. 96 Coolant Fan Control Circuit Schematic—3.1L engine

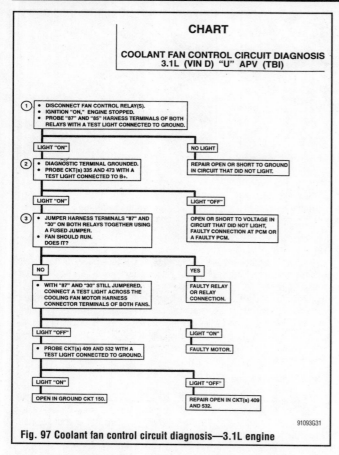

CHART

COOLANT FAN CONTROL CIRCUIT DIAGNOSIS 3.1L (VIN D) "U" APV (TBI)

① • DISCONNECT FAN CONTROL RELAY(S).
• IGNITION "ON," ENGINE STOPPED.
• PROBE "87" AND "85" HARNESS TERMINALS OF BOTH RELAYS WITH A TEST LIGHT CONNECTED TO GROUND.

LIGHT "ON" → **NO LIGHT** → REPAIR OPEN OR SHORT TO GROUND IN CIRCUIT THAT DID NOT LIGHT.

② • DIAGNOSTIC TERMINAL GROUNDED.
• PROBE CKT(s) 335 AND 473 WITH A TEST LIGHT CONNECTED TO B+.

LIGHT "ON" → **LIGHT "OFF"** → OPEN OR SHORT TO VOLTAGE IN CIRCUIT THAT DID NOT LIGHT, FAULTY CONNECTION AT PCM OR A FAULTY PCM.

③ • JUMPER HARNESS TERMINALS "87" AND "30" ON BOTH RELAYS TOGETHER USING A FUSED JUMPER.
• FAN SHOULD RUN. DOES IT?

NO → **YES** → FAULTY RELAY OR RELAY CONNECTION.

• WITH "87" AND "30" STILL JUMPERED, CONNECT A TEST LIGHT ACROSS THE COOLING FAN MOTOR HARNESS CONNECTOR TERMINALS OF BOTH FANS.

LIGHT "OFF" → **LIGHT "ON"** → FAULTY MOTOR.

• PROBE CKT(s) 409 AND 532 WITH A TEST LIGHT CONNECTED TO GROUND.

LIGHT "ON" → OPEN IN GROUND CKT 150.

LIGHT "OFF" → REPAIR OPEN IN CKT(s) 409 AND 532.

91093G31

Fig. 97 Coolant fan control circuit diagnosis—3.1L engine

The numbers used below refer to the circled numbers on the accompanying diagnostic flow chart.

1. 12 volts should be available to both terminals '87' and '85', when the ignition is "ON".

2. This test checks the ability of the PCM to ground circuit 335 and circuit 473. The MIL (Service Engine Soon) should also be flashing at this point.

3. This test checks to see if the coolant puller and pusher fan relay (circuits 409 and 532) are open. Jumping terminals '87' and '30' bypasses the relay, which should cause the fans to run, if the fan motors and wiring are OK.

➡ **If the engine is overheating and the cooling fan is ON, the cooling system should be checked.**

3.4L Engine

♦ **See Figure 98**

Power for the fan motors is supplied through two Maxifuses® in the underhood electrical center. The cooling fan relays are energized when current flows from the two Maxifuses® through the relay coils to ground through the PCM. The coolant Fan #1 Relay (Cool Fan 1 Relay) control circuit is grounded for low speed fans operation. The Coolant Fan #1 Relay control circuit and the Coolant Fan 2 Relay control circuit (Cool Fan Relay and Cool Fan 2 Relay) are grounded for high-speed fans operation.

During low speed fan operation, the PCM supplies a ground path for Cool Fan 1 Relay. This closes the Cool Fan 1 Relay contacts, allowing current to flow from the U/H Electrical center through the relay contacts to the left engine-cooling fan. During low speed operation, the ground path for the primary cooling fan is through the engine Cool Fan Relay and the right engine cooling fan motor. The result is a series circuit with both cooling fans running at low speed.

During high speed cooling fan operation, the PCM supplies a ground path for the Cool Fan 1 Relay. The PCM also supplies a ground path for Cool Fan cooling fan relays. During high speed fans operation, both the right and the left engine cooling fans are supplied current from the U/H Electrical Center and each cooling fan has its own ground path.

Testing of this system is done with a scan tool. Stored diagnostic codes may

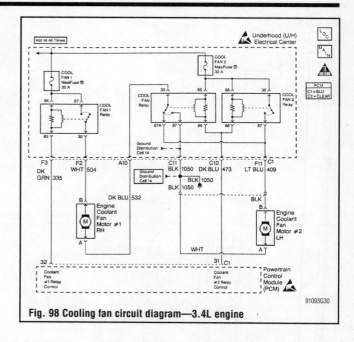

Fig. 98 Cooling fan circuit diagram—3.4L engine

affect engine cooling fans operation. Stored codes should be remedied before attempting to diagnose a cooling fan fault.

3.8L Engine

♦ **See Figure 99**

The PCM will complete the ground path for the winding of the puller fan (Fan 1) relay when it sees engine temperature above approximately 100°C (212°F) or when the A/C is requested. It turns the fan on by grounding the system through circuit '86' (the terminal number on the relay). The fans will continue to run for approximately 45 seconds after the A/C request is gone.

The cooling fans can be tested for proper operation.

Power for the fan motors comes from fusible links to terminal '87' on the relays. The relays are energized when current flows to ground through the PCM quad-driver #4.

1. Turn the ignition key to the **ON** position, but do not start the engine.

2. Disconnect the puller fan relay and probe the harness connector cavities '85' and '87' with a test light connected to ground. The test light should light.

3. If the test light does not light, trace and repair the open in the affected circuit.

4. If test light lights, jump the puller fan relay harness connector terminals '87' to '30'. The fan should run.

5. If the fan does not run, with jumper still connected, probe terminal "B" at the fan motor connector with a test light. The light should light.

6. If the light does not light, trace and repair the wire fault between the relay and the fan motor connector.

7. If test light lights, connect a test light between terminal "A" and "B" at the fan connector harness. The test light should light.

8. If the light does not light, repair wire fault in ground circuit to fan motor.

9. If test light lights, check for a loose connection at the fan; then check the fan operation.

10. Unplug the fan electrical connector.

11. Fabricate a jumper wire (using 10-gauge wire) and attach one end to terminal "A" on the fan motor.

12. Attach the other end to a good engine ground.

13. Fabricate a second, but fused, jumper wire and attach it to the other terminal of the cooling fan.

14. Now take the loose end and touch it to the positive battery terminal. The fan should spin; if it does not, replace it. Plug the fan connector back in again.

Puller fan (Fan #1) relay—The PCM energizes the relay through terminal 'WD11' when engine coolant temperature reaches a set value or when the A/C is requested.

15. Jump the puller fan relay harness connector terminals '87' to '30'. Fan should run.

16. Using a suitable Scan tool, turn Fan 1 "on". Probe the fan relay harness

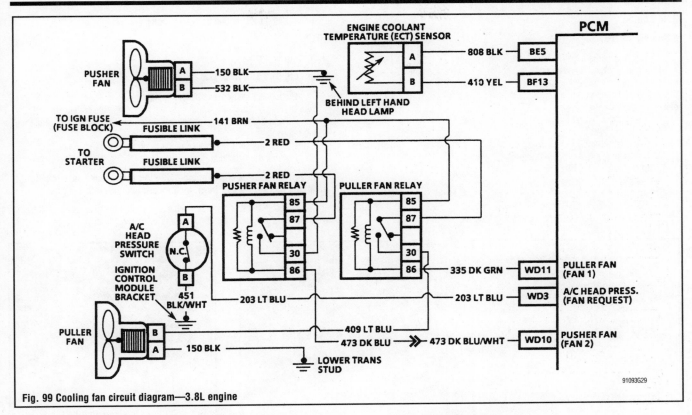

Fig. 99 Cooling fan circuit diagram—3.8L engine

connector terminal '86' with a test light connected to battery power. Test light should light.

17. If the light does not light, trace and repair wire fault between the relay and the PCM, if connections and wiring are good; replace the PCM.

18. If the test light lights, replace the fan relay.

Pusher fan (Fan #2)—The pusher fan relay is energized by the PCM if the A/C head pressure switch opens, indicating refrigerant pressure above 210 psi (1448 kPa), or when engine coolant temperature reaches 226°F (108°C). This fan is tested the same way.

Water Pump

The water pump is a centrifugal-type pump consisting of an impeller, impeller drive shaft, pulley flange, and cast housing. The serpentine belt drives the pulley that attaches to the pump. The water pump draws coolant from the radiator, through the lower hose, circulates it through the coolant jackets in the engine block, intake manifold, and cylinder heads, and then directs it back to the radiator, where it is cooled, through the upper hose.

REMOVAL & INSTALLATION

❊❊ CAUTION

Never open, service or drain the radiator or cooling system when hot; serious burns can occur from the steam and hot coolant. Also, when draining engine coolant, keep in mind that cats and dogs are attracted to ethylene glycol antifreeze and could drink any that is left in an uncovered container or in puddles on the ground. This will prove fatal in sufficient quantities. Always drain coolant into a sealable container. Coolant should be reused unless it is contaminated or is several years old.

3.1L Engine

♦ See Figure 100

1. Disconnect the negative battery cable.
2. Drain and recycle the engine coolant into a suitable container.

3. Disconnect the heater hose.
4. Remove the serpentine belt shield.
5. With a ⅜ breaker-bar, relieve tension in the serpentine belt.
6. Remove the water pump pulley.
7. Unfasten the retainers, then remove the water pump. Remove and discard the gasket.
8. Thoroughly clean the gasket mating surfaces.

To install:

9. Position a new gasket, then install the water pump. Tighten the attaching bolts to 89 inch lbs. (10 Nm).
10. Install the water pump pulley.
11. Install the serpentine belt, then replace the serpentine belt shield.
12. Connect the heater hose.
13. Refill the cooling system.
14. Connect the negative battery cable.

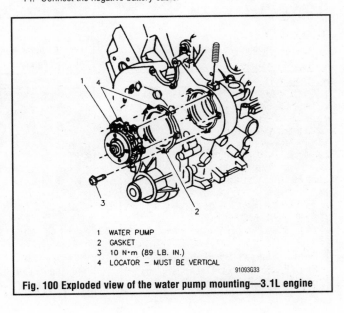

1 WATER PUMP
2 GASKET
3 10 N·m (89 LB. IN.)
4 LOCATOR – MUST BE VERTICAL

91093G33

Fig. 100 Exploded view of the water pump mounting—3.1L engine

3.4L Engine

▶ See Figure 101

1. Disconnect the negative battery cable.
2. Drain and recycle the engine coolant into a suitable container.
3. Remove the serpentine belt guard, bolts and nuts.
4. Loosen the water pump pulley bolts. Do not remove the bolts until the belt is removed.
5. Remove the serpentine belt.
6. Remove the water pump pulley.
7. Remove the water pump and gasket.
8. Thoroughly clean the gasket mating surfaces.

To install:

9. Install the water pump with a new gasket.
10. Install the water pump pulley and loosely install the attaching bolts.
11. Install the serpentine belt.
12. Tighten the water pump pulley bolts to 18 ft. lbs. (25 Nm)

13. Install the serpentine belt guard, bolts and nuts.
14. Refill the coolant system.

3.8L Engine

▶ See Figures 102 thru 112

1. Disconnect the negative battery cable.
2. Drain and recycle the engine coolant into a suitable container.
3. Loosen the water pump pulley bolts. Do not remove the bolts until the belt is removed.
4. Release the serpentine drive belt tension, then remove the belt.
5. Remove the water pump pulley.

➡**As you remove the water pump mounting bolts, make sure to note the locations that they came from, as they are two different lengths.**

6. Unfasten the retainers, then remove the water pump and gasket. If the water pump is stuck to the engine, there is a small notch in which you can

Fig. 101 Water pump mounting—3.4L engine

1 FRONT COVER
2 GASKET
3 WATER PUMP
4 BOLT/SCREW, WATER PUMP
5 LOCATOR—MUST BE IN VERTICAL POSITION

91093G34

Fig. 102 Loosen the pulley mounting bolts before releasing the belt tension

91093P02

Fig. 103 After the serpentine belt is removed, you can remove the water pump pulley

91093P03

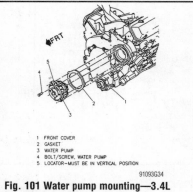

Fig. 104 Unfasten the water pump mounting bolts

91093P04

Fig. 105 Attempt to pull the water pump off the engine

91093P07

Fig. 106 If you can't pull the water pump off, there is a provision made for a small prytool. Be very careful when prying the water pump off!

91093P05

Fig. 107 It doesn't take much pressure with a prytool to release the water pump from the gasket

91093P06

Fig. 108 Use a suitable tool to scrape the gasket material from the engine . . .

91093P08

Fig. 109 . . . and from the old water pump assembly

91093P09

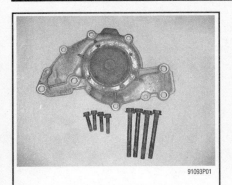

Fig. 110 Make a note, or mark the bolts, because they are two different lengths

Fig. 111 Make sure the mating surfaces are clean before affixing a new gasket to the water pump

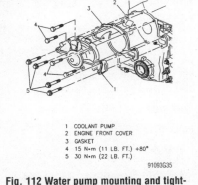

1   COOLANT PUMP
2   ENGINE FRONT COVER
3   GASKET
4   15 N•m (11 LB. FT.) +80°
5   30 N•m (22 LB. FT.)

Fig. 112 Water pump mounting and tightening specifications—3.8L engine

insert a small prytool. Be extremely carefully if you have to pry the water pump off! Discard the gasket.

7. Thoroughly clean the gasket mating surfaces.

To install:

8. Attach a new gasket to the water pump.

9. Install the water pump to the engine. Tighten the mounting bolts to the specifications given in accompanying figure.

10. Install the water pump pulley. Loosely install the mounting bolts.

11. Install the serpentine drive belt.

12. Tighten the pump pulley bolts.

13. Refill the coolant system.

14. Connect the negative battery cable.

Cylinder Head

➡️ If your vehicle is equipped with air conditioning, refer to Section 1 for information regarding the implications of servicing your A/C system yourself. Only an MVAC-trained, EPA-certified, automotive technician should service the A/C system or its components.

❄️❄️ CAUTION

Observe all applicable safety precautions when working around fuel. Whenever servicing the fuel system, always work in a well-ventilated area. Do not allow fuel spray or vapors to be exposed to a spark or open flame. Keep a dry chemical fire extinguisher near the work area. Always keep fuel in a container specifically designed for fuel storage; also, always properly seal fuel containers to avoid the possibility of fire or explosion.

❄️❄️ CAUTION

Never open, service or drain the radiator or cooling system when hot; serious burns can occur from the steam and hot coolant. Also, when draining engine coolant, keep in mind that cats and dogs are attracted to ethylene glycol antifreeze and could drink any that is left in an uncovered container or in puddles on the ground. This will prove fatal in sufficient quantities. Always drain coolant into a sealable container. Coolant should be reused unless it is contaminated or is several years old.

REMOVAL & INSTALLATION

➡️ This repair procedure requires the use of a torque angle meter.

3.1L Engine

LEFT SIDE

◆ See Figure 113

The cast iron cylinder heads have individual intake and exhaust ports for each cylinder. Rocker arms are retained on individual threaded studs.

1. Disconnect the negative battery cable.

2. Drain and recycle the engine coolant.

3. Properly relieve the fuel system pressure, as outlined in Section 5 of this manual.

4. Remove the following components, as outlined in this section:

a. Rocker arm covers

b. Intake manifold

c. Exhaust manifold and crossover pipe

5. Remove the oil level indicator and tube. Remove the engine strut bracket.

6. Loosen the rocker arms and remove the pushrods. Make sure to keep the pushrods in proper order for installation.

7. Unfasten the cylinder head mounting bolts, then remove head from the engine. Remove and discard the gasket.

8. Thoroughly clean the gasket mounting surfaces, head bolts and cylinder block threads. Once the cylinder head has been removed, it is best to clean and check the head for straightness and cracks. Refer to the engine reconditioning portion of this section for more details.

➡️ It is usually best to engage the services of a local machine shop to perform these checks.

To install:

9. Place a new gasket in position over the dowel pins, with the note "This Side Up" showing.

10. Install the cylinder head over the dowel pins.

11. Install the cylinder head bolts. Tighten in the sequence shown in the accompanying figure to 33 ft. lbs. (45 Nm), plus an additional 90 ° rotation.

12. Install the intake gasket.

13. Install the pushrods, make sure the lower ends of the pushrods are in the lifter seats.

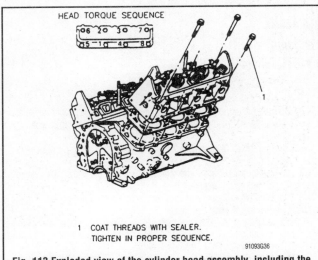

HEAD TORQUE SEQUENCE

1   COAT THREADS WITH SEALER.
    TIGHTEN IN PROPER SEQUENCE.

Fig. 113 Exploded view of the cylinder head assembly, including the tightening sequence

14. Install the rocker arms, adjust the valve lash as described in section one.
15. Replace the intake manifold, rocker arm covers, exhaust manifold, and crossover pipe.
16. Attach the oil level indicator tube and bracket to the head.
17. Install the engine strut bracket.
18. Replace coolant, change oil and filter.
19. Connect the negative battery cable.

RIGHT SIDE

♦ **See Figure 113**

1. Disconnect the negative battery cable.
2. Drain and recycle the engine coolant.
3. Remove the air cleaner and inlet hose.
4. Remove the exhaust crossover tube.
5. Raise the vehicle, remove the right side exhaust manifold and lower the vehicle.
6. Remove the alternator, as described in Section 2 of this manual.
7. Remove the rocker arm covers, and intake manifold as described in this section of the manual.
8. Loosen the rocker arms and remove the pushrods. Make sure to keep the pushrods in order for installation.
9. Remove the coil bracket.
10. Unfasten the cylinder head mounting bolts, then remove head from the engine. Remove and discard the gasket.
11. Thoroughly clean the gasket mounting surfaces, head bolts and cylinder block threads. Once the cylinder head has been removed, it is best to clean and check the head for straightness and cracks. Refer to the engine reconditioning portion of this section for more details.

To install:
12. Place a new gasket in position over the dowel pins, with the note "This Side Up" showing.
13. Install the cylinder head over the dowel pins.
14. Install the cylinder head bolts. Tighten in the sequence shown in the accompanying figure to 33 ft. lbs. (45 Nm), plus an additional 90° rotation.
15. Install the coil bracket.
16. Install the intake gasket.
17. Install the pushrods, making sure the lower ends of the pushrods are in the lifter seats.
18. Install the rocker arms.
19. Replace the intake manifold, rocker arm covers, and alternator.
20. Raise and safely support the vehicle.
21. Install the exhaust manifold, and exhaust pipe and lower the vehicle.
22. Install the crossover pipe.
23. Install the air cleaner and inlet pipe.
24. Connect the negative battery cable.
25. Adjust the valve lash as described in Section 1 of this manual.
26. Fill the fluid levels, change the oil and filter.

3.4L Engine

LEFT SIDE

♦ **See Figure 114**

1. Disconnect the negative battery cable.
2. Drain and recycle the engine coolant.
3. Remove the rocker arm covers, upper intake manifold, lower intake manifold, and exhaust manifold and crossover pipe, as described in this section of the manual.
4. Remove the oil level indicator assembly retaining bolt, and remove the indicator assembly.
5. Loosen the rocker arms and remove the pushrods. Make sure to keep the pushrods in order for installation.
6. Unfasten the cylinder head mounting bolts, then remove head from the engine. Remove and discard the gasket
7. Thoroughly clean the gasket mounting surfaces, head bolts and cylinder block threads. Once the cylinder head has been removed, it is best to clean and

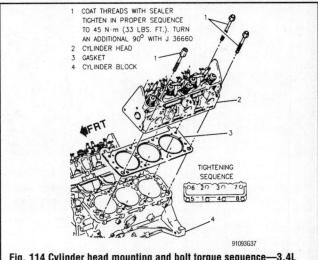

Fig. 114 Cylinder head mounting and bolt torque sequence—3.4L engine

check the head for straightness and cracks. Refer to the engine reconditioning portion of this section for more details.

➡**It is usually best to engage the services of a local machine shop to perform these checks.**

To install:
8. Place the new gasket in position over the dowel pins, with the note "This Side Up" showing.
9. Position the cylinder head over the dowel pins.
10. Install the cylinder head bolts. Tighten in the sequence shown in the accompanying figure to 33 ft. lbs. (45 Nm), plus an additional 90° rotation with the torque angle meter.
11. The remainder of installation is the reverse of the removal procedure.
12. Adjust valve lash according to the directions given in Section 1.
13. Fill fluid levels, change oil and filter.
14. Connect the negative battery cable.

RIGHT SIDE

♦ **See Figure 114**

1. Disconnect the negative battery cable.
2. Drain and recycle the engine coolant.
3. Remove the rocker arm covers, upper intake manifold, lower intake manifold, and exhaust manifold and crossover pipe, as described in this section of the manual.
4. Loosen the rocker arms and remove the pushrods. Make sure to keep the pushrods in order for installation.
5. Unfasten the cylinder head mounting bolts, then remove head from the engine. Remove and discard the gasket.
6. Thoroughly clean the gasket mounting surfaces, head bolts and cylinder block threads. Once the cylinder head has been removed, it is best to clean and check the head for straightness and cracks. Refer to the engine reconditioning portion of this section for more details.

➡**It is usually best to engage the services of a local machine shop to perform these checks.**

To install:
7. Place the new gasket in position over the dowel pins, with the note "This Side Up" showing.
8. Position the cylinder head over the dowel pins.
9. Install the cylinder head bolts. Tighten in the sequence shown in the accompanying figure to 33 ft. lbs. (45 Nm), plus an additional 90° rotation with the torque angle meter.
10. The remainder of installation is the reverse of the removal procedure.

11. Adjust valve lash according to the directions given in Section 1.
12. Fill fluid levels, change oil and filter.
13. Connect the negative battery cable.

3.8L Engine

LEFT AND RIGHT SIDE

▶ **See Figures 115 thru 127**

1. Disconnect the negative battery cable.
2. Drain and recycle the engine coolant.
3. Remove the intake manifold and the exhaust manifold, as outlined in this section.
4. Remove the rocker arm covers, loosen the rocker arms and remove the pushrods. Make sure to keep the pushrods in order for installation.
5. Remove the electronic ignition and spark plug wires.

6. Remove the alternator bracket attached from the head.
7. Remove the A/C compressor bracket from the head.
8. Unbolt the power steering pump and position it aside. Do not disconnect the fluid lines.
9. Remove the serpentine belt tensioner.
10. Remove the fuel pipe heat shield.
11. Unfasten the cylinder head mounting bolts, then remove head from the engine. Remove and discard the gasket
12. Thoroughly clean the gasket mounting surfaces, head bolts and cylinder block threads. Once the cylinder head has been removed, it is best to clean and check the head for straightness and cracks. Refer to the engine reconditioning portion of this section for more details.

➡**This engine uses special torque to yield head bolts. This design bolt requires a special tightening procedure. Failure to follow the given procedure will cause head gasket failure and possible engine damage.**

Fig. 115 Unfasten the bolts, then remove the intake manifold

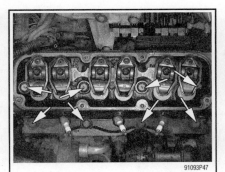

Fig. 116 Unfasten the cylinder head mounting bolts

Fig. 117 Pulling the head, with rockers intact, from the engine block

Fig. 118 View of the top of the pistons with the head removed; these pistons are dished (concave) to help in emission control. Arrows point to the pushrods

Fig. 119 Remove the cylinder head gasket from the block. Discard the old gasket and use a new one for installation

Fig. 120 In the intake valley you will see the balance shaft, used to reduce engine vibration; the valve lifter guides prevent lifters from rotating in their bores

Fig. 121 The dowel pin (arrow) makes it easy to position up a new gasket on the head, after it has been cleaned

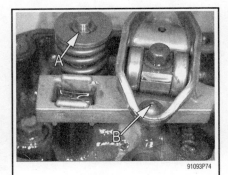

Fig. 122 View of the valve keeper (A) and the location where the pushrod seats (B)

Fig. 123 View of the valve spring (A), rocker assembly (B) and cylinder head bolt (C)

Fig. 124 Disassembling the rocker

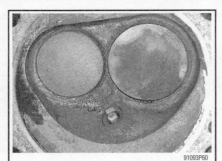

Fig. 125 With the head removed, you can see the intake (larger), and exhaust (smaller), valves. The spark plug is nestled between them

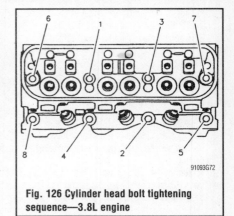

Fig. 126 Cylinder head bolt tightening sequence—3.8L engine

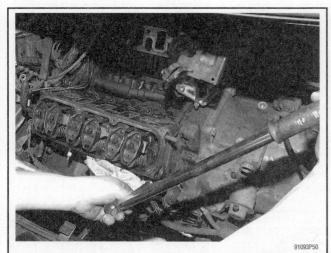

Fig. 127 Always use a torque wrench when tightening cylinder head bolts

To install:

➡️Install the head gasket with arrow pointing to front of the engine.

✳️ CAUTION

Head gaskets are not interchangeable. Failure to install with arrow pointing to front will cause gasket failure and possible engine failure. New head bolts must be used to complete installation. They are "torque to yield".

13. Apply sealant to the underside of the head bolts, and apply thread locker to the bolt threads before installation.

14. Install NEW head bolts, and tighten to 35 ft. lbs. (47 Nm) in the sequence shown in the accompanying figure.

15. Rotate each bolt an additional 130°, in sequence, using a torque angle meter.

16. Rotate the center 4 bolts an additional 30°, in sequence, using a torque angle meter.

17. Install the pushrods, guide plate and rocker arm assemblies. Apply thread lock compound to the rocker arm pedestal bolts before assembly.

18. Tighten the rocker arm pedestal bolts to 11 ft. lbs. (15 Nm), plus an additional 90° rotation.

19. The remainder of installation is the reverse of the removal procedure.

20. Adjust lash according to the procedure given in Section 1.

21. Fill fluid levels, change oil and filter.

22. Connect the negative battery cable.

Oil Pan

REMOVAL & INSTALLATION

3.1L Engine

▶ **See Figures 128 and 129**

1. Disconnect the negative battery cable.
2. Raise and safely support the vehicle.
3. Remove the crankshaft damper.
4. Drain the engine oil into a suitable container.
5. Remove the flywheel shields.
6. Remove the starter, as outlined in Section 2.
7. Support the engine from underneath, at the transaxle-mounting bracket.
8. Remove the engine mount bracket-to-engine bolts.
9. Raise the engine enough to clear the oil pan removal.
10. Unfasten the oil pan bolts, then remove the oil pan. Remove the gasket.
11. Thoroughly clean all gasket mating surfaces including the oil pan flanges, oil pan rail, front cover, rear main bearing cap and the threaded holes.

➡️**Check the oil pan for any damage, check at the drain hole, and check the drain plug for stripped threads. Repair or replace as necessary.**

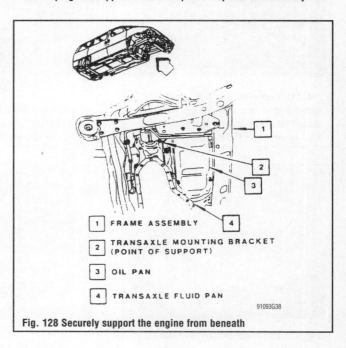

1	FRAME ASSEMBLY
2	TRANSAXLE MOUNTING BRACKET (POINT OF SUPPORT)
3	OIL PAN
4	TRANSAXLE FLUID PAN

Fig. 128 Securely support the engine from beneath

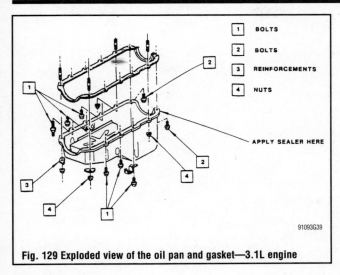

1	BOLTS
2	BOLTS
3	REINFORCEMENTS
4	NUTS

APPLY SEALER HERE

91093G39

Fig. 129 Exploded view of the oil pan and gasket—3.1L engine

To install:

12. Replace the oil pan gasket if necessary.
13. Apply sealant to the oil pan gasket tabs at the rear main bearing caps.
14. Install the oil pan, and secure with the retaining bolts. Tighten the pan bolts to 89 inch lbs. (10 Nm).
15. Lower the engine, and secure the mounting bracket.
16. Install the starter, as outlined in Section 2.
17. Replace the flywheel shields.
18. Carefully lower the vehicle.
19. Install the crankshaft damper.
20. Fill the crankcase with the proper type and amount of oil.
21. Connect the negative battery cable.

3.4L Engine

♦ **See Figure 130**

➡**Removal and installation of the oil pan in this vehicle requires the use of some special tools. Needed are the following:**

- Universal Support Fixture
- Engine Support Fixture Adapters
- Engine Support Fixture Adapter
- Torque Wrench Adapter

1. Install a suitable universal support fixture, engine support fixture adapters and the engine support fixture adapter.
2. Disconnect the negative battery cable.

3. Raise and safely support the vehicle.
4. Drain the engine oil into a suitable container.
5. Remove the oil filter drip shield, bolts and shield.
6. Disconnect the exhaust pipe from the manifold.
7. Place jackstands under the frame at the front and rear.
8. Remove the engine mount-to-frame nuts, then remove the transaxle mount-to-frame nuts.
9. Loosen, but do not remove, the rear frame bolts.
10. Remove the front frame bolts, then lower the front of the frame.
11. Remove the engine mount and bracket.
12. Remove the starter, as outlined in Section 2 of this manual.
13. Remove the oil level wiring harness connector.
14. Remove the transaxle brace.
15. Remove the oil pan side bolts, remove the oil pan bottom bolts, and remove the pan.
16. Thoroughly clean all gasket mating surfaces including the oil pan flanges, oil pan rail, front cover, rear main bearing cap and the threaded holes.

➡**Check the oil pan for any damage, check at the drain hole, and check the drain plug for stripped threads. Repair or replace as necessary.**

To install:

17. Position the oil pan gasket.
18. Apply sealant to the oil pan gasket tabs at the rear main bearing caps.
19. Install the oil pan, then tighten the pan bolts to 18 ft. lbs. (25 Nm).
20. Install the oil pan side bolts and tighten to 37 ft. lbs. (50 Nm) using a torque wrench adapter.
21. Reconnect the oil level wiring harness connector.
22. Install the transaxle brace.
23. Install the starter, as outlined in Section 2.
24. Install the engine mount bracket and mount.
25. Raise the frame to the proper position using new frame bolts.
26. Remove the jackstands.
27. Connect the exhaust pipe to the manifold.
28. Install the transaxle and engine mount nuts.
29. Install the oil filter drip shield and bolts.
30. Lower the vehicle and fill the crankcase with oil.
31. Remove the special tools installed at the beginning of this procedure.
32. Connect the negative battery cable.

3.8L Engine

♦ **See Figure 131**

1. Disconnect the negative battery cable.
2. Remove the crankshaft balancer with a suitable puller.
3. Raise and safely support the vehicle securely.
4. Drain the oil pan into a suitable container.
5. Unfasten the oil pan bolts, then remove the oil pan.

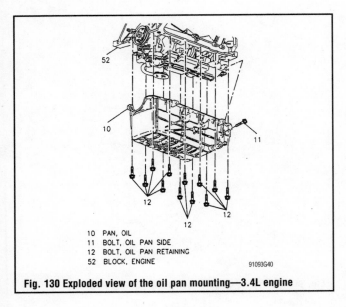

10	PAN, OIL
11	BOLT, OIL PAN SIDE
12	BOLT, OIL PAN RETAINING
52	BLOCK, ENGINE

91093G40

Fig. 130 Exploded view of the oil pan mounting—3.4L engine

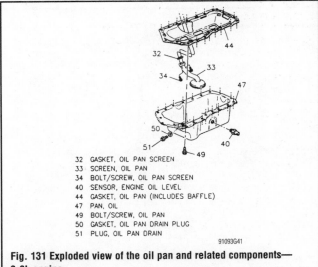

32	GASKET, OIL PAN SCREEN
33	SCREEN, OIL PAN
34	BOLT/SCREW, OIL PAN SCREEN
40	SENSOR, ENGINE OIL LEVEL
44	GASKET, OIL PAN (INCLUDES BAFFLE)
47	PAN, OIL
49	BOLT/SCREW, OIL PAN
50	GASKET, OIL PAN DRAIN PLUG
51	PLUG, OIL PAN DRAIN

91093G41

Fig. 131 Exploded view of the oil pan and related components— 3.8L engine

6. Remove the old oil pan gasket and discard. The formed rubber oil pan gasket cannot be reused. Clean the gasket mating surfaces.

To install:

7. Install the new formed rubber oil pan gasket on the oil pan flange.
8. Apply thread lock compound to the oil pan bolt threads before assembly.
9. Install the oil pan and tighten the bolts to 124 inch lbs. (14 Nm).

✳✳ WARNING

Do not overtorque pan bolts or damage to the oil pan will occur, resulting in an oil leak.

10. Install the crankshaft balancer.
11. Carefully lower the vehicle, then fill the crankcase with oil.
12. Connect the negative battery cable.

Oil Pump

REMOVAL & INSTALLATION

3.1L Engine

◆ **See Figure 132**

1. Remove the oil pan as outlined earlier in this section.
2. Remove the oil pump and drive shaft extension.

➡**Do not remove the pickup tube from the cover unless loose or broken.**

3. Installation is the reverse of the removal procedure.

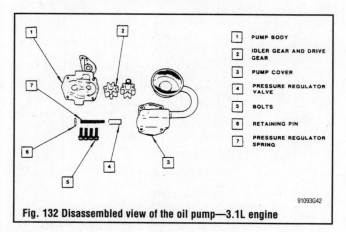

1	PUMP BODY
2	IDLER GEAR AND DRIVE GEAR
3	PUMP COVER
4	PRESSURE REGULATOR VALVE
5	BOLTS
6	RETAINING PIN
7	PRESSURE REGULATOR SPRING

91093G42

Fig. 132 Disassembled view of the oil pump—3.1L engine

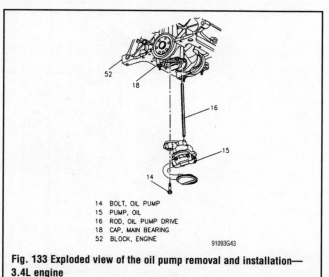

14 BOLT, OIL PUMP
15 PUMP, OIL
16 ROD, OIL PUMP DRIVE
18 CAP, MAIN BEARING
52 BLOCK, ENGINE

91093G43

Fig. 133 Exploded view of the oil pump removal and installation—3.4L engine

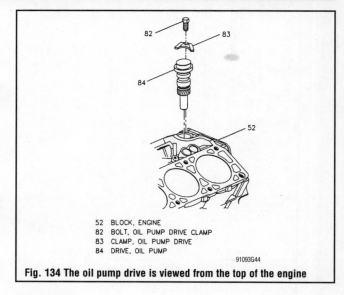

52 BLOCK, ENGINE
82 BOLT, OIL PUMP DRIVE CLAMP
83 CLAMP, OIL PUMP DRIVE
84 DRIVE, OIL PUMP

91093G44

Fig. 134 The oil pump drive is viewed from the top of the engine

3.4L Engine

◆ **See Figures 133 and 134**

1. Remove the oil pan as described earlier in this section.
2. Remove the oil pump bolt.
3. Remove the pump and drive shaft extension. Clean all parts in a suitable solvent; remove all varnish, sludge, and dirt.
4. Installation is the reverse of the removal procedure. Tighten the oil pump retaining bolt to 30 ft. lbs. (41 Nm).

3.8L Engine

◆ **See Figures 135 and 136**

1. Remove the engine front cover, as outlined in this section.
2. Remove the oil filter adapter, pressure regulator valve and spring.
3. Remove oil pump covers attaching screws and cover.
4. Remove the gears.
5. Remove the oil pan as described earlier in this section.
6. Remove the oil pump pipe and screen assembly attaching bolts.
7. Clean all parts in a suitable solvent. Remove all varnish, sludge and dirt. Remove all traces of old gasket from the front cover and engine block. Use compressed air to blow-dry the screen and housing.
8. Inspect the pump cover and front cover for cracks and scoring, porous or damaged casting, excessive wear or damaged threads.

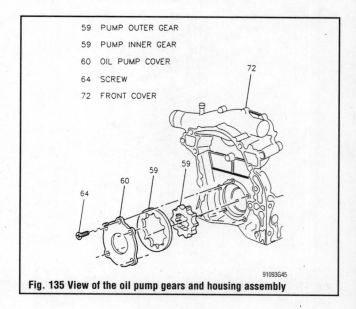

59 PUMP OUTER GEAR
59 PUMP INNER GEAR
60 OIL PUMP COVER
64 SCREW
72 FRONT COVER

91093G45

Fig. 135 View of the oil pump gears and housing assembly

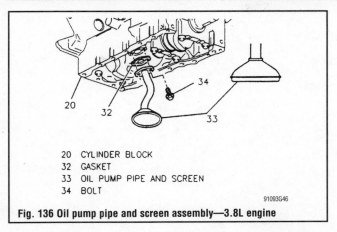

20 CYLINDER BLOCK
32 GASKET
33 OIL PUMP PIPE AND SCREEN
34 BOLT

91093G46

Fig. 136 Oil pump pipe and screen assembly—3.8L engine

9. Inspect the oil pump gears for: chipping and galling, scoring or excessive wear.

➡️**If there is a question about the integrity of any portion of the oil pump or housing, replace the cover assembly.**

To install:

10. Lubricate the gears with petroleum jelly, then assemble the gears in the housing. Pack gear cavity with petroleum jelly.

11. Install the oil pump cover and screws. Tighten the oil pump cover screws to 97 inch lbs. (11 Nm).

12. Install the pressure regulator spring and valve.

13. Install the oil filter adapter with a new gasket. Tighten the oil filter adapter bolts to 22 ft. lbs. (30 Nm).

14. Install the front cover onto the engine.

15. Install the oil pump pipe and screen with a new gasket and tighten bolts securely.

16. Install the oil pan, as outlined in this section.

17. Change the oil, install a new oil filter.

Crankshaft Damper

The inertia weight section of the crankshaft damper is assembled to the hub with a rubber sleeve. The removal and installation procedures (with the proper tools) must be followed or movement of the inertia weight section on the hub will destroy the tuning of the crankshaft damper, and the engine timing reference.

REMOVAL & INSTALLATION

3.1L Engine

▶ **See Figure 137**

➡️**The following special tools are necessary to perform this operation: a crankshaft damper/pulley puller and installation tool.**

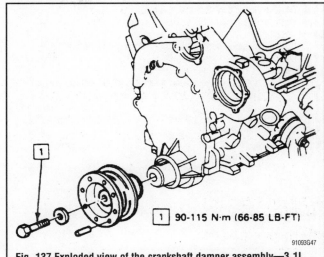

1 90-115 N·m (66-85 LB-FT)

91093G47

Fig. 137 Exploded view of the crankshaft damper assembly—3.1L engine

1. Disconnect the negative battery cable.
2. Remove the serpentine belt.
3. Raise and safely support the vehicle.
4. Remove the tire and wheel assembly. Remove the inner fender splash shield on the passenger side of the vehicle.
5. Remove the damper retaining bolt.
6. Install the crankshaft damper puller, turn the puller screw, then remove the damper.

To install:

7. Coat the front cover seal contact area (on damper) with clean engine oil.
8. Apply a suitable sealant (RTV will suffice) to the key and keyway.
9. Place the damper in position over the key on the crankshaft. Install damper onto crankshaft using a suitable crankshaft damper installation tool.
10. With damper secured on the crankshaft, remove the installer tool and install the retaining bolt. Tighten the bolt to 76 ft. lbs. (103 Nm).
11. Install the inner fender splash shield. Install the wheel assembly, if removed.
12. Lower the vehicle.
13. Install the serpentine belt
14. Connect the negative battery cable.

3.4L Engine

▶ **See Figures 138, 139 and 140**

➡️**The following special tools are necessary to perform this operation: a harmonic balancer removal tool and a harmonic balancer installation tool.**

1. Remove the serpentine belt.
2. Raise and safely support the vehicle securely.
3. Remove the right front tire and wheel.

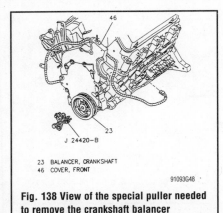

J 24420-B

23 BALANCER, CRANKSHAFT
46 COVER, FRONT

91093G48

Fig. 138 View of the special puller needed to remove the crankshaft balancer

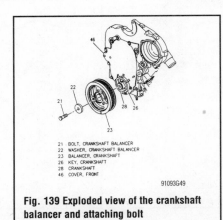

21 BOLT, CRANKSHAFT BALANCER
22 WASHER, CRANKSHAFT BALANCER
23 BALANCER, CRANKSHAFT
26 KEY, CRANKSHAFT
28 CRANKSHAFT
46 COVER, FRONT

91093G49

Fig. 139 Exploded view of the crankshaft balancer and attaching bolt

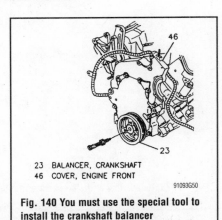

23 BALANCER, CRANKSHAFT
46 COVER, ENGINE FRONT

91093G50

Fig. 140 You must use the special tool to install the crankshaft balancer

4. Remove the right inner fender splash shield.

5. Remove the balancer bolt, you may need an assistant to keep the flywheel from turning.

6. Install the special harmonic balancer remover tool, turn the puller screw and remove the balancer.

To install:

7. Coat the front cover seal contact area (on damper) with engine oil.

8. Apply a suitable sealant (RTV will suffice) to the key and keyway.

9. Place the damper in position over the key on the crankshaft. Install the damper onto the crankshaft using a suitable damper installation tool.

10. With damper secured on the crankshaft, remove the installer tool and install the retaining bolt. Tighten the bolt to 76 ft lbs. (103 Nm). You may need assistance to keep the flywheel from turning.

11. Install the inner fender splash shield. Install the tire and wheel assembly.

12. Carefully lower the vehicle.

13. Install the serpentine belt.

3.8L Engine

▶ See Figures 141 and 142

The following special tools required for this operation are: flywheel holding tool, crankshaft balancer puller, torque angle meter.

1. Remove the serpentine belt.

2. Raise and safely support the vehicle securely.

3. Remove the right front tire and wheel.

4. Remove the right inner fender splash shield.

5. Hold flywheel with the special tool, to prevent it from turning.

6. Remove the balancer bolt.

7. Remove the crankshaft balancer with a suitable puller, using ¼ inch bolts to attach to the pulley. Screw in ¼ inch. Turn the puller screw and remove the balancer.

➡ **The balancer is serviced as an assembly. Do not attempt or separate the pulley from the balancer hub.**

To install:

8. Coat the front cover seal contact area (on damper) with clean engine oil.

9. Hold flywheel with the special tool, to prevent it from turning.

10. Place the damper in position over key on crankshaft. Install the damper onto the crankshaft.

11. With the damper secured on the crankshaft, install the retaining bolt. Tighten the bolt to 111 ft. lbs. (150 Nm), plus an additional 76° rotation, using a torque angle meter.

12. Install the inner fender splash shield. Install the wheel assembly, if removed.

13. Carefully lower the vehicle.

14. Install the serpentine belt

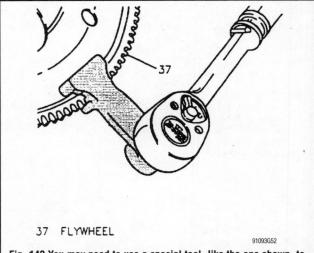

Fig. 142 You may need to use a special tool, like the one shown, to hold the flywheel stationary

37 FLYWHEEL

Timing Chain Cover and Seal

The timing chain cover may also be called the engine front cover in some instances. This cover houses the timing chain and gear assemblies (camshaft gear and crankshaft gear). If the engine employs a balancer shaft, then the balance shaft gear is also housed in the front cover. It is also the front sealing surface for the oil pan. In some cases, it may even house the oil pump.

REMOVAL & INSTALLATION

3.1L Engine

▶ See Figure 143

1. Disconnect the negative battery cable.

2. Drain and recycle the engine coolant.

3. Remove the serpentine belt and tensioner.

4. Unbolt the power steering pump and position it aside.

5. Raise and safely support the vehicle.

6. Remove the right side tire and wheel assembly, then remove the inner splash shield.

7. Remove the crankshaft damper pulley.

8. Unbolt the starter, and move it aside.

9. Place a suitable jack under the transaxle-to-engine mount.

10. Remove the engine mount bolts and mount.

11. Raise the engine for access.

12. Disconnect the radiator hose from the water pump.

13. Remove the cover bolts.

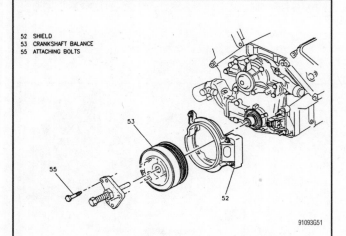

52 SHIELD
53 CRANKSHAFT BALANCE
55 ATTACHING BOLTS

Fig. 141 Exploded view of the balancer and related components—3.8L engine

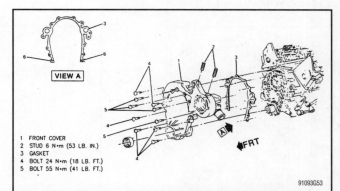

1 FRONT COVER
2 STUD 6 N•m (53 LB. IN.)
3 GASKET
4 BOLT 24 N•m (18 LB. FT.)
5 BOLT 55 N•m (41 LB. FT.)

VIEW A

FRT

Fig. 143 Exploded view of the front cover, gasket and related components

14. Lower the oil pan as outlined previously in this section.
15. Disconnect the heater coolant hose from the cooling system fill pipe.
16. Remove the bypass and overflow hoses.
17. Remove the upper front cover bolts.
18. Remove the serpentine belt pulley.
19. Remove the engine front cover. Inspect the sealing surfaces on the front cover and block; clean the surfaces with degreaser.

To install:

20. Position a new gasket, making sure not to damage sealing surfaces.
21. Apply a suitable sealant to the bottom-sealing surface of front cover
22. Place the front cover on the engine, then install the upper cover bolts.
23. Install the serpentine belt pulley.
24. Install the oil pan as described earlier in this section.
25. Install the remaining cover bolts.
26. Attach the engine mount to the engine.
27. Lower the engine into the frame, align the engine mount and install the nuts. Tighten to 35 ft. lbs. (48 Nm).
28. Install the crankshaft damper, using the special tool as required.
29. Install the flywheel cover on the transaxle.
30. Install the inner splash shield, install the tire and wheel assembly.
31. Carefully lower the vehicle.
32. Connect the radiator hose and heater hoses.
33. Install the power steering pump.
34. Install the serpentine belt tensioner and belt.
35. Fill the cooling system, change the oil.
36. Connect the negative battery cable.

3.4L Engine

▶ See Figure 144

1. Disconnect the negative battery cable.
2. Drain and recycle the engine coolant.
3. Drain the engine oil into a suitable container.
4. Remove the serpentine belt shield and belt.
5. Remove the crankshaft balancer, as described earlier in this chapter.
6. Remove the drive belt tensioner.
7. Remove the power steering pump with lines intact. Move the power steering pump aside.
8. Remove the thermostat bypass pipe from the engine front cover.
9. Disconnect the lower radiator hose from the water pump.
10. Remove the water pump pulley. For more information, refer to the water pump procedure in this section.
11. Remove the crankshaft position sensor from the engine front cover.
12. Remove the engine front cover bolts, then remove the front cover.
13. Remove the front cover gasket, clean and check the gasket mating surfaces.
14. Remove the water pump from the engine front cover.

To install:

15. Install the water pump to the engine front cover.

16. Coat both sides of the lower tabs of the engine front cover gasket with a suitable sealant.
17. Install the engine front cover gasket, then install the engine front cover. Tighten the bolts to the following specifications:
   a. Tighten the five small bolts to 20 ft. lbs. (27Nm)
   b. Tighten the three large bolts to 41 ft. lbs. (55Nm)
   c. Tighten the two long bolts to 35 ft. lbs. (47Nm)
18. Install the crankshaft position sensor to the engine front cover.
19. Install the water pump pulley.
20. Install the drive belt shield.
21. Connect the hoses that were removed.
22. Move the power steering pump into position, then tighten the bolts securely.
23. Install the crankshaft balancer.
24. Install the drive belt tensioner and the drive belt.
25. Install the crankshaft balancer.
26. Fill the fluids (oil and coolant) to the proper levels.
27. Connect the negative battery cable.

3.8L Engine

▶ See Figure 145

➡**The following special tools are required for this operation: Flywheel holding tool, crankshaft balancer puller and torque angle meter.**

1. Remove the serpentine belt.
2. Raise and safely support the vehicle securely.
3. Remove the right front tire and wheel.
4. Remove the right inner fender splash shield.
5. Hold flywheel with the special tool to prevent it from turning, then remove the balancer bolt.
6. Remove the crankshaft balancer with a suitable puller, using ¼ inch bolts to attach to the pulley. Screw in ¼ inch. Turn the puller screw and remove the balancer.

➡**The balancer is serviced as an assembly. Do not attempt or separate the pulley from the balancer hub.**

7. Remove the crankshaft sensor shield and crankshaft sensor.
8. Remove the oil pan-to-front cover bolts.
9. Remove the coolant cover bolts.
10. Unfasten the front cover attaching bolts, then remove the cover.
To install:

➡**If oil pan gasket is excessively swollen, the oil pan should be removed and the gasket replaced**

11. Install the gasket at the cylinder block
12. Apply a suitable sealant to the attaching bolt threads. Install the front cover and attaching bolts. Tighten bolts to 22 ft. lbs. (30 Nm).

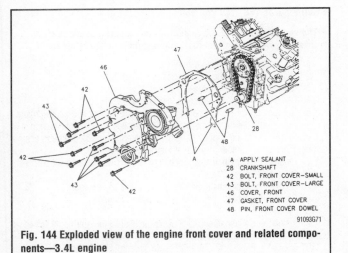

A	APPLY SEALANT
28	CRANKSHAFT
42	BOLT, FRONT COVER—SMALL
43	BOLT, FRONT COVER—LARGE
46	COVER, FRONT
47	GASKET, FRONT COVER
48	PIN, FRONT COVER DOWEL

91093G71

Fig. 144 Exploded view of the engine front cover and related components—3.4L engine

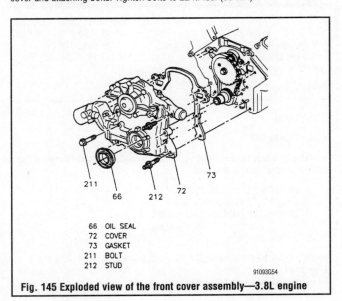

66	OIL SEAL
72	COVER
73	GASKET
211	BOLT
212	STUD

91093G54

Fig. 145 Exploded view of the front cover assembly—3.8L engine

13. Install the water pump pulley.
14. Install the oil pan-to-front cover bolts, and tighten to 10 ft. lbs. (14 Nm).
15. Install the crankshaft sensor, and the sensor shield.
16. Install the balancer and bolt. Tighten to 110 ft. lbs. (150 Nm), plus an additional 76° rotation using the torque angle meter.
17. Install the drive belt.
18. Reverse the removal process to complete the repair procedure.

SEAL REPLACEMENT

♦ See Figure 146

To remove and replace the oil seal on this vehicle, you will need a suitable front cover aligner and seal installation tool. It will not require the removal of the front cover from the engine. To remove the cover seal without removing the front cover, use the following procedure.
1. Removal the crankshaft damper as outlined earlier in this section.
2. Pry out the seal with a suitable tool, being careful not to scratch or mar any of the sealing surfaces.
To install:
3. Lubricate the seal with clean engine oil.
4. Insert the seal in the front cover with the lip facing the engine.
5. Install the special tool and drive the seal into place.
6. Install the crankshaft damper. Check for fluid leaks.

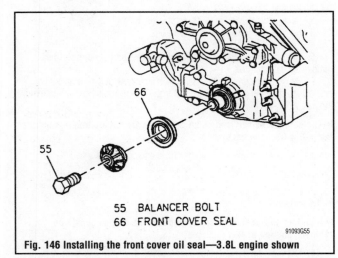

55 BALANCER BOLT
66 FRONT COVER SEAL

91093G55

Fig. 146 Installing the front cover oil seal—3.8L engine shown

Timing Chain and Gears

The timing chain is a device used to keep the camshaft operating in synchronization with the crankshaft, and consequently, the stroke of the piston coincides with the opening and closing of the valves in their proper order. The camshaft gear is precision cut to be twice as large as the crankshaft gear. For each rotation of the camshaft gear, the crankshaft gear spins twice.

REMOVAL & INSTALLATION

3.1L Engine

♦ See Figure 147

➡**This procedure requires the use of a crankshaft sprocket removal tool, and a sprocket installation tool.**

1. Bring the engine to TDC on #1 cylinder
2. Disconnect the negative battery cable.
3. Drain and recycle the engine coolant.
4. Remove the right front tire and wheel.
5. Remove the engine front cover, as outlined in this section.

➡**Align the timing marks on the cam and crank sprockets. Use the alignment marks on the damper stamping or the cast alignment marks on the cylinder and case for reference.**

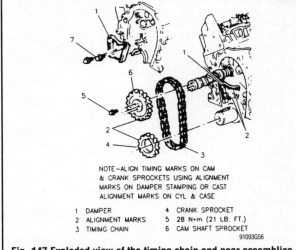

NOTE—ALIGN TIMING MARKS ON CAM
& CRANK SPROCKETS USING ALIGNMENT
MARKS ON DAMPER STAMPING OR CAST
ALIGNMENT MARKS ON CYL & CASE

1	DAMPER	4	CRANK SPROCKET
2	ALIGNMENT MARKS	5	28 N·m (21 LB. FT.)
3	TIMIMG CHAIN	6	CAM SHAFT SPROCKET

91093G56

Fig. 147 Exploded view of the timing chain and gear assemblies showing timing mark alignment

6. Place the #1 piston at top dead center with the marks on the camshaft and crankshaft sprockets aligned.
7. Unfasten the camshaft sprocket bolt, then remove the camshaft sprocket and chain.

➡**Lock the crankshaft to prevent it from turning, by freezing it with a prybar at the flywheel before attempting to remove the crank sprocket.**

8. Remove the crankshaft sprocket using a suitable sprocket removal tool.
To install:
9. Install the crankshaft sprocket with a suitable tool. Lubricate the sprocket thrust surface.
10. Hold the camshaft sprocket with the chain hanging down and around the crank sprocket.
11. Align the dowel in the camshaft with the dowel hole in the camshaft sprocket.
12. Draw the camshaft sprocket onto the camshaft using the mounting bolts. Tighten to the specifications shown in the accompanying figure. Install the crank bolt.
13. Lubricate the timing chain with engine oil.
14. Unlock the flywheel and using a socket and breaker bar, rotate the engine (crankshaft) twice. Make sure the timing marks line up again at TDC.
15. Install the engine front cover, using the directions given earlier in this section, and complete the installation procedure.
16. Connect the negative battery cable.

3.4L Engine

♦ See Figures 148, 149 and 150

➡**The special tools required to perform this repair procedure are a crankshaft sprocket removal tool, and a sprocket installation tool.**

1. Disconnect the negative battery cable.
2. Drain and recycle the engine coolant.
3. Remove the right front tire and wheel.
4. Remove the engine front cover, as outlined in this section.
5. Reinstall the crankshaft bolt, and using a breaker bar and socket, rotate the crankshaft until the timing marks on the crankshaft sprocket and camshaft sprocket locator hole are aligned to marks on the engine block or timing chain damper. This is the number 1 piston at top dead center.
6. Remove the camshaft sprocket bolt, then remove the camshaft sprocket and timing chain.
7. Remove the crankshaft sprocket by using the special tool.
8. Remove the timing chain damper bolts and damper.
To install:
9. Install the crankshaft sprocket using the special tool until fully seated on the flange of the crankshaft nose.
10. Apply a suitable lubricant to the sprocket thrust face.

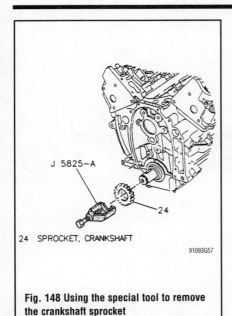

24 SPROCKET, CRANKSHAFT

91093G57

Fig. 148 Using the special tool to remove the crankshaft sprocket

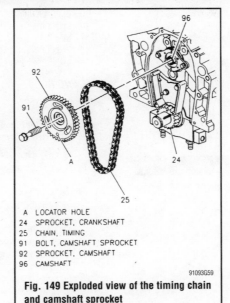

A LOCATOR HOLE
24 SPROCKET, CRANKSHAFT
25 CHAIN, TIMING
91 BOLT, CAMSHAFT SPROCKET
92 SPROCKET, CAMSHAFT
96 CAMSHAFT

91093G59

Fig. 149 Exploded view of the timing chain and camshaft sprocket

J 38612

A TIMING ALIGNMENT MARKS
24 SPROCKET, CRANKSHAFT
25 KEY, CRANKSHAFT
28 CRANKSHAFT
52 BLOCK, ENGINE

91093G58

Fig. 150 You must use a special tool to install crankshaft sprocket

11. Align the crankshaft timing mark to the timing mark on the bottom of the chain damper

12. Hold the camshaft sprocket with the chain hanging down and install the chain to the crankshaft gear.

13. Install the camshaft sprocket and timing chain. Align the timing mark on the camshaft gear (centerline of locator hole) with the timing mark on top of the chain damper. Torque the bolt to 140N.m (103lb. ft.)

14. Install the chain damper to the block.

15. Lubricate the timing chain with engine oil.

16. Replace the engine front cover, as outlined in this section. Use that procedure to complete installation.

17. Change the oil, fill the fluids.

18. Install the right front wheel and tighten the lug nuts.

19. Connect the negative battery cable.

3.8L Engine

♦ **See Figures 151 and 152**

➥You will need a torque angle meter to perform this procedure.

1. Disconnect the negative battery cable.
2. Drain and recycle the engine coolant.

3. Remove the right front wheel.

4. Using the procedure given earlier in this section, remove the engine front cover.

5. Align the timing marks on the sprockets so that they are as close together as possible.

6. Remove the timing chain damper.

7. Remove the camshaft sprocket bolt, the camshaft sprocket and timing chain, and the crankshaft sprocket.

8. If the engine has been disturbed, or the timing marks were not aligned on tear down, begin the installation process here.

9. If the balance shaft timing has been disturbed, refer to the Balance Shaft procedure.

To install:

10. Install the crank bolt, and using a socket and breaker bar, turn the engine so that the number one piston is at TDC.

11. Turn the camshaft so that, with the sprocket temporarily installed, the timing mark is straight down.

➥If engine has not been disturbed, and timing marks lined up on tear down, begin the repair procedure here.

12. Assemble the timing chain onto the sprockets with the timing marks in their closest position. Put the timing mark on the crankshaft sprocket at 12

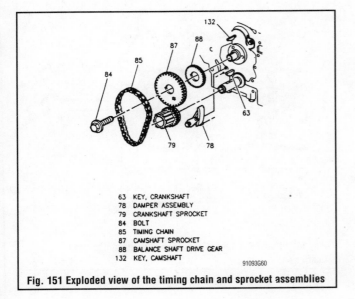

63 KEY, CRANKSHAFT
78 DAMPER ASSEMBLY
79 CRANKSHAFT SPROCKET
84 BOLT
85 TIMING CHAIN
87 CAMSHAFT SPROCKET
88 BALANCE SHAFT DRIVE GEAR
132 KEY, CAMSHAFT

91093G60

Fig. 151 Exploded view of the timing chain and sprocket assemblies

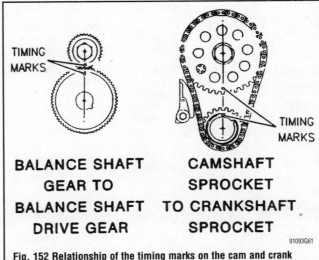

TIMING MARKS

BALANCE SHAFT GEAR TO BALANCE SHAFT DRIVE GEAR

TIMING MARKS

CAMSHAFT SPROCKET TO CRANKSHAFT SPROCKET

91093G61

Fig. 152 Relationship of the timing marks on the cam and crank sprockets

o'clock and the timing mark on the camshaft sprocket at the 6 o'clock position to line them up.

13. Install the timing chain and sprocket assemblies onto their respective shafts.

14. Install the camshaft sprocket bolt and tighten to 74 ft. lbs. (100 Nm), plus an additional 90° with a torque angle meter.

15. Install the timing chain damper. Tighten the bolt to 16 ft. lbs. (22Nm).

16. To complete the repair procedure, follow the installation directions for Timing Chain Cover, located in this section.

17. Connect the negative battery cable.

18. Install the right side wheel and tighten the lug nuts.

Camshafts, Bearings, and Lifters

Specific directions for the removal and installation of many of the following components have already been given in previous chapters. Only the basic instructions for removal of the components will be given here. For more detailed instructions on the repair procedures, and the special tools necessary to perform those procedures, refer to the separate component listings given earlier in this section of the manual.

REMOVAL & INSTALLATION

Camshaft and Bearings

3.1L ENGINE

The camshaft is cast alloy iron with tapered 13.2mm wide lobes, with the exception of lobes 2 and 10, which are 11.2mm wide. It is offset from the lifters and tapered to provide positive valve lifter rotation. The camshaft is supported by four journals and includes an oil pump drive gear and a fuel pump eccentric.

1. Remove the engine from the vehicle and place on a suitable holding fixture.

2. Remove the valve covers.

3. Remove the intake manifold.

4. Remove the valve rocker arms and pushrods.

5. Remove the valve lifters.

6. Remove the crankcase front cover.

7. Remove the timing chain and sprocket.

8. Remove the camshaft.

9. To remove the camshaft bearings use the special bearing tool (J 33049).

10. Select the proper pilot, nut and thrust washer.

11. Assemble the bearing puller. Make sure the puller nut engages a sufficient number of threads to pull out the bearings.

➡All the camshaft bearings are the same diameter and care must be taken in removing the camshaft to avoid damage to bearings. Never reuse camshaft bearings once they have been removed.

12. Inspect the camshaft sprocket, keyway and threads. Inspect the bearing surfaces and lobes for: wear, galling, and gouges, overheating (bluing) discoloration.

➡Whenever a new camshaft is installed, coat the camshaft lobes and journals with camshaft and lifter prelube.

To install:

13. Select the front, rear, and intermediate camshaft bearings to be installed.
   • Select the proper expander assembly and driving washer.
   • Assemble the installation tool according to manufacturer's recommendations.
   • Index the bearing oil holes with engine block oil passages.
   • Secure an intermediate bearing onto the tool. Drive the intermediate camshaft bearings into place.
   • Place #1 or #4 camshaft bearing onto the tool and index the oil holes. Drive the outer camshaft bearings into place.

14. With a piece of 3⁄32 inch brass rod with a 90°bend at the end, probe the bearing oil holes and verify that they are properly aligned.

✳✳ CAUTION

Proper alignment of the oil holes is critical. Restriction of the oil flow will cause severe engine damage.

15. Lubricate the camshaft journals with engine oil.

16. Install the camshaft.

17. Install the timing chain, and the crankcase front cover.

18. Install the valve lifters and attaching parts.

19. Install the remaining components, and the engine assembly.

3.4L ENGINE

◆ See Figure 153

➡The special tool required to perform this repair procedure is: Camshaft Bearing Remover/Installer

1. Remove the intake manifold.

2. Remove the rocker arm covers, rocker arms, pushrods, and lifter assemblies.

3. Remove the oil pump driven gear assembly.

4. Remove the right side tire and wheel assembly, remove the inner splash shield.

5. Remove the crankshaft pulley.

6. Remove the front cover.

7. Remove the timing chain and sprockets.

8. Remove the camshaft thrust plate, and camshaft.

9. Remove the camshaft rear cover.

10. Assemble the camshaft bearing removal tool according to the manufacturer's recommendations. Tighten the expander assembly snug against the camshaft bearing.

11. Remove the bearings (drive out) and discard; never reuse camshaft bearings once they have been removed. Always install new bearings.

➡When removing or installing a camshaft, avoid marring the bearing surfaces.

To install:

12. Select the front, rear, and intermediate camshaft bearings to be installed.
   • Select the proper expander assembly and driving washer.
   • Assemble the installation tool according to manufacturer's recommendations.
   • Index the bearing oil holes with engine block oil passages.
   • Secure the intermediate bearing onto the tool. Index the oil hole at 4 o'clock when looking from the front of the engine block. Drive the intermediate camshaft bearings into place.
   • Place #1 or #4 camshaft bearing onto the tool and index the oil holes at 3 and 6 o'clock respectively when looking from the front of the engine block. Drive the outer camshaft bearings into place.

13. With a piece of 3⁄32 inch brass rod with a 90° bend at the end, probe the bearing oil holes and verify that they are properly aligned.

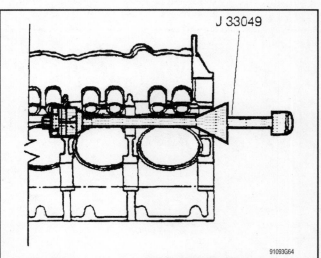

91093G64

Fig. 153 View of the special tool needed to install the camshaft bearings

✳✳ WARNING

Proper alignment of the oil holes is critical. Restriction of the oil flow will cause severe engine damage.

14. Apply a suitable sealer to the rear camshaft cover and then install the camshaft cover flush with the engine block.
15. Liberally coat the camshaft with a suitable prelube before installation.

➡ **Camshaft journals are the same diameter so care must be used when installing the camshaft to avoid bearing damage.**

16. Use of a large screwdriver inserted in the camshaft bolt hole will help ease installation of the shaft into the bearings. Rotating the camshaft back and forth will also help with the installation.
17. Install the camshaft, the camshaft thrust plate, And the timing chain and sprockets.
18. Install the front cover, the crankshaft sensor shield, and the crankshaft pulley.

➡ **Dip the valve lifters in prelube or equivalent before installation.**

19. Install the pushrods, rocker arms, and rocker arm covers.
20. Install the oil pump driven gear assembly.
21. Install the intake manifold.
22. Change the oil, and fill the fluids.

3.8L ENGINE

◗ **See Figure 154**

➡ **The special tool required to perform this repair procedure is a camshaft bearing remover/installer.**

1. Remove the intake manifold.
2. Remove the rocker arm covers, the rocker arms, and the pushrods.
3. Remove the lifter guides, and the lifters.
4. Remove the crankshaft pulley, and the crankshaft sensor shield.
5. Remove the timing chain front cover.
6. Remove the timing chain and sprockets.
7. Remove the camshaft thrust plate, then remove the camshaft.
8. Remove the camshaft rear plug.

➡ **When removing or installing the camshaft, avoid marring the bearing surfaces.**

9. Assemble the camshaft bearing tool removal tool according to the manufacturer's recommendations. Tighten the expander assembly snug against the camshaft bearing.
10. Remove the bearings (drive out) and discard; never reuse camshaft bearings once they have been removed. Always install new bearings.

To install:
11. Select the front, rear, and intermediate camshaft bearings to install.
12. Select the proper expander assembly and driving washer.
13. Assemble the installation tool according to manufacturer's recommendations.
14. Index the bearing oil holes with engine block oil passages.
15. Secure an intermediate bearing onto the tool. Index the oil hole with the engine block. Drive the intermediate camshaft bearings into place.
16. Place #1 or #4 camshaft bearing onto the tool and index the oil holes. Drive the outer camshaft bearings into place.
17. With a piece of ³⁄₃₂ inch brass rod with a 90° bend at the end, probe the bearing oil holes and verify that they are properly aligned.

✳✳ CAUTION

Proper alignment of the oil holes is critical. Restriction of the oil flow will cause severe engine damage.

18. Lubricate the camshaft journals liberally with engine oil.
19. Apply a suitable sealer to the rear camshaft cover and then install the camshaft cover flush with the engine block.
20. Liberally coat the camshaft with prelube before installation.
21. Install the camshaft, and the camshaft thrust plate.
22. Install the timing chain and sprockets, be sure the timing marks are aligned.
23. Install the front cover.
24. Install the crankshaft sensor shield, and the crankshaft pulley.
25. Dip each of the valve lifters in prelube before installation, install the lifters and lifter guides.
26. Install the pushrods, install the rocker arms, and the rocker arm covers.
27. Install the intake manifold.

Valve Lifters

3.1L ENGINE

◗ **See Figures 155, 156, 157 and 158**

If the lifters are removed, they must be reinstalled in their original location. If replacement is necessary use lifters with a narrow flat ground along the lower ¾ of the lifter. These flats provide additional oil to the cam lobe and lifter surfaces.

1. Drain and recycle the engine coolant.
2. Remove the rocker arm covers, remove the rocker assemblies, and pushrods.
3. Remove the intake manifold.
4. Remove the valve lifter.

To install:
Whenever new valve lifters are being installed, coat the base of the lifter with prelube, or soak it in oil. In addition, coat the cam lobes with oil.

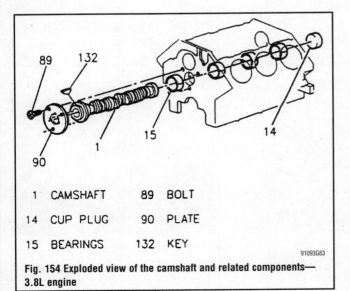

1	CAMSHAFT	89	BOLT
14	CUP PLUG	90	PLATE
15	BEARINGS	132	KEY

91093G63

Fig. 154 Exploded view of the camshaft and related components—3.8L engine

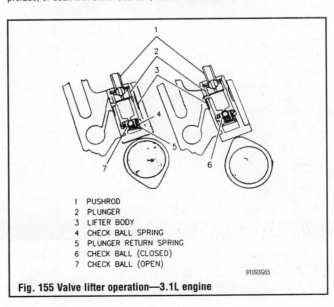

1 PUSHROD
2 PLUNGER
3 LIFTER BODY
4 CHECK BALL SPRING
5 PLUNGER RETURN SPRING
6 CHECK BALL (CLOSED)
7 CHECK BALL (OPEN)

91093G65

Fig. 155 Valve lifter operation—3.1L engine

Fig. 156 Removing the lifter lock down; it holds lifters in place and does not let them rotate

Fig. 157 Removing the lifter from its bore by pulling it straight up

Fig. 158 The bottom side of the lifter is where the roller contacts the cam

5. Install the valve lifter.
6. Install the pushrods, the rocker assemblies, and set the valve lash.
7. Install the intake manifold, and the rocker covers.
8. Replace the fluids, change the oil.

3.4L ENGINE

1. Remove the valve covers.
2. Remove the upper intake manifold, remove the lower intake manifold.
3. Remove the valve rocker arms and pushrods.
4. Remove the lifter guide bolts, remove the lifter guide, and remove the lifter.

To install:
5. Coat the lifters with prelube
6. Install the lifters to the same location from which they were removed.
7. Install the lifter guide, install the lifter guide bolts and tighten to 10N.m (89lb. in.).
8. Install the valve rocker arms and pushrods.
9. Install the lower intake manifold, install the upper intake manifold.

10. Install the valve rocker arm covers.
11. Reverse the removal process to complete the repair procedure.

3.8L ENGINE

◆ See Figures 159 thru 165

1. Remove the rocker arm covers.
2. Remove the intake manifold.
3. Remove the rocker arms and pedestals.

➡ **Be sure to keep all valve train parts in order so they may be reinstalled in their original locations and with the same mating surfaces as when removed.**

4. Remove the pushrods.
5. Remove the guide retainer bolts and retainer.
6. Remove the lifter guides, and the valve lifters.
7. Clean all gasket surfaces with degreaser. Clean the valve train parts,

Fig. 159 Unfasten the lifter guide bolt (see arrows); there are two for each side

Fig. 160 Once the bolts are removed, remove the lifter guide

Fig. 161 View into top of lifters at pushrod seat with the lifter guide and pushrods removed

Fig. 162 Pull the lifter straight up to remove it from the bore. The lifter is keyed at the top to fit in the guide without rotating

Fig. 163 The bottom of lifter rides against the cam lobe. The roller reduces friction and gives the lifter its name

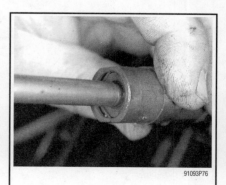

Fig. 164 The pushrod seats in the top of the lifter

Fig. 165 View of the lifter and pushrod; the hole in the pushrod carries oil for lubrication

using a suitable solvent. Inspect the valve train parts. Inspect the lifters and cam lobes for wear.

To install:

8. Dip the valve lifters in prelube before installation.

9. Install the lifter guides, and guide retainer. Tighten bolts to 27 ft. lbs. (37 Nm).

10. Install the pushrods, rocker arms, and pedestals.

11. Apply thread lock to the bolt threads to prevent them from backing out. Install the bolts and tighten to 19 ft. lbs. (25 Nm), plus an addition 70° rotation.

12. Install the intake manifold and gaskets.

13. Install the rocker arm covers and gaskets.

14. The remainder of installation is the reverse of the removal procedure.

Balance Shaft

The crankshaft is counterbalanced by the flywheel, the crankshaft pulley, and weights cast into the crankshaft. Additional counter balancing is obtained from the balance shaft, which rides in the block above the camshaft and is driven by the camshaft.

REMOVAL & INSTALLATION

3.8L Engine

♦ See Figures 166, 167, 168 and 169

This procedure requires several special tools. The are as follows:
- Slide Hammer
- Dial Indicator

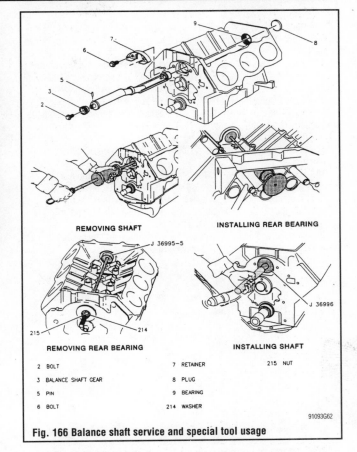

Fig. 166 Balance shaft service and special tool usage

2	BOLT	7	RETAINER	215	NUT
3	BALANCE SHAFT GEAR	8	PLUG		
5	PIN	9	BEARING		
6	BOLT	214	WASHER		

- Torque Angle Meter
- Bearing Remover/Installer
- Balance Shaft Installer

1. Remove the flywheel, as outlined in this section.
2. Remove the intake manifold
3. Remove the lifter guide retainer.
4. Remove the front cover.
5. Remove the balance shaft drive gear bolt.
6. Remove the camshaft sprocket and timing chain.
7. Remove the balance shaft retainer bolts, retainer and gear. Remove the balance shaft using the special tool J 6125-B.
8. Remove the balance shaft rear plug, and the rear bearing using the special removal tool.
9. The balance shaft and both bearings are serviced as a complete package. Use only the correct tools for bearing and shaft installation.

Inspect the balance shaft drive gear and the camshaft drive gear for nicks and burrs.

Fig. 167 The balance shaft runs from one end of the block to the other

Fig. 168 Closer view of the balance shaft. Note it's irregular and asymmetrical shape

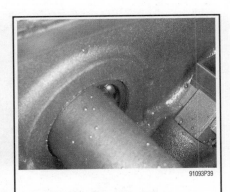

Fig. 169 View of the bearings that the shaft rides on in the front of the block

To install:

10. Dip the bearings in clean engine oil before installation. Install the bearing with the rolled edge facing into the engine and the manufacturer's markings facing the flywheel side.

11. Install the balance shaft rear bearing using the special installation tool.

12. Install the balance shaft into the block using the special installation tool.

13. Temporarily install the balance shaft bearing retainer and bolts.

14. Apply a suitable thread lock compound to bolt threads.

15. Install the balance shaft drive gear and bolt. Tighten the bolt, using the torque angle meter, to 15 ft. lbs. (20 Nm), plus an additional 35° rotation.

16. Install the balance shaft rear plug.

17. Measure the balance shaft endplay. It should be 0.000-0.008 in. (0.000-0.203mm).

18. Measure the balance shaft radial play at both the front and rear:
   a. Front radial play should be 0.000-0.0011 inch (0.000-0.028mm).
   b. Rear radial play should be 0.0005-0.0047 inch (0.0127-0.119mm).

19. Turn the camshaft so that, with the camshaft sprocket temporarily installed, the timing mark is straight down.

20. With the camshaft sprocket and the camshaft gear removed, turn the balance shaft so that the timing mark on the gear points straight down.

21. Install the camshaft gear.

22. Align the marks on the balance shaft gear and the camshaft gear by turning the balance shaft.

23. Turn the crankshaft so that number one piston is at top dead center.

24. Install the timing chain and camshaft sprocket.

25. Measure gear lash at four places, every 90° turn. Lash should be 0.002 to 0.005 inch (0.050 to 0.127mm).

26. Install the balance shaft front bearing retainer and bolts, tighten to 22 ft. lbs. (30 Nm).

27. Install the front cover.

28. Install the lifter guide retainer.

29. Install the intake manifold.

30. Install the flywheel, tighten the bolts to 11 ft. lbs. (15N.m), plus an additional 50° rotation.

31. Complete the engine installation, as outlined earlier in this section.

Flywheel/Flexplate

REMOVAL & INSTALLATION

▶ See Figure 170

The directions given for this repair can be taken as a generic process for all the different engine/transaxle combinations in this group of vehicles. The differences in procedure are minor. Where one application calls for the removal of a bolt, the next application may call for the removal of a retainer, or a clamp. However, it is always wise to double check the torque specifications against the chart, for the given year and model.

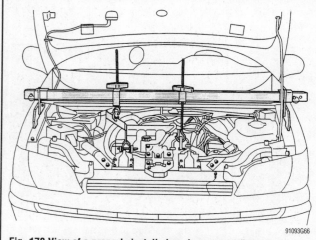

91093G66

Fig. 170 View of a properly installed engine support fixture tool

The following are some of the special tools required for this procedure:
- Engine support fixture
- Engine support fixture lift hook bracket
- Engine support fixture lift hook
- Engine support fixture swivel lift hook
- Engine support fixture lift hook wing nut

1. Obtain a suitable engine support tool.

2. Install strut tower support assemblies to the passenger and driver's side strut towers respectively.

3. Slide a cross bracket onto the strut tower tube.

4. Install the front support plate to the driver's side radiator core brace.

5. Install the inner leg and outer leg/foot into strut tower tube.

6. Install the strut tower tube into the passenger side strut tower assembly and secure with the large pin.

7. Adjust the outer leg/foot so the assembly centers securely on the front support plate.

8. Insert the radiator shelf tube through the cross bracket and secure it at the driver's side strut tower support assembly with the large pin.

9. Install the dedicated hooks to the strut tower tube and the radiator shelf tube.

10. Insert the hooks through the engine lift brackets.

11. Remove any play from the hooks and cross bracket before loosening engine mounts.

12. Disconnect the negative battery cable.

13. Remove the air cleaner assembly.

14. Tag and detach the electrical connectors from the transaxle.

15. Disconnect the electrical wiring harness retainer-to-transaxle shift cable bracket.

16. Disconnect the transaxle shift cable bracket and heat shield assembly, and the wire cable/bracket assembly from the body.

17. Disconnect the vacuum supply from modulator at the transaxle.

18. Unbolt the retaining bolt holding the transaxle indicator tube, and remove the tube assembly.

19. Remove the retaining bolt from the TV cable, and the cable from the TV link.

20. Remove the ground cable to engine/transaxle stud and the stud from the engine/transaxle.

21. Raise and safely support the vehicle.

22. Remove the front wheels, and engine splash shields.

23. Remove the wiring harness retainers at the front engine frame. Disengage the power steering cooler lines attached to the frame.

24. Disconnect both tie rod ends from the steering knuckles.

25. Remove the power steering gear heat shield from the gear assembly.

26. Remove the power steering assembly from the frame, and wire the gear assembly to the body. Do not disconnect the fluid lines.

27. Remove the front engine mount to frame retaining nuts and washers, and the front and rear transaxle mount nuts and washers.

28. Remove both lower ball joints retaining bolts and nuts.

29. Remove the flywheel covers from the engine/transaxle assembly.

30. Remove the starter.

31. Access the torque converter bolts, to remove them, by rotating the engine flywheel.

32. Drain and remove the transaxle pan.

33. Disconnect the transaxle cooler lines at the transaxle and bracket.

34. Pull both LH and RH drive axles from the transaxle, and secure them to the steering knuckle/strut assembly.

35. Detach the electrical connector from the speed sensor.

36. Support the transaxle/frame assembly with a transaxle table.

37. Remove the engine to transaxle bracket and bolts.

38. Remove the retaining bolt from transaxle to the engine.

39. Lower the assembly from the vehicle.

40. Separate the transaxle from the engine.

41. Mark the flywheel and converter to ease in installation and prevent an imbalance condition.

42. Remove the flywheel.

43. For installation, refer to the procedure under rear main seal.

Rear Main Seal

1. Remove the flywheel from the vehicle.

2. Remove the old rear main seal, with a prytool. Do not damage the surface of the crankshaft.

3. Check the inside diameter (I.D.) of the bore for nicks or burrs and correct as required. Inspect the crankshaft for burrs or nicks on the surface that contacts the seal. Repair or replace the crankshaft as required. Check for an "O" ring in the rear main bearing cap.

To install:

4. Install a new seal using a special seal installation tool.

5. Apply a light coat of oil to the inside diameter (I. D.) of the new seal and install it over the mandrill. Slide the seal onto the mandrill until the dust lip (the back of the seal) bottoms squarely against the collar of the tool.

6. Align the dowel pin of the tool with the dowel pinhole in the crankshaft and attach the tool to the crankshaft by hand .

7. Turn the "T" handle of the tool so that the collar pushes seal into the bore, turn the handle until the collar is tight against the case. This will insure that the seal is seated properly.

8. Loosen the "T" handle of the tool until it comes to a stop. This will insure that the collar will be in the proper position for installing a new seal.

9. Make sure the seal is seated squarely in the bore.

10. Install the flywheel.

11. For the 3.1L engine, tighten the bolts to 52 ft. lbs. (71 Nm)

12. For the 3.4L engine, tighten the bolts to 61 ft. lbs. (83 Nm)

13. For the 3.8L engine, tighten the bolts to 11 ft. lbs. (15 Nm), plus an additional 50° rotation.

14. Install the transaxle assembly.

15. Mount the transaxle to the frame, and raise the frame assembly to the body.

16. Install the frame-to-body bolts. Install the lower transaxle-to-engine and engine-to-transaxle bolts.

17. Install the transaxle brace, remove the transaxle table.

18. Attach the wiring harness connectors to the transaxle, including the vehicle speed sensor, and wheel speed sensors harness connectors, where applicable.

19. Insert the drive axles into the transaxle.

20. Install the transaxle cooler lines and bracket to the transaxle.

21. Tighten the converter bolts.

22. Install the starter motor.

23. Connect the lower ball joint to the steering knuckles.

24. Install the engine mount to frame retaining nuts and washers.

25. Install the power steering cooler line clamps to frame.

26. Power steering gear-to-frame retaining bolts, remove and discard the wire.

27. Install the power steering gear heat shield to the power steering gear.

28. Install both tie rod ends to the steering knuckles, install the stabilizer shaft links into the lower control arms.

29. Install the engine splash shields. Install the tires and wheels.

30. Install the fluid filler tube, use a new seal.

31. Lower the vehicle and remove the engine support fixtures.

32. Install the upper transaxle bolts and screws including the wiring harness grounds.

33. Install the transaxle range selector lever cable bracket with cable to the transaxle, and the selector lever cable to the range switch.

34. Install the solenoid harness connectors, and the electrical connectors to the transaxle range switch.

35. Install the vacuum hoses and pipe to the vacuum modulator.

36. Install the air cleaner duct, and the fuel injector sight shield.

37. Connect the negative battery cable.

38. Fill the fluids and check the toe-in.

EXHAUST SYSTEM

Inspection

▶ **See Figures 171 thru 177**

➡Safety glasses should be worn at all times when working on or near the exhaust system. Older exhaust systems will almost always be covered with loose rust particles that will shower you when disturbed. These particles are more than a nuisance and could injure your eye.

✳✳ CAUTION

DO NOT perform exhaust repairs or inspection with the engine or exhaust hot. Allow the system to cool completely before attempting any work. Exhaust systems are noted for sharp edges, flaking metal and rusted bolts. Gloves and eye protection are required. A healthy supply of penetrating oil and rags is highly recommended.

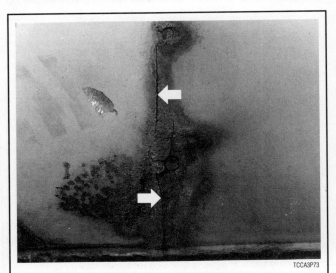

Fig. 171 Cracks in the muffler are a guaranteed leak

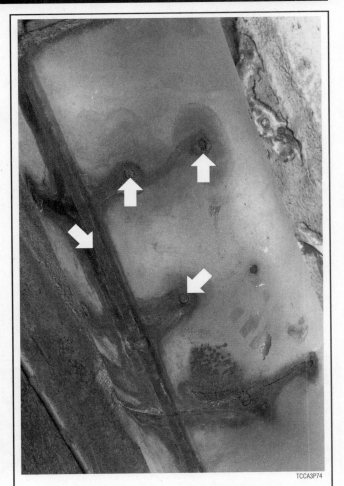

Fig. 172 Check the muffler for rotted spot welds and seams

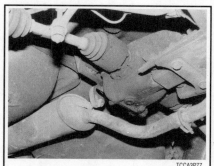

Fig. 173 Make sure the exhaust components are not contacting the body or suspension

Fig. 174 Check for overstretched or torn exhaust hangers

Fig. 175 Example of a badly deteriorated exhaust pipe

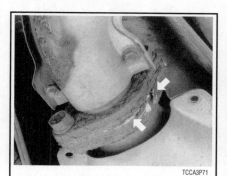

Fig. 176 Inspect flanges for gaskets that have deteriorated and need replacement

Fig. 177 Some systems, like this one, use large O-rings (doughnuts) in between the flanges

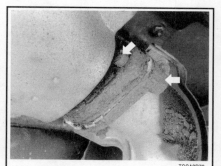

Fig. 178 Nuts and bolts will be extremely difficult to remove when deteriorated with rust

Your vehicle must be raised and supported safely to inspect the exhaust system properly. By placing 4 safety stands under the vehicle for support should provide enough room for you to slide under the vehicle and inspect the system completely. Start the inspection at the exhaust manifold or turbocharger pipe where the header pipe is attached and work your way to the back of the vehicle. On dual exhaust systems, remember to inspect both sides of the vehicle. Check the complete exhaust system for open seams, holes, loose connections, or other deterioration that could permit exhaust fumes to seep into the passenger compartment. Inspect all mounting brackets and hangers for deterioration, some models may have rubber O-rings that can be overstretched and non-supportive. These components will need to be replaced if found. It has always been a practice to use a pointed tool to poke up into the exhaust system where the deterioration spots are to see whether or not they crumble. Some models may have heat shield covering certain parts of the exhaust system , it will be necessary to remove these shields to have the exhaust visible for inspection also.

REPLACEMENT

▶ See Figure 178

There are basically two types of exhaust systems. One is the flange type where the component ends are attached with bolts and a gasket in-between. The other exhaust system is the slip joint type. These components slip into one another using clamps to retain them together.

✸✸ CAUTION

Allow the exhaust system to cool sufficiently before spraying a solvent exhaust fasteners. Some solvents are highly flammable and could ignite when sprayed on hot exhaust components.

Before removing any component of the exhaust system, ALWAYS squirt a liquid rust dissolving agent onto the fasteners for ease of removal. A lot of knuckle skin will be saved by following this rule. It may even be wise to spray the fasteners and allow them to sit overnight.

Flange Type
▶ See Figure 179

✸✸ CAUTION

Do NOT perform exhaust repairs or inspection with the engine or exhaust hot. Allow the system to cool completely before attempting any work. Exhaust systems are noted for sharp edges, flaking metal and rusted bolts. Gloves and eye protection are required. A healthy supply of penetrating oil and rags is highly recommended. Never spray liquid rust dissolving agent onto a hot exhaust component.

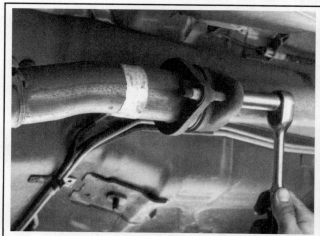

Fig. 179 Example of a flange type exhaust system joint

Before removing any component on a flange type system, ALWAYS squirt a liquid rust dissolving agent onto the fasteners for ease of removal. Start by unbolting the exhaust piece at both ends (if required). When unbolting the headpipe from the manifold, make sure that the bolts are free before trying to remove them. if you snap a stud in the exhaust manifold, the stud will have to be removed with a bolt extractor, which often means removal of the manifold itself. Next, disconnect the component from the mounting; slight twisting and turning may be required to remove the component completely from the vehicle. You may need to tap on the component with a rubber mallet to loosen the component. If all else fails, use a hacksaw to separate the parts. An oxy-acetylene cutting torch may be faster but the sparks are DANGEROUS near the fuel tank, and at the very least, accidents could happen, resulting in damage to the under-car parts, not to mention yourself.

Slip Joint Type

▶ See Figure 180

Before removing any component on the slip joint type exhaust system, ALWAYS squirt a liquid rust dissolving agent onto the fasteners for ease of removal. Start by unbolting the exhaust piece at both ends (if required). When unbolting the headpipe from the manifold, make sure that the bolts are free before trying to remove them. if you snap a stud in the exhaust manifold, the stud will have to be removed with a bolt extractor, which often means removal of the manifold itself. Next, remove the mounting U-bolts from around the exhaust pipe you are extracting from the vehicle. Don't be surprised if the U-bolts break while removing the nuts. Loosen the exhaust pipe from any mounting brackets retaining it to the floor pan and separate the components.

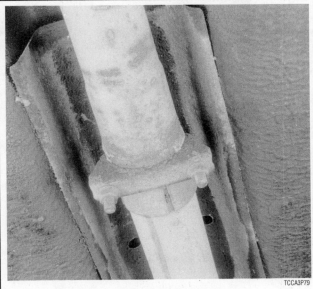
TCCA3P79

Fig. 180 Example of a common slip joint type system

ENGINE RECONDITIONING

Determining Engine Condition

Anything that generates heat and/or friction will eventually burn or wear out (for example, a light bulb generates heat, and has a limited lifespan. A running engine generates tremendous amounts of both; friction is encountered by the moving and rotating parts inside the engine and heat is created by friction and combustion of the fuel. However, the engine has systems designed to help reduce the effects of heat and friction and provide added longevity. The oiling system reduces the amount of friction encountered by the moving parts inside the engine, while the cooling system reduces heat created by friction and combustion. If either system is not maintained, a break-down will be inevitable. Therefore, you can see how regular maintenance can affect the service life of your vehicle. If you do not drain, flush and refill your cooling system at the proper intervals, deposits will begin to accumulate in the radiator, thereby reducing the amount of heat it can extract from the coolant. The same applies to your oil and filter; if not changed often enough it becomes laden with contaminates and is unable to properly lubricate the engine. This increases friction and wear.

There are a number of methods for evaluating the condition of your engine. A compression test can reveal the condition of your pistons, piston rings, cylinder bores, and head gasket(s), valves and valve seats. An oil pressure test can warn you of possible engine bearing, or oil pump failures. Excessive oil consumption, evidence of oil in the engine air intake area and/or bluish smoke from the tailpipe may indicate worn piston rings, worn valve guides and/or valve seals. As a rule, an engine that uses no more than one quart of oil every 1000 miles is in good condition. Engines that use one quart of oil or more in less than 1000 miles should first be checked for oil leaks. If any oil leaks are present, have them fixed before determining how much oil is consumed by the engine, especially if blue smoke is not visible at the tailpipe.

COMPRESSION TEST

▶ See Figure 181

A noticeable lack of engine power, excessive oil consumption, and/or poor fuel mileage measured over an extended period, is an indication of internal engine wear. Worn piston rings, scored or worn cylinder bores, blown head gaskets, sticking or burnt valves, and worn valve seats are all possible culprits. A check of the compression of each cylinder will help locate the problem.

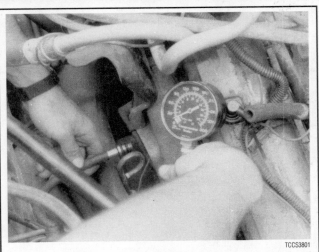
TCCS3801

Fig. 181 A screw-in type compression gauge is more accurate and easier to use without an assistant

➡A screw-in type compression gauge is more accurate than the type you simply hold against the spark plug hole. Although it takes slightly longer to use, it's worth the effort to obtain a more accurate reading.

1. Make sure that the proper amount and viscosity of engine oil is in the crankcase, then ensure the battery is fully charged.
2. Warm-up the engine to normal operating temperature, then shut the engine **OFF**.
3. Disable the ignition system.
4. Label and disconnect all of the spark plug wires from the plugs.
5. Thoroughly clean the cylinder head area around the spark plug ports, then remove the spark plugs.
6. Set the throttle plate to the fully open (wide-open throttle) position. You can block the accelerator linkage open for this, or you can have an assistant fully depress the accelerator pedal.

7. Install a screw-in type compression gauge into the No. 1 spark plug hole until the fitting is snug.

✳✳ WARNING

Be careful not to crossthread the spark plug hole.

8. According to the tool manufacturer's instructions, connect a remote starting switch to the starting circuit.

9. With the ignition switch in the **OFF** position, use the remote starting switch to crank the engine through at least five compression strokes (approximately 5 seconds of cranking) and record the highest reading on the gauge.

10. Repeat the test on each cylinder, cranking the engine approximately the same number of compression strokes and/or time as the first.

11. Compare the highest readings from each cylinder to that of the others. The indicated compression pressures are considered within specifications if the lowest reading cylinder is within 75 percent of the pressure recorded for the highest reading cylinder. For example, if your highest reading cylinder pressure was 150 psi (1034 kPa), then 75 percent of that would be 113 psi (779 kPa). Therefore, the lowest reading cylinder should be no less than 113 psi (779 kPa).

12. If a cylinder exhibits an unusually low compression reading, pour a tablespoon of clean engine oil into the cylinder through the spark plug hole and repeat the compression test. If the compression rises after adding oil, it means that the cylinder's piston rings and/or cylinder bore are damaged or worn. If the pressure remains low, the valves may not be seating properly (a valve job is needed), or the head gasket may be blown near that cylinder. If compression in any two adjacent cylinders is low, and if the addition of oil doesn't help raise compression, there is leakage past the head gasket. Oil and/or coolant in the combustion chamber, combined with blue or constant white smoke from the tailpipe, is symptoms of this problem. However, don't be alarmed by the normal white smoke emitted from the tailpipe during engine warm-up or from cold weather driving. There may be evidence of water droplets on the engine dipstick and/or oil droplets in the cooling system if a head gasket is blown.

OIL PRESSURE TEST

Check for proper oil pressure at the sending unit passage with an externally mounted mechanical oil pressure gauge (as opposed to relying on a factory installed dash-mounted gauge). A tachometer may also be needed, as some specifications may require running the engine at a specific rpm.

1. With the engine cold, locate and remove the oil pressure sending unit.

2. Following the manufacturer's instructions, connect a mechanical oil pressure gauge and, if necessary, a tachometer to the engine.

3. Start the engine and allow it to idle.

4. Check the oil pressure reading when cold and record the number. You may need to run the engine at a specified rpm, so check the specifications.

5. Run the engine until normal operating temperature is reached (upper radiator hose will feel warm).

6. Check the oil pressure reading again with the engine hot and record the number. Turn the engine **OFF**.

7. Compare your hot oil pressure reading to that given in the chart. If the reading is low, check the cold pressure reading against the chart. If the cold pressure is well above the specification, and the hot reading was lower than the specification, you may have the wrong viscosity oil in the engine. Change the oil, making sure to use the proper grade and quantity, then repeat the test.

Low oil pressure readings could be attributed to internal component wear, pump related problems, a low oil level, or oil viscosity that is too low. High oil pressure readings could be caused by an overfilled crankcase, too high of an oil viscosity or a faulty pressure relief valve.

Buy or Rebuild?

Now that you have determined that your engine is worn out, you must make some decisions. The question of whether or not an engine is worth rebuilding is largely a subjective matter and one of personal taste. Is the engine a popular one, or is it an obsolete model? Are parts available? Will it get acceptable gas mileage once it is rebuilt? Is the car it's being put into worth keeping? Would it be less expensive to buy a new engine, have your engines rebuilt by a pro, rebuild it yourself or buy a used engine from a salvage yard? On the other hand,

would it be simpler and less expensive to buy another car? If you have considered all these matters and more, and have still decided to rebuild the engine, then it is time to decide how you will rebuild it.

➡The editors at Chilton feel that most engine machining should be performed by a professional machine shop. Don't think of it as wasting money, rather, as an assurance that the job has been done right the first time. There are many expensive and specialized tools required to perform such tasks as boring and honing an engine block or having a valve job done on a cylinder head. Even inspecting the parts requires expensive micrometers and gauges to properly measure wear and clearances. In addition, a machine shop can deliver to you clean, and ready to assemble parts, saving you time and aggravation. Your maximum savings will come from performing the removal, disassembly, assembly and installation of the engine and purchasing or renting only the tools required to perform the above tasks. Depending on the particular circumstances, you may save 40 to 60 percent of the cost doing these yourself.

A complete rebuild or overhaul of an engine involves replacing all of the moving parts (pistons, rods, crankshaft, camshaft, etc.) with new ones and machining the non-moving wearing surfaces of the block and heads. Unfortunately, this may not be cost effective. For instance, your crankshaft may have been damaged or worn, but it can be machined undersize for a minimal fee.

So, as you can see, you can replace everything inside the engine, but, it is wiser to replace only those parts which are really needed, and, if possible, repair the more expensive ones. Later in this section, we will break the engine down into its two main components: the cylinder head and the engine block. We will discuss each component, and the recommended parts to replace during a rebuild on each.

Engine Overhaul Tips

Most engine overhaul procedures are a standard practice. In addition to specific replacement procedures and parts specifications for your individual engine, this section is also a guide to acceptable rebuilding procedures. Examples of standard rebuilding practice are given and should be used along with specific details concerning your particular engine.

Competent and accurate machine shop services will ensure maximum performance, reliability and engine life. In most instances it is more profitable for the do-it-yourself mechanic to remove, clean and inspect the component, buy the necessary parts and deliver these to a shop for actual machine work.

Much of the assembly work (crankshaft, bearings, piston rods, and other components) is well within the scope of the do-it-yourself mechanic's tools and abilities. You will have to decide for yourself the depth of involvement you desire in an engine repair or rebuild.

TOOLS

The tools required for an engine overhaul or parts replacement will depend on the depth of your involvement. With a few exceptions, they will be the tools found in a mechanic's tool kit (see Section 1 of this manual). More in-depth work will require some or all of the following:

- A dial indicator (reading in thousandths) mounted on a universal base
- Micrometers and telescope gauges
- Jaw and screw-type pullers
- Scraper
- Valve spring compressor
- Ring groove cleaner
- Piston ring expander and compressor
- Ridge reamer
- Cylinder hone or glaze breaker
- Plastigage®
- Engine stand

The use of most of these tools is illustrated in this section. Many can be rented for a one-time use from a local parts jobber or tool supply house specializing in automotive work.

Occasionally, the use of special tools is called for. See the information on Special Tools and the Safety Notice in the front of this book before substituting another tool.

OVERHAUL TIPS

Aluminum has become extremely popular for use in engines, due to its low weight. Observe the following precautions when handling aluminum parts:
- Never hot tank aluminum parts (the caustic hot tank solution will eat the aluminum.
- Remove all aluminum parts (identification tag, etc.) from engine parts before the tanking.
- Always coat threads lightly with engine oil or anti-seize compounds before installation, to prevent seizure.
- Never overtighten bolts or spark plugs especially in aluminum threads.

When assembling the engine, any parts that will be exposed to frictional contact must be prelubed to provide lubrication at initial start-up. Any product specifically formulated for this purpose can be used, but engine oil is not recommended as a prelube in most cases.

When semi-permanent (locked, but removable) installation of bolts or nuts is desired, threads should be cleaned and coated with Loctite• or another similar, commercial non-hardening sealant.

CLEANING

♦ **See Figures 182, 183, 184 and 185**

Before the engine and its components are inspected, they must be thoroughly cleaned. You will need to remove any engine varnish, oil sludge and/or carbon deposits from all of the components to insure an accurate inspection. A crack in the engine block or cylinder head can easily become overlooked if hidden by a layer of sludge or carbon.

Most of the cleaning process can be carried out with common hand tools

TCCS3132

Fig. 182 Use a gasket scraper to remove the old gasket material from the mating surfaces

and readily available solvents or solutions. Carbon deposits can be chipped away using a hammer and a hard wooden chisel. Old gasket material and varnish or sludge can usually be removed using a scraper and/or cleaning solvent. Extremely stubborn deposits may require the use of a power drill with a wire brush. If using a wire brush, use extreme care around any critical machined surfaces (such as the gasket surfaces, bearing saddles, cylinder bores, etc.). USE OF A WIRE BRUSH IS NOT RECOMMENDED ON ANY ALUMINUM COMPONENTS. Always follow any safety recommendations given by the manufacturer of the tool and/or solvent. You should always wear eye protection during any cleaning process involving scraping, chipping or spraying of solvents.

An alternative to the mess and hassle of cleaning the parts yourself, is to drop them off at a local garage or machine shop. They will, more than likely, have the necessary equipment to properly clean all of the parts for a nominal fee.

✳✳ CAUTION

Always wear eye protection during any cleaning process involving scraping, chipping or spraying of solvents.

Remove any oil galley plugs, freeze plugs and/or pressed-in bearings and carefully wash and degrease all of the engine components including the fasteners and bolts. Small parts such as the valves, springs, etc., should be placed in a metal basket and allowed to soak. Use pipe cleaner type brushes, and clean all passageways in the components. Use a ring expander and remove the rings from the pistons. Clean the piston ring grooves with a special tool or a piece of broken ring. Scrape the carbon off the top of the piston. You should never use a wire brush on the pistons. After preparing all of the piston assemblies in this manner, wash and degrease them again.

✳✳ WARNING

Use extreme care when cleaning around the cylinder head valve seats. A mistake or slip may cost you a new seat.

When cleaning the cylinder head, remove carbon from the combustion chamber with the valves installed. This will avoid damaging the valve seats.

REPAIRING DAMAGED THREADS

♦ **See Figures 186, 187, 188, 189 and 190**

Several methods of repairing damaged threads are available. Heli-Coil® (shown here), Keenserts® and Microdot® are among the most widely used. All involve basically the same principle—drilling out stripped threads, tapping the hole and installing a prewound insert—making welding, plugging and oversize fasteners unnecessary.

Two types of thread repair inserts are usually supplied: a standard type for most inch coarse, inch fine, metric course and metric fine thread sizes and a spark lug type to fit most spark plug port sizes. Consult the individual tool manufacturer's catalog to determine exact applications. Typical thread repair kits will contain a selection of prewound threaded inserts, a tap (corresponding to the outside diameter threads of the insert) and an installation tool. Spark plug inserts usually differ because they require a tap equipped with pilot threads and

TCCS3211

Fig. 183 Use a ring expander tool to remove the piston rings

TCCS3208

Fig. 184 Clean the piston ring grooves using a ring groove cleaner tool, or . . .

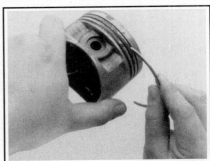

TCCS3911

Fig. 185 . . . use a piece of an old ring to clean the grooves. Be careful, the ring can be quite sharp

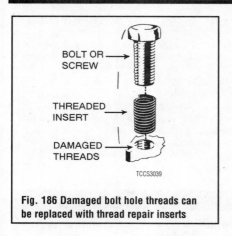

BOLT OR
SCREW

THREADED
INSERT

DAMAGED
THREADS

TCCS3039

Fig. 186 Damaged bolt hole threads can
be replaced with thread repair inserts

TANG

NOTCH

TCCS3040

Fig. 187 Standard thread repair insert
(left), and spark plug thread insert

TCCS3041

Fig. 188 Drill out the damaged threads
with the specified size bit. Be sure to drill
completely through the hole or to the bottom of a blind hole

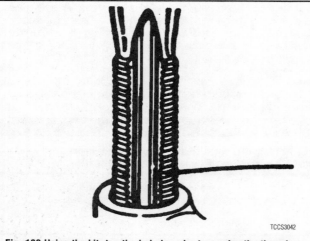

TCCS3042

Fig. 189 Using the kit, tap the hole in order to receive the thread
insert. Keep the tap well oiled and back it out frequently to avoid
clogging the threads

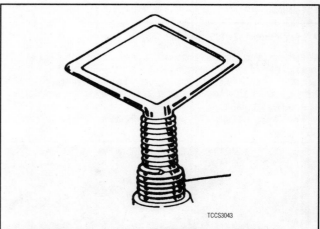

TCCS3043

Fig. 190 Screw the insert onto the installer tool until the tang
engages the slot. Thread the insert into the hole until it is ¼–½ turn
below the top surface, then remove the tool and break off the tang
using a punch

a combined reamer/tap section. Most manufacturers also supply blister-packed
thread repair inserts separately in addition to a master kit containing a variety of
taps and inserts plus installation tools.

Before attempting to repair a threaded hole, remove any snapped, broken or
damaged bolts or studs. Penetrating oil can be used to free frozen threads. The
offending item can usually be removed with locking pliers or using a screw/stud
extractor. After the hole is clear, the thread can be repaired, as shown in the
series of accompanying illustrations and in the kit manufacturer's instructions.

Engine Preparation

To properly rebuild an engine, you must first remove it from the vehicle, then
disassemble and diagnose it. Ideally, you should place your engine on an
engine stand. This affords you the best access to the engine components. Follow the manufacturer's directions for using the stand with your particular engine.
Remove the flywheel or flexplate before installing the engine to the stand.

Now that you have the engine on a stand, and if you have drained the oil and
coolant from the engine, it's time to strip it of all but the necessary components.
Before you start disassembling the engine, you may want to take a moment to
draw some pictures, or fabricate some labels or containers to mark the locations
of various components and the bolts and/or studs which fasten them. Modern
day engines use a lot of little brackets and clips which hold wiring harnesses
and such, and these holders are often mounted on studs and/or bolts that can
be easily mixed up. The manufacturer spent a lot of time and money designing
your vehicle, and they wouldn't have wasted any of it by haphazardly placing
brackets, clips or fasteners on the vehicle. If it's present when you disassemble
it, put it back when you assemble, you will regret not remembering that little
bracket which holds a wire harness out of the path of a rotating part.

You should begin by unbolting any accessories still attached to the engine,
such as the water pump, power steering pump, alternator, etc. Then, unfasten
any manifolds (intake or exhaust) which were not removed during the engine
removal procedure. Finally, remove any covers remaining on the engine such as
the rocker arm, front or timing cover and oil pan. Some front covers may require
the vibration damper and/or crank pulley to be removed beforehand. The idea is
to reduce the engine to the bare necessities (cylinder head(s), valve train,
engine block, crankshaft, pistons and connecting rods), plus any other 'in block'
components such as oil pumps, balance shafts and auxiliary shafts.

Finally, remove the cylinder head(s) from the engine block and carefully
place on a bench. Disassembly instructions for each component follow later in
this section.

Cylinder Head

There are two basic types of cylinder heads used on today's automobiles: the
Overhead Valve (OHV) and the Overhead Camshaft (OHC). The latter can also be
broken down into two subgroups: the Single Overhead Camshaft (SOHC) and
the Dual Overhead Camshaft (DOHC). Generally, if there is only a single
camshaft on a head, it is just referred to as an OHC head. In addition, an engine
with an OHV cylinder head is also known as a pushrod engine.

Most cylinder heads these days are made of an aluminum alloy due to its
light weight, durability and heat transfer qualities. However, cast iron was the
material of choice in the past, and is still used on many vehicles today.
Whether made from aluminum or iron, all cylinder heads have valves and
seats. Some use two valves per cylinder, while the more hi-tech engines will
use a multi-valve configuration using 3, 4 and even 5 valves per cylinder.
When the valve contacts the seat, it does so on precision machined surfaces,

which seals the combustion chamber. All cylinder heads have a valve guide for each valve. The guide centers the valve to the seat and allows it to move up and down within it. The clearance between the valve and guide can be critical. Too much clearance and the engine may consume oil, lose vacuum and/or damage the seat. Too little, and the valve can stick in the guide causing the engine to run poorly if at all, and possibly causing severe damage. The last components all cylinder heads have are valve springs. The spring holds the valve against its seat. It also returns the valve to this position when the valve has been opened by the valve train or camshaft. The spring is fastened to the valve by a retainer and valve locks (sometimes called keepers). Aluminum heads will also have a valve spring shim to keep the spring from wearing away the aluminum.

An ideal method of rebuilding the cylinder head would involve replacing all of the valves, guides, seats, springs, etc. with new ones. However, depending on how the engine was maintained, often this is not necessary. A major cause of valve, guide and seat wear is an improperly tuned engine. An engine that is running too rich, will often wash the lubricating oil out of the guide with gasoline, causing it to wear rapidly. Conversely, an engine, which is running too lean, will place higher combustion temperatures on the valves and seats allowing them to wear or even burn. Springs fall victim to the driving habits of the individual. A driver who often runs the engine rpm to the redline will wear out or break the springs faster then one that stays well below it. Unfortunately, mileage takes its toll on all of the parts. Generally, the valves, guides, springs and seats in a cylinder head can be machined and re-used, saving you money. However, if a valve is burnt, it may be wise to replace all of the valves, since they were all operating in the same environment. The same goes for any other component on the cylinder head. Think of it as an insurance policy against future problems related to that component.

Unfortunately, the only way to find out which components need replacing, is to disassemble and carefully check each piece. After the cylinder head(s) are disassembled, thoroughly clean all of the components.

DISASSEMBLY

OHV Heads

▶ See Figures 191 thru 196

Before disassembling the cylinder head, you may want to fabricate some containers to hold the various parts, as some of them can be quite small (such as keepers) and easily lost. Also keeping you and the components organized will aid in assembly and reduce confusion. Where possible, try to maintain a components original location; this is especially important if there is not going to be any machine work performed on the components.

1. If you haven't already removed the rocker arms and/or shafts, do so now.
2. Position the head so that the springs are easily accessed.
3. Use a valve spring compressor tool, and relieve spring tension from the retainer.

➡Due to engine varnish, the retainer may stick to the valve locks. A gentle tap with a hammer may help to break it loose.

4. Remove the valve locks from the valve tip and/or retainer. A small magnet may help in removing the locks.
5. Lift the valve spring, tool and all, off the valve stem.
6. If equipped, remove the valve seal. If the seal is difficult to remove with the valve in place, try removing the valve first, then the seal. Follow the steps below for valve removal.
7. Position the head to allow access for withdrawing the valve.

➡Cylinder heads that have seen a lot of miles and/or abuse may have mushroomed the valve lock grove and/or tip, causing difficulty in removal of the valve. If this has happened, use a metal file to carefully

Fig. 191 When removing an OHV valve spring, use a compressor tool to relieve the tension from the retainer

Fig. 192 A small magnet will help in removal of the valve locks

Fig. 193 Be careful not to lose the small valve locks (keepers)

Fig. 194 Remove the valve seal from the valve stem—O-ring type seal shown

Fig. 195 Removing an umbrella/positive type seal

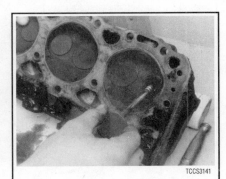

Fig. 196 Invert the cylinder head and withdraw the valve from the valve guide bore

remove the high spots around the lock grooves and/or tip. Only file it enough to allow removal.

8. Remove the valve from the cylinder head.

9. If equipped, remove the valve spring shim. A small magnetic tool or screwdriver will aid in removal.

10. Repeat Steps 3 though 9 until all of the valves have been removed.

ROCKER ARM TYPE CAMSHAFT FOLLOWERS

▶ See Figures 197 thru 205

Most cylinder heads with rocker arm-type camshaft followers are easily disassembled using a standard valve spring compressor. However, certain models may not have enough open space around the spring for the standard tool and may require you to use a C-clamp style compressor tool instead.

1. If not already removed, remove the rocker arms and/or shafts and the camshaft. If applicable, also remove the hydraulic lash adjusters. Mark their positions for assembly.

2. Position the cylinder head to allow access to the valve spring.

3. Use a valve spring compressor tool to relieve the spring tension from the retainer.

➡Due to engine varnish, the retainer may stick to the valve locks. A gentle tap with a hammer may help to break it loose.

4. Remove the valve locks from the valve tip and/or retainer. A small magnet may help in removing the small locks.

5. Lift the valve spring, tool and all, off the valve stem.

6. If equipped, remove the valve seal. If the seal is difficult to remove with the valve in place, try removing the valve first, then the seal. Follow the steps below for valve removal.

7. Position the head to allow access for withdrawing the valve.

➡Cylinder heads that have seen a lot of miles and/or abuse may have

Fig. 197 Example of the shaft mounted rocker arms on some OHC heads

Fig. 198 Another example of the rocker arm type OHC head. This model uses a follower under the camshaft

Fig. 199 Before the camshaft can be removed, all of the followers must first be removed . . .

Fig. 200 . . . then the camshaft can be removed by sliding it out (shown), or unbolting a bearing cap (not shown)

Fig. 201 Compress the valve spring . . .

Fig. 202 . . . then, remove the valve locks from the valve stem and spring retainer

Fig. 203 Remove the valve spring and retainer from the cylinder head

Fig. 204 Remove the valve seal from the guide. Some gentle prying or pliers may help to remove stubborn ones

Fig. 205 All aluminum and some cast iron heads will have these valve spring shims. Remove all of them as well

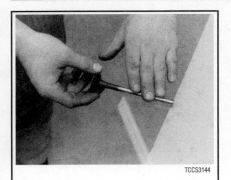

Fig. 206 Valve stems may be rolled on a flat surface to check for bends

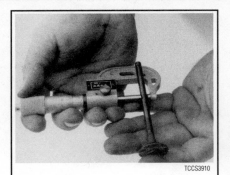

Fig. 207 Use a micrometer to check the valve stem diameter

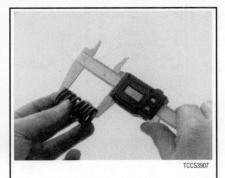

Fig. 208 Use a caliper to check the valve spring free-length

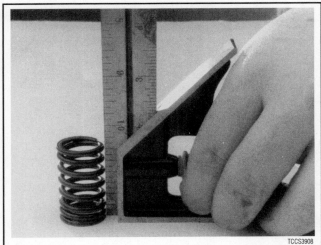

Fig. 209 Check the valve spring for squareness on a flat surface; a carpenter's square can be used

mushroomed the valve lock grove and/or tip, causing difficulty in removal of the valve. If this has happened, use a metal file to carefully remove the high spots around the lock grooves and/or tip. Only file it enough to allow removal.

8. Remove the valve from the cylinder head.
9. If equipped, remove the valve spring shim. A small magnetic tool or screwdriver will aid in removal.
10. Repeat Steps 3 though 9 until all of the valves have been removed.

INSPECTION

Now that all of the cylinder head components are clean, it's time to inspect them for wear and/or damage. To accurately inspect them, you will need some specialized tools:

- A 0–1 in. micrometer for the valves
- A dial indicator or inside diameter gauge for the valve guides
- A spring pressure test gauge

If you do not have access to the proper tools, you may want to bring the components to a shop that does.

Valves

♦ See Figures 206 and 207

The first things to inspect are the valve heads. Look closely at the head, margin and face for any cracks, excessive wear or burning. The margin is the best place to look for burning. It should have a squared edge with an even width all around the diameter. When a valve burns, the margin will look melted and the edges rounded. Also, inspect the valve head for any signs of tulipping. This will

show as a lifting of the edges or dishing in the center of the head and will usually not occur to all of the valves. All of the heads should look the same, any that seem dished more than others are probably bad. Next, inspect the valve lock grooves and valve tips. Check for any burrs around the lock grooves, especially if you had to file them to remove the valve. Valve tips should appear flat, although slight rounding with high mileage engines is normal. Slightly worn valve tips will need to be machined flat. Last, measure the valve stem diameter with the micrometer. Measure the area that rides within the guide, especially towards the tip where most of the wear occurs. Take several measurements along its length and compare them to each other. Wear should be even along the length with little to no taper. If no minimum diameter is given in the specifications, then the stem should not read more than 0.001 in. (0.025mm) below the unworn area of the valve stem. Any valves that fail these inspections should be replaced.

Springs, Retainers and Valve Locks

♦ See Figures 208 and 209

The first thing to check is the most obvious, broken springs. Next, check the free length and squareness of each spring. If applicable, insure to distinguish between intake and exhaust springs. Use a ruler and/or carpenter's square to measure the length. A carpenter's square should be used to check the springs for squareness. If a spring pressure test gauge is available, check each springs rating and compare to the specifications chart. Check the readings against the specifications given. Any springs that fail these inspections should be replaced.

The spring retainers rarely need replacing, however they should still be checked as a precaution. Inspect the spring mating surface and the valve lock retention areas for any signs of excessive wear. Also, check for any signs of cracking. Replace any retainers that are questionable.

Valve locks should be inspected for excessive wear on the outside contact area as well as on the inner notched surface. Any locks which appear worn or broken and its respective valve should be replaced.

Cylinder Head

There are several things to check on the cylinder head: valve guides, seats, cylinder head surface flatness, cracks and physical damage.

VALVE GUIDES

♦ See Figure 210

Now that you know the valves are good, you can use them to check the guides, although a new valve, if available, is preferred. Before you measure anything, look at the guides carefully and inspect them for any cracks, chips or breakage. Also, if the guide is a removable style (as in most aluminum heads), check them for any looseness or evidence of movement. All of the guides should appear to be at the same height from the spring seat. If any seem lower (or higher) from another, the guide has moved. Mount a dial indicator onto the spring side of the cylinder head. Lightly oil the valve stem and insert it into the cylinder head. Position the dial indicator against the valve stem near the tip and zero the gauge. Grasp the valve stem and wiggle towards and away from the dial indicator and observe the readings. Mount the dial indicator 90 degrees from the initial point and zero the gauge and again take a reading. Compare the two

Fig. 210 A dial gauge may be used to check valve stem-to-guide clearance; read the gauge while moving the valve stem

TCCS3142

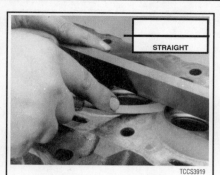

Fig. 211 Check the head for flatness across the center of the head surface using a straightedge and feeler gauge

TCCS3919

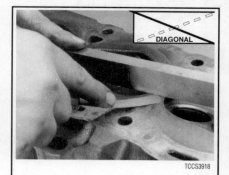

Fig. 212 Checks should also be made along both diagonals of the head surface

TCCS3918

readings for a out of round condition. Check the readings against the specifications given. An Inside Diameter (I.D.) gauge designed for valve guides will give you an accurate valve guide bore measurement. If the I.D. gauge is used, compare the readings with the specifications given. Any guides that fail these inspections should be replaced or machined.

VALVE SEATS

A visual inspection of the valve seats should show a slightly worn and pitted surface where the valve face contacts the seat. Inspect the seat carefully for severe pitting or cracks. In addition, a seat that is badly worn will be recessed into the cylinder head. A severely worn or recessed seat may need to be replaced. All cracked seats must be replaced. A seat concentricity gauge, if available, should be used to check the seat run-out. If run-out exceeds a specification the seat must be machined (if no specification is given use 0.002 in. or 0.051mm).

CYLINDER HEAD SURFACE FLATNESS

▶ See Figures 211 and 212

After you have cleaned the gasket surface of the cylinder head of any old gasket material, check the head for flatness.

Place a straightedge across the gasket surface. Using feeler gauges, determine the clearance at the center of the straightedge and across the cylinder head at several points. Check along the centerline and diagonally on the head surface. If the warpage exceeds 0.003 in. (0.076mm) within a 6.0 in. (15.2cm) span, or 0.006 in. (0.152mm) over the total length of the head, the cylinder head must be resurfaced. After resurfacing the heads of a V-type engine, the intake manifold flange surface should be checked, and if necessary, milled proportionally to allow for the change in its mounting position.

CRACKS AND PHYSICAL DAMAGE

Generally, cracks are limited to the combustion chamber, however, it is not uncommon for the head to crack in a spark plug hole, port, outside of the head or in the valve spring/rocker arm area. The first area to inspect is always the hottest: the exhaust seat/port area.

A visual inspection should be performed, but just because you don't see a crack, does not mean it is not there. Some more reliable methods for inspecting for cracks include Magnaflux®, a magnetic process or Zyglo®, a dye penetrant. Magnaflux® is used only on ferrous metal (cast iron) heads. Zyglo® uses a spray on fluorescent mixture along with a black light to reveal the cracks. It is strongly recommended to have your cylinder head checked professionally for cracks, especially if the engine was known to have overheated and/or leaked or consumed coolant. Contact a local shop for availability and pricing of these services.

Physical damage is usually very evident. For example, a broken mounting ear from dropping the head or a bent or broken stud and/or bolt. All of these defects should be fixed or, if not repairable, the head should be replaced.

REFINISHING & REPAIRING

Many of the procedures given for refinishing and repairing the cylinder head components must be performed by a machine shop. Certain steps, if the inspected part is not worn, can be performed yourself inexpensively. However,

you spent a lot of time and effort so far, why risk trying to save a couple of bucks if you might have to do it all over again?

Valves

Any valves that were not replaced should be refaced and the tips ground flat. Unless you have access to a valve grinding machine, this should be done by a machine shop. If the valves are in extremely good condition, as well as the valve seats and guides, they may be lapped in without performing machine work.

It is a recommended practice to lap the valves even after machine work has been performed and/or new valves have been purchased. This insures a positive seal between the valve and seat.

LAPPING THE VALVES

➡Before lapping the valves to the seats, read the rest of the cylinder head section to insure that any related parts are in acceptable enough condition to continue.

➡Before any valve seat machining and/or lapping can be performed, the guides must be within factory recommended specifications.

1. Invert the cylinder head.
2. Lightly lubricate the valve stems and insert them into the cylinder head in their numbered order.
3. Raise the valve from the seat and apply a small amount of fine lapping compound to the seat.
4. Moisten the suction head of a hand-lapping tool and attach it to the head of the valve.
5. Rotate the tool between the palms of both hands, changing the position of the valve on the valve seat and lifting the tool often to prevent grooving.
6. Lap the valve until a smooth, polished circle is evident on the valve and seat.
7. Remove the tool and the valve. Wipe away all traces of the grinding compound and store the valve to maintain its lapped location.

✴✴ WARNING

Do not get the valves out of order after they have been lapped. They must be put back with the same valve seat with which they were lapped.

Springs, Retainers and Valve Locks

There is no repair or refinishing possible with the springs, retainers and valve locks. If they are found to be worn or defective, they must be replaced with new (or known good) parts.

Cylinder Head

Most refinishing procedures dealing with the cylinder head must be performed by a machine shop. Read the sections below and review your inspection data to determine whether or not machining is necessary.

VALVE GUIDE

➡If any machining or replacements are made to the valve guides, the seats must be machined.

Unless the valve guides need machining or replacing, the only service to perform is to thoroughly clean them of any dirt or oil residue.

There are only two types of valve guides used on automobile engines: the replaceable-type (all aluminum heads) and the cast-in integral-type (most cast iron heads). There are four recommended methods for repairing worn guides.

- Knurling
- Inserts
- Reaming oversize
- Replacing

Knurling is a process in which metal is displaced and raised, thereby reducing clearance, giving a true center, and providing oil control. It is the least expensive way of repairing the valve guides. However, it is not necessarily the best, and in some cases, a knurled valve guide will not stand up for more than a short time. It requires a special knurlizer and precision reaming tools to obtain proper clearances. It would not be cost effective to purchase these tools, unless you plan to rebuild several of the same cylinder head.

Installing a guide insert involves machining the guide to accept a bronze insert. One style is the coil-type, which is installed into a threaded guide. Another is the thin-walled insert where the guide is reamed oversize to accept a split-sleeve insert. After the insert is installed, a special tool is then run through the guide to expand the insert, locking it to the guide. The insert is then reamed to the standard size for proper valve clearance.

Reaming for oversize valves restores normal clearances and provides a true valve seat. Most cast-in type guides can be reamed to accept a valve with an oversize stem. The cost factor for this can become quite high as you will need to purchase the reamer and new, oversize stem valves for all guides which were reamed. Oversize is generally 0.003 to 0.030 in. (0.076 to 0.762mm), with 0.015 in. (0.381mm) being the most common.

To replace cast-in type valve guides, they must be drilled out, then reamed to accept replacement guides. This must be done on a fixture which will allow centering and leveling off of the original valve seat or guide, otherwise a serious guide-to-seat misalignment may occur making it impossible to properly machine the seat.

Replaceable-type guides are pressed into the cylinder head. A hammer and a stepped drift or punch may be used to install and remove the guides. Before removing the guides, measure the protrusion on the spring side of the head and record it for installation. Use the stepped drift to hammer out the old guide from the combustion chamber side of the head. When installing, determine whether or not the guide also seals a water jacket in the head, and if it does, use the recommended sealing agent. If there is no water jacket, grease the valve guide and its bore. Use the stepped drift, and hammer the new guide into the cylinder head from the spring side of the cylinder head. A stack of washers the same thickness as the measured protrusion may help the installation process.

VALVE SEATS

➡ **Before any valve seat machining can be performed, the guides must be within factory recommended specifications.**

➡ **If any machining or replacements were made to the valve guides, the seats must be machined.**

If the seats are in good condition, the valves can be lapped to the seats, and the cylinder head assembled. See the valves section for instructions on lapping.

If the valve seats are worn, cracked or damaged, they must be serviced by a machine shop. The valve seat must be perfectly centered to the valve guide, which requires very accurate machining.

CYLINDER HEAD SURFACE

If the cylinder head is warped, it must be machined flat. If the warpage is extremely severe, the head may need to be replaced. In some instances, it may be possible to straighten a warped head enough to allow machining. In either case, contact a professional machine shop for service.

CRACKS AND PHYSICAL DAMAGE

Certain cracks can be repaired in both cast iron and aluminum heads. For cast iron, a tapered threaded insert is installed along the length of the crack. Aluminum can also use the tapered inserts, however welding is the preferred method. Some physical damage can be repaired through brazing or welding. Contact a machine shop to get expert advice for your particular dilemma.

ASSEMBLY

The first step for any assembly job is to have a clean area in which to work. Next, thoroughly clean all of the parts and components that are to be assembled. Finally, place all of the components onto a suitable work space and, if necessary, arrange the parts to their respective positions.

OHV Engines

1. Lightly lubricate the valve stems and insert all of the valves into the cylinder head. If possible, maintain their original locations.
2. If equipped, install any valve spring shims that were removed.
3. If equipped, install the new valve seals, keeping the following in mind:
- If the valve seal presses over the guide, lightly lubricate the outer guide surfaces.
- If the seal is an O-ring type, it is installed just after compressing the spring but before the valve locks.
4. Place the valve spring and retainer over the stem.
5. Position the spring compressor tool and compress the spring.
6. Assemble the valve locks to the stem.
7. Relieve the spring pressure slowly and insure that neither valve lock becomes dislodged by the retainer.
8. Remove the spring compressor tool.
9. Repeat Steps 2 through 8 until all of the springs have been installed.

ROCKER ARM TYPE CAMSHAFT FOLLOWERS

1. Lightly lubricate the valve stems and insert all of the valves into the cylinder head. If possible, maintain their original locations.
2. If equipped, install any valve spring shims that were removed.
3. If equipped, install the new valve seals, keeping the following in mind:
- If the valve seal presses over the guide, lightly lubricate the outer guide surfaces.
- If the seal is an O-ring type, it is installed just after compressing the spring but before the valve locks.
4. Place the valve spring and retainer over the stem.
5. Position the spring compressor tool and compress the spring.
6. Assemble the valve locks to the stem.
7. Relieve the spring pressure slowly and insure that neither valve lock becomes dislodged by the retainer.
8. Remove the spring compressor tool.
9. Repeat Steps 2 through 8 until all of the springs have been installed.
10. Install the camshaft(s), rockers, shafts and any other components that were removed for disassembly.

Engine Block

GENERAL INFORMATION

A thorough overhaul or rebuild of an engine block would include replacing the pistons, rings, bearings, timing belt/chain assembly and oil pump. For OHV engines also include a new camshaft and lifters. The block would then have the cylinders bored and honed oversize (or if using removable cylinder sleeves, new sleeves installed) and the crankshaft would be cut undersize to provide new wearing surfaces and perfect clearances. However, your particular engine may not have everything worn out. What if only the piston rings have worn out and the clearances on everything else are still within factory specifications? Well, you could just replace the rings and put it back together, but this would be a very rare example. Chances are, if one component in your engine is worn, other components are sure to follow, and soon. At the very least, you should always replace the rings, bearings and oil pump. This is what is commonly called a "freshen up".

Cylinder Ridge Removal

Because the top piston ring does not travel to the very top of the cylinder, a ridge is built up between the end of the travel and the top of the cylinder bore.

Pushing the piston and connecting rod assembly past the ridge can be difficult, and damage to the piston ring lands could occur. If the ridge is not removed before installing a new piston or not removed at all, piston ring breakage and piston damage may occur.

➡It is always recommended that you remove any cylinder ridges before removing the piston and connecting rod assemblies. If you know that new pistons are going to be installed and the engine block will be bored oversize, you may be able to forego this step. However, some ridges may actually prevent the assemblies from being removed, necessitating its removal.

There are several different types of ridge reamers on the market, none of which are inexpensive. Unless a great deal of engine rebuilding is anticipated, borrow or rent a reamer.

1. Turn the crankshaft until the piston is at the bottom of its travel.
2. Cover the head of the piston with a rag.
3. Follow the tool manufacturer instructions and cut away the ridge, exercising extreme care to avoid cutting too deeply.
4. Remove the ridge reamer, the rag and as many of the cuttings as possible. Continue until all of the cylinder ridges have been removed.

DISASSEMBLY

♦ **See Figures 213 and 214**

The engine disassembly instructions following assume that you have the engine mounted on an engine stand. If not, it is easiest to disassemble the engine on a bench or the floor with it resting on the bell housing or transmission mounting surface. You must be able to access the connecting rod fasteners and turn the crankshaft during disassembly. Also, all engine covers (timing, front, side, oil pan, whatever) should have already been removed. Engines, which are seized or locked up, may not be able to be completely disassembled, and a core (salvage yard) engine should be purchased.

If not done during the cylinder head removal, remove the pushrods and lifters, keeping them in order for assembly. Remove the timing gears and/or timing chain assembly, then remove the oil pump drive assembly and withdraw the camshaft from the engine block. Remove the oil pick-up and pump assembly. If equipped, remove any balance or auxiliary shafts. If necessary, remove the cylinder ridge from the top of the bore. See the cylinder ridge removal procedure earlier in this section.

Rotate the engine over so that the crankshaft is exposed. Use a number punch or scribe and mark each connecting rod with its respective cylinder number. The cylinder closest to the front of the engine is always number 1. However, depending on the engine placement, the front of the engine could either be the flywheel or damper/pulley end. Generally, the front of the engine faces the front of the vehicle. Use a number punch or scribe and also mark the main bearing caps from front to rear with the front most cap being number 1 (if there are five caps, mark them 1 through 5, front to rear).

✴✴ WARNING

Take special care when pushing the connecting rod up from the crankshaft because the sharp threads of the rod bolts/studs will score the crankshaft journal. Insure that special plastic caps are installed over them, or cut two pieces of rubber hose to do the same.

Again, rotate the engine, this time to position the number one cylinder bore (head surface) up. Turn the crankshaft until the number one piston is at the bottom of its travel, this should allow the maximum access to its connecting rod. Remove the number one connecting rods fasteners and cap and place two lengths of rubber hose over the rod bolts/studs to protect the crankshaft from damage. Using a sturdy wooden dowel and a hammer, push the connecting rod up about 1 in. (25mm) from the crankshaft and remove the upper bearing insert. Continue pushing or tapping the connecting rod up until the piston rings are out of the cylinder bore. Remove the piston and rod by hand, put the upper half of the bearing insert back into the rod, install the cap with its bearing insert installed, and hand-tighten the cap fasteners. If the parts are kept in order in this manner, they will not get lost and you will be able to tell which bearings came form what cylinder if any problems are discovered and diagnosis is necessary. Remove all the other piston assemblies in the same manner. On V-style engines, remove all of the pistons from one bank, then reposition the engine with the other cylinder bank head surface up, and remove that banks piston assemblies.

The only remaining component in the engine block should now be the crankshaft. Loosen the main bearing caps evenly until the fasteners can be turned by hand, then remove them and the caps. Remove the crankshaft from the engine block. Thoroughly clean all of the components.

TCCS3803

Fig. 213 Place rubber hose over the connecting rod studs to protect the crankshaft and cylinder bores from damage

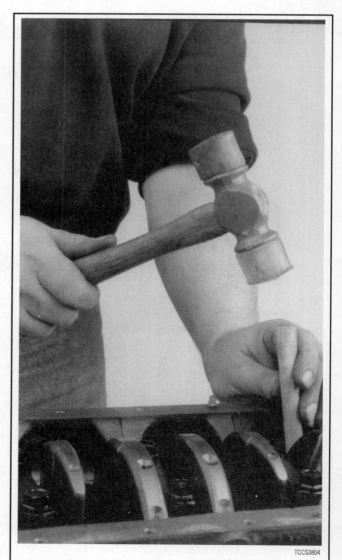

TCCS3804

Fig. 214 Carefully tap the piston out of the bore using a wooden dowel

INSPECTION

Now that the engine block and all of its components are clean, it's time to inspect them for wear and/or damage. To accurately inspect them, you will need some specialized tools:

- Two or three separate micrometers to measure the pistons and crankshaft journals
- A dial indicator
- Telescoping gauges for the cylinder bores
- A rod alignment fixture to check for bent connecting rods

If you do not have access to the proper tools, you may want to bring the components to a shop that does.

Generally, you shouldn't expect cracks in the engine block or its components unless it was known to leak, consume or mix engine fluids, it was severely overheated, or there was evidence of bad bearings and/or crankshaft damage. A visual inspection should be performed on all of the components, but just because you don't see a crack, does not mean it is not there. Some more reliable methods for inspecting for cracks include Magnaflux®, a magnetic process or Zyglo®, a dye penetrant. Magnaflux® is used only on ferrous metal (cast iron). Zyglo® uses a spray on fluorescent mixture along with a black light to reveal the cracks. It is strongly recommended to have your engine block checked professionally for cracks, especially if the engine was known to have overheated and/or leaked or consumed coolant. Contact a local shop for availability and pricing of these services.

Engine Block

ENGINE BLOCK BEARING ALIGNMENT

Remove the main bearing caps and, if still installed, the main bearing inserts. Inspect all of the main bearing saddles and caps for damage, burrs or high spots. If damage is found, and it is caused from a spun main bearing, the block will need to be align-bored or, if severe enough, replacement. Any burrs or high spots should be carefully removed with a metal file.

Place a straightedge on the bearing saddles, in the engine block, along the centerline of the crankshaft. If any clearance exists between the straightedge and the saddles, the block must be align-bored.

Align-boring consists of machining the main bearing saddles and caps by means of a flycutter that runs through the bearing saddles.

DECK FLATNESS

The top of the engine block where the cylinder head mounts is called the deck. Insure that the deck surface is clean of dirt, carbon deposits and old gasket material. Place a straightedge across the surface of the deck along its centerline and, using feeler gauges, check the clearance along several points. Repeat the checking procedure with the straightedge placed along both diagonals of the deck surface. If the reading exceeds 0.003 in. (0.076mm) within a 6.0 in. (15.2cm) span, or 0.006 in. (0.152mm) over the total length of the deck, it must be machined.

CYLINDER BORES

♦ See Figure 215

The cylinder bores house the pistons and are slightly larger than the pistons themselves. A common piston-to-bore clearance is 0.0015–0.0025 in. (0.0381mm–0.0635mm). Inspect and measure the cylinder bores. The bore should be checked for out-of-roundness, taper and size. The results of this inspection will determine whether the cylinder can be used in its existing size and condition, or a rebore to the next oversize is required (or in the case of removable sleeves, have replacements installed).

The amount of cylinder wall wear is always greater at the top of the cylinder than at the bottom. This wear is known as taper. Any cylinder that has a taper of 0.0012 in. (0.305mm) or more, must be rebored. Measurements are taken at a number of positions in each cylinder: at the top, middle and bottom and at two points at each position; that is, at a point 90 degrees from the crankshaft centerline, as well as a point parallel to the crankshaft centerline. The measurements are made with either a special dial indicator or a telescopic gauge and micrometer. If the necessary precision tools to check the bore are not available, take the block to a machine shop and have them mike it. In addition, if you don't have the tools to check the cylinder bores, chances are you will not have the necessary devices to check the pistons, connecting rods and crankshaft. Take these components with you and save yourself an extra trip.

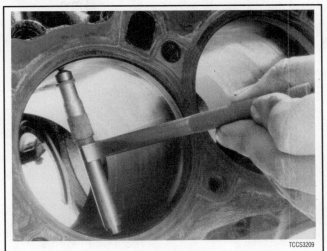

TCCS3209

Fig. 215 Use a telescoping gauge to measure the cylinder bore diameter—take several readings within the same bore

For our procedures, we will use a telescopic gauge and a micrometer. You will need one of each, with a measuring range which covers your cylinder bore size.

1. Position the telescopic gauge in the cylinder bore, loosen the gauges lock and allow it to expand.

➡**Your first two readings will be at the top of the cylinder bore, then proceed to the middle and finally the bottom, making a total of six measurements.**

2. Hold the gauge square in the bore, 90 degrees from the crankshaft centerline, and gently tighten the lock. Tilt the gauge back to remove it from the bore.
3. Measure the gauge with the micrometer and record the reading.
4. Again, hold the gauge square in the bore, this time parallel to the crankshaft centerline, and gently tighten the lock. Again, you will tilt the gauge back to remove it from the bore.
5. Measure the gauge with the micrometer and record this reading. The difference between these two readings is the out-of-round measurement of the cylinder.
6. Repeat steps 1 through 5, each time going to the next lower position, until you reach the bottom of the cylinder. Then go to the next cylinder, and continue until all of the cylinders have been measured.

The difference between these measurements will tell you all about the wear in your cylinders. The measurements, which were taken 90 degrees from the crankshaft centerline, will always reflect the most wear. That is because at this position is where the engine power presses the piston against the cylinder bore the hardest. This is known as thrust wear. Take your top, 90 degree measurement and compare it to your bottom, 90 degree measurement. The difference between them is the taper. When you measure your pistons, you will compare these readings to your piston sizes and determine piston-to-wall clearance.

Crankshaft

Inspect the crankshaft for visible signs of wear or damage. All of the journals should be perfectly round and smooth. Slight scores are normal for a used crankshaft, but you should not feel them with your fingernail. When measuring the crankshaft with a micrometer, you will take readings at the front and rear of each journal, then turn the micrometer 90 degrees and take two more readings, front and rear. The difference between the front-to-rear readings is the journal taper and the first-to-90 degree reading is the out-of-round measurement. Generally, there should be no taper or out-of-roundness found, however, up to 0.0005 in. (0.0127mm) for either can be overlooked. In addition, the readings should fall within the factory specifications for journal diameters.

If the crankshaft journals fall within specifications, it is recommended that it be polished before being returned to service. Polishing the crankshaft insures that any minor burrs or high spots are smoothed, thereby reducing the chance of scoring the new bearings.

Pistons and Connecting Rods

PISTONS

▶ **See Figure 216**

The piston should be visually inspected for any signs of cracking or burning (caused by hot spots or detonation), and scuffing or excessive wear on the skirts. The wrist pin attaches the piston to the connecting rod. The piston should move freely on the wrist pin, both sliding and pivoting. Grasp the connecting rod securely, or mount it in a vise, and try to rock the piston back and forth along the centerline of the wrist pin. There should not be any excessive play evident between the piston and the pin. If there are C-clips retaining the pin in the piston then you have wrist pin bushings in the rods. There should not be any excessive play between the wrist pin and the rod bushing. Normal clearance for the wrist pin is approx. 0.001–0.002 in. (0.025mm–0.051mm).

Use a micrometer and measure the diameter of the piston, perpendicular to the wrist pin, on the skirt. Compare the reading to its original cylinder measurement obtained earlier. The difference between the two readings is the piston-to-wall clearance. If the clearance is within specifications, the piston may be used as is. If the piston is out of specification, but the bore is not, you will need a new piston. If both are out of specification, you will need the cylinder rebored and oversize pistons installed. Generally, if two or more pistons/bores are out of specification, it is best to rebore the entire block and purchase a complete set of oversize pistons.

CONNECTING ROD

You should have the connecting rod checked for straightness at a machine shop. If the connecting rod is bent, it will unevenly wear the bearing and piston, as well as place greater stress on these components. Any bent or twisted connecting rods must be replaced. If the rods are straight and the wrist pin clearance is within specifications, then only the bearing end of the rod need be checked. Place the connecting rod into a vice, with the bearing inserts in place, install the cap to the rod and torque the fasteners to specifications. Use a telescoping gauge and carefully measure the inside diameter of the bearings. Compare this reading to the rods original crankshaft journal diameter measurement. The difference is the oil clearance. If the oil clearance is not within specifications, install new bearings in the rod and take another measurement. If the clearance is still out of specifications, and the crankshaft is not, the rod will need to be reconditioned by a machine shop.

➡You can also use Plastigage® to check the bearing clearances. The assembling section has complete instructions on its use.

Camshaft

Inspect the camshaft and lifters/followers as described earlier in this section.

Bearings

All of the engine bearings should be visually inspected for wear and/or damage. The bearing should look evenly worn all around with no deep scores or pits. If the bearing is severely worn, scored, pitted or heat blued, then the bearing, and the components that use it, should be brought to a machine shop for inspection. Full-circle bearings (used on most camshafts, auxiliary shafts, balance shafts, etc.) require specialized tools for removal and installation, and should be brought to a machine shop for service.

Oil Pump

➡The oil pump is responsible for providing constant lubrication to the whole engine and so it is recommended that a new oil pump be installed when rebuilding the engine.

Completely disassemble the oil pump and thoroughly clean all of the components. Inspect the oil pump gears and housing for wear and/or damage. Insure that the pressure relief valve operates properly and there is no binding or sticking due to varnish or debris. If all of the parts are in proper working condition, lubricate the gears and relief valve, and assemble the pump.

REFINISHING

▶ **See Figure 217**

Almost all engine block refinishing must be performed by a machine shop. If the cylinders are not to be rebored, then the cylinder glaze can be removed with a ball hone. When removing cylinder glaze with a ball hone, use a light or penetrating type oil to lubricate the hone. Do not allow the hone to run dry as this may cause excessive scoring of the cylinder bores and wear on the hone. If new pistons are required, they will need to be installed to the connecting rods. This should be performed by a machine shop as the pistons must be installed in the correct relationship to the rod or engine damage can occur.

Pistons and Connecting Rods

▶ **See Figure 218**

Only pistons with the wrist pin retained by C-clips are serviceable by the home-mechanic. Press fit pistons require special presses and/or heaters to remove/install the connecting rod and should only be performed by a machine shop.

All pistons will have a mark indicating the direction to the front of the engine and the must be installed into the engine in that manner. Usually it is a notch or arrow on the top of the piston, or it may be the letter F cast or stamped into the piston.

ASSEMBLY

Before you begin assembling the engine, first give yourself a clean, dirt free work area. Next, clean every engine component again. The key to a good assembly is cleanliness.

Mount the engine block into the engine stand and wash it one last time using water and detergent (dishwashing detergent works well). While washing it, scrub the cylinder bores with a soft bristle brush and thoroughly clean all of the oil passages. Completely dry the engine and spray the entire assembly down with an anti-rust solution such as WD-40® or similar product. Take a clean lint-free rag and wipe up any excess anti-rust solution from the bores, bearing saddles, etc. Repeat the final cleaning process on the crankshaft. Replace any freeze or oil galley plugs that were removed during disassembly.

TCCS3210

Fig. 216 Measure the piston's outer diameter, perpendicular to the wrist pin, with a micrometer

TCCS3913

Fig. 217 Use a ball type cylinder hone to remove any glaze and provide a new surface for seating the piston rings

TCCS3814

Fig. 218 Most pistons are marked to indicate positioning in the engine (usually a mark means the side facing the front)

Crankshaft

▶ **See Figures 219, 220, 221 and 222**

1. Remove the main bearing inserts from the block and bearing caps.
2. If the crankshaft main bearing journals have been refinished to a definite undersize, install the correct undersize bearing. Be sure that the bearing inserts and bearing bores are clean. Foreign material under inserts will distort bearing and cause failure.
3. Place the upper main bearing inserts in bores with tang in slot.

➡ **The oil holes in the bearing inserts must be aligned with the oil holes in the cylinder block.**

4. Install the lower main bearing inserts in bearing caps.
5. Clean the mating surfaces of block and rear main bearing cap.
6. Carefully lower the crankshaft into place. Be careful not to damage bearing surfaces.
7. Check the clearance of each main bearing by using the following procedure:

   a. Place a piece of Plastigage® or its equivalent, on bearing surface across full width of bearing cap and about ¼ in. off center.

   b. Install cap and tighten bolts to specifications. Do not turn crankshaft while Plastigage® is in place.

   c. Remove the cap. Using the supplied Plastigage® scale, check width of Plastigage® at widest point to get maximum clearance. The difference between the readings is the taper of the journal.

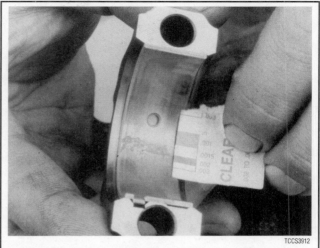

Fig. 220 After the cap is removed again, use the scale supplied with the gauging material to check the clearance

Fig. 221 A dial gauge may be used to check crankshaft end-play

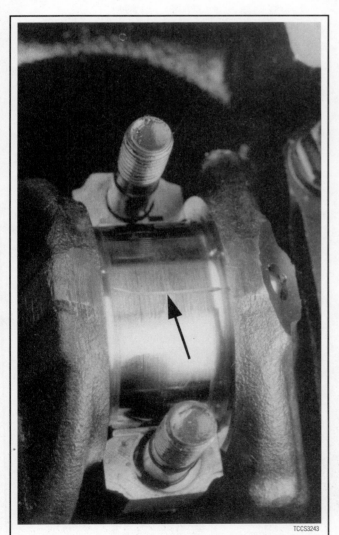

Fig. 219 Apply a strip of gauging material to the bearing journal, then install and torque the cap

Fig. 222 Carefully pry the crankshaft back and forth while reading the dial gauge for end-play

Fig. 223 Checking the piston ring-to-ring groove side clearance using the ring and a feeler gauge

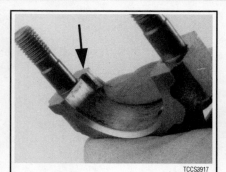

Fig. 224 The notch on the side of the bearing cap matches the tang on the bearing insert

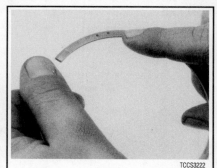

Fig. 225 Most rings are marked to show which side of the ring should face up when installed to the piston

Fig. 226 Install the piston and rod assembly into the block using a ring compressor and the handle of a hammer

d. If clearance exceeds specified limits, try a 0.001 in. or 0.002 in. undersize bearing in combination with the standard bearing. Bearing clearance must be within specified limits. If standard and 0.002 in. undersize bearing does not bring clearance within desired limits, refinish crankshaft journal, then install undersize bearings.

8. After the bearings have been fitted, apply a light coat of engine oil to the journals and bearings. Install the rear main bearing cap. Install all bearing caps except the thrust bearing cap. Be sure that main bearing caps are installed in original locations. Tighten the bearing cap bolts to specifications.

9. Install the thrust bearing cap with bolts finger-tight.

10. Pry the crankshaft forward against the thrust surface of upper half of bearing.

11. Hold the crankshaft forward and pry the thrust bearing cap to the rear. This aligns the thrust surfaces of both halves of the bearing.

12. Retain the forward pressure on the crankshaft. Tighten the cap bolts to specifications.

13. Measure the crankshaft end-play as follows:

a. Mount a dial gauge to the engine block and position the tip of the gauge to read from the crankshaft end.

b. Carefully pry the crankshaft toward the rear of the engine and hold it there while you zero the gauge.

c. Carefully pry the crankshaft toward the front of the engine and read the gauge.

d. Confirm that the reading is within specifications. If not, install a new thrust bearing and repeat the procedure. If the reading is still out of specifications with a new bearing, have a machine shop inspect the thrust surfaces of the crankshaft, and if possible, repair it.

14. Rotate the crankshaft so as to position the first rod journal to the bottom of its stroke.

15. Install the rear main seal.

Pistons and Connecting Rods

▶ See Figures 223, 224, 225 and 226

1. Before installing the piston/connecting rod assembly, oil the pistons, piston rings and the cylinder walls with light engine oil. Install connecting rod bolt protectors or rubber hose onto the connecting rod bolts/studs. Also, perform the following:

a. Select the proper ring set for the size cylinder bore.

b. Position the ring in the bore in which it is going to be used.

c. Push the ring down into the bore area where normal ring wear is not encountered.

d. Use the head of the piston to position the ring in the bore so that the ring is square with the cylinder wall. Use caution to avoid damage to the ring or cylinder bore.

e. Measure the gap between the ends of the ring with a feeler gauge. Ring gap in a worn cylinder is normally greater than specification. If the ring gap is greater than the specified limits, try an oversize ring set.

f. Check the ring side clearance of the compression rings with a feeler gauge inserted between the ring and its lower land according to specification. The gauge should slide freely around the entire ring circumference without binding. Any wear that occurs will form a step at the inner portion of the lower land. If the lower lands have high steps, the piston should be replaced.

2. Unless new pistons are installed, be sure to install the pistons in the cylinders from which they were removed. The numbers on the connecting rod and bearing cap must be on the same side when installed in the cylinder bore. If a connecting rod is ever transposed from one engine or cylinder to another, new bearings should be fitted and the connecting rod should be numbered to correspond with the new cylinder number. The notch on the piston head goes toward the front of the engine.

3. Install all of the rod bearing inserts into the rods and caps.

4. Install the rings to the pistons. Install the oil control ring first, then the second compression ring and finally the top compression ring. Use a piston ring expander tool to aid in installation and to help reduce the chance of breakage.

5. Make sure the ring gaps are properly spaced around the circumference of the piston. Fit a piston ring compressor around the piston and slide the piston and connecting rod assembly down into the cylinder bore, pushing it in with the wooden hammer handle. Push the piston down until it is only slightly below the top of the cylinder bore. Guide the connecting rod onto the crankshaft bearing journal carefully, to avoid damaging the crankshaft.

6. Check the bearing clearance of all the rod bearings, fitting them to crankshaft bearing journals. Follow the procedure in the crankshaft installation above.

7. After the bearings have been fitted, apply a light coating of assembly oil to the journals and bearings.

8. Turn the crankshaft until the appropriate bearing journal is at the bottom of its stroke, then push the piston assembly all the way down until the connecting rod bearing seats on the crankshaft journal. Be careful not to allow the bearing cap screws to strike the crankshaft bearing journals and damage them.

9. After the piston and connecting rod assemblies have been installed, check the connecting rod side clearance on each crankshaft journal.

10. Prime and install the oil pump and the oil pump intake tube.

11. Install the auxiliary/balance shaft(s)/assembly(ies).

Camshaft

1. Install the camshaft.
2. Install the lifters/followers into their bores.
3. Install the timing gears/chain assembly.

Cylinder Head(s)

1. Install the cylinder head(s) using new gaskets.
2. Assemble the rest of the valve train (pushrods and rocker arms and/or shafts).

Engine Start-up and Break-in

STARTING THE ENGINE

Now that the engine is installed and every wire and hose is properly connected, go back and double check that all coolant and vacuum hoses are connected. Check that your oil drain plug is installed and properly tightened. If not already done, install a new oil filter onto the engine. Fill the crankcase with the proper amount and grade of engine oil. Fill the cooling system with a 50/50 mixture of coolant/water.

1. Connect the vehicle battery.
2. Start the engine. Keep your eye on your oil pressure indicator; if it does not indicate oil pressure within 10 seconds of starting, turn the vehicle off.

❄❄ WARNING

Damage to the engine can result if it is allowed to run with no oil pressure. Check the engine oil level to make sure that it is full.

Check for any leaks and if found, repair the leaks before continuing. If there is still no indication of oil pressure, you may need to prime the system.

3. Confirm that there are no fluid leaks (oil or other).
4. Allow the engine to reach normal operating temperature (the upper radiator hose will be hot to the touch).
5. At this point, you can perform any necessary checks or adjustments, such as checking the ignition timing.
6. Install any remaining components or body panels that were removed.

BREAKING IT IN

Make the first miles on the new engine, easy ones. Vary the speed but do not accelerate hard. Most importantly, do not lug the engine, and avoid sustained high speeds until at least 100 miles. Check the engine oil and coolant levels frequently. Expect the engine to use a little oil until the rings seat. Change the oil and filter at 500 miles, 1500 miles, then every 3000 miles past that.

KEEP IT MAINTAINED

Now that you have just gone through all of that hard work, keep yourself from doing it all over again by thoroughly maintaining it. Not that you may not have maintained it before, heck you could have had one to two hundred thousand miles on it before doing this. However, you may have bought the vehicle used, and the previous owner did not keep up on maintenance. Which is why you just went through all of that hard work. See?

3.1L ENGINE MECHANICAL SPECIFICATIONS

Description	English Specifications	Metric Specifications
General Information		
Engine type	60° V6 IRON HEAD	
Displacement	191 cubic in.	3.1L
Bore	3.503 in.	89mm
Stroke	3.307 in.	84mm
Compression ratio	8.5:1	
Firing order	1-2-3-4-5-6	
Cylinder Head		
Flatness	0.01 in.	0.25mm
Valve seat run-out	0.0021 in.	0.0540mm
Valve seat width		
Intake	0.0610-0.0728 in.	1.55-1.85mm
Exhaust	0.0669-0.0787 in.	1.70-2.0mm
Valve seat angle	46°	
Cylinder Block		
Bore		
Diameter	3.5046-3.5053 in.	89.016-89.034mm
Out-of-round (max.)	0.0005 in.	0.013mm
Taper (max.)	0.0005 in.	0.013mm
Piston		
Clearance to bore	0.0009-0.0023 in.	0.0220-0.0580mm
Piston Rings		
Compression rings		
Groove clearance		
1st	0.0020-0.0035 in.	0.05-0.09mm
2nd	0.0020-0.0035 in.	0.05-0.09mm
Gap		
1st	0.0071-0.0161 in.	0.18-0.41mm
2nd	0.0197-0.0280 in.	0.50-0.75mm
Oil ring		
Groove clearance	0.0079 in.	0.20mm
Gap	0.098-0.0295 in.	0.25-0.75mm
Piston Pin		
Diameter	0.9052-0.9054 in.	22.9915-22.9964mm
Clearance	0.0004-0.0008 in.	0.0096-0.0215mm
Press fit in rod	0.0006-0.0018 in.	0.0165-0.0464mm
Camshaft		
Lobe Lift		
Intake	0.2306 in.	5.858mm
Exhaust	0.2620 in.	6.654mm
Journal diameter	1.8677-1.8815 in.	47.44-47.79mm
Journal clearance	0.001-0.004 in.	0.026-0.101mm
Crankshaft		
Main journal		
Diameter (all)	2.6472-2.6479 in.	67.239-67.257mm
Taper (max.)	0.0002 in.	0.005mm
Out-of-round (max.)	0.0002 in.	0.005mm
Clearance (all)	0.0013-0.00030 in.	0.032-0.077mm
Main thrust bearing	0.0013-0.00030 in.	0.032-0.077mm
Crankshaft end-play	0.0024-0.0083 in.	0.060-0.210mm
Crankpin		
Diameter	1.9994-01.9987 in.	50.784-50.768mm
Taper (max.)	0.0002 in.	0.005mm

91093C01

3.1L ENGINE MECHANICAL SPECIFICATIONS

Description	English Specifications	Metric Specifications
Crankshaft (cont.)		
Out-of-round (max.)	0.00020 in.	0.005mm
Rod bearing clearance	0.0011-0.0032 in.	0.028-0.82mm
Rod side clearance	0.0071-0.0173 in.	0.18-0.44mm
Valve System		
Lifter type	Hydraulic	
Rocker arm ratio	1.5:1	
Face angle (all)	45°	
Seat angle (all)	46°	
Seat run-out	0.0021 in.	0.054mm
Seat width		
Intake	0.0610-0.0728 in.	1.55-1.85mm
Exhaust	0.0669-0.0787 in.	1.70-2.0mm
Stem clearance-all	0.0010-0.0027 in.	0.026-0.068mm
Valve spring		
Free length	1.9094 in.	48.5mm
Load		
Closed	82 lbs. @ 1.58 in.	363N @ 40mm
Open	191 lbs. @ 1.187 in.	851N @ 30mm
Installed height	1.58 in.	40.0mm
Oil Pump		
Pressure @ 1100 rpm 150° F (65° C)	15 psi	
Gear lash	0.009-0.015 in.	0.230-0.380mm
Gear pocket		
Gear lash depth	1.201-1.203 in.	0.230-0.380mm
Gear pocket diameter	1.502-1.504 in.	38.175-38.226mm
Gear diameter		
Drive gear	1.498-1.500 in.	38.05-38.10mm
Side clearance		
Drive gear	0.001-0.003 in.	0.040-0.080mm
End clearance	0.001-0.004 in.	0.040-0.125mm
Valve-to-bore	0.0015-0.0035 in.	0.038-0.089mm

91093C02

3.4L ENGINE MECHANICAL SPECIFICATIONS

Description	English Specifications	Metric Specifications
General Information		
Engine type	60 Degree V-6	
Displacement	209 cubic in.	3.4L
Bore	3.620 in.	92mm
Stroke	3.307 in.	84mm
Compression ratio	9.5:1	
Firing order	1-2-3-4-5-6	
Oil Pump		
Gear Lash	0.0037-0.0077 in.	0.094-0.195mm
Gear Pocket Depth	1.2020-1.2040 in.	30.531-30.582mm
Gear Pocket Diameter	1.5030-1.5050 in.	38.176-38.226mm
Oil Pump Gear		
Length	1.1990-1.2000 in.	30.455-30.480mm
Diameter	1.4980-1.5000 in	38.049-38.100mm
Side clearance	0.0010-0.0030 in.	0.025-0.088mm
End clearance	0.0020-0.0050 in.	0.040-0.127mm
Valve to bore clearance	0.0015-0.0035 in.	0.038-0.089mm
Oil pressure @ operating temperature	15 psi (103 kPa)	1100 rpm-minimum
Cylinder Bore		
Diameter	3.6228-3.6235 in.	92.019-92.037mm
Out of round (max.)	0.0003 in.	0.007mm
Taper (max.)	0.004 in.	0.010mm
Piston		
Diameter-Gauged on skirt 13mm below centerline of piston pin bore	3.6209-3.6216 in.	91.970-91.988mm
Clearance ring groove width-second compression	0.0013-0.0027in.	0.032-0.068mm
Pin bore	0.9057-0.9060 in	23.006-23.013mm
Piston Rings		
Compression groove clearance		
1st	0.0016-0.0030 in.	0.040-0.075mm
2nd	0.0015-0.0035 in.	0.040-0.090mm
Gap (at 92mm)		
1st	0.0059-0.01420 in.	0.150-0.360mm
2nd	0.0189-0.0291 in.	0.480-0.740mm
Oil groove clearance (max.)	0.0080 in.	0.2020mm
Gap (segment at 92mm)	0.0098-0.0299	0.250-0.760mm
Piston Pin		
Diameter	0.9052-0.9054 in.	22.992-22.996mm
Clearance	0.00040-0.00080 in.	0.0096-0.0215mm
Fit in rod-press pin-to-rod clearance	0.0006-0.0018 in.	0.0160-0.0460mm
Crankshaft		
Main journal		
Diameter (all)	2.6473-2.6483 in.	67.239-67.257mm
Taper (max.)	0.0002 in.	0.0050mm
Out-of-round (max.)	0.0002 in.	0.0050mm
Flange Runout (max.)	0.0016 in.	0.0410mm
Cylinder block main bearing bore diameter	2.8407-2.8412 in.	72.155-72.168mm
Crankshaft main bearing inside diameter	2.6492-2.6502 in.	67.289-67.316mm
Crankshaft main bearing clearance	0.0008-0.0025 in.	0.019-0.064mm
Crankshaft main thrust bearing clearance	0.0012-0.0030 in.	0.032-0.077mm
Crankshaft end play	0.0024-0.0083 in.	0.060-0.210mm
Crankshaft flange run-out (max.)	0.0016 in.	0.0400mm

9109C03

3.4L ENGINE MECHANICAL SPECIFICATIONS

Description	English Specifications	Metric Specifications
Connecting Rod		
Diameter	1.9987-1.9994 in.	50.768-50.784mm
Taper (max.)	0.0002 in.	0.0050mm
Out of round (max.)	0.0002 in.	0.0050mm
Rod bearing bore diameter	2.1245-2.1253 in.	53.962-53.984mm
Rod inside bearing diameter	2.000-2.002 in.	21.90-22.10mm
Rod bearing clearance	0.0007-0.0024 in.	0.0180-0.0620mm
Rod side clearance	0.007-0.017 in.	0.178-0.432mm
Camshaft		
Lobe lift		
Intake	0.2727 in.	6.926mm
Exhaust	0.2727 in.	6.926mm
Journal diameter	1.8677-1.8696 in.	47.440-47.488mm
Camshaft bearing bore diameter		
Front and rear	2.0090-2.0110 in.	51.029-51.079mm
Middle #2 and #3	1.9990-2.0010 in.	50.775-50.825mm
Camshaft bearing inside diameter	1.8710-1.8720 in.	47.523-47.549mm
Journal clearance	0.001-0.0040 in.	0.026-0.101mm
Journal runout (max.)	0.0010 in.	0.025mm
Valve System		
Roller lifter		Hydraulic
Rocker arm ratio		1.60:1
Valves		
Face angle		45°
Seat angle		46°
Seat runout (max.)	0.0014 in.	0.035mm
Seat width		
Intake	0.0610-0.0710 in.	1.549-1.803mm
Exhaust	0.0670-0.0790 in.	10702-2.006mm
Valve margin minimum		
Intake	0.0830 in.	2.108mm
Exhaust	0.1060 in.	2.692mm
Stem clearance-all	0.0010-0.0027 in.	0.026-0.068mm
Valve Springs		
Free length	1.91 in.	48.5mm
Load-closed	72 lbs. @ 1.701 in.	320 N @43.20mm
Load-open	230 lbs. @ 1.260 in.	1036 N @ 32.00mm
Installed height		
Intake	1.7010 in.	43.180mm
Exhaust	1.7010 in.	43.180mm

9109C04

3.8L ENGINE MECHANICAL SPECIFICATIONS

Description	English Specifications	Metric Specifications
General Information		
Engine type	90° V6	
Displacement	231 cubic in.	3.8L
Bore	3.8 in.	96.52mm
Stroke	3.4 in.	86.36mm
Compression ratio	9.0:1	
Firing order	1-6-5-4-3-2	
Lubrication System		
Oil capacity (without filter change)	4 qts.	3.75L
Oil pressure	414 kPa (60psi) @ 1850 RPM	
Oil pump		
Gear pocket depth	0.461-0.4625 in.	11.71-11.75mm
Gear pocket diameter	3.508-3.512 in.	89.10-89.20mm
Inner gear tip clearance	0.006 in.	0.152mm
Outer gear diameter clearance	0.001-0.015 in.	0.203-0.381mm
End clearance	0.001-0.0035 in.	0.025-0.089mm
Valve to bore clearance	0.0015-0.003 in.	0.038-0.076mm
Cylinder Bore		
Diameter	3.8 in.	96.5mm
Out-of-round (max.)	0.0004 in.	0.010mm
Taper (max.)	0.0005 in.	0.013mm
Piston		
Clearance (44 mm from top of piston)	0.0004-0.0022 in.	0.010-0.056mm
Piston Rings		
Ring groove depth		
Top compression	0.169-0.174 in.	4.294-4.424mm
2nd compression	0.173-0.178 in.	4.389-4.519mm
End gap		
Top compression	0.012-0.022 in.	0.305-0.559mm
2nd compression	0.030-0.040 in.	0.762-1.016mm
Oil control	0.010-0.030 in.	0.254-0.762mm
Side clearance		
Top compression	0.0013-0.0031 in.	0.033-0.079mm
2nd compression	0.0013-0.0031 in.	0.033-0.079mm
Oil control	0.011-0.0081 in.	0.028-0.206mm
Ring width		
Top compression	0.463-0.471 in.	1.176-1.197mm
Second compression	0.0581-0.0589 in.	1.476-1.497mm
Oil control	0.1122-0.1182 in.	2.850-3.002mm
Piston Pin		
Diameter	0.9053-0.9055 in.	22.995-23.000mm
Fit in Piston	0.0003-0.0006 in.	0.018-0.0155mm
Fit in Rod	0.0007-0.0017 in.	0.018-0.043mm
Crankshaft-Main Bearings		
Journal		
Diameter (all)	2.4988-2.4998 in.	63.470-63.495mm
Taper (max.)	0.0003 in.	0.008mm
Runout (max.)	0.0003 in.	0.008mm
Bearing to Journal Clearance	0.0008-0.0022 in.	0.020-0.055mm
Main bearing bore inside diameter	2.687-2.688 in.	68.250-68.275mm
Crankshaft end play	0.003-0.011 in.	0.076-0.279mm

91093C05

3.8L ENGINE MECHANICAL SPECIFICATIONS

Description	English Specifications	Metric Specifications
Connecting Rod Bearings		
Connecting rod bearing		
Diameter (all)	2.2487-2.2499 in.	57.117-57.147mm
Taper (max.)	0.0003 in.	0.008mm
Runout (max.)	0.0003 in.	0.008mm
Bearing to journal clearance	0.0008-0.0022 in.	0.020-0.055mm
Rod side clearance	0.003-0.015 in.	0.076-0.381mm
Connecting rod		
Large end bore inside diameter	2.3738-2.3745 in.	60.295-60312mm
Camshaft		
Lobe lift		
Intake	0.250 in.	6.43mm
Exhaust	0.255 in.	6.48mm
Journal diameter	1.785-1.786 in.	45.339-45.364mm
Bearing inside diameter	1.7865-1.7885 in.	45.377-45.428mm
Bearing to journal clearance	0.0005-0.0035 in.	0.013-0.089mm
Balance shaft		
End play	0.0-0.008 in.	0.0-0.203mm
Radial play		
Front	0.0-0.0011 in.	0.028mm
Rear	0.0005-0.0047 in.	0.0127-0.119mm
Drive gear lash	0.002-0.005 in.	0.050-0.127mm
Bearing bore diameter		
Front	2.0462-2.0472 in.	51.973-51.999mm
Rear	1.950-1.952 in.	49.530-49580mm
Valve System		
Rocker Arm Ratio	1.6:1	
Lifters	Hydraulic	
Valves		
Face angle	45°	
Seat angle	45°	
Minimum margin	0.025 in.	0.635mm
Seat runout (max.)	0.002 in.	0.050mm
Seat width		
Intake	0.060-0.800 in.	1.53-2.03mm
Exhaust	0.090-0.110 in.	2.29-2.79mm
Stem height-all	1.935-1.975 in.	49.15-50.17mm
Stem clearance		
Intake	0.0015-0.0032 in.	0.038-0.089mm
Exhaust	0.0015-0.0035 in.	0.038-0.089mm
Valve springs		
Free length	1.981 in.	50.32mm
Load-closed	80lbs. @ 1.75 in.	356 N @43.69 mm
Load-open	210 lbs. @ 1.315 in.	935 N @ 33.4 mm
Seat width	0.0370-0.0748 in.	0.940-1.900 mm
Installed height	1.690-1.720 in.	42.93-44.45mm

91093C06

3.1L ENGINE TORQUE SPECIFICATIONS

Components	English	Metric
Rocker Arm (Valve) Cover		
Throttle cable bracket bolts	89 inch lbs.	10 Nm
Throttle body nuts	18 ft. lbs.	25 Nm
Rocker Arms and Pushrods		
Valve cover nut	80 inch lbs	9 Nm
Rocker arm retaining nuts	18 ft. lbs.	24 Nm
Thermostat		
Thermostat housing pipe retaining bolt	18 ft. lbs.	25 Nm
Thermostat outlet retainers	18 ft. lbs.	25 Nm
Intake Manifold		
Intake manifold bolt		
1st pass	13 ft. lbs.	18 Nm
2nd pass	22 ft. lbs.	30 Nm
Intake manifold nuts	22 ft. lbs.	30 Nm
Alternator bracket retaining nut	37 ft. lbs.	50 Nm
Alternator bracket retaining stud	37 ft. lbs.	50 Nm
EGR valve retaining bolt	18 ft. lbs.	25 Nm
Distributor clamp bolt	25 ft. lbs.	34 Nm
Exhaust Manifold		
Exhaust crossover pipe stud	89 inch lbs.	10 Nm
Exhaust manifold nuts	25 ft. lbs.	34 Nm
Water Pump		
Drive belt tensioner bolt	37 ft. lbs.	50 Nm
Water pump bolts	89 inch lbs.	10 Nm
Cylinder Head		
Cylinder head bolts	Refer to procedure	
Oil Pan		
Oil pan bolts	89 inch lbs.	10 Nm
Oil Pump		
Oil pump bolts	40 ft. lbs.	54 Nm
Oil filter adapter connector	50 ft. lbs.	68 Nm
Crankshaft Damper/Pulley		
Crankshaft main bearing cap bolt	78 ft. lbs.	105 Nm
Crankshaft balancer bolt	76 ft. lbs.	103 Nm
Damper bolt	76 ft. lbs.	103 Nm
Timing Chain Cover and Seal		
Timing cover bolts	15 ft. lbs.	21 Nm
Timing Chain and Gears		
Timing chain damper bolt	15 ft. lbs.	21 Nm
Crankshaft (torsional) damper bolt	76 ft. lbs.	103 Nm
Timing indicator bolt	89 inch lbs.	10 Nm
Camshaft		
Camshaft sprocket bolt	18 ft. lbs.	25 Nm
Thrust plate bolts	106 inch lbs.	12 Nm
Flywheel		
Flywheel bolts	57 ft. lbs.	80 Nm

91093C07

3.4L ENGINE TORQUE SPECIFICATIONS

Components	English	Metric
Camshaft		
Camshaft position sensor bolt	89 inch lbs.	10 Nm
Camshaft sprocket bolt	81 ft. lbs.	110 Nm
Camshaft thrust plate bolt	89 inch lbs.	10 Nm
Coolant System		
Coolant drain plug	14 ft. lbs.	19 Nm
Coolant pump pulley bolt	25 ft. lbs.	18 Nm
Coolant pump bolt	89 inch lbs.	10 Nm
Coolant outlet bolt	25 ft. lbs.	18 Nm
Coolant temperature sensor	17 ft. lbs.	23 Nm
Crankshaft Damper/Pulley		
Crankshaft balancer bolt	76 ft. lbs.	103 Nm
Crankshaft bearing cap bolt	37 ft. lbs + 77°	50 Nm + 77°
Crankshaft bearing cap stud	37 ft. lbs + 77°	50 Nm + 77°
Crankshaft position sensor		
Front cover bolt	89 inch lbs.	10 Nm
Side of block bolt	98 inch lbs.	11 Nm
Connecting rod cap nut	15 ft. lbs + 75°	20 Nm + 75°
Cylinder Head		
Cylinder head bolts	37 ft. lbs. + 90°	50 ft. lbs. + 90°
Exhaust manifold retaining nuts	12 ft. lbs.	16 Nm
Heat shield	89 inch lbs.	10 Nm
Exhaust manifold stud	12 ft. lbs.	16 Nm
Drive belt tensioner bolt	37 ft. lbs.	50 Nm
Knock sensor	14 ft. lbs.	19 Nm
Accelerator control cable bracket		
Bolt	125 inch lbs.	14 Nm
Nut	89 inch lbs.	10 Nm
Oil Pan		
Oil pan side bolts	37 ft. lbs.	50 Nm
Oil pan drain plug	18 ft. lbs.	25 Nm
Oil pan retaining bolts	18 ft. lbs.	25 Nm
Oil Pump		
Oil pressure switch	115 inch lbs.	13 Nm
Oil pump cover bolts	89 inch lbs.	10 Nm
Oil pump drive assembly bolts	27 ft. lbs.	36 Nm
Oil pump bolts	30 ft. lbs.	41 Nm
Rocker Arm Assembly		
Rocker arm bolt	89 inch lbs. + 30°	10 Nm + 30°
Rocker arm (valve) cover bolt - hand tighten first	89 inch lbs.	10 Nm
Valve lifter guide bolt	89 inch lbs.	10 Nm
Spark plug	15 ft. lbs.	20 Nm
Timing Chain		
Timing chain dampener bolts	15 ft. lbs.	20 Nm
Intake Manifold		
Upper intake manifold bolt	18 ft. lbs.	25 Nm
Upper intake manifold stud	18 ft. lbs.	25 Nm
Lower intake manifold stud	115 inch lbs.	13 Nm
Flywheel		
Flywheel bolts	12 ft. lbs.	16 Nm

91093C08

3.8L ENGINE TORQUE SPECIFICATIONS

Components	English	Metric
Camshaft		
Camshaft sensor front cover bolt	88 inch lbs.	10 Nm
Camshaft sprocket bolt	74 ft. lbs. + 90°	100 Nm + 90°
Balance shaft retainer	22 ft. lbs.	30 Nm
Coolant System		
Coolant drain plug	14 ft. lbs.	19 Nm
Coolant pump pulley bolt	10 ft. lbs.	13 Nm
Coolant pump bolt to front cover	11 ft. lbs. + 80°	15 Nm + 80°
Coolant outlet bolt (thermostat housing)	20 ft. lbs.	27 Nm
Coolant temperature sensor	15 ft. lbs.	20 Nm
Crankshaft Damper/Pulley		
Crankshaft balancer bolt	110 ft. lbs. + 76°	150 Nm + 76°
Crankshaft bearing caps to cylinder block bolt	26 ft. lbs.+ 50°	35 Nm. + 50°
Crankshaft position sensor bolt - front cover	22 ft. lbs.	30 Nm
Crankshaft sensor clamp bolt	40 inch lbs.	4.5 Nm
Connecting rod bolts	20 ft. lbs.+ 50°	27 Nm + 50°
Cylinder Head		
Cylinder head bolts	Refer to Procedure	
Knock sensor	13 ft. lbs.	18 Nm
Rocker arm cover to head bolts (hand tighten first)	89 inch lbs.	10 Nm
Spark plug	20 ft. lbs.	27 Nm
Exhaust manifold to cylinder head	38 ft. lbs.	52 Nm
Oxygen sensor to exhaust manifold	31 ft. lbs.	42 Nm
Generator suppport to cylinder head	37 ft. lbs.	50 Nm
Generator suppport through generator	37 ft. lbs.	50 Nm
Front cover to block	22 ft. lbs.	30 Nm
Oil Pan		
Oil pan to block bolts	10 ft.lbs.	14 Nm
Oil pan to front cover	10 ft.lbs.	14 Nm
Oil filter adapter to front cover	22 ft.lbs.	30 Nm
Oil Pump		
Oil pressure switch	24 ft.lbs.	32 Nm
Oil pump cover to front cover	8 ft.lbs.	11 Nm
Oil screen housing to cylinder block	11 ft. lbs.	15 Nm
Drain plug	30 ft. lbs.	40 Nm
Rocker Valve Assembly		
Rocker arm pedestal to head	18 ft. lbs. + 70°	25 Nm + 70°
Rocker arm (valve) cover (hand tighten first)	89 inch lbs.	10 Nm
Valve lifter guide retainer bolt	22 ft. lbs.	30 Nm
Timing Chain		
Timing chain damper bolt (special bolt)	16 ft. lbs.	22 Nm
Intake Manifold		
Coolant temperature sensor to intake	15 ft. lbs	20 Nm
Intake manifold to cylinder head (lower)	89 inch lbs.	10 Nm
Upper to lower intake manifold bolts	22 ft. lbs.	30 Nm
Throttle body to intake manifold bolts	11 ft. lbs.	15 Nm
Flywheel		
Flywheel bolts	11 ft. lbs.+ 50°	15 Nm + 50°

91093C09

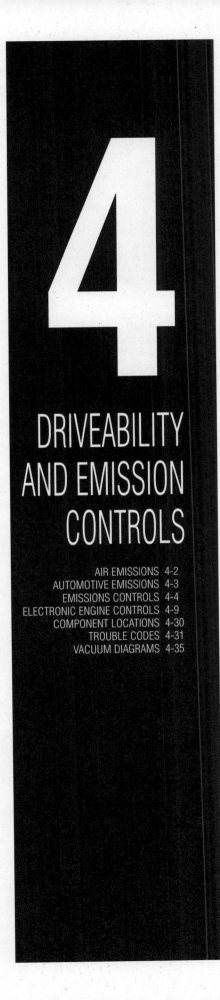

4

DRIVEABILITY AND EMISSION CONTROLS

AIR EMISSIONS

Air Pollution

The earth's atmosphere, at or near sea level, consists approximately of 78 percent nitrogen, 21 percent oxygen and 1 percent other gases. If it were possible to remain in this state, 100 percent clean air would result. However, many varied sources allow other gases and particulates to mix with the clean air, causing our atmosphere to become unclean or polluted.

Some of these pollutants are visible while others are invisible, with each having the capability of causing distress to the eyes, ears, throat, skin and respiratory system. Should these pollutants become concentrated in a specific area and under certain conditions, death could result due to the displacement or chemical change of the oxygen content in the air. These pollutants can also cause great damage to the environment and to the many man made objects that are exposed to the elements.

To better understand the causes of air pollution, the pollutants can be categorized into 3 separate types, natural, industrial and automotive.

Natural Pollutants

Natural pollution has been present on earth since before man appeared and continues to be a factor when discussing air pollution, although it causes only a small percentage of the overall pollution problem. It is the direct result of decaying organic matter, wind born smoke and particulates from such natural events as plain and forest fires (ignited by heat or lightning), volcanic ash, sand and dust which can spread over a large area of the countryside.

Such a phenomenon of natural pollution has been seen in the form of volcanic eruptions. The resulting plume of smoke, steam and volcanic ash blotting out the rays of the sun as it spreads and rises higher into the atmosphere. As it travels into the atmosphere the upper air currents catch and carry the smoke and ash, while condensing the steam back into water vapor. As the water vapor, smoke and ash travel on their journey, the smoke dissipates into the atmosphere while the ash and moisture settle back to earth in a trail hundreds of miles long. In some cases, lives are lost and millions of dollars of property damage result.

Industrial Pollutants

Industrial pollution is caused primarily by industrial processes, the burning of coal, oil and natural gas, which in turn produce smoke and fumes. Because the burning fuels contain large amounts of sulfur, the principal ingredients of smoke and fumes are sulfur dioxide and particulate matter. This type of pollutant occurs most severely during still, damp and cool weather, such as at night. Even in its less severe form, this pollutant is not confined to just cities. Because of air movements, the pollutants move for miles over the surrounding countryside, leaving in its path a barren and unhealthy environment for all living things.

Working with Federal, State and Local mandated regulations and by carefully monitoring emissions, big business has greatly reduced the amount of pollutant introduced from its industrial sources, striving to obtain an acceptable level. Because of the mandated industrial emission clean up, many land areas and streams in and around the cities that were formerly barren of vegetation and life, have now begun to move back in the direction of nature's intended balance.

Automotive Pollutants

The third major source of air pollution is automotive emissions. The emissions from the internal combustion engines were not an appreciable problem years ago because of the small number of registered vehicles and the nation's small highway system. However, during the early 1950's, the trend of the American people was to move from the cities to the surrounding suburbs. This caused an immediate problem in transportation because the majority of suburbs were not afforded mass transit conveniences. This lack of transportation created an attractive market for the automobile manufacturers, which resulted in a dramatic increase in the number of vehicles produced and sold, along with a marked increase in highway construction between cities and the suburbs. Multi-vehicle families emerged with a growing emphasis placed on an individual vehicle per family member. As the increase in vehicle ownership and usage occurred, so did pollutant levels in and around the cities, as suburbanites drove daily to their businesses and employment, returning at the end of the day to their homes in the suburbs.

It was noted that a smoke and fog type haze was being formed and at times, remained in suspension over the cities, taking time to dissipate. At first this

"smog," derived from the words "smoke" and "fog," was thought to result from industrial pollution but it was determined that automobile emissions shared the blame. It was discovered that when normal automobile emissions were exposed to sunlight for a period of time, complex chemical reactions would take place.

It is now known that smog is a photochemical layer that develops when certain oxides of nitrogen (NOx) and unburned hydrocarbons (HC) from automobile emissions are exposed to sunlight. Pollution was more severe when smog would become stagnant over an area in which a warm layer of air settled over the top of the cooler air mass, trapping and holding the cooler mass at ground level. The trapped cooler air would keep the emissions from being dispersed and diluted through normal airflow. This type of air stagnation was given the name "Temperature Inversion."

TEMPERATURE INVERSION

In normal weather situations, surface air is warmed by heat radiating from the earth's surface and the sun's rays. This causes it to rise upward, into the atmosphere. Upon rising, it will cool through a convection type heat exchange with the cooler upper air. As warm air rises, the surface pollutants are carried upward and dissipated into the atmosphere.

When a temperature inversion occurs, we find the higher air is no longer cooler, but is warmer than the surface air, causing the cooler surface air to become trapped. This warm air blanket can extend from above ground level to a few hundred or even a few thousand feet into the air. As the surface air is trapped, so are the pollutants, causing a severe smog condition. Should this stagnant air mass extend to a few thousand feet high, enough air movement with the inversion takes place to allow the smog layer to rise above ground level but the pollutants still cannot dissipate. This inversion can remain for days over an area, with the smog level only rising or lowering from ground level to a few hundred feet high. Meanwhile, the pollutants level increases, causing eye irritation, respiratory problems, reduced visibility, plant damage and in some cases, even disease.

This inversion phenomenon was first noted in the Los Angeles, California area. The city lies in terrain resembling a basin and with certain weather conditions, a cold air mass is held in the basin while a warmer air mass covers it like a lid.

Because this type of condition was first documented as prevalent in the Los Angeles area, this type of trapped pollution was named Los Angeles Smog, although it occurs in other areas where a large concentration of automobiles are used and the air remains stagnant for any length of time.

HEAT TRANSFER

Consider the internal combustion engine as a machine in which raw materials must be placed so a finished product comes out. As in any machine operation, a certain amount of wasted material is formed. When we relate this to the internal combustion engine, we find that through the input of air and fuel, we obtain power during the combustion process to drive the vehicle. The by-product or waste of this power is, in part, heat and exhaust gases with which we must dispose.

The heat from the combustion process can rise to over 4000°F (2204°C). The dissipation of this heat is controlled by a ram air effect, the use of cooling fans to cause air flow and a liquid coolant solution surrounding the combustion area to transfer the heat of combustion through the cylinder walls and into the coolant. The coolant is then directed to a thin-finned, multi-tube radiator, from which the excess heat is transferred to the atmosphere by 1 of the 3 heat transfer methods, conduction, convection or radiation.

The cooling of the combustion area is an important part in the control of exhaust emissions. To understand the behavior of the combustion and transfer of its heat, consider the air/fuel charge. It is ignited and the flame front burns progressively across the combustion chamber until the burning charge reaches the cylinder walls. Some of the fuel in contact with the walls is not hot enough to burn, thereby snuffing out or quenching the combustion process. This leaves unburned fuel in the combustion chamber. This unburned fuel is then forced out of the cylinder and into the exhaust system, along with the exhaust gases.

Many attempts have been made to minimize the amount of unburned fuel in the combustion chambers due to quenching, by increasing the coolant temperature and lessening the contact area of the coolant around the combustion area. However, design limitations within the combustion chambers prevent the complete burning of the air/fuel charge, so a certain amount of the unburned fuel is still expelled into the exhaust system, regardless of modifications to the engine.

w.nile

er name: Litwin, Sta

te charged: 9/10/2016,15:59
em ID: 31491007640612
ll number: 629.28734 G3261u 1990/1999
tle: Chilton's General Motors Lumina/Sil
uette/Trans
te due: 10/1/2016,23:59

tal checkouts for session:1
tal checkouts:1

n-Thu 9-9, Fri 9-7
t 9-5, Sun 1-5
new online
w.nileslibrary.org
ve a nice day

AUTOMOTIVE EMISSIONS

Before emission controls were mandated on internal combustion engines, other sources of engine pollutants were discovered along with the exhaust emissions. It was determined that engine combustion exhaust produced approximately 60 percent of the total emission pollutants, fuel evaporation from the fuel tank and carburetor vents produced 20 percent, with the final 20 percent being produced through the crankcase as a by-product of the combustion process.

Exhaust Gases

The exhaust gases emitted into the atmosphere are a combination of burned and unburned fuel. To understand the exhaust emission and its composition, we must review some basic chemistry.

When the air/fuel mixture is introduced into the engine, we are mixing air, composed of nitrogen (78 percent), oxygen (21 percent) and other gases (1 percent) with the fuel, which is 100 percent hydrocarbons (HC), in a semi-controlled ratio. As the combustion process is accomplished, power is produced to move the vehicle while the heat of combustion is transferred to the cooling system. The exhaust gases are then composed of nitrogen, a diatomic gas (N_2), the same as was introduced in the engine, carbon dioxide (CO_2), the same gas that is used in beverage carbonation, and water vapor (H_2O). The nitrogen (N_2), for the most part, passes through the engine unchanged, while the oxygen (O_2) reacts (burns) with the hydrocarbons (HC) and produces the carbon dioxide (CO_2) and the water vapors (H_2O). If this chemical process would be the only process to take place, the exhaust emissions would be harmless. However, during the combustion process, other compounds are formed which are considered dangerous. These pollutants are hydrocarbons (HC), carbon monoxide (CO), oxides of nitrogen (NOx) oxides of sulfur (SOx) and engine particulates.

HYDROCARBONS

Hydrocarbons (HC) are essentially fuel which was not burned during the combustion process or which has escaped into the atmosphere through fuel evaporation. The main sources of incomplete combustion are rich air/fuel mixtures, low engine temperatures and improper spark timing. The main sources of hydrocarbon emission through fuel evaporation on most vehicles used to be the fuel tank and carburetor float bowl of the vehicle.

To reduce combustion hydrocarbon emission, engine modifications were made to minimize dead space and surface area in the combustion chamber. In addition, the air/fuel mixture was made leaner through the improved control which feedback carburetors and fuel injection offer and by the addition of external controls to aid in further combustion of the hydrocarbons outside the engine. Two such methods were the addition of air injection systems, to inject fresh air into the exhaust manifolds and the installation of catalytic converters, units that are able to burn traces of hydrocarbons without affecting the internal combustion process or fuel economy.

To control hydrocarbon emissions through fuel evaporation, modifications were made to the fuel tank to allow storage of the fuel vapors during periods of engine shutdown. Modifications were also made to the air intake system so that at specific times during engine operation, these vapors may be purged and burned by blending them with the air/fuel mixture.

CARBON MONOXIDE

Carbon monoxide is formed when not enough oxygen is present during the combustion process to convert carbon (C) to carbon dioxide (CO_2). An increase in the carbon monoxide (CO) emission is normally accompanied by an increase in the hydrocarbon (HC) emission because of the lack of oxygen to completely burn all of the fuel mixture.

Carbon monoxide (CO) also increases the rate at which the photo chemical smog is formed by speeding up the conversion of nitric oxide (NO) to nitrogen dioxide (NO_2). To accomplish this, carbon monoxide (CO) combines with oxygen (O_2) and nitric oxide (NO) to produce carbon dioxide (CO_2) and nitrogen dioxide (NO_2). ($CO + O_2 + NO = CO_2 + NO_2$).

The dangers of carbon monoxide, which is an odorless and colorless toxic gas are many. When carbon monoxide is inhaled into the lungs and passed into the blood stream, oxygen is replaced by the carbon monoxide in the red blood cells, causing a reduction in the amount of oxygen supplied to the many parts of the body. This lack of oxygen causes headaches, lack of coordination, reduced mental alertness and, should the carbon monoxide concentration be high enough, death could result.

NITROGEN

Normally, nitrogen is an inert gas. When heated to approximately 2500°F (1371°C) through the combustion process, this gas becomes active and causes an increase in the nitric oxide (NO) emission.

Oxides of nitrogen (NOx) are composed of approximately 97–98 percent nitric oxide (NO). Nitric oxide is a colorless gas but when it is passed into the atmosphere, it combines with oxygen and forms nitrogen dioxide (NO_2). The nitrogen dioxide then combines with chemically active hydrocarbons (HC) and when in the presence of sunlight, causes the formation of photochemical smog.

Ozone

To further complicate matters, some of the nitrogen dioxide (NO_2) is broken apart by the sunlight to form nitric oxide and oxygen. ($NO_2 +$ sunlight $= NO + O$). This single atom of oxygen then combines with diatomic (meaning 2 atoms) oxygen (O_2) to form ozone (O_3). Ozone is one of the smells associated with smog. It has a pungent and offensive odor, irritates the eyes and lung tissues, affects the growth of plant life and causes rapid deterioration of rubber products. Ozone can be formed by sunlight as well as electrical discharge into the air.

The most common discharge area on the automobile engine is the secondary ignition electrical system, especially when inferior quality spark plug cables are used. As the surge of high voltage is routed through the secondary cable, the circuit builds up an electrical field around the wire, which acts upon the oxygen in the surrounding air to form the ozone. The faint glow along the cable with the engine running that may be visible on a dark night, is called the "corona discharge." It is the result of the electrical field passing from a high along the cable, to a low in the surrounding air, which forms the ozone gas. The combination of corona and ozone has been a major cause of cable deterioration. Recently, different and better quality insulating materials have lengthened the life of the electrical cables.

Although ozone at ground level can be harmful, ozone is beneficial to the inhabitants of the earth. By having a concentrated ozone layer called the "ozonosphere," between 10 and 20 miles (16–32 km) up in the atmosphere, much of the ultra violet radiation from the sun's rays are absorbed and screened. If this ozone layer were not present, much of the surface of the earth would be burned, dried and unfit for human life.

OXIDES OF SULFUR

Oxides of sulfur (SOx) were initially ignored in the exhaust system emissions, since the sulfur content of gasoline as a fuel is less than $\frac{1}{10}$ of 1 percent. Because of this small amount, it was felt that it contributed very little to the overall pollution problem. However, because of the difficulty in solving the sulfur emissions in industrial pollution and the introduction of catalytic converters to automobile exhaust systems, a change was mandated. The automobile exhaust system, when equipped with a catalytic converter, changes the sulfur dioxide (SO_2) into sulfur trioxide (SO_3).

When this combines with water vapors (H_2O), a sulfuric acid mist (H_2SO_4) is formed and is a very difficult pollutant to handle since it is extremely corrosive. The sulfuric acid mist that is formed, is the same mist that rises from the vents of an automobile battery when an active chemical reaction takes place within the battery cells.

When a large concentration of vehicles equipped with catalytic converters are operating in an area, this acid mist may rise and be distributed over a large ground area causing land, plant, crop, paint and building damage.

PARTICULATE MATTER

A certain amount of particulate matter is present in the burning of any fuel, with carbon constituting the largest percentage of the particulates. In gasoline, the remaining particulates are the burned remains of the various other compounds used in its manufacture. When a gasoline engine is in good internal condition, the particulate emissions are low but as the engine wears internally, the particulate emissions increase. By visually inspecting the tail pipe emissions, a determination can be made as to where an engine defect may exist. An engine with light gray or blue smoke emitting from the tail pipe normally indicates an increase in the oil consumption through burning due to internal engine wear. Black smoke would indicate a defective fuel delivery system, causing the engine to operate in a rich mode. Regardless of the color of the smoke, the internal part of the engine or the fuel delivery system should be repaired to prevent excess particulate emissions.

Diesel and turbine engines emit a darkened plume of smoke from the exhaust system because of the type of fuel used. Emission control regulations are mandated for this type of emission and more stringent measures are being used to prevent excess emission of the particulate matter. Electronic components are being introduced to control the injection of the fuel at precisely the proper time of piston travel, to achieve the optimum in fuel ignition and fuel usage. Other particulate after-burning components are being tested to achieve a cleaner emission.

Good grades of engine lubricating oils should be used, which meet the manufacturer's specification. Cut-rate oils can contribute to the particulate emission problem because of their low flash or ignition temperature point. Such oils burn prematurely during the combustion process causing emission of particulate matter.

The cooling system is an important factor in the reduction of particulate matter. The optimum combustion will occur, with the cooling system operating at a temperature specified by the manufacturer. The cooling system must be maintained in the same manner as the engine oiling system, as each system is required to perform properly in order for the engine to operate efficiently for a long time.

Crankcase Emissions

Crankcase emissions are made up of water, acids, unburned fuel, oil fumes and particulates. These emissions are classified as hydrocarbons (HC) and are formed by the small amount of unburned, compressed air/fuel mixture entering the crankcase from the combustion area (between the cylinder walls and piston rings) during the compression and power strokes. The head of the compression and combustion help to form the remaining crankcase emissions.

Since the first engines, crankcase emissions were allowed into the atmosphere through a road draft tube, mounted on the lower side of the engine block. Fresh air came in through an open oil filler cap or breather. The air passed through the crankcase mixing with blow-by gases. The motion of the vehicle and the air blowing past the open end of the road draft tube caused a low pressure area (vacuum) at the end of the tube. Crankcase emissions were simply drawn out of the road draft tube into the air.

To control the crankcase emission, the road draft tube was deleted. A hose and/or tubing was routed from the crankcase to the intake manifold so the blow-by emission could be burned with the air/fuel mixture. However, it was found that intake manifold vacuum, used to draw the crankcase emissions into the manifold, would vary in strength at the wrong time and not allow the proper emission flow. A regulating valve was needed to control the flow of air through the crankcase.

Testing, showed the removal of the blow-by gases from the crankcase as quickly as possible, was most important to the longevity of the engine. Should large accumulations of blow-by gases remain and condense, dilution of the engine oil would occur to form water, soot, resins, acids and lead salts, resulting in the formation of sludge and varnishes. This condensation of the blow-by gases occurs more frequently on vehicles used in numerous starting and stopping conditions, excessive idling or when the engine is not allowed to attain normal operating temperature through short runs.

Evaporative Emissions

Gasoline fuel is a major source of pollution, before and after it is burned in the automobile engine. From the time the fuel is refined, stored, pumped and transported, again stored until it is pumped into the fuel tank of the vehicle, the gasoline gives off unburned hydrocarbons (HC) into the atmosphere. Through the redesign of storage areas and venting systems, the pollution factor was diminished, but not eliminated, from the refinery standpoint. However, the automobile remained the primary source of vaporized, unburned hydrocarbon (HC) emissions.

Fuel pumped from an underground storage tank is cool but when exposed to a warmer ambient temperature, will expand. Before controls were mandated, an owner might fill the fuel tank with fuel from an underground storage tank and park the vehicle for some time in warm area, such as a parking lot. As the fuel would warm, it would expand and should no provisions or area be provided for the expansion, the fuel would spill out of the filler neck and onto the ground, causing hydrocarbon (HC) pollution and creating a severe fire hazard. To correct this condition, the vehicle manufacturers added overflow plumbing and/or gasoline tanks with built in expansion areas or domes.

However, this did not control the fuel vapor emission from the fuel tank. It was determined that most of the fuel evaporation occurred when the vehicle was stationary and the engine not operating. Most vehicles carry 5–25 gallons (19–95 liters) of gasoline. Should a large concentration of vehicles be parked in one area, such as a large parking lot, excessive fuel-vapor emissions would take place, increasing as the temperature increases.

To prevent the vapor emission from escaping into the atmosphere, the fuel systems were designed to trap the vapors while the vehicle is stationary, by sealing the system from the atmosphere. A storage system is used to collect and hold the fuel vapors from the carburetor (if equipped) and the fuel tank when the engine is not operating. When the engine is started, the storage system is then purged of the fuel vapors, which are drawn into the engine and burned with the air/fuel mixture.

EMISSIONS CONTROLS

Crankcase Ventilation System

OPERATION

▶ **See Figures 1 and 2**

All vehicles are equipped with Positive Crankcase Ventilation (PCV) or Crankcase Ventilation (CV) System to control crankcase blow-by vapors.

A crankcase ventilation system is used to consume crankcase vapors in the combustion process instead of venting them to atmosphere. Fresh, filtered air is supplied to the crankcase, mixed with blow-by gases and then passed through a PCV valve into the intake manifold. The crankcase ventilation system must be operating correctly to provide complete scavenging of the crankcase vapors.

The PCV valve meters the flow at a rate depending upon the manifold vacuum. To maintain idle quality, the PCV valve restricts the flow when inlet vacuum is high. If abnormal operating conditions occur, excessive amounts of internal exhaust gases back flow through the crankcase vent tube into the air filter to be burned by normal combustion.

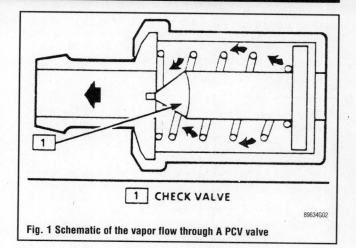

| 1 | CHECK VALVE

89634G02

Fig. 1 Schematic of the vapor flow through A PCV valve

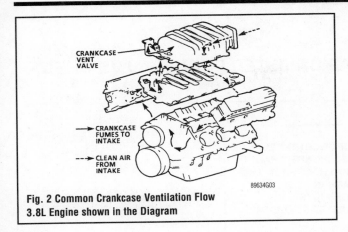

Fig. 2 Common Crankcase Ventilation Flow
3.8L Engine shown in the Diagram

COMPONENT TESTING

♦ See Figure 3

A plugged valve or hose may cause the following conditions.
- Rough idle
- Stalling or slow idle speed
- Oil leaks
- Sludge in engine
- Oil in air cleaner

A leaking valve or hose may cause the following conditions.
- Rough idle, possibly a rolling idle
- Stalling
- High idle speed

If the engine is idling roughly, a quick check of the PCV valve can be made. While the engine is idling, pull the PCV valve from the valve cover, place your thumb over the end of the PCV valve and check for vacuum. If no vacuum exists, check for a plugged PCV valve, manifold port, collapsed vacuum hose, or deteriorated hoses. Turn the engine OFF, remove the PCV valve and shake it. Listen for the rattle of the check needle inside the valve. If it does not rattle, replace the valve.

The PCV system should be checked at every oil change, and serviced every 30,000 miles (48,000km).

Fig. 3 Remove and shake the PCV valve; if a rattling noise is heard, the valve is OK

Evaporative Emission Controls

OPERATION

♦ See Figure 4

The basic Evaporative Emission (EVAP) control system used on all vehicles is the charcoal canister storage method. This method transfers fuel vapor from the fuel tank to an activated carbon (charcoal) storage device (canister) to hold

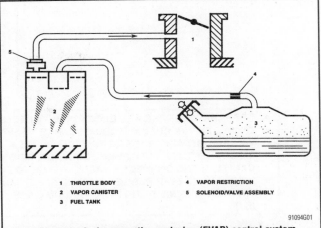

1	THROTTLE BODY	4	VAPOR RESTRICTION
2	VAPOR CANISTER	5	SOLENOID/VALVE ASSEMBLY
3	FUEL TANK		

Fig. 4 Shows typical evaporative emission (EVAP) control system schematic. Remember the fuel cap is also part of the system

the vapors when the vehicle is not operating. When the engine is running, the fuel vapor is purged from the carbon element by intake airflow and consumed in the normal combustion process.

Gasoline vapors from the fuel tank flow into the tube labeled tank. These vapors are absorbed into the carbon. The canister is purged by the PCM control when the engine has been running for a specified amount of time. Air is drawn into the canister and mixed with the vapor and then is drawn into the intake manifold.

The fuel tank filler cap is an integral part of the system in that it was designed to seal in fuel vapors. If it is lost or damaged, make sure the replacement is the correct size and fit so a proper seal can be obtained.

COMPONENT TESTING

♦ See Figures 5 and 6

The PCM operates a normally closed solenoid valve that allows vacuum to purge the canister when energized. The PCM supplies a Pulse Width Modulated (PWM) ground to energize the solenoid (purge ON).

Preliminary checks
- Inspect the canister for cracks or fuel saturation.
- Inspect the fuel vapor lines from the fuel tank or intake for leaks, disconnected hoses, or sharp bends blocking the vapor flow.

Chart Test Description: Numbers below refer to the circled numbers on the diagnostic chart.

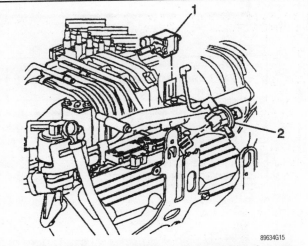

Fig. 5 Typical location of the EVAP Purge Solenoid (1) and vacuum switch (2) mounting 3.8L Engine

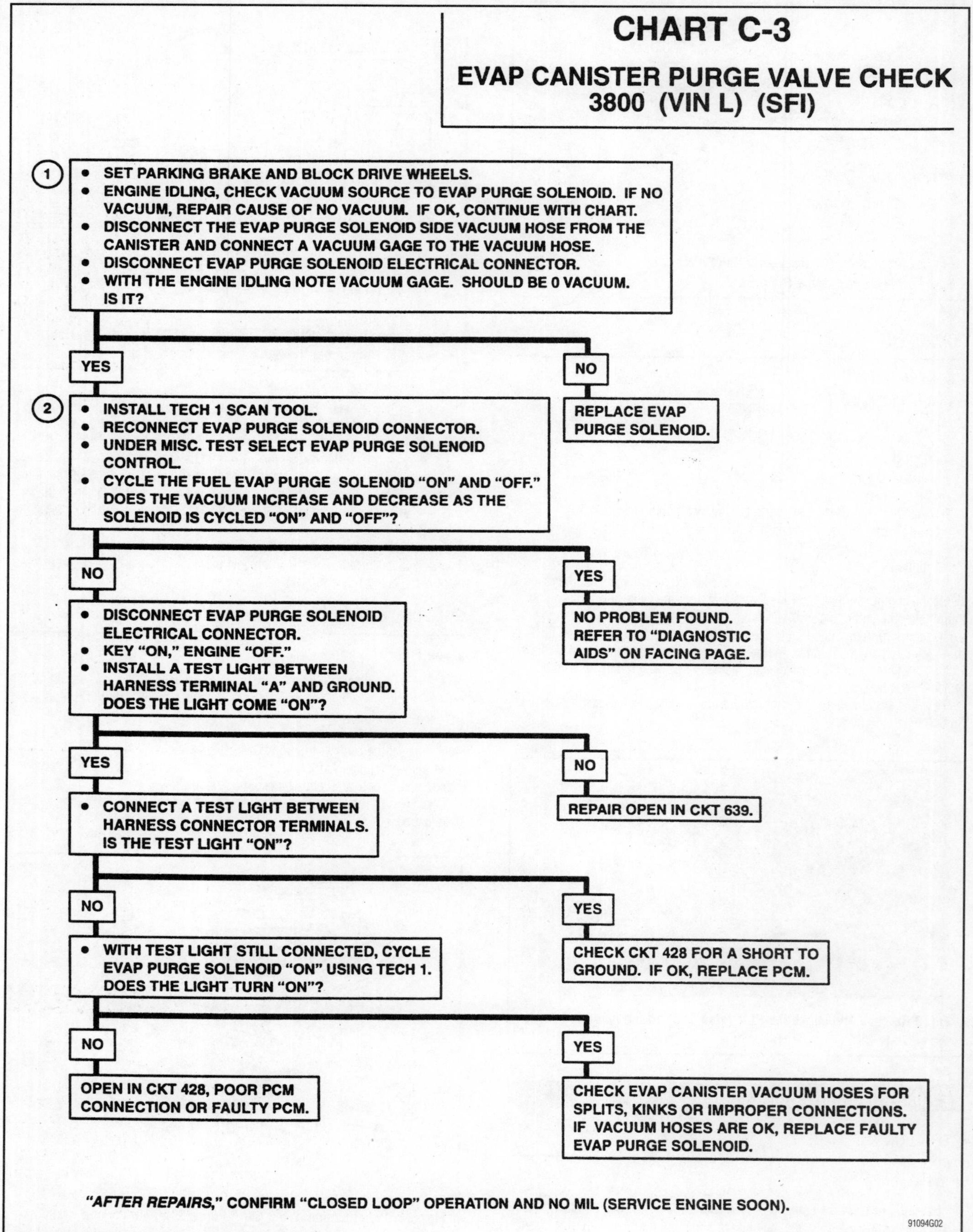

CHART C-3

EVAP CANISTER PURGE VALVE CHECK
3800 (VIN L) (SFI)

1
- SET PARKING BRAKE AND BLOCK DRIVE WHEELS.
- ENGINE IDLING, CHECK VACUUM SOURCE TO EVAP PURGE SOLENOID. IF NO VACUUM, REPAIR CAUSE OF NO VACUUM. IF OK, CONTINUE WITH CHART.
- DISCONNECT THE EVAP PURGE SOLENOID SIDE VACUUM HOSE FROM THE CANISTER AND CONNECT A VACUUM GAGE TO THE VACUUM HOSE.
- DISCONNECT EVAP PURGE SOLENOID ELECTRICAL CONNECTOR.
- WITH THE ENGINE IDLING NOTE VACUUM GAGE. SHOULD BE 0 VACUUM. IS IT?

YES

NO

REPLACE EVAP PURGE SOLENOID.

2
- INSTALL TECH 1 SCAN TOOL.
- RECONNECT EVAP PURGE SOLENOID CONNECTOR.
- UNDER MISC. TEST SELECT EVAP PURGE SOLENOID CONTROL.
- CYCLE THE FUEL EVAP PURGE SOLENOID "ON" AND "OFF." DOES THE VACUUM INCREASE AND DECREASE AS THE SOLENOID IS CYCLED "ON" AND "OFF"?

NO

YES

NO PROBLEM FOUND. REFER TO "DIAGNOSTIC AIDS" ON FACING PAGE.

- DISCONNECT EVAP PURGE SOLENOID ELECTRICAL CONNECTOR.
- KEY "ON," ENGINE "OFF."
- INSTALL A TEST LIGHT BETWEEN HARNESS TERMINAL "A" AND GROUND. DOES THE LIGHT COME "ON"?

YES

NO

REPAIR OPEN IN CKT 639.

- CONNECT A TEST LIGHT BETWEEN HARNESS CONNECTOR TERMINALS. IS THE TEST LIGHT "ON"?

NO

YES

CHECK CKT 428 FOR A SHORT TO GROUND. IF OK, REPLACE PCM.

- WITH TEST LIGHT STILL CONNECTED, CYCLE EVAP PURGE SOLENOID "ON" USING TECH 1. DOES THE LIGHT TURN "ON"?

NO

YES

OPEN IN CKT 428, POOR PCM CONNECTION OR FAULTY PCM.

CHECK EVAP CANISTER VACUUM HOSES FOR SPLITS, KINKS OR IMPROPER CONNECTIONS. IF VACUUM HOSES ARE OK, REPLACE FAULTY EVAP PURGE SOLENOID.

"AFTER REPAIRS," CONFIRM "CLOSED LOOP" OPERATION AND NO MIL (SERVICE ENGINE SOON).

91094G02

Fig. 6 Diagnostic flow chart for EVAP Canister Purge

1. Checks to see if the valve is opened or closed. The solenoid is normally de-energized in this step, so it should be closed.

2. This step completes the functional check. This should normally energize the solenoid and allow vacuum to the gauge (purge "ON")

REMOVAL & INSTALLATION

Canister Purge Valve

▶ See Figure 7

1. To replace the canister purge valve, label and detach the electrical connector and hoses from the valve.
2. Remove the valve assembly from the bracket.

To install:

3. Mount the valve to the bracket.
4. Connect the electrical connector and hoses to the valve.

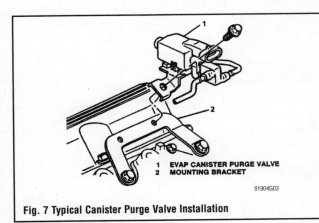

1   EVAP CANISTER PURGE VALVE
2   MOUNTING BRACKET

91904G03

Fig. 7 Typical Canister Purge Valve Installation

Fuel Vapor Canister

▶ See Figure 8

1. Label and disconnect the hoses from the canister.
2. Loosen and/or remove the hold down strap.
3. Remove the canister.

To install:

4. Install the canister.
5. Secure with the hold down strap.
6. Install the hoses. Make sure that the connections are correct.

Exhaust Gas Recirculation System

OPERATION

The EGR system is used to lower NOx (oxides of nitrogen) emission levels caused by high combustion temperatures. The main element of the system is the EGR valve The EGR valve feeds small amounts of exhaust gas back into the combustion chamber. This dilutes the air/fuel mixture and consequently reduces combustion temperatures.

The EGR valve used on the 3.1L (VIN D) engine is a negative backpressure valve. It varies the amount of exhaust gas flow into the manifold depending on manifold vacuum and variations in exhaust backpressure. The diaphragm on this EGR valve has an internal vacuum bleed hole that is held closed by a small spring when there is no exhaust backpressure. The amount of vacuum to the valve is controlled buy a PCM controlled solenoid valve, called an Electronic Vacuum Regulator Valve (EVRV).

The linear EGR valve, used on the 3.8L and the 3.4L engine, is designed to accurately supply the engine with an EGR flow independent of intake manifold vacuum. The valve controls EGR flow from the exhaust to the intake manifold through an orifice with a PCM controlled pintle. PCM control means the EGR valve is usually activated when the engine is warm and operating above idle speed.

Fig. 8 The EVAP canister is usually mounted low along the frame rail

91091P10

COMPONENT TESTING

▶ See Figure 9

Incorrect operation of the EGR system causing too much EGR flow at idle, cruise, or cold operation can cause any of the following condition to occur:

- Engine stalls after a cold start.
- Engine stalls at idle after deceleration.
- Vehicle surges at a steady cruise.
- Vehicle exhibits a rough idle.

The EGR valve should always be closed at wide-open throttle and idle. Too little or no EGR flow may allow combustion temperatures to get too high. This could cause:

- Spark knock (pinging), and if carried to the extreme, detonation.
- The engine to overheat.
- Emission test failure.

REMOVAL & INSTALLATION

▶ See Figures 10 thru 15

1. Disconnect the negative battery cable.
2. If equipped, detach the electrical connector at the solenoid.
3. Remove the two base to flange nuts and lift the EGR valve assembly from its mount.

To install:

4. Thoroughly clean the gasket mounting surfaces. Replace the gasket.
5. Install the EGR assembly, install the two nuts and tighten to 22 ft. lbs. (30Nm).
6. If necessary, attach the electrical connector.
7. Connect the negative battery cable.

Emission Service Light

OPERATION

A Power Train Control Module (PCM) is the heart of this control system. A network of sensors provides the PCM with information about engine operation and the various systems that it controls. The on-board diagnostic system check verifies the system is functioning correctly. The PCM has the ability to do some diagnosis of itself, as well as other parts of the system. When the PCM finds a problem, it lights a Malfunction Indicator Light (MIL) on the instrument panel (Check Engine or Service Engine Soon) and a trouble code is stored in the PCM memory. The MIL does not indicate that the engine should be stopped right away, but that the vehicle should be checked as soon as reasonably possible.

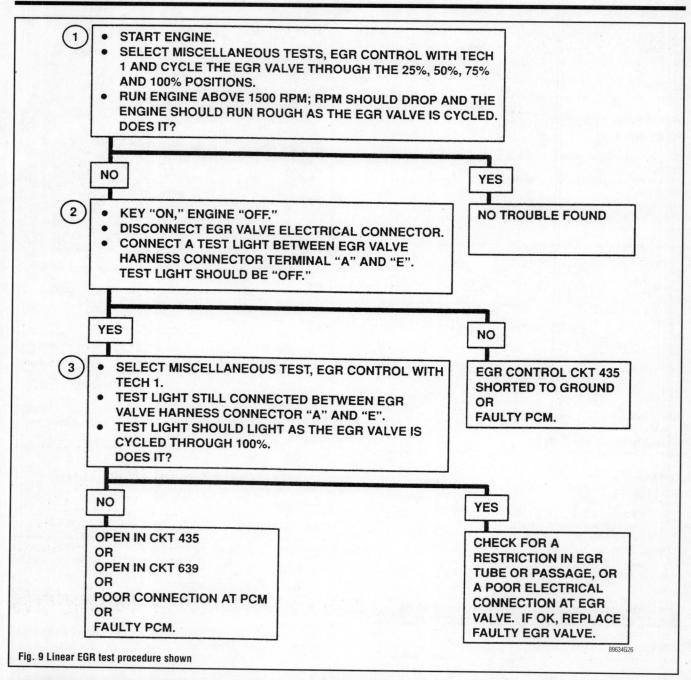

1
- START ENGINE.
- SELECT MISCELLANEOUS TESTS, EGR CONTROL WITH TECH 1 AND CYCLE THE EGR VALVE THROUGH THE 25%, 50%, 75% AND 100% POSITIONS.
- RUN ENGINE ABOVE 1500 RPM; RPM SHOULD DROP AND THE ENGINE SHOULD RUN ROUGH AS THE EGR VALVE IS CYCLED. DOES IT?

NO | YES

NO TROUBLE FOUND

2
- KEY "ON," ENGINE "OFF."
- DISCONNECT EGR VALVE ELECTRICAL CONNECTOR.
- CONNECT A TEST LIGHT BETWEEN EGR VALVE HARNESS CONNECTOR TERMINAL "A" AND "E". TEST LIGHT SHOULD BE "OFF."

YES | NO

EGR CONTROL CKT 435 SHORTED TO GROUND OR FAULTY PCM.

3
- SELECT MISCELLANEOUS TEST, EGR CONTROL WITH TECH 1.
- TEST LIGHT STILL CONNECTED BETWEEN EGR VALVE HARNESS CONNECTOR "A" AND "E".
- TEST LIGHT SHOULD LIGHT AS THE EGR VALVE IS CYCLED THROUGH 100%. DOES IT?

NO | YES

**OPEN IN CKT 435
OR
OPEN IN CKT 639
OR
POOR CONNECTION AT PCM
OR
FAULTY PCM.**

CHECK FOR A RESTRICTION IN EGR TUBE OR PASSAGE, OR A POOR ELECTRICAL CONNECTION AT EGR VALVE. IF OK, REPLACE FAULTY EGR VALVE.

89634G26

Fig. 9 Linear EGR test procedure shown

91094P22

Fig. 10 Typical EGR Valve installation and location for 3.8L engine

91094P23

Fig. 11 EGR Valve with electrical connector removed

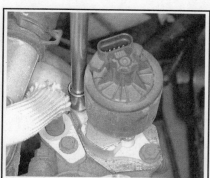

91094P24

Fig. 12 Remove the two retaining bolts for the EGR valve

Fig. 13 Remove the EGR valve

Fig. 14 Removing and checking the gasket

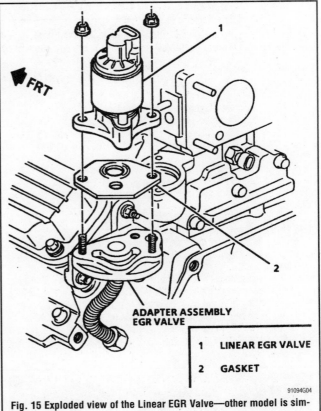

ADAPTER ASSEMBLY
EGR VALVE

| 1 | LINEAR EGR VALVE |
| 2 | GASKET |

Fig. 15 Exploded view of the Linear EGR Valve—other model is similar

RESETTING

The Malfunction Indicator Lamp (MIL) will illuminate when the key is turned to the **ON** position as a systems check, but will extinguish shortly after the engine is started. If the computer control module detects a malfunction in one of the monitored circuits, a trouble code will be set and the lamp will be illuminated to indicate a fault.

When the computer module sets a code, the MIL will remain illuminated as long as the fault is detected. If the problem is intermittent, the light will extinguish approximately ten seconds after the fault goes away. However, the code will stay in the memory for fifty starts or until the code is cleared.

Obviously, the MIL cannot be reset until the malfunction is corrected (or at least not present if it is an intermittent fault) and the computer memory is cleared of the fault. Codes may be cleared using a suitable scan tool or by removing power from the computer control module. If the latter method is chosen power must be removed from the module for a minimum for thirty seconds. The lower the ambient temperature, the longer period of time the power must be removed.

ELECTRONIC ENGINE CONTROLS

The fuel injection system is operated along with the ignition system to obtain optimum performance and fuel economy while producing a minimum of exhaust emissions. There are various sensors used by the computer control module for feedback to determine proper engine operating conditions.

When dealing with the electronic engine control system, keep in mind that the system is sensitive to improperly connected electrical and vacuum circuits. The condition and connection of all hoses and wires should always be the first step when attempting to diagnose a driveability problem. Worn or deteriorated hoses and damaged or corroded wires may well make a good component appear faulty.

Diagnosis of the electronic control systems used in today's vehicles requires some special tools. To diagnose the on-board systems used in these vehicles, a TECH 1® (or equivalent) scan tool will be necessary. If the proper tester is not available, the vehicle should be taken to a reputable service facility that has the appropriate equipment.

Powertrain Control Module

The PCM is responsible for maintaining proper spark and fuel injection timing for all driving conditions. Ignition Control (IC) spark timing is the PCM method of controlling spark advance and ignition dwell. To provide optimum driveability and emissions, the PCM monitors input signals from the following components in calculating Ignition Control (IC) spark timing:

- Igniition Control Module (ICM).
- Engine Coolant Temperature (ECT) sensor.
- Intake Air Temperature (IAT) sensor.
- Transmission Range (TR) and/or Park/Neutral Position (PNP) switch.
- Manifold Absolute Pressure (MAP) sensor.
- Mass Air Flow (MAF) sensor.
- Throttle Position (TP) switch.
- Vehicle Speed Sensor (VSS)/Trans Output Speed Sensor (TOSS).

To allow one model of PCM to be used for many different vehicles, a device called a PROM (Programmable Read Only Memory) is used .The PROM is located inside the PCM and has information on the vehicle's weight, engine, transmission, axle ratio, and several other distinguishing characteristics. While one PCM can be used by many vehicle lines a PROM is very specific and must be used for the right vehicle.

Service of the PCM should normally consist of either replacement of the PCM or a PROM change. If the diagnostic procedures call for the PCM to be replaced, the engine "calibrator" (PROM) and the PCM should be checked first to see if they are the correct parts. If they are, remove the PROM from the faulty PCM and install it in the new PCM.

REMOVAL & INSTALLATION

➡In order to prevent electrostatic discharge damage to the PCM, do not touch the connector pins or soldered components in the circuit board.

3.1L and 3.8L Engines

♦ See Figure 16

1. Make sure the ignition is switched off.
2. Disconnect the negative battery cable.
3. Locate the PCM.
4. Carefully detach the harness connectors from the PCM (use hand tools only).
5. Remove the PCM from the bracket.
6. Since the new PCM is supplied without a PROM, care should be used when removing it from the defective PCM because it will be reused in the new PCM.
7. Using two fingers, push both retaining clips back away from the PROM. At the same time, grasp it at both ends and lift it up out of the socket.
8. Note the position of the PROM for proper installation in the new PCM. Do not remove the cover of the PROM.

To install:

9. When replacing the PROM, align the small notches in the PROM socket, and gently press down on the ends of the PROM until the clips are against the sides of the PROM. Now, press inward on the clips until they snap into place.
10. Attach the harness connectors to the PCM (use hand tools only).
11. Install the PCM to the bracket.
12. Connect the negative battery cable.

91094P03

Fig. 16 Location of the PCM for 3.1L and 3.8L engines is in the right hand side of the dash, behind the convenience center

3.4L Engine

♦ See Figure 17

With the advent of the 3.4L engine, the location of the Powertrain Control Module (PCM), was moved into the air cleaner housing.

1. Make sure the ignition is switched off.
2. Disconnect the negative battery cable.
3. Remove the coolant reservoir.
4. Remove the SMCC module bracket.
5. Remove the left front strut brace.
6. Remove the PCM cover from the air cleaner housing.
7. Remove the PCM from the air cleaner housing.

To install:

8. If a new PCM is being installed, install the KS module from the original PCM.
9. Install the PCM into the air cleaner housing.
10. Install the PCM cover to the air cleaner housing.

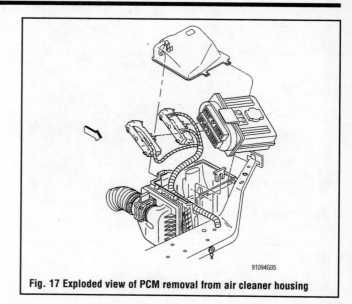

91094G05

Fig. 17 Exploded view of PCM removal from air cleaner housing

11. Install the left front strut brace.
12. Install the SMCC module bracket.
13. Install the SMCC module to the SMCC module bracket.
14. Install the coolant reservoir, correct the coolant level.
15. Connect the negative battery cable.
16. If a new PCM is being installed, program the EEPROM.

Oxygen Sensor (O2)

OPERATION

The exhaust Oxygen (O2) Sensor is mounted in the exhaust system, ahead of the catalytic converters, where it can monitor the oxygen content of the exhaust gas stream. There are two types of Oxygen sensors in use today. They are the single wire Oxygen Sensor (O2S) and the Heated Oxygen Sensor (HO2S), usually a three or four wire lead. The PCM constantly monitors the O2 signal during closed loop operation and compensates for a rich or lean condition by decreasing or increasing injector pulse width as necessary. The PCM will not go into "closed loop" operation if it can't read the O2 sensor.

Oxygen Sensors generate a voltage signal dependant upon the amount of oxygen reaching the element. This voltage should constantly fluctuate from approximately 1 volt (1000 mV), when reading a rich exhaust, to .01 (100mV) volt if the exhaust is lean. Oxygen sensors can be monitored using a scan tool. By monitoring the voltage output of the oxygen sensor, the PCM calculates what fuel mixture command (pulse width) to give to the injectors. The sensor is like an open circuit and produces no voltage when it is below about 360°C (600°F).

TESTING

♦ See Figures 18 and 19

This type oxygen sensor is found on the earlier model vehicles. Later years went to a heated O2 sensor because it would react quicker, allowing the PCM to switch into closed loop operation faster.

1. Visually inspect the pigtail for proper routing and connection.
2. Check for an adequate air supply, and a clean unclogged air filter.
3. Poor PCM to engine block grounds.
4. Fuel Injectors; faulty or sticky fuel injectors can cause a false reading or false DTC indicating an O2 sensor problem.
5. Fuel pressure; the system will go lean if pressure is too low. The PCM can compensate for some decrease. Likewise, the system will go rich if pressure is too high. The PCM can compensate for some increase. However, if fuel pressure is not in spec, a DTC may be set.
6. Vacuum leaks. Check for disconnected or damaged vacuum hoses and for vacuum leaks at the intake manifold, throttle body, EGR system, and crankcase ventilation system.

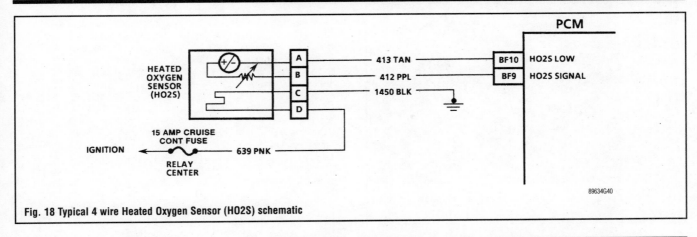

Fig. 18 Typical 4 wire Heated Oxygen Sensor (HO2S) schematic

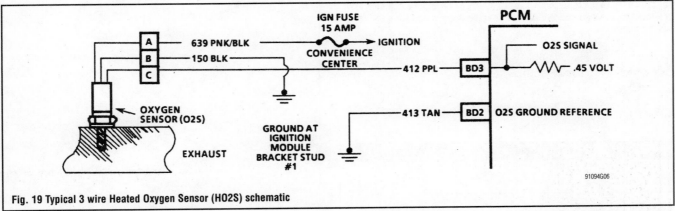

Fig. 19 Typical 3 wire Heated Oxygen Sensor (HO2S) schematic

7. Exhaust leaks. An exhaust leak may cause outside air to enter the exhaust gas stream going past the O2 sensor, causing the system to appear lean. Check for exhaust leaks that may cause a false lean condition.

8. Fuel contamination; Water, even in small amounts, can be delivered to the fuel injectors. The water passing through the system can cause a lean exhaust. Excessive alcohol in the fuel can also cause this condition.

9. Check the EVAP canister for fuel saturation. If the canister is full of fuel, check the canister control and hoses.

10. Check for a leaking fuel pressure regulator diaphragm by checking the vacuum line to the regulator for the presence of fuel.

11. An intermittent TP sensor output will cause the system to go rich due to a false indication of engine acceleration.

12. Mass Air Flow sensor; disconnect the MAF sensor and see if the condition is corrected. A faulty MAF sensor can give a false reading (lean or rich) to the O2 sensor.

13. A faulty Manifold Absolute Pressure (MAP) Sensor can affect O2 operation.

14. For single wire O2 sensors, check the following:

a. Connect a DVOM between the signal wire and ground. With the engine at normal operating temperature and the engine running (1200 to 1500) RPM, the O2 sensor should be generating a fluctuating signal between zero and 1 volt. If the reading stays above or below .5 volts and does not fluctuate, the sensor could be bad. If the sensor is slow in switching, or acts lazy in changing it's voltage reading, it could be bad.

15. For heated O2 sensors, check the following:

a. An internally shorted Heated Oxygen Sensor will indicate voltage output of over 1 volt.

b. Unplug the sensor connector and check the resistance between terminals C and D. Resistance values should be about 10–15 ohms at about 80°F. If the resistance is not within specification, the heater is faulty.

c. If resistance is within specification, check for battery voltage between connector terminals C and D with the key on, engine off.

d. Check the O2 sensor voltage between terminals A and B with the engine off. The voltage should be within the 350–500 mV range. If the voltage reading is off, the sensor is faulty. If the reading is good, run the engine

while reading the scale. The voltage should vary between 100–1000 mV (0 to 1 volt).

16. If the sensor is operating within specifications, check the circuits to the PCM for continuity.

17. If the sensor and circuits are functioning properly, the PCM may be faulty.

REMOVAL & INSTALLATION

▸ **See Figures 20 and 21**

1. Disconnect the negative battery cable.
2. Detach the sensors pigtail electrical connector.
3. Unscrew the O2 sensor.

To install:

➥**A special anti-seize compound is used on the oxygen sensor threads. The compound consists of liquid graphite and glass beads. The graphite will burn away, but the glass beads will remain, making the sensor eas-**

Fig. 20 There is a special socket available to ease removal of the O2 sensor, however most can be removed with a open end, or line wrench

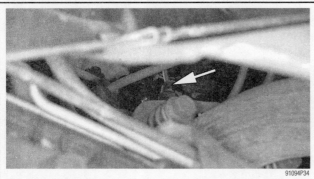

Fig. 21 Location of Oxygen Sensor (shown by arrow) in rear exhaust manifold

ier to remove. Most replacement sensors already have the compound on the threads, however you will need to coat the threads if reusing an old sensor.

4. If necessary, coat the sensor threads with the anti-seize compound liberally. GM compound #5613695 or equivalent. This is not a conventional anti-seize paste. It is an electrically conductive compound.

5. Screw the sensor into the mounting hole in the exhaust system. Torque to 30 ft. lbs. (41Nm).

6. Attach the sensors pigtail connector.

7. Connect the negative battery cable.

Idle Air Control Valve

OPERATION

♦ **See Figures 22, 23 and 24**

The PCM controls engine idle speed by adjusting the position of the Idle Air Control (IAC) motor pintle. The IAC is a bi-directional motor driven by two

coils. The pintle movement controls the air flow bypassing the throttle valves, which in turn, controls engine idle speed. The PCM pulses current to the IAC coils in steps (counts) to extend the IAC pintle into a passage in the throttle body to decrease air flow. The PCM reverses the current pulses to retract the pintle, increasing air flow. This method allows highly accurate control of idle speed and quick response to changes in engine load.

"Controlled" idle speed is programmed into the PCM, which determines the correct IAC valve pintle position to maintain the desired idle speed for all engine operating conditions and loads. "Minimum" idle air rate is set at the factory with a stop screw. This setting allows enough air flow by the throttle valves to cause the IAC valve pintle to be positioned a calibrated number of steps (counts), from the seat, during "controlled" idle operation. It also helps prevent the throttle plate(s) from binding in the fully closed position in the throttle housing. The throttle stop screw is covered over at the factory.

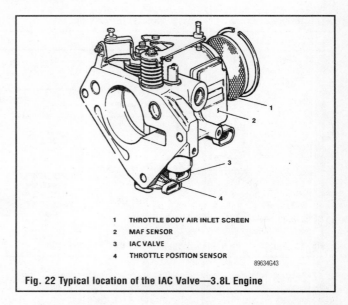

1	THROTTLE BODY AIR INLET SCREEN
2	MAF SENSOR
3	IAC VALVE
4	THROTTLE POSITION SENSOR

Fig. 22 Typical location of the IAC Valve—3.8L Engine

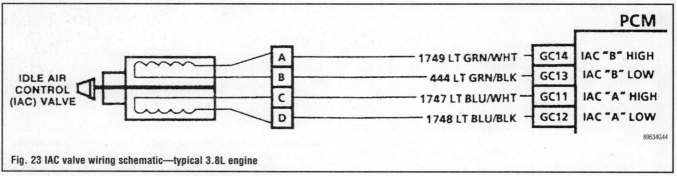

Fig. 23 IAC valve wiring schematic—typical 3.8L engine

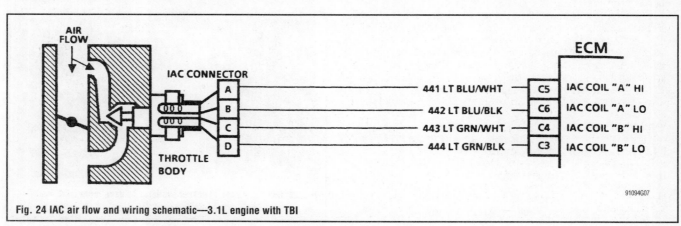

Fig. 24 IAC air flow and wiring schematic—3.1L engine with TBI

TESTING

▶ **See Figures 25, 26, 27, 28 and 29**

Preliminary tests for an IAC related problem include checking for the following conditions:

• Poor connection at PCM or IAC motor. Inspect the harness connectors for backed out terminals, improper mating, broken locks, improperly formed or damaged terminals, and poor terminal to wire connection.

• Inspect the wire harness for damage, including; proper routing, broken insulation, rub through, or broken wires.

• A restricted air intake system. Check for a possible collapsed air intake duct, restricted air filter element or foreign objects blocking the air intake system.

• Check the throttle body for objects blocking the IAC passage or throttle bore, excessive deposits in the IAC passage and on the IAC pintle, and excessive deposits in the throttle bore and on the throttle plate. Check for a sticking throttle plate. Also inspect the IAC passage for deposits or objects which will not allow the IAC pintle to fully extend.

• Check for a condition that causes a vacuum leak, such as disconnected or damaged hoses, leaks at the EGR valve or EGR pipe to intake manifold, leaks at the throttle body, faulty or incorrectly installed PCV valve, leaks at the intake manifold, a brake booster hose that leaks or is disconnected, or a faulty component that uses engine vacuum to operate.

1. If a scan tool is available, connect it to the system, and start the engine.

a. Turn all accessories **OFF** (A/C, Heater, Rear Defroster, etc.).

b. Using the scan tool, command RPM up to 1500, down to 650, and then up to 1500 while monitoring Engine Speed on the scan tool. If the IAC valve follows these commands and holds the commanded engine speed, then it is good.

2. If a scan tool is unavailable, then try the following test procedure:

a. Unplug the IAC connector and check resistance between the IAC terminals. Resistance between terminals A & B and terminals C & D should be 40–to 80 ohms. If resistance is not within specification, the IAC valve should be replaced.

b. Check the resistance between the IAC terminals A to C, A to D, B to C and B to D. Resistance should be infinite. If not the IAC is faulty.

c. If the resistances are within specifications, check the IAC circuits for continuity back to the PCM. If the valve and circuits are functional, the PCM may be faulty.

3. If intermittent poor driveability or idle symptoms are resolved by disconnecting the IAC, carefully re-check connections, and the IAC valve terminal resistance or replace the IAC.

REMOVAL & INSTALLATION

Both original and replacement IAC valves have a special factory applied thread-locking compound applied to the screw threads. If the valve removed from the throttle body is being reinstalled, do not remove any of the thread locking compound that may remain on the threads.

3.1L Engine (VIN D)

▶ **See Figure 30**

1. Disconnect the negative battery cable.
2. Remove the air cleaner assembly.
3. Detach the IAC valve electrical connector.
4. Remove the IAC valve assembly and gasket.

✳✳ CAUTION

If the IAC valve has been in service, do not push or pull on the IAC valve pintle. The force required to move the pintle may damage the threads on the worm drive. Also, do not soak the IAC valve in any liquid cleaner or solvent, as damage may result. If installing a new IAC valve, be sure to replace with an identical part. IAC valve pintle shape and diameter are designed for the specific application. Measure the distance between the tip of the IAC pintle and the mounting surface, and if it measures greater than 1⅛ in. (28mm), use finger pressure to slowly retract the pintle. The force required to retract the pintle of a new valve will not cause damage to the valve.

Fig. 25 Unplug the connector to the sensor

91091P10

Fig. 26 Read the resistance of terminals A and B in the IAC

89634P05

89634P06

Fig. 27 When the IAC Terminals B and C are jumped, the reading should be infinity (Open Circuit)

91094P09

Fig. 28 The sensor plug is labeled/lettered for easy reference

91094P11

Fig. 29 Measure the resistance at the sensor prongs, check for corrosion and/or looseness

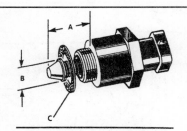

A DISTANCE OF PINTLE EXTENSION

B DIAMETER AND SHAPE OF PINTLE

C IAC VALVE GASKET

91094G08

Fig. 30 Idle Air Control Valve (IAC) and gasket

To install:

5. Clean the IAC valve gasket sealing surface, pintle valve seat and air passage. Use carburetor cleaner to remove carbon deposits. Shiny spots on the pintle or seat are normal, and do not indicate misalignment or a bent pintle shaft.

❊❊ WARNING

Do not use a cleaner that contains methyl ethyl ketone, an extremely strong solvent, and one that is not necessary for this type of deposit.

6. Install the new gasket and valve assembly.
7. Using a box wrench or socket, tighten the valve to 13 ft. lbs. (18Nm)
8. Attach the electrical connector.
9. Install the air cleaner assembly.
10. Connect the negative battery cable.
11. To reset the IAC pintle position.
   a. With the key **OFF**; depress the accelerator pedal slightly.
   b. Start and run the engine for five seconds.
   c. Turn the ignition **OFF** for ten seconds.
   d. Restart the engine and check for proper idle operation.

3.4L Engines

▶ See Figure 31

❊❊ WARNING

The IAC Valve may be damaged if installed with the cone (pintle) extended more than 1⅛ in. (28mm). Measure the distance that the valve is extended before installing a new valve. The distance from the idle air control valve motor housing to the end of the idle air control valve pintle should be less than 1⅛ in. (28mm). If it is longer, manually compress the pintle until the extension is retracted to less than 1⅛ in. (28mm).

1. Detach the electrical connector from the Idle Air Control (IAC) valve and, if necessary for clearance, Throttle Position (TP) sensor.
2. Remove the two screws attaching the IAC valve to the intake manifold.
3. Remove the IAC.
4. Remove the IAC valve O-ring.

To install:

5. Install a new O-ring seal onto the IAC Valve.
6. Install the new IAC in the intake manifold.
7. Install the two screws into the IAC. Tighten them to 27 inch lbs. (3 Nm).
8. Reconnect the electrical connector to the IAC and to the TP sensor.
9. The IAC resets when the key is cycled **ON** then **OFF**.

3.8L Engines

➡ The repair procedure for the 3.8L engine is the same as the 3.1L engine with the following exceptions:

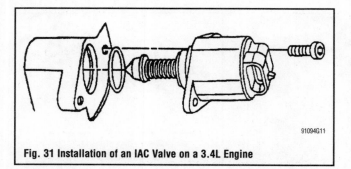

Fig. 31 Installation of an IAC Valve on a 3.4L Engine

91094G11

1. If the IAC valve is disconnected and reconnected with the engine running, the idle RPM will be wrong. In this case, the IAC has to be reset.
2. The IAC resets when the key is cycled **ON** then **OFF**.

Coolant Temperature Sensor

OPERATION

The engine coolant temperature sensor is a thermistor (a resistor which changes value based on temperature) mounted in the engine coolant stream. Low coolant temperature produces a high resistance (100,000 ohms {100K ohms} at -40°F/-40°C) While high temperature causes low resistance (70 ohms at 266°F/130°C).

The PCM supplies a 5 volt signal to the engine coolant temperature sensor through a resistor in the PCM and measures the voltage. The voltage will be high when the engine is cold, and low when the engine is hot. By measuring the voltage, the PCM calculates the engine coolant temperature. The scan tool displays engine coolant temperature in degrees. After engine start-up, the temperature should rise steadily to about 194°F (90°C) then stabilize when the thermostat open. If the engine has not been run for several hours (overnight), the engine coolant temperature and intake air temperature displays should be close to each other.

Engine coolant temperature affects most systems the PCM controls.

TESTING

Sensor in Vehicle

▶ See Figures 32 and 33

1. The Engine Coolant Temperature (ECT) sensor is located in the intake manifold, in a tapped and threaded hole in a water jacket.
2. Disconnect the electrical connector.
3. Attach an ohmmeter to the sensor terminals and then measure the resistance and compare with the accompanying chart on a cold engine. Measure the coolant temperature in the radiator or overflow bottle. Compare the resistance and temperature on the chart.
4. Tape an automotive thermometer tightly to the upper radiator hose. Start and run the engine to normal operating temperature, comparing the temperature on the thermometer to the resistance reading on the ohm meter. The readings should coincide with the chart.
5. If the sensor is not in specification, replace it.

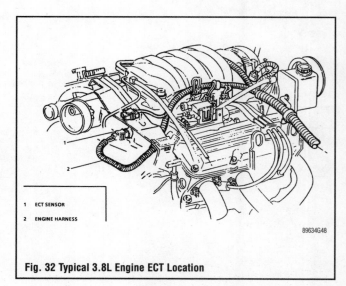

1 ECT SENSOR
2 ENGINE HARNESS

89634G48

Fig. 32 Typical 3.8L Engine ECT Location

DIAGNOSTIC AID

TEMPERATURE VS. RESISTANCE VALUES (APPROXIMATE)		
°C	°F	OHMS
100	212	177
90	194	241
80	176	332
70	158	467
60	140	667
50	122	973
45	113	1188
40	104	1459
35	95	1802
30	86	2238
25	77	2796
20	68	3520
15	59	4450
10	50	5670
5	41	7280
0	32	9420
-5	23	12300
-10	14	16180
-15	5	21450
-20	-4	28680
-30	-22	52700
-40	-40	100700

89634G47

Fig. 33 Engine Coolant Temperature (ECT) and Intake Air Temperature (IAT) Sensor Resistance Values vs. Temperature Readings

Sensor Removed From Vehicle

1. Remove the ECT from the vehicle.
2. Immerse the tip of the sensor in a container of icy water (32°F/0°C), as measured with a calibrated thermometer.
3. Attach an Ohm meter to the sensor connector. The Ohms value should read approximately 9400 to 9500 Ohms.
4. Using the thermometer readings, compare the resistance of the sensor to the temperature of the water.
5. Repeat the test at two other temperature readings, heating the water as necessary.
6. Refer to the resistance value chart; if the sensor is not within specification, replace it.

REMOVAL & INSTALLATION

▶ **See Figures 34 and 35**

➡ **Use care when handling the ECT sensor. Damage to the coolant sensor will affect the operation of the fuel control system.**

1. Disconnect the negative battery cable.
2. Drain the coolant level below the height of the ECT and recycle the engine coolant.
3. Disconnect the electrical connector at the sensor.
4. Remove any obstruction to access the ECT.
5. Using a deep well socket, remove the sensor.
To install:
6. Coat the threads of the new sensor with a suitable thread sealant and install it in the engine. Tighten to 17 ft. lbs. (23Nm).
7. Install the electrical connector.
8. Refill the system with coolant.
9. Connect the negative battery cable.

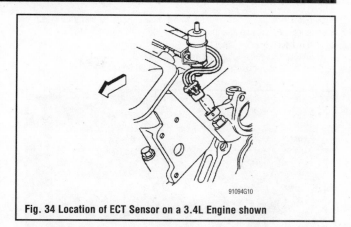

Fig. 34 Location of ECT Sensor on a 3.4L Engine shown

91093P34

Fig. 35 The Engine Coolant Temperature Sensor is tapped into the intake manifold and is able to transmit engine coolant temperature to the PCM

Intake Air Temperature Sensor

OPERATION

The Intake Air Temperature (IAT) sensor is a thermistor, which changes value based on the temperature of air entering the engine. Low temperature produces a high resistance (100,000 ohms{100K ohms} at -40°C/-40°F), while high temperature causes low resistance (70 ohms at 130°C/266°F). The PCM supplies a 5 volt signal to the sensor through a resistor in the PCM and measures the voltage the voltage will be high when the incoming air is cold, and low when the air is hot. By measuring the voltage, the PCM calculates the incoming air temperature.

The IAT sensor signal is used to adjust spark timing according to incoming air density. The scan tool displays temperature of the air entering the engine, which should read close to ambient air temperature when the engine is cold, and rise as underhood temperature increases. If the engine has not been run for several hours (overnight) the IAT sensor temperature and engine coolant temperature should read close to each other.

TESTING

▶ **See Figures 36, 37 and 38**

1. Access the IAT; if necessary, remove it from the vehicle.
2. Connect a digital ohmmeter to the terminals of the IAT.
3. On a cold engine, compare the resistance of the sensor to the temperature of the ambient air.
4. With the DVOM connected to the IAT sensor, and a thermometer at the

sensor end, heat the sensor slightly, with a blow dryer or similar tool. Watch as the temperature goes up and the resistance goes down. Check the temperature against resistance on the chart.

5. Allow the sensor to cool, then repeat the test.
6. If the sensor does not meet specs, it should be replaced.

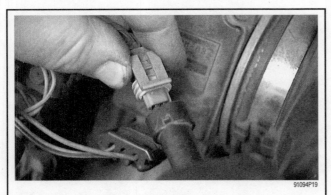

Fig. 36 Disconnect the Intake Air Temperature sensor connector

Fig. 37 The resistance of the IAT reads high because the engine is cold

Fig. 38 Just the heat from a blow dryer can cause a drastic drop in resistance. This IAT sensor tests good

REMOVAL & INSTALLATION

➡**Vehicles with a 3.1L engine employed a TBI unit and a Thermostatic Air Cleaner (Thermac) unit. This system heated the air before it was ingested by the engine. Inside the air cleaner is a temperature sensor that reacts to air intake temperature and controls the amount of vacuum going to the diaphragm motor that controls the damper door.**

3.4L Engine

▶ **See Figure 39**

1. Disconnect the electrical connector.
2. Carefully remove the IAT sensor (snaps into place).
To install:
3. Installation is the reversal of the removal procedure.

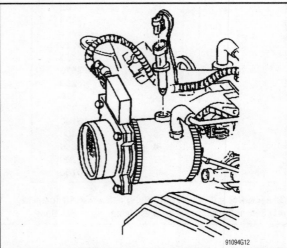

Fig. 39 IAT Location for a 3.4L engine. The IAT sensor is mounted in the rear air intake duct

3.8L Engine

▶ **See Figure 40**

1. Remove the air intake cover and filter element, to access the IAT, if necessary.
2. Disconnect the electrical connector.
3. Remove the retaining clip from the IAT sensor, if equipped, and remove the sensor.
To install:
4. Installation is the reversal of the removal procedure.

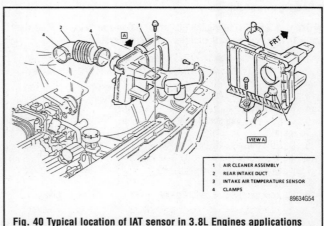

1	AIR CLEANER ASSEMBLY
2	REAR INTAKE DUCT
3	INTAKE AIR TEMPERATURE SENSOR
4	CLAMPS

Fig. 40 Typical location of IAT sensor in 3.8L Engines applications

Mass Air Flow Sensor

♦ See Figure 41

OPERATION

. The Mass Air Flow (MAF) sensor measures the amount of air, which passes through the throttle body. The PCM uses this information to determine the operating condition of the engine., to control fuel delivery. A large quantity of air indicates acceleration, while a small quantity indicates deceleration or idle.

The Scan Tool reads the MAF value and displays it to grams per second (gm/s). At idle, it should read between 4gm/s—7gm/s on a fully warmed up engine. Values should change rather quickly on acceleration but values should remain stable at any given RPM. A failure in the MAF sensor or circuit should set a DTC.

TESTING

♦ See Figures 42, 43, 44 and 45

1. Visually check the connector and make sure it is secure, clean and tight.
2. Bring the engine to normal operating conditions, lightly tap on the MAF sensor (with a suitable tool), and wiggle the wires at the connector while watching for a change in the idle speed. A common problem is MAF sensor wire damage.
3. Backprobe the sensor connector using a DVOM set to the Hertz scale. Attach the leads to A and B while simulating driving conditions by blowing air across the wire in the sensor. There should be a frequency swing from air crossing the wire in the sensor. A normal flow signal will be close to 1200 Hertz. If the frequency does not register, or is not proportional to the air flow across the sensing wire, then the sensor is faulty.
4. Check for battery positive (source voltage) on terminal C and ground on terminal B. If voltage or ground do not register, check the circuits to the PCM for continuity.
5. If voltage checks are good at the electrical connector and a driveability problem still exists, it may be the MAF sensor.
6. If the sensor and circuits are functional, the PCM may be at fault.

REMOVAL & INSTALLATION

3.4L Engine

♦ See Figure 46

1. Disconnect the negative battery cable.
2. Detach the MAF sensor electrical connector.
3. Remove the air inlet duct from the MAF sensor.
4. Remove the MAF sensor from the air filter housing.

To install:
Installation is the reverse of the removal procedure.

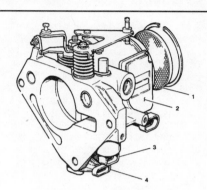

1	THROTTLE BODY AIR INLET SCREEN
2	MAF SENSOR
3	IAC VALVE
4	THROTTLE POSITION SENSOR

89634G58

Fig. 41 Location of MAF sensor on typical 3.8L engine, 3.4L engine similar

89634P12

Fig. 42 Attach a DVOM to the MAF sensor electrical connector's top and middle terminals and check for a 5-volt reference signal

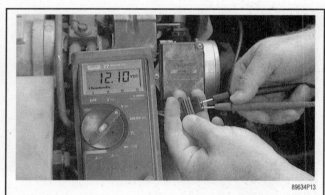

89634P13

Fig. 43 Check the middle and bottom connector for battery voltage

89634P14

Fig. 44 Connect a DVOM to the MAF sensor and check the air flow's corresponding voltage

89634P15

Fig. 45 Try having a hair dryer blow across the MAF and check for a voltage fluctuation as the air speed changes

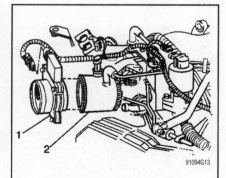

91094G13

Fig. 46 This Diagram Shows #1 as the MAF and #2 as the Air Duct

3.8L Engine

▶ See Figures 47, 48, 49 and 50

1. Disconnect the negative battery cable.
2. Loosen the clamps on the air duct, and remove the duct.
3. Disconnect the electrical connector.
4. Remove the retaining screws holding the MAF sensor to the throttle body.
5. Remove the MAF sensor.

✳ CAUTION

The MAF sensor gasket is not removable or serviceable. If it is damaged or altered, the entire throttle body may need to be replaced.

To install:

6. Install the MAF sensor to the throttle body using the retaining screws.
7. Connect the electrical connector,

Fig. 47 Loosen the clamp, and remove the air duct

Fig. 48 Disconnect the MAF sensor plug

Fig. 49 Remove the retaining bolts and remove the MAF sensor

Fig. 50 Typical mounting hole locations for MAF sensor

8. Install the air duct, and tighten the clamps.
9. Connect the negative battery cable.

Manifold Absolute Pressure Sensor

OPERATION

The Manifold Absolute Pressure (MAP) Sensor responds to changes in intake manifold pressure which result from engine load (intake manifold vacuum) and RPM changes; and converts these to a voltage output. The PCM sends a 5 volt reference voltage to the MAP sensor. As the manifold pressure changes, the output signal voltage of the sensor also changes. By monitoring the sensor output voltage, the PCM knows the manifold pressure. A lower pressure (low voltage) output voltage will be about 1–2 volts at idle. While higher pressure (high voltage) output voltage will be about 4–4.8 volts at Wide Open Throttle, (WOT). The MAP sensor is also used under certain conditions, to measure barometric pressure, allowing the PCM to make adjustments for different altitudes. The PCM uses the MAP sensor to control fuel delivery and ignition timing.

If the PCM detects a voltage that is lower than the possible range of the MAP sensor, a DTC will be set. A signal voltage higher than the possible range of the sensor will also set a DTC. The PCM will recognize an intermittent lower or higher voltage than possible as a fault and will set a code. The PCM can also detect a shifted MAP sensor. The PCM compares the MAP sensor signal to a calculated MAP based on throttle position and various engine load factors. If the detects A map signal that varies excessively above or below the calculated value a DTC will be set.

TESTING

▶ See Figures 51 and 52

The MAP sensor voltage reading is the opposite of a vacuum gauge reading. When manifold pressure is high, the MAP sensor value is high and vacuum is low.

Altitude—Meters	Altitude—Feet	Pressure—kPa	Voltage Range
Below 305	Below 1000	100–98	3.8–5.5V
305–610	1000–2000	98–95	3.6–5.3V
610–914	2000–3000	95–92	3.5–5.1V
914–1219	3000–4000	92–89	3.3–5.0V
1219–1524	4000–5000	89–86	3.2–4.8V
1524–1829	5000–6000	86–83	3.0–4.6V
1829–2133	6000–7000	83–80	2.9–4.5V
2133–2438	7000–8000	80–77	2.8–4.3V
2438–2743	8000–9000	77–74	2.6–4.2V
2743–3948	9000–10,000	74–71	2.5–4.0V

Fig. 51 MAP Sensor specifications—voltage and altitude

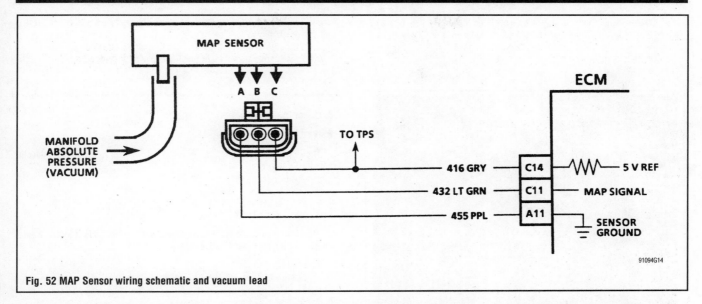

Fig. 52 MAP Sensor wiring schematic and vacuum lead

1. Using the accompanying chart as a guide, determine the height above sea level and the comparative voltage range.

2. Now, backprobe the MAP connector between terminals A and B.

3. Key On, Engine Off, the voltage reading obtained should coincide with the chart; voltage and altitude should match.

4. Now apply 10" Hg (34 kPa) vacuum to the MAP sensor, it should cause the voltage to be 1.5 to 2.1 volts less than the voltage at Step 1. Upon applying vacuum to the sensor, the change in voltage should be instantaneous. A slow voltage change indicates a faulty sensor.

5. Check the voltage between terminal C and ground, you should read reference voltage (about 5 volts).

6. If the reference voltage is right, and the sensor voltage is not within specs, replace the sensor.

7. If the sensor and the circuits are functional, the PCM may be faulty.

8. Be sure to test the vacuum hose for leaks or restrictions. This source must supply vacuum to the MAP sensor only.

REMOVAL & INSTALLATION

▶ See Figures 53 and 54

1. On early model vehicles with a TBI unit, the MAP sensor plugs into the side of the air cleaner.

2. On later models, the MAP is bolted in, on top of the engine.

3. Disconnect the negative battery cable.

4. Detach the electrical connector from the sensor.

5. Unplug the vacuum line.

6. Remove the locking clip and remove the sensor.

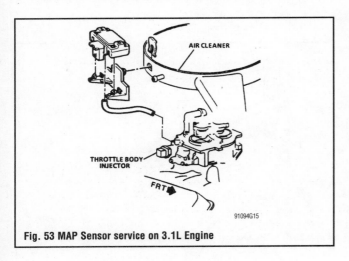

Fig. 53 MAP Sensor service on 3.1L Engine

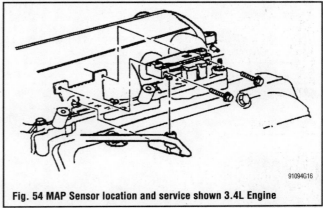

Fig. 54 MAP Sensor location and service shown 3.4L Engine

Throttle Position Sensor

OPERATION

The Throttle Position (TP) Sensor is a potentiometer that provides a voltage signal that changes relative to the throttle blade angle. It is connected to the throttle shaft on the throttle body. By monitoring the voltage on the signal line, the PCM calculates throttle position. As the throttle blade angle is changed (accelerator pedal moved), the TP sensor signal also changes. At a closed throttle position, the output or the TPL sensor is low. As the throttle blade opens the TP sensor voltage increases so that at Wide Open Throttle (WOT), The TP sensor voltage should be above 4 volts. The PCM calculates fuel delivery based on throttle blade angle (driver demand).

TESTING

▶ See Figures 55, 56 and 57

A broken or loose TP sensor may cause intermittent bursts of fuel from and injector and unstable idle because the PCM thinks the throttle is moving. A hard failure in the TP sensor 5 volts reference or signal circuits should set a DTC. A hard fault in the ground circuit will also set a DTC. Once a DTC is set, the PCM will use an artificial flow for throttle position and some vehicle performance will return. A high idle may result when there is a hard fault in the system.

1. Visually check the connector for cracks, or looseness, and that the connector is corrosion free.

2. With the key on, engine not running, measure the voltage at Terminal B. The voltage should read about .5 volts

3. Operate the throttle smoothly to wide open throttle (WOT), the voltage reading should follow the lever action, but not exceed 5 volts. If it does, or the voltage reading jumps, then replace the sensor.

4. Check terminal A for a proper ground signal.

Fig. 55 Attach a DVOM (1) to the TP sensor terminal (2) and measure the resistance of the sensor with the throttle closed. . . .

Fig. 56 . . . .then move the lever to the wide-open throttle (WOT) position slowly, while watching the change in resistance

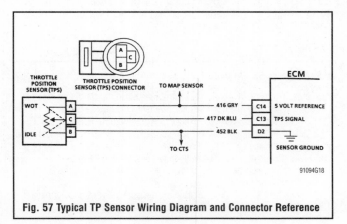

Fig. 57 Typical TP Sensor Wiring Diagram and Connector Reference

5. Check terminal C for a 5 volt reference signal. If the signals are correct, the sensor is faulty.

6. If the signals are not correct, check the circuits for continuity.

7. If the circuits are not faulty, the PCM may be at fault.

REMOVAL & INSTALLATION

3.1L Engine (VIN D)

▶ **See Figure 58**

The TP sensor is mounted on the side of the TBI unit and is attached directly onto the throttle shaft.

1. Remove the air cleaner assembly.
2. Disconnect the TP sensor electrical connector.
3. Remove the attaching screws·and remove the sensor.
4. Remove the TP Seal.

➡**The TP sensor is an electrical component. Do not soak it in any liquid cleaner or solvent, as damage may result.**

To install:

5. Install the TP sensor seal and then the TP sensor.
6. Align the TP sensor lever with the TP sensor drive lever on the throttle body.
7. If there is no thread locking material left on the attaching screws, apply Loctite 262® or equivalent, then install the screws.

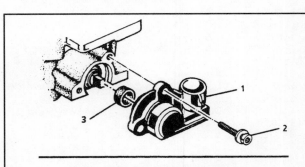

1	SENSOR -THROTTLE POSITION (TPS)
2	SCREW ASSEMBLY - TPS ATTACHING
3	SEAL - THROTTLE POSITION SENSOR

Fig. 58 Diagram of Throttle Body mounted TP sensor

3.4L Engine

▶ **See Figure 59**

1. Remove the air inlet tube.
2. Remove the TP sensor electrical connector.
3. Remove the two TP attaching screws, and remove the sensor.

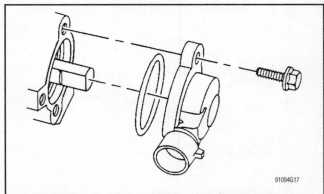

Fig. 59 The TP Sensor mounts directly onto the throttle shaft

To install:

4. With the throttle blade in the normal closed idle position, install the TP sensor on the throttle body assembly, making sure the TP sensor pickup lever is located **ABOVE** the tang on the throttle actuator lever.

5. Install the two TP sensor attaching screws, using a thread-locking compound on the screws. Use Loctite® or equivalent.

6. Tighten the TP sensor attaching screws to 18 inch lbs. (20 Nm).

3.8L Engine

1. Disconnect the IAT and the TP sensor electrical connectors.
2. Remove the two TP sensor attaching screws.

To install:

3. With the throttle blade in the normal closed idle position, install the throttle position sensor on the throttle body assembly, making sure the TP sensor pickup lever is located **ABOVE** the tang on the throttle actuator lever.

4. Install the two screws using a thread-locking compound on the screws, as necessary.

5. Connect the IAT and TP sensor electrical connectors.

Camshaft Position Sensor

The 3.1L Engine uses a Distributor.

OPERATION

During cranking, the Ignition control Module (ICM) monitors the 7X-crankshaft (3.4L Engine) position sensor signal. Once the ICM determines spark synchronization, 3X reference signals are sent to the PCM. The PCM will command all six injectors **ON** for one priming shot of fuel in all cylinders. After the priming, the injectors are left **OFF** for the next six fuel control reference signals (two crankshaft revolutions). This allows each cylinder a chance to use the fuel from the priming shot. During this waiting period, a cam pulse will have been received by the PCM. The PCM uses the Cam signal pulses to initiate sequential fuel injection. The PCM constantly monitors the number of pulses on the Cam signal circuit and compares the number of Cam pulses to the number of 24X reference pulses and the number of 3X reference pulses being received. If the PCM receives and incorrect number of pulses on the Cam reference circuit, the PCM will initiate injector sequence without the Cam signal with a one in six chance that injector sequence is correct. The engine will continue to start and run normally, although the misfire diagnostic will be affected if a misfiring condition occurs. It will also set a DTC.

TESTING

3.8L Engine

⬥ See Figures 60, 61, 62 and 63

Diagnostic Aids—check for:
- Incorrect harness routing near secondary ignition components.
- Ignition coil arcing to the wiring harness or to the Ignition Control Module. Check the ignition coils for cracks, carbon tracking, or other signs of damage.
- Secondary ignition wire(s) arcing to the wiring harness.
- Check for a poor connection or damaged harness: Inspect the PCM harness connectors for backed out terminals, improper mating, broken locks, improperly formed or damaged terminals, poor terminal to wire connections and damaged harnesses.
- An intermittent may be caused by a poor connection, rubbed through wire insulation or a wire broken inside the insulation.

Fig. 60 Location of the CMP sensor shown (water pump removed for clarity)

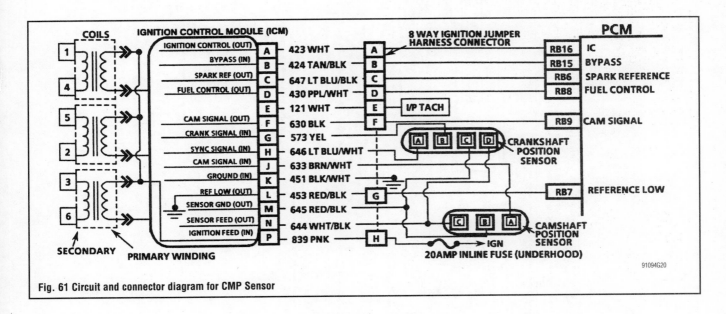

Fig. 61 Circuit and connector diagram for CMP Sensor

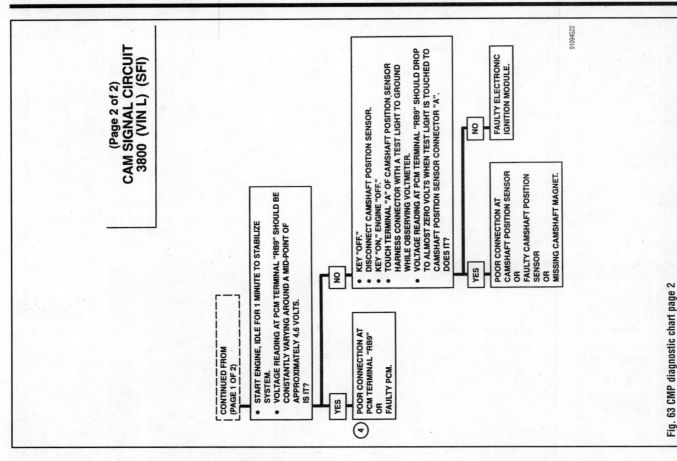

(Page 2 of 2)
CAM SIGNAL CIRCUIT
3800 (VIN L) (SFI)

Fig. 63 CMP diagnostic chart page 2

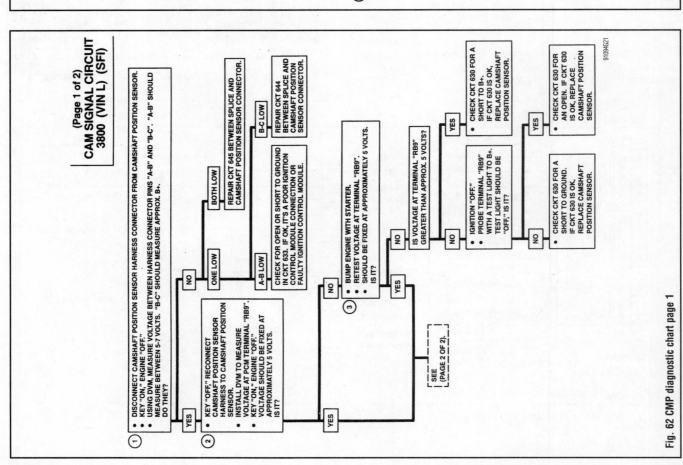

(Page 1 of 2)
CAM SIGNAL CIRCUIT
3800 (VIN L) (SFI)

Fig. 62 CMP diagnostic chart page 1

• Perform an intermittent test: If connections and harnesses check OK, monitor a digital voltmeter connected from the PCM terminal "RB9"(cam signal) to ground while moving related connectors and wiring harnesses. If the failure is induced, the voltage reading will change. This may help to isolate the location of the malfunction.

If necessary to perform a test on the camshaft sensor, use the diagnostic tree and the connector diagram given here for the 3.8L Engine.

3.4L Engine

▶ See Figures 64 and 65

Diagnostic Aids—check for:
• Incorrect harness routing near secondary ignition components.
• Ignition coil arcing to the wiring harness or to the Ignition Control Module. Check the ignition coils for cracks, carbon tracking, or other signs of damage.
• Secondary ignition wire(s) arcing to the wiring harness.
• Check for a poor connection or damaged harness: Inspect the PCM harness connectors for backed out terminals, improper mating, broken locks, improperly formed or damaged terminals, poor terminal to wire connections and damaged harnesses.
• An intermittent may be caused by a poor connection, rubbed through wire insulation or a wire broken inside the insulation.
• Perform an intermittent test: If connections and harnesses check OK, monitor a digital voltmeter connected from the PCM terminal "RB9"(cam signal) to ground while moving related connectors and wiring harnesses. If the failure

is induced, the voltage reading will change. This may help to isolate the location of the malfunction.

If necessary to perform a test on the camshaft sensor, use the diagnostic repair chart and the wire and connector diagram given here for the 3.4L Engine.

REMOVAL & INSTALLATION

▶ See Figures 66 and 67

Although different in appearance, the camshaft sensor, on both the 3.8L and the 3.4L engines, is located on the timing cover behind the water pump near the camshaft sprocket.
1. Disconnect the negative battery cable.
2. Remove the serpentine belt.
3. Remove the water pump pulley, if necessary.
4. Remove the power steering pump assembly, if necessary.
5. Detach the electrical connector.
6. Remove the retaining bolt, and extract the sensor.

To install:
7. Install the sensor and bolt and tighten to 8 ft. lbs. (10Nm).
8. The remainder of the installation is the reverse of the removal procedure.

Crankshaft Position Sensor

The 3.1L Engine uses a Distributor.

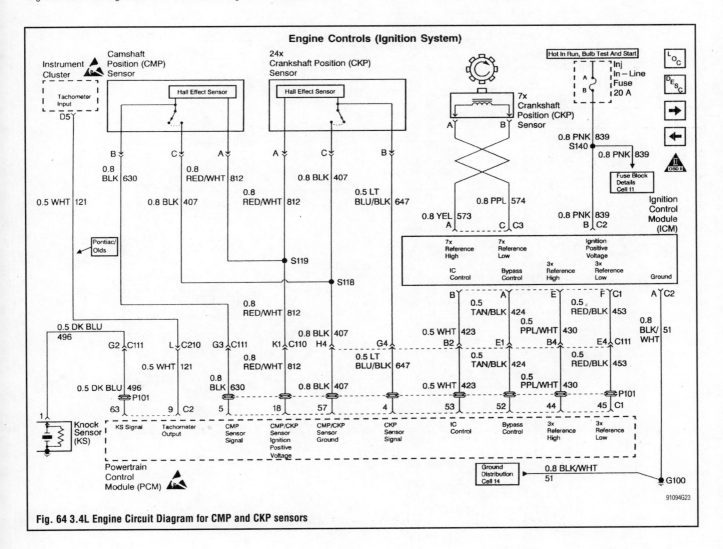

Fig. 64 3.4L Engine Circuit Diagram for CMP and CKP sensors

DTC P0341 CMP Sensor Circuit Performance

Step	Action	Value(s)	Yes	No
1	Was the Powertrain On–Board Diagnostic (OBD) System Check performed?	—	Go to Step 2	Go to the *Powertrain OBD System Check*
2	1. Turn ON the ignition switch, review and record scan tool Fail Records data. 2. Operate vehicle within Fail Records conditions as noted. 3. Using a scan tool, monitor Specific DTC info for DTC P0341 until the DTC P0341 test runs. Note test result; does scan tool indicate DTC P0341 failed this ign?	—	Go to Step 3	Refer to Diagnostic Aids
3	1. Turn OFF the ignition switch. 2. Disconnect the PCM connector. 3. Probe the sensor feed terminal with a test light to B+. Is the testlight ON?	—	Go to Step 4	Go to Step 6
4	1. With the test light connected, disconnect the CMP sensor connector from the CMP sensor 2. Observe the test light. Is the testlight ON?	—	Go to Step 5	Go to Step 11
5	1. Check for the following circuit conditions: • A short to ground in the Camshaft Position Sensor feed wire. • Short to ground in the 24X CKP sensor and/or feed wire. 2. If a problem is found, repair as necessary. Refer to Repair Procedures in Electrical Diagnosis. Was a problem found?	—	Go to Step 14	Refer to Diagnostic Aids
6	1. Connect a fused jumper between the sensor feed terminal in the PCM connector and B+. 2. Connect a DVM between the CMP signal terminal in the PCM connector and ground. Does the DVM display a voltage near the specified value?	B+	Go to Step 7	Go to Step 8
7	With the fused jumper connected to the sensor feed terminal, connect a DVM between the sensor ground terminal and engine ground. Does the DVM display a voltage near the specified value?	B+	Go to Step 12	Go to Step 10
8	1. Check for an open in the CMP sensor feed circuit. 2. If a problem is found, repair as necessary. Refer to Repair Procedures in Electrical Diagnosis. 3. Was a problem found?	—	Go to Step 14	Go to Step 9
9	1. Check CMP sensor signal wire for an open or short to ground. 2. If a problem is found, repair as necessary. Refer to Repair Procedures in Electrical Diagnosis. Was a problem found?	—	Go to Step 14	Go to Step 11
10	1. Check CMP sensor ground wire for an open. 2. If a problem is found, repair as necessary. Refer to Repair Procedures in Electrical Diagnosis. Was a problem found?	—	Go to Step 14	Go to Step 11
11	Replace the camshaft position sensor. Refer to *Camshaft Position Sensor.* Is action complete?	—	Go to Step 14	—
12	Check connections at the PCM. Replace terminals if necessary. Refer to Repair Procedures in Electrical Diagnosis. Was a problem found?	—	Go to Step 14	Go to Step 13
13	Replace the PCM. **Important:** Replacement PCM must be programmed. Refer to *PCM Replacement/Programming.* Is action complete?	—	Go to Step 14	—
14	1. Review and record scan tool Fail Records data. 2. Clear DTCs. 3. Operate vehicle within Fail Records conditions as noted. 4. Using a scan tool, monitor Specific DTC info for DTC P0341 until the DTC P0341 test runs. Note test result; does scan tool indicate DTC P0341 failed this ign?	—	Go to Step 2	System OK

91094G24

Fig. 65 CMP Sensor circuit performance testing

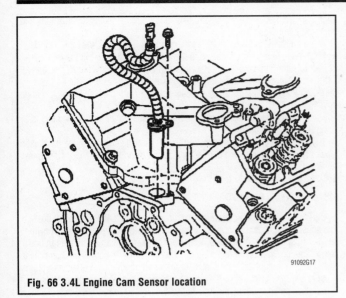

Fig. 66 3.4L Engine Cam Sensor location

OPERATION

3.8L Engine

▶ See Figures 68, 69, and 70

The dual Hall-effect crank sensor is the most critical part of the ignition system. If the sensor is damaged so that the crank sensor pulses are not generated, the engine will not start. There are four circuit wires connecting the dual crankshaft position sensor to the ignition control module. If there is a problem with any of the four, the engine will not start (no spark and no injector pulses).

The circuits are:
- Source voltage (10 to 12 volts) operating power supply for the Hall-effect switches from the ignition control module.
- 18X sensor pulse signal to the ignition control module.
- 3X sensor pulse signal to the ignition control module.
- Ground circuit for both Hall-effect switches. Equally important is the crankshaft reference (fuel control) signal generated by the ignition control module. If the PCM does not receive this signal, it will not pulse the injectors.

If the 3x crankshaft position sensor pulses stop while the engine is running, the engine will keep running. It will not restart after being shut "OFF".

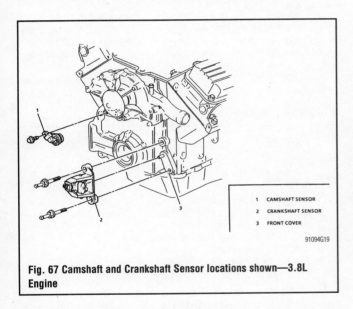

1	CAMSHAFT SENSOR
2	CRANKSHAFT SENSOR
3	FRONT COVER

91094G19

Fig. 67 Camshaft and Crankshaft Sensor locations shown—3.8L Engine

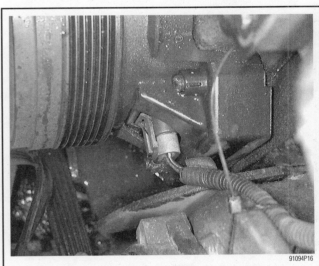

Fig. 68 Crankshaft position sensor connector and cover shown

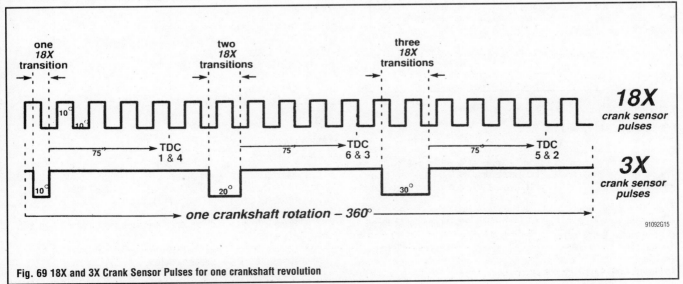

Fig. 69 18X and 3X Crank Sensor Pulses for one crankshaft revolution

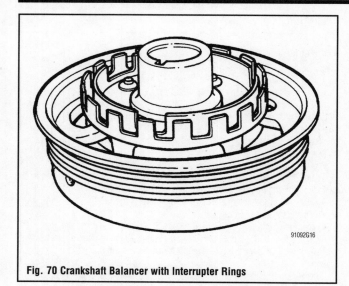

Fig. 70 Crankshaft Balancer with Interrupter Rings

91092G16

If the 18X crankshaft position sensor pulses stop while the engine is running, the engine will stop running and will not restart.

➡**Crankshaft Position (CKP) Sensor clearance is very important! The sensor must not contact the rotating interrupter rings at any time, or sensor damage will result.**

Ignition timing is not adjustable.—The firing order is 1-6-5-4-3-2.

3.4L Engine

3X reference PCM input
From the ignition control module, the PCM uses this signal to calculate engine Rpm and crankshaft position at engine speeds above 1200 RPM .The PCM also uses the pulses on this circuit to initiate injector pulses. If the PCM receives no pulses on this circuit, it will use the 24X reference signal circuit for fuel and ignition control. The engine will continue to start and run using the 24X reference signal only.

24X reference PCM input
From the ignition control module, the DPCM uses this signal to calculate engine RPM and crankshaft position at engine speeds below 1200 RPM. The PCM also uses the pulses on this circuit to initiate injector pulses. If the PCM receives no pulses on this circuit, the PCM will use the 3X reference signal circuit at all times for fuel and ignition control. The engine will continue to start and run using the 3X reference signal only.

7X Crankshaft Position (CKP) Sensor
the 7X crankshaft position sensor provides a signal used by the ignition control module to calculate ignition sequence. The ignition control module also uses the crankshaft position sensor signals to initiate 3X reference pulses that the PCM uses as reference to calculate RPM and crankshaft position.

Ignition timing is not adjustable.—The firing order is 1-2-3-4-5-6.

TESTING

3.4L Engine

▶ **See Figures 71, 72 and 73**

Diagnostic Aids—check for:
• Incorrect harness routing near secondary ignition components.
• Ignition coil arcing to the wiring harness or to the Ignition Control Module. Check the ignition coils for cracks, carbon tracking, or other signs of damage.
• Secondary ignition wire(s) arcing to the wiring harness.
• An intermittent fault may be caused by a poor connection, rubbed through wire insulation or a wire broken inside the insulation.
• Check for a poor connection or damaged harness: Inspect the PCM harness connectors for backed out terminals, improper mating, broken locks,

improperly formed or damaged terminals, poor terminal to wire connections and damaged harnesses.
• If harness appears to be OK, disconnect the PCM, turn the ignition ON and observe a voltmeter connected to the 24X reference circuit at the PCM harness connector while moving connectors and wiring harnesses related to the 24X Crankshaft Position Sensor and Camshaft Position Sensor. The 24X and Camshaft Position sensors share the same sensor feed from the PCM. A change in voltage will indicate the location of the fault.
• If the 24X sensor feed is open, the tachometer on the dash (if vehicle is equipped) will not operate.
1. If necessary to perform a test on the crankshaft sensor, use the diagnostic repair chart and the wire and connector diagram given here for the 3.4L Engine.

3.8L Engine

▶ **See Figures 74 and 75**

During cranking, the ignition control module monitors the crankshaft position sensor sync signal. The sync signal is used to determine the correct cylinder pair to spark first. After the sync signal has been processed by the ignition control module, it sends a reference pulse to the PCM. If there is an intermittent fault, a code may not set immediately or under all conditions. Certain symptoms experienced may help isolate the cause of the condition. A poor connection or fault in the camshaft position sensor circuits or a faulty camshaft position sensor may cause the PCM to re-initialize injector sequence when the fault occurs, causing a possible stumble or miss. A poor connection or fault in the fuel control circuit, crankshaft position sensor circuits, the 18X portion of the crankshaft position sensor or damaged vanes on the harmonic balancer interrupter rings will cause the PCM to stop pulsing the injectors when the fault occurs, causing an intermittent stumble or stall.

If the CKP sensor is suspect, use the accompanying charts to help diagnose the problem.

REMOVAL & INSTALLATION

▶ **See Figure 65**

3.4L Engine

7X CKP SENSOR

1. Disconnect the negative battery cable.
2. Raise and safely support the vehicle securely on jackstands.
3. Remove the intermediate exhaust pipe.
4. Remove the rack and pinion heat shield.
5. Detach the sensor electrical connector.
6. Remove the crankshaft Position sensor shield retaining nut.
7. Extract the 7X CKP sensor from the engine block.

To install:

➡**Before installing the new crankshaft sensor, lubricate new O-ring with clean oil.**

8. Install the crankshaft sensor in the block.
9. Install the sensor retainer and bolt. Tighten the bolt to 70 inch lbs. (8Nm).
10. Install the rack and pinion heat shield.
11. Install the intermediate exhaust pipe.
12. Lower the vehicle.
13. Connect the negative battery cable.

24X CKP SENSOR

▶ **See Figure 65**

1. Disconnect the negative battery cable.
2. Remove the serpentineentine belt form the crankshaft pulley.
3. Raise and safely support the vehicle securely on jackstands.
4. Remove the right front tire and wheel assembly.
5. Remove the right inner fender access cover.
6. Remove the crankshaft harmonic balancer retaining bolt and harmonic balancer using a suitable tool.
7. Remove the CKP sensor harness clip, the electrical connector, and remove the sensor from the engine block face.

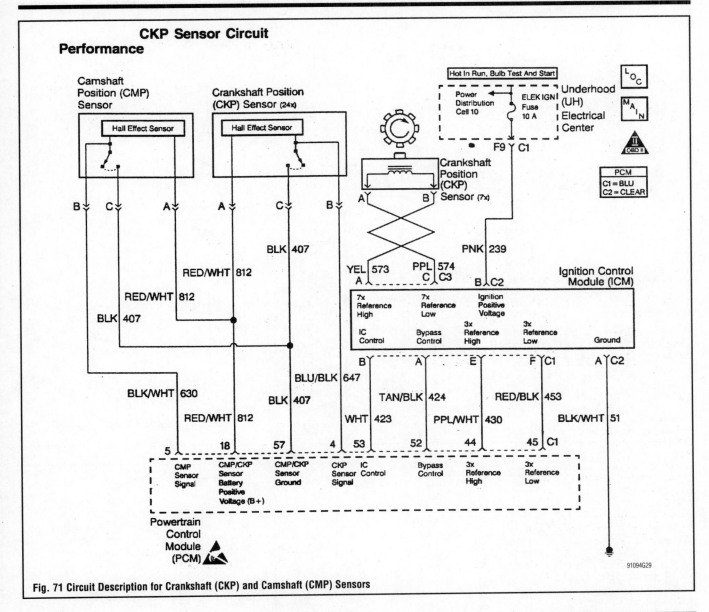

Fig. 71 Circuit Description for Crankshaft (CKP) and Camshaft (CMP) Sensors

	DTC P0336 CKP Sensor Circuit Performance			
Step	Action	Value(s)	Yes	No
1	Was the *Powertrain OBD System Check* performed?	—	Go to Step 2	Go to *Powertrain OBD System Check*
2	Attempt to start the engine. Does the engine start?	—	Go To Step 3	Go To *Engine Cranks but Does Not Run*
3	1. Clear DTC P0336. 2. Start the engine and idle. 3. Observe DTC(s). Is DTC P0336 set?	—	Go To Step 4	Go to Diagnostic Aids
4	With DMM Check for voltage at Crankshaft Position and Camshaft Position Sensor Feed circuit. Does the DMM display a voltage near the specified value?	B+	Go to Step 8	Go to Step 5
5	Disconnect PCM. 1. With fused jumper apply battery positive voltage to Sensor Feed circuit. 2. Check for voltage at Reference Signal circuit. Does the DMM display a voltage near the specified value?	B+	Go To Step 14	Go To Step 6

Fig. 72 CKP Sensor circuit performance testing

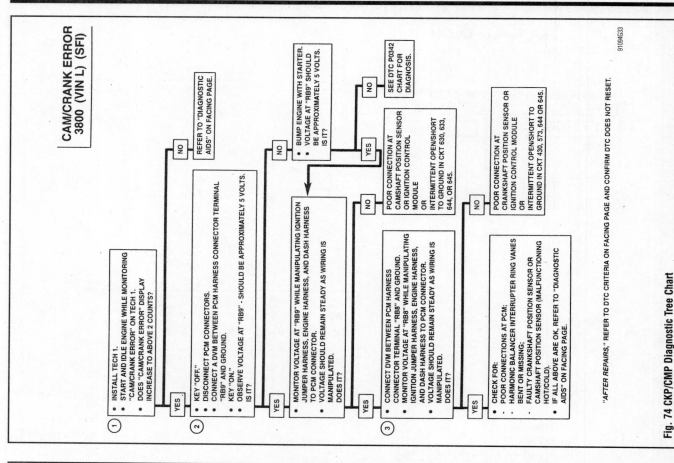

CAM/CRANK ERROR 3800 (VIN L) (SFI)

"AFTER REPAIRS," REFER TO DTC CRITERIA ON FACING PAGE AND CONFIRM DTC DOES NOT RESET.

Fig. 74 CKP/CMP Diagnostic Tree Chart

DTC P0336 CKP Sensor Circuit Performance (cont'd)

Step	Action	Value(s)	Yes	No
6	Check for the following circuit conditions: • Open or short to ground in Sensor Feed circuit. • Check connection at PCM. • Check connections at 24X Crankshaft Position Sensor and Camshaft Position Sensor. If a problem is found, repair as necessary. Refer to *Repair procedures in Electrical Diagnosis.* Is action Complete?	—	Go To Step 15	—
7	Check connections at the PCM and replace terminals if necessary. Refer to *Repair procedures in Electrical Diagnosis.* Did any terminals require replacement?	—	Go To Step 15	Go To Step 8
8	1. Check reference signal circuit connections at the Crankshaft Position Sensor. 2. Replace terminals if necessary, Refer to *Repair procedures in Electrical Diagnosis.* Did any terminals require replacement?	—	Go To Step 15	Go To Step 9
9	1. Check Reference Signal circuit for open or short to ground. 2. If a problem is found, repair as necessary. Refer to *Repair procedures in Electrical Diagnosis.* Was a problem found?	—	Go To Step 15	Go To Step 10
10	1. Disconnect 24X Crankshaft Position and Camshaft Position Sensors. 2. Check for continuity from CMP harness Reference Low to CKP harness Reference Low circuit. 3. Check for continuity from CKP harness Reference Low to PCM. Does DMM indicate continuity?	0 Ω	Go To Step 15	Go To Step 11
11	Check for the following circuit conditions: • Open in Reference Low circuit for 24X Crankshaft Position Sensor. • Open in splice for Reference Low circuit. • Check connections at PCM and sensors. 2. If a problem is found, repair as necessary. Refer to *Repair procedures in Electrical Diagnosis.* Is the action complete?	—	Go To Step 15	—
12	1. Ignition OFF. 2. Disconnect 24X Crankshaft Position Sensor connector. 3. Ignition ON. 4. Probe Reference Low circuit at sensor harness connector with test light to battery voltage. Is test light ON?	—	Go To Step 13	—
13	Replace 24X crankshaft Position Sensor. Is action complete?	—	Go To Step 15	Go To Step 14
14	Check connections at PCM, if OK replace the PCM. **Important:** Replacement PCM must be programmed. Refer to *PCM Replacement/Programming.* Is the action complete?	—	Go To Step 15	—
15	1. Review and record scan tool Fail Records data. 2. Clear DTCs. 3. Operate vehicle within Fail Records conditions as noted. 4. Using a scan tool, monitor SPECIFIC DTC info for DTC P0336 until the DTC P0336 test runs. Does scan tool indicate DTC P0336 failed this ignition?	—	Go to Step 2	Repair Complete

Fig. 73 CKP Sensor circuit performance testing—continued

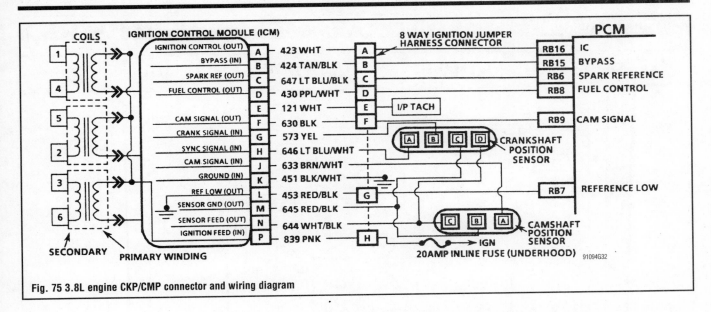

Fig. 75 3.8L engine CKP/CMP connector and wiring diagram

To install:

8. Install the sensor to the block, connect the electrical connector, and install the sensor harness clip.

9. Torque the sensor mounting bolts to 8 ft. lbs. (10Nm)

10. Apply sealer to the keyway of the balancer.

11. Install the balancer onto the crankshaft.

12. Apply thread sealer to the threads of the crankshaft balancer bolt and tighten to 79 ft. lbs. (107Nm).

13. Install the serpentineentine belts.

14. Install the right inner fender access cover.

15. Install the right side tire and wheel assembly.

16. Lower the vehicle.

17. Connect the negative battery cable.

3.8L Engine

▶ **See Figures 76, 77 and 78**

1. Disconnect the negative battery cable.

2. Remove the serpentineentine belt from the crank pulley.

3. Raise and safely support the vehicle securely on jackstands.

4. Remove the right front tire and wheel assembly.

5. Remove the right inner fender access cover.

6. Remove crankshaft harmonic balancer retaining bolt, and harmonic balancer using a suitable puller.

7. Remove the CKP sensor shield, do not use a pry bar.

8. Detach the sensor electrical connector.

9. Remove the sensor and pedestal from the engine block face.

10. Remove the sensor from the pedestal.

To install:

11. Loosely install the CKP sensor on the pedestal.

12. Position the sensor with pedestal attached using the appropriate tool.

13. Position the CKP sensor alignment tool onto the crankshaft and install the bolts to hold the pedestal to the block face. Torque to 14–28 ft. lbs. (20–40 Nm). Torque the pedestal pinch bolt to 36–40 inch lbs. (4–4.5 Nm).

14. Remove the CKP sensor alignment tool.

15. Replace the crankcase position shield.

16. Connect the electrical connector.

17. Place the CKP sensor alignment tool on the harmonic balancer and turn. If any of the vanes on the harmonic balancer contacts the tool, replace the balancer assembly.

18. Install the balancer to the crankshaft, apply sealer to the threads, and torque the crankshaft bolt to 110 ft. lbs. (150Nm) + 76°.

19. Install the inner fender shield, and the tire and wheel assembly.

20. Lower the vehicle, and install the serpentine belt.

21. Connect the negative battery cable.

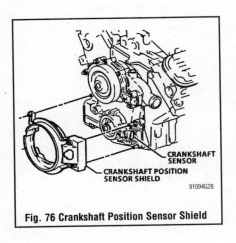

Fig. 76 Crankshaft Position Sensor Shield

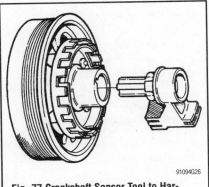

Fig. 77 Crankshaft Sensor Tool to Harmonic Balancer Alignment

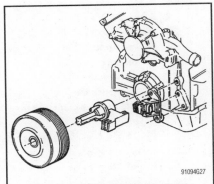

Fig. 78 Crankshaft Sensor Tool to Crankshaft Alignment

COMPONENT LOCATIONS

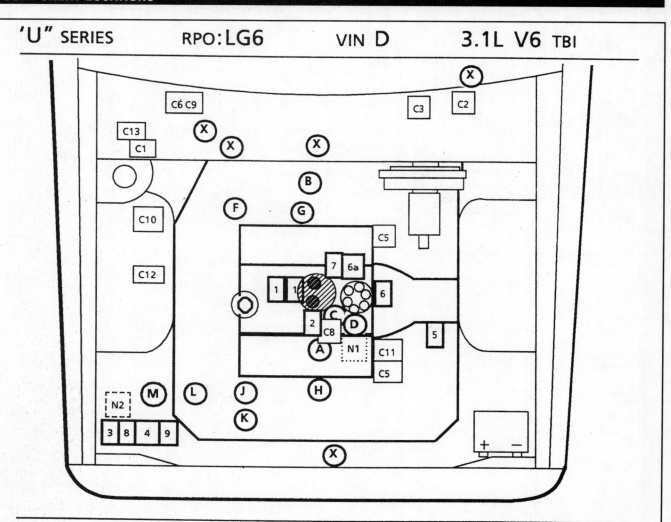

'U" SERIES   RPO: LG6   VIN D   3.1L V6 TBI

☐ COMPUTER HARNESS

- C1 Powertrain Control Module
- C2 DLC diagnostic connector
- C3 Malfunction Indicator Lamp
- C5 PCM harness grounds
- C6 Fuse panel
- C8 Fuel pump prime connector
- C9 Fuel pump fuse & PCM power
- C10 Set timing connector
- C11 Engine Grounds
- C12 Knock Sensor Module
- C13 Vehicle Speed Sensor Buffer

☐ NOT PCM CONNECTED

- N1 Crankcase ventilation valve
- N2 Evaporative Emission Canister

◯ INFORMATION SENSORS

- A Manifold Absolute Pressure (MAP) (attached to air cleaner)
- B Oxygen Sensor (O2S)
- C Throttle Position (TP) Sensor
- D Engine Coolant Temperature (ECT) Sensor
- F Vehicle Speed Sensor (VSS)
- G Knock Sensor (KS)
- H Fuel Pump/Engine Oil Pressure Indicator switch
- J A/C low compressor pressure cutoff switch (C67)
- K A/C high compressor pressure cutoff switch (C67)
- L Intermediate pressure A/C fan switch
- M A/C pressure cycling switch (C34)

☐ CONTROLLED DEVICES

- 1 Fuel injectors
- 2 Idle Air Control (IAC) valve
- 3 Fuel pump relay
- 4 Coolant pusher fan relay
- 5 Torque Converter Clutch (TCC) connector
- 6 Distributor
- 6a Ignition coil
- 7 EGR control solenoid valve
- 8 Coolant puller fan relay
- 9 A/C compressor relay

(X) SIR SYSTEM COMPONENTS:

 Exhaust Gas Recirculation valve

ELECTRONIC ENGINE CONTROL AND EMISSION COMPONENT LOCATIONS—3.4L ENGINE

1. Camshaft position sensor
2. Manifold absolute pressure sensor (near ignition coils)
3. EGR valve
4. Idle air control valve (mounted on throttle body)
5. Throttle position sensor (mounted on throttle body)
6. Powertrain control module (in air cleaner housing)
7. Mass air flow sensor
8. Engine coolant temperature sensor
9. PCV valve
10. Knock sensor (in engine block, near oil pan)

ELECTRONIC ENGINE CONTROL AND EMISSION COMPONENT LOCATIONS—3.8L ENGINE

1. Powertrain control module
2. Crankshaft position sensor
3. Camshaft position sensor
4. Crankcase ventilation valve
5. Oxygen sensor, mounted in exhaust manifold
6. Throttle position sensor (mounted on throttle body)
7. Idle air control valve (mounted on throttle body)
8. Mass air flow sensor (mounted on throttle body)
9. Intake Air Temperature (IAT) sensor (in air intake pipe)
10. Linear EGR valve
11. Knock sensor (in engine block, near oil pan)

91094PA2

TROUBLE CODES

General Information

Since the computer control module is programmed to recognize the presence and value of electrical inputs, it will also note the lack of a signal or a radical change in values. It will, for example, react to the loss of signal from the vehicle speed sensor or note that engine coolant temperature has risen beyond acceptable (programmed) limits. Once a fault is recognized, a numeric code is assigned and held in memory. The dashboard warning lamp: CHECK ENGINE or SERVICE ENGINE SOON (SES), will illuminate to advise the operator that the system has detected a fault. This lamp is also known as the Malfunction Indicator Lamp (MIL).

More than one code may be stored. Keep in mind not every engine uses every code. Additionally, the same code may carry different meanings relative to each engine or engine family.

In the event of an computer control module failure, the system will default to a pre-programmed set of values. These are compromise values which allow the engine to operate, although possibly at reduced efficiency. This is variously known as the default, limp-in or back-up mode. Driveability is almost always affected when the ECM enters this mode.

SCAN TOOLS

▶ **See Figures 79 and 80**

On most early models, the stored codes may be read with only the use of a small jumper wire, however the use of a hand-held scan tool such as GM's TECH-1® or equivalent is recommended. On some 1994 vehicles (equipped with a 16-pin Data Link Connector), and all 1995–99 models, an OBD-II compliant scan tool must be used. There are many manufacturers of these tools; a purchaser must be certain that the tool is proper for the intended use. If you own a scan type tool, it probably came with comprehensive instructions on proper use. Be sure to follow the instructions that came with your unit if they differ from what is given here; this is a general guide with useful information included.

The scan tool allows any stored codes to be read from the ECM or PCM memory. The tool also allows the operator to view the data being sent to the computer control module while the engine is running. This ability has obvious diagnostic advantages; the use of the scan tool is frequently required for component testing. The scan tool makes collecting information easier; the data must be correctly interpreted by an operator familiar with the system.

An example of the usefulness of the scan tool may be seen in the case of a temperature sensor which has changed its electrical characteristics. The ECM is reacting to an apparently warmer engine (causing a driveability problem), but the sensor's voltage has not changed enough to set a fault code. Connecting the scan tool, the voltage signal being sent to the ECM may be viewed; comparison to normal values or a known good vehicle reveals the problem quickly.

ELECTRICAL TOOLS

▶ **See Figure 81**

The most commonly required electrical diagnostic tool is the digital multimeter, allowing voltage, ohmage (resistance) and amperage to be read by one instrument. The multimeter must be a high-impedance unit, with 10 megohms of impedance in the voltmeter. This type of meter will not place an additional load on the circuit it is testing; this is extremely important in low voltage circuits. The multimeter must be of high quality in all respects. It should be handled carefully and protected from impact or damage. Replace batteries frequently in the unit.

Other necessary tools include an unpowered test light, a quality tachometer with an inductive (clip-on) pick up, and the proper tools for releasing GM's Metri-Pack, Weather Pack and Micro-Pack terminals as necessary. The Micro-Pack connectors are used at the ECM electrical connector. A vacuum pump/gauge may also be required for checking sensors, solenoids and valves.

Diagnosis and Testing

Diagnosis of a driveability and/or emissions problems requires attention to detail and following the diagnostic procedures in the correct order. Resist the temptation to perform any repairs before performing the preliminary diagnostic steps. In many cases this will shorten diagnostic time and often cure the problem without electronic testing.

The proper troubleshooting procedure for these vehicles is as follows:

VISUAL/PHYSICAL INSPECTION

This is possibly the most critical step of diagnosis and should be performed immediately after retrieving any codes. A detailed examination of connectors, wiring and vacuum hoses can often lead to a repair without further diagnosis. Performance of this step relies on the skill of the technician performing it; a careful inspector will check the undersides of hoses as well as the integrity of hard-to-reach hoses blocked by the air cleaner or other component. Wiring should be checked carefully for any sign of strain, burning, crimping, or terminal pull-out from a connector. Checking connectors at components or in harnesses is required; usually, pushing them together will reveal a loose fit.

INTERMITTENTS

If a fault occurs intermittently, such as a loose connector pin breaking contact as the vehicle hits a bump, the ECM will note the fault as it occurs and energize the dash warning lamp. If the problem self-corrects, as with the terminal pin again making contact, the dash lamp will extinguish after 10 seconds but a code will remain stored in the computer control module's memory.

When an unexpected code appears during diagnostics, it may have been set during an intermittent failure that self-corrected; the codes are still useful in diagnosis and should not be discounted.

CIRCUIT/COMPONENT REPAIR

The fault codes and the scan tool data will lead to diagnosis and checking of a particular circuit. It is important to note that the fault code indicates a fault or loss of signal in an ECM-controlled system, not necessarily in the specific component.

Refer to the appropriate Diagnostic Code chart to determine the codes meaning.

89634G86

Fig. 79 A TECH 1®, or equivalent scan tool is recommended for reading trouble codes

TCCS4P12

Fig. 80 Inexpensive scan tools, such as this Auto Xray®, are available to interface with your General Motors vehicle

89634G87

Fig. 81 A quality digital multimeter is an extremely useful piece of diagnostic equipment to have in your tool box

The component may then be tested following the appropriate component test procedures found in this section. If the component is OK, check the wiring for shorts or opens. Further diagnoses should be left to an experienced driveability technician.

If a code indicates the ECM to be faulty and the ECM is replaced, but does not correct the problem, one of the following may be the reason:

• There is a problem with the ECM terminal connections: The terminals may have to be removed from the connector in order to check them properly.

• The ECM or PROM is not correct for the application: The incorrect ECM or PROM may cause a malfunction and may or may not set a code.

• The problem is intermittent: This means that the problem is not present at the time the system is being checked. In this case, make a careful physical inspection of all portions of the system involved.

• Shorted solenoid, relay coil or harness: Solenoids and relays are turned on and off by the ECM using internal electronic switches called drivers. Each driver is part of a group of four called Quad-Drivers. A shorted solenoid, relay coil or harness may cause an ECM to fail, and a replacement ECM to fail when it is installed. Use a short tester, J34696, BT 8405, or equivalent, as a fast, accurate means of checking for a short circuit.

• The Programmable Read Only Memory (PROM) or MEM-CAL may be faulty: Although the PROM rarely fails, it operates as part of the ECM. Therefore, it could be the cause of the problem. Substitute a known good PROM/MEM-CAL.

• The replacement ECM may be faulty: After the ECM is replaced, the system should be rechecked for proper operation. If the diagnostic code again indicates the ECM is the problem, substitute a known good ECM. Although this is a very rare condition, it could happen.

Reading Codes

1990–94 VEHICLES EXCEPT 1994 MODELS WITH 16-PIN DLC

▶ See Figures 82 and 83

Listings of the trouble for the various engine control system covered in this manual are located in this section. Remember that a code only points to the faulty circuit, NOT necessarily to a faulty component. Loose, damaged or corroded connections may contribute to a fault code on a circuit when the sensor or component is operating properly. Be sure that the components are faulty before replacing them, especially the expensive ones.

The Assembly Line Diagnostic Link (ALDL) or Data Link Connector (DLC) may be located under the dashboard, and is sometimes covered with a plastic cover labeled DIAGNOSTIC CONNECTOR.

DTC	DESCRIPTION	ILLUMINATE MIL
13	Oxygen Sensor (O2S) - open circuit	YES
14	Engine Coolant Temperature (ECT) Sensor - high temp. indicated	YES
15	Engine Coolant Temperature (ECT) Sensor - low temp. indicated	YES
16	System Voltage high or low	YES
17	Spark Reference Circuit	NO
18	Cam/Crank Error	YES
21	Throttle Position (TP) Sensor voltage high	YES
22	Throttle Position (TP) Sensor voltage low	YES
23	Intake Air Temperature (IAT) Sensor - low temp. indicated	NO
24	Vehicle Speed Sensor Circuit	YES
25	Intake Air Temperature (IAT) Sensor - high temp. indicated	NO
26	QDM "A" Circuit	YES
31	PRNDL Input Circuit	NO
34	Mass Air Flow (MAF) Sensor - low gm/sec indicated	YES
36	Transaxle Shift Problem	NO
38	Brake Input Circuit	NO
39	Torque Convertor Clutch (TCC) Problem	NO
41	Cam Sensor Circuit	YES
42	Ignition Control (IC) Circuit	YES
43	Knock Sensor (KS)	YES
44	Oxygen Sensor (O2S) - lean exhaust indicated	YES
45	Oxygen Sensor (O2S) - rich exhaust indicated	YES
51	PROM Error	YES
53, 54, 55	EGR Problem	YES
56	QDM "B" Circuit	YES
61	Cruise Vent Solenoid Circuit	NO
62	Cruise Vacuum Solenoid Circuit	NO
63	Cruise System Problem (SPS Indicated Low)	NO
65	Cruise Servo Position Sensor (SPS) Circuit (open/grounded)	NO
66	Excessive A/C Cycling (low refrigerant charge)	NO
67	Cruise Switches Circuit	NO
68	Cruise System Problem (SPS Indicated High)	NO
69	A/C Head Pressure Switch Circuit	NO
99	Power Management	NO

If a DTC not listed above appears on Tech 1, ground DLC Diagnostic Request Terminal "B" and observe flashed codes. If DTC does not reappear, Tech 1 data may be faulty. If DTC does reappear, check for incorrect or faulty PROM.

89634G90

Fig. 82 Engine diagnostic trouble codes—1990–93 vehicles, and 1994 vehicles with a 12-pin DLC connector

1. The diagnostic trouble codes can be read by grounding test terminal **B**. The terminal is most easily grounded by connecting it to terminal **A** (internal ECM ground). This is the terminal to the right of terminal **B** on the top row of the ALDL connector.

2. Once the terminals have been connected, the ignition switch must be moved to the **ON** position with the engine not running.

3. The Service Engine Soon or Check Engine light should be flashing. If it isn't, turn the ignition switch **OFF** and remove the jumper wire. Turn the ignition **ON** and confirm that the light is now on. If it is not, replace the bulb and try again. If the bulb still will not light, or if it does not flash with the test terminal grounded, the system should be diagnosed by an experienced driveability technician. If the light is OK, proceed as follows.

4. The code(s) stored in memory may be read through counting the flashes of the dashboard warning lamp. The dash warning lamp should begin to flash Code 12. The code will display as one flash, a pause and two flashes. Code 12 is not a fault code. It is used as a system acknowledgment or handshake code; its presence indicates that the ECM can communicate as requested. Code 12 is used to begin every diagnostic sequence. Some vehicles also use Code 12 after all diagnostic codes have been sent.

5. After Code 12 has been transmitted 3 times, the fault codes, if any, will each be transmitted 3 times. The codes are stored and transmitted in numeric order from lowest to highest.

➡ **The order of codes in the memory does not indicate the order of occurrence.**

6. If there are no codes stored, but a driveability or emissions problem is evident, the system should be diagnosed by an experienced driveability technician.

7. If one or more codes are stored, record them. Refer to the applicable Diagnostic Code chart in this section.

8. Switch the ignition **OFF** when finished with code retrieval or scan tool readings.

➡ **After making repairs, clear the trouble codes and operate the vehicle to see if it will reset, indicating further problems.**

1994 VEHICLES WITH 16-PIN DLC & ALL 1995–99 MODELS

◢ See Figures 84, 85, 86, 87 and 88

On 1994–95 3.4L and 3.8L engines, and all 1996 models, an OBD-II compliant scan tool must be used to retrieve the trouble codes. Follow the scan tool

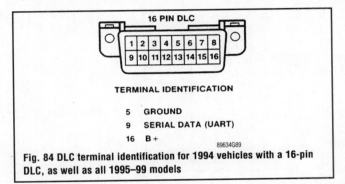

TERMINAL IDENTIFICATION

A	GROUND	F	TCC (IF USED)
B	DIAGNOSTIC TERMINAL	M	SERIAL DATA
E	SERIAL DATA (IF USED)	E	

89634G88

Fig. 83 ALDL/DLC terminal identification for 1990–94 vehicles, except 1994 models with a 16-pin DLC

16 PIN DLC

```
1  2  3  4  5  6  7  8
9 10 11 12 13 14 15 16
```

TERMINAL IDENTIFICATION

5   GROUND
9   SERIAL DATA (UART)
16 B +

89634G89

Fig. 84 DLC terminal identification for 1994 vehicles with a 16-pin DLC, as well as all 1995–99 models

DTC	Description	Illuminate MIL
P0101	Mass Air Flow System Performance	Yes
P0102	MAF Sensor Circuit Low Frequency	Yes
P0103	MAF Sensor Circuit High Frequency	Yes
P0107	MAP Sensor Circuit Low Voltage	Yes
P0108	MAP Sensor Circuit High Voltage	Yes
P0112	IAT Sensor Circuit Low Voltage	Yes
P0113	IAT Sensor Circuit High Voltage	Yes
P0117	ECT Sensor Circuit Low Voltage	Yes
P0118	ECT Sensor Circuit High Voltage	Yes
P0121	TP Sensor Performance	Yes
P0122	TP Sensor Circuit Low Voltage	Yes
P0123	TP Sensor Circuit High Voltage	Yes
P0125	ECT Excessive Time to Closed Loop	Yes
P0131	HO2S Circuit Low Voltage Bank 1 Sensor 1	Yes
P0132	HO2S Circuit High Voltage Bank 1 Sensor 1	Yes
P0133	HO2S Circuit Slow Response Bank 1 Sensor 1	Yes
P0134	HO2S CKT Insufficient Activity Bank 1 Sensor 1	Yes
P0135	HO2S Heater Circuit Bank 1 Sensor 1	Yes
P0143	HO2S Circuit Low Voltage Bank 1 Sensor 3 (Post-Converter)	Yes
P0144	HO2S Circuit High Voltage Bank 1 Sensor 3 (Post-Converter)	Yes
P0146	HO2S Circuit Insufficient Activity Bank 1 Sensor 3 (Post-Converter)	Yes
P0147	HO2S Heater Circuit Bank 1 Sensor 3 (Post-Converter)	Yes
P0151	HO2S Circuit Low Voltage Bank 2 Sensor 1	Yes
P0152	HO2S Circuit High Voltage Bank 2 Sensor 1	Yes
P0153	HO2S Circuit Slow Response Bank 2 Sensor 1	Yes
P0154	HO2S Circuit Insufficient Activity Bank 2 Sensor 1	Yes
P0155	HO2S Heater Circuit Bank 2 Sensor 1	Yes
P0171	Fuel Trim System Lean Bank 1	Yes

89634G91

Fig. 85 Engine diagnostic trouble codes (1 of 4)—1994 vehicles with a 16-pin DLC and all 1995–99 vehicles

DTC	Description	Illuminate MIL
P0719	Brake Switch Circuit Low.	No
P0724	Brake Switch Circuit High.	No
P0730	Incorrect Gear Ratio.	No
P0741	Torque Converter Clutch System Stuck Off.	Yes
P0742	Torque Converter Clutch System Stuck On.	Yes
P0748	Pressure Control Solenoid Valve Circuit Malfunction.	Yes
P0751	Shift Solenoid 1 - Performance/Stuck Off.	Yes
P0753	Shift Solenoid 1 - Electrical.	Yes
P0756	Shift Solenoid 2 - Performance/Stuck Off.	Yes
P0758	Shift Solenoid 2 - Electrical.	Yes
P1106	MAP Sensor CKT Intermittent High Voltage	No
P1107	MAP Sensor CKT Intermittent Low Voltage	No
P1111	IAT Sensor CKT Intermittent High Voltage	No
P1112	IAT Sensor CKT Intermittent Low Voltage	No
P1114	ECT Sensor CKT Intermittent Low Voltage	No
P1115	ECT Sensor CKT Intermittent High Voltage	No
P1121	TP Sensor CKT Intermittent High Voltage	No
P1122	TP Sensor CKT Intermittent Low Voltage	No
P1133	HO2S Insufficient Switching Bank 1 Sensor 1	Yes
P1134	HO2S Transition Time Ratio Bank 1 Sensor 1	Yes
P1153	HO2S Insufficient Switching Bank 2 Sensor 1	Yes
P1154	HO2S Transition Time Ratio Bank 2 Sensor 1	Yes
P1336	CKP System Variation Not Learned	Yes
P1351	IC Circuit Open	Yes
P1352	Bypass Circuit Open	Yes
P1361	IC Circuit Not Toggling	Yes
P1362	Bypass Circuit Shorted	Yes
P1374	3X Reference Circuit	Yes
P1380	EBCM DTC Rough Data Unstable	No
P1381	Misfire Detected No EBCM/PCM Serial Data	No
P1404	EGR Valve Closed Pintle Position	Yes
P1441	EVAP System Flow During Non-Purge	Yes
P1554	Cruise Control Status Circuit	No
P1626	Theft Deterrent System Fuel Enable CKT	No
P1629	Theft Deterrent Crank Signal Malfunction	No
P1635	5 Volt Reference (A) Circuit	Yes
P1639	5 Volt Reference (B) Circuit	Yes

89634G93

Fig. 87 Engine diagnostic trouble codes (3 of 4)—1994 vehicles with a 16-pin DLC and all 1995–99 vehicles

DTC	Description	Illuminate MIL
P0172	Fuel Trim System Rich Bank 1	Yes
P0174	Fuel Trim System Lean Bank 2	Yes
P0175	Fuel Trim System Rich Bank 2	Yes
P0201	Injector 1 Control Circuit	Yes
P0202	Injector 2 Control Circuit	Yes
P0203	Injector 3 Control Circuit	Yes
P0204	Injector 4 Control Circuit	Yes
P0205	Injector 5 Control Circuit	Yes
P0206	Injector 6 Control Circuit	Yes
P0300	Engine Misfire Detected	Yes
P0325	Knock Sensor System	Yes
P0327	Knock Sensor Circuit Bank 1	No
P0332	Knock Sensor Circuit Bank 2	No
P0336	18X Reference Signal Circuit	Yes
P0341	CMP Sensor Circuit Performance	Yes
P0401	EGR System Flow Insufficient	Yes
P0403	EGR Solenoid Control Circuit	Yes
P0404	EGR System Performance	Yes
P0405	EGR Pintle Position Circuit Low Voltage	Yes
P0420	TWC System Low Efficiency	Yes
P0440	EVAP System	Yes
P0442	EVAP Control System Small Leak Detected	Yes
P0446	EVAP Canister Vent Blocked	Yes
P0452	Fuel Tank Pressure Sensor Circuit Low Voltage	Yes
P0453	Fuel Tank Pressure Sensor Circuit High Voltage	Yes
P0500	Vehicle Speed Sensor Circuit	Yes
P0506	Idle Control System Low RPM	Yes
P0507	Idle Control System High RPM	Yes
P0530	A/C Refrigerant Pressure Sensor Circuit	No
P0560	System Voltage	No
P0601	PCM Memory	Yes
P0602	PCM Not Programmed	Yes
P0704	Clutch Anticipate Switch Circuit	No
P0705	Trans Range Switch Circuit	No
P0706	Trans Range Switch Performance	No
P0711	Transaxle Fluid Temperature (TFT) Sensor Circuit	No
P0712	Transaxle Fluid Temperature (TFT) Sensor Circuit - Low Signal.	No
P0713	Transaxle Fluid Temperature (TFT) Sensor Circuit - High Signal Voltage.	No
P0716	Automatic Transmission Input (Shaft) Speed Sensor Circuit Performance.	Yes
P0717	Automatic Transmission Input (Shaft) Speed Sensor No Input. Refer	Yes

89634G92

Fig. 86 Engine diagnostic trouble codes (2 of 4)—1994 vehicles with a 16-pin DLC and all 1995–99 vehicles

DTC	Description	Illuminate MIL
P1641	A/C Relay Control Circuit	No
P1651	Fan 1 Relay Control Circuit	Yes
P1652	Fan 2 Relay Control Circuit	Yes
P1653	Fuel Level Output Control Circuit	No
P1662	Cruise Control Inhibit Control Circuit	No
P1663	Generator Lamp Control Circuit	No
P1665	EVAP Vent Solenoid Control Circuit	Yes
P1671	MIL Control Circuit	No
P1672	Low Engine Oil Level Lamp Control Circuit	No
P1676	EVAP Canister Purge Solenoid Control CKT	Yes
P1810	Automatic Transmission Fluid Pressure Manual Valve Position Switch Malfunction.	Yes
P1811	Maximum Adapt and Long Shift.	No
P1860	Torque Converter Clutch PWM Solenoid Circuit.	Yes
P1887	TCC Release Switch Malfunction.	Yes

89634G94

Fig. 88 Engine diagnostic trouble codes (4 of 4)—1994 vehicles with a 16-pin DLC and all 1995–99 vehicles

manufacturer's instructions on how to connect the scan tool to the vehicle and how to retrieve the codes.

Clearing Codes

Stored fault codes may be erased from memory at any time by using a suitable scan tool, or removing power from the ECM for at least 30 seconds. It may be necessary to clear stored codes during diagnosis to check for any recurrence during a test drive, but the stored codes must be written down when retrieved. The codes may still be required for subsequent troubleshooting. Whenever a repair is complete, the stored codes must be erased and the vehicle test driven to confirm correct operation and repair.

☀☀ WARNING

The ignition switch must be OFF any time power is disconnected or restored to the ECM. Severe damage may result if this precaution is not observed.

When using a scan tool to clear the codes, make sure to follow all of the instructions provided by the manufacturer.

Depending on the electrical distribution of the particular vehicle, power to the ECM may be disconnected by removing the ECM fuse in the fuse box, disconnecting the in-line fuse holder near the positive battery terminal or disconnecting the ECM power lead at the battery terminal. Disconnecting the negative battery cable to clear codes is not recommended as this will also clear other memory data in the vehicle such as radio presets.

VACUUM DIAGRAMS

▶ See Figures 89 thru 104

Following are vacuum diagrams for most of the engine and emissions package combinations covered by this manual. Because vacuum circuits will vary based on various engine and vehicle options, always refer first to the vehicle emission control information label, if present. Should the label be missing, or should the vehicle be equipped with a different engine from the vehicle's original equipment, refer to the following diagrams for the same or similar configuration.

If you wish to obtain a replacement emissions label, most manufacturers make the labels available for purchase. The labels can usually be ordered from a local dealer.

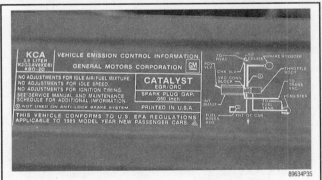

89634P35

Fig. 89 The VECI sticker, affixed to the radiator panel, includes important emission information regarding your vehicle

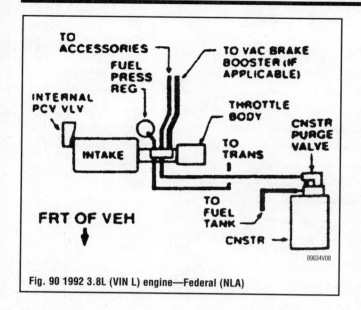

Fig. 90 1992 3.8L (VIN L) engine—Federal (NLA)

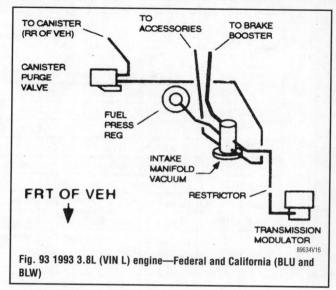

Fig. 93 1993 3.8L (VIN L) engine—Federal and California (BLU and BLW)

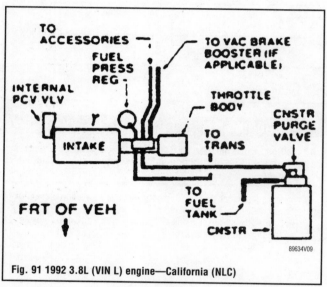

Fig. 91 1992 3.8L (VIN L) engine—California (NLC)

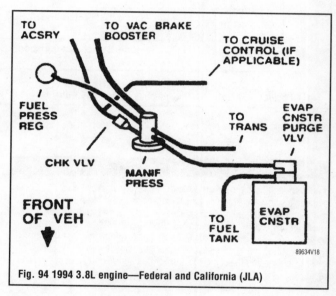

Fig. 94 1994 3.8L engine—Federal and California (JLA)

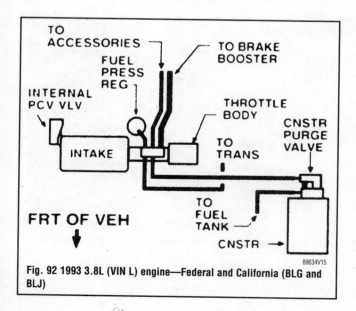

Fig. 92 1993 3.8L (VIN L) engine—Federal and California (BLG and BLJ)

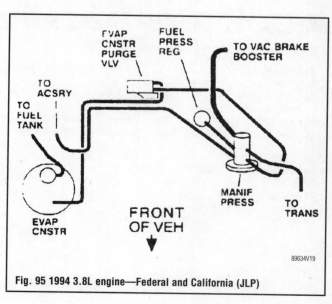

Fig. 95 1994 3.8L engine—Federal and California (JLP)

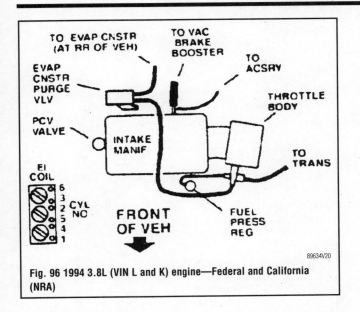

Fig. 96 1994 3.8L (VIN L and K) engine—Federal and California (NRA)

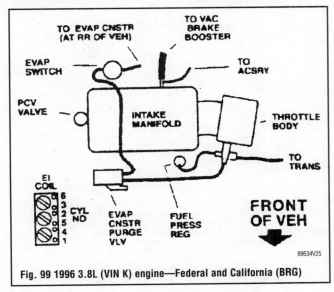

Fig. 99 1996 3.8L (VIN K) engine—Federal and California (BRG)

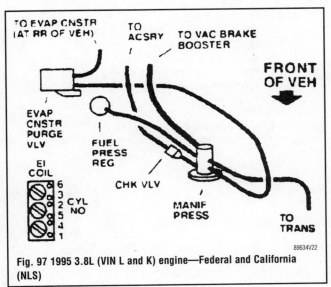

Fig. 97 1995 3.8L (VIN L and K) engine—Federal and California (NLS)

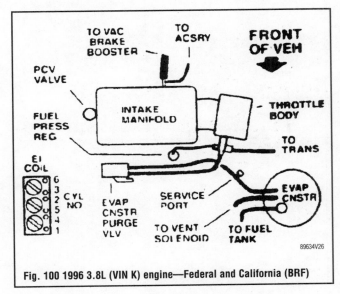

Fig. 100 1996 3.8L (VIN K) engine—Federal and California (BRF)

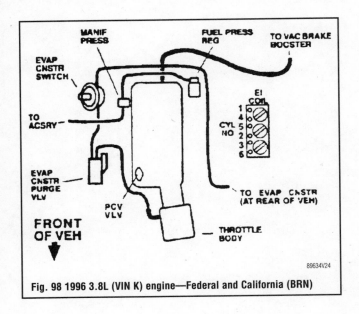

Fig. 98 1996 3.8L (VIN K) engine—Federal and California (BRN)

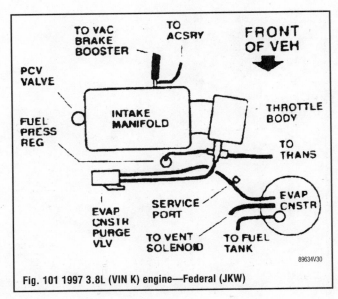

Fig. 101 1997 3.8L (VIN K) engine—Federal (JKW)

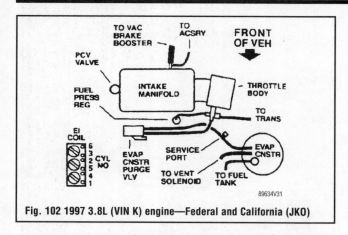

Fig. 102 1997 3.8L (VIN K) engine—Federal and California (JKO)

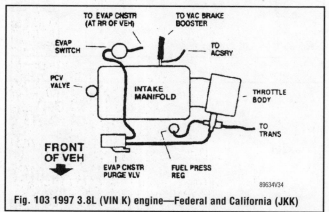

Fig. 103 1997 3.8L (VIN K) engine—Federal and California (JKK)

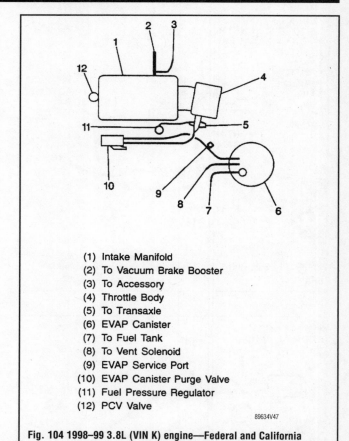

(1) Intake Manifold
(2) To Vacuum Brake Booster
(3) To Accessory
(4) Throttle Body
(5) To Transaxle
(6) EVAP Canister
(7) To Fuel Tank
(8) To Vent Solenoid
(9) EVAP Service Port
(10) EVAP Canister Purge Valve
(11) Fuel Pressure Regulator
(12) PCV Valve

Fig. 104 1998–99 3.8L (VIN K) engine—Federal and California

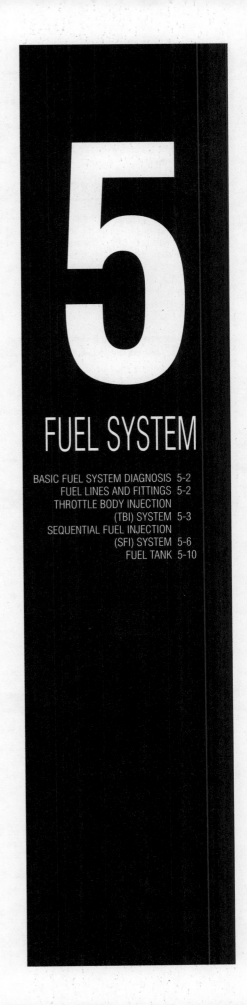

5

FUEL SYSTEM

BASIC FUEL SYSTEM DIAGNOSIS

When there is a problem starting or driving a vehicle, two of the most important checks involve the ignition and the fuel systems. The questions most mechanics attempt to answer first, "is there spark?" and "is there fuel?" will often lead to solving most basic problems. For ignition system diagnosis and testing, please refer to the information on engine electrical components and ignition systems found earlier in this manual. If the ignition system checks out (there is spark), then you must determine if the fuel system is operating properly (is there fuel?).

FUEL LINES AND FITTINGS

The fuel supply is stored in the fuel tank. An electric fuel pump, attached to the fuel sender assembly (inside the fuel tank) pumps fuel through an in-line filter to the throttle body unit or fuel rail. The pump is designed to provide fuel at a pressure above the regulated pressure needed by the throttle body unit or fuel rail. Unused fuel is returned to the fuel tank by a separate pipe.

Unleaded fuel must be used with all gasoline engines for proper emission control system operation. Using unleaded fuel will also decrease spark plug fouling and extend engine oil life. Leaded fuel can damage the emission control system, and its use can result in loss of emission warranty cover-age.

Quick-Connect Fittings

Some early model vehicles do not have quick-connect fuel line fittings. They use a threaded union with a hex head fitting. On these vehicles, just make sure to use a back-up wrench on the fuel lines when disconnecting them.

➡️**If your vehicle is equipped with metal quick-connect fittings, a special tool will be required to service the fittings.**

REMOVAL & INSTALLATION

▶ See Figures 1 and 2

⚜️ CAUTION

Observe all applicable safety precautions when working around fuel. Whenever servicing the fuel system, always work in a well ventilated area. Do not allow fuel spray or vapors to come in contact with a spark or open flame. Keep a dry chemical fire extinguisher near the work area. Always keep fuel in a container specifically designed for fuel storage; also, always properly seal fuel containers to avoid the possibility of fire or explosion.

1. Disconnect the negative battery cable.
2. Properly relieve the fuel system pressure.
3. If equipped, slide the dust cover back to access the fuel line fitting.

Grasp both ends of the fitting, Twist the female connector ¼ turn in each direction to loosen any dirt within the fittings. If available, use compressed air to blow out any dirt from the quick-connect fittings.

⚜️ WARNING

Safety glasses are recommended when trying to clean debris from an enclosed area with compressed air.

4. If the fittings are metal:
   a. Choose the correct size releasing tool and insert it into the female connector.
   b. Push inward to release the locking tabs.
   c. Pull the connector apart.

➡️**It may be necessary to remove rust or burrs from the male end of a quick-connect fitting. If this is the case, use an emery cloth to clean the tube by rotating the cloth in a radial motion.**

5. For plastic type fittings, which are hand releasable:
   a. Squeeze the plastic retainer release tabs.
   b. Pull the connection apart.
6. Using a clean shop towel, wipe off the male ends of the tube.

To install:

➡️**Apply a few drops of lubricant (clean engine oil), to the male end of the tube before reconnecting the fittings.**

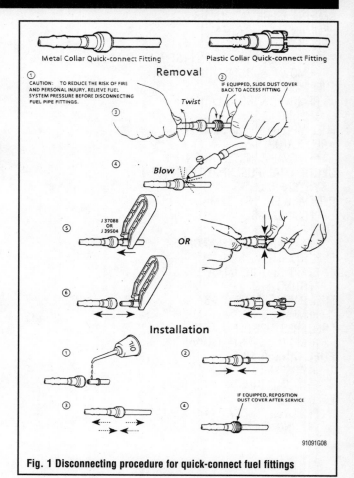

Fig. 1 Disconnecting procedure for quick-connect fuel fittings

Fig. 2 Slide the fuel line fitting release tool into the connection

7. Push the connectors together until you can hear an audible click, indicating they have locked.

8. Once installed, pull on both ends of the connection to make sure it is secure.

THROTTLE BODY INJECTION (TBI) SYSTEM

General Information

♦ **See Figure 3**

The function of the fuel metering system is to deliver the correct amount of fuel to the engine under all operating conditions. Fuel is delivered by the Throttle Body Fuel Injection (TBI) unit, which is controlled by the Powertrain Control module (PCM).

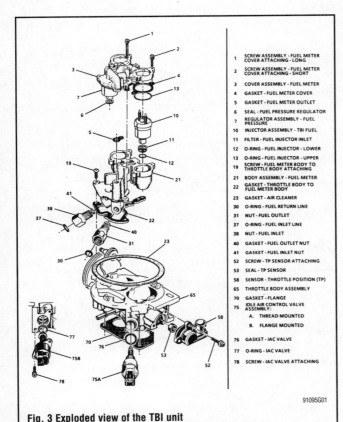

1	SCREW ASSEMBLY - FUEL METER COVER ATTACHING - LONG
2	SCREW ASSEMBLY - FUEL METER COVER ATTACHING - SHORT
3	COVER ASSEMBLY - FUEL METER
4	GASKET - FUEL METER COVER
5	GASKET - FUEL METER OUTLET
6	SEAL - FUEL PRESSURE REGULATOR
7	REGULATOR ASSEMBLY - FUEL PRESSURE
10	INJECTOR ASSEMBLY - TBI FUEL
11	FILTER - FUEL INJECTOR INLET
12	O-RING - FUEL INJECTOR - LOWER
13	O-RING - FUEL INJECTOR - UPPER
19	SCREW - FUEL METER BODY TO THROTTLE BODY ATTACHING
21	BODY ASSEMBLY - FUEL METER
22	GASKET - THROTTLE BODY TO FUEL METER BODY
23	GASKET - AIR CLEANER
30	O-RING - FUEL RETURN LINE
31	NUT - FUEL OUTLET
37	O-RING - FUEL INLET LINE
38	NUT - FUEL INLET
40	GASKET - FUEL OUTLET NUT
41	GASKET - FUEL INLET NUT
52	SCREW - TP SENSOR ATTACHING
53	SEAL - TP SENSOR
58	SENSOR - THROTTLE POSITION (TP)
65	THROTTLE BODY ASSEMBLY
70	GASKET - FLANGE
75	IDLE AIR CONTROL VALVE ASSEMBLY:
	A. THREAD MOUNTED
	B. FLANGE MOUNTED
76	GASKET - IAC VALVE
77	O-RING - IAC VALVE
78	SCREW - IAC VALVE ATTACHING

91095G01

Fig. 3 Exploded view of the TBI unit

Relieving Fuel System Pressure

✳✳ CAUTION

Observe all applicable safety precautions when working around fuel. Whenever servicing the fuel system, always work in a well ventilated area. Do not allow fuel spray or vapors to come in contact with a spark or open flame. Keep a dry chemical fire extinguisher near the work area. Always keep fuel in a container specifically designed for fuel storage; also, always properly seal fuel containers to avoid the possibility of fire or explosion.

1. Disconnect negative battery terminal to avoid possible fuel discharge if an accidental attempt is made to start the engine.

2. Loosen fuel filler cap to relieve tank vapor pressure.

3. The internal constant bleed feature of the TBI relieves fuel pump system pressure when the engine is turned **OFF**. Therefore, no further pressure relief procedure is required, other than allowing 5–10 minutes for system pressure to dissipate.

9. If equipped, slide the fuel fitting dust cover back into place.

10. Connect the negative battery cable.

11. Cycle the ignition key **ON** for two seconds, then turn it **OFF**. Check the connections for any leaks.

Throttle Body Injection Unit

REMOVAL & INSTALLATION

♦ **See Figure 4**

✳✳ CAUTION

Observe all applicable safety precautions when working around fuel. Whenever servicing the fuel system, always work in a well ventilated area. Do not allow fuel spray or vapors to come in contact with a spark or open flame. Keep a dry chemical fire extinguisher near the work area. Always keep fuel in a container specifically designed for fuel storage; also, always properly seal fuel containers to avoid the possibility of fire or explosion.

➡It is recommended to replace all gaskets and O-rings on disconnected fuel system components. Read the procedure first to ensure that you will have the necessary parts to complete the repair.

1. Disconnect the negative battery cable.
2. Properly relieve the fuel system pressure.
3. Remove the air cleaner.
4. Unplug the electrical connectors from the idle air control valve, throttle position sensor and fuel injectors.
5. Disengage the injector wiring harness from the throttle body.
6. Disconnect the throttle and the transmission control cables from the throttle body.
7. If equipped, disconnect the cruise control cable.
8. Remove the cables from the support bracket and/or remove the cable support bracket from the throttle body.
9. Label and disconnect the vacuum and PCV hoses from the throttle body.
10. Place a rag under the fuel line-to-throttle body connections (to catch any excess fuel), then disconnect the fuel lines from the throttle body.

➡Use a back-up wrench on the TBI fuel nuts to prevent them from turning.

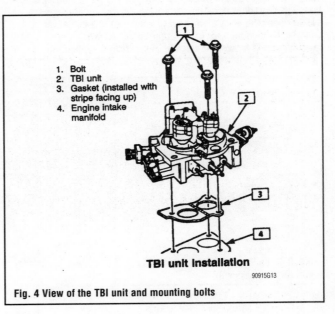

1. Bolt
2. TBI unit
3. Gasket (installed with stripe facing up)
4. Engine intake manifold

TBI unit Installation

90915G13

Fig. 4 View of the TBI unit and mounting bolts

11. Remove the fuel line O-rings and discard.

12. Remove the TBI attaching bolts and nuts and remove the TBI unit. Discard the gasket.

To install:

13. Place a cloth in the intake manifold to prevent dirt from entering the engine.

14. Thoroughly clean the gasket mounting surfaces using a gasket scraper, if necessary. Remove the Cloth.

15. Position a new gasket onto the mounting flange. Install the throttle body and mounting bolts. Torque the throttle body-to-intake manifold nuts/bolts to 18 lbs. ft. (25 Nm).

16. Install new O-rings onto the fuel lines and connect them to the throttle body. Use a back-up wrench and tighten the nuts to 20 lbs. ft. (27 Nm).

17. Connect the vacuum hoses to the throttle body.

18. If removed, install the cable support bracket and tighten the screws to 88 lbs. in..

19. Install the throttle, transmission control and, if equipped, cruise control cables.

20. Plug in the electrical connectors to the idle air control valve, throttle position sensor and fuel injectors. Make sure all the connectors are fully seated and latched.

21. Connect the negative battery cable.

22. Turn the ignition switch to the **ON** position for 2 seconds then turn to the **OFF** position for 10 seconds. Again turn the switch to the **ON** position and check for leaks.

23. With the engine **OFF**, depress the accelerator pedal to the floor and release it. Ensure that the pedal returns freely.

24. Install the air cleaner assembly.

25. If necessary, reset the IAC valve pintle position as follows:

   a. Depress the accelerator pedal slightly.

   b. Start and run the engine for 3 seconds.

   c. Turn the ignition OFF for 10 seconds.

   d. Restart the engine and check for proper idle operation,

Fuel Injectors

REMOVAL & INSTALLATION

▸ See Figures 5, 6 and 7

✳✳ CAUTION

Observe all applicable safety precautions when working around fuel. Whenever servicing the fuel system, always work in a well ventilated area. Do not allow fuel spray or vapors to come in contact with a spark or open flame. Keep a dry chemical fire extinguisher near the work area. Always keep fuel in a container specifically designed for fuel storage; also, always properly seal fuel containers to avoid the possibility of fire or explosion.

✳✳ WARNING

When removing the injector(s), be careful not to damage the electrical connector pins (on top of the injector), the injector fuel filter and the nozzle. The fuel injector is serviced as a complete assembly ONLY, it is an electrical component and should not be immersed in any kind of cleaner.

➡**It is recommended to replace all gaskets and O-rings on disconnected fuel system components. Read the procedure first to ensure that you will have the necessary parts to complete the repair.**

1. Disconnect the negative battery terminal from the battery. Remove the air cleaner.

2. Properly relieve the fuel system pressure.

3. Unplug the electrical connectors at the injectors by squeezing the two tabs together and pulling it straight up.

4. Remove the fuel meter cover.

➡**When removing the fuel meter cover screws, note the location of the two short screws.**

5. Using a small pry tool and support bar, carefully pry up on the injector until it is free from the fuel meter body.

6. Remove the lower small O-ring from the nozzle end of the injector and discard.

7. Discard the fuel meter cover gasket.

8. Remove the upper, large O-ring from the top of the injector cavity and discard.

To install:

9. Lubricate the new upper (large) O-ring with clean engine oil, and install in the counterbore of the fuel meter body. Make sure it is seated properly.

✳✳ CAUTION

When installing an injector, install the upper O-ring before the injector to ensure proper seating of the O-ring. Reversing these steps could result in a fuel leak and possible fire.

10. Lubricate the new lower (small) O-ring with clean engine oil, and install on the nozzle end of the injector. Push the O-ring on far enough to contact the filter.

11. Install the fuel injector as follows:

   a. Align the raised lug on the injector base with the notch on the fuel meter body cavity.

   b. Push down on the injector until it is fully seated in the fuel meter body.

➡**The electrical terminals of the injector should be parallel with the throttle shaft.**

12. Install the fuel meter cover assembly.

13. Install the electrical connectors to the injectors.

14. Connect the negative battery cable.

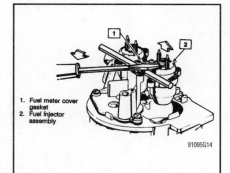

1. Fuel meter cover gasket
2. Fuel injector assembly

91095G14

Fig. 5 Carefully pry the injector from the throttle body assembly

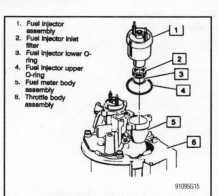

1. Fuel injector assembly
2. Fuel injector inlet filter
3. Fuel injector lower O-ring
4. Fuel injector upper O-ring
5. Fuel meter body assembly
6. Throttle body assembly

91095G15

Fig. 6 Exploded view of the injector and O-rings

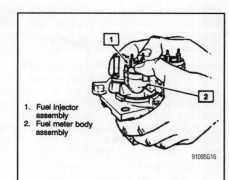

1. Fuel injector assembly
2. Fuel meter body assembly

91095G16

Fig. 7 Firmly press the injector into the throttle body

15. Turn the ignition switch to the **ON** position for 2 seconds then turn to the **OFF** position for 10 seconds. Again turn the switch to the **ON** position and check for leaks.

16. Install the air cleaner assembly.

TESTING

✷✷ CAUTION

Observe all applicable safety precautions when working around fuel. Whenever servicing the fuel system, always work in a well ventilated area. Do not allow fuel spray or vapors to come in contact with a spark or open flame. Keep a dry chemical fire extinguisher near the work area. Always keep fuel in a container specifically designed for fuel storage; also, always properly seal fuel containers to avoid the possibility of fire or explosion.

1. Ensure that the vehicle's ignition system is operating properly.
2. Perform a fuel pump test to ensure that fuel is getting to the injectors.
3. Remove the air cleaner assembly.
4. Have an assistant crank the engine and observe the fuel injectors.
5. There should be a fuel spray below the injectors, into the throttle body.
6. If there is no fuel spray coming from the injectors, perform the following steps:
   a. Turn the ignition switch **OFF**.
   b. Detach the electrical connector(s) from the fuel injector(s).
   c. Attach a suitable test light to the A terminal of each harness and to ground.
   d. Crank the engine and observe the test light.
   e. If the light blinks, the injector is probably faulty. Replace the injector with a known good one and repeat the tests.
   f. If the light fails to blink, there is a problem with the wiring harness or engine control module.
7. If fuel sprays from the injector, perform the following steps:
   a. Turn the ignition **OFF**.
   b. Detach the electrical connector(s) from the injector(s).
   c. Crank the engine and observe any fuel spray or drip from the injector.
   d. If there is no fuel spray or drips from the injectors, the injectors are fine.
   e. If fuel spray or drips are visible, the injectors are leaking internally and must be replaced.

Fuel Meter Cover/Pressure Regulator

REMOVAL & INSTALLATION

▶ See Figure 8

➡The fuel meter cover and pressure regulator are serviced as a complete assembly only.

✷✷ CAUTION

Do not remove the screws securing the pressure regulator to the fuel meter cover. The regulator includes a spring, which if released,

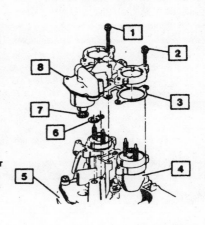

1. Fuel meter cover attaching screw assembly (long)
2. Fuel meter cover attaching screw assembly (short)
3. Fuel meter cover gasket
4. Fuel meter body assembly
5. Throttle body assembly
6. Fuel meter outlet gasket
7. Pressure regulator seal
8. Fuel meter cover assembly

91095G17

Fig. 8 Exploded view of the fuel meter cover/pressure regulator assembly and related components

could cause personal injury. Disassembly might also result in a fuel leak between the diaphragm and the regulator container.

1. Disconnect the negative battery cable.
2. Properly relieve the fuel system pressure.
3. Remove the air cleaner assembly.
4. Unplug the electrical connectors at the injectors by squeezing the two tabs together and pulling it straight up.
5. Remove the fuel meter cover attaching screws and remove the fuel meter cover.

➡When removing the fuel meter cover screws, note the location of the two short screws.

To install:

6. Clean the gasket sealing surfaces and install a new pressure regulator dust seal, fuel meter outlet passage gasket and cover gasket.

✷✷ WARNING

Do not immerse the fuel meter cover (with pressure regulator) in cleaner, as damage to the pressure regulator diaphragm could occur.

7. Install the fuel meter cover. Apply Loctite® 262 or equivalent to the screw threads and install and torque the screws to 27 inch lbs. (3.0 Nm).

➡Install the short screws next to the injectors.

8. Reconnect the injector electrical plugs.
9. Connect the negative battery cable.
10. Turn the ignition switch to the **ON** position for 2 seconds then turn to the **OFF** position for 10 seconds. Again turn the switch to the **ON** position and check for leaks.
11. Install the air cleaner assembly.

SEQUENTIAL FUEL INJECTION (SFI) SYSTEM

Relieving Fuel System Pressure

1. Disconnect the negative battery terminal to avoid possible fuel discharge if an accidental attempt is made to start the engine.
2. Loosen the fuel filler cap to relieve tank vapor pressure.
3. Connect a suitable fuel gauge to the fuel pressure connection. Wrap a shop towel around the fitting while connecting the gauge to avoid spillage.
4. Install the bleed hose into an approved container and open the valve to bleed the system pressure. Fuel connections are now safe for servicing.
5. Drain any fuel remaining in the gauge into an approved container.

Throttle Body

REMOVAL & INSTALLATION

♦ See Figures 9, 10 and 11

1. Drain and recycle the engine coolant.
2. Disconnect the air intake tube from the throttle body.
3. Disconnect and remove the throttle cable, and any other cables, from the throttle body. Remove the throttle cable bracket.
4. Unplug the Idle Air Control (IAC), Idle Air Temperature (IAT), Throttle Position Sensor (TPS), and Mass Air Flow (MAF) sensor electrical connectors.
5. Remove the three nuts retaining the throttle body support to the intake and the throttle body; remove the throttle body support.

6. Remove the two nuts and the stud holding the throttle body to the intake manifold.
7. Remove the throttle body assembly.

To install:

8. Thoroughly clean the gasket surface on the intake manifold and the throttle body.
9. Install a new gasket, if necessary.
10. Install the throttle body assembly, the stud, and the two retaining nuts.
11. Tighten the retaining nuts and the stud to 11 ft. lbs. (15 Nm).
12. Install the throttle body support and retaining nuts and tighten to 11 ft. lbs. (15 Nm).
13. Install the throttle cable bracket, and the throttle and other cables.

❊❊ CAUTION

Make sure the throttle linkage does not hold the throttle open.

14. Install the IAC, IAT, TP, and MAF sensor electrical connectors.
15. Reconnect the air intake tube.
16. Refill the radiator.

Fuel Injectors

♦ See Figures 12, 13 and 14

The SFI fuel injector is a solenoid-operated device controlled by the PCM. The PCM energizes the solenoid, which opens a valve to allow fuel delivery.

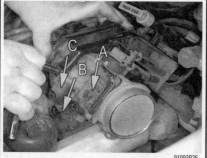

Fig. 9 Disconnect the MAF (A), TPS (B), and IAC (C) sensors, then remove the retaining bolts

91093P26

Fig. 10 Carefully pull the throttle body off of its mounting studs (arrows)

91093P27

Fig. 11 Clean the gasket mating surfaces thoroughly

91093P29

Fig. 12 This is a typical ported fuel injector with its two O-rings and retaining clip

91095P10

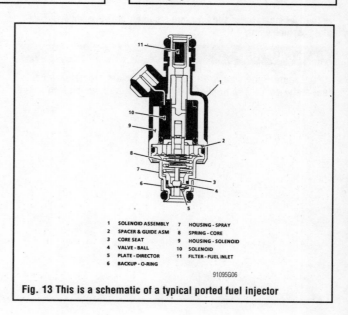

1	SOLENOID ASSEMBLY	7	HOUSING - SPRAY
2	SPACER & GUIDE ASM	8	SPRING - CORE
3	CORE SEAT	9	HOUSING - SOLENOID
4	VALVE - BALL	10	SOLENOID
5	PLATE - DIRECTOR	11	FILTER - FUEL INLET
6	BACKUP - O-RING		

91095G06

Fig. 13 This is a schematic of a typical ported fuel injector

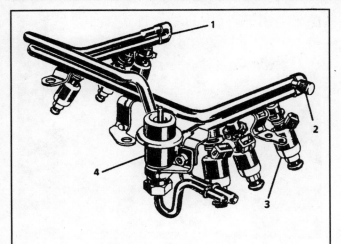

1 RAIL ASSEMBLY - MFI FUEL

2 CONNECTION ASSEMBLY - FUEL PRESSURE

3 INJECTOR ASSEMBLY - MFI FUEL

4 REGULATOR ASSEMBLY - FUEL PRESSURE

91095G07

Fig. 14 Typical fuel rail assembly for a V-6 engine shown

Fuel is injected, under pressure, in a conical spray pattern at the opening of the intake valve. Excess fuel not used by the injectors passes through the pressure regulator before being returned to the fuel tank.

The fuel injector is serviced as a complete assembly only and should never be immersed in any type of cleaner. Support the fuel rail to avoid damaging other components while removing the injector. Be sure to note that different injectors are calibrated for different flow rates. When replacing fuel injectors, be sure to get an exact replacement.

REMOVAL & INSTALLATION

▶ See Figures 15 thru 22

➡ The fuel injector is serviced as a complete assembly only. If the injector fails the leak test, the engine oil may be contaminated with fuel. It would be recommended to change the oil and filter.

1. Properly relieve the fuel system pressure.
2. Disconnect the negative battery cable.
3. Remove the fuel rail from the vehicle; remove the fuel feed and return pipes from the fuel rail.
4. Remove the fuel injector retaining clips, separate the injector from the fuel rail.

➡ When ordering new fuel injectors, be sure to order the correct injector for the applications being serviced. The fuel injector lower O-ring (brown) uses a nylon collar, called the O-ring backup, to properly position the O-ring on the injector. Be sure to reinstall the O-ring backup, or the sealing O-ring may move on the injector when installing the fuel rail and result in a possible vacuum leak and driveability complaints will occur.

To install:

5. Install the new injectors using new O-rings. Coat the O-rings with clean engine oil.
6. Install the injector retaining clips.
7. Install the fuel rail, injectors are retained by the fuel rail.
8. Plug in the electrical connectors to the injectors.

91095P01

Fig. 15 Unplug the injector harness from the injector

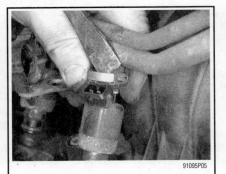

91095P18

Fig. 16 Remove the fuel rail hold-down bolts . . .

91095P03

Fig. 17 . . . which can be difficult to see under layers of accumulated dirt

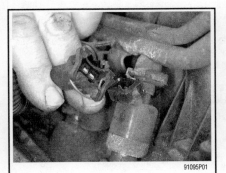

91095P04

Fig. 18 Using an even force, raise the fuel rail, pulling the injectors from their mounting holes (arrows) in the manifold

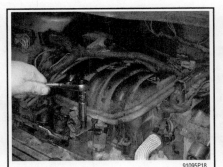

91095P05

Fig. 19 Using a small pry tool, pry the injector lock from the injector

91095P06

Fig. 20 Gently pull the injector from the rail. A slight twisting motion may help ease removal

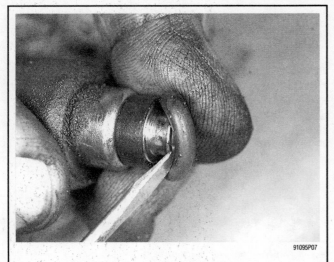

Fig. 21 The injector O-rings can be removed easily

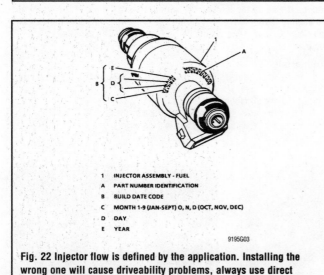

1 INJECTOR ASSEMBLY - FUEL
A PART NUMBER IDENTIFICATION
B BUILD DATE CODE
C MONTH 1-9 (JAN-SEPT) O, N, D (OCT, NOV, DEC)
D DAY
E YEAR

9195G03

Fig. 22 Injector flow is defined by the application. Installing the wrong one will cause driveability problems, always use direct replacement parts

TESTING

▶ See Figure 23

The injector circuit can be can be tested by installing a "noid light", into the injector electrical harness connector. The light confirms a voltage feed when it flashes, as though the injector was firing.

1. Start the engine and listen to each fuel injector individually for a clicking sound.

2. Turn the engine **OFF** and detach the electrical connector from the injector that did not have a clicking sound.

3. Check the injector for continuity across the terminals. Compare the injector the resistance value to a known good injector. The readings should be similar, if so proceed to the next test. If readings differ greatly, replace the injector.

4. Check between each injector terminal and ground. If continuity exists, replace the injector.

5. Detach the fuel injector connector and connect a noid light to the wiring harness connector. Crank the engine, while observing the light. Perform this test on at least two injectors before proceeding. If the light does not flash, check the injector power supply and ground control circuitry. If the light flashes, proceed to the next step.

6. If the light flashes remove the fuel rail from the engine and following the procedure given, check the injector operation.

Fig. 23 Use an ohmmeter to check injector resistance. Compare readings with a known good injector

a. Using mechanic's wire, secure the injector to the fuel rail.
b. Place a clear plastic container around each injector.

✳✳ CAUTION

Before performing this test, all fuel safety precaution must be followed. Make certain the container is approved to handle fuel and is securely positioned around the injector. Do not use a glass container. Glass containers can be easily damaged, resulting in a serious fire hazard.

c. With the help of an assistant or using a remote starter button, crank the engine for 15 seconds while observing the injector operation. The injector should produce a cone shaped spray pattern and all containers should contain equal amounts of fuel.

d. Once the cranking test is complete, leave the fuel rail pressurized and observe the injectors for leakage.

7. Replace any injector that leaks or fails to provide a good spray pattern.

Fuel Rail Assembly

▶ See Figures 24 and 25

When servicing the fuel rail assembly, precautions must be taken to prevent dirt and other contaminants from entering the fuel passages. It is recommended that fittings are capped and holes plugged during servicing.

REMOVAL & INSTALLATION

1. Properly relieve the fuel system pressure.
2. Clean the fuel rail assembly and connections. Use a spray type (carburetor) cleaner. Never immerse the fuel rail or components in a liquid solvent.
3. Remove the fuel feed and return pipes from the fuel rail.
4. Remove the vacuum line from the pressure regulator.
5. Disconnect the injector electrical connectors.
6. Remove the fuel rail hold-down bolts.
7. Pull with equal force on both sides of the rail to remove it.
To install:
8. O-rings must be replaced on all components that are replaced.
9. Lightly oil the injector O-rings with clean motor oil.
10. Place the rail assembly on the manifold and seat the injectors by hand.
11. Torque the fuel rail hold down bolts to 22 ft. lbs. (30Nm).
12. Install the fuel feed and return lines by pushing the pipes onto the fuel rail tubes.
13. Reconnect the fuel injector electrical connectors, and plug in the vacuum line to the pressure regulator.

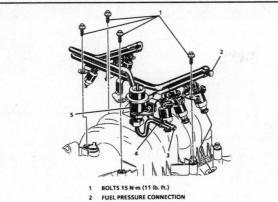

1 BOLTS 15 N·m (11 lb. ft.)
2 FUEL PRESSURE CONNECTION
3 FUEL FEED
4 FUEL RETURN
5 FUEL PRESSURE REGULATOR

91095G08

Fig. 24 View of the fuel rail and pressure regulator assemblies mounted on the intake manifold

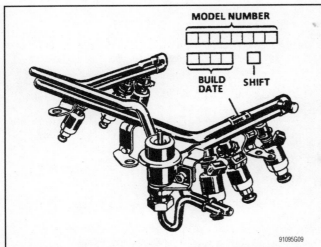

MODEL NUMBER

BUILD DATE   SHIFT

91095G09

Fig. 25 Note the fuel rail identification plate. When replacing parts you may need the numbers for a replacement part

Fuel Pressure Regulator

REMOVAL & INSTALLATION

▶ **See Figures 26 and 27**

1. Bleed the fuel pressure from the fuel system.
2. Clean the dirt from the pressure regulator assembly.
3. Remove the fuel return pipe from the return tube by squeezing the tab and pulling the pipe off.
4. Disconnect the vacuum line from the regulator.
5. Remove the regulator attaching screw from the bracket.
6. Pull with an even force to remove the pressure regulator..
7. Cover or plug the regulator housing fuel outlet to prevent contamination.
8. Remove the fuel return tube assembly from the pressure regulator

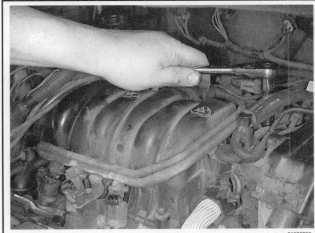

91093P23

Fig. 26 Remove the hold-down bolts for the fuel regulator, located towards the back of the engine compartment

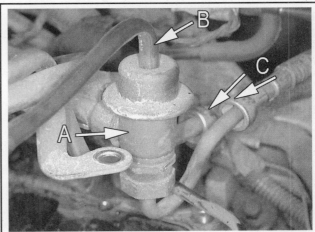

91095P14

Fig. 27 View of the fuel pressure regulator (A), vacuum hose (B) and fuel feed/return lines with quick connect fittings (C)

➡If the fuel pressure regulator is to be reinstalled, inspect the filter screen for contamination. If contaminated, remove and discard.

To install:
9. If the pressure regulator is not to be replaced with a new one, both O-rings must be replaced.
10. Lubricate both of the O-rings lightly with clean motor oil.
11. Install the fuel return tubes assembly to the pressure regulator, and tighten the tube nut to 13 ft. lbs. (17 Nm).
12. Install the filter screen into the fuel rail, and seat the regulator with an even pressure.
13. Install the regulator attaching screw.

✷✷ CAUTION

Compressed air must never be used to test or clean a pressure regulator. If needed, the filter screen should be cleaned with gasoline. The pressure regulator should not be immersed in solvent.

FUEL TANK

Tank Assembly

REMOVAL & INSTALLATION

♦ See Figures 28 and 29

1. Disconnect the negative battery cable.
2. Relieve the fuel system pressure.
3. Block the front wheels and raise and support the rear of the vehicle safely. Make sure the rear is high enough to accommodate the removal of the fuel cell.
4. Loosen the fuel filler neck connecting tube clamp at the tank.
5. Wrap a shop towel around the fuel filter neck connecting tube and slowly remove the fuel filler neck connecting tube from the fuel tank.
6. Position a siphon hose into the fuel tank through the fuel filler opening. Place the other end into an approved container with enough capacity to hold the fuel in the tank. Siphon the fuel.
7. Raise the vehicle to gain access to the fuel tank. Make sure the vehicle is safely supported.
8. Disconnect the tail pipe hanger attaching bolt.
9. Remove the muffler hanger attaching bolts and remove the muffler hanger.

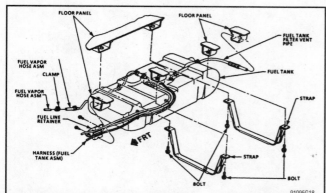

Fig. 28 Exploded view of the fuel tank mounting and related components

91095G18

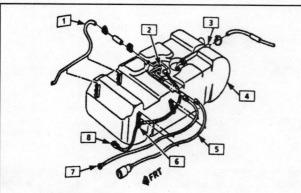

1. Fuel tank vapor line
2. Fuel level meter assembly
3. Fuel tank vent line
4. Fuel tank
5. Fuel feed line
6. Fuel tank mounting clips
7. Fuel return line
8. Fuel level meter electrical connection

91095G19

Fig. 29 View of the fuel tank hoses and electrical connections

10. Loosen the converter hanger attaching nuts.
11. Remove the two heat shield attaching screws and note the position for reassembly.
12. Support the exhaust and move the heat shield to gain the access to the right side of the fuel tank retaining strap attaching bolts.
13. Remove the in-line fuel filter body clips.

➡If the nylon fuel feed or return lines becomes kinked, and cannot be straightened, they must be replaced. Do not attempt to repair sections of the nylon fuel lines.

14. Disconnect the quick-connect fitting at the fuel filter, and return line fitting.
15. Disconnect the fuel tank electrical connector.
16. Disconnect the vapor hose at the fuel tank.
17. Disconnect the vent hose at the fuel tank.
18. With the aid of an assistant, support the fuel tank, remove the left and right tank retaining strap attaching bolts, and remove the tank.
19. As necessary, remove the fuel sending unit (which includes the fuel pump), as outlined, in this section.

To install:

20. If the fuel tank is replaced, transfer the fuel feed and return lines from the mounting clips, the vapor hose from the mounting clips and the vent hose from the vent hose fitting.
21. Check the fuel filler neck for cracks and holes and replace as necessary.
22. Install the fuel sending unit.
23. With the aid of an assistant, position and support the fuel tank and install the left and right tank retaining strap attaching bolts and tighten to 18 ft. lbs.
24. Connect the vent and vapor hoses.
25. Connect the fuel sending unit electrical connector.
26. Connect the quick-connect fittings as outlined.
27. Position the fuel sending unit electrical connector and fuel return line under the in-line fuel filter bracket.
28. Install the in-line fuel filter and new body clips.
29. Reposition the heat shield as noted during removal and tighten the retaining screws to 18 lbs. ft.
30. Tighten the converter hanger attaching bolts to 20 lbs. ft.
31. Install the muffler hanger and attaching bolts and tighten to 18 lbs. ft.
32. Install the tailpipe hanger attaching bolt and tighten to 20 lbs. ft.
33. Lower the vehicle, add fuel and install the fuel filler cap.
34. Connect the negative battery cable.
35. Turn the ignition switch to the **ON** position for 3 seconds, then turn to the **OFF** position for 5 seconds. Repeat this procedure two or three times to pressurize the system. Again turn the switch to the **ON** position and check for leaks.

Fuel Pump

♦ See Figure 30

There are two different electric fuel pumps used:
• A medium pressure twin turbine pump for vehicles equipped with Throttle Body Injection (TBI).
• A high pressure roller vane pump for vehicles equipped with Sequential Fuel Injection (SFI).

The fuel pump is mounted to the fuel sender assembly inside the fuel tank. The fuel is pumped to the engine at a specified flow and pressure by the fuel pump. Excess fuel is returned to the fuel tank by the return pipe. The fuel pump delivers a constant flow of fuel to the engine even during low fuel conditions and aggressive vehicle maneuvers.

❈❈ CAUTION

When working on or near the fuel tank, be sure to observe the information molded on the bottom of the tank.

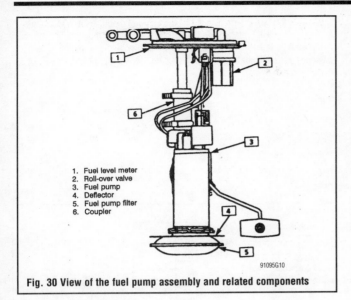

1. Fuel level meter
2. Roll-over valve
3. Fuel pump
4. Deflector
5. Fuel pump filter
6. Coupler

Fig. 30 View of the fuel pump assembly and related components

REMOVAL & INSTALLATION

▶ See Figures 31, 32 and 33

1. Disconnect the negative battery cable.
2. Properly relieve the fuel system pressure.
3. Drain and remove the fuel tank.
4. Remove the fuel sender assembly, by rotating the lock ring counterclockwise.
5. Disassemble the fuel pump strainer and the fuel pump: Note the position of the strainer in relation to the pump.
6. Support the fuel pump in one hand, and grab the strainer in the other hand.
   a. Rotate strainer in one direction and pull off pump. Discard strainer.
   b. Remove deflector.
7. Disconnect the fuel pump electrical connector.
8. Loosen the two connecting clamps, if equipped.
9. Place the fuel sender assembly upside down on the work bench.
   a. Pull the fuel pump downward to remove it from the mounting bracket, then tilt the pump outward and remove it from the connecting hose or the fuel pulse dampener.
10. It is recommended to replace the hose and clamps, if equipped.

✳✳ CAUTION

Do not run the pump unless submerged in fuel

To install:

11. Push the fuel pump assembly into the attaching hose. Attach the pump electrical wires and fasten the hose clamps to the attaching hose and around the pump body, where equipped.

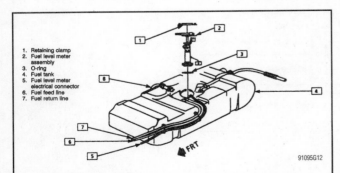

1. Retaining clamp
2. Fuel level meter assembly
3. O-ring
4. Fuel tank
5. Fuel level meter electrical connector
6. Fuel feed line
7. Fuel return line

Fig. 31 Exploded view of the fuel pump-to-tank mounting components

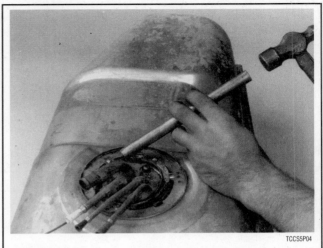

Fig. 32 Remove the fuel tank locking ring with a non-sparking (brass) punch

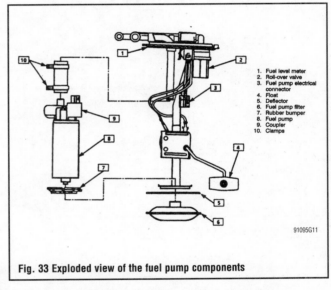

1. Fuel level meter
2. Roll-over valve
3. Fuel pump electrical connector
4. Float
5. Deflector
6. Fuel pump filter
7. Rubber bumper
8. Fuel pump
9. Coupler
10. Clamps

Fig. 33 Exploded view of the fuel pump components

12. Place the fuel tank sender and pump assembly into the fuel tank. Use a new O-ring seal during assembly.

TESTING

▶ See Figures 34, 35 and 36

1. Properly relieve the fuel system pressure and install a pressure test gauge according to the tool manufacturers instructions.
2. Turn the ignition switch to the **ON** position for 3 seconds, then turn to the **OFF** position for 5 seconds. Repeat this procedure two or three times to pressurize the system. Again turn the switch to the **ON** position.
   a. On TBI equipped vehicles, the gauge should read a static pressure of between 9 and 13 psi (6289kPa)
   b. On SFI equipped vehicles, the gauge should read a static pressure of between 41 and 47 psi (248325kPa)
   c. If not, check for a clogged fuel filter, a kinked fuel line, or an inoperative fuel pump.
3. On TBI equipped vehicles, the fuel pressure will drop after the fuel pump stops running due to a controlled bleed in the fuel system. Use of the fuel pressure gauge will determine if the fuel system pressure is enough for the engine to start and run.
4. No fuel spray from the injector indicates a faulty fuel or ignition system or no PCM control of the injector.

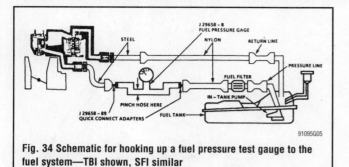

Fig. 34 Schematic for hooking up a fuel pressure test gauge to the fuel system—TBI shown, SFI similar

5. This test will determine if the ignition control module is not generating the reference pulse or if the wiring or PCM are at fault. By touching and removing a test light to B+ on CKT 430 (purple/white wire from the ignition system), a reference pulse should be generated. If the injector test light blinks, the PCM and wiring are OK.

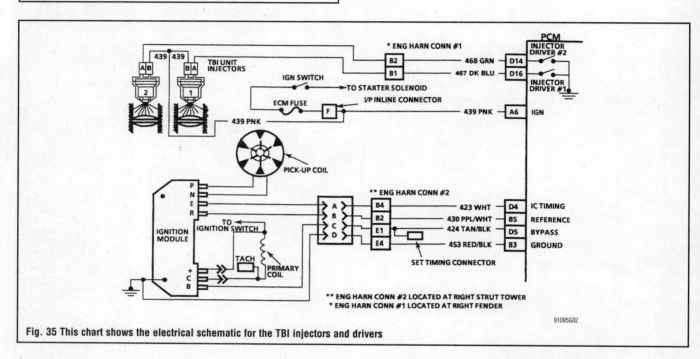

Fig. 35 This chart shows the electrical schematic for the TBI injectors and drivers

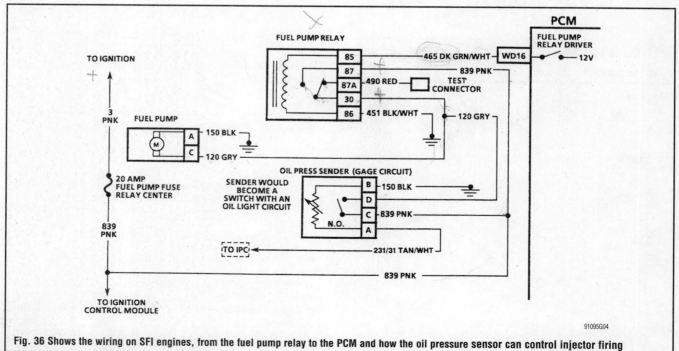

Fig. 36 Shows the wiring on SFI engines, from the fuel pump relay to the PCM and how the oil pressure sensor can control injector firing

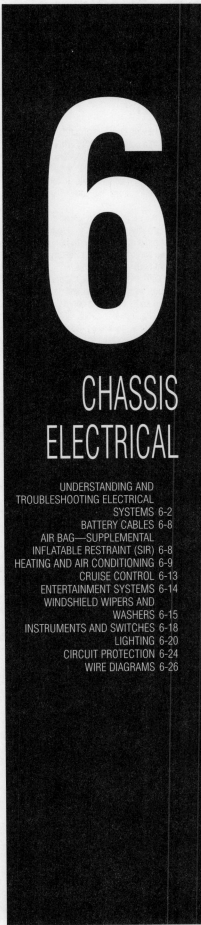

6

CHASSIS ELECTRICAL

UNDERSTANDING AND TROUBLESHOOTING ELECTRICAL SYSTEMS

Basic Electrical Theory

▶ **See Figure 1**

For any 12 volt, negative ground, electrical system to operate, the electricity must travel in a complete circuit. This simply means that current (power) from the positive (+) terminal of the battery must eventually return to the negative (-) terminal of the battery. Along the way, this current will travel through wires, fuses, switches and components. If, for any reason, the flow of current through the circuit is interrupted, the component fed by that circuit will cease to function properly.

Perhaps the easiest way to visualize a circuit is to think of connecting a light bulb (with two wires attached to it) to the battery—one wire attached to the negative (-) terminal of the battery and the other wire to the positive (+) terminal. With the two wires touching the battery terminals, the circuit would be complete and the light bulb would illuminate. Electricity would follow a path from the battery to the bulb and back to the battery. It's easy to see that with longer wires on our light bulb, it could be mounted anywhere. Further, one wire could be fitted with a switch so that the light could be turned on and off.

The normal automotive circuit differs from this simple example in two ways. First, instead of having a return wire from the bulb to the battery, the current travels through the frame of the vehicle. Since the negative (-) battery cable is attached to the frame (made of electrically conductive metal), the frame of the vehicle can serve as a ground wire to complete the circuit. Secondly, most automotive circuits contain multiple components that receive power from a single circuit. This lessens the amount of wire needed to power components on the vehicle.

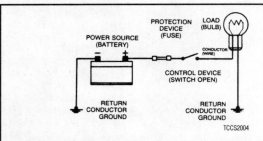

TCCS2004

Fig. 1 This example illustrates a simple circuit. When the switch is closed, power from the positive (+) battery terminal flows through the fuse and the switch, and then to the light bulb. The light illuminates and the circuit is completed through the ground wire back to the negative (-) battery terminal. In reality, the two ground points shown in the illustration are attached to the metal frame of the vehicle, which completes the circuit back to the battery

HOW DOES ELECTRICITY WORK: THE WATER ANALOGY

Electricity is the flow of electrons—the subatomic particles that constitute the outer shell of an atom. Electrons spin in an orbit around the center core of an atom. The center core is comprised of protons (positive charge) and neutrons (neutral charge). Electrons have a negative charge and balance out the positive charge of the protons. When an outside force causes the number of electrons to unbalance the charge of the protons, the electrons will split off the atom and look for another atom to balance out. If this imbalance is kept up, electrons will continue to move and an electrical flow will exist.

Many people were taught electrical theory using an analogy with water. In a comparison with water flowing through a pipe, the electrons would be the water and the wire is the pipe.

The flow of electricity can be measured much like the flow of water through a pipe. The unit of measurement used is amperes, frequently abbreviated as amps (a). You can compare amperage to the volume of water flowing through a pipe. When connected to a circuit, an ammeter will measure the actual amount of current flowing through the circuit. When relatively few electrons flow through a circuit, the amperage is low. When many electrons flow, the amperage is high.

Water pressure is measured in units such as pounds per square inch (psi);

the electrical pressure is measured in units called volts (v). When a voltmeter is connected to a circuit, it is measuring the electrical pressure.

The actual flow of electricity depends not only on voltage and amperage, but also on the resistance of the circuit. The higher the resistance, the higher the force necessary to push the current through the circuit. The standard unit for measuring resistance is an ohm. Resistance in a circuit varies depending on the amount and type of components used in the circuit. The main factors that determine resistance are:

- Material—some materials have more resistance than others. Those with high resistance are said to be insulators. Rubber materials (or rubber-like plastics) are some of the most common insulators used in vehicles as they have a very high resistance to electricity. Very low resistance materials are said to be conductors. Copper wire is among the best conductors. Silver is actually a superior conductor to copper and is used in some relay contacts, but its high cost prohibits its use as common wiring. Most automotive wiring is made of copper.
- Size—the larger the wire size being used, the less resistance the wire will have. This is why components that use large amounts of electricity usually have large wires supplying current to them.
- Length—for a given thickness of wire, the longer the wire, the greater the resistance. The shorter the wire, the less the resistance. When determining the proper wire for a circuit, both size and length must be considered to design a circuit that can handle the current needs of the component.
- Temperature—with many materials, the higher the temperature, the greater the resistance (positive temperature coefficient). Some materials exhibit the opposite trait of lower resistance with higher temperatures (negative temperature coefficient). These principles are used in many of the sensors on the engine.

OHM'S LAW

There is a direct relationship between current, voltage and resistance. The relationship between current, voltage and resistance can be summed up by a statement known as Ohm's law.

Voltage (E) is equal to amperage (I) times resistance ®: $E = I \times R$

Other forms of the formula are $R = E/I$ and $I = E/R$

In each of these formulas, E is the voltage in volts, I is the current in amps and R is the resistance in ohms. The basic point to remember is that as the resistance of a circuit goes up, the amount of current that flows in the circuit will go down, if voltage remains the same.

The amount of work that the electricity can perform is expressed as power. The unit of power is the watt (w). The relationship between power, voltage and current is expressed as:

Power (w) is equal to amperage (I) times voltage (E): $W = I \times E$

This is only true for direct current (DC) circuits; the alternating current formula is a tad different, but since the electrical circuits in most vehicles are DC types, we need not get into AC circuit theory.

Electrical Components

POWER SOURCE

Power is supplied to the vehicle by two devices: The battery and the alternator. The battery supplies electrical power during starting or during periods when the current demand of the electrical system of the vehicle exceeds the output capacity of the alternator. The alternator supplies electrical current when the engine is running. Not only does the alternator supply the current needs of the vehicle, but also it recharges the battery.

The Battery

In most modern vehicles, the battery is a lead/acid electrochemical device consisting of six two volt subsections (cells) connected in series, so that the unit is capable of producing approximately 12 volts of electrical pressure. Each subsection consists of a series of positive and negative plates held a short distance apart in a solution of sulfuric acid and water.

The two types of plates are of dissimilar metals. This sets up a chemical reaction, and it is the reaction that produces current flow from the battery when its positive and negative terminals are connected to an electrical load. The power removed from the battery is replaced by the alternator, restoring the battery to its original chemical state.

The Alternator

On some vehicles, there isn't an alternator, but a generator. The difference is that an alternator supplies alternating current, which is then changed to direct current for use on the vehicle, while a generator produces direct current. Alternators tend to be more efficient and that is why they are used.

Alternators and generators are devices that consist of coils of wires wound together making big electromagnets. One group of coils spins within another set and the interaction of the magnetic fields causes a current to flow. This current is then drawn off the coils and fed into the vehicles electrical system.

GROUND

Two types of grounds are used in automotive electric circuits. Direct ground components are grounded to the frame through their mounting points. All other components use some sort of ground wire, which is attached to the frame or chassis, of the vehicle. The electrical current runs through the chassis of the vehicle and returns to the battery through the ground (-) cable; if you look, you'll see that the battery ground cable connects between the battery and the frame or chassis of the vehicle.

➡ **It should be noted that a good percentage of electrical problems could be traced to bad grounds.**

PROTECTIVE DEVICES

◆ **See Figure 2**

It is possible for large surges of current to pass through the electrical system of your vehicle. If this surge of current were to reach the load in the circuit, the surge could burn it out or severely damage it. It can also overload the wiring, causing the harness to get hot and melt the insulation. To prevent this, fuses, circuit breakers and/or fusible links are connected into the supply wires of the electrical system. These items are nothing more than a built-in weak spot in the system. When abnormal amounts of current flows through the system, these protective devices work as follows to protect the circuit:

• Fuse—when an excessive electrical current passes through a fuse, the fuse "blows" (the conductor melts) and opens the circuit, preventing the passage of current.

• Circuit Breaker—a circuit breaker is a self-repairing fuse. It will open the circuit in the same fashion as a fuse, but when the surge subsides, the circuit breaker can be reset and does not need replacement.

• Fusible Link—a fusible link (fuse link or main link) is a short length of special, high temperature insulated wire that acts as a fuse. When an excessive electrical current passes through a fusible link, the thin gauge wire inside the link melts, creating an intentional open to protect the circuit. To repair the circuit, the link must be replaced. Some newer type fusible links are housed in plug-in modules, which are simply replaced like a fuse, while older type fusible links must be cut and spliced if they melt. Since this link is very early in the electrical path, it's the first place to look if nothing on the vehicle works, yet the battery seems to be charged and is properly connected.

✳✳ CAUTION

Always replace fuses, circuit breakers and fusible links with identically rated components. Under no circumstances should a component of higher or lower amperage rating be substituted.

SWITCHES & RELAYS

◆ **See Figures 3 and 4**

Switches are used in electrical circuits to control the passage of current. The most common use is to open and close circuits between the battery and the various electric devices in the system. Switches are rated according to the amount of amperage they can handle. If a sufficient amperage rated switch is not used in a circuit, the switch could overload and cause damage.

Some electrical components, which require a large amount of current to operate use a special switch, called a relay. Since these circuits carry a large amount of current, the thickness of the wire in the circuit is also greater. If this large wire were connected from the load to the control switch, the switch would have to carry the high amperage load and the dash would be twice as large to accommodate the increased size of the wiring harness. To prevent these problems, a relay is used.

Relays are composed of a coil and a set of contacts. When the coil has a current passed though it, a magnetic field is formed and this field causes the contacts to move together, completing the circuit. Most relays are normally open, preventing current from passing through the circuit, but they can take any electrical form depending on the job they are intended to do. Relays can be considered "remote control switches." They allow a smaller current to operate devices that require higher amperages. When a small current operates the coil, a larger current is allowed to pass by the contacts. Some common circuits, which may use relays, are the horn, headlights, starter, electric fuel pump and other high draw circuits.

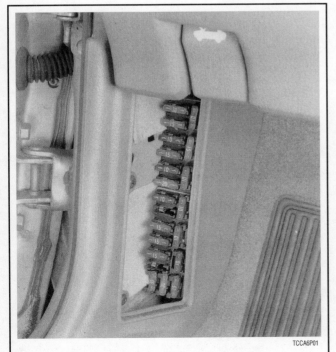

TCCA6P01

Fig. 2 Most vehicles use one or more fuse panels. This one is located on the driver's side kick panel

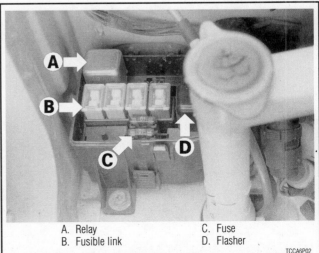

A. Relay   C. Fuse
B. Fusible link   D. Flasher

TCCA6P02

Fig. 3 The underhood fuse and relay panel usually contains fuses, relays, flashers and fusible links

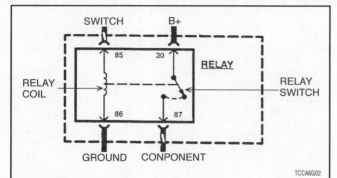

SWITCH B+

85 30 **RELAY**

RELAY COIL

RELAY SWITCH

86 87

GROUND CONPONENT

TCCA6G02

Fig. 4 Relays are composed of a coil and a switch. These two components are linked together so that when one operates, the other operates at the same time. The large wires in the circuit are connected from the battery to one side of the relay switch (B+) and from the opposite side of the relay switch to the load (component). Smaller wires are connected from the relay coil to the control switch for the circuit and from the opposite side of the relay coil to ground

LOAD

Every electrical circuit must include a "load" (something to use the electricity coming from the source). Without this load, the battery would attempt to deliver its entire power supply from one pole to another. This is called a "short circuit." All this electricity would take a short cut to ground and cause a great amount of damage to other components in the circuit by developing a tremendous amount of heat. This condition could develop sufficient heat to melt the insulation on all the surrounding wires and reduce a multiple wire cable to a lump of plastic and copper.

WIRING & HARNESSES

The average vehicle contains meters and meters of wiring, with hundreds of individual connections. To protect the many wires from damage and to keep them from becoming a confusing tangle, they are organized into bundles, enclosed in plastic or taped together and called wiring harnesses. Different harnesses serve different parts of the vehicle. Individual wires are color coded to help trace them through a harness where sections are hidden from view.

Automotive wiring or circuit conductors can be either single strand wire, multi-strand wire or printed circuitry. Single strand wire has a solid metal core and is usually used inside such components as alternators, motors, relays and other devices. Multi-strand wire has a core made of many small strands of wire twisted together into a single conductor. Most of the wiring in an automotive electrical system is made up of multi-strand wire, either as a single conductor or grouped together in a harness. All wiring is color coded on the insulator, either as a solid color or as a colored wire with an identification stripe. A printed circuit is a thin film of copper or other conductor that is printed on an insulator backing. Occasionally, a printed circuit is sandwiched between two sheets of plastic for more protection and flexibility. A complete printed circuit, consisting of conductors, insulating material and connectors for lamps or other components is called a printed circuit board. Printed circuitry is used in place of individual wires or harnesses in places where space is limited, such as behind instrument panels.

Since automotive electrical systems are very sensitive to changes in resistance, the selection of properly sized wires is critical when systems are repaired. A loose or corroded connection or a replacement wire that is too small for the circuit will add extra resistance and an additional voltage drop to the circuit.

The wire gauge number is an expression of the cross-section area of the conductor. Vehicles from countries that use the metric system will typically describe the wire size as its cross-sectional area in square millimeters. In this method, the larger the wire, the greater the number. Another common system for expressing wire size is the American Wire Gauge (AWG) system. As gauge number increases, area decreases and the wire becomes smaller. An 18 gauge wire is smaller than a four gauge wire. A wire with a higher gauge number will carry less current than a wire with a lower gauge number. Gauge wire size refers to the size of the strands of the conductor, not the size of the complete wire with

insulator. It is possible, therefore, to have two wires of the same gauge with different diameters because one may have thicker insulation than the other.

It is essential to understand how a circuit works before trying to figure out why it doesn't. An electrical schematic shows the electrical current paths when a circuit is operating properly. Schematics break the entire electrical system down into individual circuits. In a schematic, usually no attempt is made to represent wiring and components as they physically appear on the vehicle; switches and other components are shown as simply as possible. Face views of harness connectors show the cavity or terminal locations in all multi-pin connectors to help locate test points.

CONNECTORS

♦ **See Figures 5 and 6**

Three types of connectors are commonly used in automotive applications—weatherproof, molded and hard shell.

• Weatherproof—these connectors are most commonly used where the connector is exposed to the elements. Terminals are protected against moisture and dirt by sealing rings, which provide a weathertight seal. All repairs require the use of a special terminal and the tool needed in servicing it. Unlike standard blade type terminals, these weatherproof terminals cannot be straightened once they are bent. Make certain that the connectors are properly seated and all of the sealing rings are in place when connecting leads.

• Molded—these connectors require complete replacement of the connector if found to be defective. This means splicing a new connector assembly into

TCCA6P03

Fig. 5 Hard shell (left) and weatherproof (right) connectors have replaceable terminals

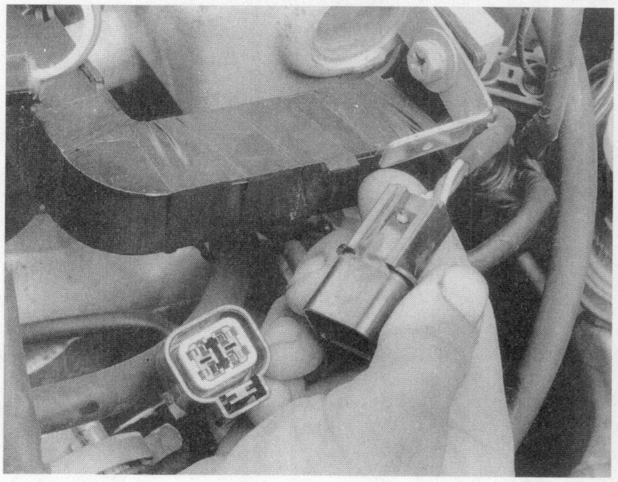

TCCA6P04

Fig. 6 Weatherproof connectors are most commonly used in the engine compartment, or where the connector is exposed to the elements

the harness. All splices should be soldered to insure proper contact. Use care when probing the connections or replacing terminals in them, as it is possible to create a short circuit between opposite terminals. If this happens to the wrong terminal pair, it is possible to damage certain components. Always use jumper wires between connectors for circuit checking and NEVER probe through weatherproof seals.

• Hard Shell—unlike molded connectors, the terminal contacts in hard-shell connectors can be replaced. Replacement usually involves the use of a special terminal removal tool that depresses the locking tangs (barbs) on the connector terminal and allows the connector to be removed from the rear of the shell. The connector shell should be replaced if it shows any evidence of burning, melting, cracks, or breaks. Replace individual terminals that are burnt, corroded, distorted or loose.

Test Equipment

Pinpointing the exact cause of trouble in an electrical circuit is most times accomplished by the use of special test equipment. The following describes different types of commonly used test equipment and briefly explains how to use them in diagnosis. In addition to the information covered below, the tool manufacturer's instructions booklet (provided with the tester) should be read and clearly understood before attempting any test procedures.

JUMPER WIRES

✳✳ CAUTION

Never use jumper wires made from a thinner gauge wire than the circuit being tested. If the jumper wire is of too small a gauge, it may overheat and possibly melt. Never use jumpers to bypass high resistance loads in a circuit. Bypassing resistances, in effect, creates a short circuit. This may, in turn, cause damages and fires. Jumper wires should only be used to bypass lengths of wire or to simulate switches.

Jumper wires are simple, yet extremely valuable, pieces of test equipment. They are test wires, which are used to bypass sections of a circuit. Although jumper wires can be purchased, they are usually fabricated from lengths of standard automotive wire and whatever types of connector (alligator clip, spade connector or pin connector) that is required for the particular application being tested. In cramped, hard-to-reach areas, it is advisable to have insulated boots over the jumper wire terminals in order to prevent accidental grounding. It is also advisable to include a standard automotive fuse in any jumper wire. This is commonly referred to as a "fused jumper". By inserting an in-line fuse holder between a set of test leads, a fused jumper wire can be used for bypassing open circuits. Use a five amp fuse to provide protection against voltage spikes.

Jumper wires are used primarily to locate open electrical circuits, on either the ground (-) side of the circuit or on the power (+) side. If an electrical component fails to operate, connect the jumper wire between the component and a good ground. If the component operates only with the jumper installed, the ground circuit is open. If the ground circuit is good, but the component does not operate, the circuit between the power feed and component may be open. By moving the jumper wire successively back from the component toward the power source, you can isolate the area of the circuit where the open is located. When the component stops functioning, or the power is cut off, the open is in the segment of wire between the jumper and the point previously tested.

You can sometimes connect the jumper wire directly from the battery to the "hot" terminal of the component, but first make sure the component uses 12 volts in operation. Some electrical components, such as fuel injectors or sensors, are designed to operate on about 4 to 5 volts, and running 12 volts directly to these components will cause damage.

TEST LIGHTS

▶ See Figure 7

The test light is used to check circuits and components while electrical current is flowing through them. It is used for voltage and ground tests. To use a 12 volt test light, connect the ground clip to a good ground and probe wherever necessary with the pick. The test light will illuminate when voltage is detected. This does not necessarily mean that 12 volts (or any particular amount of volt-

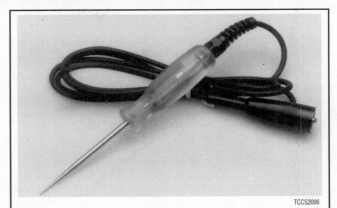

TCCS2006

Fig. 7 A 12 volt test light is used to detect the presence of voltage in a circuit

age) is present; it only means that some voltage is present. It is advisable before using the test light to touch its ground clip and probe across the battery posts or terminals to make sure the light is operating properly.

✳✳ WARNING

Do not use a test light to probe electronic ignition, spark plug or coil wires. Never use a pick-type test light to probe wiring on computer controlled systems unless specifically instructed to do so. Any wire insulation that is pierced by the test light probe should be taped and sealed with silicone after testing.

Like the jumper wire, the 12 volt test light is used to isolate opens in circuits. However, whereas the jumper wire is used to bypass the open to operate the load, the 12 volt test light is used to locate the presence of voltage in a circuit. If the test light illuminates, there is power up to that point in the circuit; if the test light does not illuminate, there is an open circuit (no power). Move the test light in successive steps back toward the power source until the light in the handle illuminates. The open is between the probe and a point, which was previously probed.

The self-powered test light is similar in design to the 12 volt test light, but contains a 1.5 volt penlight battery in the handle. It is most often used in place of a multimeter to check for open or short circuits when power is isolated from the circuit (continuity test).

The battery in a self-powered test light does not provide much current. A weak battery may not provide enough power to illuminate the test light even when a complete circuit is made (especially if there is high resistance in the circuit). Always make sure that the test battery is strong. To check the battery, briefly touch the ground clip to the probe; if the light glows brightly, the battery is strong enough for testing.

➡ A self-powered test light should not be used on any computer controlled system or component. The small amount of electricity transmitted by the test light is enough to damage many electronic automotive components.

MULTIMETERS

Multimeters are an extremely useful tool for troubleshooting electrical problems. They can be purchased in either analog or digital form and have a price range to suit any budget. A multimeter is a voltmeter, ammeter and ohmmeter (along with other features) combined into one instrument. It is often used when testing solid state circuits because of its high input impedance (usually 10 megaohms or more). A brief description of the multimeter main test functions follows:

• Voltmeter—the voltmeter is used to measure voltage at any point in a circuit, or to measure the voltage drop across any part of a circuit. Voltmeters usually have various scales and a selector switch to allow the reading of different voltage ranges. The voltmeter has a positive and a negative lead. To avoid damage to the meter, always connect the negative lead to the negative (-) side of the circuit (to ground or nearest the ground side of the circuit) and connect the positive lead to the positive (+) side of the circuit (to the power source or the nearest power source). Note that the negative voltmeter lead will always be black and that the positive voltmeter will always be some color other than black (usually red).

• Ohmmeter—the ohmmeter is designed to read resistance (measured in ohms) in a circuit or component. Most ohmmeters will have a selector switch which permits the measurement of different ranges of resistance (usually the selector switch allows the multiplication of the meter reading by 10, 100, 1,000 and 10,000). Some ohmmeters are "auto-ranging" which means the meter itself will determine which scale to use. Since the meters are powered by an internal battery, the ohmmeter can be used like a self-powered test light. When the ohmmeter is connected, current from the ohmmeter flows through the circuit or component being tested. Since the ohmmeter's internal resistance and voltage are known values, the amount of current flow through the meter depends on the resistance of the circuit or component being tested. The ohmmeter can also be used to perform a continuity test for suspected open circuits. In using the meter for making continuity checks, do not be concerned with the actual resistance readings. Zero resistance, or any ohm reading, indicates continuity in the circuit. Infinite resistance indicates an opening in the circuit. A high resistance reading where there should be none indicates a problem in the circuit. Checks for short circuits are made in the same manner as checks for open circuits, except that the circuit must be isolated from both power and normal ground. Infinite resistance indicates no continuity, while zero resistance indicates a dead short.

⁕⁕ WARNING

Never use an ohmmeter to check the resistance of a component or wire while there is voltage applied to the circuit.

• Ammeter—an ammeter measures the amount of current flowing through a circuit in units called amperes or amps. At normal operating voltage, most circuits have a characteristic amount of amperes, called "current draw" which can be measured using an ammeter. By referring to a specified current draw rating, then measuring the amperes and comparing the two values, one can determine what is happening within the circuit to aid in diagnosis. An open circuit, for example, will not allow any current to flow, so the ammeter reading will be zero. A damaged component or circuit will have an increased current draw, so the reading will be high. The ammeter is always connected in series with the circuit being tested. All of the current that normally flows through the circuit must also flow through the ammeter; if there is any other path for the current to follow, the ammeter reading will not be accurate. The ammeter itself has very little resistance to current flow and, therefore, will not affect the circuit, but it will measure current draw only when the circuit is closed and electricity is flowing. Excessive current draw can blow fuses and drain the battery, while a reduced current draw can cause motors to run slowly, lights to dim and other components to not operate properly.

Troubleshooting Electrical Systems

When diagnosing a specific problem, organized troubleshooting is necessary. The complexity of a modern automotive vehicle demands that you approach any problem in a logical, organized manner. There are certain troubleshooting techniques, however, which are standard:
• Establish when the problem occurs. Does the problem appear only under certain conditions? Were there any noises, odors or other unusual symptoms? Isolate the problem area. To do this, make some simple tests and observations, then eliminate the systems that are working properly. Check for obvious problems, such as broken wires and loose or dirty connections. Always check the obvious before assuming something complicated is the cause.
• Test for problems systematically to determine the cause once the problem area is isolated. Are all the components functioning properly? Is there power going to electrical switches and motors. Performing careful, systematic checks will often turn up most causes on the first inspection, without wasting time checking components that have little or no relationship to the problem.
• Test all repairs after the work is done to make sure that the problem is fixed. Some causes can be traced to more than one component, so a careful verification of repair work is important in order to pick up additional malfunctions that may cause a problem to reappear or a different problem to arise. A blown fuse, for example, is a simple problem that may require more than another fuse to repair. If you don't look for a problem that caused a fuse to blow, a shorted wire (for example) may go undetected.

Experience has shown that most problems tend to be the result of a fairly simple and obvious cause, such as loose or corroded connectors, bad grounds or damaged wire insulation that causes a short. This makes careful visual inspection of components during testing essential to quick and accurate troubleshooting.

Testing

OPEN CIRCUITS

▶ See Figure 8

This test already assumes the existence of an open in the circuit and it is used to help locate the open portion.
1. Isolate the circuit from power and ground.
2. Connect the self-powered test light or ohmmeter ground clip to the ground side of the circuit and probe sections of the circuit sequentially.
3. If the light is out or there is infinite resistance, the open is between the probe and the circuit ground.
4. If the light is on or the meter shows continuity, the open is between the probe and the end of the circuit toward the power source.

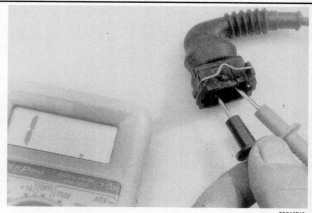

TCCA6P10

Fig. 8 The infinite reading on this multimeter indicates that the circuit is open

SHORT CIRCUITS

➡**Never use a self-powered test light to perform checks for opens or shorts when power is applied to the circuit under test. The test light can be damaged by outside power.**

1. Isolate the circuit from power and ground.
2. Connect the self-powered test light or ohmmeters ground clip to a good ground and probe any easy-to-reach point in the circuit.
3. If the light comes on or there is continuity, there is a short somewhere in the circuit.
4. To isolate the short, probe a test point at either end of the isolated circuit (the light should be on or the meter should indicate continuity).
5. Leave the test light probe engaged and sequentially open connectors or switches, remove parts, etc. until the light goes out or continuity is broken.
6. When the light goes out, the short is between the last two circuit components that were opened.

VOLTAGE

This test determines voltage available from the battery and should be the first step in any electrical troubleshooting procedure after visual inspection. Many electrical problems, especially on computer controlled systems, can be caused by a low state of charge in the battery. Excessive corrosion at the battery cable terminals can cause poor contact that will prevent proper charging and full battery current flow.
1. Set the voltmeter selector switch to the 20V position.
2. Connect the multimeter negative lead to the battery's negative (-) post or terminal and the positive lead to the battery's positive (+) post or terminal.
3. Turn the ignition switch **ON** to provide a load.
4. A well charged battery should register over 12 volts. If the meter reads below 11.5 volts, the battery power may be insufficient to operate the electrical system properly.

VOLTAGE DROP

▶ **See Figure 9**

When current flows through a load, the voltage beyond the load drops. This voltage drop is due to the resistance created by the load and also by small resistances created by corrosion at the connectors and damaged insulation on the wires. The maximum allowable voltage drop under load is critical, especially if there is more than one load in the circuit, since all voltage drops are cumulative.

1. Set the voltmeter selector switch to the 20 volt position.
2. Connect the multimeter negative lead to a good ground.
3. Operate the circuit and check the voltage before the first component (load).
4. There should be little or no voltage drop in the circuit before the first component. If a voltage drop exists, the wire or connectors in the circuit are suspect.
5. While operating the first component in the circuit, probe the ground side of the component with the positive meter lead and observe the voltage readings. A small voltage drop should be noticed. This voltage drop is caused by the resistance of the component.
6. Repeat the test for each component (load) down the circuit.
7. If a large voltage drop is noticed, the preceding component, wire or connector is suspect.

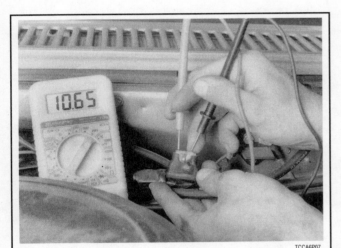

Fig. 9 This voltage drop test revealed high resistance (low voltage) in the circuit

RESISTANCE

▶ **See Figures 10 and 11**

✱✱ WARNING

Never use an ohmmeter with power applied to the circuit. The ohmmeter is designed to operate on its own power supply. The normal 12 volt electrical system voltage could damage the meter!

1. Isolate the circuit from the power source of the vehicle.
2. Ensure that the ignition key is **OFF** when disconnecting any components or the battery.
3. Where necessary, also isolate at least one side of the circuit to be checked, in order to avoid reading parallel resistances. Parallel circuit resistances will always give a lower reading than the actual resistance of either of the branches.
4. Connect the meter leads to both sides of the circuit (wire or component) and read the actual measured ohms on the meter scale. Make sure the selector switch is set to the proper ohm scale for the circuit being tested, to avoid misreading the ohmmeter test value.

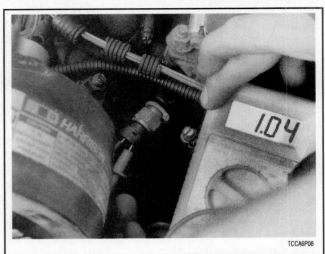

Fig. 10 Checking the resistance of a coolant temperature sensor with an ohmmeter. Reading is 1.04 kilohms

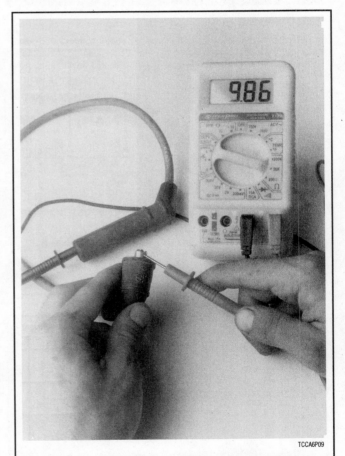

Fig. 11 Spark plug wires can be checked for excessive resistance using an ohmmeter

Wire and Connector Repair

Almost anyone can replace damaged wires, as long as the proper tools and parts are available. Wire and terminals are available to fit almost any need. Even the specialized weatherproof, molded and hard shell connectors are now available from aftermarket suppliers.

Be sure the ends of all the wires are fitted with the proper terminal hardware and connectors. Wrapping a wire around a stud is never a permanent solution and will only cause trouble later. Replace wires one at a time to avoid confusion. Always route wires the same as the factory.

BATTERY CABLES

Disconnecting the Cables

When working on any electrical component on the vehicle, it is always a good idea to disconnect the negative (-) battery cable. This will prevent potential damage to many sensitive electrical components such as the Engine Control Module (ECM), radio, alternator, etc.

➡Any time you disengage the battery cables, it is recommended that you disconnect the negative (-) battery cable first. This will prevent your accidentally grounding the positive (+) terminal to the body of the vehicle when disconnecting it, thereby preventing damage to the above mentioned components.

➡If connector repair is necessary, only attempt it if you have the proper tools. Weatherproof and hard shell connectors require special tools to release the pins inside the connector. Attempting to repair these connectors with conventional hand tools will damage them.

Before you disconnect the cable(s), first turn the ignition to the **OFF** position. This will prevent a draw on the battery which could cause arcing (electricity trying to ground itself to the body of a vehicle, just like a spark plug jumping the gap) and, of course, damaging some components such as the alternator diodes.

When the battery cable(s) are reconnected (negative cable last), be sure to check that your lights, windshield wipers and other electrically operated safety components are all working correctly. If your vehicle contains an Electronically Tuned Radio (ETR), don't forget to also reset your radio stations. Ditto for the clock.

AIR BAG—SUPPLEMENTAL INFLATABLE RESTRAINT (SIR)

General Information

▶ See Figures 12 and 13

➡General Motors calls their air bag system a Supplemental Inflatable Restraint (SIR). Most other Manufacturers refer to it as a Supplemental Restraint System (SRS). SRS is also widely accepted as the industry standard nomenclature for the system. This manual may use SIR or SRS when referring to the air bag system.

The Supplemental Inflatable Restraint (SIR) system helps supplement the protection offered by the driver and front passenger seat belts by deploying an air bag from the center of the steering wheel and from the top of the right side of the instrument panel. The air bag deploys when the vehicle is involved in a frontal crash of sufficient force up to 30 degrees off the centerline of the vehicle.

The SIR system consists of the following components:
- An inflatable restraint sensing and diagnostic module (SDM).
- An inflatable restraint steering wheel module.
- An inflatable restraint steering wheel module coil.
- An inflatable restraint I/P module
- An **AIR BAG** warning lamp in the instrument cluster.

SERVICE PRECAUTIONS

The Sensing Diagnostic Module (SDM) maintains a reserve energy supply with sufficient voltage to cause a deployment for up to ten minutes after the ignition switch is turned "OFF", the battery is disconnected or the fuse powering the SDM is removed. Many of the service procedures require removal of the inflater module fuse and disconnection of the deployment loops to avoid an accidental deployment .

✳✳ CAUTION

Proper operation of the Supplemental Inflatable Restraint (SIR) sensing system requires that any repairs to the vehicle structure return the vehicle structure to the original production configuration. Not properly repairing the vehicle structure could cause non-deployment of the air bag in a frontal collision or deployment of the air bag for conditions less severe than intended.

DISARMING THE SYSTEM

1. Turn the steering wheel to the straight ahead position.
2. Remove the key from the ignition switch.
3. Remove the SIR fuse from the Instrument Panel (I/P) fuse block.
4. Remove the left side I/P sound insulator.
5. Disconnect the Connector Position Assurance (CPA) and the driver side yellow 2-way connector located at the base of the steering column.
6. Remove the right hand I/P sound insulator.
7. Disconnect the Connector Position Assurance (CPA) and the passenger side yellow 2-way connector located near the base of the steering column.

➡With the SIR fuse removed and the ignition switch in the RUN position, the AIR BAG warning lamp illuminates. This is normal operation and does not indicate a SIR system malfunction.

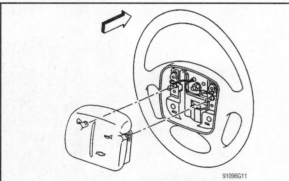

91096G11

Fig. 12 View of the Inflatable Restraint steering wheel module—Chevrolet shown, other models similar

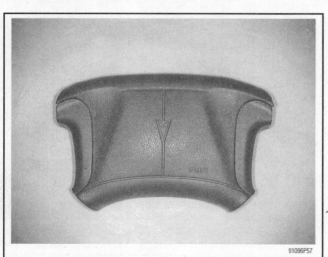

91096P57

Fig. 13 This is the driver's side air bag assembly. If storing or transporting an air bag, only store it in this position

ARMING THE SYSTEM

1. Connect the Connector Position Assurance (CPA) and the passenger yellow 2-way connector located near the base of the steering column.
2. Install the right hand I/P sound insulator.
3. Connect the connector position assurance (CPA) and the driver yellow 2-way connector located at the base of the steering column.

4. Install the left side I/P sound insulator.
5. Install the SIR fuse from the I/P fuse block.
6. Staying well away from both air bags, turn the ignition switch to the RUN position. Verify that the AIR BAG warning lamp flashes seven times and then stays off. If the AIR BAG warning lamp does not operate as described, the system will have to be diagnosed.

HEATING AND AIR CONDITIONING

➡ **If your vehicle is equipped with air conditioning, refer to Section 1 for information regarding the implications of servicing your A/C system yourself. Only a MVAC-trained, EPA-certified, automotive technician should service the A/C system or its components.**

Front Blower Motor

The blower motor location can change from year-to-year. It can also change with the trim level of the vehicle. A vehicle that has front and rear climate controls may be configured differently than a vehicle that has front controls only. The following are two different repair procedures. One is for blower motors located and accessed in the engine compartment, the other is for blower motors mounted inside the vehicle.

REMOVAL & INSTALLATION

Engine Compartment Mounted

▶ **See Figures 14, 15, 16, 17 and 18, 19**

1. Disconnect the negative battery cable.
2. Remove the engine air cleaner assembly.

3. If necessary for clearance, remove the left hand wiper arm linkage.
4. Detach the wire harness connector from the blower motor.
5. Disconnect the motor cooling hose.
6. Remove the blower motor assembly retaining screws
7. Carefully pull the blower motor assembly out from the firewall.
To install:
8. Installation of the blower motor is a reversal of the removal procedure.
9. Connect the negative battery cable.

Interior Mounted

1. Disconnect the negative battery cable.
2. Remove the right-side instrument panel insulator.
3. Disconnect the blower motor cooling hose.
4. Detach the blower motor electrical connector.
5. Remove the blower motor-to-air housing mounting screws.
6. Pull the blower motor out of the air housing.
To install:
7. Installation of the blower motor is a reverse of the removal procedure.
8. Connect the negative battery cable.

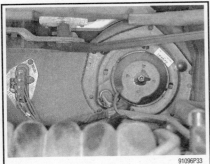

Fig. 14 The blower motor is mounted in the engine compartment, behind the wiper linkage on this model

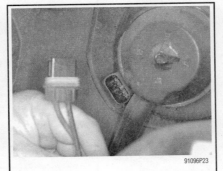

Fig. 15 Detach the electrical connector from the blower motor

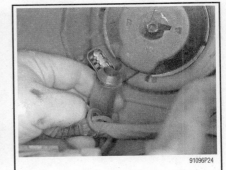

Fig. 16 Disconnect the blower motor cooling hose

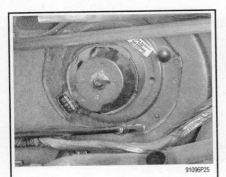

Fig. 17 Remove the attaching screws

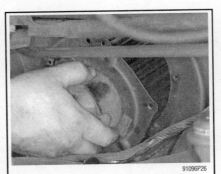

Fig. 18 It may be necessary to rotate the blower motor to clear the surrounding obstructions

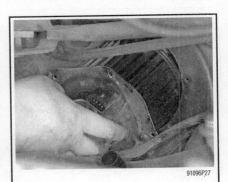

Fig. 19 Remove the blower motor and "squirrel cage" fan as an assembly

Rear Auxiliary Blower Motor

REMOVAL & INSTALLATION

1. Disconnect the negative battery cable.
2. Remove the left hand side rear quarter access panel.
3. Remove the blower motor electrical connector.
4. Lift the tabs on blower motor and turn counter clockwise.
5. Remove the blower motor.

To install:

6. Install the blower motor and turn it clockwise until the tabs lock into position.
7. Connect the electrical connector.
8. Install the left-hand side access panel rear quarter.
9. Connect the negative battery cable.

Heater Core

REMOVAL & INSTALLATION

▶ **See Figures 20, 21, 22, 23 and 24**

1. Disconnect the negative battery cable.
2. Remove the air cleaner and duct assembly.
3. Drain and recycle the engine coolant.

Fig. 20 You must disconnect the wiper linkage to allow clearance for removing the heater core coolant hoses

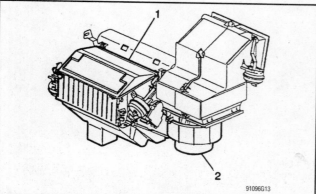

Fig. 21 View of the HVAC module—1 is the A/C module, two is the front blower motor (interior mount style)

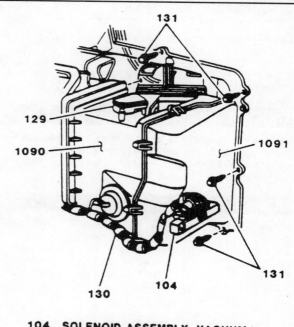

104	SOLENOID ASSEMBLY, VACUUM/ ELECTRIC
129	ACTUATOR, TEMPERATURE VALVE
130	HARNESS, HEATER CONTROL VACUUM
131	SCREW, 7 N·m (62 lb.in.)
1090	CASE, TEMPERATURE
1091	COVER, HEATER CORE

Fig. 22 View of the heater core cover and related components

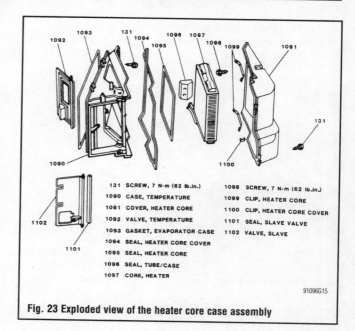

131	SCREW, 7 N·m (62 lb.in.)	1098	SCREW, 7 N·m (62 lb.in.)
1090	CASE, TEMPERATURE	1099	CLIP, HEATER CORE
1091	COVER, HEATER CORE	1100	CLIP, HEATER CORE COVER
1092	VALVE, TEMPERATURE	1101	SEAL, SLAVE VALVE
1093	GASKET, EVAPORATOR CASE	1102	VALVE, SLAVE
1094	SEAL, HEATER CORE COVER		
1095	SEAL, HEATER CORE		
1096	SEAL, TUBE/CASE		
1097	CORE, HEATER		

Fig. 23 Exploded view of the heater core case assembly

CHASSIS ELECTRICAL 6-11

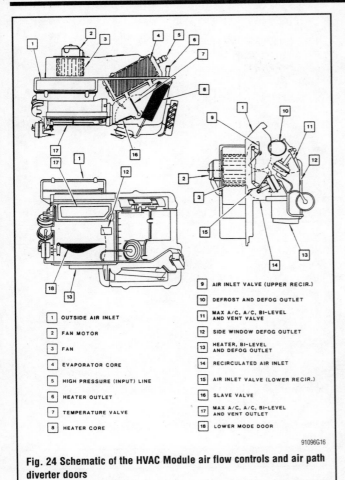

Fig. 24 Schematic of the HVAC Module air flow controls and air path diverter doors

1 OUTSIDE AIR INLET	9 AIR INLET VALVE (UPPER RECIR.)
2 FAN MOTOR	10 DEFROST AND DEFOG OUTLET
3 FAN	11 MAX A/C, A/C, BI-LEVEL AND VENT VALVE
4 EVAPORATOR CORE	12 SIDE WINDOW DEFOG OUTLET
5 HIGH PRESSURE (INPUT) LINE	13 HEATER, BI-LEVEL AND DEFOG OUTLET
6 HEATER OUTLET	14 RECIRCULATED AIR INLET
7 TEMPERATURE VALVE	15 AIR INLET VALVE (LOWER RECIR.)
8 HEATER CORE	16 SLAVE VALVE
	17 MAX A/C, A/C, BI-LEVEL AND VENT OUTLET
	18 LOWER MODE DOOR

4. Disconnect the wiper linkage from the wiper motor.
5. Detach both heater hoses at the heater core.
6. Remove the lower center console.
7. Remove both instrument panel insulators.
8. Remove the heater outlet module screws, and the heater cover.
9. Remove the heater core mounting clip screw, and the heater core line clamp screw.
10. Carefully pull the heater core from the case.
11. If necessary, remove the foam seals on the heater core module for transfer to the replacement core.
12. If necessary, remove the heater core line clamp for transfer to the replacement core.
To install:
13. Installation is the reversal of the removal process. Tighten the mounting screws to 27 inch lbs. (3 Nm).

Air Conditioning Components

REMOVAL & INSTALLATION

Repair or service of air conditioning components is not covered by this manual, because of the risk of personal injury or death, and because of the legal ramifications of servicing these components without the proper EPA certification and experience. Cost, personal injury or death, environmental damage, and legal considerations (such as the fact that it is a federal crime to vent refrigerant into the atmosphere), dictate that the A/C components on your vehicle should be serviced only by a Motor Vehicle Air Conditioning (MVAC) trained, and EPA certified automotive technician.

➡ If the A/C system of your vehicle uses R-12 refrigerant and is in need of recharging, the A/C system can be converted over to R-134a refriger-

ant (less environmentally harmful and expensive). Refer to Section 1 for additional information on R-12 to R-134a conversions, and for additional considerations dealing with the A/C system of your vehicle.

Control Panel

REMOVAL & INSTALLATION

▶ **See Figures 25 thru 34**

1. Disconnect the negative battery cable.
2. Remove the steering column lower trim cover.
3. Remove the center console mounting screws and then remove the center console.
4. Loosen and remove the two retaining screws on the heater control (HVAC) assembly.
5. Slide the control assembly out of its mounting bracket.
6. Detach the two wire harness electrical connectors from the rear side of the heater control assembly.
7. Remove the heater control assembly.
To install:
8. Installation is the reversal of the removal process.

Fig. 25 Remove the driver side and . . .

Fig. 26 . . . passenger side lower dash panels

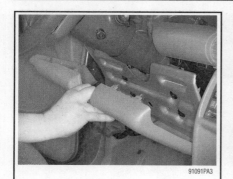

Fig. 27 Remove the lower steering column trim panel . . .

Fig. 28 . . . then, remove the center console retaining screws

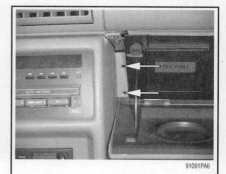

Fig. 29 Including the two hidden behind the glove box door

Fig. 30 Slide the center console off . . .

Fig. 31 . . . to gain access to the mounting screws on the control panel

Fig. 32 Remove the fasteners holding the control panel in place and pull the panel out

Fig. 33 Detach the wire harness connectors from the control panel

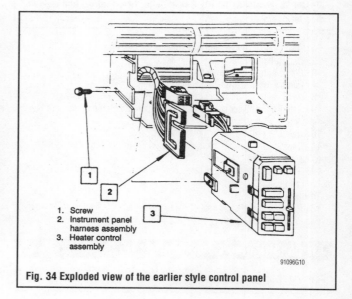

1. Screw
2. Instrument panel harness assembly
3. Heater control assembly

Fig. 34 Exploded view of the earlier style control panel

CRUISE CONTROL

▶ See Figure 35

Some models covered by this manual may be equipped with a Supplemental Inflatable Restraint (SIR), which uses an air bag. Whenever working near any of the SIR components, such as the impact sensors, the air bag module, steering column and instrument panel, disable the SIR, as described in this section.

Cruise control is a speed control system that maintains a desired vehicle speed under normal driving conditions. However, steep grades up or down may cause variations in the selected speeds. The cruise control system has the capability to cruise, resume speed, accelerate, tap-up and tap-down. The main parts of the cruise control system are the turn signal and multi-function switch, the cruise control module, the cruise control cable, the vehicle speed sensor, the cruise control release switch and the stoplamp switch.

On vehicles equipped with the 3.1L (LG6) engine, cruise control functions are controlled by a cruise control module mounted under the I/P. On vehicles equipped with the 3800 (L27) engine, cruise control functions are controlled by the powertrain control module (PCM).

The cruise control system, on vehicles equipped with a 3.4L engine, uses a cruise control module to obtain and hold any desired vehicle cruise speed above a minimum speed of 40 km/h (25mph).

The cruise control system uses vacuum to operate a throttle servo unit. The servo unit maintains the desired vehicle speed by trapping vacuum at the proper servo position. The control module monitors vehicle speed and servo position and operates the vacuum and vent valves in the servo to maintain desired speed. The control module contains a low speed limit, which prevents system engagement below a minimum speed of about 25 mph. Operation of the control

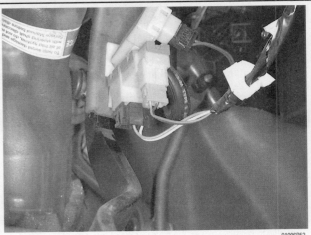
91096P52

Fig. 35 Example of the brake/stoplight switches mounted on the pedal bracket

module is achieved with mode control switches located in the end of the turn signal lever. Two release switches are provided to disengage the system. An electrical release switch mounted on the brake pedal bracket disengages the system electrically when the brake pedal is depressed. A vacuum release valve, mounted on the brake pedal bracket, vents the trapped vacuum in the servo to atmosphere when the brake pedal is depressed, allowing the servo unit to quickly return the throttle to idle position.

CRUISE CONTROL TROUBLESHOOTING

Problem	Possible Cause
Will not hold proper speed	Incorrect cable adjustment
	Binding throttle linkage
	Leaking vacuum servo diaphragm
	Leaking vacuum tank
	Faulty vacuum or vent valve
	Faulty stepper motor
	Faulty transducer
	Faulty speed sensor
	Faulty cruise control module
Cruise intermittently cuts out	Clutch or brake switch adjustment too tight
	Short or open in the cruise control circuit
	Faulty transducer
	Faulty cruise control module
Vehicle surges	Kinked speedometer cable or casing
	Binding throttle linkage
	Faulty speed sensor
	Faulty cruise control module
Cruise control inoperative	Blown fuse
	Short or open in the cruise control circuit
	Faulty brake or clutch switch
	Leaking vacuum circuit
	Faulty cruise control switch
	Faulty stepper motor
	Faulty transducer
	Faulty speed sensor
	Faulty cruise control module

Note: Use this chart as a guide. Not all systems will use the components listed.

TCCA6C01

ENTERTAINMENT SYSTEMS

⚹⚹ CAUTION

Some models covered by this manual may be equipped with a Supplemental Inflatable Restraint (SIR), which uses an air bag. Whenever working near any of the SIR components, such as the impact sensors, the air bag module, steering column and instrument panel, disable the SIR, as described in this section.

Radio Receiver/Player in Dash

REMOVAL & INSTALLATION

⬥ **See Figures 25 thru 30 and 36, 37, 38, and 39**

1. Disconnect the negative battery cable.
2. Remove the steering column opening filler panel.
3. Remove the right side sound insulator panel.
4. Remove the accessory trim panel.
5. Loosen the two nuts at the bottom of the radio.
6. Remove the two screws attaching the radio bracket to the instrument panel lower trim pad assembly.
7. Slide the radio assembly out from the accessory housing.
8. Disconnect the antenna lead-in cable from the radio.
9. Disconnect the instrument panel electrical harness connectors from the radio and remove the radio assembly.

To install:

10. Connect the instrument panel electrical harness connectors and the antenna lead-in cable to the radio.
11. Slide the radio assembly into the accessory housing.
12. Install the two screws attaching the radio bracket to the instrument panel lower trim pad assembly.
13. Tighten the two nuts at the bottom of the radio.
14. Install the accessory trim panel.
15. Install the right side sound insulator panel.
16. Install the steering column opening filler panel.
17. Connect the negative battery cable.

Speakers

REMOVAL & INSTALLATION

Front Door

⬥ **See Figures 40, 41, 42 and 43**

1. Disconnect the negative battery cable.
2. Remove the front door trim panel.
3. Remove the front door water deflector.
4. To remove the speaker from the door frame, depress the retaining clip and pull the speaker forward.
5. Detach the wire harness connector from the speaker.

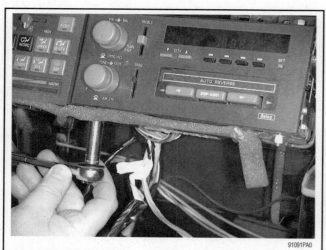

Fig. 36 . . . to gain access to the radio attaching hardware. Loosen the two nuts at the bottom of the radio

Fig. 37 Remove the two screws attaching the radio bracket to the instrument panel lower trim pad assembly

Fig. 38 Slide the radio out of the dash

Fig. 39 Detach the electrical connector and the antenna plug

Fig. 40 To remove the front speaker, first remove the door panel . . .

Fig. 41 . . . as well as the weather sheet to access the inner door

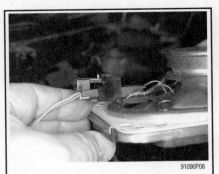

Fig. 42 After unclipping the speaker, carefully pull the speaker forward to gain access to the harness connector

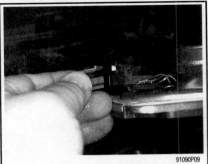

Fig. 43 Detach the speaker's electrical connector and remove the speaker from the door

6. Remove the speaker.

To install:

7. Attach the wire harness connector and install the speaker to the door.
8. Install the weather sheet (duct tape can help if it's torn).
9. Install the door panel.

Rear Liftgate

▶ See Figure 44

1. Disconnect the negative battery cable.
2. Remove the liftgate trim panel.
3. Remove the rear radio speaker by pushing on the top tab and pulling the speaker form the liftgate.
4. Detach the electrical connector from the rear radio speaker.

To install:

5. Install the electrical connector to the rear radio speaker.
6. Install the rear radio speaker by inserting the tabs into the lower slots and pushing the upper tab into the slot.
7. Install the liftgate trim panel.
8. Connect the negative battery cable.

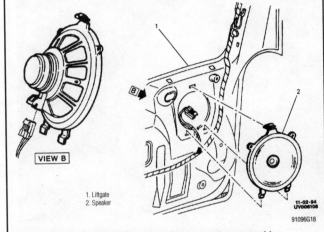

1. Liftgate
2. Speaker

VIEW B

Fig. 44 Exploded view of the rear liftgate speaker assembly

WINDSHIELD WIPERS AND WASHERS

Windshield Wiper Blade and Arm

REMOVAL & INSTALLATION

Front

▶ See Figures 45 thru 51

➡This procedure requires the use of a wiper arm puller tool or equivalent and a pin or pop rivet for articulated wiper arms.

1. Disconnect the washer hoses.
2. Remove the nut cover from the wiper arm nut by twisting slightly with a 17mm socket. Try to gently pull the cover off. The cover may crack or break and need to be replaced.
3. Loosen and remove the retaining nut from the wiper arm.
4. Lift the wiper arm and insert a suitable pin or pop rivet completely through the two holes located next to the pivot of the arm, where applicable. A heavy duty battery terminal puller can be substituted to pull the wiper arm from the stud, in most cases.

To install:

5. Run and park the wiper motor.
6. Install the wiper arm on the drive shaft.
7. Install the nut on the drive shaft finger tight, then remove the pin, that was inserted near the pivot arm.

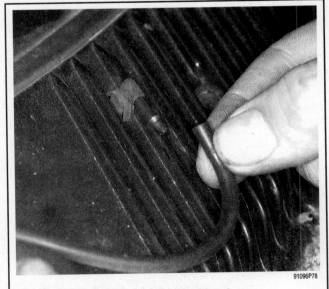

Fig. 45 Disconnect the washer hose, if equipped

Fig. 46 Remove the wiper arm attaching nut trim cover, then remove the nut

Fig. 47 After removing the nut, match mark the stud . . .

Fig. 48 . . . to the wiper arm for easier alignment during assembly

Fig. 49 Use a small puller to pop the wiper arm off the stud—a battery terminal puller worked well for this

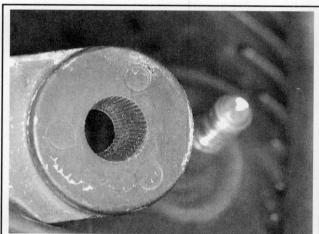

Fig. 50 The wiper arm removed from the stud. Note the tapered splines

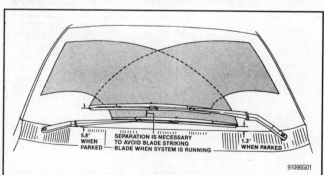

Fig. 51 Windshield wiper arm alignment and wipe pattern

➡It may be necessary to allow for some movement of the arm when the nut is being tightened. If the arm moves away from the desired alignment mark, loosen the nut and reposition the arm by moving the blade tip. Retighten the tip.

8. If installing the driver's side wiper arm and blade, measure from the tip of blade to the bottom edge of the glass. This must be approximately 5.8 in. (147mm).

9. If installing the passenger's side wiper arm and blade, measure from the tip of blade to the bottom edge of the glass. This must be approximately 1.3 in. (33mm).

10. Tighten the wiper arm nut to 29.5 ft. lbs. (40 Nm).

11. Install the nut cover and connect the washer hose.

Rear

1. Lift the wiper arm from the window and pull the retaining latch.
2. Remove the wiper arm from the pivot shaft.

To install:

3. Run the wiper motor to the park position.
4. Install the head of the wiper arm on the serrated wiper pivot shaft in position where the wiper blade will rest in the proper parked position.
5. Lift the arm extension and push in the retaining latch when the head is fully seated on the pivot shaft.

Windshield Wiper Motor

REMOVAL & INSTALLATION

Front Wiper Motor

1990 MODELS

1. Remove the wiper module assembly.
2. Using a 8mm socket, loosen the two crank arm socket screw and lockwashers until the socket releases from the crank arm ball.
3. Run the wipers to the park position.
4. Remove the three wiper motor retaining screws and remove the wiper motor from the frame.

To install:

5. Make sure the wiper motor is in the park position.

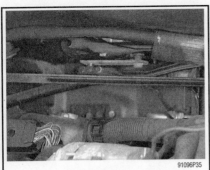

Fig. 52 The wiper motor is located in the engine compartment, above the engine, offset to the passenger side

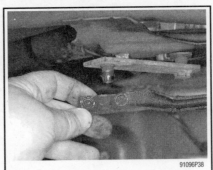

Fig. 53 Loosen the two attaching bolts to disconnect the wiper transmission linkage from the pivot

Fig. 54 Note that this is a cinch type connection. Lube it on reassembly

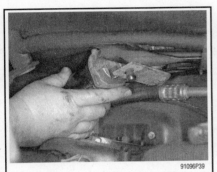

Fig. 55 After removing the wiper motor retaining bolts, carefully lower it from its position

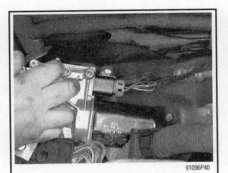

Fig. 56 It's easier to remove the motor from it's mount and then disconnect the electrical connectors

Fig. 57 To detach the electrical connector, first push up on the locking tab . . .

Fig. 58 . . . then, pull the tab out of the lock slot

Fig. 59 Separate the electrical connector from the motor

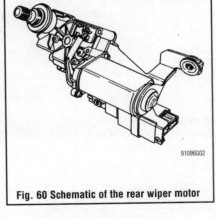

Fig. 60 Schematic of the rear wiper motor

6. Position the wiper motor to the frame and install the three wiper motor retaining screws.

7. Using an 8mm socket, tighten the two crank arm socket screw and lockwashers.

8. Install the wiper module assembly as outlined in this section.

1991—1999 MODELS

▶ See Figures 52 thru 59

➡Because of a new wiper motor bracket design, the wiper motor can be removed from the vehicle without removing the complete wiper module.

1. Disconnect the negative battery cable.
2. Disconnect the harness from the wiper motor.
3. Using a 8mm socket, loosen the two crank arm socket screw and lockwashers until the socket releases from the crank arm ball.

➡Do not remove the crank arm from the motor.

4. Using a 10mm socket, remove the three motor retaining screws.
5. Slide the motor out of the slot in the bracket.

To install:

6. Make sure the wipers are in the park position.
7. Slide the motor into the slot in the bracket.
8. Using a 10mm socket, install the three motor retaining screws and tighten to 49-80 inch lbs. (5.5-9.0 Nm).
9. Using a 8mm socket, tighten the two crank arm socket screw and lockwashers.
10. Connect the harness to the wiper motor.
11. Connect the negative battery cable.

Rear Wiper Motor

▶ See Figure 60

1. Disconnect the negative battery cable.
2. Remove the rear wiper arm.

3. Remove the tailgate inner trim finish panel as outlined in Section 10.
4. Detach the wiring harness connector from the wiper motor.
5. Remove the two motor retaining screws from the grommets and the retaining nut at the pivot and spacer on the tailgate.
6. Remove the motor from the vehicle.
7. Installation is the reverse of removal.

Windshield Washer Pump

REMOVAL & INSTALLATION

♦ **See Figure 61**

➡ **Front and rear washer pump replacement procedures are the same.**

1. Disconnect the negative battery cable.
2. Remove the connector (1) from the front washer pump (2).
3. Remove the hose (5) from the front washer pump (2).
4. Remove the front washer pump (2) from the washer solvent container assembly (7).
5. Pull the top of the front washer pump (2) out from the side of the washer solvent container assembly (7).
6. Pull the front washer pump (2) up out of the washer solvent container assembly (7).
   To install:

➡ **Using windshield washer solvent, lubricate the washer pump where it's installed in the rubber grommet.**

7. Install the front washer pump (2) into the washer solvent container assembly (7).

8. Push the front washer pump (2) down into the washer solvent container assembly (7).
9. Push the top of front washer pump (2) into the side of the washer solvent container assembly (7).
10. Connect the hose (5) to the front washer pump (2).
11. Attach the connector (1) to the front washer pump(2).
12. Connect the negative battery cable.

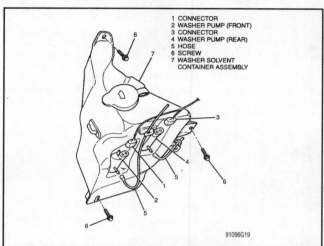

1 CONNECTOR
2 WASHER PUMP (FRONT)
3 CONNECTOR
4 WASHER PUMP (REAR)
5 HOSE
6 SCREW
7 WASHER SOLVENT
  CONTAINER ASSEMBLY

91096G19

Fig. 61 This diagram shows the numbered steps and connections for the front and rear pumps

INSTRUMENTS AND SWITCHES

❊❊ CAUTION

Some models covered by this manual may be equipped with a Supplemental Inflatable Restraint (SIR), which uses an air bag. Whenever working near any of the SIR components, such as the impact sensors, the air bag module, steering column and instrument panel disable the SIR, as described in this section.

Many solid state electrical components can be damaged by electrostatic discharge (ESD). Some will display a label indicating this sensitivity. Many electrical components, which are ESD sensitive, will not, however, display a label.

Instrument Cluster

The instrument panel assembly contains the instruments used by the driver during vehicle operation, the ventilation and sound system controls, many vehicle convenience items and most of the HVAC outlets. The panel has been designed to facilitate removal of all switches and instruments.

REMOVAL & INSTALLATION

♦ **See Figures 62 thru 77**

1. Disconnect the negative battery cable.
2. Remove the instrument panel insulator.
3. Remove the knee bolster.
4. Remove the instrument panel accessory trim plate.
5. Tilt steering wheel to lowest position.
6. Start near the headlamp switch and work toward the center of the vehicle instrument panel cluster trim plate by pulling the release clips securing the instrument panel cluster trim plate to the dash board.
7. Remove the instrument panel cluster trim plate from the instrument panel.
8. Remove the screws from the gauge cluster to the instrument panel, and detach the electrical connectors.
   To install:
9. installation is the reverse of the removal procedure.

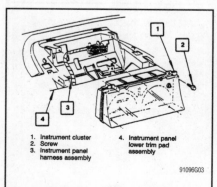

1. Instrument cluster
2. Screw
3. Instrument panel harness assembly
4. Instrument panel lower trim pad assembly

91096G03

Fig. 62 Exploded view of the instrument cluster

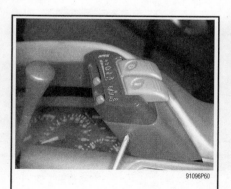

91096P60

Fig. 63 Remove this screw . . .

91096P62

Fig. 64 . . . and the switch will snap out, revealing other fasteners

Fig. 65 When both switches are removed . . .

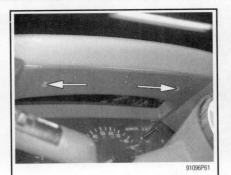

Fig. 66 . . . remove these two screws to remove the trim pad . . .

Fig. 67 . . . and access the mounting adapter for the switches

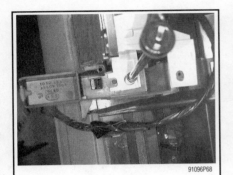

Fig. 68 Remove the two fasteners on each side . . .

Fig. 69 . . . to remove the mounting stands from the cluster

Fig. 70 Unplug the switches

Fig. 71 Use a small screwdriver to unscrew the bulb . . .

Fig. 72 . . . then remove the bulb for replacement

Fig. 73 Unplug the harness from the instrument cluster

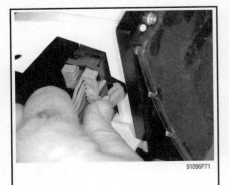

Fig. 74 The connector is a positive lock

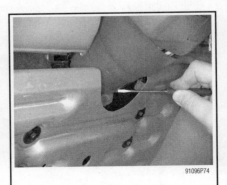

Fig. 75 Don't forget to disconnect the small cable for the PRNDL indicator

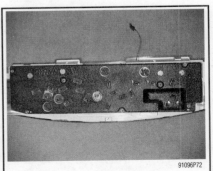

Fig. 76 Once removed, the gauge cluster is serviceable as a unit, along with the instrument cluster lamps that . . .

Fig. 77 . . . are serviceable from the rear of the cluster with a simple twist

LIGHTING

❊❊ CAUTION

Halogen bulbs contain a gas under pressure. Handling a bulb improperly could cause it to shatter into flying glass fragments.

Headlights

REMOVAL & INSTALLATION

Sealed Beam Type

1. Disconnect the negative battery cable.
2. Remove the headlamp capsule screws.
3. Remove the headlamp capsule from the bracket.
4. Remove the lamp socket from the headlamp capsule.
5. Disconnect the bulb from the lamp socket.

To install:

6. Install the bulb into the lamp socket.
7. Install the lamp socket into the headlamp capsule.
8. Install the headlamp capsule to bracket with screws.
9. Connect the negative battery cable.

Composite Type

▶ See Figure 78

➡**This procedure only applies to replaceable halogen headlight bulbs (such as Nos. 9004 and 9005); it does not pertain to sealed beam units.**

1. Open the hood of the vehicle and secure it in an upright position.
2. Unscrew the locking ring, which secures the bulb, and socket assembly, then withdraw the assembly rearward.
3. If necessary, gently pry the socket's retaining clip over the projection on the bulb (use care not to break the clip.) Pull the bulb from the socket.

To install:

4. Before installing a light bulb into the socket, ensure that all electrical contact surfaces are free of corrosion or dirt.
5. Line up the replacement headlight bulb with the socket. Firmly push the bulb onto the socket until the spring clip latches over the projection of the bulb.

❊❊ WARNING

Do not touch the glass bulb with your fingers. Oil from your fingers can severely shorten the life of the bulb. If necessary, wipe off any

Back-up Light Switch

REMOVAL & INSTALLATION

1. Remove the automatic transaxle range selector lever cable from the automatic transaxle range selector lever .
2. Remove the automatic transaxle range selector lever nut, and remove the selector lever.
3. Installation is the reversal of the removal process.

Fig. 78 Carefully pull the halogen headlight bulb from its socket. If applicable, release the retaining clip

dirt or oil from the bulb with rubbing alcohol before completing installation.

6. To ensure that the replacement bulb functions properly, activate the applicable switch to illuminate the bulb which was just replaced. (If this is a combination low and high beam bulb, be sure to check both intensities.) If the replacement light bulb does not illuminate, either it too is faulty or there is a problem in the bulb circuit or switch. Correct as necessary.
7. Position the headlight bulb and secure it with the locking ring.
8. Close the hood of the vehicle.

AIMING THE HEADLIGHTS

▶ See Figures 79 thru 85

The headlights must be properly aimed to provide the best, safest road illumination. The lights should be checked for proper aim and adjusted as necessary. Certain state and local authorities have requirements for headlight aiming; these should be checked before adjustment is made.

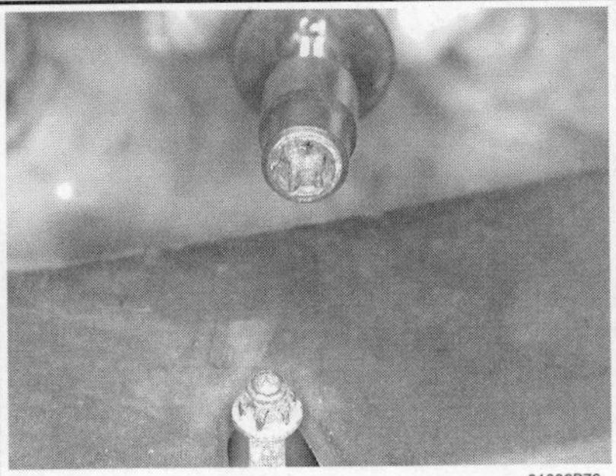

Fig. 79 Using this special inverted Torx®socket to make adjustments . . .

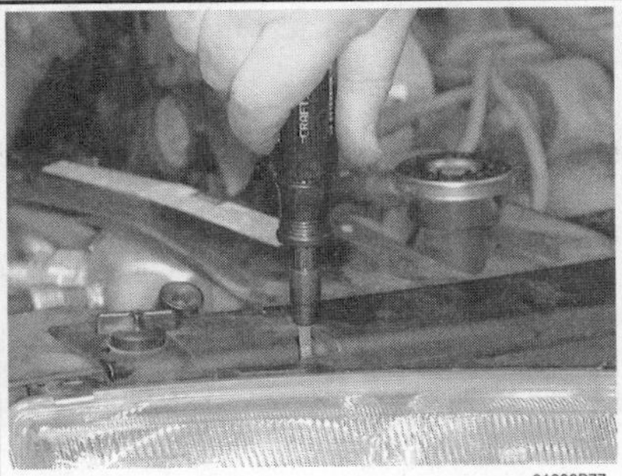

Fig. 80 . . . that can still be made to aim the headlamps correctly

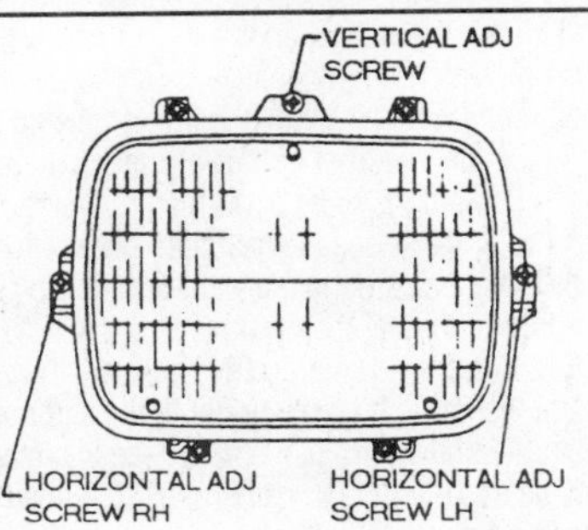

Fig. 81 Location of the aiming screws on most vehicles with sealed beam headlights

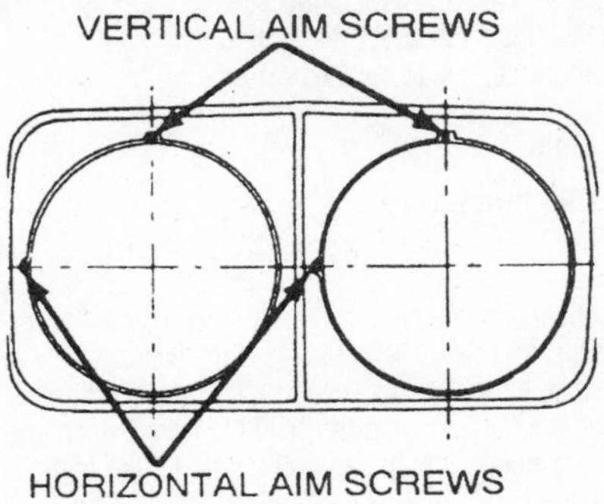

Fig. 82 Dual headlight adjustment screw locations—one side shown here (other side should be mirror image)

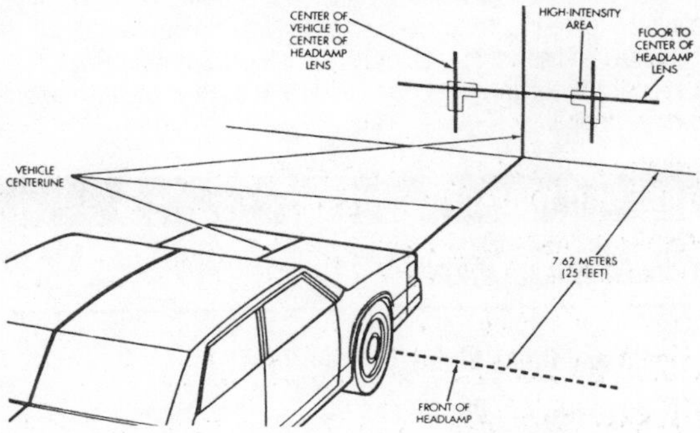

Fig. 84 Low-beam headlight pattern alignment

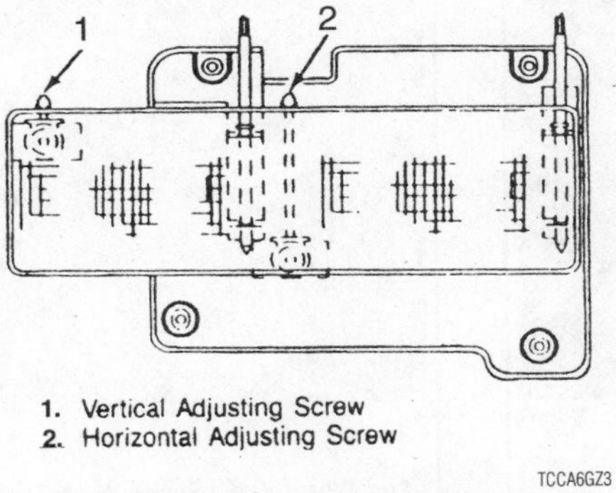

Fig. 83 Example of headlight adjustment screw location for composite headlamps

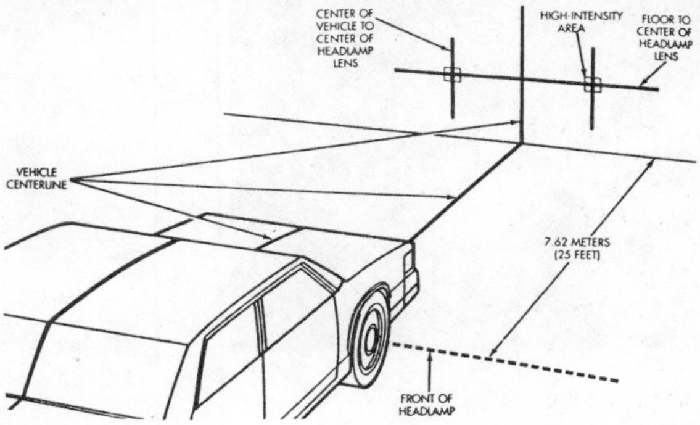

Fig. 85 High-beam headlight pattern alignment

CAUTION

About once a year, when the headlights are replaced or any time front-end work is performed on your vehicle, the headlight should be accurately aimed by a reputable repair shop using the proper equipment. Headlights not properly aimed can make it virtually impossible to see and may blind other drivers on the road, possibly causing an accident. Note that the following procedure is a temporary fix, until you can take your vehicle to a repair shop for a proper adjustment.

Headlight adjustment may be temporarily made using a wall, as described below, or on the rear of another vehicle. When adjusted, the lights should not glare in oncoming car or truck windshields, nor should they illuminate the passenger compartment of vehicles driving in front of you. These adjustments are rough and should always be fine-tuned by a repair shop that is equipped with headlight aiming tools. Improper adjustments may be both dangerous and illegal.

For most of the vehicles covered by this manual, horizontal and vertical aiming of each sealed beam unit is provided by two adjusting screws which move the retaining ring and adjusting plate against the tension of a coil spring. There is no adjustment for focus; this is done during headlight manufacturing.

➡Because the composite headlight assembly is bolted into position, no adjustment should be necessary or possible. Some applications, however, may be bolted to an adjuster plate or may be retained by adjusting screws. If so, follow this procedure when adjusting the lights, BUT always have the adjustment checked by a reputable shop.

Before removing the headlight bulb or disturbing the headlamp in any way, note the current settings in order to ease headlight adjustment upon reassembly. If the high or low beam setting of the old lamp still works, this can be done using the wall of a garage or a building:

1. Park the vehicle on a level surface, with the fuel tank about ½ full and with the vehicle empty of all extra cargo (unless normally carried). The vehicle should be facing a wall that is no less than 6 feet (1.8m) high and 12 feet (3.7m) wide. The front of the vehicle should be about 25 feet from the wall.

2. If aiming is to be performed outdoors, it is advisable to wait until dusk in order to properly see the headlight beams on the wall. If done in a garage, darken the area around the wall as much as possible by closing shades or hanging cloth over the windows.

3. Turn the headlights **ON** and mark the wall at the center of each light's low beam, then switch on the bright lights and mark the center of each light's high beam. A short length of masking tape that is visible from the front of the vehicle may be used. Although marking all four positions is advisable, marking one position from each light should be sufficient.

4. If neither beam on one side is working, and if another like-sized vehicle is available, park the second one in the exact spot where the vehicle was and mark the beams using the same-side light. Then switch the vehicles so the one to be aimed is back in the original spot. It must be parked no closer to or farther away from the wall than the second vehicle.

5. Perform any necessary repairs, but make sure the vehicle is not moved, or is returned to the exact spot from which the lights were marked. Turn the headlights **ON** and adjust the beams to match the marks on the wall.

6. Have the headlight adjustment checked as soon as possible by a reputable repair shop.

Signal and Marker Lights

REMOVAL & INSTALLATION

Turn Signal and Brake Lights

▶ **See Figures 86, 87, 88, 89 and 90**

1. Depending on the vehicle and bulb application, either unscrew or remove the lens or disengage the bulb and socket assembly from the rear of the lens housing.

2. To remove a light bulb with retaining pins from its socket, grasp the bulb, then gently depress and twist it 1/8 turn counterclockwise, and pull it from the socket.

To install:

3. Before installing a light bulb into the socket, ensure that all electrical contact surfaces are free of corrosion or dirt.

➡**Before installing the light bulb, note the positions of the two retaining pins on the bulb. They will likely be at different heights on the bulb, to ensure that the bulb is installed correctly. If, when installing the bulb, it does not turn easily, do not force it. Remove the bulb and rotate it 180 ° from its former position, then reinsert it into the bulb socket.**

4. Insert the light bulb into the socket and, while depressing the bulb, twist it 1/8 turn clockwise until the two pins on the light bulb are properly engaged in the socket.

5. To ensure that the replacement bulb functions properly, activate the applicable switch to illuminate the bulb which was just replaced. If the replacement light bulb does not illuminate, either it too is faulty or there is a problem in the bulb circuit or switch. Correct if necessary.

6. If applicable, install the socket and bulb assembly into the rear of the lens housing; otherwise, install the lens over the bulb.

Side Marker Light

▶ **See Figures 91 thru 95**

TYPE 1

On some applications, the side marker lamp bulbs can be replaced without any component disassembly. The bulbs are directly accessible from inside the front bumper fascia. If they are not, use the Type 2 procedure.

1. Disengage the bulb and socket assembly from the lens housing.

2. Gently grasp the light bulb and pull it straight out of the socket.

To install:

3. Before installing the light bulb into the socket, ensure that all electrical contact surfaces are free of corrosion or dirt.

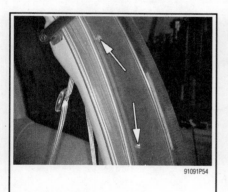

91091P54

Fig. 86 Remove the two screws . . .

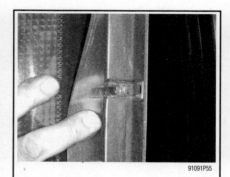

91091P55

Fig. 87 . . . release the two latches . . .

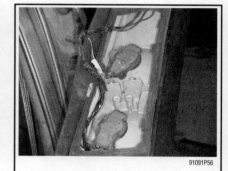

91091P56

Fig. 88 . . . to expose the bulb sockets and . . .

91091P57

Fig. 89 . . . to release the rear lens assembly

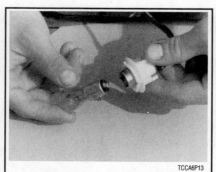

TCCA6P13

Fig. 90 Depress and twist this type of bulb counterclockwise, then pull the bulb straight from its socket

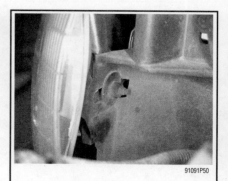

91091P50

Fig. 91 This retaining nut must be removed

Fig. 92 Using a small socket and ratchet is easiest

Fig. 93 Slide the lamp assembly forward to free it from the slot

Fig. 94 A simple twist will remove the bulb holder from the lens assembly

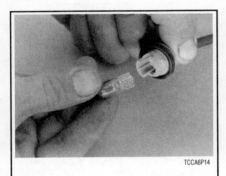

Fig. 95 Simply pull this side marker light bulb straight from its socket

Fig. 96 The reflector houses the brake bulb

Fig. 97 Remove the two screws to get to the bulb

4. Line up the base of the light bulb with the socket, then insert the light bulb into the socket until it is fully seated.

5. To ensure that the replacement bulb functions properly, activate the applicable switch to illuminate the bulb which was just replaced. If the replacement light bulb does not illuminate, either it too is faulty or there is a problem in the bulb circuit or switch. Correct as necessary.

6. Install the socket and bulb assembly into the lens housing.

TYPE 2

On this application, the bulb is not directly replaceable without removing some parts. It is necessary to remove the front parking/turn signal lamp bulbs by removing the headlamp capsule screws, pulling the headlamp capsule forward, and accessing the lamp sockets.

1. Remove the side marker lamp assembly.
2. Remove the front parking/turn signal lamp assembly retaining nuts.
3. Disengage lamp assembly from slots in fascia and pull assembly away from fascia.
4. Remove the socket and bulb, as described in Type 1.

To install:
5. Install the bulb and socket, as described in Type 1.
6. Engage the lamp assembly to slots in fascia.
7. Install the front parking/turn signal lamp assembly retaining nuts.
8 Install the front parking/turn signal lamp socket to lamp assembly, and install the side marker lamp assembly.

High-Mount Brake Light

♦ See Figures 96 and 97

To replace the high-mount brake light bulb, unfasten the retaining screws, then remove the bulb.

Dome Light

♦ See Figures 98 and 99

1. Using a small prytool, carefully remove the cover lens from the lamp assembly.

2. Remove the bulb from its retaining clip contacts. If the bulb has tapered ends, gently depress the spring clip/metal contact and disengage the light bulb, then pull it free of the two metal contacts.

To install:
3. Before installing the light bulb into the metal contacts, ensure that all electrical conducting surfaces are free of corrosion or dirt.
4. Position the bulb between the two metal contacts. If the contacts have small holes, be sure that the tapered ends of the bulb are situated in them.
5. To ensure that the replacement bulb functions properly, activate the applicable switch to illuminate the bulb which was just replaced. If the replace-

Fig. 98 Disengage the spring clip, which retains one tapered end of this dome light bulb, then withdraw the bulb

Fig. 99 Pulling the double ended light bulb out of the dome socket

91091P88

ment light bulb does not illuminate, either it is faulty or there is a problem in the bulb circuit or switch. Correct as necessary.

6. Install the cover lens until its retaining tabs are properly engaged.

License Plate Lights

See Figures 100, 101, and 102

1. Remove the two Torx® screws and remove the light assembly.
2. Remove the socket from the lamp assembly and replace the bulb as necessary.
To install:
3. Installation is the reverse of removal.

Fog/Driving Lights

REMOVAL & INSTALLATION

Fog lamp bulb replacement does not require any disassembly. The fog lamp sockets are directly accessible from behind the front bumper fascia. To replace a bulb, pull the rubber seal back from the lamp socket. Squeeze the lamp socket retainer and pull the socket out from behind the fog lamp assembly. Replace the bulb, squeeze, insert the lamp socket into the lamp assembly, and pull the rubber seal forward over the lamp socket.

Fig. 100 Use a longer screwdriver (preferably magnetic) to remove the retaining screws

91091P84

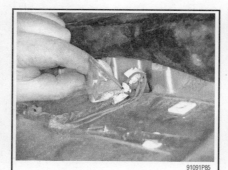

Fig. 101 Pull the whole light assembly out

91091P85

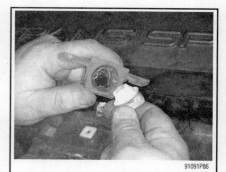

Fig. 102 Disassemble the holder and replace the bulb

91091P86

CIRCUIT PROTECTION

✳✳ CAUTION

Some models covered by this manual may be equipped with a Supplemental Inflatable Restraint (SIR), which uses an air bag. Whenever working near any of the SIR components, such as the impact sensors, the air bag module, steering column and instrument panel, disable the SIR, as described in this section.

The power distribution system of the vehicle consists of fuses, fusible links, circuit breakers, and the ignition switch. Fusible links are short pieces of wire several sizes smaller than the circuit wire to which they supply power. They are covered with special high temperature insulation. When conducting an improperly high current flow, they will melt and stop current flow. They are designed to protect the vehicle's electrical system from electrical shorts in circuits that are not protected by circuit breakers or fuses.

Fuses

The fuses are of the miniaturized (compact) size and are located on a fuse block, they provide increased circuit protection and reliability. Access to the fuse block is gained through the glove box opening. Each fuse receptacle is marked as to the circuit it protects and the correct amperage of the fuse.

REPLACEMENT

1. Pull the fuse from the fuse block.
2. Inspect the fuse element (through the clear plastic body) to the blade terminal for defects.

➡**When replacing the fuse, DO NOT use one of higher amperage.**

3. To install, reverse the removal procedures.

Fusible Links

In addition to fuses, the wiring harness incorporates fusible links (in the battery feed circuits) to protect the wiring. Fusible links are 4 in. (102mm) sections of copper wire, 4 gauges smaller than the circuit(s) they are protecting, designed to melt under electrical overload. There are four different gauge sizes used. The fusible links are color coded so that they may be installed in their original positions.

1. Fusible link B—Rust colored, charging and starting circuit, connected to the starter solenoid.
2. Fusible link C—Rust colored, TBI circuit, located at junction block, in the engine compartment, on the left side wheelhouse opening.
3. Fusible link H—Rust colored, charging and starting circuit, connected to the starter solenoid.

4. Fusible link J—RUST colored, coolant fan circuit, connected to the starter solenoid.

5. Fusible link Y—Rust colored, headlight circuit, located at junction block, in the engine compartment, on the left side wheelhouse opening.

6. Fusible link X—Rust colored, heater circuit, located at junction block, in the engine compartment, on the left side wheelhouse opening.

7. Fusible link X—Rust colored, TBI circuit, located at junction block, in the engine compartment, on the left side wheelhouse opening.

8. Fusible link X—Rust colored, charging and starting circuit, located at junction block, in the engine compartment, on the left side wheelhouse opening.

REPLACEMENT

1. Disconnect the negative battery terminal from the battery.
2. Locate the cause of the problem and repair before replacing the link.
3. Locate the burned out link.
4. Strip away the melted insulation and cut the burned link ends from the wire.
5. Strip the wire back ½. (13mm) to allow soldering of the new link.
6. Using a new fusible link 4 gauges smaller than the protected circuit and approximately 10 in. (254mm) long, solder it into the circuit.

➡**Whenever splicing a new wire, always bond the splice with rosin core solder, then cover with electrical tape. Using acid core solder may cause corrosion.**

7. Tape and seal all splices with silicone to weatherproof repairs.
8. After taping the wire, tape the electrical harness leaving an exposed 5 in. (127mm) loop of wire.
9. Reconnect the battery.

Circuit Breakers

1. A circuit breaker is an electrical switch, which breaks the circuit in case of an overload. The rear defogger, power accessories, power windows and Daytime Running Light (DRL) circuit breakers are located in the convenience center. The circuit breaker will remain open until the short or overload condition in the circuit is corrected.

RESETTING AND/OR REPLACEMENT

1. Locate the circuit breaker in the convenience center, then push the circuit breaker in until it locks. If the circuit breaker kicks itself Off again, locate and correct the problem in the electrical circuit.

Flashers

REPLACEMENT

▶ **See Figures 103 and 104**

1. Disconnect the negative battery cable.
2. Remove the sound insulator panel.
3. Remove the I/P steering column opening filler from the I/P lower trim pad by disengaging the four upper clips.

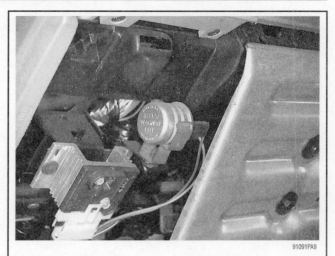

Fig. 103 The turn signal flasher is serviceable by removing the trim panels under the steering column

Fig. 104 The hazard flasher is serviceable by removing the right side trim panels

4. Remove the turn signal flasher from the retaining clip and unplug it.
To install:
5. Installation is the reverse of removal.

The hazard flasher is mounted in the convenience center. The convenience center is located behind the glove compartment. The repair procedure is the same as the T/S flasher.

WIRE DIAGRAMS

INDEX OF WIRING DIAGRAMS

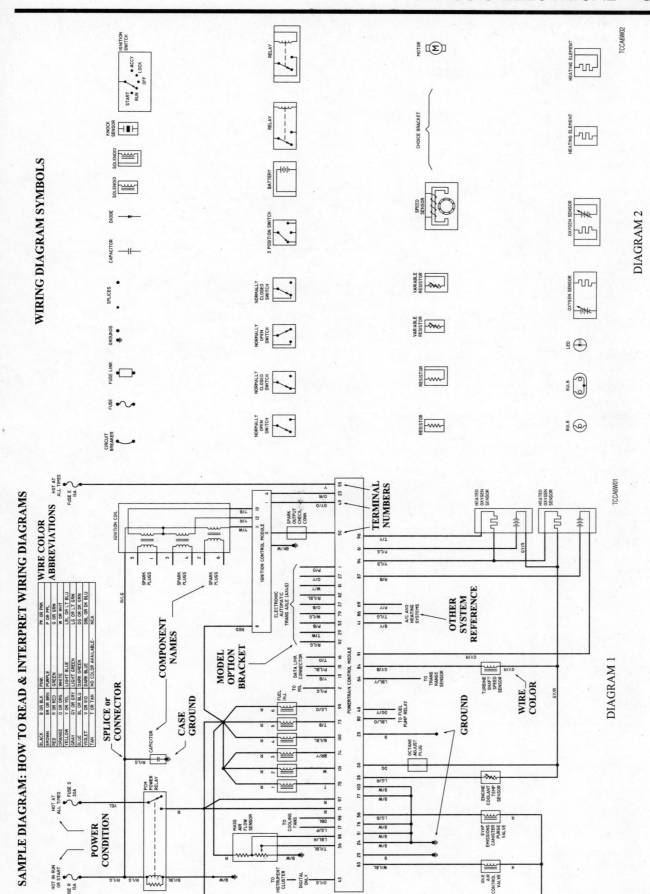

WIRING DIAGRAM SYMBOLS

SAMPLE DIAGRAM: HOW TO READ & INTERPRET WIRING DIAGRAMS

DIAGRAM 1

DIAGRAM 2

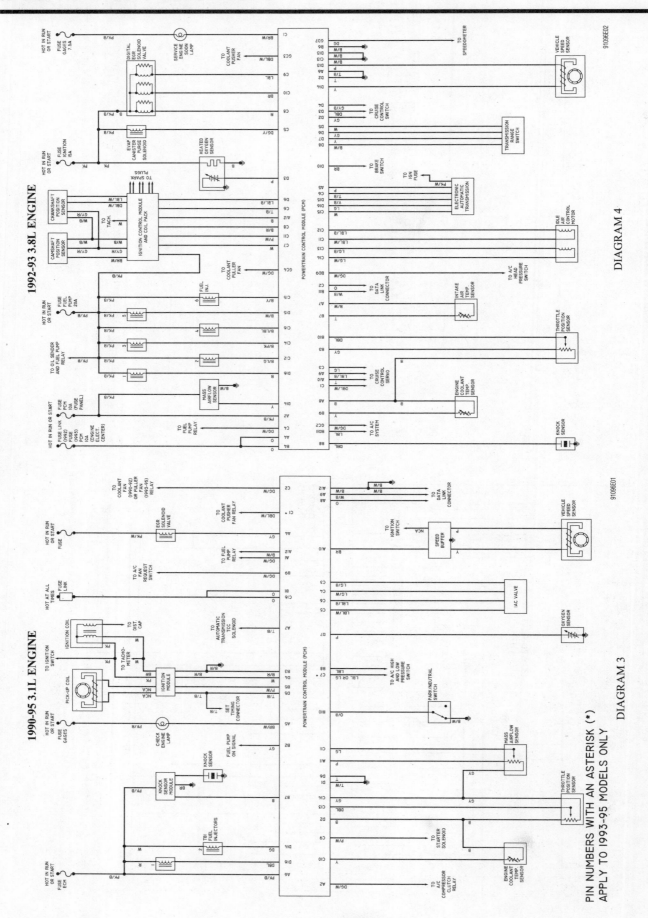

1992-93 3.8L ENGINE

1990-95 3.1L ENGINE

DIAGRAM 4

DIAGRAM 3

PIN NUMBERS WITH AN ASTERISK (*)
APPLY TO 1993-95 MODELS ONLY

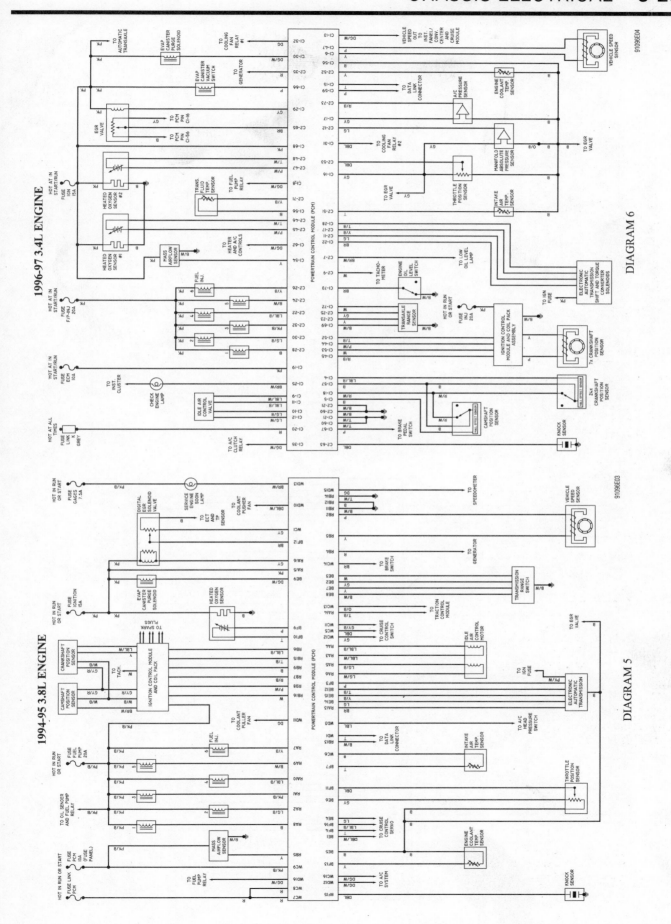

DIAGRAM 6

DIAGRAM 5

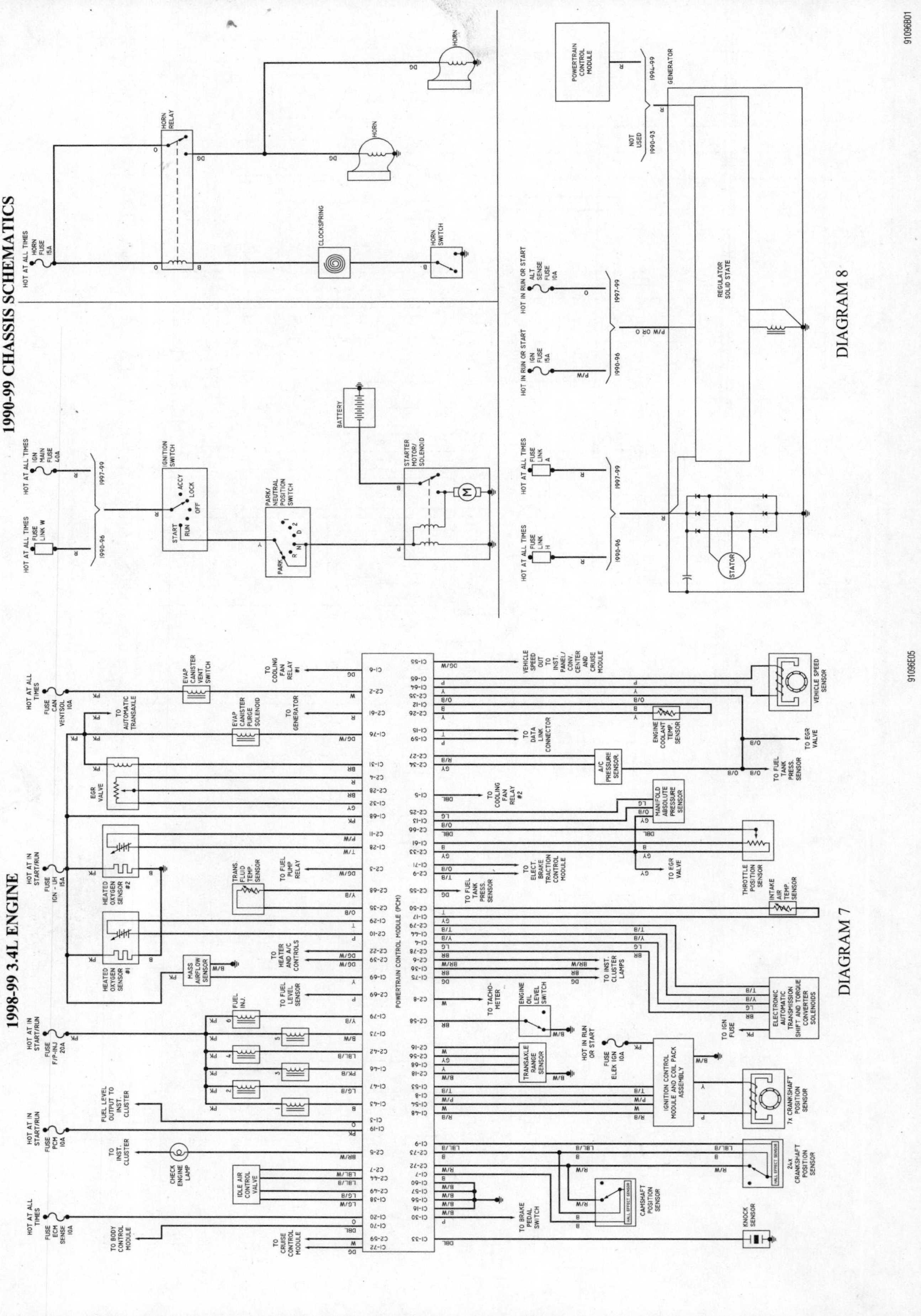

1990-99 CHASSIS SCHEMATICS

DIAGRAM 8

1998-99 3.4L ENGINE

DIAGRAM 7

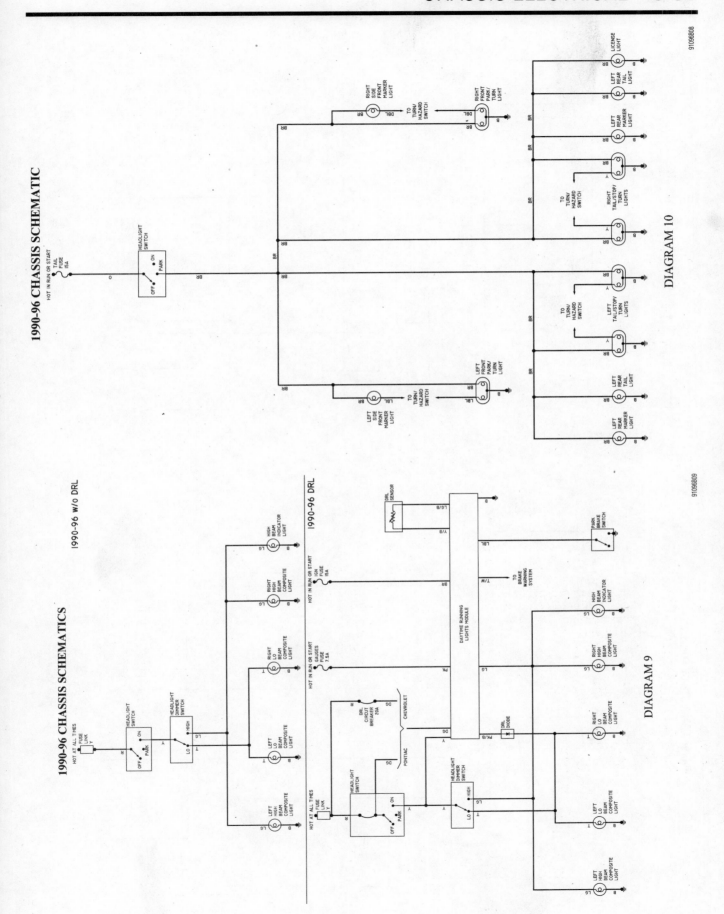

1990-96 CHASSIS SCHEMATIC

DIAGRAM 10

1990-96 CHASSIS SCHEMATICS

DIAGRAM 9

1997-99 CHASSIS SCHEMATIC

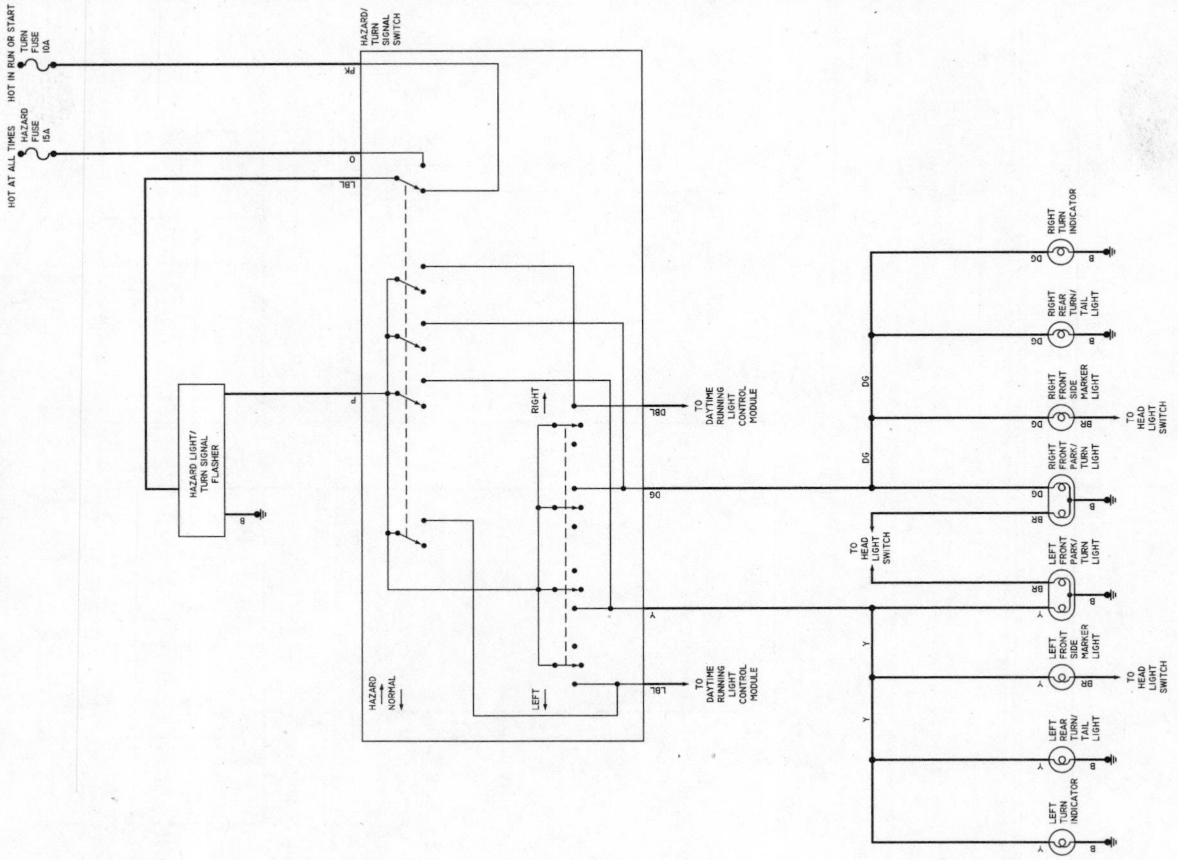

HAZARD/TURN SIGNAL SWITCH

HOT IN RUN OR START
TURN FUSE 10A

HOT AT ALL TIMES
HAZARD FUSE 15A

HAZARD LIGHT/TURN SIGNAL FLASHER

TO DAYTIME RUNNING LIGHT CONTROL MODULE

RIGHT

LEFT

HAZARD
NORMAL

TO DAYTIME RUNNING LIGHT CONTROL MODULE

RIGHT TURN INDICATOR

RIGHT REAR TAIL LIGHT

RIGHT FRONT SIDE MARKER LIGHT

TO HEAD LIGHT SWITCH

RIGHT FRONT PARK/TURN LIGHT

TO HEAD LIGHT SWITCH

LEFT FRONT PARK/TURN LIGHT

LEFT FRONT SIDE MARKER LIGHT

TO HEAD LIGHT SWITCH

LEFT REAR TURN/TAIL LIGHT

LEFT TURN INDICATOR

DIAGRAM 12

1990-96 CHASSIS SCHEMATIC

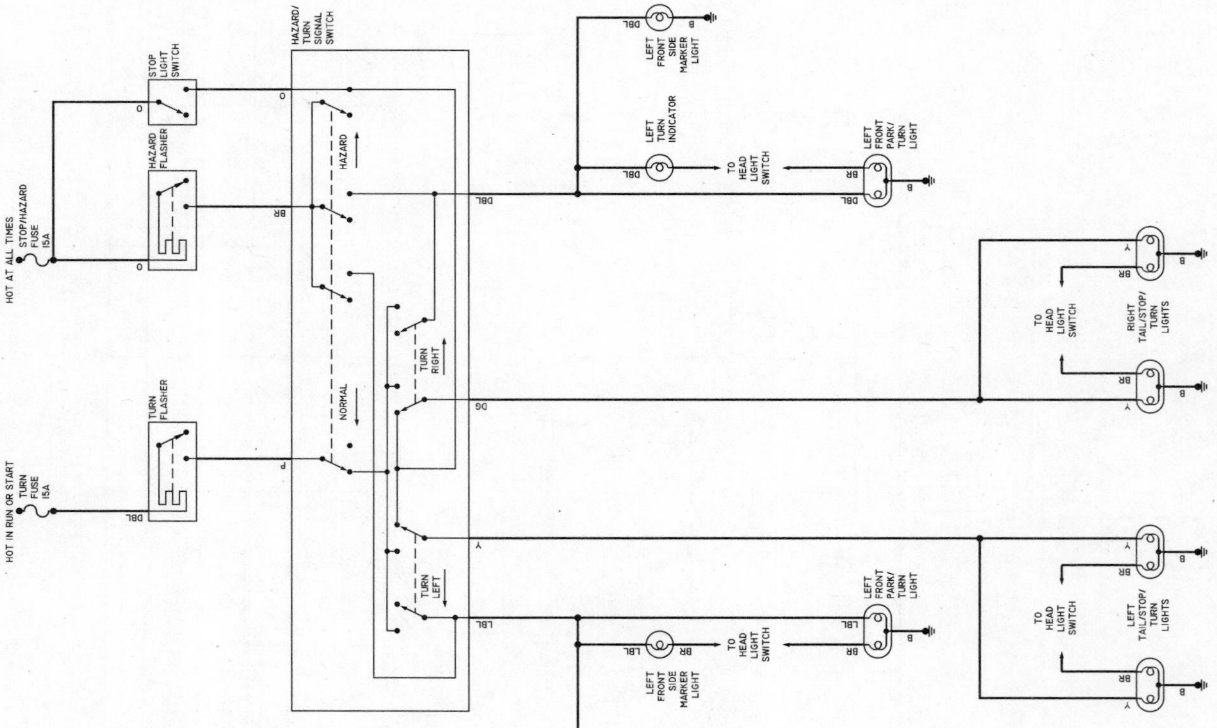

STOP LIGHT SWITCH

HAZARD/TURN SIGNAL SWITCH

HOT AT ALL TIMES
STOP/HAZARD FUSE 15A

HAZARD FLASHER

HAZARD

TURN RIGHT

NORMAL

TURN LEFT

TURN FLASHER

HOT IN RUN OR START
TURN FUSE 15A

LEFT FRONT SIDE MARKER LIGHT

LEFT TURN INDICATOR

TO HEAD LIGHT SWITCH

LEFT FRONT PARK/TURN LIGHT

RIGHT TAIL/STOP/TURN LIGHTS

TO HEAD LIGHT SWITCH

LEFT FRONT SIDE MARKER LIGHT

TO HEAD LIGHT SWITCH

LEFT FRONT PARK/TURN LIGHT

TO HEAD LIGHT SWITCH

LEFT TAIL/STOP/TURN LIGHTS

LEFT TURN INDICATOR

DIAGRAM 11

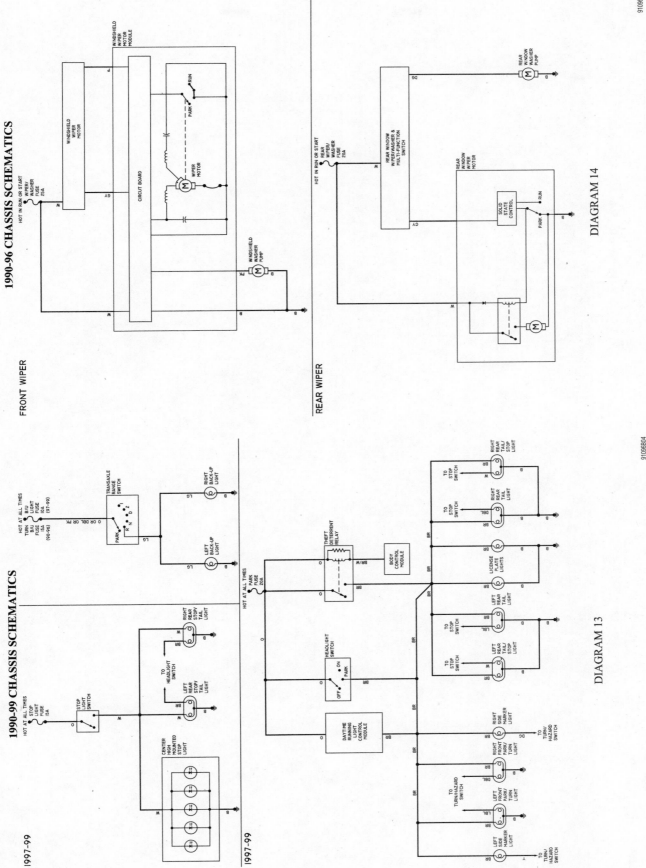

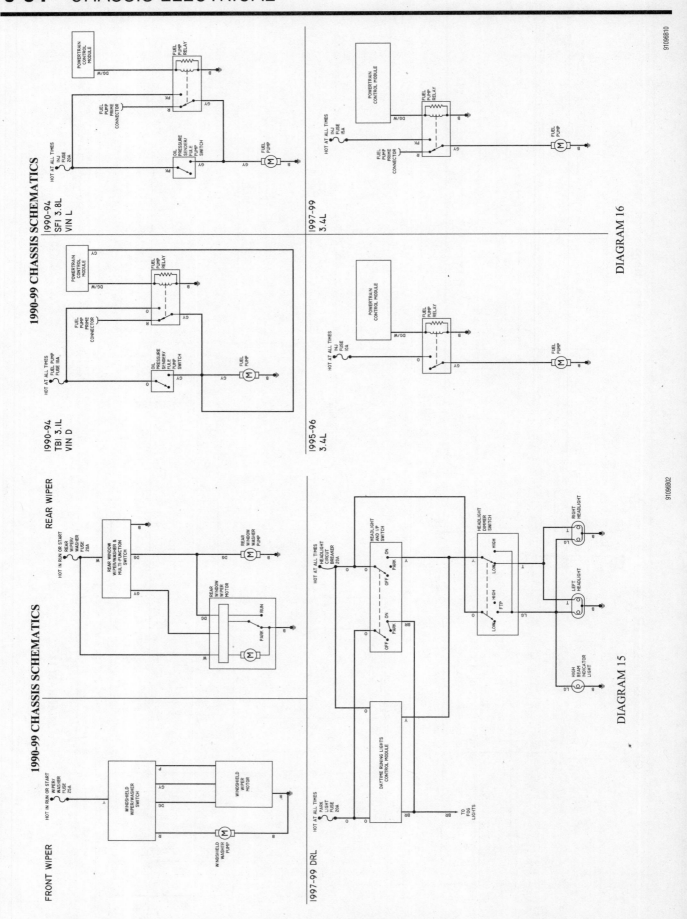

1990-99 CHASSIS SCHEMATICS

1990-94
SFI 3.8L
VIN L

1990-94
TBI 3.1L
VIN D

1997-99
3.4L

1995-96
3.4L

DIAGRAM 16

REAR WIPER

FRONT WIPER

1990-99 CHASSIS SCHEMATICS

1997-99 DRL

DIAGRAM 15

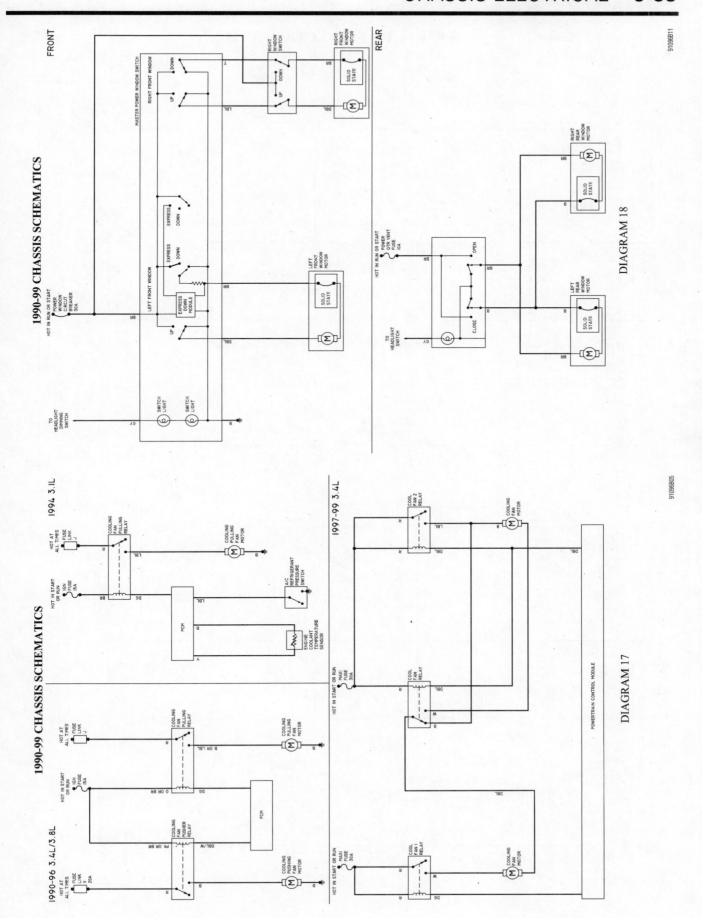

1990-99 CHASSIS SCHEMATICS

DIAGRAM 18

1990-99 CHASSIS SCHEMATICS

DIAGRAM 17

1990-99 CHASSIS SCHEMATICS

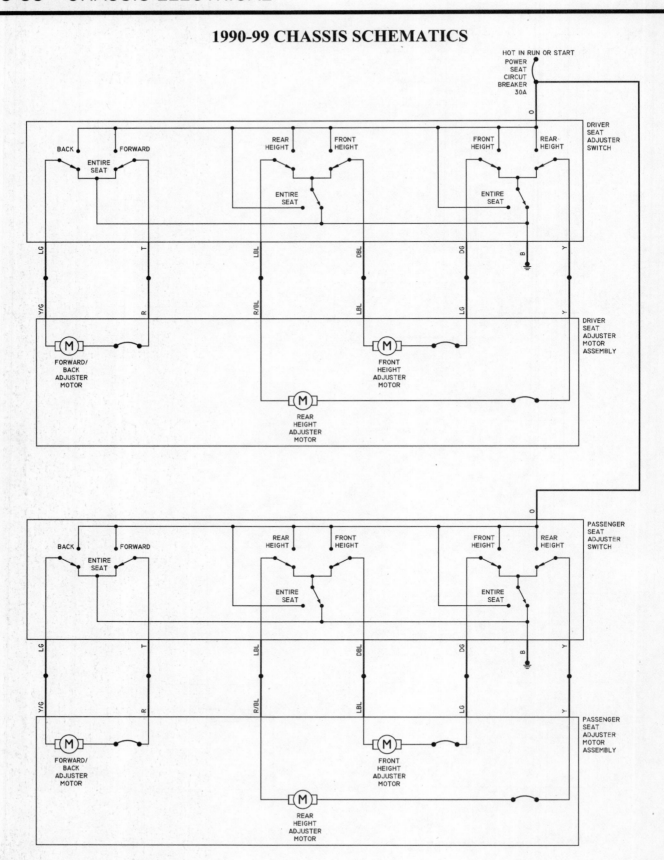

DIAGRAM 19

91096B12

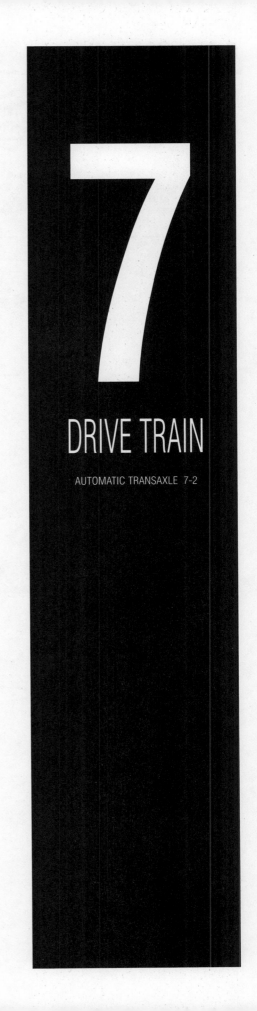

7

DRIVE TRAIN

AUTOMATIC TRANSAXLE 7-2

AUTOMATIC TRANSAXLE

Understanding the Automatic Transaxle

♦ **See Figure 1**

The automatic transaxle allows engine torque and power to be transmitted to the front wheels within a narrow range of engine operating speeds. It will allow the engine to turn fast enough to produce plenty of power and torque at very low speeds, while keeping it at a sensible rpm at high vehicle speeds

(and it does this job without driver assistance). The transaxle uses a light fluid as the medium for the transmission of power. This fluid also works in the operation of various hydraulic control circuits and as a lubricant. Because the transaxle fluid performs all of these functions, trouble within the unit can easily travel from one part to another. For this reason, and because of the complexity and unusual operating principles of the transaxle, a very sound understanding of the basic principles of operation will simplify troubleshooting.

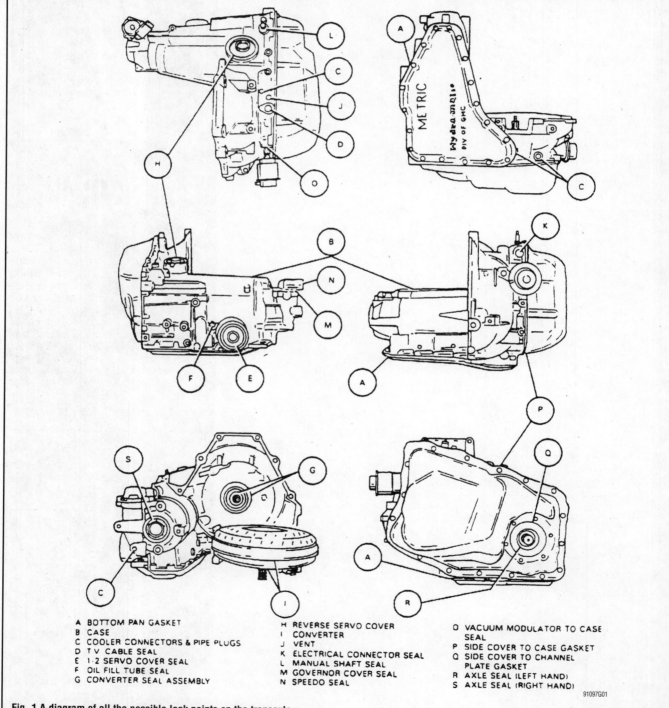

A	BOTTOM PAN GASKET
B	CASE
C	COOLER CONNECTORS & PIPE PLUGS
D	T V CABLE SEAL
E	1-2 SERVO COVER SEAL
F	OIL FILL TUBE SEAL
G	CONVERTER SEAL ASSEMBLY

H	REVERSE SERVO COVER
I	CONVERTER
J	VENT
K	ELECTRICAL CONNECTOR SEAL
L	MANUAL SHAFT SEAL
M	GOVERNOR COVER SEAL
N	SPEEDO SEAL

O	VACUUM MODULATOR TO CASE SEAL
P	SIDE COVER TO CASE GASKET
Q	SIDE COVER TO CHANNEL PLATE GASKET
R	AXLE SEAL (LEFT HAND)
S	AXLE SEAL (RIGHT HAND)

91097G01

Fig. 1 A diagram of all the possible leak points on the transaxle

TORQUE CONVERTER

▶ **See Figure 2**

The torque converter replaces the conventional clutch. It has three functions:

1. It allows the engine to idle with the vehicle at a standstill, even with the transmission in gear.

2. It allows the transmission to shift from range-to-range smoothly, without requiring that the driver close the throttle during the shift.

3. It multiplies engine torque to an increasing extent as vehicle speed drops and throttle opening is increased. This has the effect of making the transmission more responsive and reduces the amount of shifting required.

The torque converter is a metal case, which is shaped like a sphere that has been flattened on opposite sides. It is bolted to the rear end of the engine's crankshaft. Generally, the entire metal case rotates at engine speed and serves as the flywheel of the engine.

The case contains three sets of blades. One set is attached directly to the case. This set forms the torus or pump. Another set is directly connected to the output shaft, and forms the turbine. The third set is mounted on a hub which, in turn, is mounted on a stationary shaft through a one-way clutch. This third set is known as the stator.

A pump, which is driven by the converter hub at engine speed, keeps the torque converter full of transmission fluid at all times. Fluid flows continuously through the unit to provide cooling.

Under low speed acceleration, the torque converter functions as follows:

The torus is turning faster than the turbine. It picks up fluid at the center of the converter and, through centrifugal force, slings it outward. Since the outer edge of the converter moves faster than the portions at the center, the fluid picks up speed.

The fluid then enters the outer edge of the turbine blades. It then travels back toward the center of the converter case along the turbine blades. In impinging upon the turbine blades, the fluid loses the energy picked up in the torus.

If the fluid was now returned directly into the torus, both halves of the converter would have to turn at approximately the same speed at all times, and torque input and output would both be the same.

In flowing through the torus and turbine, the fluid picks up two types of flow, or flow in two separate directions. It flows through the turbine blades, and it spins with the engine. The stator, whose blades are stationary when the vehicle is being accelerated at low speeds, converts one type of flow into another. Instead of allowing the fluid to flow straight back into the torus, the stator's curved blades turn the fluid almost 90° toward the direction of rotation of the engine. Thus the fluid does not flow as fast toward the torus, but is already spinning when the torus picks it up. This has the effect of allowing the torus to turn much faster than the turbine. This difference in speed may be compared to the difference in speed between the smaller and larger gears in any gear train. The result is that engine power output is higher, and engine torque is multiplied.

As the speed of the turbine increases, the fluid spins faster and faster in the direction of engine rotation. Consequently, the ability of the stator to redirect the fluid flow is reduced. Under cruising conditions, the stator is eventually forced to rotate on its one-way clutch in the direction of engine rotation. Under these conditions, the torque converter begins to behave almost like a solid shaft, with the torus and turbine speeds being almost equal.

PLANETARY GEARBOX

▶ **See Figures 3, 4 and 5**

The ability of the torque converter to multiply engine torque is limited. In addition, the unit tends to be more efficient when the turbine is rotating at relatively high speeds. Therefore, a planetary gearbox is used to carry the power output of the turbine to the driveshaft.

Planetary gears function very similarly to conventional transmission gears. However, their construction is different in that three elements make up one gear system, and, in that, all three elements are different from one another. The three elements are: an outer gear that is shaped like a hoop, with teeth cut into the inner surface; a sun gear, mounted on a shaft and located at the very center of the outer gear; and a set of three planet gears, held by pins in a ring-like planet carrier, meshing with both the sun gear and the outer gear. Either the outer gear or the sun gear may be held stationary, providing more than one possible torque multiplication factor for each set of gears. In addition, if all three gears are forced to rotate at the same speed, the gearset forms, in effect, a solid shaft.

Most automatics use the planetary gears to provide various reductions ratios. Bands and clutches are used to hold various portions of the gearsets to the transmission case or to the shaft on which they are mounted. Shifting is accomplished, then, by changing the portion of each planetary gearset that is held to the transmission case or to the shaft.

SERVOS & ACCUMULATORS

▶ **See Figure 6**

The servos are hydraulic pistons and cylinders. They resemble the hydraulic actuators used on many other machines, such as bulldozers. Hydraulic fluid

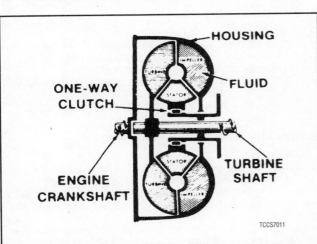

Fig. 2 The torque converter housing is rotated by the engine's crankshaft, and turns the impeller—The impeller then spins the turbine, which gives motion to the turbine shaft, driving the gears

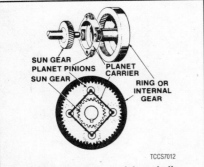

Fig. 3 Planetary gears work in a similar fashion to manual transmission gears, but are composed of three parts

Fig. 4 Planetary gears in the maximum reduction (low) range. The ring gear is held and a lower gear ratio is obtained

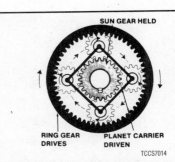

Fig. 5 Planetary gears in the minimum reduction (drive) range. The ring gear is allowed to revolve, providing a higher gear ratio

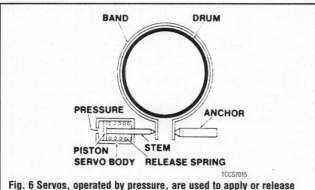

Fig. 6 Servos, operated by pressure, are used to apply or release the bands, to either hold the ring gear or allow it to rotate

enters the cylinder, under pressure, and forces the piston to move to engage the band or clutches.

The accumulators are used to cushion the engagement of the servos. The transmission fluid must pass through the accumulator on the way to the servo. The accumulator housing contains a thin piston, which is sprung away from the discharge passage of the accumulator. When fluid passes through the accumulator on the way to the servo, it must move the piston against spring pressure, and this action smoothes out the action of the servo.

HYDRAULIC CONTROL SYSTEM

The hydraulic pressure used to operate the servos comes from the main transmission oil pump. This fluid is channeled to the various servos through the shift valves. There is generally a manual shift valve, which is operated by the transmission selector lever, and an automatic shift valve for each automatic upshift the transmission provides.

➡**Many new transmissions are electronically controlled. On these models, electrical solenoids are used to better control the hydraulic fluid. Usually, the solenoids are regulated by an electronic control module.**

There are two pressures that affect the operation of these valves. One is the governor pressure, which is effected by vehicle speed. The other is the modulator pressure, which is affected by intake manifold vacuum or throttle position. Governor pressure rises with an increase in vehicle speed, and modulator pressure rises as the throttle is opened wider. By responding to these two pressures, the shift valves cause the upshift points to be delayed with increased throttle opening to make the best use of the power output of the engine.

Most transmissions also make use of an auxiliary circuit for downshifting. This circuit may be actuated by the throttle linkage the vacuum line which actuates the modulator, by a cable or by a solenoid. It applies pressure to a special downshift surface on the shift valve or valves.

The transmission modulator also governs the line pressure, used to actuate the servos. In this way, the clutches and bands will be actuated with a force matching the torque output of the engine.

Fluid Pan

REMOVAL & INSTALLATION

▶ See Figures 7, 8, 9, 10

1. Raise the vehicle and support it safely.
2. Place a drain pan under the transaxle fluid pan.
3. Remove the trans pan bolts from the front and sides only.
4. Loosen the rear trans pan bolts approximately four turns.
5. Lightly tap on the trans pan with a rubber mallet to allow the fluid to drain.
6. Remove the remaining trans pan bolts, then remove the trans pan and gasket.

To install:

7. Thoroughly clean the pan and magnet. Clean the gasket surfaces with a suitable solvent and allow to dry completely. All traces of gasket material must be removed.
8. Install the trans pan with either a new gasket or the reusable gasket, as applicable, and secure with the pan retaining bolts. Tighten the bolts to 15 ft. lbs. (20 Nm).
9. Lower the vehicle and fill the transaxle to the proper level with DEXRON II® fluid.
10. Check the cold fluid level for the initial fill. Do not overfill.
11. Check the fluid level as outlined in Section 1.
12. Check the trans pan for leaks.

FILTER SERVICE

▶ See Figures 11 and 12

1. Raise the vehicle and support it safely.
2. Place a drain pan under the transaxle fluid pan.
3. Remove the trans pan bolts from the front and sides only.
4. Loosen the rear trans pan bolts approximately four turns.
5. Lightly tap on the trans pan with a rubber mallet to allow the fluid to drain.
6. Remove the remaining trans pan bolts, oil pan and gasket.
7. Remove the trans filter and O-ring using a slight twisting and pulling motion.

➡**The trans filter O-ring may be stuck in the case.**

To install:

8. Coat the O-ring with a small amount of Transjel®, or equivalent.
9. Install the new filter into the case.
10. Thoroughly clean the pan and magnet. Clean the gasket surfaces with a suitable solvent and allow to dry completely. All traces of gasket material must be removed.
11. Install the trans pan with either a new gasket or the reusable gasket, as applicable, and secure with the pan retaining bolts. Tighten the bolts to 15 ft. lbs. (20 Nm).
12. Lower the vehicle and fill the transaxle to the proper level with DEXRON® II.

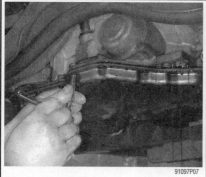

Fig. 7 Remove the bolts from the trans pan

Fig. 8 With the trans pan removed, the filter is visible and accessible

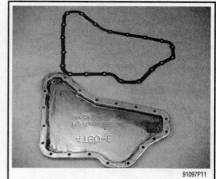

Fig. 9 Some trans pan gaskets were designed to be reusable; this is one of them

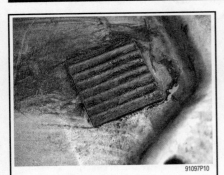

Fig. 10 The magnet in this trans pan catches a lot of debris, but it is not removable. It must be cleaned along with the pan

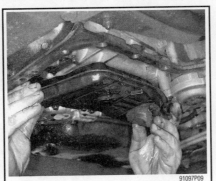

Fig. 11 Remove the filter with a slight twist and pull

Fig. 12 This transaxle seepage (from the cooler lines) is not enough of a leak to repair. All it did was stain the bottom of the trans. No drops of fluid were visible

13. Check the cold fluid level for the initial fill. Do not overfill.
14. Check the fluid level as outlined in Section 1.
15. Check the trans pan for leaks.

Neutral Safety and Back-up Light Switch

REMOVAL, INSTALLATION & ADJUSTMENT

♦ See Figure 13

1. Disconnect the negative battery cable.
2. Disconnect the shift linkage, lever and nut.
3. Unplug the electrical connector.
4. Remove the mounting bolts, then remove the switch, cable and nut.
To install:
5. To install the old switch, perform the following:
    a. Place the shift shaft in NEUTRAL.
    b. Align the flats of the shift shaft with the switch.
    c. Loosely assemble the mounting bolts to the case.
    d. Insert a gauge pin in the service adjustment hole and rotate the switch until the pin drops in to a depth of 1/8 in.(3mm).
    e. Remove the gauge pin and verify that the engine will only start in PARK or NEUTRAL. If it starts in any other position, readjust the switch.

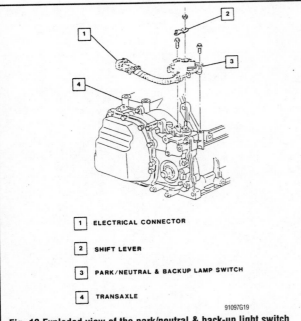

1 ELECTRICAL CONNECTOR

2 SHIFT LEVER

3 PARK/NEUTRAL & BACKUP LAMP SWITCH

4 TRANSAXLE

91097G19

Fig. 13 Exploded view of the park/neutral & back-up light switch mounting

6. To install a new switch, perform the following:
    a. Place the shift shaft in NEUTRAL.
    b. Align the flats of the shift shaft with the switch.

➡If the switch has been rotated and the pin broken, the switch can be adjusted using the old switch procedure.

    c. Install the mounting bolts and torque to 22 ft. lbs. (30 Nm). If the holes do not align with the mounting boss on the transaxle, verify that the shift shaft is in NEUTRAL position; do not rotate the switch. The switch is pinned in the NEUTRAL position.

➡If the switch has been rotated and the pin broken, the switch can be adjusted using the old switch procedure.

7. Adjust the switch as follows:
    a. Place the transaxle in the N position.
    b. Loosen the switch attaching screws.
    c. Rotate the switch on the shifter assembly to align the service hole in the switch with the hole in the carrier.
    d. Insert a 3/32 in. (2.4mm) gauge pin into the hole.
    e. Tighten the mounting bolts/screw to 20 ft. lbs. (27 Nm). Remove the gauge pin.
8. Attach the electrical connector and shift linkage.
9. Connect the negative battery cable.

Automatic Transaxle Assembly

REMOVAL & INSTALLATION

♦ See Figures 14, 15 and 16

✷✷ CAUTION

Some models covered by this manual may be equipped with a Supplemental Restraint System (SRS), which uses an air bag. Whenever working near any of the SRS components, such as the impact sensors, the air bag module, steering column and instrument panel, disable the SRS, as described in Section 6.

➡If your vehicle is equipped with air conditioning, refer to Section 1 for information regarding the implications of servicing your A/C system yourself. Only an MVAC-trained, EPA-certified, automotive technician should service the A/C system or its components.

The automatic transaxle in these vehicles can only be removed by removing the engine and transaxle/sub-frame as an assembly.
1. Disconnect the negative battery cable.
2. Drain and recycle the engine coolant. Disconnect the airflow tube from the air cleaner.
3. Unplug the electrical connector from the PCM and push it through to the engine compartment. Disconnect the harness from the clips on the body and lay it across the engine.

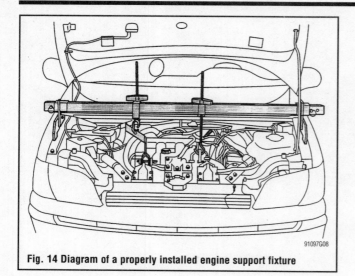

Fig. 14 Diagram of a properly installed engine support fixture

91097G08

→On later model vehicles, the PCM is located in the air filter housing. Disconnect the wiring harness connectors from the transaxle.

4. Disconnect the engine harness at the bulkhead connector. Disconnect the throttle and TV cables.

✳✳ CAUTION

Observe all applicable safety precautions when working around fuel. Whenever servicing the fuel system, always work in a well ventilated area. Do not allow fuel spray or vapors to be exposed to a spark or open flame. Keep a dry chemical fire extinguisher near the work area. Always keep fuel in a container specifically designed for fuel storage; also, always properly seal fuel containers to avoid the possibility of fire or explosion.

5. Disconnect the fuel lines. Disconnect the transaxle shift linkage.

✳✳ CAUTION

Never open, service or drain the radiator or cooling system when hot; serious burns can occur from the steam and hot coolant. In

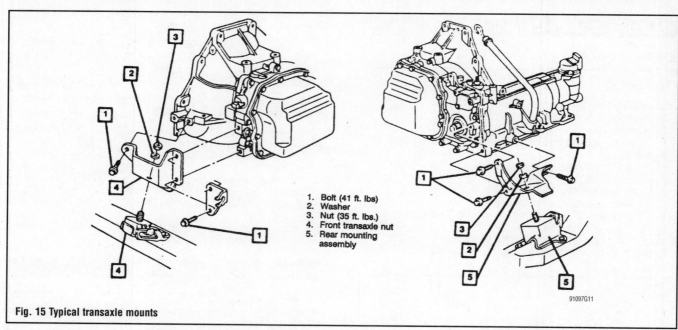

1. Bolt (41 ft. lbs)
2. Washer
3. Nut (35 ft. lbs.)
4. Front transaxle nut
5. Rear mounting assembly

91097G11

Fig. 15 Typical transaxle mounts

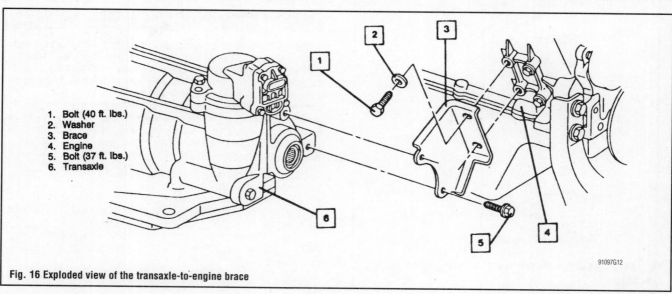

1. Bolt (40 ft. lbs.)
2. Washer
3. Brace
4. Engine
5. Bolt (37 ft. lbs.)
6. Transaxle

91097G12

Fig. 16 Exploded view of the transaxle-to-engine brace

addition, when draining engine coolant, keep in mind that cats and dogs are attracted to ethylene glycol antifreeze and could drink any that is left in an uncovered container or in puddles on the ground. This will prove fatal in sufficient quantities. Always drain coolant into a sealable container. Coolant should be reused unless it is contaminated or is several years old.

6. Disconnect the cooler lines at the radiator. Disconnect the radiator and heater hoses.
7. Remove the air conditioning compressor from the bracket and support it out of the way. Remove the upper engine support strut.
8. Raise and safely support the vehicle. Remove the front wheel and tire assemblies.
9. Remove the stabilizer bar. Disconnect the tie rod ends. Separate the lower control arm ball joints.
10. Disconnect the halfshafts and support them out of the way. Disconnect the steering shaft pinch bolt.
11. Remove the starter.
12. Disconnect the exhaust pipe at the manifold. Support the engine and sub-frame with a suitable jack.
13. Remove the sub-frame bolts and lower the engine/transaxle and sub-frame from the vehicle.

To install:
14. Raise the engine assembly into position and install the subframe bolts. Tighten the bolts to 35 ft. lbs. (47 Nm).
15. Connect the exhaust pipe at the rear manifold. Install the starter.
16. Connect the steering shaft and install the pinch bolt. Connect the halfshafts to the transaxle.
17. Connect the lower control arm ball joints to the steering knuckles.
18. Install the stabilizer bar. Install the upper engine strut.
19. Install the wheel and tire assemblies. Lower the vehicle. Install the radiator and heater hoses.
20. Install the shift linkage. Connect the fuel lines and the throttle and TV cables.
21. Attach the harness to bulkhead connector. Connect the PCM harness to the PCM.
22. Connect the air cleaner hose and the radiator upper support.
23. Fill the cooling system. Install the air conditioning compressor.
24. Connect the negative battery cable.

ADJUSTMENTS

Throttle Linkage

TV CABLE

▶ See Figures 17, 18 and 19

1. As required, remove the air cleaner assembly.
2. Depress and hold down the metal readjust tab at the engine end of the throttle valve cable.
3. Move the slider until it stops against the fitting. Release the readjustment tab.
4. Rotate the throttle lever to its full travel position. The slider must move toward the lever when the lever is rotated to its full travel position.
5. Check for proper operation. When the engine is cold, the cable may appear to be functioning properly, check the cable when the engine is hot.
6. Road test the vehicle.

SHIFT CONTROL CABLE

▶ See Figures 20, 21, 22 and 23

1. Place the shift lever in NEUTRAL. Neutral can be found by rotating the selector shaft clockwise from PARK through REVERSE to NEUTRAL.
2. Place the shift control assembly in NEUTRAL.
3. Push the tab on the cable adjuster to adjust the cable in the cable mounting bracket.

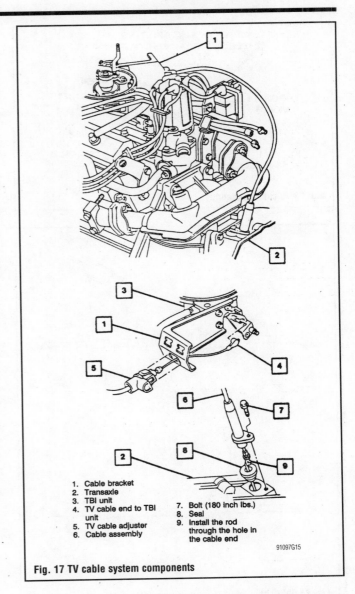

1. Cable bracket
2. Transaxle
3. TBI unit
4. TV cable end to TBI unit
5. TV cable adjuster
6. Cable assembly
7. Bolt (180 inch lbs.)
8. Seal
9. Install the rod through the hole in the cable end

Fig. 17 TV cable system components

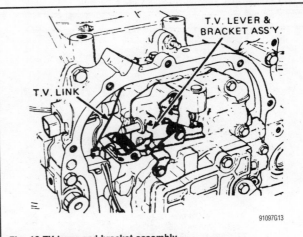

Fig. 18 TV lever and bracket assembly

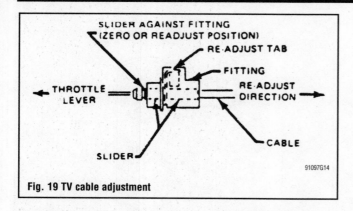

Fig. 19 TV cable adjustment

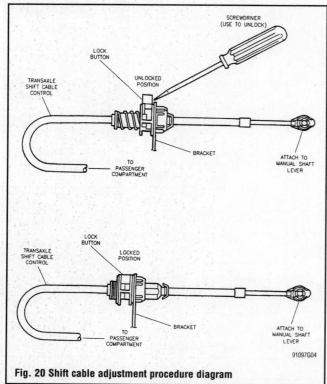

Fig. 20 Shift cable adjustment procedure diagram

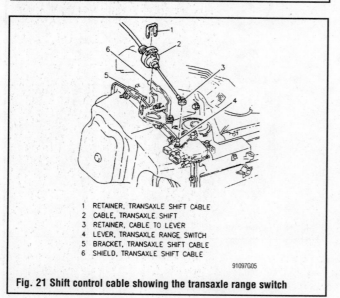

1 RETAINER, TRANSAXLE SHIFT CABLE
2 CABLE, TRANSAXLE SHIFT
3 RETAINER, CABLE TO LEVER
4 LEVER, TRANSAXLE RANGE SWITCH
5 BRACKET, TRANSAXLE SHIFT CABLE
6 SHIELD, TRANSAXLE SHIFT CABLE

Fig. 21 Shift control cable showing the transaxle range switch

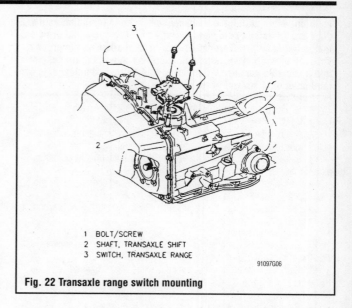

1 BOLT/SCREW
2 SHAFT, TRANSAXLE SHIFT
3 SWITCH, TRANSAXLE RANGE

Fig. 22 Transaxle range switch mounting

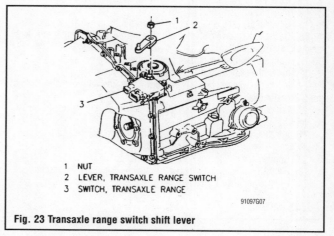

1 NUT
2 LEVER, TRANSAXLE RANGE SWITCH
3 SWITCH, TRANSAXLE RANGE

Fig. 23 Transaxle range switch shift lever

Vacuum Modulator

The vacuum modulator system on the Hydra-Matic 4T60-E transaxle controls shift feel (may be soft or firm shifts) by sensing changes in engine load, which is indicated by engine vacuum. The vacuum modulator does this by controlling main line pressure boost. The vacuum modulator system may be suspect for firm or slipping shift conditions.

INSPECTION & DIAGNOSIS

◗ See Figures 24 and 25

For proper operation, the transaxle requires 13-17 in. Hg (44-57 kPa) of engine vacuum at hot engine idle checked at the modulator with the transaxle in "D". An incorrect vacuum signal at the modulator can cause shifting problems.

1. To check for proper vacuum, disconnect the vacuum supply line at the modulator and install a vacuum gauge to the line. Check for the proper vacuum signal, if there is less, locate the cause and correct as required. The gauge reading must respond in less than $\frac{1}{10}$ of a second delay to throttle movement.

2. Remove the modulator and modulator valve. Connect a hand operated vacuum pump. Pump the device until 15-20 in. Hg (51-68 kPa) of vacuum is reached. At the same time, observe the modulator plunger; it should be drawn in as the vacuum pump is operated. After reaching the 15-20 in. Hg (51-68 kPa) the vacuum should not bleed down for at least 30 seconds.

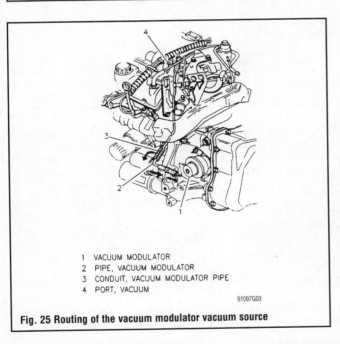

30 BOLT, MODULATOR TO CASE, M8 X 1.25 X 20.0, (1)
31 RETAINER, MODULATOR
32 MODULATOR ASSEMBLY, TRANSMISSION
33 SEAL, O-RING
34 VALVE, MODULATOR

91097G02

Fig. 24 The vacuum modulator and O-ring assembly diagram are mounted into the side of the transaxle case

1 VACUUM MODULATOR
2 PIPE, VACUUM MODULATOR
3 CONDUIT, VACUUM MODULATOR PIPE
4 PORT, VACUUM

91097G03

Fig. 25 Routing of the vacuum modulator vacuum source

REMOVAL & INSTALLATION

▶ **See Figures 26, 27, 28 and 29**

1. Slide the conduit back from the vacuum modulator hose.
2. Remove the vacuum line from the vacuum modulator.
3. Remove the bolt holding the torque converter clutch wiring harness shield and the clamp holding the vacuum modulator.
4. Remove the vacuum modulator and O-ring.

To install:

5. Install the vacuum modulator, using a new O-ring.
6. Install the clamp, torque converter clutch wiring harness and shield. Install the retaining bolt and tighten to 20 ft. lbs. (27 Nm).
7. Connect the vacuum line to the vacuum modulator.
8. Slide the conduit back over the hose and the vacuum modulator.

Halfshafts

REMOVAL & INSTALLATION

▶ **See Figures 30 thru 40**

✳✳ WARNING

Care must be exercised to prevent Tri-Pot joints from being over-extended. When either end of the shaft is disconnected, over-extension of the joint could result in separation of the internal components and possible joint failure. Drive axle joint seal protectors should be used any time service is performed on or near the

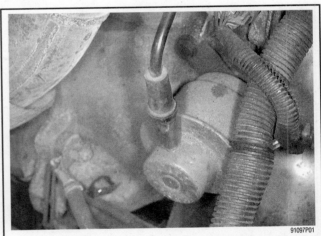

91097P01

Fig. 26 The vacuum modulator determines the shift harshness of the transaxle

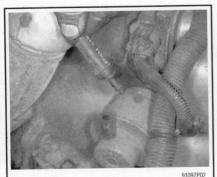

91097P02

Fig. 27 Disconnect the vacuum line from the modulator

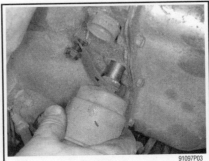

91097P03

Fig. 28 After unplugging the modulator wiring harness and removing the bolt, pull the vacuum modulator straight out . . .

91097P04

Fig. 29 . . . and remove the vacuum modulator from the transaxle case. Make sure no debris falls into the opening left by the modulator

drive axles. Failure to observe this can result in interior joint or seal damage and possible joint failure.

1. Raise and safely support the vehicle.
2. Remove the tire and wheel assemblies.
3. Insert a drift or other suitable tool into the caliper and rotor to prevent the rotor from turning and remove the halfshaft retaining nut and washer. Remove and discard the cotter pin.
4. Remove the brake caliper from the rotor and support it aside.
5. Remove the brake rotor from the hub.
6. Disconnect the lower ball joint pinch bolt.
7. Install a suitable drive axle seal protector. It may be necessary to modify the protector for installation.

➡ When servicing suspension components in the area in the area of the outer drive axle seal or when removing a drive axle, always install a suitable drive axle seal protector, after modifying it if necessary.

8. Remove the ball joint from the steering knuckle.
9. Remove the halfshafts from the hub and bearing assembly using a suitable puller.
10. Remove the halfshafts from the spindle, using a suitable spindle removal tool.
11. Remove the halfshafts from the transaxle using a suitable tool with a slide hammer attachment.

To install:
12. Install the a suitable tear away axle seal protector tool, to the right side of the transaxle in a position so it can be pulled out after the drive axle is installed (approximately between 5 and 7 o'clock position).
13. Install the a suitable axle seal protector to the drive axle.
14. Install the axle into transaxle.
15. Remove and discard the tear away axle seal protector tool. Make sure that there are no pieces of the tool left inside of the transaxle, if so, repeat the steps necessary to remove the drive axle and correct the condition.

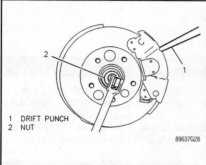

1 DRIFT PUNCH
2 NUT

89637G28

Fig. 30 Prevent the rotor from turning by inserting a drift through the caliper and into the rotor

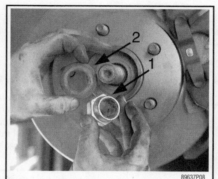

89637P08

Fig. 31 Remove the hub nut (1) and the washer (2)

89637P09

Fig. 32 Pull the cotter pin and discard it

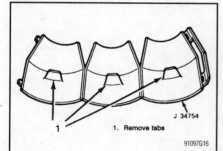

1. Remove tabs

91097G16

Fig. 33 It is necessary to install a modified drive axle seal protector to prevent the seal from being damaged

89637P07

Fig. 34 Pull the hub, bearing, and knuckle assembly away from the halfshaft

89637P02

Fig. 35 Although you can use a large pry tool to separate the inner CV-joint from the transaxle case, it is better to use the proper tool and slide hammer

89637P06

Fig. 36 Carefully remove the halfshaft from the vehicle

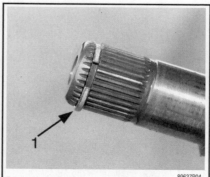

89637P04

Fig. 37 The end of the halfshaft is grooved and has a retaining circlip (1)

89637P05

Fig. 38 While the halfshaft is removed, be sure not to get any dirt or other debris in the transaxle case

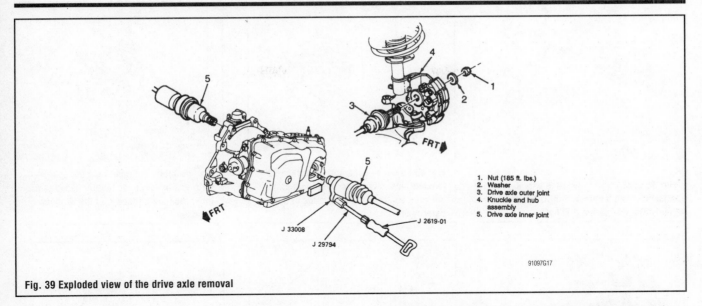

1. Nut (185 ft. lbs.)
2. Washer
3. Drive axle outer joint
4. Knuckle and hub assembly
5. Drive axle inner joint

J 33008
J 29794
J 2619-01

91097G17

Fig. 39 Exploded view of the drive axle removal

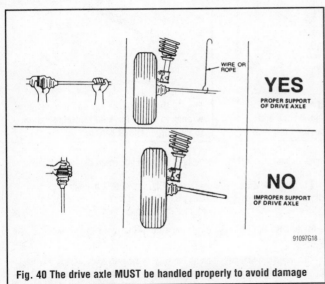

YES
PROPER SUPPORT OF DRIVE AXLE

NO
IMPROPER SUPPORT OF DRIVE AXLE

WIRE OR ROPE

91097G18

Fig. 40 The drive axle MUST be handled properly to avoid damage

16. Install the axle shaft in the hub.
17. Install the lower control arm ball joint to the steering knuckle.
18. Install the lower ball joint pinch bolt, then tighten the ball joint pinch bolt nut to 33 lb. ft. (45 Nm).
19. Install the brake rotor and brake caliper.

20. Install a drift or other suitable tool to hold the caliper and rotor stationary, and prevent them from rotating.
21. Install the drive axle washer and a new nut. Tighten the nut to 185 ft. lbs. (260 Nm).
22. Remove the drift or other suitable tool from the caliper and rotor.
23. Remove the modified axle seal protector tool.
24. Seat the drive axle into the transaxle by placing a suitable tool into the groove on the joint housing and tapping it until properly seated.
25. Verify that the drive axle is seated into the transaxle by grasping on the housing and pulling outboard.

➡ **Do not grasp and pull on the axle shaft.**

26. Install the tire and wheel assembly.
27. Lower the vehicle.

OVERHAUL

Outer CV-Joint and Seal

▶ See Figures 41 thru 51

1. Remove the halfshaft from the vehicle and mount in a suitable vise.
2. Remove the large seal retaining clamp from the CV-joint with side cutters. Discard the clamp.
3. Remove the small seal retaining clamp with side cutters or, for swage ring removal, use a hand grinder to cut through the ring (being careful not to damage the halfshaft).
4. Separate the joint seal from the CV-joint race at the large diameter end and slide the seal away from the joint along the axle shaft.
5. Wipe off the grease from the face of the CV inner race.

TCCS7030

Fig. 41 Check the CV-boot for wear

TCCS7034

Fig. 42 Clean the CV-joint housing prior to removing the boot

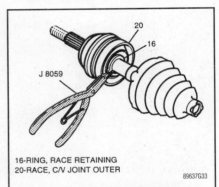

J 8059

20
16

16-RING, RACE RETAINING
20-RACE, C/V JOINT OUTER

89637G33

Fig. 43 Use a pair of snapring pliers to spread the ears on the race retaining ring

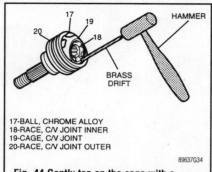

17-BALL, CHROME ALLOY
18-RACE, C/V JOINT INNER
19-CAGE, C/V JOINT
20-RACE, C/V JOINT OUTER

89637G34

Fig. 44 Gently tap on the cage with a brass drift and hammer, until it is tilted enough to remove the first ball

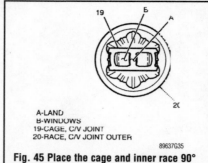

A-LAND
B-WINDOWS
19-CAGE, C/V JOINT
20-RACE, C/V JOINT OUTER

89637G35

Fig. 45 Place the cage and inner race 90° to centerline of the outer race, and align the cage windows with the lands of the outer race

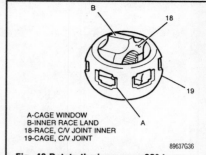

A-CAGE WINDOW
B-INNER RACE LAND
18-RACE, C/V JOINT INNER
19-CAGE, C/V JOINT

89637G36

Fig. 46 Rotate the inner race 90° to centerline of the cage, so that the lands of the inner race are aligned with the windows of the cage

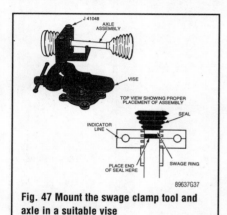

89637G37

Fig. 47 Mount the swage clamp tool and axle in a suitable vise

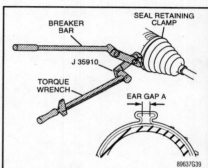

15-SEAL, DRIVE AXLE OUTBOARD
16-CLAMP, SEAL RETAINING
21-RACE, C/V JOINT OUTER

89637G38

Fig. 48 Slide the large end of the seal over the outside of the CV-joint race and seat the seal lip in the groove on the race

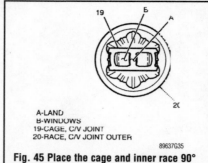

89637G39

Fig. 49 Use a breaker bar and torque wrench to crimp the seal retaining clamp to the proper specifications

6. Spread the ears on the race retaining ring with a suitable pair of snapring pliers and remove the CV-joint from the axle shaft.

7. Remove the joint seal from the axle shaft.

8. Use a brass drift and hammer to gently tap on the CV-joint cage until it is tilted enough to remove the first ball.

9. Tilt the cage in the opposite direction and remove the opposing ball.

10. Repeat until all the ball are removed. There are usually 6 balls.

11. Position cage and inner race 90° to centerline of the outer race, and align cage windows with the lands of the outer race.

12. Remove the cage and inner race from the outer race.

13. Rotate the inner race 90° to centerline of the cage so that the lands of the inner race are aligned with the windows of the cage.

14. Pivot the inner race into cage window and remove the inner race.

15. Clean the inner and outer race assemblies, cage and balls thoroughly with a suitable solvent. All traces of old grease and contaminants must be removed. Thoroughly dry all parts.

To install:

16. If equipped, install a new swage ring on the neck of the seal. Do not swage.

17. Slide the seal onto the axle shaft on position the neck of the seal in the seal groove on the axle shaft.

18. For the swage ring, mount a suitable swage clamp tool in a vise and proceed as follows:

    a. Position the outboard end of the halfshaft in the tool.

    b. Align the top of the seal neck on the bottom die using the indicator line.

    c. Place the top half of the tool on the lower half of the tool.

    d. Make sure there are no pinch points on the seal before continuing. Any pinching could damage the seal.

    e. Install the bolts and tighten by hand until snug.

    f. Make sure that the seal, housing and swage ring all stay in alignment. Continue to tighten each bolt 180°, alternating until both sides are bottomed.

19. Put a light coat of grease from the service kit on the ball grooves of the inner race and outer race.

20. Hold the inner race 90° to centerline of the cage with the lands of the

inner race aligned with the windows of the cage and insert the inner race into the cage.

21. Hold the cage and inner race 90° to centerline of the outer race and align the cage windows with the lands of the outer race.

22. Install the cage and inner race into the outer race.

➡**Make sure that the retaining ring side of the inner race faces the axle shaft.**

23. Insert the first ball, then tilt the cage in the opposite direction to install the opposing ball. Repeat this process until the remaining balls are installed.

24. Place about half the grease from the service kit inside the seal and pack the CV-joint with the remaining grease.

25. Push the CV joint onto the axle shaft until the retaining ring is seated in the groove on the axle shaft.

26. Slide the large diameter of the seal with the large seal retaining clamp in place over the outside of the CV joint race and locate the seal lip in the groove on the race.

✶✶ WARNING

The seal must not be dimpled, stretched or out of shape in any way. IF the seal is NOT shaped correctly, equalize pressure in seal and shape seal properly by hand or replace.

27. Crimp the retaining clamp to 130 ft. lbs. (176 Nm).

28. Install the halfshaft into the vehicle.

Inner Tri-Pot Joint and Seal

◆ **See Figures 47, 49 and 52 thru 55**

1. Remove the halfshaft from the vehicle and mount in a suitable vise.

2. If equipped, remove the swage ring from the axle shaft using a hand grinder to cut through the ring (being careful not to damage the halfshaft).

3. Remove the large retaining clamp from tri-pot joint with side cutter, and discard.

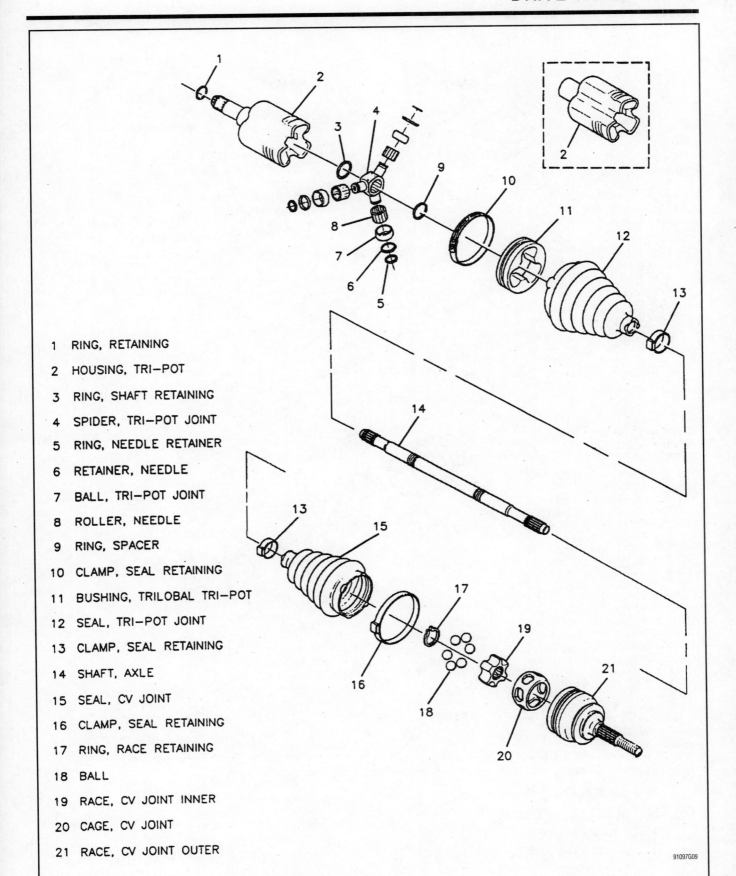

1   RING, RETAINING

2   HOUSING, TRI–POT

3   RING, SHAFT RETAINING

4   SPIDER, TRI–POT JOINT

5   RING, NEEDLE RETAINER

6   RETAINER, NEEDLE

7   BALL, TRI–POT JOINT

8   ROLLER, NEEDLE

9   RING, SPACER

10 CLAMP, SEAL RETAINING

11 BUSHING, TRILOBAL TRI–POT

12 SEAL, TRI–POT JOINT

13 CLAMP, SEAL RETAINING

14 SHAFT, AXLE

15 SEAL, CV JOINT

16 CLAMP, SEAL RETAINING

17 RING, RACE RETAINING

18 BALL

19 RACE, CV JOINT INNER

20 CAGE, CV JOINT

21 RACE, CV JOINT OUTER

91097G09

Fig. 50 Exploded view of the halfshaft assembly—1992 vehicle shown

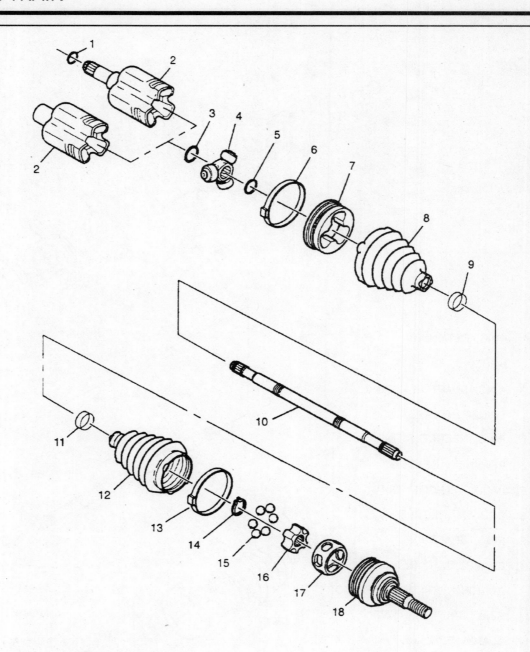

(1) Retaining Ring
(2) Retainer and Housing Assembly
(3) Shaft Retaining Ring
(4) Tripot Joint Spider
(5) Spacer Ring
(6) Seal Retaining Clamp
(7) Tripot Trilobal Bushing
(8) Drive Axle Inboard Seal
(9) Seal Retaining Ring

(10) Axle Shaft
(11) Seal Retaining Ring
(12) Drive Axle Outboard Seal
(13) Seal Retaining Clamp
(14) Race Retaining Ring
(15) Chrome Alloy Ball
(16) CV Joint Inner Race
(17) CV Joint Cage
(18) CV Joint Outer Race

91097G10

Fig. 51 Exploded view of the halfshaft assembly—1998 vehicle shown

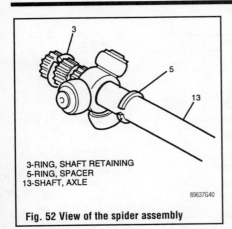

3-RING, SHAFT RETAINING
5-RING, SPACER
13-SHAFT, AXLE

89637G40

Fig. 52 View of the spider assembly

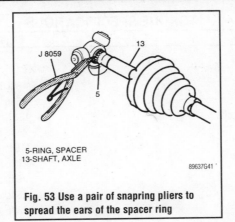

5-RING, SPACER
13-SHAFT, AXLE

89637G41

Fig. 53 Use a pair of snapring pliers to spread the ears of the spacer ring

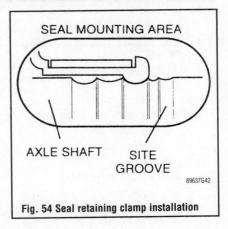

89637G42

Fig. 54 Seal retaining clamp installation

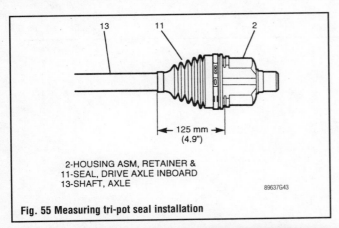

125 mm
(4.9")

2-HOUSING ASM, RETAINER &
11-SEAL, DRIVE AXLE INBOARD
13-SHAFT, AXLE

89637G43

Fig. 55 Measuring tri-pot seal installation

✳✳ WARNING

Do not cut through the seal and damage the sealing surface of tri-pot housing and trilobal tri-pot bushing.

4. If necessary, remove the small seal retaining clamp using side cutters.

5. Separate the seal from the trilobal tri-pot bushing at large diameter and slide seal away from the joint.

6. Remove the tri-pot housing from the spider and shaft. Remove the trilobal tri-pot bushing from the housing.

7. Spread the spacer ring with a pair of snapring pliers and slide space ring and tri-pot spider back on axle shaft.

8. Remove the shaft retaining ring from the groove on the axle shaft, then slide the spider from the shaft. Clean the tri-pot balls, needle rollers and housing thoroughly with suitable solvent. All traces of old grease and contaminants must be removed. Thoroughly dry all parts.

9. Remove the trilobal tripot bushing from the tripot housing.

10. Remove the spacer ring and seal from the axle shaft.

11. Inspect the joint balls and needle rollers for damage or wear. Handle with care, and don't reuse them if there is any sign of damage.

To install:

12. Install a new small seal retaining clamp, or swage, as applicable. Do NOT crimp/swage.

13. Slide the seal onto the axle shaft and position neck of seal in groove on the axle shaft.

14. For the swage ring, mount the swage clamp tool, J 41048 or equivalent, in a vise and proceed as follows:

a. Position the outboard end of the halfshaft in the tool.

b. Align the top of the seal neck on the bottom die using the indicator line.

c. Place the top half of the tool on the lower half of the tool.

d. Make sure there are no pinch points on the seal before continuing. Any pinching could damage the seal.

e. Install the bolts and tighten by hand until snug.

f. Make sure that the seal, housing and swage ring all stay in alignment. Continue to tighten each bolt 180°, alternating until both sides are bottomed.

15. If equipped, crimp the seal using a breaker bar and torque wrench to 100 ft. lbs. (136 Nm).

16. Install the spacer ring onto the axle shaft and beyond the second groove.

17. Slide the tri-pot spider toward the spacer ring as far as it will go on the shaft. Make sure the counterbored face of the tri-pot spider faces the end of the axle shaft.

18. Use snapring pliers to install the shaft retaining ring in the groove of the axle shaft.

19. Slide the tri-pot spider towards the end of the axle shaft and reseat the spacer ring in the groove on shaft.

20. Place about half the grease provided with the repair kit into the seal and use the remainder to repack the tri-pot housing.

21. Install the trilobal tri-pot bushing to the housing. Make sure the bushing is flush with the face of the housing.

22. Position the new large clamp on the seal.

23. Slide tri-pot housing over the tri-pot spider on axle shaft and remove the slotted sheet metal plate.

24. Slide large diameter end of seal with large clamp in place, over the outside of the trilobal bushing, and locate the lip of seal in the bushing groove.

25. Position the tri-pot at the proper vehicle dimension, 4.9 inches (125mm).

✳✳ WARNING

The seal must not be dimpled, stretched or out of shape in any way. If the seal is NOT shaped correctly, carefully insert a thin, flat, blunt tool (no sharp edges) into the between the large seal opening and trilobal tri-pot bushing to equalize pressure. Shape the seal properly by hand and remove the tool.

26. Use a breaker bar and torque wrench to crimp retaining clamp to 130 ft. lbs. (176 Nm).

27. Make certain the seal, housing and large clamp all remain in alignment while crimping.

28. Install the halfshaft in the vehicle.

TORQUE SPECIFICATIONS

Components	English	Metric
Automatic transaxle		
Shift cable bracket		
Retaining bolt	18 ft. lbs.	25 Nm
Retaining nut	15 ft. lbs.	20 Nm
Drivetrain and Front Suspension Frame bolts	133 ft. lbs.	180 Nm
Flywheel to Torque Converter Bolts	46 ft. lbs.	63 Nm
Fluid Filler Tube Bracket Bolt	115 in. lbs.	13 Nm
Oil Pan Bolts	13 ft. lbs.	17 Nm
Transaxle Mount to Frame Nut	35 ft. lbs.	47Nm
Transaxle to Engine Bolts	55 ft. lbs.	75 Nm
Transaxle Range Switch Bolts	18 ft. lbs.	25 Nm
Transaxle Bracket to Transaxle Bolt	70 ft. lbs.	95 Nm
Transaxle-to-Engine bolts	32 ft. lbs.	43 Nm
Case Side Cover Bolt	17 ft. lbs	24 Nm

91097C01

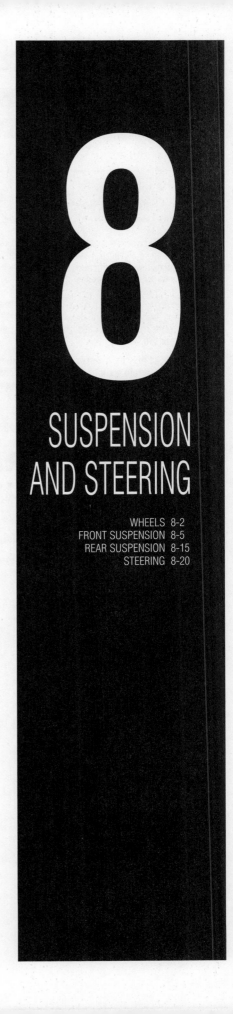

8

SUSPENSION AND STEERING

WHEELS

Wheels

REMOVAL & INSTALLATION

▶ **See Figures 1 thru 7**

1. Park the vehicle on a level surface.
2. Remove the jack, tire iron and, if necessary, the spare tire from their storage compartments.
3. Check the owner's manual or refer to Section 1 of this manual for the jacking points on your vehicle. Then, place the jack in the proper position.
4. If equipped with lug nut trim caps, remove them by either unscrewing or pulling them off the lug nuts, as appropriate. Consult the owner's manual, if necessary.
5. If equipped with a wheel cover or hubcap, insert the tapered end of the tire iron in the groove and pry off the cover.
6. Apply the parking brake and block the diagonally opposite wheel with a wheel chock or two.

➡ **Wheel chocks may be purchased at your local auto parts store, or a block of wood cut into wedges may be used. If possible, keep one or two of the chocks in your tire storage compartment, in case any of the tires has to be removed on the side of the road.**

7. Place the selector lever in **P** or Park.
8. With the tires still on the ground, use the tire iron/wrench to break the lug nuts loose. Do not remove them at this time.

✴✴ WARNING

If a nut is stuck, never use heat to loosen it or damage to the wheel and bearings may occur. If the nuts are seized, one or two heavy

hammer blows directly on the end of the bolt usually loosens the rust. Be careful, as continued pounding will likely damage the brake drum or rotor.

➡ **Sometimes wheels can be difficult to remove from the vehicle due to foreign material or a tight fit between the wheel center hole and the hub or rotor. These wheels can be removed without damage as follows:**

- Tighten all of the wheel nuts on the affected wheel, then loosen each wheel nut two turns.
- Lower the vehicle onto the floor or ground.
- Rock the vehicle from side to side as possible using 1 or more person's body weight to loosen the wheel and/or rock the vehicle from DRIVE to REVERSE allowing the vehicle to move several feet in each direction. Apply quick hard jabs on the brake pedal to loosen the wheel.
- Raise the vehicle, remove the wheel nuts and the wheel.

To install:

➡ **Before installing the wheels, remove any build up of corrosion on the wheel mounting surface by scraping and wire brushing.**

- Install the wheel into position and screw the wheel nuts onto the studs with the cone shaped ends toward the wheel.
- Tighten the wheel retaining nuts in sequence to 100 ft. lbs. (140 Nm).

➡ **The wheel nuts must be tightened in sequence and to the proper torque to avoid bending the wheel, brake drum or rotor.**

9. Using the jack, raise the vehicle until the tire is clear of the ground. Support the vehicle safely using jackstands.
10. Remove the lug nuts, then remove the tire and wheel assembly.

To install:

11. Make sure the wheel and hub mating surfaces, as well as the wheel lug studs, are clean and free of all foreign material. Always remove rust from the

Fig. 1 Place the jack at the proper lifting point on your vehicle

Fig. 2 Before jacking the vehicle, block the diagonally opposite wheel with one or, preferably, two chocks

Fig. 3 With the vehicle still on the ground, break the lug nuts loose using the wrench end of the tire iron

Fig. 4 After the lug nuts have been loosened, raise the vehicle using the jack until the tire is clear of the ground

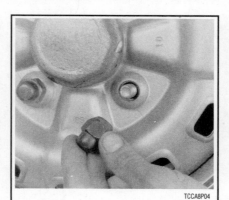

Fig. 5 Remove the lug nuts from the studs

Fig. 6 Remove the wheel and tire assembly from the vehicle

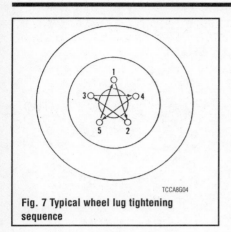

Fig. 7 Typical wheel lug tightening sequence

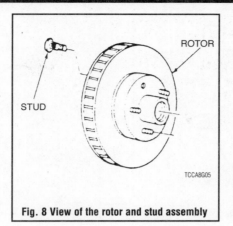

Fig. 8 View of the rotor and stud assembly

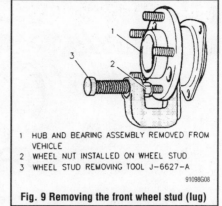

1 HUB AND BEARING ASSEMBLY REMOVED FROM VEHICLE
2 WHEEL NUT INSTALLED ON WHEEL STUD
3 WHEEL STUD REMOVING TOOL J-6627-A

Fig. 9 Removing the front wheel stud (lug)

wheel mounting surface and the brake rotor or drum. Failure to do so may cause the lug nuts to loosen in service.

12. Install the tire and wheel assembly and hand-tighten the lug nuts.

13. Using the tire wrench, tighten all the lug nuts, in a crisscross pattern, (for 4 lug) or a 'star' pattern (for 5 lug) until they are snug.

14. Raise the vehicle and withdraw the jackstands, then lower the vehicle.

15. Using a torque wrench, tighten the lug nuts in a crisscross pattern to 100 ft. lbs. (140 Nm). Check your owner's manual or refer to Section 1 of this manual for the proper tightening sequence.

✳✳ WARNING

Do not overtighten the lug nuts, as this may cause the wheel studs to stretch or the brake disc (rotor) to warp.

16. If so equipped, install the wheel cover or hubcap. Make sure the valve stem protrudes through the proper opening before tapping the wheel cover into position.

17. If equipped, install the lug nut trim caps by pushing them or screwing them on, as applicable.

18. Remove the jack from under the vehicle, and place the jack and tire iron/wrench in their storage compartments. Remove the wheel chock(s).

19. If you have removed a flat or damaged tire, place it in the storage compartment of the vehicle and take it to your local repair station to have it fixed or replaced as soon as possible.

INSPECTION

Inspect the tires for lacerations, puncture marks, nails and other sharp objects. Repair or replace as necessary. Also, check the tires for treadwear and air pressure as outlined in Section 1 of this manual.

Check the wheel assemblies for dents, cracks, rust and metal fatigue. Repair or replace as necessary.

Wheel Lug Studs

REPLACEMENT

With Disc Brakes

▶ See Figures 8, 9, 10, 11 and 12

1. Raise and support the appropriate end of the vehicle safely using jackstands, then remove the wheel.

2. Unbolt the caliper assembly and support it aside with a piece of wire or coat hanger. Do not disconnect the brake fluid line. For more details, please refer to Section 9 of this manual.

3. Remove the outer wheel bearing and lift off the rotor. For details on wheel bearing removal, installation and adjustment, please refer to Section 1 of this manual.

4. Properly support the rotor using press bars, then drive the stud out using an arbor press.

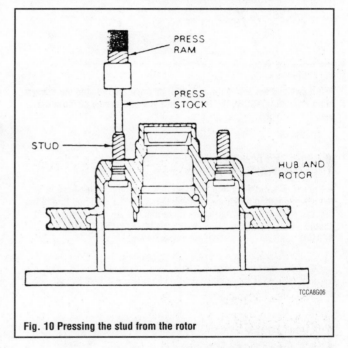

Fig. 10 Pressing the stud from the rotor

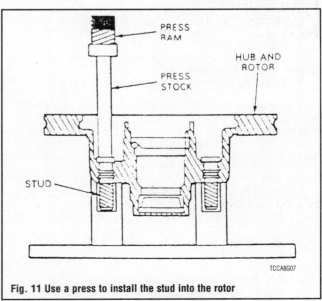

Fig. 11 Use a press to install the stud into the rotor

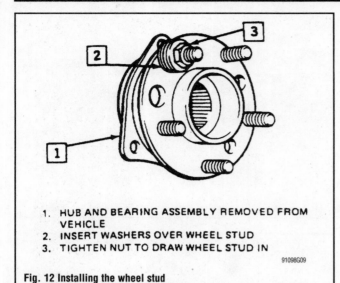

1. HUB AND BEARING ASSEMBLY REMOVED FROM VEHICLE
2. INSERT WASHERS OVER WHEEL STUD
3. TIGHTEN NUT TO DRAW WHEEL STUD IN

91098G09

Fig. 12 Installing the wheel stud

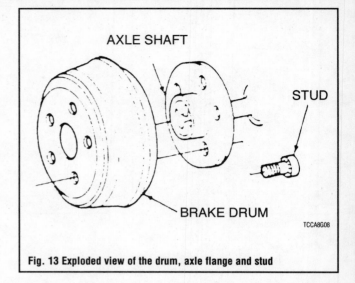

AXLE SHAFT

STUD

BRAKE DRUM

TCCA8G08

Fig. 13 Exploded view of the drum, axle flange and stud

➡If a press is not available, CAREFULLY drive the old stud out using a blunt drift. MAKE SURE the rotor is properly and evenly supported or it may be damaged.

To install:

5. Clean the stud hole with a wire brush and start the new stud with a hammer and drift pin. Do not use any lubricant or thread sealer.
6. Finish installing the stud with the press.

➡If a press is not available, start the lug stud through the bore in the hub, then position about four flat washers over the stud and thread the lug nut. Hold the hub/rotor while tightening the lug nut, and the stud should be drawn into position. MAKE SURE THE STUD IS FULLY SEATED, then remove the lug nut and washers.

7. Install the rotor and adjust the wheel bearings.
8. Install the brake caliper and pads.
9. Install the wheel, then remove the jackstands and carefully lower the vehicle.
10. Tighten the lug nuts to the proper torque.

With Drum Brakes

◆ See Figures 13, 14 and 15

1. Raise the vehicle and safely support it with jackstands, then remove the wheel.
2. Remove the brake drum.
3. If necessary to provide clearance, remove the brake shoes, as outlined in Section 9 of this manual.
4. Using a large C-clamp and socket, press the stud from the axle flange.
5. Coat the serrated part of the stud with liquid soap and place it into the hole.

To install:

6. Position about four flat washers over the stud and thread the lug nut. Hold the flange while tightening the lug nut, and the stud should be drawn into position. MAKE SURE THE STUD IS FULLY SEATED, then remove the lug nut and washers.
7. If applicable, install the brake shoes.
8. Install the brake drum.
9. Install the wheel, then remove the jackstands and carefully lower the vehicle.
10. Tighten the lug nuts to the proper torque.

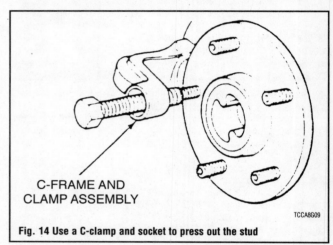

C-FRAME AND CLAMP ASSEMBLY

TCCA8G09

Fig. 14 Use a C-clamp and socket to press out the stud

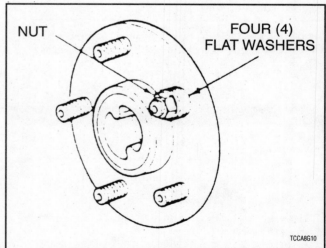

NUT

FOUR (4) FLAT WASHERS

TCCA8G10

Fig. 15 Force the stud onto the axle flange using washers and a lug nut

FRONT SUSPENSION

♦ See Figures 16 and 17

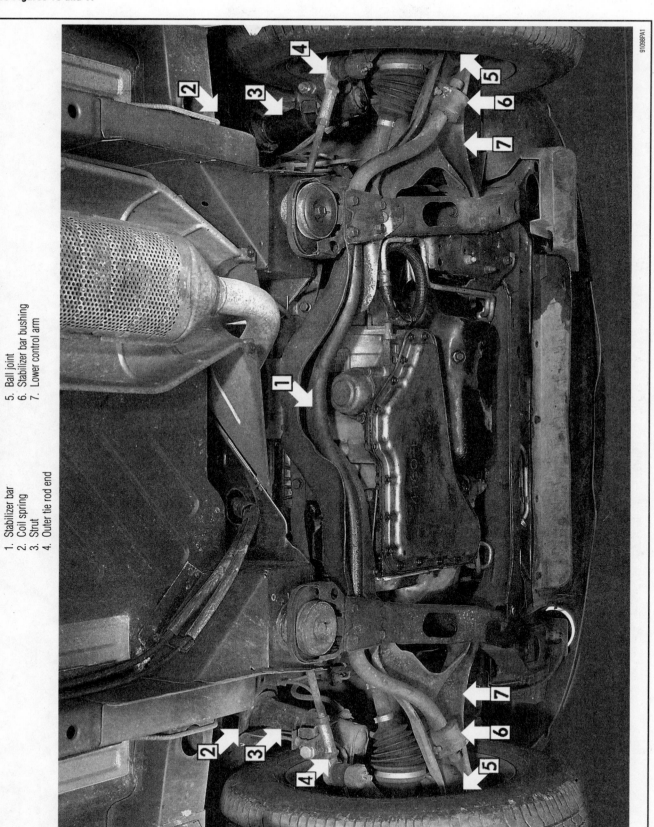

FRONT SUSPENSION COMPONENT LOCATIONS—EARLY MODEL

1. Stabilizer bar
2. Coil spring
3. Strut
4. Outer tie rod end
5. Ball joint
6. Stabilizer bar bushing
7. Lower control arm

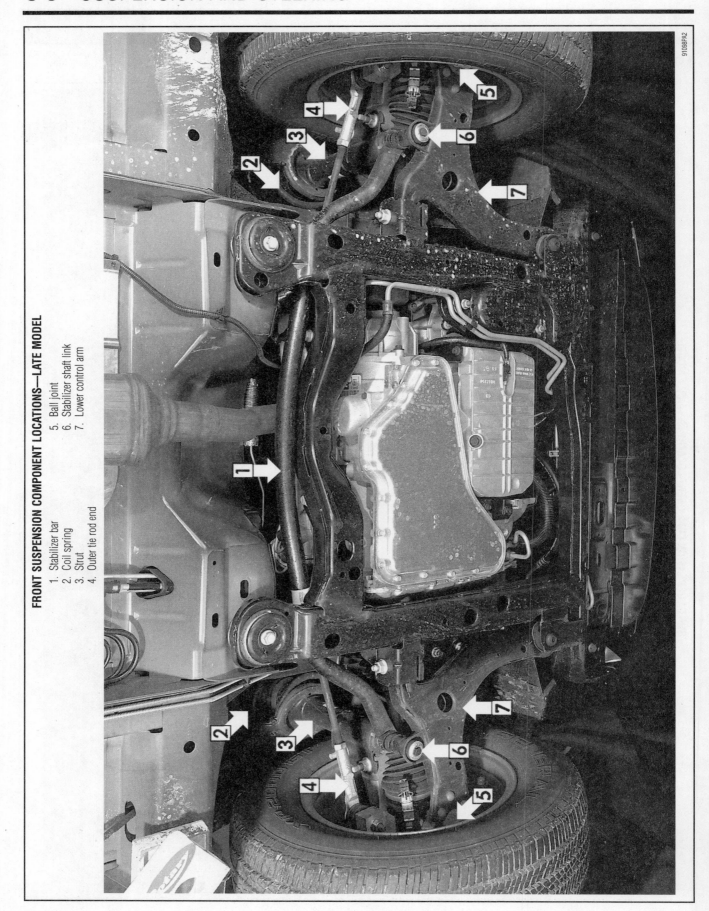

FRONT SUSPENSION COMPONENT LOCATIONS—LATE MODEL

1. Stabilizer bar
2. Coil spring
3. Strut
4. Outer tie rod end
5. Ball joint
6. Stabilizer shaft link
7. Lower control arm

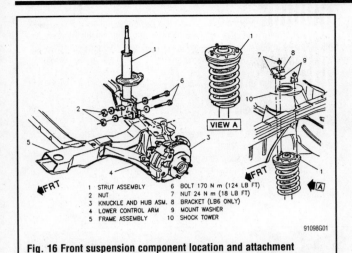

1 STRUT ASSEMBLY 6 BOLT 170 N·m (124 LB FT)
2 NUT 7 NUT 24 N·m (18 LB FT)
3 KNUCKLE AND HUB ASM. 8 BRACKET (LB6 ONLY)
4 LOWER CONTROL ARM 9 MOUNT WASHER
5 FRAME ASSEMBLY 10 SHOCK TOWER

91098G01

Fig. 16 Front suspension component location and attachment

All suspension and steering fasteners are important attaching parts in that they can affect the performance of vital components and systems, and can result in major repair expense. They must be replaced with one of the same part number or with an equivalent part if replacement becomes necessary. Do not use a replacement part of lesser quality or substitute design. Torque values must be used as specified during reassembly to assure proper retention of these parts. Observe all nut and bolt tightening specifications.

MacPherson Struts

REMOVAL & INSTALLATION

▶ **See Figures 18 thru 26**

 1. Remove the three nuts attaching the top of the strut to the body.
 2. Raise and safely support the vehicle.
 3. Place jackstands under the frame.
 4. Lower the vehicle slightly so the weight of the vehicle rests on the jackstands and not on the control arms.
 5. Remove the wheel and tire assembly.

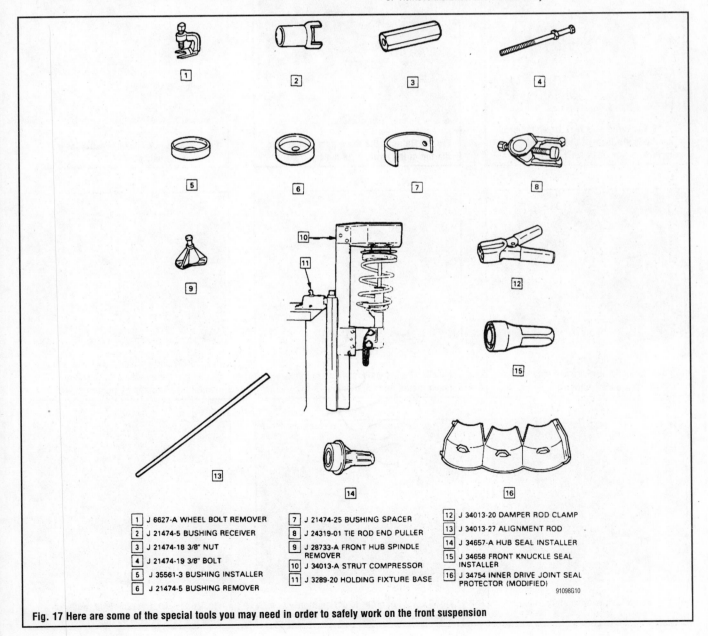

1	J 6627-A WHEEL BOLT REMOVER	7	J 21474-25 BUSHING SPACER	12	J 34013-20 DAMPER ROD CLAMP
2	J 21474-5 BUSHING RECEIVER	8	J 24319-01 TIE ROD END PULLER	13	J 34013-27 ALIGNMENT ROD
3	J 21474-18 3/8" NUT	9	J 28733-A FRONT HUB SPINDLE REMOVER	14	J 34657-A HUB SEAL INSTALLER
4	J 21474-19 3/8" BOLT	10	J 34013-A STRUT COMPRESSOR	15	J 34658 FRONT KNUCKLE SEAL INSTALLER
5	J 35561-3 BUSHING INSTALLER	11	J 3289-20 HOLDING FIXTURE BASE	16	J 34754 INNER DRIVE JOINT SEAL PROTECTOR (MODIFIED)
6	J 21474-5 BUSHING REMOVER				

91098G10

Fig. 17 Here are some of the special tools you may need in order to safely work on the front suspension

✳✳ WARNING

Drive axle joint seal protectors should be used anytime service is performed on or near the drive axles. Failure to observe this could result in joint or seal failure.

6. Place a suitable modified inner drive joint seal protector on the drive axle joints.

7. Remove the brake line bracket from the strut mount.

✳✳ WARNING

Before removing the strut lower mounting bolts, the steering knuckle must be supported to prevent axle joint overextension.

8. Support the steering knuckle with a suitable piece of wire or equivalent.

9. Use a paint marker to equivalent to matchmark the relation of the lower bolts to the strut housing. Remove the lower strut to knuckle mounting bolts.

10. Remove the strut from the vehicle.

To install:

11. Position the strut assembly in the vehicle. Install the three upper strut-to-body attaching nuts and tighten to 18 ft. lbs. (25 Nm).

12. Install the steering knuckle to strut assembly bolts and tighten to 140 ft. lbs. (190 Nm).

13. Install the brake line bracket and secure with the retaining bolts. Tighten the bolts to 13 ft. lbs. (17 Nm).

14. Remove the axle shaft seal protectors.

15. Install the tire and wheel assembly.

16. Raise the vehicle slightly to allow removal of the jackstands, then carefully lower the vehicle.

Fig. 18 The three nuts that attach the strut to the body are located in the engine compartment

Fig. 19 Remove the three nuts that secure the top of the strut to the body

Fig. 20 Save the spacer washer for installation of the new strut

Fig. 21 Unfasten the retainers, then remove the brake line bracket which is mounted on the strut housing

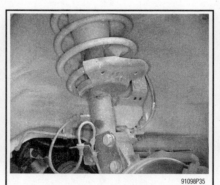

Fig. 22 The two bolts shown are the strut lower mount attaching points

Fig. 23 Matchmark the installation position of the bolts to the strut housing. Bolt position determines alignment angles

Fig. 24 Use a long wrench on the lower nut as a backup . . .

Fig. 25 . . . in order to obtain more of an advantage when loosening the strut bolts

Fig. 26 The strut assembly is removed from the vehicle as a complete unit

OVERHAUL

▶ **See Figures 27 thru 41**

1. Remove the strut assembly from the vehicle, as outlined earlier in this section.
2. Mount a suitable strut compressor or equivalent, into a strut holding fixture.

3. Mount the strut into the strut compressor, if available. Note that most strut compressors have strut mounting holes drilled for specific car manufacturers.

➡**Other variations of strut compressor tools that are suitable for performing this procedure are available. Make sure the compressor you have is correct for the vehicle you are working on.**

Fig. 27 This tool is an alternative to a wall mounted strut compressor

Fig. 28 Assemble the tool, mount the U-clamps around the spring . . .

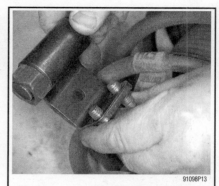

Fig. 29 . . . and through the mounting boss on the tool

Fig. 30 Secure the U-clamp with the supplied nuts . . .

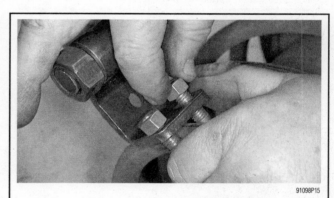

Fig. 31 . . . making sure to tighten the nuts down evenly

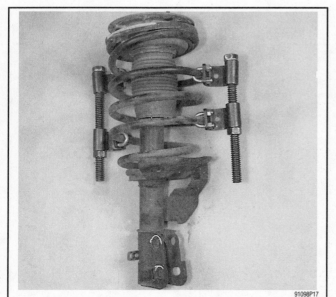

Fig. 32 This is the proper assembled view of the strut and tool. It is important to mount the legs of the tool 180° apart

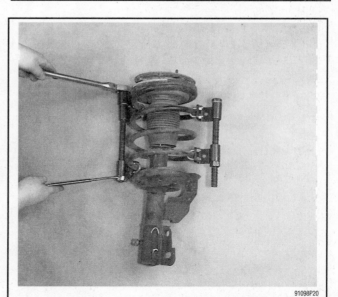

Fig. 33 Tighten the legs down carefully, a little at a time on each side. Compress the spring only as much as is needed to relieve the pressure against the mounts

Fig. 34 The top strut nut must be removed for complete overhaul and/or parts replacement

Fig. 35 Removal of the nut requires the use of a deep offset wrench to turn the nut, and a thin wall socket to hold the shaft

Fig. 36 Removing the nut and bearing cap

4. Carefully compress the spring by tightening the legs down in small increments on each side. Make sure to keep spring pressure as even as possible. Compress the strut at least ½ its height after initial contact with the top cap.

✳✳ WARNING

Never bottom out the spring or dampener rod.

5. Remove the nut from the strut dampener shaft and place a suitable guiding rod on top of the dampener shaft. Use this rod to guide the dampener shaft straight down through the bearing cap while decompressing the spring.

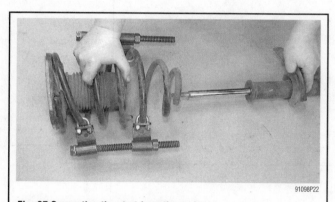

Fig. 37 Separating the strut from the spring

Fig. 38 Removing the top mount and dust cover/shield

6. Unfasten the top strut nut, then remove the components from above the spring and remove the spring from the strut. See the accompanying figures for details.

✳✳ WARNING

Care should be taken to avoid chipping or cracking the spring coating when handling the front suspension coil spring.

To install:

7. Install the bearing cap into the strut compressor, if previously removed.

8. Mount the strut into the strut compressor using the bottom locking pin only. Extend the dampener shaft and install the clamp on the dampener shaft.

9. Install the spring over the dampener and swing the assembly up so the upper locking pin can be installed. Install the upper insulator, shield, bumper and upper spring seat. Be sure the flat on the upper spring seat is facing in the proper direction. The spring seat flat should be 10° forward of the centerline of the strut assembly spindle.

10. Install the guiding rod and turn the forcing screw while the guiding rod centers the assembly. When the threads on the dampener shaft are visible, remove the guiding rod and install the nut.

11. Use a crowfoot wrench while holding the dampener shaft with the socket to tighten the nut to 65 ft. lbs. (85 Nm).

12. Remove the clamp from the strut assembly.

13. Install the strut assembly in the vehicle, as outlined earlier in this section.

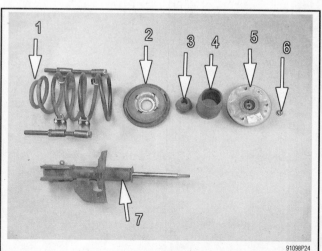

Fig. 39 View of a disassembled strut. 1 = Spring; 2 = Bearing plate; 3 = Jounce bumper; 4 = Dust cover; 5 = Top plate (cap); 6 = Top mounting nut; 7 = Strut

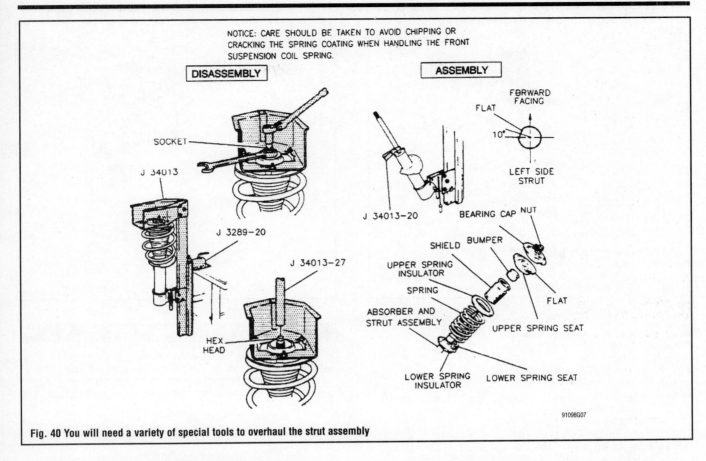

NOTICE: CARE SHOULD BE TAKEN TO AVOID CHIPPING OR CRACKING THE SPRING COATING WHEN HANDLING THE FRONT SUSPENSION COIL SPRING.

Fig. 40 You will need a variety of special tools to overhaul the strut assembly

Fig. 41 When installing the spring, make sure it seats properly on the mounts

Lower Ball Joint

INSPECTION

Front lower control arm ball stud tightness in the knuckle boss should be checked when inspecting the front lower control arm ball stud (ball joint). Raise the vehicle, allowing the front suspension to hang free. Grasp the tire at the top and bottom and move the bottom of the tire in an in-and-out motion while checking for movement of the stud end or castellated nut at the knuckle boss. Observe any horizontal movement of the knuckle relative to the control arm. Ball joints/studs must be replaced if any looseness is detected in the joint, or the ball joint seal is cut. Worn or damaged parts must be replaced with the correct service parts. Failure to use the correct front lower control arm ball stud and specified fastener torque may eventually cause a loose joint and may result in loss of steering control which could result in personal injury.

REMOVAL & INSTALLATION

◆ See Figure 42

1. Raise and safely support the vehicle.
2. Place jackstands under the frame.
3. Lower the vehicle slightly so the weight of the vehicle rests on the jackstands and not on the control arms.
4. Remove the wheel and tire assembly.

✳✳ WARNING

Drive axle joint seal protectors should be used anytime service is performed on or near the drive axles. Failure to observe this could result in joint or seal failure.

5. Place a modified inner drive joint seal protector on the drive axle joints.
6. Remove the pinch bolt from the vehicle.
7. Remove the rag joint from the steering knuckle.
8. Use a ⅛ in. (3mm) drill bit to make a pilot hole through the rivets, then finish drilling the rivets out with a ½ in. (13 mm) drill bit.

✳✳ WARNING

Be careful not to damage the drive axle seals when drilling out the ball joint rivets.

9. Loosen the stabilizer shaft bushing assembly nut.
10. Remove the ball joint from the steering knuckle and control arm.

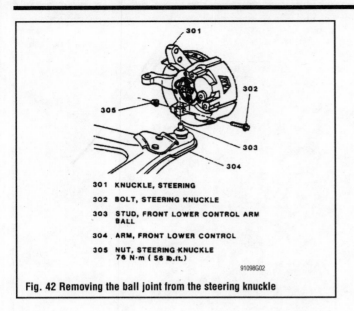

301 KNUCKLE, STEERING

302 BOLT, STEERING KNUCKLE

303 STUD, FRONT LOWER CONTROL ARM BALL

304 ARM, FRONT LOWER CONTROL

305 NUT, STEERING KNUCKLE 76 N·m (56 lb.ft.)

91098G02

Fig. 42 Removing the ball joint from the steering knuckle

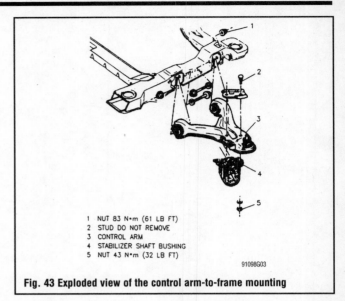

1 NUT 83 N·m (61 LB FT)
2 STUD DO NOT REMOVE
3 CONTROL ARM
4 STABILIZER SHAFT BUSHING
5 NUT 43 N·m (32 LB FT)

91098G03

Fig. 43 Exploded view of the control arm-to-frame mounting

To install:

11. Position the ball joint in the control arm.

12. Install the three ball joint bolts and nuts and tighten to specification as specified in the ball joint kit.

13. Install the ball joint to the knuckle, install a new pinch bolt and nut, and tighten to 33 ft. lbs. (45 Nm).

14. Install the stabilizer shaft bushing clamp bolts to 33 ft. lbs. (45 Nm).

15. Remove the seal protectors.

16. Install the tire and wheel assembly.

17. Raise the vehicle slightly to allow removal of the jackstands, then carefully lower the vehicle.

Stabilizer (Sway) Bar

REMOVAL & INSTALLATION

1. Raise and safely support the front of the vehicle so that the suspension hangs free.

2. Remove the stabilizer shaft insulator clamp and insulator at the control arms; do not remove the studs from the control arms.

3. Remove the plate from each side of the frame.

4. Remove the stabilizer shaft and insulator bushings.

To install:

5. Install the insulator bushings to the stabilizer shaft.

6. Install the stabilizer shaft and insulator bushings to the frame.

7. Install the plate to each side of the frame and tighten the bolts to 40 ft. lbs. (55 Nm).

8. Install the insulator clamp to the control arms and tighten the nuts to 33 ft. lbs. (45 Nm).

Lower Control Arm

The lower control arm is a two-piece welded unit with a riveted ball joint. A conventional rubber bushing is used for the rear lower control arm pivot. The front lower control arm bushing is mounted vertically.

REMOVAL & INSTALLATION

◗ See Figure 43

Some special tools are required to perform this operation including, a front hub spindle removal tool and a suitable ball joint separator tool.

⁂ WARNING

Do not hammer or pry ball joint from knuckle. Failure to use recommended tools may cause damage to the ball joint and seal.

1. Raise the vehicle and suitably support by the frame allowing the control arms to hang free.

2. Remove the wheel and tire assembly.

3. Remove the steering gear outer tie rod from the steering knuckle.

4. Remove the stabilizer shaft link from the control arm.

5. Remove the front drive axle shaft nut and washer.

6. Use a suitable front hub spindle removal tool to Push the axle splines back out of the front wheel drive shaft bearing.

7. Remove the drive axle from the transaxle.

➡Drive axle joint seal protectors should be used anytime service is performed on or near the drive axles. Failure to observe this could result in joint or seal failure.

8. Place a modified inner drive joint seal protector on the drive axle joints.

9. If equipped, remove the ABS wheel speed sensor jumper harness.

10. Remove and discard the cotter pin, then loosen the nut from the ball stud.

11. Remove the pinch bolt and the control arm mounting bolts, then remove the control arm from the vehicle.

To install:

12. If equipped, install the ABS wheel speed sensor jumper harness, if equipped.

13. Install the control arm to the frame and install the mounting bolts but do not tighten at this time.

14. Install the drive axle into the transaxle and the front drive axle shaft splines into the front wheel drive shaft bearing, Tighten the axle nut to 96 lb. ft. (130 Nm).

15. Install the ball joint to the steering knuckle using a NEW pinch bolt and nut, then tighten to 33 ft. lbs. (45 Nm). Install a new cotter pin.

16. Raise the vehicle slightly so the weight of the vehicle is supported by the control arms.

➡The weight of the vehicle must be supported by the control arms when tightening the control arm mounting bolts.

17. Tighten the stabilizer shaft bushing clamp nuts to 32 ft. lbs. (43 Nm) and the control arm pivot bolt nut to 61 ft. lbs. (83 Nm).

18. Remove the seal protectors.

19. Install the tire and wheel assembly.

20. Raise the vehicle slightly to allow removal of the jackstands and lower the vehicle.

Front Hub and Bearings

REMOVAL & INSTALLATION

♦ **See Figures 44, 45 and 46**

1. Raise and safely support the vehicle.
2. Place jackstands under the frame.
3. Lower the vehicle slightly so the weight of the vehicle rests on the jackstands and not on the control arms.
4. Remove the wheel and tire assembly.

✳✳ WARNING

Drive axle joint seal protectors should be used anytime service is performed on or near the drive axles. Failure to observe this could result in joint or seal failure.

5. Place a modified inner drive joint seal protector on the drive axle joints.
6. Insert a drift punch through the rotor to keep it from moving, then remove the hub nut and washer.

➡ **Clean all of the dirt and lubricant from the drive axle threads.**

7. Unbolt the caliper and support it out of the way with a suitable piece of wire. Do not disconnect the brake fluid line. For more details, refer to Section 9 of this manual.
8. Remove the rotor.

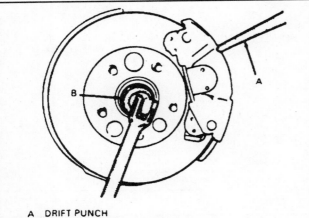

A DRIFT PUNCH
B 6 POINT DEEP WELL SOCKET

91098G05

Fig. 44 Removal and installation of the front wheel hub/drive shaft nut

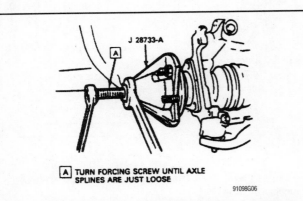

J 28733-A

A TURN FORCING SCREW UNTIL AXLE SPLINES ARE JUST LOOSE

91098G06

Fig. 45 Use the proper tool to separate the drive axle from the hub

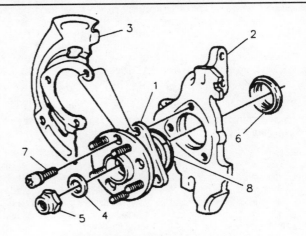

1 HUB AND BEARING ASSEMBLY
2 STEERING KNUCKLE
3 SHIELD
4 WASHER
5 HUB NUT 145 N·m (107 LB FT)
6 SEAL
7 HUB AND BEARING RETAINING BOLT (55 TORX) 95 N·m (70 LB FT)
8 "O" RING

91098G04

Fig. 46 The hub and bearing assembly is attached to the knuckle with retaining bolts

9. Install a suitable front hub spindle removal tool, then separate the hub and drive axle.
10. Unfasten the three hub-and-bearing retaining bolts, then remove the shield, hub and bearing assembly and O-ring.
11. To remove the seal, use a punch and tap the seal toward the engine. When the seal is removed from the steering knuckle, cut it off the drive axle using side cutters.

➡ **The factory seal is installed from the engine side of the steering knuckle. The service replacement seal is installed from the wheel side of the steering knuckle.**

To install:

12. Install the new hub and bearing seal in the steering knuckle using the proper installer.
13. Lubricate the hub and bearing seal with grease.
14. Install a new O-ring around the hub and bearing assembly.
15. Install the hub and bearing assembly into the steering knuckle. Tighten the hub and bearing retaining bolts to 70 ft. lbs. (95 Nm).
16. Install the rotor and caliper. Tighten the caliper retaining bolts to 38 ft. lbs. (51 Nm).
17. Install the hub nut and washer.
18. Insert a drift punch through the rotor and caliper to keep the rotor from moving.
19. Tighten the hub nut to 185 ft. lbs. (260 Nm).
20. Remove the seal protectors.
21. Install the tire and wheel assembly.
22. Raise the vehicle slightly to allow removal of the jackstands, then carefully lower the vehicle.

Wheel Alignment

If the tires are worn unevenly, if the vehicle is not stable on the highway or if the handling seems uneven in spirited driving, the wheel alignment should be checked. If an alignment problem is suspected, first check for improper tire inflation and other possible causes. These can be worn suspension or steering components, accident damage or even unmatched tires. If any worn or damaged components are found, they must be replaced before the wheels can be properly aligned. Wheel alignment requires very expensive equipment and involves minute adjustments, which must be accurate; a trained technician should perform it. Take your vehicle to a properly equipped shop.

Following is a description of the alignment angles, which are adjustable on most vehicles and how they affect vehicle handling. Although these angles can apply to both the front and rear wheels, usually only the front suspension is adjustable.

CASTER

▶ **See Figure 47**

Looking at a vehicle from the side, caster angle describes the steering axis rather than a wheel angle. The steering knuckle is attached to a control arm or strut at the top and a control arm at the bottom. The wheel pivots around the line between these points to steer the vehicle. When the upper point is tilted back, this is described as positive caster. Having a positive caster tends to make the wheels self-centering, increasing directional stability. Excessive positive caster makes the wheels hard to steer, while an uneven caster will cause a pull to one side. Overloading the vehicle or sagging rear springs will affect caster, as will raising the rear of the vehicle. If the rear of the vehicle is lower than normal, the caster becomes more positive.

CAMBER

▶ **See Figure 48**

Looking from the front of the vehicle, camber is the inward or outward tilt of the top of wheels. When the tops of the wheels are tilted in, this is negative camber; if they are tilted out, it is positive. In a turn, a slight amount of negative camber helps maximize contact of the tire with the road. However, too much negative camber compromises straight-line stability, increases bump steer and torque steer.

TOE

▶ **See Figure 49**

Looking down at the wheels from above the vehicle, toe angle is the distance between the front of the wheels, relative to the distance between the back of the wheels. If the wheels are closer at the front, they are said to be toed-in or to have negative toe. A small amount of negative toe enhances directional stability and provides a smoother ride on the highway.

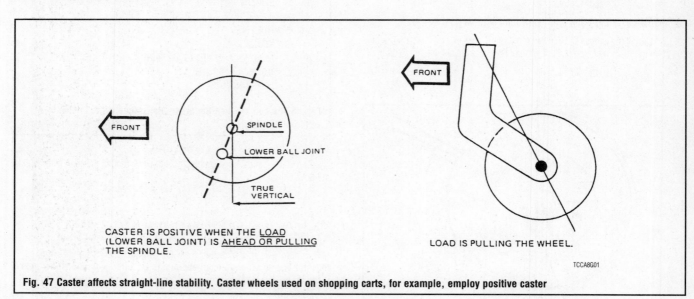

CASTER IS POSITIVE WHEN THE <u>LOAD</u> (LOWER BALL JOINT) IS <u>AHEAD OR PULLING</u> THE SPINDLE.

LOAD IS PULLING THE WHEEL.

TCCA8G01

Fig. 47 Caster affects straight-line stability. Caster wheels used on shopping carts, for example, employ positive caster

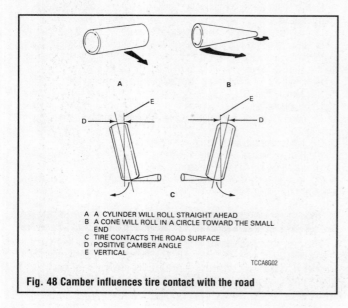

A A CYLINDER WILL ROLL STRAIGHT AHEAD
B A CONE WILL ROLL IN A CIRCLE TOWARD THE SMALL END
C TIRE CONTACTS THE ROAD SURFACE
D POSITIVE CAMBER ANGLE
E VERTICAL

TCCA8G02

Fig. 48 Camber influences tire contact with the road

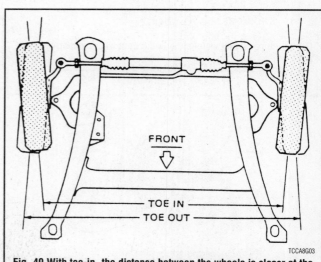

TCCA8G03

Fig. 49 With toe-in, the distance between the wheels is closer at the front than at the rear

REAR SUSPENSION

REAR SUSPENSION COMPONENT LOCATIONS—EARLY MODEL

1. Track bar
2. Coil spring
3. Shock absorber
4. Rear axle assembly

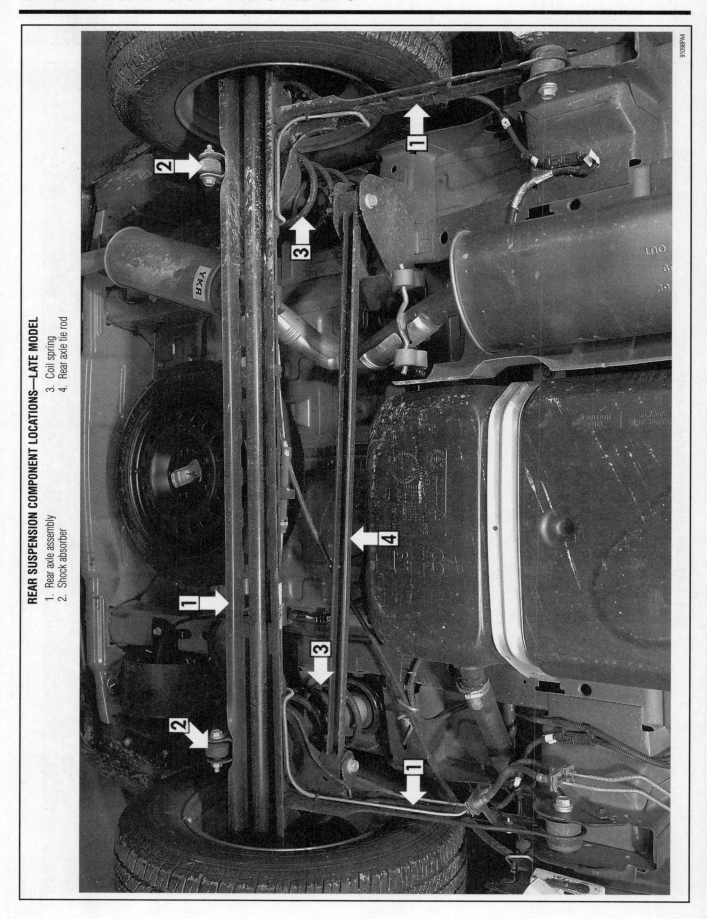

REAR SUSPENSION COMPONENT LOCATIONS—LATE MODEL

1. Rear axle assembly
2. Shock absorber
3. Coil spring
4. Rear axle tie rod

Coil Springs

REMOVAL & INSTALLATION

▶ **See Figure 50**

✳✳ CAUTION

When removing the rear springs do not use a twin-post type hoist. The swing arc tendency of the rear axle assembly when certain fasteners are removed may cause it to slip from the hoist, which may cause personal injury. Perform operation on floor, if necessary.

➥When reassembling rear axle components, make sure that the bolts attaching the axle to the supports are inserted from inboard to outboard side of chassis. Position the leg of the upper coil on each spring parallel to the axle assembly and towards the side of vehicle.

1. Support the rear axle and safely raise the vehicle.
2. Remove the right and left brake line bracket attaching screws from the frame. Allow the brake line to hang freely.
3. Disconnect the track bar attaching nut and bolt at the rear axle.
4. Remove the right and left shock absorber lower attaching bolts.

✳✳ WARNING

Do not suspend the rear axle by the brake hoses or damage to the hoses could result.

5. Carefully lower the rear axle, then remove the springs and insulators.
To install:
6. Position the springs and insulators in the seats and raise the rear axle. The leg of the upper coil on the springs must be parallel to the axle assembly and face outboard.
7. Install the shocks to the rear axle and tighten the nuts to 44 ft. lbs. (59 Nm).
8. Install the track bar to the rear axle and tighten the nut to 44 ft. lbs. (59 Nm).

9. Install the brake line brackets to the frame and tighten the retaining screws to 8 ft. lbs. (11 Nm).
10. Remove the rear axle support jack and carefully lower the vehicle.

Track Bar

The track bar, in combination with the shock absorbers and control arms, maintain the relationship of the rear axle to the body, oppose torque reaction on acceleration and braking and provide for the best possible handling. The track bar was only available on early models.

REMOVAL & INSTALLATION

▶ **See Figure 51**

1. Support the rear axle and safely raise the vehicle.
2. Remove the nut and bolt from both the rear axle and body attachments, then remove the track bar.
To install:
3. Position the track bar at the axle mounting bracket and loosely install the bolt and nut.
4. Place the other end of the track bar in the body reinforcement and install the bolt and nut. Tighten the nut at the axle bracket to 44 ft. lbs. (60 Nm). Tighten the nut at the underbody reinforcement to 35 ft. lbs. (47 Nm).
5. Remove the rear axle support and carefully lower the vehicle.

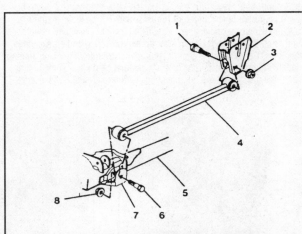

1. BOLT, TRACK BAR TO UPPER BODY MOUNT 65 N·m (48 LB.FT.)
2. MOUNT, TRACK BAR UPPER BODY
3. NUT, TRACK BAR TO UPPER BODY MOUNT
4. TRACK BAR
5. AXLE ASSEMBLY
6. BOLT, TRACK BAR TO AXLE MOUNT 85 N·m (63 LB.FT.)
7. MOUNT, TRACK BAR TO AXLE
8. NUT, TRACK BAR TO AXLE

91098G12

Fig. 51 Exploded view of the track bar-to-body mount attachment

Shock Absorbers

TESTING

▶ **See Figure 52**

The purpose of the shock absorber is simply to limit the motion of the spring during compression and rebound cycles. If the vehicle is not equipped with these motion dampers, the up and down motion would multiply until the vehicle was alternately trying to leap off the ground and to pound itself into the pavement.

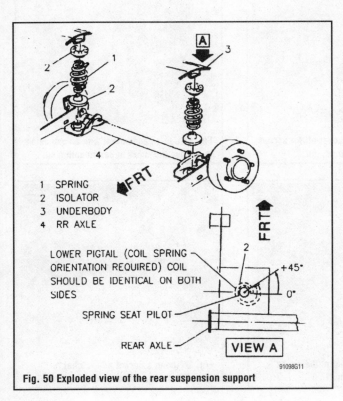

1. SPRING
2. ISOLATOR
3. UNDERBODY
4. RR AXLE

LOWER PIGTAIL (COIL SPRING ORIENTATION REQUIRED) COIL SHOULD BE IDENTICAL ON BOTH SIDES

SPRING SEAT PILOT

REAR AXLE

VIEW A

+45°

0°

91098G11

Fig. 50 Exploded view of the rear suspension support

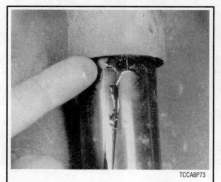

Fig. 52 When fluid is seeping out of the shock absorber, it's time to replace it

TCCA8P73

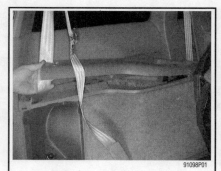

Fig. 53 The trim cover is held in place by snaps and can be removed by carefully lifting it off

91098P01

Fig. 54 The cover can be completely removed to get it out of the way

91098P02

Contrary to popular rumor, the shocks do not affect the ride height of the vehicle. This is controlled by other suspension components such as springs and tires. Worn shock absorbers can affect handling; if the front of the vehicle is rising or falling excessively, the "footprint" of the tires changes on the pavement and steering is affected.

One of the simplest tests of shock absorbers is to simply push down on one corner of an unladen vehicle and release it. Observe the motion of the body as it is released. In most cases, it will come up beyond it original rest position, dip back below it and settle quickly to rest. This shows that the damper is controlling the spring action. Any tendency to excessive pitch (up-and-down) motion or failure to return to rest within 2-3 cycles is a sign of poor function within the shock absorber. Oil-filled shocks may have a light film of oil around the seal, resulting from normal breathing and air exchange. This should NOT be taken as a sign of failure, but any sign of thick or running oil definitely indicates failure. Gas filled shocks may also show some film at the shaft; if the gas has leaked out, the shock will have almost no resistance to motion.

While each shock absorber can be replaced individually, it is recommended that they be changed as a pair (both front or both rear) to maintain equal response on both sides of the vehicle. Chances are quite good that if one has failed, its mate is weak also.

REMOVAL & INSTALLATION

▶ **See Figures 53 thru 64**

1. Open the lift gate, remove the trim cover and remove the upper shock attaching nut.
2. Support the rear axle and safely raise the vehicle.
3. If equipped with electronic level control, disconnect the air hose.
4. Remove the lower attaching bolt and nut and remove the shock.
To install:
5. Position the shock at the lower attachment, feed the bolt through the holes, and loosely install the nut.

Fig. 55 There is a rubber bumper cover over the top mount of the shock

91098P03

Fig. 56 Pull the rubber cover off for access to the shock upper retaining nut

91098P04

Fig. 57 Use a deep socket with an extension to remove the shock upper mounting nut

91098P05

Fig. 58 This is the top of the shock as viewed inside the wheel housing

91098P34

Fig. 59 The bottom mount of the shock is secured with a nut and bolt

91098P07

Fig. 60 Using a socket and ratchet to loosen the bottom mounting bolt

91098P09

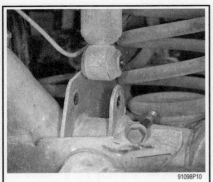
Fig. 61 Remove the shock from the bottom mount . . .

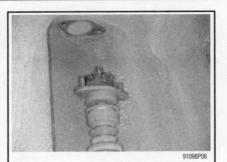
Fig. 62 . . . then lower the shock and remove it from the vehicle. Remove the upper mounting brace with the shock, to inspect for wear

Fig. 63 Standard rear shock absorber, with attaching parts

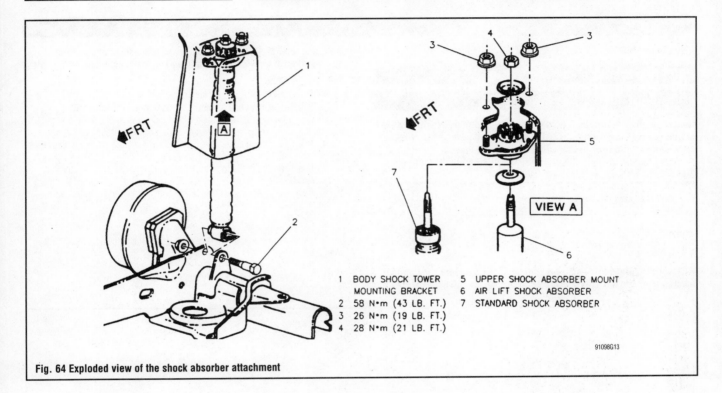

1	BODY SHOCK TOWER	5	UPPER SHOCK ABSORBER MOUNT
	MOUNTING BRACKET	6	AIR LIFT SHOCK ABSORBER
2	58 N•m (43 LB. FT.)	7	STANDARD SHOCK ABSORBER
3	26 N•m (19 LB. FT.)		
4	28 N•m (21 LB. FT.)		

Fig. 64 Exploded view of the shock absorber attachment

6. If equipped with electronic level control, connect the air hose.

7. Lower the vehicle enough to guide the upper stud through the body opening and install the nut loosely.

8. Tighten the lower nut to 44 ft. lbs. (59 Nm).

9. Lower the vehicle the rest of the way, then tighten the upper nut to 16 ft. lbs. (22 Nm).

10. Install the rubber bumper and trim cover.

Hub and Bearing

REMOVAL & INSTALLATION

▶ **See Figures 65, 66 and 67**

1. Raise and support the vehicle safely.
2. Remove the tire and wheel assembly.

❊❊ WARNING

Do not hammer on the brake drum or damage to the bearing could result.

3. Remove the brake drum.

❊❊ WARNING

The bolts, which attach the hub and bearing assembly support the brake assembly. When removing these bolts, support the brake assembly with a wire or other means.

4. Remove the attaching bolts, then remove the hub and bearing assembly from the axle.

To install:

5. Install the hub and bearing assembly to the rear axle and tighten the retaining bolts to 45 ft. lbs. (60 Nm).

6. Install the brake drum.

7. Install the tire and wheel assembly, then carefully lower the vehicle.

Fig. 65 A deep socket fits through the opening in the hub flange to . . .

Fig. 66 . . . unbolt the hub from the axle

Fig. 67 The rear hub and bearing is attached with four bolts. Some vehicles use Torx® bolts, so you will need the proper tools for removal

STEERING

♦ See Figure 68

Steering Wheel

❋❋ CAUTION

Some models covered by this manual may be equipped with a Supplemental Restraint System (SRS), which uses an air bag. Whenever working near any of the SRS components, such as the impact sensors, the air bag module, steering column and instrument panel, disable the SRS, as described in Section 6.

REMOVAL & INSTALLATION

Without Air Bags

♦ See Figure 69

➡This procedure is for vehicles that do not have a driver's side air bag incorporated into the steering wheel. Please see the following procedure, and refer to Section 6 for disarming procedures and additional SRS warnings if the vehicle you are working on is equipped with an air bag

1. Disconnect the negative battery cable.
2. Remove the horn pad by gently prying with a thin bladed tool.
3. Disconnect the horn electrical lead. Push down on the horn lead and turn left; the wire and spring will then come out of the canceling cam tower.
4. Matchmark the steering wheel and the shaft using a marker or equivalent.
5. Remove the steering wheel retainer and nut.
6. Use a suitable puller to remove the steering wheel from the shaft.

To install:

7. Position the steering wheel on the shaft, aligning the matchmarks made during removal. Install the steering wheel retaining nut and tighten it to 30 ft. lbs. (40 Nm).
8. Install the retainer.
9. Attach the horn lead electrical connection. Push down on the horn lead and turn right into a lock position.
10. Install the horn pad.
11. Connect the negative battery cable.

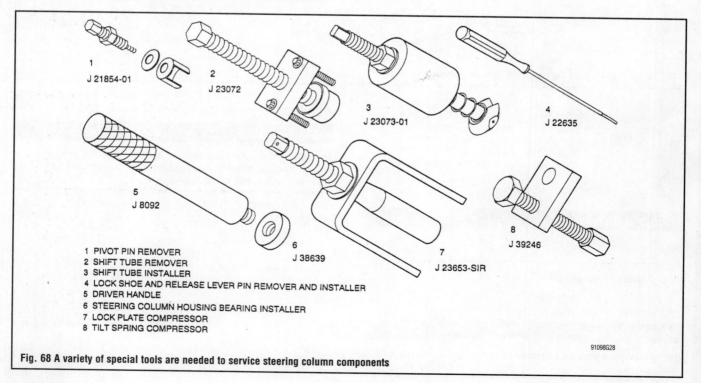

1 PIVOT PIN REMOVER
2 SHIFT TUBE REMOVER
3 SHIFT TUBE INSTALLER
4 LOCK SHOE AND RELEASE LEVER PIN REMOVER AND INSTALLER
5 DRIVER HANDLE
6 STEERING COLUMN HOUSING BEARING INSTALLER
7 LOCK PLATE COMPRESSOR
8 TILT SPRING COMPRESSOR

1 J 21854-01
2 J 23072
3 J 23073-01
4 J 22635
5 J 8092
6 J 38639
7 J 23653-SIR
8 J 39246

Fig. 68 A variety of special tools are needed to service steering column components

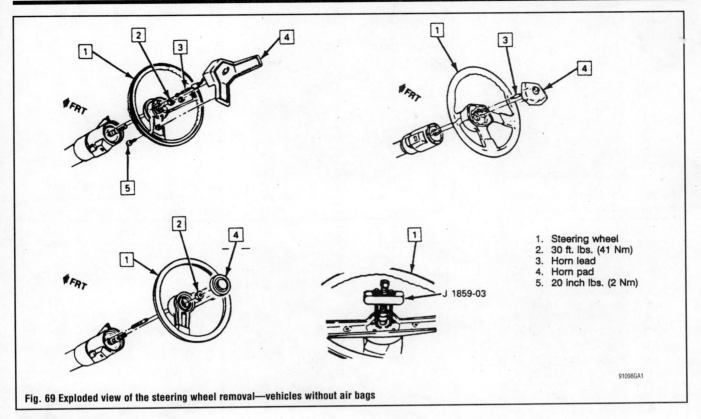

Fig. 69 Exploded view of the steering wheel removal—vehicles without air bags

1. Steering wheel
2. 30 ft. lbs. (41 Nm)
3. Horn lead
4. Horn pad
5. 20 inch lbs. (2 Nm)

91098GA1

With Air Bags

◆ **See Figures 70 thru 78**

1. Properly disarm the Supplemental Retraint System (SRS), as outlined in Section 6 of this manual.

2. If not already done, disconnect the negative battery cable.

3. Remove the steering wheel inflatable restraint module. The module is either secured with retaining bolts/screws on the backside of the module, or by leaf springs which are also located on the rear side of the module. To remove this type, use a suitable flat bladed tool to release the springs while gently pulling on the module.

4. Detach the electrical connector from the steering wheel inflatable module, then remove the module and place it in a safe location with the pad facing up.

5. Matchmark the steering wheel and the shaft.

6. Loosen the steering wheel shaft nut and unthread it until it is flush with the end of the shaft.

7. Use a suitable puller to pull the steering wheel loose from the shaft.

8. Remove the steering wheel shaft nut, then remove the steering wheel from the shaft.

To install:

9. Route the SRS electrical connector through the steering wheel.

10. Align the matchmarks made during removal and tighten the steering wheel retaining nut to 33 ft. lbs. (45 Nm).

11. Attach the electrical connector to the steering wheel inflatable module.

12. Install the inflator module, using a reverse of the removal procedure.

13. Enable the SRS system, as outlined in Section 6 of this manual.

14. If not already done, connect the negative battery cable.

Turn Signal Switch

REMOVAL & INSTALLATION

◆ **See Figures 79, 80, 81, 82 and 83**

✷✷ CAUTION

Some models covered by this manual may be equipped with a Supplemental Restraint System (SRS), which uses an air bag. When-

Fig. 70 Unfasten the module retaining screws

91096P53

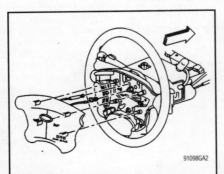

Fig. 71 Exploded view of the inflatable restraint steering wheel module—Silhouette shown

91098GA2

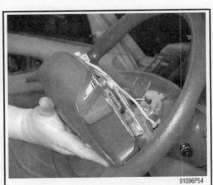

Fig. 72 Pull the inflator module partially away from the steering wheel . . .

91096P54

Fig. 73 . . . then remove the Connector Position Assurance (CPA) clip . . .

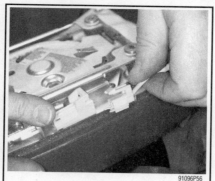

Fig. 74 . . . and detach the module electrical connector

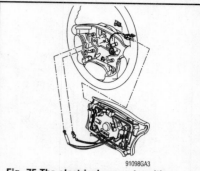

Fig. 75 The electrical connector either attaches to either the module or the steering wheel, depending upon the model

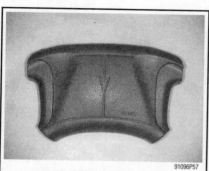

Fig. 76 Make sure to place the inflator module on a suitable workbench the pad facing up

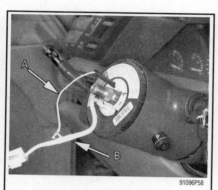

Fig. 77 View of the horn lead (A) and inflator module electrical connector (B)

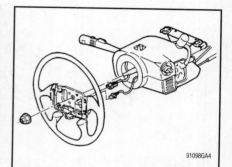

Fig. 78 Once the puller loosens the steering wheel from the shaft, you can remove the nut and then the steering wheel

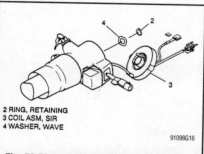

2 RING, RETAINING
3 COIL ASM, SIR
4 WASHER, WAVE

Fig. 79 Place the ignition in the "LOCK" position to prevent losing the center on the coil assembly. Diagrams shows removing the coil assembly from the shaft

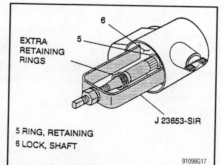

EXTRA RETAINING RINGS

J 23653-SIR

5 RING, RETAINING
6 LOCK, SHAFT

Fig. 80 Use a suitable lock plate compressor tool to remove the shaft lock retaining ring

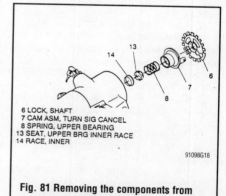

6 LOCK, SHAFT
7 CAM ASM, TURN SIG CANCEL
8 SPRING, UPPER BEARING
13 SEAT, UPPER BRG INNER RACE
14 RACE, INNER

Fig. 81 Removing the components from the upper shaft to obtain access

ever working near any of the SRS components, such as the impact sensors, the air bag module, steering column and instrument panel, disable the SRS, as described in Section 6.

➡This procedure requires the use of two special tools; a steering wheel puller and a lock plate compressor.

1. If equipped with an air bag, disable the system as outlined in Section 6 of this manual.

2. If not done already, disconnect the negative battery cable.

3. Remove the steering wheel as outlined earlier in this section.

4. Remove the shaft lock cover.

5. Remove the shaft lock retaining ring using a suitable lock plate compressor tool to press down the shaft lock. Dispose of the ring.

6. Remove the shaft lock.

7. Remove the turn signal canceling cam assembly.

8. On vehicles without tilt columns, remove the upper bearing spring and thrust washer.

9. On vehicles with tilt columns, remove the upper bearing spring, inner race seat and inner race.

10. Move the turn signal lever up, into the "right turn" position.

11. Remove the multi-function lever.

12. Remove the hazard knob assembly and the turn signal switch arm retaining screw.

13. Remove the turn signal switch screws.

14. Remove the wire protector and gently pull the wire harness through the gearshift bowl shroud, gearshift lever bowl, and the steering column housing assembly, and remove the switch assembly.

To install:

15. Feed the turn signal switch wiring harness through the steering column housing assembly, gearshift lever bowl and the gearshift bowl shroud.

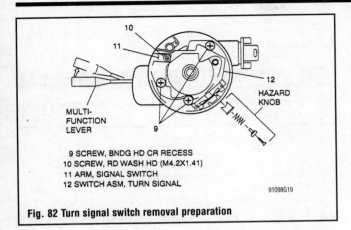

Fig. 82 Turn signal switch removal preparation

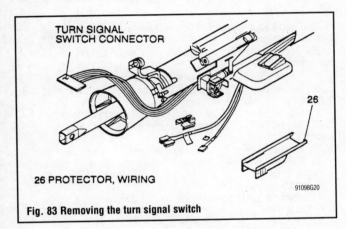

TURN SIGNAL
SWITCH CONNECTOR

26 PROTECTOR, WIRING

Fig. 83 Removing the turn signal switch

16. Install the turn signal switch and retaining screws and tighten to 31 inch lbs. (3.5 Nm).
17. Install the wire protector shield.
18. Install the turn signal switch arm and secure with the retaining screw. Tighten the screw to 20 inch lbs. (2.3 Nm).
19. Install the hazard knob assembly.
20. Install the multi-function lever.
21. On vehicles without tilt columns, install the upper bearing spring, and thrust washer and on vehicles with tilt columns, install the upper bearing spring, inner race seat and inner race.
22. Lubricate with synthetic grease and install the turn signal canceling cam assembly.
23. Install the shaft lock.
24. Install a new shaft lock retaining ring. Align it to the block tooth on the shaft, using a lock plate compressor tool to press down the shaft lock.
25. Install the shaft lock cover.
26. Install the steering wheel, as outlined earlier in this section.
27. Connect the negative battery cable. If equipped, enable the SRS system as outlined in Section 6 of this manual.

Ignition Switch and Dimmer Switch

✳✳ CAUTION

Some models covered by this manual may be equipped with a Supplemental Restraint System (SRS), which uses an air bag. Whenever working near any of the SRS components, such as the impact sensors, the air bag module, steering column and instrument panel, disable the SRS, as described in Section 6.

REMOVAL & INSTALLATION

Standard Column

▶ See Figures 84 and 85

➥This procedure requires the use of two special tools; a steering wheel puller and a lock plate compressor.

1. If equipped with an air bag, disable the system as outlined in Section 6 of this manual.
2. If not done already, disconnect the negative battery cable.
3. Remove the steering wheel, as outlined earlier in this section.
4. Remove the shaft lock cover.
5. Remove the shaft lock retaining ring using a suitable lock plate compressor tool to press down the shaft lock. Dispose of the ring.
6. Remove the shaft lock.
7. Remove the turn signal canceling cam assembly.
8. Remove the upper bearing spring.
9. Remove the thrust washer.
10. Move the turn signal lever up, into the "right turn" position.
11. Remove the multi-function lever.
12. Remove the turn signal switch arm retaining screw.
13. Remove the turn signal switch screws and let the switch hang freely.
14. Remove the key from the lock cylinder set.
15. Remove the buzzer switch assembly.
16. Reinsert the key in the lock cylinder.
17. Turn the key to the **LOCK** position.
18. Remove the lock retaining screw and remove the lock cylinder.
19. If equipped with cruise control, remove the housing cover end cap, unplug the cruise control connector and gently pull through the shroud, bowl, and steering column housing assembly.

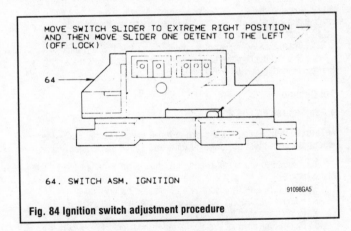

MOVE SWITCH SLIDER TO EXTREME RIGHT POSITION
AND THEN MOVE SLIDER ONE DETENT TO THE LEFT
(OFF LOCK)

64

64. SWITCH ASM. IGNITION

Fig. 84 Ignition switch adjustment procedure

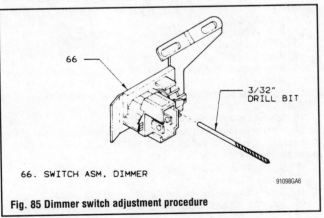

66

3/32"
DRILL BIT

66. SWITCH ASM. DIMMER

Fig. 85 Dimmer switch adjustment procedure

20. Remove the washer head screw, the hex nut and dimmer switch.
21. Remove the mounting stud and ignition switch.

To install:

22. If equipped with cruise control, gently pull the connector through the steering column housing assembly, bowl and shroud and connect the plug.
23. Install the housing cover end cap and screw and tighten to 17 inch lbs. (1.9 Nm).
24. Install the ignition switch and mounting stud and tighten the stud to 35 inch lbs. (4.0 Nm). Adjust the ignition switch by moving the switch slider to the extreme left position and then move the slider 1 detent to the right (off lock).
25. Install the dimmer switch hex nut, screw, and tighten to 35 inch lbs. (4.0 Nm). Adjust the dimmer switch.
26. To adjust the dimmer switch, depress the switch slightly to allow insertion of a 3/32 in. drill bit into the hole above the actuator rod. Force the switch upward then tighten the screw.
27. Install the switch using the original screws. Use of screws that are too long could prevent the column from collapsing on impact.
28. Install the lock cylinder and retaining screws and tighten to 40 inch lbs. (4.5 Nm).
29. Turn the key to the RUN position.
30. Install the buzzer switch assembly.
31. Install the turn signal switch and retaining screws and tighten to 31 inch lbs. (3.5 Nm).
32. Install the wire protector shield.
33. Install the turn signal switch arm and retaining screw and tighten to 29 inch lbs. (2.3 Nm).
34. Install the hazard knob assembly.
35. Install the multi-function lever.
36. Install the thrust washer and upper bearing spring.
37. Lubricate with synthetic grease and install the turn signal canceling cam assembly.
38. Install the shaft lock.
39. Install a new shaft lock retaining ring. Align it to the block tooth on the shaft, using a lock plate compressor tool to press down the shaft lock.
40. Install the shaft lock cover.
41. Install the steering wheel, as outlined earlier in this section.
42. Connect the negative battery cable. If equipped, enable the air bag system as outlined in Section 6 of this manual.

Tilt Column

▶ **See Figures 84 and 85**

➥This procedure requires the use of three special tools; a steering wheel puller, a pivot pin removal tool, and a lock plate compressor.

1. If equipped with an air bag, disable the system as outlined in Section 6 of this manual.
2. If not done already, disconnect the negative battery cable.
3. Remove the steering wheel, as outlined earlier in this section.
4. Remove the shaft lock cover.
5. Remove the shaft lock retaining ring using a lock plate compressor tool, or equivalent to press down the shaft lock. Dispose of the ring.
6. Remove the shaft lock.
7. Remove the turn signal canceling cam assembly.
8. Remove the upper bearing spring.
9. Remove the inner race seat and inner race.
10. Move the turn signal lever up, into the "right turn" position.
11. Remove the multi-function lever.
12. Remove the hazard knob assembly and the turn signal switch arm retaining screw.
13. Remove the turn signal switch screws.
14. Remove the wire protector and gently pull the wire harness through the gearshift bowl shroud, gearshift lever bowl, and the steering column housing assembly, and remove the switch assembly.
15. Remove the screws and remove the lock housing cover assembly.
16. Remove the tilt wheel lever.
17. Remove the cover end cap and the dimmer switch rod actuator.
18. Gently pull the pivot switch wire harness through the bowl assembly and column housing.
19. Remove the tilt wheel spring retainer and spring.
20. Remove the pivot pins, using a suitable pivot pin removal tool.

21. Reinstall the tilt lever.
22. Pull back on the tilt lever and pull the column housing down and away from the column.
23. Remove the column from the vehicle.

Once the column is removed from the vehicle, it is extremely susceptible to damage.

24. Remove the bearing and seal retainer.
25. Remove the lower spring retainer and dispose of the retainer.
26. Remove the lower bearing spring and seat.
27. Remove the hex head screws and remove the adapter and bearing assembly.
28. Remove the column shaft assembly and check for accident damage.

➡Mark the upper and lower shaft assembly to ensure proper assembly. Failure to assemble properly wig cause the steering wheel to be turned 180°.

29. Disconnect the upper shaft from the lower shaft assembly. Tilt 90° to each other and disengage.
30. Disconnect the centering sphere from the upper shaft assembly. Rotate 90° and slip out.
31. Remove the housing support retaining screws.
32. Remove the column housing support assembly and dimmer switch rod from the steering column jacket assembly.
33. Remove the rod from the column housing support assembly.
34. Remove the two screws and remove the shift lever gate from the support assembly.
35. Remove the hex nut and screw and remove the dimmer switch assembly.
36. Remove the mounting stud and remove the ignition switch assembly and actuator rod.

To install:

37. Install the gate to the support assembly and tighten the retaining screws to 33 inch lbs. (3.7 Nm).
38. Install the dimmer switch rod to the support assembly.
39. Install the column housing support assembly and tighten the retaining screws to 78 inch lbs. (8.8 Nm).
40. Install the actuator assembly to the track housing support assembly.
41. Install the joint preload spring to the two centering spheres.
42. Install the centering sphere. Lubricate with lithium grease and slip into the upper shaft assembly and rotate 90°.

➡The marks on the upper and lower shaft assembly must line up after assembled. Failure to assemble properly will cause the steering wheel to be turned 180°.

43. Connect the upper shaft to the lower shaft assembly. Line up the mark tilt the assemblies 90° to each other and engage.
44. Lubricate the column shaft assembly with lithium grease and install the jacket assembly.
45. Install the lock cylinder and retaining screws and tighten to 40 inch lbs. (4.5 Nm).
46. Turn the key to the RUN position.
47. Install the buzzer switch assembly.
48. Feed the turn signal switch wiring harness through the steering column housing assembly, gearshift lever bowl and the gearshift bowl shroud.
49. Install the turn signal switch and retaining screws. Tighten the screws to 31 inch lbs. (3.5 Nm).
50. Install the wire protector shield.
51. Install the turn signal switch arm and secure with the retaining screw. Tighten to 20 inch lbs. (2.3 Nm).
52. Install the hazard knob assembly.
53. Install the multi-function lever.
54. Install the upper bearing spring, inner race seat and inner race.
55. Lubricate with synthetic grease and install the turn signal canceling cam assembly.
56. Install the shaft lock.
57. Install a new shaft lock retaining ring. Align it to the block tooth on the shaft, using a lock plate compressor tool to press down the shaft lock.
58. Install the shaft lock cover.

59. Install the steering wheel, as outlined earlier in this section.

60. Install the locking nut and retaining ring.

61. Install the horn contact into the horn tower. Push down on the horn lead and turn right into a lock position.

62. Install the horn pad and the screws from the back of the steering wheel.

63. Coat the inner surface with lithium grease and install the adapter and bearing assembly. Tighten the screws to 30 inch lbs. (3.4 Nm).

64. Install the lower bearing seat and spring. Press the retainer onto the shaft to compress the shaft. Spring height must be 1.0 in. (25.4 mm).

65. Install the bearing and seal retainer.

66. Install the ignition switch and mounting stud and tighten to 35 inch lbs. (4.0 Nm).

67. Install the dimmer switch and adjust as follows:

    a. Depress the switch slightly to allow insertion of a ³⁄₃₂ in. drill bit into the hole above the actuator rod.

    b. Force the switch upward then tighten the screw. Tighten the screw to 35 inch lbs. (4.0 Nm).

68. Install the switch using the original screws. Using screws that are too long could prevent the column from collapsing on impact.

69. Install the column to the instrument panel.

70. Connect the negative battery cable. If equipped, enable the air bag system as outlined in Section 6 of this manual.

Ignition Lock Cylinder

REMOVAL & INSTALLATION

♦ See Figures 86 thru 93

❊❊ CAUTION

Some models covered by this manual may be equipped with a Supplemental Restraint System (SRS), which uses an air bag. When-

ever working near any of the SRS components, such as the impact sensors, the air bag module, steering column and instrument panel, disable the SRS, as described in Section 6.

➡**This procedure requires the use of two special tools; a steering wheel puller and a lock plate compressor.**

1. If equipped with an air bag, disable the system as outlined in Section 6 of this manual.

2. If not done already, disconnect the negative battery cable.

3. Remove the steering wheel, as outlined earlier in this section.

4. For vehicles without air bags, remove the shaft lock cover.

5. For vehicles with air bags, perform the following:

    a. Remove the coil assembly retaining ring.

    b. Remove the inflatable restraint coil assembly, allowing the coil to hang freely if removal is not needed.

    c. Remove the wave washer.

6. Remove the shaft lock retaining ring using a lock plate compressor tool to press down the shaft lock. Dispose of the ring.

7. Remove the shaft lock.

8. Remove the turn signal canceling cam assembly.

9. On vehicles without tilt columns, remove the upper bearing spring and thrust washer.

10. On vehicles with tilt columns, remove the upper bearing spring, inner race seat and inner race.

11. Move the turn signal lever up, into the "right turn" position.

12. Remove the multi-function lever.

13. Remove the turn signal switch arm retaining screw.

14. Remove the turn signal switch screws and let the switch hang freely.

➡**On vehicles with air bags, the coil will become uncentered if the steering column is separated from the steering gear and is allowed to rotate, or the centering spring is pushed down, allowing the hub to rotate while the coil is remove the steering column.**

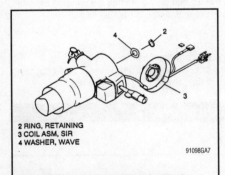

2 RING, RETAINING
3 COIL ASM, SIR
4 WASHER, WAVE

91098GA7

Fig. 86 For vehicles equipped with air bags, remove the coil assembly from the steering shaft

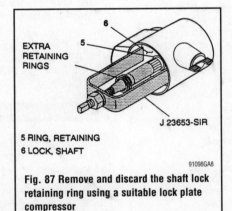

EXTRA RETAINING RINGS

J 23653-SIR

5 RING, RETAINING
6 LOCK, SHAFT

91098GA8

Fig. 87 Remove and discard the shaft lock retaining ring using a suitable lock plate compressor

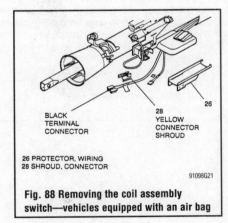

BLACK TERMINAL CONNECTOR

YELLOW CONNECTOR SHROUD

26 PROTECTOR, WIRING
28 SHROUD, CONNECTOR

91098G21

Fig. 88 Removing the coil assembly switch—vehicles equipped with an air bag

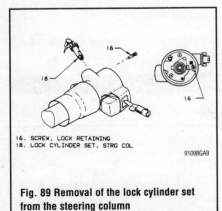

16. SCREW, LOCK RETAINING
18. LOCK CYLINDER SET, STRG COL

91098GA9

Fig. 89 Removal of the lock cylinder set from the steering column

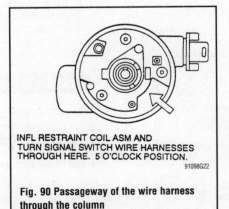

INFL RESTRAINT COIL ASM AND TURN SIGNAL SWITCH WIRE HARNESSES THROUGH HERE. 5 O'CLOCK POSITION.

91098G22

Fig. 90 Passageway of the wire harness through the column

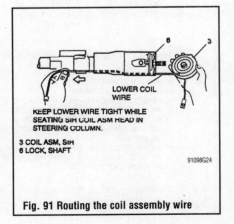

LOWER COIL WIRE

KEEP LOWER WIRE TIGHT WHILE SEATING SIR COIL ASM HEAD IN STEERING COLUMN.

3 COIL ASM, SIR
6 LOCK, SHAFT

91098G24

Fig. 91 Routing the coil assembly wire

15. If equipped with air bags, remove the coil assembly with the wire from the column as follows:

 a. Remove the wiring protector.

 b. Attach a piece of mechanics wire to the coil terminal connector to aid in reassembly.

 c. Gently pull the wire through the column.

16. Remove the key from the lock cylinder set.

17. Remove the buzzer switch assembly.

18. Reinsert the key in the lock cylinder.

19. Turn the key to the LOCK position.

20. Unfasten the retaining screw, then remove the lock cylinder.

To install:

21. Install the lock cylinder and retaining screws and tighten to 40 inch lbs. (4.5 Nm).

22. Turn the key to the RUN position.

23. Install the buzzer switch assembly.

24. Route the turn signal switch assembly wire harness through the steering column. Let the switch hang freely. Attach the switch connector through the bulkhead connector.

25. If equipped with air bags, route the coil assembly wire harness through the column, allowing the coil to hang freely.

26. Install the turn signal switch and retaining screws and tighten to 31 inch lbs. (3.5 Nm).

27. Install the wire protector shield.

28. Install the turn signal switch arm and retaining screw and tighten to 29 inch lbs. (2.3 Nm).

29. Install the hazard knob assembly.

30. Install the multi-function lever.

31. On vehicles without tilt columns, install the upper bearing spring and thrust washer. On vehicles with tilt columns, install the upper bearing spring, inner race seat and inner race.

32. Lubricate with synthetic grease, then install the turn signal canceling cam assembly.

33. Install the shaft lock.

34. Install a new shaft lock retaining ring. Align it to the block tooth on the shaft, using a lock plate compressor tool to press down the shaft lock.

35. On vehicles with air bags, perform the following:

 a. Set the steering shaft so that the block tooth on the race & upper steering shaft is at the 12 o'clock position, wheels on the vehicle should be straight ahead.

 b. Place the ignition switch in the LOCK position to ensure that the coil will not be damaged.

 c. Install the wave washer.

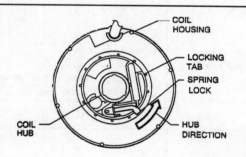

PERFORM THE FOLLOWING STEPS TO CENTER COIL ASSEMBLY

A. WHEELS STRAIGHT AHEAD.
B. REMOVE COIL ASSEMBLY.
C. HOLD COIL ASSEMBLY WITH BOTTOM UP.
D. WHILE HOLDING COIL ASSEMBLY, DEPRESS SPRING LOCK TO ROTATE HUB IN DIRECTION OF ARROW UNTIL IT STOPS.
E. THE COIL RIBBON SHOULD BE WOUND UP SNUG AGAINST CENTER HUB.
F. ROTATE COIL HUB IN OPPOSITE DIRECTION APPROXIMATELY TWO AND A HALF (2-1/2) TURNS. RELEASE SPRING LOCK BETWEEN LOCKING TABS.

91098G23

Fig. 92 If necessary, follow this procedure to center the coil assembly

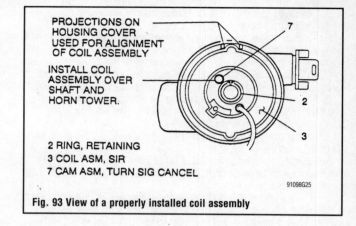

2 RING, RETAINING
3 COIL ASM, SIR
7 CAM ASM, TURN SIG CANCEL

91098G25

Fig. 93 View of a properly installed coil assembly

➡**On vehicles with air bags, the coil will become uncentered if the steering column is separated from the steering gear and is allowed to rotate, or the centering spring is pushed down, allowing the hub to rotate while the coil is remove the steering column.**

 d. If a new coil is being installed, assembly the pre-centered coil to the steering column. Remove and discard the centering tab.

 e. Make sure the coil assembly hub is centered.

36. For vehicles with air bags, install the coil as follows:

 a. Pull the wire tight while position the coil to the steering shaft.

 b. Align the opening in the coil with the horn tower and the locating bump between the 2 housing cover tabs.

 c. Seat the coil assembly into the steering column.

37. If equipped with an air bag, install the coil assembly retaining ring. Make sure the ring is firmly seated in the groove on the shaft.

➡**Gently pull on the lower coil assembly, turn signal and pivot & pulse wires to remove any wire kinks that may be inside the steering column assembly. Failure to do this may damage the wiring harness.**

38. If removed, install the wiring protector.

39. For vehicles without air bags, install the shaft lock cover.

40. Install the steering wheel, as outlined earlier in this section.

41. Connect the negative battery cable. If equipped, enable the air bag system as outlined in Section 6 of this manual.

Multi-Function Switch Lever

REMOVAL & INSTALLATION

▶ **See Figures 94 and 95**

1. Disconnect the negative battery cable.
2. Remove the wiring protector cover underneath the column.
3. Disconnect the multi-function switch.
4. If equipped, detach the cruise control electrical connector.
5. For vehicles with cruise control, attach a piece of mechanic's wire to the connector and pull the harness through the column.
6. Remove the switch.
7. Installation is the reverse of removal. Use the piece of wire to feed the cruise control wire into the column using.

Steering Linkage

REMOVAL & INSTALLATION

Tie Rod Ends

▶ **See Figures 96 thru 102**

1. Raise and support the vehicle safely. Remove the tire and wheel assemblies.
2. Remove the cotter pin and castellated nut. Discard the cotter pin.

3. Use a suitable puller to separate the outer tie rod from the steering knuckle.

4. Loosen the jam hex nut at the inner tie rod and remove the outer tie rod end from the inner tie rod.

To install:

5. Installation is the reverse of the removal procedure.

6. Tighten the outer tie rod to knuckle hex slotted nut to 35 ft. lbs. (50 Nm). If necessary, tighten up to an additional 1/6 turn to align the cotter pin in the slot, but do not exceed 45 ft. lbs. (60 Nm). The toe is adjusted by turning the inner tie rod end. Once it is set, then tighten the jam nut to 50 ft. lbs. (70 Nm).

7. Have the front end alignment adjusted, as required.

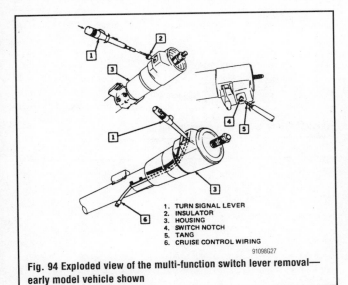

1. TURN SIGNAL LEVER
2. INSULATOR
3. HOUSING
4. SWITCH NOTCH
5. TANG
6. CRUISE CONTROL WIRING

Fig. 94 Exploded view of the multi-function switch lever removal—early model vehicle shown

Fig. 95 View of the multi-function switch lever—late model vehicle with cruise control shown

Fig. 96 The outer tie rod end connects the power steering rack to the steering knuckle

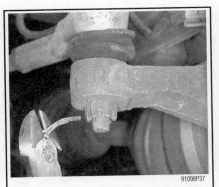

Fig. 97 Remove the cotter pin using a side cutter (pliers)

Fig. 98 Install the puller and tighten it down by hand

Fig. 99 Use a ratchet and socket to tighten down on the nut and . . .

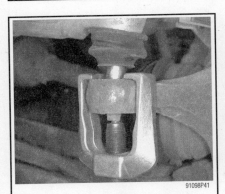

Fig. 100 . . . separate the tie rod end from the steering knuckle

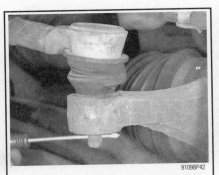

Fig. 101 When installing the tie rod rotate the stud to make it easy to install the cotter pin

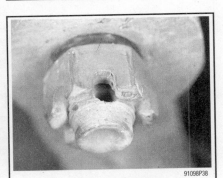

Fig. 102 The cut out in the nut and the hole in the stud must line up to be able to install a new cotter pin

Power Steering Rack and Pinion

REMOVAL & INSTALLATION

▶ **See Figures 103 and 104**

1. Disconnect the negative battery cable.
2. Remove the air cleaner assembly.
3. Remove the dust boot from the steering gear.
4. Remove the intermediate shaft lower pinch bolt and disconnect the intermediate shaft from the lower stub shaft.
5. Remove the fluid line retaining clips at the pump, then disconnect the lines.
6. Raise and safely support the vehicle.
7. Remove the wheel and tire assemblies. Disconnect the tie rod ends from the steering knuckle.
8. Remove the remaining brackets and clips at the crossmember. Support the body safely with the appropriate equipment, to allow lowering of the subframe.
9. Remove the rear subframe mounting bolts and carefully lower the rear of the subframe approximately 5 in. (12.7cm).
10. Remove the rack and pinion mounting bolts, then remove the steering gear by maneuvering it through the left wheel opening.

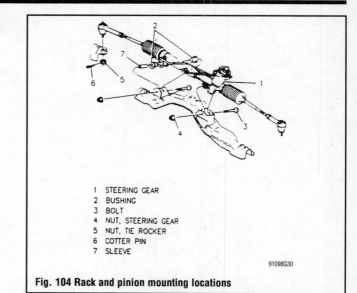

1	STEERING GEAR
2	BUSHING
3	BOLT
4	NUT, STEERING GEAR
5	NUT, TIE ROCKER
6	COTTER PIN
7	SLEEVE

91098G30

Fig. 104 Rack and pinion mounting locations

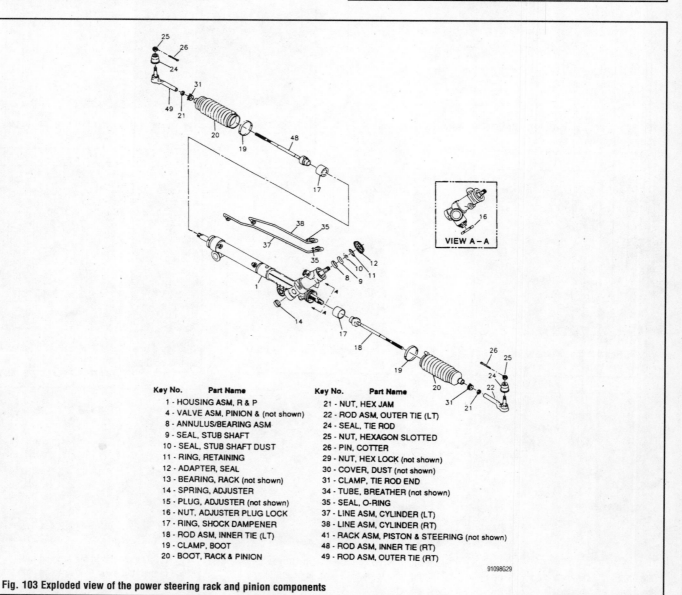

Key No.	Part Name	Key No.	Part Name
1 -	HOUSING ASM, R & P	21 -	NUT, HEX JAM
4 -	VALVE ASM, PINION & (not shown)	22 -	ROD ASM, OUTER TIE (LT)
8 -	ANNULUS/BEARING ASM	24 -	SEAL, TIE ROD
9 -	SEAL, STUB SHAFT	25 -	NUT, HEXAGON SLOTTED
10 -	SEAL, STUB SHAFT DUST	26 -	PIN, COTTER
11 -	RING, RETAINING	29 -	NUT, HEX LOCK (not shown)
12 -	ADAPTER, SEAL	30 -	COVER, DUST (not shown)
13 -	BEARING, RACK (not shown)	31 -	CLAMP, TIE ROD END
14 -	SPRING, ADJUSTER	34 -	TUBE, BREATHER (not shown)
15 -	PLUG, ADJUSTER (not shown)	35 -	SEAL, O-RING
16 -	NUT, ADJUSTER PLUG LOCK	37 -	LINE ASM, CYLINDER (LT)
17 -	RING, SHOCK DAMPENER	38 -	LINE ASM, CYLINDER (RT)
18 -	ROD ASM, INNER TIE (LT)	41 -	RACK ASM, PISTON & STEERING (not shown)
19 -	CLAMP, BOOT	48 -	ROD ASM, INNER TIE (RT)
20 -	BOOT, RACK & PINION	49 -	ROD ASM, OUTER TIE (RT)

91098G29

Fig. 103 Exploded view of the power steering rack and pinion components

To install:

11. Install the rack and pinion through the left wheel opening.

12. Install the rack and pinion mounting nuts, then tighten them to 70 ft. lbs. (95 Nm).

13. Raise the subframe assembly and install the rear mounting bolts.

14. Remove any supports, then install the brackets and clips to the cross-member.

15. Install the wheel and tire assemblies. Carefully lower the vehicle.

16. Connect the fluid lines at the pump and tighten to 18 ft. lbs. (25 Nm).

17. Install the line retaining clips. Connect the intermediate shaft to the stub shaft.

18. Install the dust boot over the steering gear.

19. Install the air cleaner assembly and connect the negative battery cable.

20. Fill and bleed the steering system.

Power Steering Pump

REMOVAL & INSTALLATION

♦ **See Figures 105, 106 and 107**

1. Disconnect the negative battery cable.

2. Disconnect and cap the power steering pump hoses.

3. Remove the accessory drive belt.

4. Remove the power steering pump pulley using a suitable puller tool.

5. Remove the pump mounting bolts and remove the pump from the vehicle.

6. Installation is the reverse of the removal procedure. Tighten the pump mounting bolts to 18 ft. lbs. (25 Nm).

7. Bleed the power steering system to remove trapped air. Air in the system could cause noise and or damage to the pump.

BLEEDING

♦ **See Figure 108**

➡**This procedure requires the help of an assistant.**

1. With the engine **OFF**, the wheels off the ground and turned all the way to the left, fill the fluid reservoir to the FULL COLD mark on the fluid level indicator.

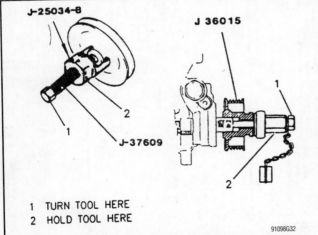

1 TURN TOOL HERE
2 HOLD TOOL HERE

91098G32

Fig. 105 On some vehicles, you must use a puller to remove the power steering pump pulley

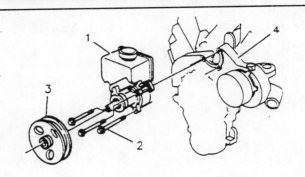

1 POWER STEERING PUMP
2 BOLT, POWER STEERING PUMP
3 PULLY
4 COVER

91098G31

Fig. 106 Power steering pump mounting—early model vehicle shown

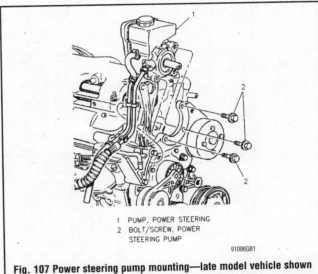

1 PUMP, POWER STEERING
2 BOLT/SCREW, POWER STEERING PUMP

91098GB1

Fig. 107 Power steering pump mounting—late model vehicle shown

2. With an assistant checking the fluid level and condition, bleed the system by turning the wheels from side to side without hitting the stops. You should repeat this at least 20 times, making sure to keep the fluid level at the FULL COLD mark.

➡**Fluid with air in it has a light tan appearance. This air must be eliminated from the fluid before normal steering action can be obtained.**

3. Start the engine, and while it is idling, recheck the fluid level and add as necessary to reach the FULL COLD mark.

4. Return the wheels to the center position. Lower the front wheels to the ground and continue running the engine for 2 or 3 minutes.

5. Road test the vehicle to make sure the steering functions properly and is free of noises.

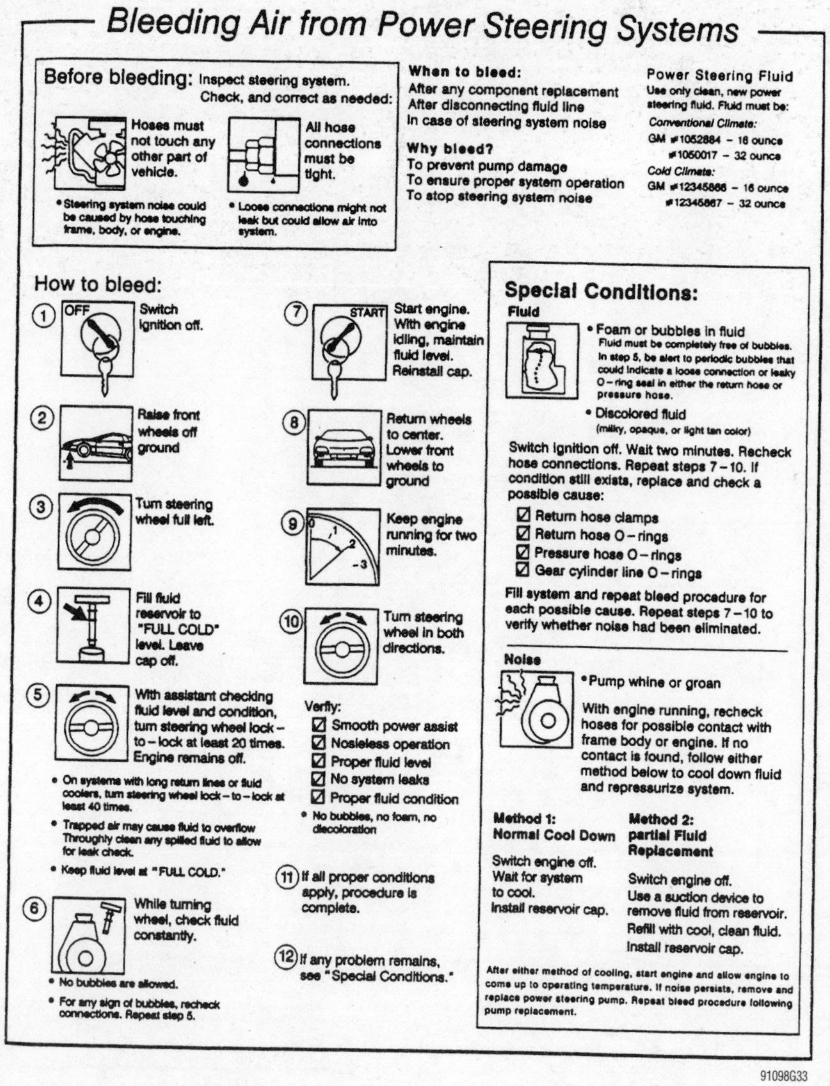

TORQUE SPECIFICATIONS

Components	English	Metric
Air bag retaining screws	14 lbs.ft.	20 Nm
Front Suspension		
Strut Assembly to Body Nuts	18 lb. ft.	25Nm
Steering Knuckle to Strut Assembly Bolts	126 ft. lbs.	170 Nm
Brake Line Bracket Bolt	13 ft. lbs.	17 Nm
Stabilizer Shaft Bushing Clamp Nuts	33 ft. lbs.	45 Nm
Control Arm Pivot Bolt Nut	61 ft. lbs.	83 Nm
Steering Knuckle Bolt and Nut	56 lb. ft.	76 Nm
Hub and Bearing Retaining Bolt	70 ft. lbs.	95 Nm
Caliper Bolts	38 ft. lbs.	51 Nm
Strut Dampener Shaft Nut (without nylon insert)	65 ft. lbs.	85 Nm
Strut Dampener Shaft Nut (with nylon insert)	80 ft. lbs.	66 Nm
Wheel nut	100 ft. lbs.	140 Nm
Tie-rod Pinch Bolts	41 ft. lbs.	55 Nm
Wheel hub retaining nut	185 ft. lbs.	260 Nm
Power rack and pinion		
Inner tie rod-to-rack and pinion	92 ft. lbs.	125 Nm
Intermediate steering shaft upper pinch bolt	35 ft. lbs.	47 Nm
Outer tie rod jam nut	50 ft. lbs.	70 Nm
Rack-to-subframe retaining bolts	70 ft. lbs.	95 Nm
Steering shaft-to-rack and pinion flange lower pinch bolt	35 ft. lbs.	47Nm
Power steering pump		
O-ring Union Fitting	55 ft. lbs.	75 Nm
Pump retaining bolts	29 ft. lbs.	39 Nm
Rear suspension		
Track Bar		
Axle Mount attaching Nut and Bolt	63 ft. lbs.	85 Nm
Underbody Reinforcement attaching Nut and Bolt	48 ft. lbs.	65 Nm
Control Arm to Underbody Bracket Nut	199 ft. lbs.	270 Nm
Upper Shock Nut	21 ft. lb.	28 Nm
Lower Shock Bolt	43 ft. lbs.	58 Nm
Brake line bracket mounting bolts	97 inch lbs.	11 Nm
Wheel hub mounting bolts	61 ft. lbs.	82 Nm
Steering wheel center nut	30 ft. lbs.	41 Nm
Wheel lug nuts	100 ft. lbs.	140 Nm

Fig. 108 Power steering bleeding procedure

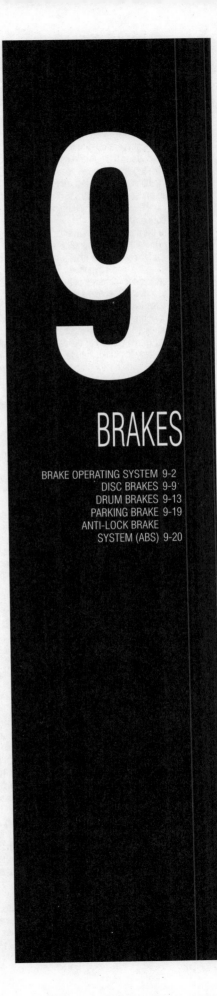

BRAKES

BRAKE OPERATING SYSTEM

Basic Operating Principles

Hydraulic systems are used to actuate the brakes of all modern automobiles. The system transports the power required to force the frictional surfaces of the braking system together from the pedal to the individual brake units at each wheel. A hydraulic system is used for two reasons.

First, fluid under pressure can be carried to all parts of an automobile by small pipes and flexible hoses without taking up a significant amount of room or posing routing problems.

Second, a great mechanical advantage can be given to the brake pedal end of the system. The foot pressure required to actuate the brakes can be reduced by making the surface area of the master cylinder pistons smaller than that of any of the pistons in the wheel cylinders or calipers.

The master cylinder consists of a fluid reservoir along with a double cylinder and piston assembly. Double reservoir master cylinders are designed to split braking systems hydraulically in case of a leak. The master cylinder converts mechanical motion from the pedal into hydraulic pressure within the lines. This pressure is translated back into mechanical motion at the wheels by either the wheel cylinder (drum brakes) or the caliper (disc brakes).

Steel lines carry the brake fluid to a junction near each of the vehicle's wheels. The fluid is then carried to the calipers and wheel cylinders by flexible tubes in order to allow for suspension and steering movements.

In drum brake systems, each wheel cylinder contains two pistons, one at either end, which push outward in opposite directions and force the brake shoe into contact with the drum.

In disc brake systems, the cylinders are part of the calipers. At least one cylinder in each caliper is used to force the brake pads against the disc.

All pistons employ some type of seal, usually made of rubber, to minimize fluid leakage. A rubber dust boot seals the outer end of the cylinder against dust and dirt. The boot fits around the outer end of the piston on disc brake calipers, and around the brake actuating rod on wheel cylinders.

The hydraulic system operates as follows: When at rest, the entire system, from the piston(s) in the master cylinder to those in the wheel cylinders or calipers, is full of brake fluid. Upon application of the brake pedal, fluid trapped in front of the master cylinder piston(s) is forced through the lines to the wheel cylinders. Here, it forces the pistons outward, in the case of drum brakes, and inward toward the disc, in the case of disc brakes. The motion of the pistons is opposed by return springs mounted outside the cylinders in drum brakes, and by piston seals, in disc brakes.

Upon release of the brake pedal, a spring located inside the master cylinder immediately returns the master cylinder pistons to the normal position. The pistons contain check valves and the master cylinder has compensating ports drilled in it. These are uncovered as the pistons reach their normal position. The piston check valves allow fluid to flow toward the wheel cylinders or calipers as the pistons withdraw. Then, as the return springs force the brake pads or shoes into the released position, the excess fluid reservoir through the compensating ports. It is during the time the pedal is in the released position that any fluid that has leaked out of the system will be replaced through the compensating ports.

Dual circuit master cylinders employ two pistons, located one behind the other, in the same cylinder. The primary piston is actuated directly by mechanical linkage from the brake pedal through the power booster. The secondary piston is actuated by fluid trapped between the two pistons. If a leak develops in front of the secondary piston, it moves forward until it bottoms against the front of the master cylinder, and the fluid trapped between the pistons will operate the rear brakes. If the rear brakes develop a leak, the primary piston will move forward until direct contact with the secondary piston takes place, and it will force the secondary piston to actuate the front brakes. In either case, the brake pedal moves farther when the brakes are applied, and less braking power is available.

All dual circuit systems use a switch to warn the driver when only half of the brake system is operational. This switch is usually located in a valve body, which is mounted on the firewall or the frame below the master cylinder. A hydraulic piston receives pressure from both circuits, each circuit's pressure being applied to one end of the piston. When the pressures are in balance, the piston remains stationary. When one circuit has a leak, however, the greater pressure in that circuit during application of the brakes will push the piston to one side, closing the switch and activating the brake warning light.

In disc brake systems, this valve body also contains a metering valve and, in some cases, a proportioning valve. The metering valve keeps pressure from traveling to the disc brakes on the front wheels until the brake shoes on the rear wheels have contacted the drums, ensuring that the front brakes will never be used alone. The proportioning valve controls the pressure to the rear brakes to lessen the chance of rear wheel lock-up during very hard braking.

Warning lights may be tested by depressing the brake pedal and holding it while opening one of the wheel cylinder bleeder screws. If this does not cause the light to go on, substitute a new lamp, make continuity checks, and, finally, replace the switch as necessary.

The hydraulic system may be checked for leaks by applying pressure to the pedal gradually and steadily. If the pedal sinks very slowly to the floor, the system has a small leak. This is not to be confused with a springy or spongy feel due to the compression of air within the lines. If the system leaks, there will be a gradual change in the position of the pedal with a constant pressure.

Check for leaks along all lines and at wheel cylinders. If no external leaks are apparent, the problem is inside the master cylinder.

DISC BRAKES

Instead of the traditional expanding brakes that press outward against a circular drum, disc brake systems use a disc (rotor) with brake pads positioned on either side of it. An easily-seen analogy is the hand brake arrangement on a bicycle. The pads squeeze onto the rim of the bike wheel, slowing its motion. Automobile disc brakes use the identical principle but apply the braking effort to a separate disc instead of the wheel.

The disc (rotor) is a casting, usually equipped with cooling fins between the two braking surfaces. This enables air to circulate between the braking surfaces making them less sensitive to heat buildup and more resistant to fade. Dirt and water do not drastically affect braking action since contaminants are thrown off by the centrifugal action of the rotor or scraped off the by the pads. In addition, the equal clamping action of the two brake pads tends to ensure uniform, straight line stops. Disc brakes are inherently self-adjusting. There are three general types of disc brake:

1. A fixed caliper.
2. A floating caliper.
3. A sliding caliper.

The fixed caliper design uses two pistons mounted on either side of the rotor (in each side of the caliper). The caliper is mounted rigidly and does not move.

The sliding and floating designs are quite similar. In fact, these two types are often lumped together. In both designs, the pad on the inside of the rotor is moved into contact with the rotor by hydraulic force. The caliper, which is not held in a fixed position, moves slightly, bringing the outside pad into contact with the rotor. There are various methods of attaching floating calipers. Some pivot at the bottom or top, and some slide on mounting bolts. In any event, the result is the same.

DRUM BRAKES

Drum brakes employ two brake shoes mounted on a stationary backing plate. These shoes are positioned inside a circular drum that rotates with the wheel assembly. The shoes are held in place by springs. This allows them to slide toward the drums (when they are applied) while keeping the linings and drums in alignment. The shoes are actuated by a wheel cylinder that is mounted at the top of the backing plate. When the brakes are applied, hydraulic pressure forces the wheel cylinder's actuating links outward. Since these links bear directly against the top of the brake shoes, the tops of the shoes are then forced against the inner side of the drum. This action forces the bottoms of the two shoes to contact the brake drum by rotating the entire assembly slightly (known as servo action). When pressure within the wheel cylinder is relaxed, return springs pull the shoes back away from the drum.

Most modern drum brakes are designed to self-adjust themselves during application when the vehicle is moving in reverse. This motion causes both shoes to rotate very slightly with the drum, rocking an adjusting lever, thereby causing rotation of the adjusting screw. Some drum brake systems are designed to self-adjust during application whenever the brakes are applied. This on-board adjustment system reduces the need for maintenance adjustments and keeps both the brake function and pedal feel satisfactory.

POWER BOOSTERS

Virtually all modern vehicles use a vacuum assisted power brake system to multiply the braking force and reduce pedal effort. Since vacuum is always available when the engine is operating, the system is simple and efficient. A vacuum diaphragm is located on the front of the master cylinder and assists the driver in applying the brakes, reducing both the effort and travel he must put into moving the brake pedal.

The vacuum diaphragm housing is normally connected to the intake manifold by a vacuum hose. A check valve is placed at the point where the hose enters the diaphragm housing, so that during periods of low manifold vacuum brakes assist will not be lost.

Depressing the brake pedal closes off the vacuum source and allows atmospheric pressure to enter on one side of the diaphragm. This causes the master cylinder pistons to move and apply the brakes. When the brake pedal is released, vacuum is applied to both sides of the diaphragm and springs return the diaphragm and master cylinder pistons to the released position.

If the vacuum supply fails, the brake pedal rod will contact the end of the master cylinder actuator rod and the system will apply the brakes without any power assistance. The driver will notice that much higher pedal effort is needed to stop the car and that the pedal feels harder than usual.

Vacuum Leak Test

1. Operate the engine at idle without touching the brake pedal for at least one minute.
2. Turn off the engine and wait one minute.
3. Test for the presence of assist vacuum by depressing the brake pedal and releasing it several times. If vacuum is present in the system, light application will produce less and less pedal travel. If there is no vacuum, air is leaking into the system.

System Operation Test

1. With the engine **OFF**, pump the brake pedal until the supply vacuum is entirely gone.
2. Put light, steady pressure on the brake pedal.
3. Start the engine and let it idle. If the system is operating correctly, the brake pedal should fall slightly toward the floor if a constant pressure is maintained.

Power brake systems may be tested for hydraulic leaks just as ordinary systems are tested.

✳✳ WARNING

Clean, high quality brake fluid is essential to the safe and proper operation of the brake system. You should always buy the highest quality brake fluid that is available. If the brake fluid becomes contaminated, drain and flush the system, then refill the master cylinder with new fluid. Never reuse any brake fluid. Any brake fluid that is removed from the system should be discarded.

Stoplamp Switch

REMOVAL & INSTALLATION

▶ **See Figure 1**

1. Disconnect the negative battery cable.
2. Remove any necessary instrument panel sound insulators.
3. Detach the electrical and vacuum connectors from the switch, as applicable.
4. Remove any necessary retainers, then remove the switch from the brake pedal bracket.
5. Installation is the reverse of the removal procedure.

ADJUSTMENT

With the brake pedal in the fully released position, the stoplamp switch plunger should be fully depressed against the brake pedal shank.

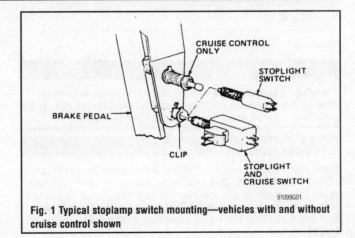

Fig. 1 Typical stoplamp switch mounting—vehicles with and without cruise control shown

1. Insert the switch into the tubular clip until the switch body seats on the tube clip.
2. Pull the brake pedal to the rear, against the internal pedal stop. The stoplamp switch will be moved in the tubular clip giving the proper adjustment.

➡**If no clicks are heard when the pedal is pulled up and the brake lamps do not stay on without the brakes being applied, the switch is properly adjusted.**

Master Cylinder

▶ **See Figure 2**

On newer vehicles (including those with ABS), the master cylinder is a composite design (plastic reservoir and aluminum body). It is used in a diagonally split system (one front and one diagonally opposite rear brake served by the primary piston, and opposite front and rear brakes served by the secondary piston). Left front and right rear are on the same circuit, and the right front and left rear are on the same circuit.

The functions of a standard dual master cylinder are incorporated; in addition, it has a fluid level sensor and integral proportioners. The proportioners are designed to provide better front to rear braking balance with heavy brake application.

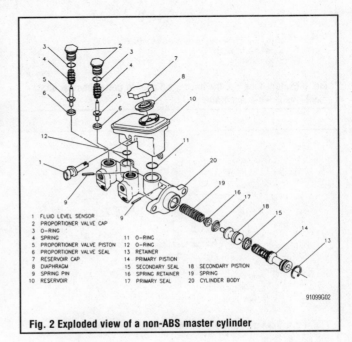

1 FLUID LEVEL SENSOR		
2 PROPORTIONER VALVE CAP		
3 O-RING		
4 SPRING	11 O-RING	
5 PROPORTIONER VALVE PISTON	12 O-RING	
6 PROPORTIONER VALVE SEAL	13 RETAINER	
7 RESERVOIR CAP	14 PRIMARY PISTON	
8 DIAPHRAGM	15 SECONDARY SEAL	18 SECONDARY PISTON
9 SPRING PIN	16 SPRING RETAINER	19 SPRING
10 RESERVOIR	17 PRIMARY SEAL	20 CYLINDER BODY

Fig. 2 Exploded view of a non-ABS master cylinder

REMOVAL & INSTALLATION

♦ See Figures 3 and 4

⁜ WARNING

For vehicles equipped with ABS, the entire Hydraulic Assembly must be removed along with the master cylinder. Please refer to the procedure, located under the ABS system in this section.

⁜ CAUTION

Brake fluid contains polyglycol ethers and polyglycols. Avoid contact with the eyes and wash your hands thoroughly after handling brake fluid. If you do get brake fluid in your eyes, flush your eyes with clean, running water for 15 minutes. If eye irritation persists, or if you have taken brake fluid internally, IMMEDIATELY seek medical assistance.

If your vehicle is equipped with ABS, please refer to the Hydraulic Modulator replacement procedure
1. Disconnect the negative battery cable.
2. Use a turkey baster or equivalent tool to siphon the brake fluid from the master cylinder into a suitable container.

⁜ WARNING

Clean, high quality brake fluid is essential to the safe and proper operation of the brake system. You should always buy the highest quality brake fluid that is available. If the brake fluid becomes contaminated, drain and flush the system, then refill the master cylinder with new fluid. Never reuse any brake fluid. Any brake fluid that is removed from the system should be discarded. Also, do not allow any brake fluid to come in contact with a painted surface; it will damage the paint.

3. Unplug the electrical connection from the fluid sensor.
4. Use a flare nut wrench to disconnect the hydraulic lines from the master cylinder. Plug or cap the lines to avoid contaminating the system.
5. Unfasten the two master cylinder-to-power booster retaining nuts or bolts, then remove the master cylinder from the vehicle.
   To install:
6. If installing a new master cylinder, bench bleed the master cylinder, as per the procedure located later in this section.
7. Place the master cylinder in position on the booster. Connect the booster pushrod.
8. Install the master cylinder retaining bolts and tighten to 20 ft. lbs. (27 Nm).
9. Unplug and connect the fluid lines to the master cylinder.
10. Attach the electrical connector to the fluid level sensor.
11. Connect the negative battery cable.
12. Fill the master cylinder to the proper level, then bleed the brake system, as outlined later in this section.

Power Brake Booster

The power brake booster used on these vehicles is a tandem vacuum unit. In a normal operating mode, with the service brakes in the released position, the tandem vacuum suspended booster operates with vacuum on both sides of its diaphragms. When the brakes are applied, air at atmospheric pressure is admitted to one side of each diaphragm to provide the power assist. When the service brake is released, the atmospheric air is shut off from one side of each diaphragm. The air is then drawn from the booster through the vacuum check valve to the vacuum source.

REMOVAL & INSTALLATION

♦ See Figure 5

➡ It may be necessary to remove other components to gain access to the booster assembly.

1. From inside the vehicle, remove the vacuum booster pushrod from the brake pedal.

➡ When disconnecting the pushrod from the brake pedal, The brake pedal must be held stationary or damage to the brake switch may result.

2. Support the brake pedal out of the way.
3. Remove the mounting nuts, which secure the vacuum booster to the firewall.
4. From under the hood, disconnect the negative battery cable.
5. Disconnect the vacuum hose from the booster assembly.
6. Do not disconnect the master cylinder fluid lines, unless there is a clearance problem. Unbolt the master cylinder from the booster unit and position it to the side, to gain clearance to remove the booster.

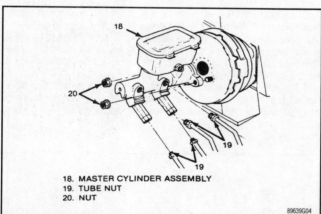

18. MASTER CYLINDER ASSEMBLY
19. TUBE NUT
20. NUT

89639G04

Fig. 3 Exploded view of the master cylinder-to-power booster attachment—vehicles without ABS

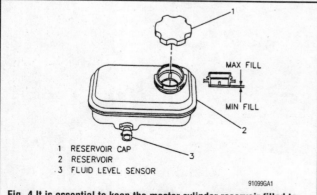

MAX FILL

MIN FILL

1 RESERVOIR CAP
2 RESERVOIR
3 FLUID LEVEL SENSOR

91099GA1

Fig. 4 It is essential to keep the master cylinder reservoir filled to the proper level

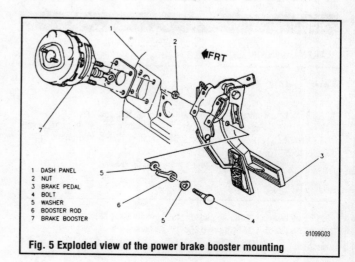

▲FRT

1 DASH PANEL
2 NUT
3 BRAKE PEDAL
4 BOLT
5 WASHER
6 BOOSTER ROD
7 BRAKE BOOSTER

91099G03

Fig. 5 Exploded view of the power brake booster mounting

7. Pull the booster away from the cowl, to clear the mounting studs, and remove it from the vehicle.

To install:

8. Position the booster and secure with the retainers. Tighten the attaching nuts to 15 ft. lbs. (21 Nm).

9. Install the booster pushrod to the brake pedal and adjust the brake switch as necessary.

10. Install the master cylinder to the booster and tighten the attaching nuts to 20 ft. lbs. (27 Nm).

11. If necessary, add fluid to the master cylinder and bleed the system. This should only be necessary if you had to disconnect the fluid lines for access.

12. Connect the negative battery cable.

Proportioning Valve

The proportioning valves, which are threaded into the master cylinder, limit outlet pressure to the rear brakes after a predetermined rear input pressure has been reached. This is used when less rear apply force is needed, and to obtain optimum braking and to prevent rear wheel lock-up on vehicles with light rear wheel loads.

REMOVAL & INSTALLATION

▶ **See Figures 2 and 6**

1. Disconnect the negative battery cable.
2. Use a turkey baster or equivalent tool to siphon the brake fluid from the master cylinder into a suitable container.
3. Detach the electrical connector from the master cylinder.
4. Remove the master cylinder reservoir.
5. Remove the proportioning valve caps from the master cylinder.
6. Remove the O-rings, springs and the valve pistons. Be very careful not to scratch the valves in any way.
7. Remove the valve seals from the valve pistons.

To install:

8. Lubricate the new seals and the pistons with a suitable silicone grease. Place the seals on the valve pistons.

9. Install the valve pistons and O-rings into the master cylinder.
10. Install the valve cap assemblies and tighten to 20 ft. lbs. (27 Nm).
11. Install the reservoir assembly. Attach the electrical leads.
12. Connect the negative battery cable. Fill the master cylinder reservoir, then bleed the brake system as outlined later in this section.

Brake Hoses and Lines

Metal lines and rubber brake hoses should be checked frequently for leaks and external damage. Metal lines are particularly prone to crushing and kinking under the vehicle. Any such deformation can restrict the proper flow of fluid and therefore impair braking at the wheels. Rubber hoses should be checked for cracking or scraping; such damage can create a weak spot in the hose and it could fail under pressure.

Any time the lines are removed or disconnected, extreme cleanliness must be observed. Clean all joints and connections before disassembly (use a stiff bristle brush and clean brake fluid); be sure to plug the lines and ports as soon as they are opened. New lines and hoses should be flushed clean with brake fluid before installation to remove any contamination.

REMOVAL & INSTALLATION

▶ **See Figures 7 thru 15**

1. Disconnect the negative battery cable.
2. Raise and safely support the vehicle on jackstands.
3. Remove any wheel and tire assemblies necessary for access to the particular line you are removing.
4. Thoroughly clean the surrounding area at the joints to be disconnected.
5. Place a suitable catch pan under the joint to be disconnected.

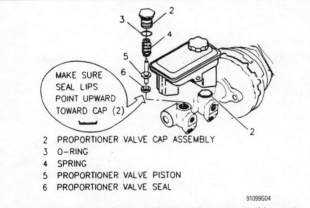

Fig. 6 Exploded view of the proportioning valves, mounted in master cylinder

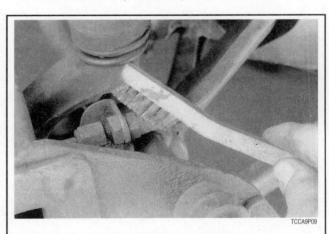

Fig. 7 Use a brush to clean the fittings of any debris

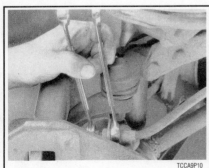

Fig. 8 Use two wrenches to loosen the fitting. If available, use flare nut type wrenches

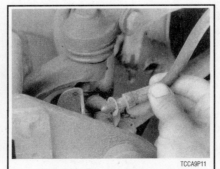

Fig. 9 Any gaskets/crush washers should be replaced with new ones during installation

Fig. 10 Tape or plug the line to prevent contamination

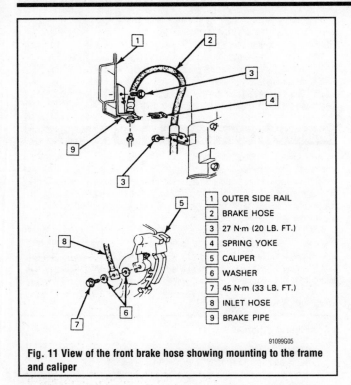

Fig. 11 View of the front brake hose showing mounting to the frame and caliper

1 OUTER SIDE RAIL
2 BRAKE HOSE
3 27 N·m (20 LB. FT.)
4 SPRING YOKE
5 CALIPER
6 WASHER
7 45 N·m (33 LB. FT.)
8 INLET HOSE
9 BRAKE PIPE

91099G05

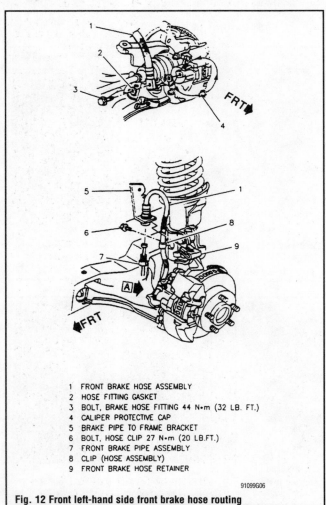

1 FRONT BRAKE HOSE ASSEMBLY
2 HOSE FITTING GASKET
3 BOLT, BRAKE HOSE FITTING 44 N·m (32 LB. FT.)
4 CALIPER PROTECTIVE CAP
5 BRAKE PIPE TO FRAME BRACKET
6 BOLT, HOSE CLIP 27 N·m (20 LB.FT.)
7 FRONT BRAKE PIPE ASSEMBLY
8 CLIP (HOSE ASSEMBLY)
9 FRONT BRAKE HOSE RETAINER

91099G06

Fig. 12 Front left-hand side front brake hose routing

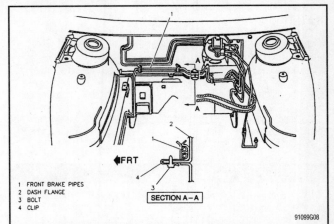

1 FRONT BRAKE PIPES
2 DASH FLANGE
3 BOLT
4 CLIP

SECTION A–A

91099G08

Fig. 13 Diagram of the front brake pipe routing (inside engine compartment)

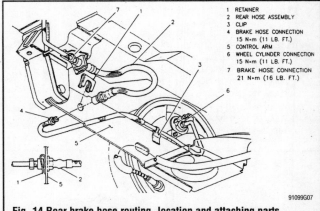

1 RETAINER
2 REAR HOSE ASSEMBLY
3 CLIP
4 BRAKE HOSE CONNECTION
  15 N·m (11 LB. FT.)
5 CONTROL ARM
6 WHEEL CYLINDER CONNECTION
  15 N·m (11 LB. FT.)
7 BRAKE HOSE CONNECTION
  21 N·m (16 LB. FT.)

91099G07

Fig. 14 Rear brake hose routing, location and attaching parts

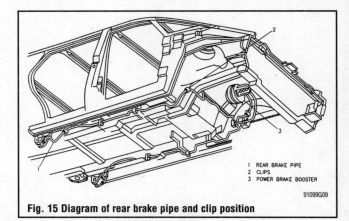

1 REAR BRAKE PIPE
2 CLIPS
3 POWER BRAKE BOOSTER

91099G09

Fig. 15 Diagram of rear brake pipe and clip position

6. Using two wrenches (one to hold the joint and one to turn the fitting), disconnect the hose or line to be replaced.

7. Disconnect the other end of the line or hose, moving the drain pan if necessary. Always use a back-up wrench to avoid damaging the fitting.

8. Disconnect any retaining clips or brackets holding the line and remove the line from the vehicle.

→If the brake system is to remain open for more time than it takes to swap lines, tape or plug each remaining clip and port to keep contaminants out and fluid in.

To install:

9. Install the new line or hose, starting with the end farthest from the master cylinder. Connect the other end, then confirm that both fittings are correctly

threaded and turn smoothly using finger pressure. Make sure the new line will not rub against any other part. Brake lines must be at least ½ (13mm) from the steering column and other moving parts. Any protective shielding or insulators must be reinstalled in the original location.

✴✴ WARNING

Make sure the hose is NOT kinked or touching any part of the frame or suspension after installation. These conditions may cause the hose to fail prematurely.

10. Using two wrenches as before, tighten each fitting.
11. Install any retaining clips or brackets on the lines.
12. If removed, install the wheel and tire assemblies, then carefully lower the vehicle to the ground.
13. Refill the brake master cylinder reservoir with clean, fresh brake fluid, meeting DOT 3 specifications. Properly bleed the brake system.
14. Connect the negative battery cable.

Bleeding Brake System

✴✴ CAUTION

Brake fluid contains polyglycol ethers and polyglycols. Avoid contact with the eyes and wash your hands thoroughly after handling brake fluid. If you do get brake fluid in your eyes, flush your eyes with clean, running water for 15 minutes. If eye irritation persists, or if you have taken brake fluid internally, IMMEDIATELY seek medical assistance.

✴✴ WARNING

Clean, high quality brake fluid is essential to the safe and proper operation of the brake system. You should always buy the highest quality brake fluid that is available. If the brake fluid becomes contaminated, drain and flush the system, then refill the master cylinder with new fluid. Never reuse any brake fluid. Any brake fluid that is removed from the system should be discarded. Also, do not allow any brake fluid to come in contact with a painted surface; it will damage the paint.

When any part of the hydraulic system has been disconnected for repair or replacement, air may get into the lines and cause spongy pedal action (because air can be compressed and brake fluid cannot). To correct this condition, it is necessary to bleed the hydraulic system so to be sure all air is purged.

When bleeding the brake system, bleed one brake cylinder at a time, beginning at the cylinder with the longest hydraulic line (farthest from the master cylinder) first. ALWAYS keep the master cylinder reservoir filled with brake fluid during the bleeding operation. Never use brake fluid that has been drained from the hydraulic system, no matter how clean it is.

The primary and secondary hydraulic brake systems are separate and are bled independently. During the bleeding operation, do not allow the reservoir to run dry. Keep the master cylinder reservoir filled with brake fluid.

➡**On vehicles equipped with ABS, before bleeding the brakes, the front, and rear displacement cylinder pistons must be returned to the topmost position. Refer to the procedure located under the ABS portion of this section. After that procedure is complete, the brakes may be bled using either the manual or pressure procedures below.**

MANUAL BLEEDING

▶ **See Figures 16, 17, 18, 19 and 20**

✴✴ CAUTION

Never reuse brake fluid which has been bled from the brake system. Brake fluid should be changed every few years. It wears out due to moisture being absorbed, which lowers the boiling point.

Fig. 16 To bleed the rear brakes, remove the cap from the wheel cylinder bleeder screw (see arrow)

Fig. 17 Attach a hose to the bleeder valve with the other end submerged in a container of clean brake fluid

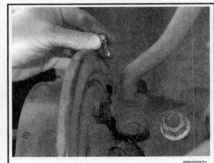

Fig. 18 If necessary, you can remove the bleeder valve from the wheel cylinder by unscrewing it

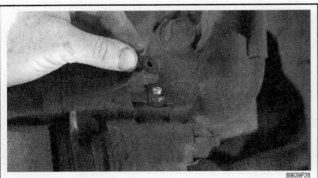

Fig. 19 To bleed the front brakes, remove the protective cap covering the bleeder screw

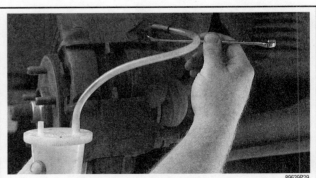

Fig. 20 Attach a brake bleeder line to the bleeder screw, then submerge the line in a container of brake fluid, and open the valve

➥Old brake fluid is often the cause of spongy brakes returning a week or so after bleeding the system. If all parts check good. Change the fluid by repeated bleeding.

1. Deplete the booster reserve by applying the brakes a few times with the engine **OFF** until all reserve is depleted.

2. Fill the master cylinder reservoir to the full level mark with brake fluid from a fresh, sealed container. You must maintain the fluid level during the bleeding procedure.

❈❈ WARNING

Clean, high quality brake fluid is essential to the safe and proper operation of the brake system. You should always buy the highest quality brake fluid that is available. If the brake fluid becomes contaminated, drain and flush the system, then refill the master cylinder with new fluid. Never reuse any brake fluid. Any brake fluid that is removed from the system should be discarded. Also, do not allow any brake fluid to come in contact with a painted surface; it will damage the paint.

3. If the master cylinder is known or suspected to have air in the bore, bleed it as follows before bleeding any of the wheel cylinders or calipers:
   a. Loosen the forward brake line connection and the master cylinder.
   b. Fill the master cylinder until fluid begins to flow from the front pipe connector port, maintaining the fluid level.
   c. Tighten the front brake pipe on the master cylinder securely.

❈❈ WARNING

Make sure the master cylinder reservoir cap is installed before the brake pedal is pressed. This prevents brake fluid from spraying out of the reservoir.

   d. Have an assistant depress the brake pedal slowly one time, and hold. Loosen the forward brake pipe connection again to purge air from the bore. Tighten the connection and then slowly released the brake pedal. Wait 15 seconds. Repeat the sequence, including the 15 second wait, until all air is removed from the bore.
   e. Tighten the brake pipe connection to 11 ft. lbs. (15 Nm).
4. After all the air has been removed from the front connection, repeat the same procedure at the rear connection of the master cylinder.
5. Individual wheel cylinders and calipers are bled only after all the air has been removed from the master cylinder.

❈❈ WARNING

Make sure the master cylinder reservoir cap is installed before the brake pedal is pressed. This prevents brake fluid from spraying out of the reservoir.

6. If all of the wheel circuits must be bled, use the following two sequence:
   a. Right rear
   b. Left front
   c. Left rear
   d. Right front
7. Fill the master cylinder reservoir with brake fluid. Keep the level at least ½ full during the bleeding operation.
8. Raise and support the vehicle safely.
9. Remove the bleeder valve cap, and place a proper size box end wrench, or suitable bleeder wrench, over the bleeder valve.
10. Attach a transparent tube to the bleeder valve, and submerge the other end of the tube in a clear container, partially filled with clean brake fluid.
11. Have an assistant slowly depress the brake pedal one time, and hold.
12. Loosen the bleeder valve to purge the air from the cylinder.
13. Tighten the bleeder screw, then slowly release the brake pedal. Wait 15 seconds.
14. Repeat this sequence until all the air is removed. Depending upon the amount of air in the system, you may have to repeat the sequence at least 10 times to remove all of the air from the system.
15. Lower the vehicle and refill the master cylinder.
16. Check the brake pedal for sponginess. If the pedal is spongy, repeat the entire bleeding procedure.

PRESSURE BLEEDING

▶ See Figure 21

The pressure bleeding equipment you use MUST be of the diaphragm type. It must have a rubber diaphragm between the air supply and the brake fluid to prevent air, moisture, oil and all other contaminants from entering the system.
1. Fill the master cylinder reservoir to the full mark with the proper type of brake fluid from a fresh, sealed container.
2. Install a suitable bleeder adapter tool to the master cylinder. The proper adapter must be installed on the master cylinder to avoid damaging the reservoir.
3. Charge the bleeder ball to 20-25 psi (140-172 kPa).
4. Connect the line/hose to the adapter, then open the line valve. The bleeder adapter has a bleed valve on top of the adapter to help eliminate air from the adapter.
5. Raise and safely support the vehicle.
6. Use the following bleeding sequence:
   a. Right rear
   b. Left front
   c. Left rear
   d. Right front
7. Remove the bleeder valve cap, and place a proper size box end wrench, or suitable bleeder wrench, over the bleeder valve.
8. Attach a transparent bleeder hose to the bleeder valve, and submerge the other end of the of the hose in a clean container partially filled with clean brake fluid.
9. Open the bleeder valve ½ to ¾ of a turn, then allow the fluid to flow until no air is seen in the fluid.
10. Tighten the wheel cylinder bleeder valve to 88 inch lbs. (10 Nm) or the caliper bleeder valve to 115 inch lbs. (13 Nm).
11. Repeat the bleeding steps until all of the calipers/cylinders have been bled. Then, install the bleeder valve caps.
12. Carefully lower the vehicle. Check the brake pedal for sponginess. If the pedal is spongy, repeat the entire bleeding procedure.
13. Remove the bleeder ball and adapter.
14. Fill the master cylinder reservoir to the full mark.

BENCH BLEEDING THE MASTER CYLINDER

❈❈ WARNING

All new master cylinders should be bench bled prior to installation. Bleeding a new master cylinder on the vehicle is not a good idea. With air trapped inside, the master cylinder piston may bottom in the bore and possibly cause internal damage.

1. Remove the master cylinder from the vehicle, and plug the outlet ports.
2. Secure the master cylinder in a soft jawed bench vise, with the front end slightly down.
3. Remove the master cylinder reservoir cap.

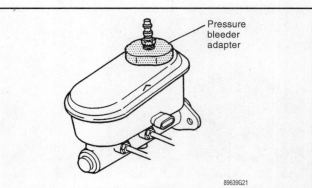

Pressure bleeder adapter

89639G21

Fig. 21 View of the pressure bleeding adapter used on later model vehicles

4. Fill the master cylinder reservoir with clean, fresh brake fluid.
5. Use a blunt tipped rod (a long socket extension works well) to slowly depress the master cylinder primary piston about 1 in. (25mm). Make sure the piston travels full its full stroke. As air bleeds from the master cylinder, the primary piston will not travel the full inch.
6. Reposition the master cylinder in the vise with the front end tilted slightly up.
7. Stroke the primary piston about 1 in. (25mm) several times again.
8. Reposition the master cylinder in the vise, so it is level.

9. Loosen the plugs in the outlet ports on at a time. Then push the piston into the bore in order to force the air from the cylinder.
10. Tighten the plugs before allowing the piston to return to its original position. This prevents air from being drawn back into the cylinder.
11. Fill the master cylinder reservoir with clean brake fluid, then install the master cylinder reservoir cap.
12. Install the master cylinder on the vehicle, then follow normal bleeding procedures.

DISC BRAKES

✳✳ CAUTION

Older brake pads or shoes may contain asbestos, which has been determined to be a cancer causing agent. Never clean the brake surfaces with compressed air! Avoid inhaling any dust from any brake surface! When cleaning the brake surfaces, use a commercially available brake cleaning fluid.

Brake Pads

➡**Always replace all pads on both front wheels at the same time. Failure to do so will result in uneven braking action and premature wear.**

REMOVAL & INSTALLATION

♦ **See Figures 22 thru 31**

1. Disconnect the negative battery cable.
2. Remove ⅔ of the brake fluid from the master cylinder reservoir using a clean syringe or equivalent. Install the reservoir cap.
3. Raise and safely support the vehicle with jackstands.
4. Mark the relationship of the wheel to the hub and bearing assembly.

5. Remove the tire and wheel assembly.
6. Remove the caliper, as outlined later, and suspend from the strut with a wire hook or suitable piece of wire. Do NOT disconnect the brake hose or allow the caliper to hang from the brake line!
7. Remove the outboard shoe and lining (pad) by using a prytool to disengage the buttons on the shoe from the holes in the caliper housing.
8. Remove the inboard shoe and lining (pad) from the caliper.
9. Before installing new pads, clean the outside surface of the caliper boot with denatured alcohol, or equivalent.
To install:
10. Lubricate the sleeves and bushings with silicone lubricant and install them in the caliper.
11. One method of pushing the piston back into the bore is to use a large pair of adjustable pliers over the caliper housing and bottom the piston into the caliper bore. Another is to use the special disc brake tool available at most part stores, or even a large C-clamp will work.

➡**Be careful not to damage the piston or piston boot with the pliers.**

12. After bottoming the piston into the caliper bore, fit the inner edge of the boot next to the piston and press out any trapped air. The boot must lay flat.
13. Clip the retaining spring onto the back of the inboard pad and install the pad in the caliper. The shoe must lie flat against the caliper.
14. Install the outboard pad into the caliper with the wear sensor at the lead-

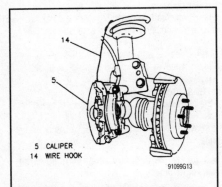
Fig. 22 Properly suspending the caliper, using a wire hook

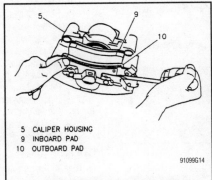
Fig. 23 Use a prytool to release the outboard pad retaining buttons

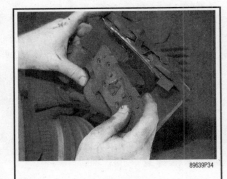
Fig. 24 Remove the inboard brake pad from the caliper

Fig. 25 Slide the outboard pad outward, disengaging the retaining clip ears . . .

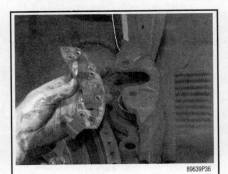
Fig. 26 . . . and remove the outboard pad from the caliper

Fig. 27 You can use a large pair of channel type slip joint pliers to compress the caliper piston into its bore

Fig. 28 There is a special tool available to compress the caliper piston into its bore . . .

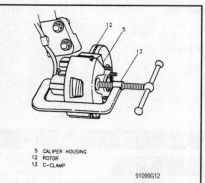

5 CALIPER HOUSING
12 ROTOR
13 C-CLAMP

Fig. 29 . . . or you can use a large C-clamp to compress the piston into the bore

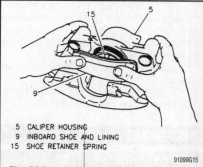

5 CALIPER HOUSING
9 INBOARD SHOE AND LINING
15 SHOE RETAINER SPRING

Fig. 30 Install the inboard pad, making sure the retainer spring is fastened securely in the caliper piston

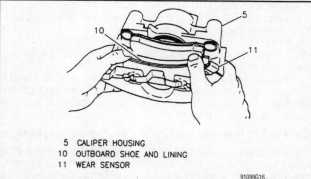

5 CALIPER HOUSING
10 OUTBOARD SHOE AND LINING
11 WEAR SENSOR

Fig. 31 The outboard brake pad must be installed with the wear sensor at the trailing edge of the pad

ing edge of the shoe during forward wheel rotation. The back of the shoe must lie flat against the caliper.

15. Install the caliper, as outlined later in this section.

16. Install the wheel and tire assembly, then carefully lower the vehicle. Tighten the wheel lug nuts to 100 ft. lbs. (136 Nm).

17. Fill the master cylinder with the proper amount of brake fluid from a fresh, sealed container. Install the reservoir cap.

18. Apply about 175 lbs. (778 N) of force to the brake pedal, three times, to seat the pads.

INSPECTION

▶ **See Figures 32 and 33**

The pad thickness should be inspected every time that the tires are removed for rotation. The outer pad has a wear sensor which will make a squealing noise when the pads wear to the point required replacement.

When the pad thickness is worn to within 1/32 in. (0.76mm) of the shoe or rivet, at either end of the pad, replace the pads in axle sets. This is the factory recommended measurement; however, your state's automobile inspection laws may not agree with this.

When checking the disc brakes, check both ends of the outer pads by looking in at each end of the caliper. These are the points at which the highest rate of wear occurs. The inner pad can be checked for premature wear by looking down through the inspection hole in the top of the caliper. Some inboard pads have a thermal layer against the shoe, integrally molded with the lining. Do not confuse this extra layer with uneven inboard/outboard pad wear.

Brake Caliper

REMOVAL & INSTALLATION

▶ **See Figures 34 thru 40**

1. Disconnect the negative battery cable.

2. Remove the master cylinder reservoir cap, then remove the 2/3 of the fluid from the reservoir with a clean syringe and place it in a suitable container. Install the reservoir cap.

3. Raise and safely support the vehicle with jackstands.

4. Mark the relationship of the wheel to the hub and bearing assembly.

5. Remove the tire and wheel assembly.

6. Reinstall two of the lug nuts to retain the rotor.

7. Push the pistons into the caliper bore to provide clearance between the linings and the rotor, as follows:

   a. Install a large C-clamp over the top of the caliper housing and against the back of the outboard shoe.

➡ **If the C-clamp is tightened too far, the outboard shoe retaining spring will be deformed and require replacement.**

   b. Slowly tighten the C-clamp until the pistons are pushed into the caliper bore enough to slide the caliper assembly off the rotor.

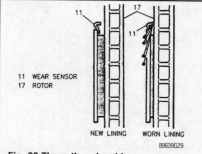

11 WEAR SENSOR
17 ROTOR

NEW LINING   WORN LINING

Fig. 32 The outboard pad has a wear sensor that will make a screeching noise against the rotor when the pad is worn to a certain limit

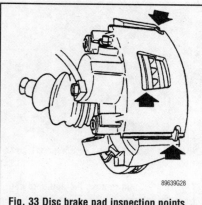

Fig. 33 Disc brake pad inspection points

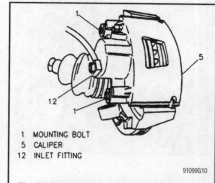

1 MOUNTING BOLT
5 CALIPER
12 INLET FITTING

Fig. 34 Installed view of the brake caliper and related components

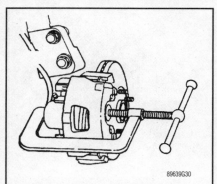

Fig. 35 Bottom the caliper piston in its bore using a large C-clamp

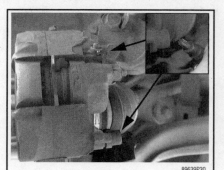

Fig. 36 Unfasten the 2 caliper mounting bolts. On some vehicles, you may need to use a Torx® driver to unfasten the bolts

Fig. 37 Pull the caliper mounting bolts from their sleeves

Fig. 38 Lift the caliper up and off the rotor

Fig. 39 Lubricate the caliper mounting bolts with a suitable grease

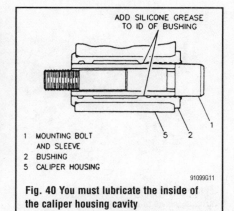

ADD SILICONE GREASE TO ID OF BUSHING

1 MOUNTING BOLT
   AND SLEEVE
2 BUSHING
5 CALIPER HOUSING

Fig. 40 You must lubricate the inside of the caliper housing cavity

8. If the caliper is going to be replaced or removed for overhaul, disconnect and plug the brake hose.

❋ WARNING

Do NOT allow the caliper to hang from the brake hose!

9. Unfasten the caliper mounting bolts and sleeves, then pull the caliper from the mounting bracket and rotor. Support the caliper with a suitable piece wire from the strut, if not removing.

10. Inspect the mounting bolts and sleeves for corrosion and the support bushings for cuts or damage; replace if necessary.

To install:

11. Fill both of the cavities in the caliper housing between the bushings with silicone grease. If removed, install the pads in the caliper.

12. Position the caliper and brake pad assembly over the rotor.

13. Install the mounting bolts and sleeves. The bolts and sleeves should slide through the bushings with only hand pressure. If greater force or mechanical assistance is necessary, perform the following:

a. Remove the bolts and sleeves, along with the bushings.

b. Inspect the mounting bores for corrosion. If the bores are corroded, remove it using a 1 in. (25mm) wheel cylinder honing brush.

c. Clean the bores with denatured alcohol.

d. Install the bushings and relubricate.

14. Tighten the caliper mounting bolts to 38 ft. lbs. (51 Nm).

15. If removed, unplug and connect the brake hose. Tighten the inlet fitting to 33 ft. lbs. (45 Nm).

16. Remove the two wheel lugs, and install the wheel and tire assembly.

17. Carefully lower the vehicle.

18. Fill the master cylinder. If the brake line was disconnected, bleed the brake system as outlined in this section.

19. Check for hydraulic leaks. Pump the brake pedal a few times before moving the vehicle.

OVERHAUL

▶ **See Figures 41 thru 48**

➡Some vehicles may be equipped dual piston calipers. The procedure to overhaul the caliper is essentially the same with the exception of multiple pistons, O-rings and dust boots.

1. Remove the caliper from the vehicle and place on a clean workbench.

❋ CAUTION

NEVER place your fingers in front of the pistons in an attempt to catch or protect the pistons when applying compressed air. This could result in personal injury!

➡Depending upon the vehicle, there are two different ways to remove the piston from the caliper. Refer to the brake pad replacement procedure to make sure you have the correct procedure for your vehicle.

2. The first method is as follows:

a. Stuff a shop towel or a block of wood into the caliper to catch the piston.

b. Remove the caliper piston using compressed air applied into the caliper inlet hole. Inspect the piston for scoring, nicks, corrosion and/or worn or damaged chrome plating. The piston must be replaced if any of these conditions are found.

3. For the second method, you must rotate the piston to retract it from the caliper.

4. If equipped, remove the anti-rattle clip.

5. Use a prytool to remove the caliper boot, being careful not to scratch the housing bore.

6. Remove the piston seals from the groove in the caliper bore.

7. Carefully loosen the brake bleeder valve cap and valve from the caliper housing.

Fig. 41 For some types of calipers, use compressed air to drive the piston out of the caliper, but make sure to keep your fingers clear

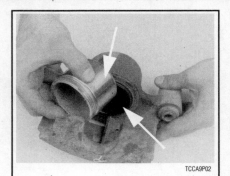

Fig. 42 Withdraw the piston from the caliper bore

Fig. 43 On some vehicles, you must remove the anti-rattle clip

Fig. 44 Use a prytool to carefully pry around the edge of the boot . . .

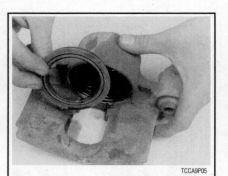

Fig. 45 . . . then remove the boot from the caliper housing, taking care not to score or damage the bore

Fig. 46 Use extreme caution when removing the piston seal; DO NOT scratch the caliper bore

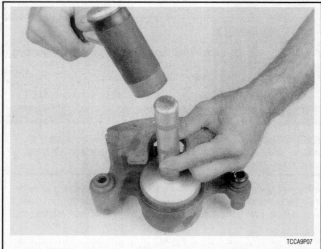

Fig. 47 Use the proper size driving tool and a mallet to properly seal the boots in the caliper housing

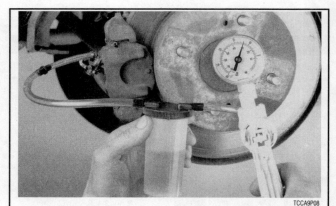

Fig. 48 There are tools, such as this Mighty-Vac, available to assist in proper brake system bleeding

8. Inspect the caliper bores, pistons and mounting threads for scoring or excessive wear.

9. Use crocus cloth to polish out light corrosion from the piston and bore.

10. Clean all parts with denatured alcohol and dry with compressed air.

To assemble:

11. Lubricate and install the bleeder valve and cap.

12. Install the new seals into the caliper bore grooves, making sure they are not twisted.

13. Lubricate the piston bore.

14. Install the pistons and boots into the bores of the calipers and push to the bottom of the bores.

15. Use a suitable driving tool to seat the boots in the housing.

16. Install the caliper in the vehicle.

17. Install the wheel and tire assembly, then carefully lower the vehicle.

18. Properly bleed the brake system.

Brake Rotor

REMOVAL & INSTALLATION

♦ See Figure 49

1. Disconnect the negative battery cable.

2. Remove ⅔ of the brake fluid from the brake reservoir using a clean syringe or equivalent.

3. Raise and safely support the vehicle with jackstands.
4. Mark the relationship of the wheel to the hub and bearing assembly.
5. Remove the tire and wheel assembly.
6. Remove the caliper and suspend it from the strut with a wire hook or suitable piece of wire. Do NOT disconnect the brake hose or allow the caliper to hang from the brake line!

➡ **If the original rotor is still on the vehicle, it may be retained with star washers, so you must remove and discard these retaining washers.**

7. Remove the rotor assembly by sliding it off the hub. If it is stuck on, use penetrating oil and tap lightly until free.

To install:

8. Install the brake rotor over the hub assembly.
9. Install the brake caliper as outlined in this section.
10. Install the wheel and tire assembly.
11. Carefully lower the vehicle. Tighten the wheel lug nuts to 100 ft. lbs. (136 Nm). If the lug nuts aren't tightened properly, the rotor will warp from heat, causing premature wear and noise.
12. Fill the master cylinder reservoir to the FULL level with the correct type of DOT 3 brake fluid from a clean, unsealed container.

13. Firmly depress the brake pedal three times to seat the brakes before moving the vehicle.

INSPECTION

◆ **See Figures 50 and 51**

Check the rotor surface for wear or scoring. Deep scoring, grooves or rust pitting can be removed by refacing, a job to be referred to your local machine shop or garage. All rotors have a minimum thickness dimension cast into them. This dimension is the minimum wear specification, and NOT a refinish dimension.

Do not use a rotor, that after refinishing, will not meet the specifications stamped into the rotor.

Check the rotor parallelism; it must vary less than 0.0005 in. (0.013mm) measured at four or more points around the circumference. Make all measurements at the same distance in from the edge of the rotor. Refinish the rotor if it fails to meet this specification.

1. Measure the disc run-out with a dial indicator. If run-out exceeds 0.003 in. (0.080mm), the rotor must be refaced or replaced as necessary.

Fig. 49 The rotor can be removed by sliding it straight off the hub

89639P39

Fig. 50 A rotor with grooves this deep will have to be resurfaced or, more likely, replaced

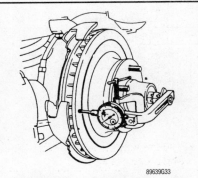

89639G33

Fig. 51 Checking rotor run-out with a dial indicator

DRUM BRAKES

◆ **See Figure 52**

✳✳ CAUTION

Older brake pads or shoes may contain asbestos, which has been determined to be a cancer causing agent. Never clean the brake surfaces with compressed air! Avoid inhaling any dust from any brake surface! When cleaning the brake surfaces, use a commercially available brake cleaning fluid.

The drum brake assembly used on these vehicles is an advanced leading/trailing shoe design. It operates with fewer parts, yet is equivalent to other drum brakes in performance while providing improved reliability.

In this assembly, a single universal spring holds both shoe and lining assemblies to the backing plate, and acts as a retractor spring for the shoe and lining assemblies.

When the brakes are applied, the wheel cylinder moves both shoes out to contact the drum. With forward wheel rotation, the leading (forward) brake shoe will wrap into the drum and become self-energized.

With reverse wheel rotation, the trailing (rear) brake shoe will wrap into the drum and become self-energized.

Force from the brake shoes is transferred through the fixed anchor and backing plate to the axle flange. Adjustment is automatic and occurs on any service brake application.

With leading/trailing brakes, the leading shoe wears at a faster rate than the trailing shoe. DO NOT switch the position of the shoes that have been in service as this may render the self-adjustment feature inoperative, resulting in increased pedal travel.

Brake Drums

REMOVAL & INSTALLATION

◆ **See Figures 53 and 54**

1. Mark the relationship of the wheel to the axle flange to help maintain wheel balance after assembly.
2. Remove the tire and wheel assembly.
3. Mark the relationship of the brake drum to the axle flange.

➡ **Do not pry against the splash shield that surrounds the backing plate in an attempt to free the drum. This will bend the splash shield.**

4. If difficulty is encountered in removing the brake drum, the following steps may be of assistance.
   a. Make sure the parking brake is released.
   b. Back off the parking brake cable adjustment.
   c. Remove the access hole plug from the backing plate.
   d. Using a screwdriver, back off the adjusting screw.
   e. Reinstall the access hole plug to prevent dirt or contamination from entering the drum brake assembly.
   f. Use a small amount of penetrating oil applied around the brake drum pilot hole.
   g. Carefully remove the brake drum from the vehicle.
5. After removing the brake drum it should be checked for the following:
   a. Inspecting for cracks and deep grooves.

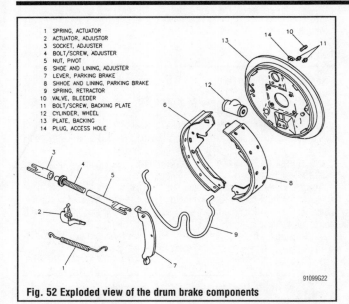

```
1   SPRING, ACTUATOR
2   ACTUATOR, ADJUSTOR
3   SOCKET, ADJUSTER
4   BOLT/SCREW, ADJUSTER
5   NUT, PIVOT
6   SHOE AND LINING, ADJUSTER
7   LEVER, PARKING BRAKE
8   SHHOE AND LINING, PARKING BRAKE
9   SPRING, RETRACTOR
10  VALVE, BLEEDER
11  BOLT/SCREW, BACKING PLATE
12  CYLINDER, WHEEL
13  PLATE, BACKING
14  PLUG, ACCESS HOLE
```

Fig. 52 Exploded view of the drum brake components

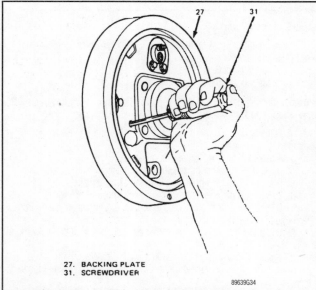

Fig. 53 The brake drum can usually be pulled straight off the lug studs

27. BACKING PLATE
31. SCREWDRIVER

Fig. 54 If the drum is hard to remove, remove the access plug, then back off the adjusting screw

b. Inspect for out of round and taper.
c. Inspecting for hot spots (black in color).

To install:

6. Install the brake drum onto the vehicle aligning the reference marks on the axle flange.

7. Install the tire and wheel assembly and hand-tighten the lug nuts.

8. Carefully lower the vehicle, then tighten the lug nuts to 100 ft. lbs. (136 Nm).

9. Road test the vehicle for proper brake operation.

INSPECTION

▶ **See Figure 55**

1. After removing the brake drum, wipe out the accumulated dust with a damp cloth.

✳✳ WARNING

Do not blow the brake dust out of the drums with compressed air or lung-power. Brake linings contain asbestos, a known cancer causing substance. Dispose of the cloth used to clean the parts after use.

2. Inspect the drums for cracks, deep grooves, roughness, scoring, or out-of-roundness. Replace any drum which is cracked; do not try to weld it up.

3. Smooth any slight scores by polishing the friction surface with fine emery cloth. Heavy or extensive scoring will cause excessive lining wear and should be removed from the drum through resurfacing, a job to be referred to your local machine shop or garage. The maximum refinished diameter of the drums is 8.880 in. (225.5mm). The drum must be replaced if the diameter is 8.909 in. (226.30mm).

Fig. 55 Most vehicles will have their maximum wear specification stamped into the brake drum

Brake Shoes

➡When servicing drum brakes, only disassemble and assemble one side at a time, leaving the remaining side intact for reference.

INSPECTION

After removing the brake drum, inspect the brake shoes. If the lining is worn down to within 1/32 in. (0.8mm) above the rivet, the shoes must be replaced.

➡This figure may disagree with your state's automobile inspection laws. If the brake lining is soaked with brake fluid or grease, it must be replaced. If this is the case, the brake drum should be sanded with crocus cloth to remove all traces of brake fluid, and the wheel cylinders should be rebuilt. Clean all grit from the friction surface of the drum before replacing it.

If the lining is chipped, cracked or otherwise damaged, it must be replaced with a new lining.

➤**Always replace the brake linings in sets of two on both ends of the axle. Never replace just one shoe or both shoes on one side.**

Check the condition of the shoes, retracting springs and hold-down springs for signs of overheating. If the shoes or springs have a slight blue color, this indicates overheating, then replacement of the shoes and springs is recommended. The wheel cylinders should be rebuilt as a precaution against future problems.

REMOVAL & INSTALLATION

▶ **See Figures 56 thru 66**

➤**To remove the brake shoes, you will need a suitable brake shoe spanner and spring removal tool. This tool will make removing the actuator spring much easier.**

1. Raise and safely support the vehicle.
2. Remove the wheel and tire assembly.
3. Remove the brake drum.
4. Remove the actuator spring, as follows:
   a. Use a suitable brake shoe spanner/spring removal tool to pry the loop end of the spring from the adjuster actuator,.

➤**The actuator spring can also be called the adjuster spring.**

   b. Disconnect the spring from the web of the parking brake shoe.
5. Lift the end of the retractor spring from the adjuster shoe and lining assembly

➤**The retractor spring is also commonly referred to as the return spring.**

6. Insert the hook end of the brake spring removal tool between the retractor spring and the adjuster shoe web.
7. Pry or twist the spring removal tool to lift the end of the spring out of the shoe web hole.

8. Pry the end of the retractor spring toward the axle with the flat edge of the tool until lit snaps down off the shoe web onto the backing plate.
9. Remove the adjuster shoe and lining assembly, the adjuster actuator, and the adjusting screw assembly.
10. Do not remove the parking brake cable from the parking brake lever unless the parking brake lever is to be replaced.
11. Lift the end of the retractor spring from the parking brake shoe and lining assembly.
12. Insert the hook end of the spring remover between the retractor spring and the park brake shoe web.
13. Pry the end of the retractor spring toward the axle with the flat edge of the tool until lit snaps down off the shoe web onto the backing plate.
14. Remove the park brake shoe and lining assemblies.
15. Remove the retractor spring from the anchor plate.

➤**If only shoe and lining are being serviced, it is not necessary to remove the retractor spring.**

To install:

➤**Before reinstalling the adjusting screw assembly, disassemble the adjusting screw and thoroughly clean and lubricate the adjusting screw threads and adjuster socket inside diameter with a brake lubricant.**

16. Apply brake lubricant to the six raised shoe pads on the backing plate assembly
17. If the retractor spring was removed, reinstall it, hooking the center spring section under the tab on the anchor.
18. Install the shoe and lining assembly as follows:
   a. Position shoe and lining on the backing plate.
   b. Using the brake shoe spanner/spring removal tool, pull the end of the retractor spring up to rest on the web of the brake shoe.
   c. Use the spring removal tool to pull the end of the retractor spring over until it snaps into the slot in the brake shoe.
19. Install the parking brake lever to the parking brake shoe and linings assemblies.

Fig. 56 View of the rear brakes with the drum removed

Fig. 57 Diagram of brakes, with the rear hub removed

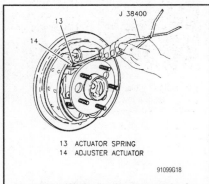

13 ACTUATOR SPRING
14 ADJUSTER ACTUATOR

91099G18

Fig. 58 Use the brake shoe spanner/spring removal tool to remove the actuator spring

Fig. 59 Once it is disengaged, remove the actuator spring from the actuator

Fig. 60 View of the adjuster actuator assembly

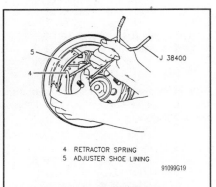

4 RETRACTOR SPRING
5 ADJUSTER SHOE LINING

91099G19

Fig. 61 Disengaging the retractor, or return, spring

Fig. 62 View of the brake adjuster assembly

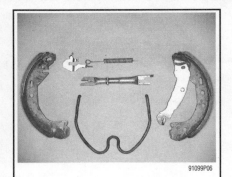

Fig. 63 This is a diagram of the brake parts, removed from the backing plate

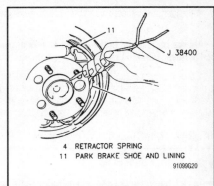

4 RETRACTOR SPRING
11 PARK BRAKE SHOE AND LINING

Fig. 64 Pulling the spring end onto the shoe web

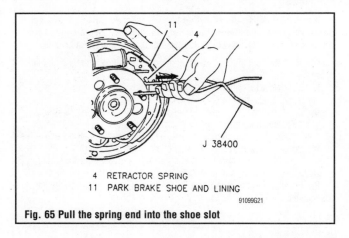

4 RETRACTOR SPRING
11 PARK BRAKE SHOE AND LINING

Fig. 65 Pull the spring end into the shoe slot

20. Reconnect the parking brake cable to the parking brake lever, if it was disconnected.

21. Install the adjusting screw assembly and adjuster shoe lining assembly.

   a. Engage the pivot nut with the web of the parking brake shoe and lining and parking brake lever.

   b. Position the adjuster shoe and lining so the shoe web engages the deep slot in the adjuster socket.

22. Install the retractor spring into the adjuster shoe and lining assembly, as follows:

   a. Using the brake spring removal tool, pull the end of the retractor spring up to rest on the web of the brake shoe.

   b. Use the brake spring removal tool to pull the end of the retractor spring over until it snaps into the slot in the brake shoe.

23. Install the adjuster actuator, lubricate the tab, and pivot point on the adjuster actuator with brake lubricant.

   a. Using the brake spanner/spring removal tool, spread the brake shoes while working the adjuster actuator into position.

24. Install the actuator spring.

   a. Engage the U-shaped end of the spring into the hole in the web of the park brake shoe.

   b. Use the brake spring tool to stretch the spring and engage the loop end over the tab on the adjuster actuator.

➡Check the arm of the adjuster actuator; it should be resting freely on the star wheel teeth of adjuster screw, not trapped under the teeth in a downward angle.

25. Pull apart the upper ends of the shoe and lining assemblies, and watch for the proper rotation of the star wheel.

26. Install the brake drum in position.

27. Install the wheel and tire assemblies.

28. Check the adjustment of the brakes by turning the star wheel so that the shoe and lining diameter is 0.050 in. (1.3mm) less than inside drum diameter.

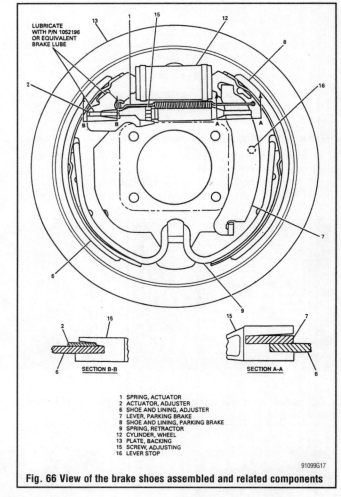

LUBRICATE WITH P/N 1052196 OR EQUIVALENT BRAKE LUBE

SECTION B-B

SECTION A-A

1 SPRING, ACTUATOR
2 ACTUATOR, ADJUSTER
6 SHOE AND LINING, ADJUSTER
7 LEVER, PARKING BRAKE
8 SHOE AND LINING, PARKING BRAKE
9 SPRING, RETRACTOR
12 CYLINDER, WHEEL
13 PLATE, BACKING
15 SCREW, ADJUSTING
16 LEVER STOP

Fig. 66 View of the brake shoes assembled and related components

The brakes should drag just slightly. If the wheel will not turn, loosen the adjuster slightly.

ADJUSTMENTS

▸ See Figures 67 and 68

The drum brakes self-adjust anytime the brakes are applied, with no vehicle motion required. This system works well and no manual adjustment is usually necessary. Adjustment will be required when new brake shoes are installed. The following procedure is with the brake drum removed.

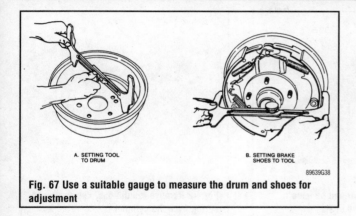

Fig. 67 Use a suitable gauge to measure the drum and shoes for adjustment

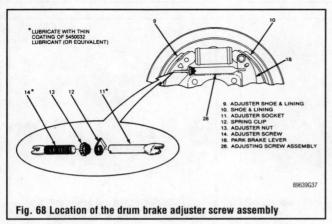

*LUBRICATE WITH THIN COATING OF 5450032 LUBRICANT (OR EQUIVALENT)

9. ADJUSTER SHOE & LINING
10. SHOE & LINING
11. ADJUSTER SOCKET
12. SPRING CLIP
13. ADJUSTER NUT
14. ADJUSTER SCREW
18. PARK BRAKE LEVER
28. ADJUSTING SCREW ASSEMBLY

Fig. 68 Location of the drum brake adjuster screw assembly

1. Raise and support the car safely.
2. Mark the relation of wheel to studs, so you install it in the same location.
3. Remove the wheel and tire assembly.
4. Remove the brake drum.
5. Make certain the parking brake is off and the brake shoes are sitting against the stops. If not readjust the parking brake, as outlined later in this section.
6. Measure the drum inside diameter using a suitable drum-to-brake shoe clearance gauge.
7. Turning the adjuster nut (star wheel on the adjuster), adjust the shoe and lining diameter to be 0.050 in. (1.27mm) less than the inside drum diameter for each rear wheel. Go slowly and don't overtighten or force the drum on. It's very difficult to remove the drum on an overadjusted system.
8. If you've over-adjusted or the drum is hard to remove; remove the access hole plug from the backing plate. Insert a flat tool though the hole and press in to push the park brake lever off its stop. This allows the lining to retract. You must not remove the drum and reassemble the brakes. Don't pry on the backing plate. If necessary, insert a punch through the hole at the bottom of the splash shield and tap gently to loosen drum.
9. After adjustment, install the drum and the tire and wheel assembly.
10. Perform the adjustment procedure at the other rear wheel and tire assembly.
11. Carefully lower the vehicle, then tighten the lug nuts to 100 ft. lbs. (136 Nm).
12. Apply and release the brakes about 30-35 times with normal pedal force, pausing about one second between pedal applications.

Wheel Cylinder

REMOVAL & INSTALLATION

♦ **See Figure 69**

1. Raise and safely support the vehicle.
2. Remove the wheel and tire assemblies.

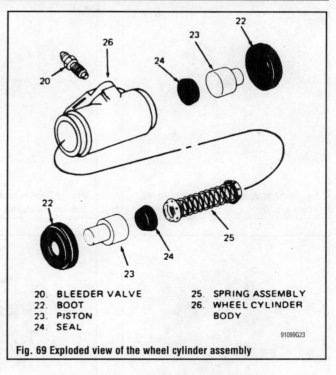

20. BLEEDER VALVE
22. BOOT
23. PISTON
24. SEAL
25. SPRING ASSEMBLY
26. WHEEL CYLINDER BODY

Fig. 69 Exploded view of the wheel cylinder assembly

3. Remove the brake drum and remove the brake shoes.
4. Disconnect and plug the brake fluid line from the wheel cylinder.
5. Remove the wheel cylinder retaining bolt.
6. Remove the wheel cylinder from the backing plate.

To install:

7. Install the wheel cylinder in position on the backing plate.
8. Install the retaining bolts and tighten to 15 ft. lbs. (20 N.).
9. Connect the brake line to the wheel cylinder.
10. Install the brake linings and the brake drum.
11. Install the wheel and tire assembly. Lower the vehicle.
12. Bleed the brake system.

OVERHAUL

♦ **See Figures 70 thru 79**

Wheel cylinder overhaul kits may be available, but often at little or no savings over a reconditioned wheel cylinder. It often makes sense with these components to substitute a new or reconditioned part instead of attempting an overhaul.

If no replacement is available, or you would prefer to overhaul your wheel cylinders, the following procedure may be used. When rebuilding and installing wheel cylinders, avoid getting any contaminants into the system. Always use clean, new, high quality brake fluid. If dirty or improper fluid has been used, it will be necessary to drain the entire system, flush the system with proper brake fluid, replace all rubber components, then refill and bleed the system.

1. Remove the wheel cylinder from the vehicle and place on a clean workbench.
2. First remove and discard the old rubber boots, then withdraw the pistons. Piston cylinders are equipped with seals and a spring assembly, all located behind the pistons in the cylinder bore.
3. Remove the remaining inner components, seals and spring assembly. Compressed air may be useful in removing these components. If no compressed air is available, be VERY careful not to score the wheel cylinder bore when removing parts from it. Discard all components for which replacements were supplied in the rebuild kit.
4. Wash the cylinder and metal parts in denatured alcohol or clean brake fluid.

⁕⁕ WARNING

Never use a mineral-based solvent such as gasoline, kerosene or paint thinner for cleaning purposes. These solvents will swell rubber components and quickly deteriorate them.

Fig. 70 Remove the outer boots from the wheel cylinder

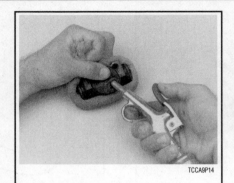

Fig. 71 Compressed air can be used to remove the pistons and seals

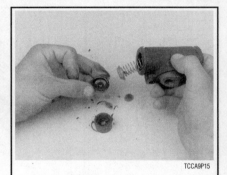

Fig. 72 Remove the pistons, cup seals and spring from the cylinder

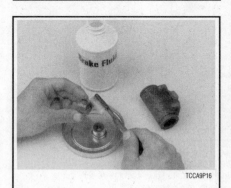

Fig. 73 Use brake fluid and a soft brush to clean the pistons . . .

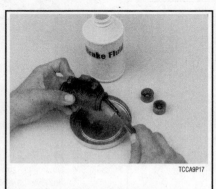

Fig. 74 . . . and the bore of the wheel cylinder

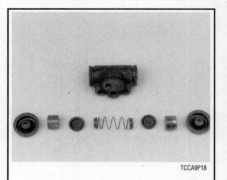

Fig. 75 Once cleaned and inspected, the wheel cylinder is ready for assembly

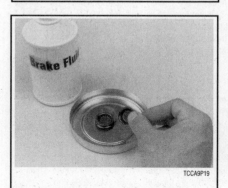

Fig. 76 Lubricate the cup seals with brake fluid

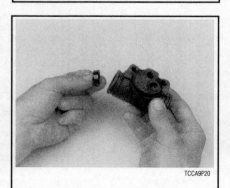

Fig. 77 Install the spring, then the cup seals in the bore

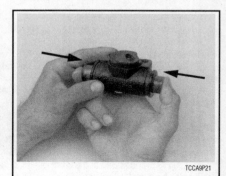

Fig. 78 Lightly lubricate the pistons, then install them

Fig. 79 The boots can now be installed over the wheel cylinder ends

5. Allow the parts to air dry or use compressed air. Do not use rags for cleaning, since lint will remain in the cylinder bore.
6. Inspect the piston and replace it if it shows scratches.
7. Lubricate the cylinder bore and seals using clean brake fluid.
8. Position the spring assembly.
9. Install the inner seals, then the pistons.
10. Insert the new boots into the counterbore by hand. Do not lubricate the boots.
11. Install the wheel cylinder.
12. Bleed the brake system.

PARKING BRAKE

Cables

REMOVAL & INSTALLATION

Front

▸ **See Figures 80, 81, 82, 83 and 84**

1. Raise and support the vehicle safely.
2. Loosen the adjuster nut and disconnect the front cable from the connector.
3. Disconnect the cable from the clip at the frame and the hanger.
4. Lower the vehicle. Unfasten the retaining screws and nut, then lower the driver's side sound insulator panel to gain access to the parking brake pedal assembly.
5. Remove the carpet finish molding and lift the carpet.
6. Remove the cable retaining clip at the lever assembly.
7. Disconnect the cable from the parking brake pedal by compressing the retainer fingers. Remove the cable from the vehicle.

To install:

8. Insert the cable through the floor pan and grommet and seat the grommet.
9. Install the grommet retainer to the floor pan.
10. Install the cable in the retaining clips.
11. Connect the cable and casing to the control assembly and seat the retaining tangs.
12. Install the cable retaining clip at the lever assembly.
13. Place the carpet in position and install the carpet finish molding.
14. Install the driver's side insulator panel screws and nuts.
15. Raise and support the vehicle safely.

16. Install the cable to the hanger and clip at the frame.
17. Connect the cable to the equalizer and connector.
18. Adjust the parking brake cable and lower the vehicle.

Rear

▸ **See Figures 85, 86, 87 and 88**

➡ **There is a special tool available which is designed to compress the rear parking brake cable retaining tangs for removal from the brake backing plate; however, another method is illustrated in the accompanying figures.**

1. Raise and support the vehicle safely.
2. Loosen the equalizer nut.
3. Disconnect the cable at the equalizer and connector.
4. Remove the tire and wheel assembly.
5. Remove the brake drum.
6. Disconnect the cable from the parking brake lever.
7. Disconnect the cable and spring from the bracket at the caliper.
8. Use the proper tool, or follow the procedure shown in the accompanying figure to depress the retaining tangs and remove the cable and casing from the backing plate.

To install:

9. Install the cable and casing to the backing plate and seat the retaining tangs.
10. Connect the cable and spring to the bracket at the caliper.
11. Connect the cable at the parking brake lever.
12. Install the brake drum and the tire and wheel assembly.
13. Connect the cable at the equalizer and connector.
14. Adjust the parking brake cable and lower the vehicle.

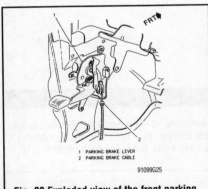

1 PARKING BRAKE LEVER
2 PARKING BRAKE CABLE

91099G25

Fig. 80 Exploded view of the front parking brake cable and lever coupling

91099P01

Fig. 81 Use a suitable pair of pliers to disconnect the front parking brake cable . . .

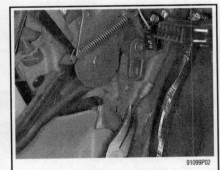

91099P02

Fig. 82 . . . from the parking brake mechanism

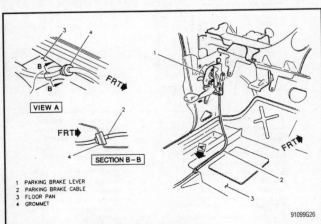

1 PARKING BRAKE LEVER
2 PARKING BRAKE CABLE
3 FLOOR PAN
4 GROMMET

91099G26

Fig. 83 Front parking brake cable routing

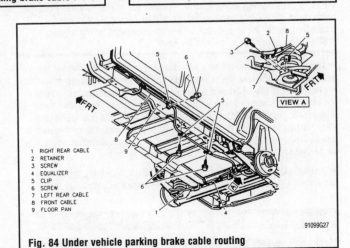

1 RIGHT REAR CABLE
2 RETAINER
3 SCREW
4 EQUALIZER
5 CLIP
6 SCREW
7 LEFT REAR CABLE
8 FRONT CABLE
9 FLOOR PAN

91099G27

Fig. 84 Under vehicle parking brake cable routing

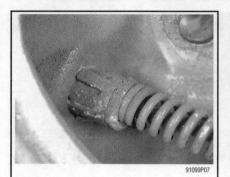

Fig. 85 View of the rear parking brake cable attachment to the backing plate

Fig. 86 To remove the rear cable from the backing plate, slide a small screw clamp partially over the conduit fitting

Fig. 87 Use a screwdriver to tighten the clamp screw snugly, in order to compress the retaining tangs

Fig. 88 Once the tangs, or fingers, are compressed, you can push the conduit through the backing plate and remove the cable from the vehicle

ADJUSTMENT

1. Set the parking brake pedal three clicks.
2. Raise and support the vehicle safely.
3. Lubricate the threaded adjusting rod on both sides of the nut.
4. Tighten the equalizer nut until the right rear wheel can just be turned rearward with 2 hands but cannot be turned forward.
5. Release the parking brake.
6. Rotate the rear wheels in the forward motion. There should be no brake drag.
7. Lower the vehicle.

ANTI-LOCK BRAKE SYSTEM (ABS)

System Operation

▶ See Figures 89 and 90

❊❊ CAUTION

Certain components in the ABS are not intended to be serviced individually. Attempting to remove or disconnect certain system components may result in personal injury and/or improper system operation. Only those components with approved removal and installation procedures should be serviced.

➡The use of rubber hoses or parts other than those specified for the Antilock Brake System (ABS) may lead to functional problems requiring replacement of the hydraulic parts. Replace all components included in the repair kits used to service this system. Lubricate the rubber parts with clean, fresh brake fluid to ease assembly, Do not use lubricated shop air on brake parts as damage to rubber components may result. If any hydraulic component is removed or brake line disconnected, it may be necessary to bleed all or part of the brake system.

➡Use only DOT 3 brake fluid. The use of DOT 5 (silicone) brake fluid is not recommended. Reduced braking performance or durability may result.

❊❊ WARNING

Clean, high quality brake fluid is essential to the safe and proper operation of the brake system. You should always buy the highest quality brake fluid that is available. If the brake fluid becomes contaminated, drain and flush the system, then refill the master cylinder with new fluid. Never reuse any brake fluid. Any brake fluid that is

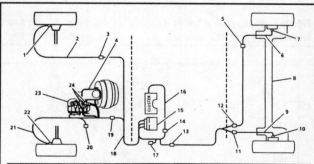

1	RIGHT FRONT WHEEL SPEED SENSOR	13	ABS TO BODY HARNESS CONNECTOR
2	RIGHT FRONT ABS JUMPER HARNESS	14	ABS TO I/P HARNESS CONNECTOR
3	ABS TO RIGHT FRONT WHEEL SPEED JUMPER HARNESS CONNECTOR	15	ELECTRONIC BRAKE CONTROL MODULE
4	MASTER CYLINDER	16	I/P HARNESS
5	REAR ABS TO RIGHT REAR ABS JUMPER HARNESS CONNECTOR	17	LAMP DRIVER MODULE
6	RIGHT REAR ABS JUMPER HARNESS	18	ABS HARNESS
7	RIGHT REAR WHEEL SPEED SENSOR	19	ABS TO LEFT FRONT WHEEL SPEED JUMPER HARNESS
8	REAR AXLE	20	ABS ENABLE RELAY AND JUNCTION
9	LEFT REAR ABS JUMPER HARNESS	21	LEFT FRONT ABS JUMPER HARNESS
10	LEFT REAR WHEEL SPEED SENSOR	22	LEFT FRONT WHEEL SPEED SENSOR
11	BODY TO LEFT REAR ABS JUMPER HARNESS CONNECTOR	23	ABS HYDRAULIC MODULATOR ASSEMBLY
12	BODY TO REAR ABS HARNESS CONNECTOR	24	ISOLATION SOLENOIDS

Fig. 89 View of the Anti-lock Brake System (ABS) components

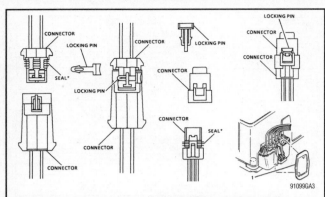

Fig. 90 Some ABS components have electrical connectors equipped with a Connector Position Assurance (CPA) lock to make sure they fasten securely

removed from the system should be discarded. Also, do not allow any brake fluid to encounter a painted surface; it will damage the paint.

Under normal operating conditions, the brake systems will operate using conventional braking by means of brake pedal force, the vacuum booster, and the compact master cylinder. Each front channel consists of a motor, solenoid ESB, ball screw piston, and check valve. Under normal operating conditions (base brakes), the piston is held in the upmost (or "home") position and the solenoid is open (not energized). This is accomplished by turning the ball screw via the motor to drive the nut upwards. Once at the upmost position, the piston is held by an Expansion Spring Brake (ESB). Two paths are available to transfer braking pressure to the wheel: (1) through the modulator, around the check valve, and out to the wheel, (2) through the modulator, past the normally open solenoid, and out to the wheel. The solenoids in the front circuits provides an alternate brake pressure path to the wheel. With this arrangement, if the ABS were to lose power or malfunction with the piston not in its home position, a redundant brake fluid path is available. The rear channels operate in a similar manner except that no solenoid exists.

ABS has been deigned to improve the controllability and steerability of a vehicle during braking. ABS accomplishes this objective by controlling the hydraulic pressure applied to each wheel brake. Antilock braking occurs only when the brake switch is closed and a microprocessor, located in the Electronic Brake Control Module (EBCM), determines one or more wheels is about to lose traction during braking. The ECBM will then allow the ABS hydraulic modulator to change the brake pressures several times each second to keep the wheel(s) from locking and provide the driver with maximum vehicle controllability. ABS does not necessarily decrease the stopping distance of the vehicle; it allows you to steer the vehicle with more control than you would have if the wheels were locked up.

➡**ABS cannot increase the brake pressure above the master cylinder pressure applied by the driver, and cannot apply the brakes by itself.**

System Testing

TESTING AND DIAGNOSTICS

The EBCM contains sophisticated on-board diagnostics that, when accessed with a Tech 1® or equivalent scan tool, are designed to identify the source of any system malfunction as specifically as possible, including whether or not the malfunction is intermittent. There are no provisions for "Flash Code" diagnostics.

VISUAL INSPECTION

Before any system diagnosis is begun, the brake system should be inspected visually for common faults, which could disable the ABS or cause a code to set. Check the vehicle carefully for any sign of: a binding parking brake cable, or a faulty parking brake switch, low brake fluid. Check the system for fluid leaks including the pump/motor area, failed fuses or fusible links, failed ABS relay, loose or damaged wiring including connectors, harnesses, and insulation wear. Check the mounting and function of the brake calipers at each wheel. Carefully inspect the multi-pin connectors at the EBCM for pin pushouts or poor connections.

FUNCTIONAL CHECK

Once the visual check has been performed, perform the functional check to determine if the problem is truly ABS related or arising from common faults.

DISPLAYING ABS TROUBLE CODES

▶ **See Figures 91, 92, 93 and 94**

Only certain ABS malfunctions will cause the EBCM to store diagnostic trouble codes. Failures causing a code will generally involve wheel speed sensors, main valve, or the inlet and outlet valves. Conditions affecting the pump/motor assembly, the accumulator, pressure switch or fluid level sensor usually do not cause a code to set.

Diagnostic fault codes can only be read through the use of a bi-directional scan tool, such as GM's Tech 1® or equivalent. There are no provisions for "Flash Code" diagnostics. Make sure to follow the scan tool manufacturer's instructions completely.

The EBCM will store trouble codes in a non-volatile memory. These codes remain in memory until erased through use of the correct procedure. The codes are NOT erased by disconnecting the EBCM, disconnecting the battery cable or turning off the ignition. Always be sure to clear the codes from the memory after repairs are made. To read stored ABS trouble codes perform the following:

1. Turn the ignition switch **ON**. Allow the pump to charge the accumulator; if fully discharged the dash warning lights may stay on up to 30 seconds. If the ANTI-LOCK warning light does not go off within 30 seconds, note it.
2. Turn the ignition switch **OFF**.
3. Remove the cover from the ALDL connector. Enter the diagnostic mode using a Tech 1® or equivalent scan tool.

The system is capable of storing and displaying codes; the ANTI-LOCK warning light will stay on continuously when all codes have been displayed.

4. After recording each code, replace the cover and proceed.

➡**The ABS trouble codes are not specifically designated current or history codes. If the ANTI-LOCK light is on before entering the ABS diagnostic mode, at least one of the stored codes is current. It is impossible**

TROUBLE CODE	DESCRIPTION
A011	ABS Warning Light Circuit Open or Shorted to Ground
A013	ABS Warning Light Circuit Shorted to Battery
A014	Enable Relay Contacts or Fuse Open
A015	Enable Relay Contacts Shorted to Battery
A016	Enable Relay Coil Circuit Open
A017	Enable Relay Coil Circuit Shorted to Ground
A018	Enable Relay Coil Circuit Shorted to Battery
A021	Left Front Wheel Speed = 0 (1 of 2)
A022	Right Front Wheel Speed = 0 (1 of 2)
A023	Left Rear Wheel Speed = 0 (1 of 2)
A024	Right Rear Wheel Speed = 0 (1 of 2)
A025	Left Front Excessive Wheel Speed Variation (1 of 2)
A026	Right Front Excessive Wheel Speed Variation (1 of 2)
A027	Left Rear Excessive Wheel Speed Variation (1 of 2)
A028	Right Rear Excessive Wheel Speed Variation (1 of 2)
A031	Two Wheel Speeds = 0 (1 of 2)
A032	Left Front Wheel Sensor Shorted to Battery or Ground
A033	Right Front Wheel Sensor Shorted to Battery or Ground
A034	Left Rear Wheel Sensor Shorted to Battery or Ground
A035	Right Rear Wheel Sensor Shorted to Battery or Ground
A036	Low System Voltage
A037	High System Voltage
A038	Left Front ESB Will Not Hold Motor
A041	Right Front ESB Will Not Hold Motor
A042	Rear Axle ESB Will Not Hold Motor
A044	Left Front Channel Will Not Move
A045	Right Front Channel Will Not Move
A046	Rear Axle Channel Will Not Move
A047	Left Front Motor Free Spins
A048	Right Front Motor Free Spins
A051	Rear Axle Motor Free Spins
A052	Left Front Channel In Release Too Long
A053	Right Front Channel In Release Too Long
A054	Rear Axle Channel In Release Too Long
A055	Motor Driver Fault Detected
A056	Left Front Motor Circuit Open
A057	Left Front Motor Circuit Shorted to Ground

Fig. 91 ABS trouble codes (1 of 2)—1992-94 vehicles

ABS SYMPTOM AND TROUBLE CODE TABLE

TROUBLE CODE	DESCRIPTION
A058	Left Front Motor Circuit Shorted to Battery or Motor Shorted
A061	Right Front Motor Circuit Open
A062	Right Front Motor Circuit Shorted to Ground
A063	Right Front Motor Circuit Shorted to Battery or Motor Shorted
A064	Rear Axle Motor Circuit Open
A065	Rear Axle Motor Circuit Shorted to Ground
A066	Rear Axle Motor Circuit Shorted to Battery or Motor Shorted
A076	Left Front Solenoid Circuit Shorted to Battery or Open
A077	Left Front Solenoid Circuit Shorted to Ground or Driver Open
A078	Right Front Solenoid Circuit Shorted to Battery or Open
A081	Right Front Solenoid Circuit Shorted to Ground or Driver Open
A082	Calibration Memory Failure
A086	Red Brake Warning Light Activated by ABS
A087	Red Brake Warning Light Circuit Open
A088	Red Brake Warning Light Circuit Shorted to Battery
A091	Open Brake Switch Contacts During Deceleration
A092	Open Brake Switch Contacts When ABS Was Required
A093	Code A091 or A092 Set in Current or Previous Ignition Cycle
A094	Brake Switch Contacts Always Closed
A095	Brake Switch Circuit Open
A096	Brake Lights Circuit Open

91099GA5

Fig. 92 ABS trouble codes (2 of 2)—1992-94 vehicles

DIAGNOSTIC TROUBLE CODE	DESCRIPTION
C1211	ABS Warning Indicator Circuit Malfunction
C1213	ABS Active Circuit Malfunction
C1214	Electronic Brake Control Relay Contact Circuit Open
C1215	Electronic Brake Control Relay Contact Circuit Always Active
C1216	Electronic Brake Control Relay Coil Circuit Open
C1217	Electronic Brake Control Relay Coil Circuit Shorted to Ground
C1218	Electronic Brake Control Relay Coil Circuit Shorted to Voltage
C1221	Left Front Wheel Speed Sensor Input Signal = 0
C1222	Right Front Wheel Speed Sensor Input Signal = 0
C1223	Left Rear Wheel Speed Sensor Input Signal = 0
C1224	Right Rear Wheel Speed Sensor Input Signal = 0
C1225	Left Front Excessive Wheel Speed Sensor Variation
C1226	Right Front Excessive Wheel Speed Sensor Variation
C1227	Left Rear Excessive Wheel Speed Sensor Variation
C1228	Right Rear Excessive Wheel Speed Sensor Variation
C1232	Left Front Wheel Speed Sensor Circuit Open or Shorted
C1233	Right Front Wheel Speed Sensor Circuit Open or Shorted
C1234	Left Rear Wheel Speed Sensor Circuit Open or Shorted
C1235	Right Rear Wheel Speed Sensor Circuit Open or Shorted
C1236	Low System Supply Voltage
C1237	High System Supply Voltage
C1238	Left Front ESB Will Not Hold Motor
C1241	Right Front ESB Will Not Hold Motor
C1242	Rear ESB Will Not Hold Motor
C1244	Left Front ABS Channel Will Not Move
C1245	Right Front ABS Channel Will Not Move
C1246	Rear ABS Channel Will Not Move
C1247	Left Front ABS Motor Free Spins
C1248	Right Front ABS Motor Free Spins
C1251	Rear ABS Motor Free Spins
C1252	Left Front ABS Channel in Release Too Long
C1253	Right Front ABS Channel in Release Too Long
C1254	Rear ABS Channel in Release Too Long
C1255	EBCM/EBTCM Internal Malfunction
C1256	Left Front ABS Motor Circuit Open

91099GA6

Fig. 93 ABS trouble codes (1 of 2)—1995-99 vehicles

to tell which code is current. If the ANTI-LOCK light is off before entering the diagnostic mode, none of the codes are current.

INTERMITTENTS

Although the ABS trouble codes stored by the EBCM are not identified as current or history codes, these codes may still be useful in diagnosing intermittent conditions. If an intermittent condition is being diagnosed perform the following:

DIAGNOSTIC TROUBLE CODE	DESCRIPTION
C1257	Left Front ABS Motor Circuit Shorted to Ground
C1258	Left Front ABS Motor Circuit Shorted to Voltage
C1261	Right Front ABS Motor Circuit Open
C1262	Right Front ABS Motor Circuit Shorted to Ground
C1263	Right Front ABS Motor Circuit Shorted to Voltage
C1264	Rear ABS Motor Circuit Open
C1265	Rear ABS Motor Circuit Shorted to Ground
C1266	Rear ABS Motor Circuit Shorted to Voltage
C1275	Serial Data Malfunction
C1276	Left Front Solenoid Circuit Open or Shorted to Ground
C1277	Left Front Solenoid Circuit Shorted to Voltage
C1278	Right Front Solenoid Circuit Open or Shorted to Ground
C1281	Right Front Solenoid Circuit Shorted to Voltage
C1282	Calibration Malfunction
C1286	EBCM/EBTCM Turned On the Red BRAKE Warning Indicator
C1287	Red Brake Warning Indicator Circuit Open or Short To Voltage
C1291	Open Brake Lamp Switch Circuit During Deceleration
C1292	Open Brake Lamp Switch Circuit When ABS Was Required
C1293	DTC C1291 or C1292 Set in Current or Previous Ignition Cycle
C1294	Brake Switch Contacts Always Active
C1295	Brake Lamp Switch Circuit Open
C1311	ABS Warning, TCS Warning, or ABS/TCS Active Indicator CKT Malfunction
C1323	PCM to EBTCM Delivered Torque Circuit Malfunction
C1324	EBTCM to PCM Requested Torque Circuit Malfunction
C1344	Left TCS Channel Will Not Move
C1345	Right TCS Channel Will Not Move
C1347	Left TCS Motor Free Spins
C1348	Right TCS Motor Free Spins
C1355	EBTCM Internal Malfunction
C1356	Left TCS Motor Circuit Open
C1357	Left TCS Motor Circuit Shorted to Ground
C1358	Left TCS Motor Circuit Shorted to Voltage
C1361	Right TCS Motor Circuit Open
C1362	Right TCS Motor Circuit Shorted to Ground
C1363	Right TCS Motor Circuit Shorted to Voltage

91099GA7

Fig. 94 ABS trouble codes (2 of 2)—1995-99 vehicles

1. Obtain an accurate description of the circumstances in which the failure occurs.

2. Display and clear any ABS trouble codes which may be present in the EBCM.

3. Test drive the vehicle, attempting to duplicate the failure condition exactly.

4. After duplicating the condition(s), stop the vehicle and display any ABS codes that have set.

5. If no codes have been stored. A good description of vehicle behavior can be helpful in determining a most likely circuit.

Most intermittent problems are caused by faulty electrical connections or wiring. Always check for poor mating of connector halves or terminals not fully seated in connector bodies, deformed, or damaged terminals and poor terminal to wire connections.

Most failures within the ABS will disable the anti-lock function for the entire ignition cycle, even if the fault clears before the next key–off occurrence. Three situations will allow the ABS to re-engage if the condition corrects during the ignition cycle. Each of these will illuminate one or both dash warning lights.

Low system voltage: If the EBCM detects low voltage, the ANTI-LOCK warning lamp is illuminated. If correct minimum voltage is restored to the EBCM, normal ABS function resumes.

Low brake fluid level: Once detected by the fluid level sensor, this condition illuminates both the BRAKE and ANTI-LOCK warning lights; when the sensor indicates acceptable fluid level, the normal ABS function resumes.

Low accumulator pressure: Should the accumulator lose or not develop correct pressure, both the BRAKE and ANTI-LOCK warning lights will illuminate. Full function is restored when the correct pressure is achieved

CLEARING TROUBLE CODES

The trouble codes in EBCM memory can be erased in one of two ways. The first method requires a Tech 1® or equivalent scan tool. The second method is called ignition cycle default. The EBCM will not let you clear any codes until all of the codes have been displayed.

To clear the codes with a Tech 1®, or equivalent, scan tool, use the "Clear DTCs" function of the scan tool. If a scan tool is not available, when no diagnostic fault codes occur for 100 drive cycles (a drive cycle is anytime the ignition is turned **ON**) and the vehicle is driven faster than 10 mph, any codes that exist are cleared from the EBCM memory.

Make sure to check for proper system operation and absence of DTCs when the clearing procedure is completed. The DTCs cannot be cleared by unplugging the EBCM, disconnecting the battery cables, or turning the ignition **OFF**.

ABS Service

PRECAUTIONS

Failure to observe the following precautions may result in system damage.
• Performing diagnostic work on the ABS requires the use of a Tech 1® Scan diagnostic tool or equivalent. If unavailable, please refer diagnostic work to a qualified technician.
• Before performing electric arc welding on the vehicle, disconnect the Electronic Brake Control Module (EBCM) and the hydraulic modulator connectors.
• When performing painting work on the vehicle, do not expose the Electronic Brake Control Module (EBCM) to temperatures in excess of 185°F (85°C) for longer than 2 hours. The system may be exposed to temperatures up to 200°F (95°C) for less than 15 minutes.
• Never disconnect or connect the Electronic Brake Control Module (EBCM) or hydraulic modulator connectors with the ignition switch **ON** or damage to the system will occur.
• Never disassemble any component of the Anti-Lock Brake System (ABS) which is designated non-serviceable; the component must be replaced as an assembly.
• When filling the master cylinder, always use Delco Supreme 11 brake fluid or equivalent, which meets DOT 3 specifications; petroleum-based fluid will destroy the rubber parts.

ABS Hydraulic Modulator Assembly

The ABS hydraulic modulator/motor pack assembly controls hydraulic pressure to the front and rear calipers or rear wheel cylinders by modulating hydraulic pressure to prevent wheel lock-up. The ABS motor pack consists of three motors, three drive gears, and three Expansion Spring Brakes (ESBs).

REMOVAL & INSTALLATION

♦ **See Figure 95**

✳✳ CAUTION

To help avoid personal injury, due to a retained load on the hydraulic modulator, the gear tension relief function of the Tech 1®, or equivalent, scan tool must be performed prior to removal of the ABS hydraulic modulator/master cylinder assembly.

1. Using a Tech 1® or equivalent scan tool, perform the "Gear Tension Relief Sequence".
2. Unplug the two solenoid electrical connectors.
3. Detach the fluid level sensor electrical connector.
4. Disengage the 6-way ABS motor pack electrical connector.
5. Use a flare nut wrench to disconnect the four brake pipes. Plug the lines to avoid allowing debris to enter and contaminate the system.
6. Unfasten the two nuts attaching the ABS hydraulic modulator/master cylinder assembly to the vacuum booster.
7. Remove the ABS hydraulic modulator/master cylinder assembly from the vehicle.
To install:
8. Install the ABS hydraulic modulator/master cylinder assembly.
9. Install the two nuts attaching ABS hydraulic modulator/master cylinder assembly to vacuum booster. Tighten the nuts to 20 ft. lbs. (27 Nm).
10. Unplug and connect the four brake pipes. Tighten the tube nuts to 18 ft. lbs. (25 Nm).
11. Attach the 6-way ABS motor pack electrical connector.
12. Reconnect the fluid level sensor electrical connector.
13. Attach the two solenoid electrical connectors.
14. Properly bleed the ABS system, as outlined later in this section.

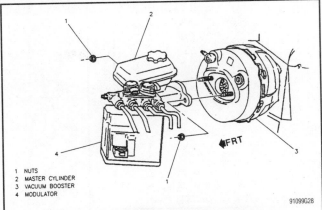

1 NUTS
2 MASTER CYLINDER
3 VACUUM BOOSTER
4 MODULATOR

91099G28

Fig. 95 The ABS hydraulic modulator and master cylinder are removed as an assembly

Electronic Brake Control Module (EBCM)

The controlling element of the ABS system is a microprocessor based Electronic Brake Control Module (ECBM). Inputs to the system include four speed sensors, the brake switch, ignition switch and unswitched battery voltage. Outputs include three bi-directional motor controls, two lamp controls, two solenoid controls, and the system enable relay. A serial data line located in terminal "9" of the Data Link Connector (DLC), is provided for service diagnostic tools (scan tools) and the assembly plant.

➡**In later model vehicles that are equipped with traction control, the control module may be referred to as the Electronic Brake and Traction Control Module (EBTCM).**

The EBCM monitors the speed of each wheel and the electrical status of the hydraulic unit. The EBCM's primary functions are to detect wheel lockup, control the brake system while in anti-lock mode, and monitor the system for proper electrical operation. When one or more wheels approach lockup during a stop, the EBCM will command appropriate valve positions to modulate brake fluid pressure and provide optimum braking. It will continue to command pressure changes in the system until a locking tendency is no longer noted.

The EBCM is a separate computer used exclusively for control of the anti-lock brake system. The unit also controls the retention and display of the ABS trouble codes when in the diagnostic mode. As the EBCM monitors the system or performs a self-check, it can react to a fault by disabling all or part of the ABS system and illuminating the amber ANTILOCK warning light.

REMOVAL & INSTALLATION

♦ **See Figures 96 and 97**

1. Disconnect the negative battery cable.
2. Remove the retainers, then remove the lower instrument panel sound insulator panel, under the steering column.

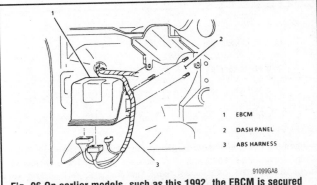

1 EBCM
2 DASH PANEL
3 ABS HARNESS

91099GA8

Fig. 96 On earlier models, such as this 1992, the EBCM is secured with hex head screws

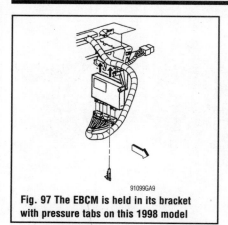

Fig. 97 The EBCM is held in its bracket
with pressure tabs on this 1998 model

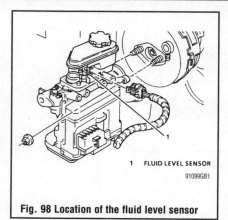

1 FLUID LEVEL SENSOR

Fig. 98 Location of the fluid level sensor

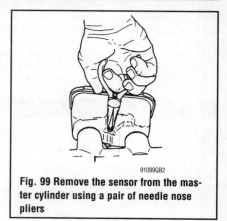

Fig. 99 Remove the sensor from the master cylinder using a pair of needle nose
pliers

3. The EBCM is secured with either hex head screws or retaining tabs. If
secured with screws, unfasten the screws securing the EBCM to the dash panel.
If equipped with pressure tabs, use the tabs to release the EBCM from its
mounting bracket.

4. Unplug the EBCM electrical connectors, then remove the EBCM from the
vehicle.

5. Installation is the reverse of the removal procedure.

Fluid Level Sensor

Found in the fluid reservoir, this sensor is a float, which operates two reed
switches when low fluid level is detected. One switch will cause the red BRAKE
warning light to illuminate; the other signals the EBCM and possibly other computers of the low fluid situation. Depending on model and equipment, other
messages may be displayed to the driver. The EBCM will engage the amber
ANTILOCK warning light and disable the ABS function.

REMOVAL & INSTALLATION

▶ **See Figures 98 and 99**

1. Disconnect the negative battery cable.
2. Detach the electrical connector from the fluid level sensor.
3. Use a pair of needle nose pliers to compress the locking tabs at the
inboard side of the master cylinder, then remove the switch.
4. Installation is the reverse of the removal procedure.

Front Wheel Speed Sensor

The front wheel speed sensors are of a variable reluctance type. Each sensor
is attached to the knuckle assembly in close proximity to a toothed ring. This
produces an AC voltage with a frequency proportional to the speed of the wheel.
The magnitude of the voltage and frequency increase with increasing speed. The
sensor is not repairable, nor is the air gap adjustable.

REMOVAL & INSTALLATION

▶ **See Figure 100**

1. Disconnect the negative battery cable.
2. Raise and safely support the vehicle.
3. Remove the tire and wheel assembly.
4. Unplug the wheel speed sensor electrical connector.
5. Remove the hub and bearing assembly. For more information, refer to
Section 8 of this manual.
6. Remove the wheel speed sensor from the hub and bearing assembly
using a suitable prytool or equivalent tool.

➡When the wheel speed sensor is removed it must be replaced. The
speed sensor is damaged when it is removed and cannot be reused.
There are two parts to the wheel speed sensor. These parts are replaced
as an assembly. They cannot be replaced individually. In addition,

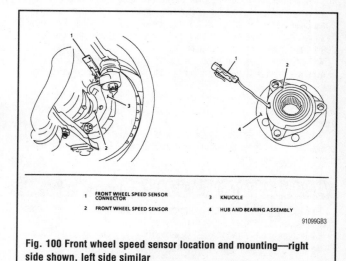

| 1 | FRONT WHEEL SPEED SENSOR CONNECTOR | 3 | KNUCKLE |
| 2 | FRONT WHEEL SPEED SENSOR | 4 | HUB AND BEARING ASSEMBLY |

Fig. 100 Front wheel speed sensor location and mounting—right
side shown, left side similar

inspect the bearing for signs of water intrusion, if intrusion is noted, the
entire bearing assembly must be replaced.

To install:

7. Apply Loctite® 620 to the mating surfaces of the wheel speed sensor that
contacts the hub and bearing assembly.
8. Use a suitable press to press the new wheel speed sensor on to the hub
and bearing assembly.
9. Install the hub and bearing assembly, as outlined in Section 8 of this
vehicle.
10. Attach the wheel speed sensor electrical connector.
11. Install the tire and wheel assembly.
12. Carefully lower the vehicle, then connect the negative battery cable.

Rear Wheel Speed Sensor

▶ **See Figure 101**

The rear wheel speed sensors operate in the same manner as the front wheel
speed sensors. However, the wheel speed sensor and toothed ring are contained
within the dust cap of the integral rear wheel bearing. The sensor and toothed
ring are not repairable and no provision for air gap adjustment exists. If a rear
wheel speed sensor fails, the entire integral bearing and speed sensor assembly
must be replaced. For replacement procedures, please refer to Section 8 of this
manual.

ABS Enable Relay

The ABS enable relay is a normally open contact type, and has special contact material to handle the high currents required for ABS operation.

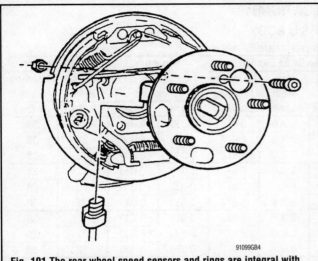

Fig. 101 The rear wheel speed sensors and rings are integral with the hub and bearing assemblies

REMOVAL & INSTALLATION

▸ **See Figure 102**

1. Disconnect the negative battery cable.
2. Remove the relay cover, then unplug and remove the ABS enable relay.

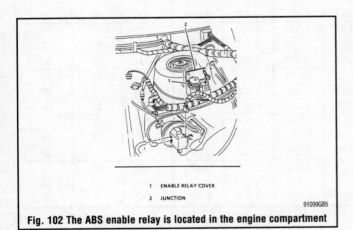

1   ENABLE RELAY COVER
2   JUNCTION

Fig. 102 The ABS enable relay is located in the engine compartment

To install:
3. Plug in the new relay; replace the cover.
4. Connect the negative battery cable.

Bleeding the ABS System

If any brake component is repaired or replaced such that air is allowed to enter the brake system, the entire bleeding procedure MUST be followed. On vehicles equipped with ABS, before bleeding the brakes, the front and rear displacement cylinder pistons must be returned to the topmost position. The preferred method uses a Tech 1®, or equivalent, scan tool to perform the re-homing procedure, If a Tech 1® is not available, the second procedure may be used, but it is extremely important that the procedure be followed exactly as outlined.

Fluid may be added to either reservoir in normal fashion. The ignition must be **OFF**. Carefully wipe the reservoir cap and surrounding area free of dirt and debris before removing the cap. Use only DOT 3 brake fluid from an unopened container. The use of DOT 5 or silicone brake fluid is specifically prohibited in this system. Fill the reservoir only to the MAX mark; do not overfill. Make certain the reservoir cap is securely installed.

RE-HOME PROCEDURE WITH TECH 1®

1. Using a Tech 1® or equivalent scan tool, select "F5: Motor Re-home." The motor re-home function cannot be performed if current DTCs are present. If DTCs are present, the vehicle must be repaired and the codes cleared before performing the motor re-home function.
2. The entire brake system should now be bled following either the "Pressure Bleeding" or "Manual Bleeding" procedure outlined earlier in this section.

WITHOUT TECH 1®

➡**This method can only be used if the ABS warning lamp is not illuminated and no DTCs are present.**

➡**Do not place your foot on the brake pedal through this entire procedure unless specifically directed to do so.**

1. Start the engine and allow it to run for at least ten seconds while observing the ABS warning lamp.
2. If the ABS warning lamp turns ON and stays ON after about ten seconds, the bleeding procedure must be stopped and a Tech 1® must be used to diagnose the ABS malfunction.
3. If the ABS warning lamp turns ON for approximately 3 seconds, then turns OFF and stays OFF, turn the ignition **OFF**.
4. Repeat these steps one more time.
5. The entire brake system should now be bled following either the "Pressure Bleeding" or "Manual Bleeding" procedure outlined earlier in this section.

BRAKE SPECIFICATIONS
GENERAL MOTORS U BODY
All measurements in inches unless noted

Year	Model	Master Cylinder Bore	Brake Disc Original Thickness	Brake Disc Minimum Thickness	Brake Disc Maximum Runout	Brake Drum Diameter Original Inside Diameter	Brake Drum Diameter Max. Wear Limit	Brake Drum Diameter Maximum Machine Diameter	Minimum Lining Thickness Front	Minimum Lining Thickness Rear	Brake Caliper Bracket Bolts (ft. lbs.)	Brake Caliper Mounting Bolts (ft. lbs.)
1990	Lumina	0.944	1.043	0.957	0.004	8.863	8.909	8.877	0.030	0.030	32	38
	Trans Sport	0.944	1.043	0.957	0.004	8.863	8.909	8.877	0.030	0.030	32	38
	Silhouette	0.944	1.043	0.957	0.004	8.863	8.909	8.877	0.030	0.030	32	38
1991	Lumina	0.944	1.043	0.957	0.004	8.863	8.909	8.877	0.030	0.030	32	38
	Trans Sport	0.944	1.043	0.957	0.004	8.863	8.909	8.877	0.030	0.030	32	38
	Silhouette	0.944	1.043	0.957	0.004	8.863	8.909	8.877	0.030	0.030	32	38
1992	Lumina	0.944	1.043	0.957	0.004	8.863	8.909	8.877	0.030	0.030	32	38
	Trans Sport	0.944	1.043	0.957	0.004	8.863	8.909	8.877	0.030	0.030	32	38
	Silhouette	0.944	1.043	0.957	0.004	8.863	8.909	8.877	0.030	0.030	32	38
1993	Lumina	0.944	1.043	0.957	0.004	8.863	8.909	8.877	0.030	0.030	32	38
	Trans Sport	0.944	1.043	0.957	0.004	8.863	8.909	8.877	0.030	0.030	32	38
	Silhouette	0.944	1.043	0.957	0.004	8.863	8.909	8.877	0.030	0.030	32	38
1994	Lumina	0.944	1.043	0.957	0.004	8.863	8.920	8.909	0.030	0.030	32	38
	Trans Sport	0.944	1.043	0.957	0.004	8.863	8.920	8.909	0.030	0.030	32	38
	Silhouette	0.944	1.043	0.957	0.004	8.863	8.920	8.909	0.030	0.030	32	38
1995	Lumina	0.944	1.043	0.957	0.004	8.863	8.920	8.909	0.030	0.030	32	38
	Trans Sport	0.944	1.043	0.957	0.004	8.863	8.920	8.909	0.030	0.030	32	38
	Silhouette	0.944	1.043	0.957	0.004	8.863	8.920	8.909	0.030	0.030	32	38
1996	Lumina	0.944	1.260	1.209	0.002	8.863	8.920	8.909	0.030	0.030	32	38
	Trans Sport	0.944	1.260	1.209	0.002	8.863	8.920	8.909	0.030	0.030	32	38
	Silhouette	0.944	1.260	1.209	0.002	8.863	8.920	8.909	0.030	0.030	32	38
1997	Venture	1.000	1.270	1.210	0.003	8.863	8.920	8.909	0.030	0.030	32	38
	Trans Sport	1.000	1.270	1.210	0.003	8.863	8.920	8.909	0.030	0.030	32	38
	Silhouette	1.000	1.270	1.210	0.003	8.863	8.920	8.909	0.030	0.030	32	38
1998	Venture	1.000	1.270	1.210	0.003	8.863	8.920	8.909	0.030	0.030	32	38
	Trans Sport	1.000	1.270	1.210	0.003	8.863	8.920	8.909	0.030	0.030	32	38
	Silhouette	1.000	1.270	1.210	0.003	8.863	8.920	8.909	0.030	0.030	32	38
1999	Venture	1.000	1.270	1.210	0.003	8.863	8.920	8.909	0.030	0.030	32	38
	Montana	1.000	1.270	1.210	0.003	8.863	8.920	8.909	0.030	0.030	32	38
	Silhouette	1.000	1.270	1.210	0.003	8.863	8.920	8.909	0.030	0.030	32	38

91099C01

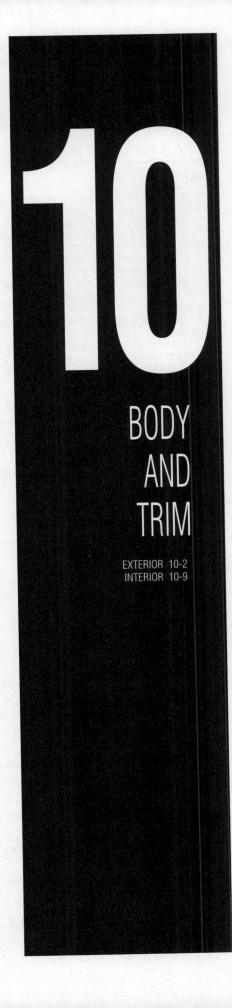

10

BODY AND TRIM

EXTERIOR

Front Doors

REMOVAL & INSTALLATION

▶ See Figure 1

1. If equipped with power door components, disconnect the negative battery cable.
2. Remove the inner door trim panels.
3. If so equipped, unplug the electrical connectors from the power door components and remove the electrical harness from the door.
4. Using a suitable tool, etch the position of the door, relative to the hinges, to aid when reinstalling.
5. With an assistant supporting the door, unfasten the hinge-to-door bolts, then remove the door from the vehicle.

To install:

6. With the aid of an assistant, reposition the door and reinstall the hinge to door bolts.
7. If so equipped, install the electrical harness to the door and attach the electrical connectors to the power door components.
8. Install the inner trim door panel.
9. Adjust the door for proper fit.
10. Connect the negative battery cable.

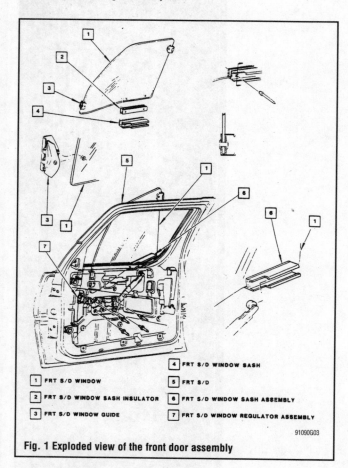

1	FRT S/D WINDOW	4	FRT S/D WINDOW SASH
2	FRT S/D WINDOW SASH INSULATOR	5	FRT S/D
3	FRT S/D WINDOW GUIDE	6	FRT S/D WINDOW SASH ASSEMBLY
		7	FRT S/D WINDOW REGULATOR ASSEMBLY

91090G03

Fig. 1 Exploded view of the front door assembly

ADJUSTMENT

▶ See Figure 2

1. Adjust the door so that all gaps between the door and body panel are equal and the door closes easily.

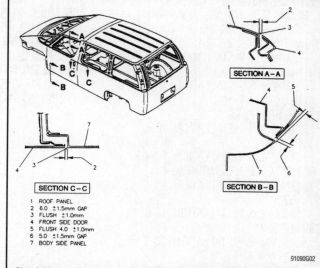

SECTION C-C
1 ROOF PANEL
2 6.0 ±1.5mm GAP
3 FLUSH ±1.0mm
4 FRONT SIDE DOOR
5 FLUSH 4.0 ±1.0mm
6 5.0 ±1.5mm GAP
7 BODY SIDE PANEL

91090G02

Fig. 2 View of the measurements necessary to align the door for a proper fit to the body

2. Make sure the door surface is flush with the body surface.
3. Refer to the accompanying figure for alignment specifications.

Front Door Hinges

REMOVAL & INSTALLATION

▶ See Figure 3

1. Remove the front door.
2. Unfasten the hinge-to-pillar bolts, then remove the hinges.
3. Installation is the reverse of the removal procedure. Adjust the door as necessary.

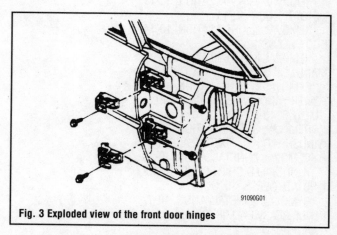

91090G01

Fig. 3 Exploded view of the front door hinges

Sliding Door

REMOVAL & INSTALLATION

▶ See Figures 4 and 5

1. Unfasten any necessary retainers, then remove the inner door trim panel and the door garnish panel.

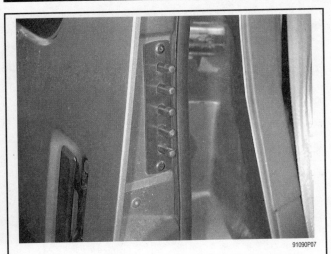

Fig. 4 View of the electrical switches that are activated by the opening and closing of the sliding door

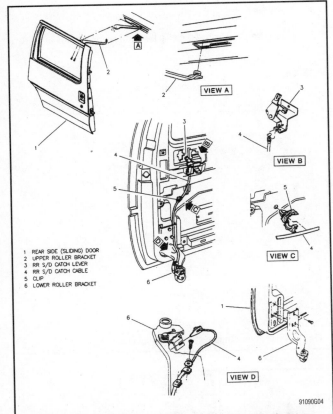

1 REAR SIDE (SLIDING) DOOR
2 UPPER ROLLER BRACKET
3 RR S/D CATCH LEVER
4 RR S/D CATCH CABLE
5 CLIP
6 LOWER ROLLER BRACKET

VIEW A
VIEW B
VIEW C
VIEW D

91090G04

Fig. 5 Exploded views of the sliding side door, including the upper and lower roller bracket

2. Remove the center track roller bracket from the door.
3. Remove the upper track roller bracket from the door.
4. Remove the lower track roller bracket from the door, then remove the sliding door from the vehicle.

To install:
5. Reposition the sliding door.
6. Install the lower track roller bracket to the door.
7. Install the upper track roller bracket to the door.
8. Install the center roller bracket to the door and align the door as necessary.
9. Install the door trim panel and the door garnish panel.

ADJUSTMENT

▶ See Figure 6

The ideal sliding door alignment is one where a parallel gap of equal proportion exists along the top and bottom edges of the door. Raising or lowering the front or rear of the door makes adjustments. The center roller bracket and the lower roller bracket are used to adjust the height of the rear and the front of the sliding door respectively. To adjust, simply loosen the bracket-to-door bolts and adjust as necessary.

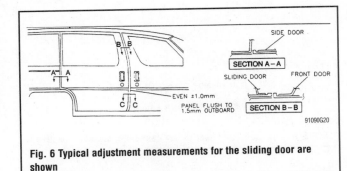

SIDE DOOR
SECTION A–A
SLIDING DOOR   FRONT DOOR
EVEN ±1.0mm
PANEL FLUSH TO
1.5mm OUTBOARD   SECTION B–B

91090G20

Fig. 6 Typical adjustment measurements for the sliding door are shown

Roller Brackets

REMOVAL & INSTALLATION

Center

▶ See Figures 7 and 8

1. Scribe the location of the existing brackets on the door.
2. Support the door, remove the bracket bolts from the door, and remove the bracket and roller assembly.
3. Remove the pin from the bracket and roller assembly and remove the bracket.

To install:
4. Install the pin to the bracket and roller assembly.
5. Install the bracket and roller assembly to the track.
6. Install the bracket bolts to the door, adjust the door to properly fit the door frame and tighten the bolts to 20 ft. lbs. (27 Nm).

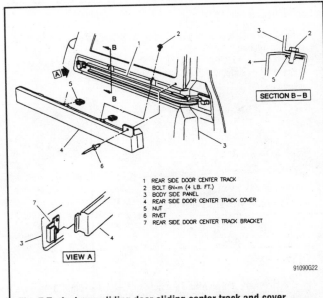

1 REAR SIDE DOOR CENTER TRACK
2 BOLT 6N•m (4 LB. FT.)
3 BODY SIDE PANEL
4 REAR SIDE DOOR CENTER TRACK COVER
5 NUT
6 RIVET
7 REAR SIDE DOOR CENTER TRACK BRACKET

SECTION B–B
VIEW A

91090G22

Fig. 7 Typical rear sliding door sliding center track and cover

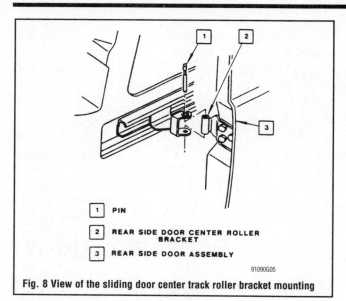

Fig. 8 View of the sliding door center track roller bracket mounting

Upper

▶ See Figure 5

1. Remove the inner door trim panel and garnish molding.
2. Support the door, remove the bracket to door screws, and remove the bracket.
3. Installation is the reverse of the removal procedure.

Lower

▶ See Figure 5

1. Remove the door inner trim panel, as outlined later in this section.
2. Scribe the location of the existing bracket on the door.
3. Remove the bracket-to-door bolts.
4. Disconnect the catch cable from the bracket.
5. Remove the lower striker, then remove the lower roller bracket.
6. Installation is the reverse of the removal procedure.

Hood

REMOVAL & INSTALLATION

▶ See Figures 9 and 10

1. Raise the hood and place protective coverings over the fenders to protect the paint and moldings.
2. Use a suitable paint marker or equivalent to matchmark the position of the hinges on the hood to aid in alignment when installing the hood.

3. With an assistant supporting the hood, unfasten the hood-to-hinge retaining bolts, then remove the hood.
4. Installation is the reverse of the removal procedure.

Rear Liftgate Assembly

The rear liftgate assembly is formed from an inner and outer plastic panel bonded together with structure adhesives. The liftgate has a stationary glass window. The liftgate's hinges are welded to the body spaceframe and bolted to the formed liftgate panels.

REMOVAL & INSTALLATION

▶ See Figures 11 thru 17

1. Disconnect the negative battery cable.
2. Open the liftgate and support it securely.
3. Remove the right and left side window garnish moldings.
4. Remove the liftgate trim finish panel.
5. Unplug the electrical connectors from the following components:
- Rear speakers
- Liftgate ajar switch
- License plate lamp
- Back-up lamps
- Window release actuator harness connector.
6. Use a small prytool to carefully pry out and remove the strut retaining clip. Pull the end of the strut from the stud.
7. Unfasten the shoulder bolt securing the upper end of the strut to the strut bracket.
8. With the aid of a helper, remove the liftgate hinge bolts and remove the liftgate assembly.
9. Installation is the reverse of the removal procedure.

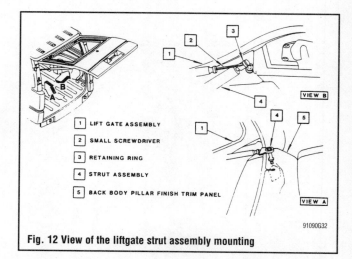

Fig. 12 View of the liftgate strut assembly mounting

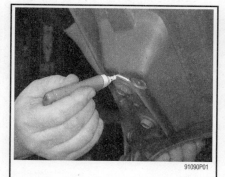

Fig. 9 Matchmark the installed position of the hood before beginning removal

Fig. 10 Remove the screw holding the hood to the angle bracket

Fig. 11 Use a suitable support tool, such as this safety stand (used here with a blanket to avoid scratches) to support the liftgate in the open position

91090P04

Fig. 13 Slide a small prytool under the retaining clip to remove it from the strut

91090P05

Fig. 14 Once the clip is removed, the strut can be pulled from the stud

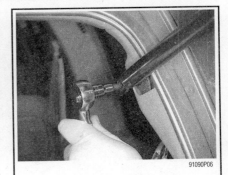

91090P06

Fig. 15 Remove the shoulder bolt from the mounting bracket to release the strut

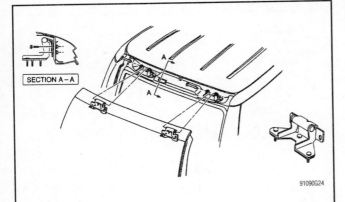

SECTION A – A

91090G24

Fig. 16 Liftgate hinge attachment and proper alignment of the hatch cover

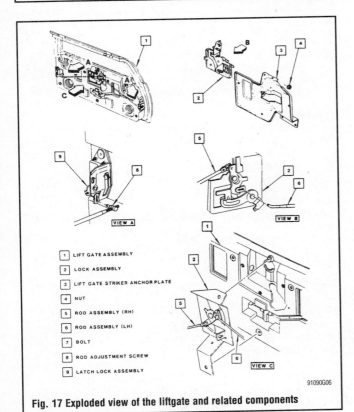

VIEW A

VIEW B

VIEW C

1 LIFT GATE ASSEMBLY
2 LOCK ASSEMBLY
3 LIFT GATE STRIKER ANCHOR PLATE
4 NUT
5 ROD ASSEMBLY (RH)
6 ROD ASSEMBLY (LH)
7 BOLT
8 ROD ADJUSTMENT SCREW
9 LATCH LOCK ASSEMBLY

91090G06

Fig. 17 Exploded view of the liftgate and related components

Bumpers

REMOVAL & INSTALLATION

Front

▶ **See Figures 18 thru 23**

1. Remove the right and left wheel well housing.
2. Remove the right and left fascia-to-fender bolts.

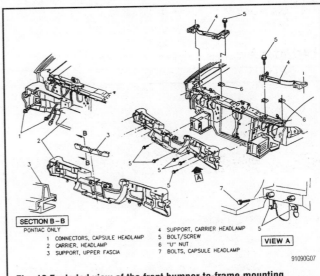

SECTION B – B
PONTIAC ONLY

1 CONNECTORS, CAPSULE HEADLAMP
2 CARRIER, HEADLAMP
3 SUPPORT, UPPER FASCIA
4 SUPPORT, CARRIER HEADLAMP
5 BOLT/SCREW
6 "U" NUT
7 BOLTS, CAPSULE HEADLAMP

VIEW A

91090G07

Fig. 18 Exploded view of the front bumper-to-frame mounting

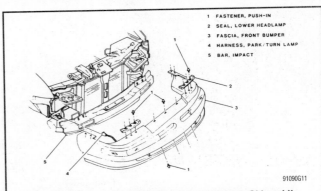

1 FASTENER, PUSH-IN
2 SEAL, LOWER HEADLAMP
3 FASCIA, FRONT BUMPER
4 HARNESS, PARK/TURN LAMP
5 BAR, IMPACT

91090G11

Fig. 19 Common front fascia and bumper mounting—Oldsmobile shown

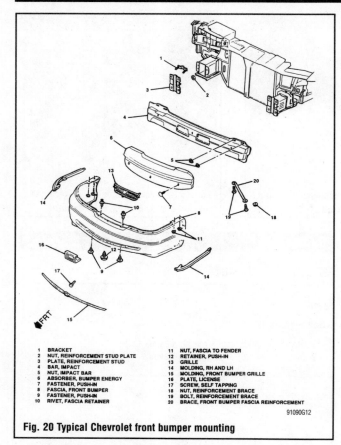

1. BRACKET
2. NUT, REINFORCEMENT STUD PLATE
3. PLATE, REINFORCEMENT STUD
4. BAR, IMPACT
5. NUT, IMPACT BAR
6. ABSORBER, BUMPER ENERGY
7. FASTENER, PUSH-IN
8. FASCIA, FRONT BUMPER
9. FASTENER, PUSH-IN
10. RIVET, FASCIA RETAINER
11. NUT, FASCIA TO FENDER
12. RETAINER, PUSH-IN
13. GRILLE
14. MOLDING, RH AND LH
15. MOLDING, FRONT BUMPER GRILLE
16. PLATE, LICENSE
17. SCREW, SELF TAPPING
18. NUT, REINFORCEMENT BRACE
19. BOLT, REINFORCEMENT BRACE
20. BRACE, FRONT BUMPER FASCIA REINFORCEMENT

91090G12

Fig. 20 Typical Chevrolet front bumper mounting

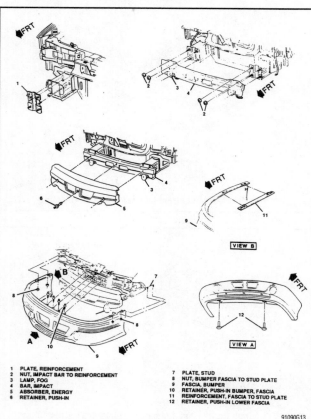

1. PLATE, REINFORCEMENT
2. NUT, IMPACT BAR TO REINFORCEMENT
3. LAMP, FOG
4. BAR, IMPACT
5. ABSORBER, ENERGY
6. RETAINER, PUSH-IN
7. PLATE, STUD
8. NUT, BUMPER FASCIA TO STUD PLATE
9. FASCIA, BUMPER
10. RETAINER, PUSH-IN BUMPER, FASCIA
11. REINFORCEMENT, FASCIA TO STUD PLATE
12. RETAINER, PUSH-IN LOWER FASCIA

91090G13

Fig. 21 Exploded view of the front bumper assembly—Pontiac

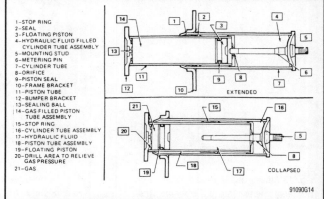

1. STOP RING
2. SEAL
3. FLOATING PISTON
4. HYDRAULIC FLUID FILLED CYLINDER TUBE ASSEMBLY
5. MOUNTING STUD
6. METERING PIN
7. CYLINDER TUBE
8. ORIFICE
9. PISTON SEAL
10. FRAME BRACKET
11. PISTON TUBE
12. BUMPER BRACKET
13. SEALING BALL
14. GAS FILLED PISTON TUBE ASSEMBLY
15. STOP RING
16. CYLINDER TUBE ASSEMBLY
17. HYDRAULIC FLUID
18. PISTON TUBE ASSEMBLY
19. FLOATING PISTON
20. DRILL AREA TO RELIEVE GAS PRESSURE
21. GAS

91090G14

Fig. 22 Cross-sectional view of the energy absorbing device which is mounted to the front bumper

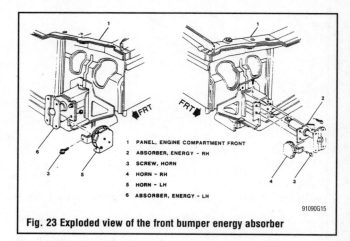

1. PANEL, ENGINE COMPARTMENT FRONT
2. ABSORBER, ENERGY - RH
3. SCREW, HORN
4. HORN - RH
5. HORN - LH
6. ABSORBER, ENERGY - LH

91090G15

Fig. 23 Exploded view of the front bumper energy absorber

3. Remove the headlights.

4. Remove the right and left headlight frame-to-fascia fasteners, then remove the front fascia.

5. Detach the parking lamp connectors.

6. Remove the radiator airflow shields.

7. Unfasten the bumper-to-energy absorber bolts, then remove the front bumper.

To install:

8. Position the bumper to the vehicle and secure with the bumper-to-energy absorber bolts. Tighten the bolts to 20 ft. lbs. (27 Nm).

9. Install the radiator air flow shields.

10. Attach the parking lamp electrical connectors.

11. Install the front fascia.

12. Install the right and left headlamp frame to fascia fasteners.

13. Install the headlamps.

14. Install the right and left fascia to fender bolts and tighten to 53 inch lbs. (6 Nm).

15. Install the right and left wheel well housing.

Rear

▶ See Figures 24 and 25

1. Remove the lower fascia-to-bumper fasteners.

2. Remove the upper fascia-to-bumper screws.

3. Unfasten the right and left bolts securing the fascia to the rear quarter panel, then remove the fascia.

4. Unfasten the bumper retaining bolts, then remove the bumper from the vehicle.

5. Installation is the reverse of the removal procedure.

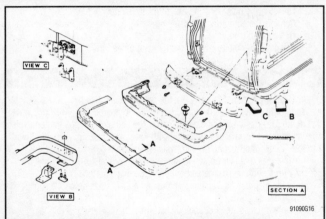

Fig. 24 Exploded view of the rear bumper/fascia assembly—Oldsmobile shown

Grille

REMOVAL & INSTALLATION

➡These are general procedures; they may vary slightly from vehicle to vehicle depending on year and trim level. Read through both procedures and decide which best fits your vehicle.

Two Piece Grille

1. Raise and support the hood.
2. Pop out the upper grille.
3. Remove the lower grille-to-fascia screws, then remove the lower grille.
4. Installation is the reverse of the removal procedure.

One Piece Grille

1. Remove the right and left wheel well housing.
2. Remove the right and left fascia-to-fender bolts.

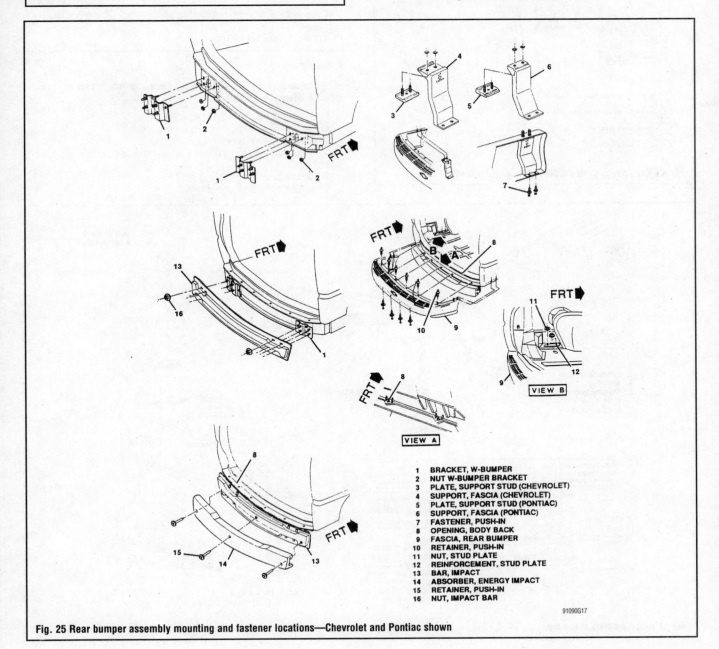

1	BRACKET, W-BUMPER
2	NUT W-BUMPER BRACKET
3	PLATE, SUPPORT STUD (CHEVROLET)
4	SUPPORT, FASCIA (CHEVROLET)
5	PLATE, SUPPORT STUD (PONTIAC)
6	SUPPORT, FASCIA (PONTIAC)
7	FASTENER, PUSH-IN
8	OPENING, BODY BACK
9	FASCIA, REAR BUMPER
10	RETAINER, PUSH-IN
11	NUT, STUD PLATE
12	REINFORCEMENT, STUD PLATE
13	BAR, IMPACT
14	ABSORBER, ENERGY IMPACT
15	RETAINER, PUSH-IN
16	NUT, IMPACT BAR

Fig. 25 Rear bumper assembly mounting and fastener locations—Chevrolet and Pontiac shown

3. Remove the headlights.

4. Remove the right and left headlight frame-to-fascia fasteners, then remove the front fascia.

5. Remove the grille-to-front fascia fasteners, then remove the grille from the vehicle.

6. Installation is the reverse of the removal procedure.

Outside Mirrors

REMOVAL & INSTALLATION

♦ See Figure 26

1. Remove the door inside trim panel, as outlined later in this section.
2. Remove the front garnish moldings.

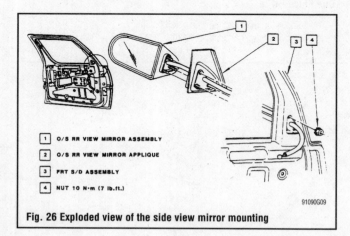

1	O/S RR VIEW MIRROR ASSEMBLY
2	O/S RR VIEW MIRROR APPLIQUE
3	FRT S/D ASSEMBLY
4	NUT 10 N·m (7 lb.ft.)

91090G09

Fig. 26 Exploded view of the side view mirror mounting

3. Unfasten the nuts securing the mirror to the door.

4. Remove the controller and cable or electrical connector through the door, then remove the mirror.

5. Installation is the reverse of the removal procedure.

Antenna

On 1992 and later model vehicles, the radio antenna has been integrated into the headlining panel and is designed to provide improved signal reception over that of the previously utilized fixed antenna. The use of this type of antenna also eliminates other drawbacks associated with fixed antennas such as wind noise and their inherent susceptibility to physical damage.

The antennae that is mounted to the headliner consists of a thin sheet of copper with a short coaxial cable bonded to the metal surface.

The roof antenna lead-in cables provide a connection between the roof antenna and the radio.

There are three sections of antenna lead-in cable that feed the radio:
- A radio-to-intermediate cable (under the instrument panel).
- An intermediate cable (running from the instrument panel to the top of the side rail).
- An intermediate to antenna cable (providing a tap to the copper foil).

REMOVAL & INSTALLATION

♦ See Figure 27

➡**This procedure is for vehicles with a fixed antenna, not for vehicles with the integral antenna.**

1. Disconnect the steel antenna out of the base.
2. Remove the trim cover from the antenna housing.
3. Remove the three antenna mounting screws.
4. Disconnect the antenna lead-in cable and remove it from the engine compartment.
5. Remove the antenna base assembly.
6. Installation is the reverse of removal

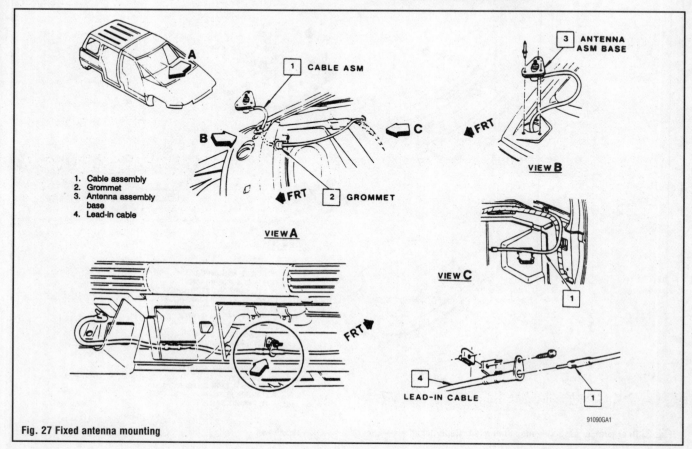

1. Cable assembly
2. Grommet
3. Antenna assembly base
4. Lead-in cable

91090GA1

Fig. 27 Fixed antenna mounting

Fender

REMOVAL & INSTALLATION

▶ See Figures 28 and 29

1. Open and properly support the hood.
2. Disconnect the side marker lamp wiring. Remove the side marker lamp.
3. Unfasten the retainers, then remove the wheel well housing.

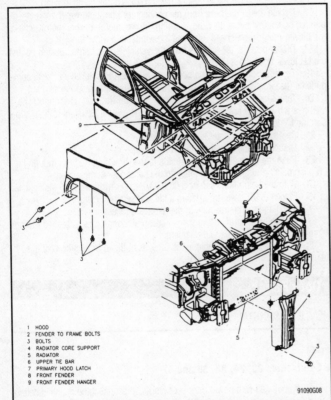

1 HOOD
2 FENDER TO FRAME BOLTS
3 BOLTS
4 RADIATOR CORE SUPPORT
5 RADIATOR
6 UPPER TIE BAR
7 PRIMARY HOOD LATCH
8 FRONT FENDER
9 FRONT FENDER HANGER

91090G08

Fig. 28 Exploded view of the fender panel. Note the hood latch support fastener locations

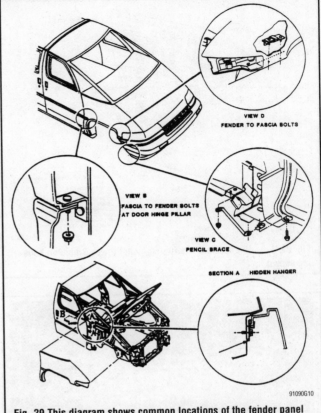

VIEW D
FENDER TO FASCIA BOLTS

VIEW B
FASCIA TO FENDER BOLTS
AT DOOR HINGE PILLAR

VIEW C
PENCIL BRACE

SECTION A   HIDDEN HANGER

91090G10

Fig. 29 This diagram shows common locations of the fender panel hidden hangers

4. Remove the fender-to-bumper fascia bolts.
5. Remove the fender to fascia bolt from the lower door hinge pillar.
6. Unfasten the fender attaching screws, then remove the fender.

To install:

7. Reposition the fender and install the attaching screws.
8. Install the fender-to-fascia bolt at the lower door hinge pillar.
9. Install the fender-to-bumper fascia bolts.
10. Install the wheel well housing.
11. Install the side marker lamp assembly and attach the wiring.
12. Close the hood.

INTERIOR

Instrument Panel and Pad

The instrument panel (I/P) contains the instruments used by the driver during vehicle operation, the ventilation and sound system controls, many vehicle convenience items, and most of the HVAC outlets. The panel has been designed to facilitate removal of all switches and instruments.

The instrument panel lower trim pad bears the load of the entire instrument panel. It is supported by the lower steering column support, a center support bracket and two outer support brackets attached to the LH and RH body side hinge (A) pillars.

To remove and replace the instrument panel lower trim pad, several of the instrument panel electrical harness, crosscar and engine harness connectors must be unplugged.

REMOVAL & INSTALLATION

▶ See Figures 30, 31 and 32

✳✳ CAUTION

Some models covered by this manual may be equipped with a Supplemental Restraint System (SRS), which uses an air bag. When- ever working near any of the SRS components, such as the impact sensors, the air bag module, steering column, and instrument panel, disable the SRS, as described in Section 6.

1. If equipped with an air bag, properly disable the SRS as outlined in Section 6 of this manual.
2. If not done already, disconnect the negative battery cable.
3. To remove the instrument panel upper trim panel, perform the following:
   a. Remove the I/P trim pad.
   b. Remove the defogger vent grilles from the I/P upper trim panel.
   c. Remove the RH front radio speaker.
   d. Loosen the upper edge of the I/P lower trim panel by removing the two hex screws.
   e. Remove the five screws retaining I/P upper trim panel and remove the panel.

➡The following steps outline removal of the instrument panel (I/P) lower trim pad.

4. Remove the front passenger seat.
5. Remove the push-in retainers securing the dash panel upper insulator.
6. Remove the dash panel upper insulator.

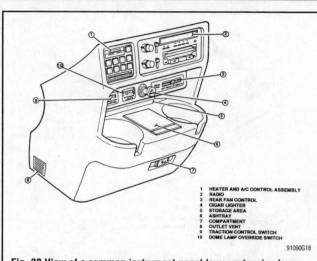

1	HEATER AND A/C CONTROL ASSEMBLY
2	RADIO
3	REAR FAN CONTROL
4	CIGAR LIGHTER
5	STORAGE AREA
6	ASHTRAY
7	COMPARTMENT
8	OUTLET VENT
9	TRACTION CONTROL SWITCH
10	DOME LAMP OVERRIDE SWITCH

91090G18

Fig. 30 View of a common instrument panel lower extension housing shown

91090P19

Fig. 31 View of the instrument panel in partial disassembly—steering wheel removed for clarity

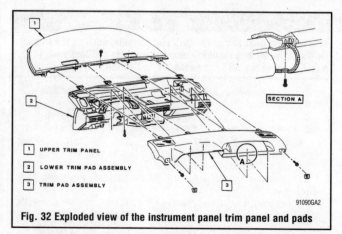

1 UPPER TRIM PANEL
2 LOWER TRIM PAD ASSEMBLY
3 TRIM PAD ASSEMBLY

SECTION A

91090GA2

Fig. 32 Exploded view of the instrument panel trim panel and pads

7. Remove the I/P sound insulators by removing the attaching screws and pins and removing the floor courtesy lamps from the insulator panel.

8. Disengage the four upper retaining clips, then remove the I/P steering column opening filler from I/P lower trim pad.

9. Remove the I/P upper trim panel

10. Remove the hood latch cable-to-hood release handle.

11. Remove the hood release handle.

12. Remove the LH and RH lower cowl side panels.

13. Tag and detach the I/P harness to the crosscar harness (J-block) connectors.

14. Label and unplug the I/P harness from the body harness (J-block) connectors.

15. Carefully lower the steering column to rest on driver's seat in order to allow clearance when removing and replacing the I/P lower trim pad. Make sure to remove or disconnect components that would interfere with this procedure.

16. Disconnect the I/P harness from the engine and forward lamp harnesses (J-block connector near the LH shock tower in the engine compartment).

17. Detach the I/P harness from the connectors from both wiper solvent pumps, brake (low hydraulic fluid) warning, blower motor, blower motor resistor, blower motor high-speed relay and the windshield wiper motor.

18. Disconnect the I/P harness from the vehicle space frame (located behind the LH lower cowl side panel).

19. Tag and detach the I/P harness from the steering column electrical components (hazard switch, ignition switch, turn signals, SIR components, etc.)

20. Temporarily provide support for the I/P lower trim pad. Disconnect the load bearing support braces. You will need the help of an assistant to help support the I/P lower trim pad during removal.

21. Remove the I/P center support bracket.

22. Disconnect the steering column lower support.

23. Push the engine compartment side of the I/P wiring harness though the LH dash panel grommet access hole into the passenger compartment.

24. With the help of an assistant, lift the I/P lower trim pad from the vehicle.

25. Place the I/P lower trim pad in a flat and secure location.

26. Installation is the reversal of the removal process.

27. During installation, make sure to attach all connectors as tagged during removal, and properly fasten all retainers.

28. If equipped, properly enable the SRS, as outlined in Section 6 of this manual.

Door Panels

REMOVAL & INSTALLATION

Front

♦ See Figures 33, 34, 35, 36 and 37

1. If equipped with power door accessories, disconnect the negative battery cable.

2. If equipped, remove the power door lock and window controls.

3. Using a suitable door window handle clip removal tool, remove the retaining clip and handle from the door.

4. Remove the door handle bezel.

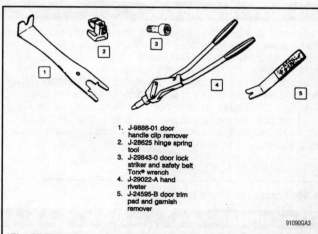

1. J-9886-01 door handle clip remover
2. J-28625 hinge spring tool
3. J-29843-0 door lock striker and safety belt Torx® wrench
4. J-29022-A hand riveter
5. J-24595-B door trim pad and garnish remover

91090GA3

Fig. 33 There are a variety of special tools available that make door and trim panel removal much easier

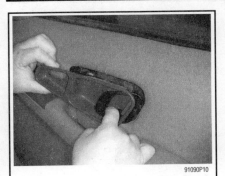

Fig. 34 Removing the door handle bezel to gain access

Fig. 35 Pull the power door lock and window switch up, then detach and feed the connectors through the door panel

Fig. 36 For 2-piece door panels, you must remove the lower panel first for access to the upper panel retainers

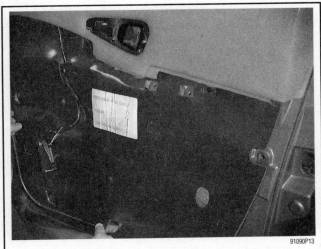

Fig. 37 The weather sheet is located under the trim panel and is designed to keep water out of the passenger compartment

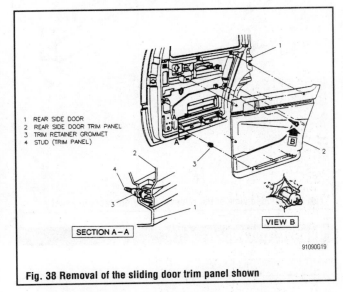

1 REAR SIDE DOOR
2 REAR SIDE DOOR TRIM PANEL
3 TRIM RETAINER GROMMET
4 STUD (TRIM PANEL)

SECTION A–A

VIEW B

Fig. 38 Removal of the sliding door trim panel shown

5. Remove the fasteners in the armrest and lower panel.

6. Detach and feed the electrical connectors through the door panel, if so equipped.

7. Unfasten the trim panel retainers, then carefully pry the trim panel from the door frame at the window seal to remove it from the vehicle.

To install:

8. Install the trim panel to the door, placing the window seal portion of the panel over the door frame.

9. If equipped, feed the electrical connectors through the door panel.

10. Install the fasteners in the armrest and lower panel.

11. Install the door handle bezel.

12. Install the door window handle.

13. Install the power door lock and window controls, if so equipped.

14. Connect the negative battery cable.

Sliding

▶ **See Figure 38**

1. Remove the inside door handle, bezel-to-door screws, then remove the bezel.

2. Remove the door trim panel fasteners by prying with a suitable trim panel removal tool, then remove the trim panel.

To install:

3. Replace any broken retainers and push the door panel with the retainers into the door.

4. Install the door inside handle bezel cover.

5. Install the inside handle and bezel to door screws.

Liftgate Trim Panel

REMOVAL & INSTALLATION

▶ **See Figure 39**

1. Open the liftgate.

2. Remove the speaker grilles from the trim finish panel by carefully releasing the plastic clips at the top of each grille.

3. Remove both speakers.

4. Unfasten the screws under the grilles retaining the upper end of the trim panel to the lift gate inner panel.

5. Remove the four screws along the bottom and the two at each end of the trim panel.

6. Remove the pull strap.

7. Disengage the two plastic retaining studs from the grommets in the inner panel using a garnish clip removal tool.

8. Remove the trim panel from the liftgate.

9. Installation is the reverse of the removal procedure. Align the finish panel retaining studs with rings in the inner panel, then with the palm of hand; tap the retainers into the rings.

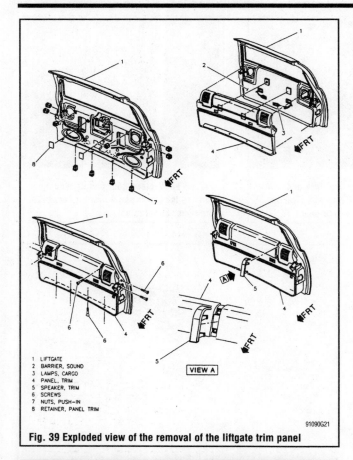

1 LIFTGATE
2 BARRIER, SOUND
3 LAMPS, CARGO
4 PANEL, TRIM
5 SPEAKER, TRIM
6 SCREWS
7 NUTS, PUSH-IN
8 RETAINER, PANEL TRIM

91090G21

Fig. 39 Exploded view of the removal of the liftgate trim panel

Quarter Trim Panels

REMOVAL & INSTALLATION

Right or Left Side

♦ **See Figures 40 and 41**

1. Remove any seats necessary to gain access to the trim panel.
2. Unfasten the upper and lower E-pillar safety belt bolts, if so equipped.
3. Remove the back body pillar finishing panel.
4. Remove the quarter trim rear finish molding assembly.
5. Remove the upper trim assembly.
6. Unfasten the upper and lower lock pillar safety belt bolts, if so equipped.

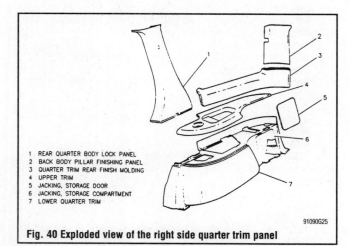

1 REAR QUARTER BODY LOCK PANEL
2 BACK BODY PILLAR FINISHING PANEL
3 QUARTER TRIM REAR FINISH MOLDING
4 UPPER TRIM
5 JACKING, STORAGE DOOR
6 JACKING, STORAGE COMPARTMENT
7 LOWER QUARTER TRIM

91090G25

Fig. 40 Exploded view of the right side quarter trim panel

1 PANEL, BODY LOCK PILLAR FINISHING BACK

2 MOLDING, QUARTER TRIM REAR FINISHING

3 PANEL, BODY LOCK PILLAR TRIM FINISHING

4 PANEL, QUARTER UPPER TRIM FINISHING

5 PANEL, CENTER PILLAR TRIM FINISHING

6 PANEL, QUARTER LOWER TRIM FINISHING

7 TRIM, REAR WHEELHOUSE LOWER

8 BRACKET, INFLATOR AIR SOLENOID VALVE
   AND RELAY

9 COVER, INFLATOR/ACCESSORY POWER OUTLET

10 PANEL, REAR WHEELHOUSE TRIM FINISHING

11 PANEL, CENTER PILLAR/QUARTER LOWER
    TRIM FINISHING

C34 / C36 ONLY

91090G26

Fig. 41 Left side quarter trim panel assembly—disassembled view

7. Remove the rear quarter body lock panel screws.
8. To remove the right side quarter trim panel, remove the jack assembly.
9. To remove the left side quarter trim panel, perform the following:
   a. Remove the stowage compartment access panel.
   b. Remove the Electronic Level Control (ELC) unit, if so equipped.
10. Unfasten the lower quarter trim assembly-to-space frame screws, then remove the right or left side lower quarter trim assembly, as applicable.

To install:

11. Install the lower quarter trim assembly and retaining screws to the space frame.
12. To install the left side quarter trim panel, perform the following:
    a. Install the Electronic Level Control (E.L.C) unit, if so equipped.
    b. Remove the stowage compartment access panel.
13. If installing the right side quarter trim panel, install the jack assembly.
14. Install the rear quarter body lock panel.
15. If equipped, install the upper and lower lock pillar safety belt bolts.
16. Install the upper trim assembly.
17. Install the quarter trim rear finish molding assembly.
18. Install the back body pillar finishing panel.
19. If equipped, install the upper and lower E-pillar safety belt bolts.
20. If removed, install the seats as necessary.

Left Side Forward

The quarter trim finish panel assembly and the C-pillar trim finish panel assembly are mated at the assembly plant and are collectively referred to as the left side forward quarter trim assembly.

1. Remove any seats necessary to gain access to the trim panel.
2. Unfasten the upper and lower body lock pillar safety belt bolts, if so equipped.
3. Remove the two body lock panel screws and remove the body lock panel.
4. Remove the back body pillar finishing panel.
5. Remove the rear quarter upper trim assembly.
6. Unfasten the 2 lower quarter trim assembly-to-space frame screws as necessary to disengage the clips that secure the forward trim assembly to the rear quarter trim assembly.

7. If equipped, remove the upper and lower C-pillar safety belt bolts.
8. Remove the C-pillar garnish screws, then push the seat belt through the C-pillar garnish.
9. Remove the C-pillar molding and the forward quarter trim assembly.

To install:
10. Push the seat belt through the C-pillar garnish.
11. Install the C-pillar molding and the forward quarter trim assembly.
12. Install the two C-pillar garnish screws.
13. Install the upper and lower C-pillar safety belt bolts, if so equipped.
14. Reattach the forward trim assembly to the rear trim assembly,
15. Install the 2 quarter trim assembly to space frame screws.
16. Install the rear quarter upper trim assembly.
17. Install the back body pillar-finishing panel.
18. Install the body lock panel.
19. If equipped, install the upper and lower body lock pillar safety belt bolts.
20. Install any seats that were removed to gain access to the trim panel.

Door Locks

REMOVAL & INSTALLATION

Front Door

▶ See Figures 42, 43 and 44

1. Remove the inside door trim panel, as outlined earlier in this section.
2. Disconnect the outside handle-to-lock assembly rod.
3. Disconnect the lock cylinder-to-lock assembly rod.
4. Disconnect the inside handle-to-lock assembly rod.
5. Unfasten the lock assembly screws, then remove the lock from the door.

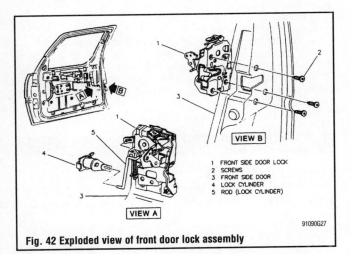
Fig. 42 Exploded view of front door lock assembly

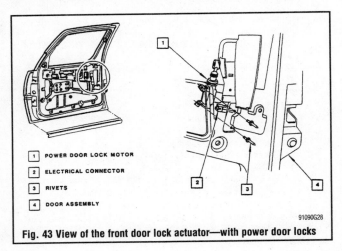
Fig. 43 View of the front door lock actuator—with power door locks

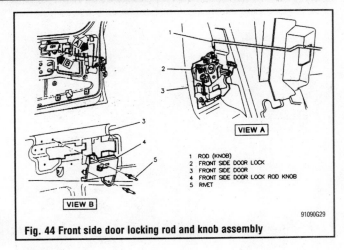
Fig. 44 Front side door locking rod and knob assembly

To install:
6. Position the lock assembly to the door and install the retaining screws.
7. Connect the inside handle-to-lock assembly rod.
8. Attach the lock cylinder-to-lock assembly rod.
9. Connect the outside handle-to-lock assembly rod.
10. Install the inside door trim panel, as outlined earlier in this section..

Sliding Door

▶ See Figures 45 and 46

1. Remove the sliding door trim panel, as outlined earlier in this section.
2. Disconnect the control rods from the lock assembly by prying the clip anchor out of the hole and pushing the clip away from the lever.
3. Support the door and remove the center roller bracket to door screws.

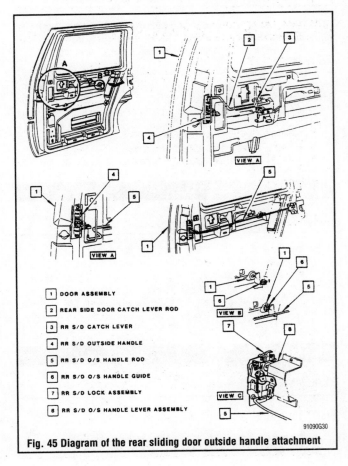
Fig. 45 Diagram of the rear sliding door outside handle attachment

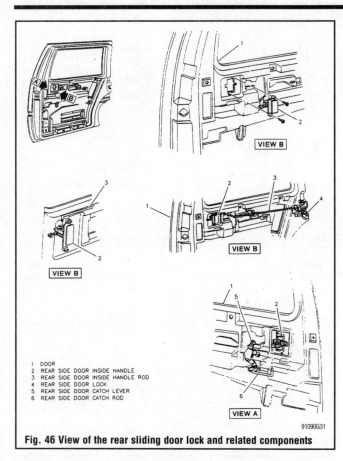

1 DOOR
2 REAR SIDE DOOR INSIDE HANDLE
3 REAR SIDE DOOR INSIDE HANDLE ROD
4 REAR SIDE DOOR LOCK
5 REAR SIDE DOOR CATCH LEVER
6 REAR SIDE DOOR CATCH ROD

91090G31

Fig. 46 View of the rear sliding door lock and related components

4. Using a ¼ in. drill bit, drill out the rod guide to door rivets. Remove the rod guide from the door.
5. Unfasten the lock assembly retaining screws, then remove the lock assembly.
To install:
6. Position the lock assembly to the door and secure with the retaining screws.
7. Attach the guide rod to the door using ¼ in. diameter bolts, ½ in. long, with a spring washer and nut.
8. Install the control rods to the lock assembly.
9. Install the center roller bracket to door screws.
10. Install the door trim panel, as outlined earlier in this section.

Liftgate Lock

REMOVAL & INSTALLATION

1. Open the liftgate and remove the speaker grilles.
2. Remove the liftgate trim finish panel as outlined earlier in this section.
3. Unfasten the bolts attaching the lock assembly to the inner door panel, then remove the lock assembly through the access hole.
4. Detach the electrical connector from the door ajar switch, then remove the lock assembly and switch.
5. Installation is the reverse of the removal procedure.

Door Glass

REMOVAL & INSTALLATION

Front

1. Remove the door trim panel, as outlined earlier in this section.
2. Remove the front and rear garnish moldings.

3. Remove the lower run channel.
4. Remove the outer window sealing strip.
5. Drill out the rivet and remove the window run channel from the door.
6. Drop the window out of the rear run channel and pull the window up and out of the vehicle.

✳✳ CAUTION

To avoid personal injury, always wear heavy gloves when handling window glass!

To install:
7. Install the window to the door frame and bolt or rivet in place.
8. Install the lower run channel.
9. Install the outer window-sealing strip.
10. Install the garnish moldings and the door trim panel.

Manual Window Regulator

REMOVAL & INSTALLATION

1. Remove the door trim panel, as outlined earlier in this section.
2. Roll the window up, and apply fabric backed body tape from the window over the top of the door to the other side of the window. This will hold the window in position when the regulator is removed.
3. Using a ³⁄₁₆ drill bit, drill the rivet heads from the regulator to door rivets.
4. Push the regulator into the door and slide it forward then rearward to remove the regulator arms from the sash and the regulator rail.
5. Fold the regulator arms together and remove the regulator from the door access hole.
To install:
6. Place the regulator into the door through the access hole.
7. Place the regulator arm rollers into the sash and the regulator rail.
8. Push the regulator through the regulator door opening and align the holes in the regulator with the holes in the door.
9. If the proper size rivets are unavailable, or a rivet gun isn't handy, then use ¼ in. bolts, about a ½ in. long, with a spring washer and nut to reattach the regulator to the door.
10. Install the trim panel, as outlined earlier in this section.

Power Window Regulator and Motor

REMOVAL & INSTALLATION

▶ **See Figures 47, 48, 49 and 50**

1. Disconnect the negative battery cable.
2. Remove the door trim panel, as outlined earlier in this section.
3. Roll the window up, and apply fabric backed body tape from the window over the top of the door to the other side of the window. This will hold the window in position when the regulator is removed.
4. Disconnect the wiring harness from the motor.
5. Use a ¼ in. drill bit to drill the rivet heads, then remove the regulator from the door.
6. Drill out the motor to regulator rivets, then remove the regulator from the motor.
To install:
7. Lubricate the motor drive gear and the regulator sector teeth, check the mesh of the motor to the regulator and rivet the motor to the regulator.
8. Place the regulator through the access opening and position the regulator arm roller into the sash and regulator rail.
9. Push the regulator through the regulator door opening and align the holes in the regulator with the holes in the door.
10. Use ¼ in. diameter bolts, ½ in. long, with nylon inserted nuts to reattach the regulator to the door, if the proper size rivets and rivet gun are unavailable.
11. Install the wiring harness from the regulator to the motor.
12. Install the trim panel as outlined earlier in this section, then reconnect the battery cable.

Fig. 47 Location of the window regulator (transmission) and door lock actuator

Fig. 48 The window regulator and motor are riveted to inner door panel

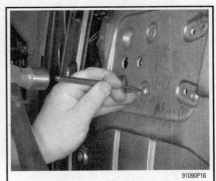

Fig. 49 Use a hammer and a punch to knock the steel center pin from the rivet

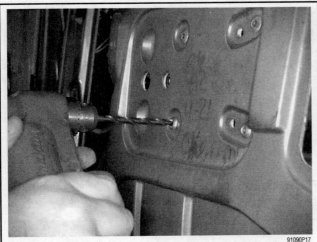

Fig. 50 You must drill out the rivets that secure the window regulator to the door

Windshield and Fixed Glass

REMOVAL & INSTALLATION

If your windshield, or other fixed window, is cracked or chipped, you may decide to replace it with a new one yourself. However, there are two main reasons why replacement windshields and other window glass should be installed only by a professional automotive glass technician: safety and cost.

The most important reason a professional should install automotive glass is for safety. The glass in the vehicle, especially the windshield, is designed with safety in mind in case of a collision. The windshield is specially manufactured from two panes of specially-tempered glass with a thin layer of transparent plastic between them. This construction allows the glass to "give" in the event that a part of your body hits the windshield during the collision, and prevents the glass from shattering, which could cause lacerations, blinding and other harm to passengers of the vehicle. The other fixed windows are designed to be tempered so that if they break during a collision, they shatter in such a way that there are no large pointed glass pieces. The professional automotive glass technician knows how to install the glass in a vehicle so that it will function optimally during a collision. Without the proper experience, knowledge, and tools, installing a piece of automotive glass you could lead to additional harm if an accident should ever occur.

Cost is also a factor when deciding to install automotive glass you. Perform-

ing this could cost you much more than a professional may charge for the same job. Since the windshield is designed to break under stress, an often life saving characteristic, windshields tend to break VERY easily when an inexperienced person attempts to install one. Do-it-yourselfers buying two, three or even four windshields from a salvage yard because they have broken them during installation are common stories. Also, since the automotive glass is designed to prevent the outside elements from entering your vehicle, improper installation can lead to water and air leaks. Annoying whining noises at highway speeds from air leaks or inside body panel rusting from water leaks can add to your stress level and subtract from your wallet. After buying two or three windshields, installing them and ending up with a leak that produces a noise while driving and water damage during rainstorms, the cost of having a professional do it correctly the first time may be much more alluring. We here at Chilton, therefore, advise that you have a professional automotive glass technician service any broken glass on your vehicle.

WINDSHIELD CHIP REPAIR

▶ See Figures 51 thru 65

➡Check with your state and local authorities on the laws for state safety inspection. Some states or municipalities may not allow chip repair as a viable option for correcting stone damage to your windshield.

Although severely cracked or damaged windshields must be replaced, there

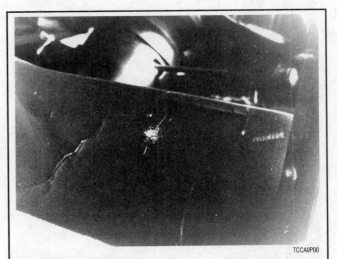

Fig. 51 Small chips on your windshield can be fixed with an aftermarket repair kit, such as the one from Loctite®

Fig. 52 To repair a chip, clean the windshield with glass cleaner and dry it completely

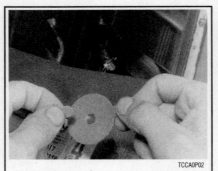

Fig. 53 Remove the center from the adhesive disc and peel off the backing from one side of the disc . . .

Fig. 54 . . . then, press it on the windshield so that the chip is centered in the hole

Fig. 55 Be sure that the tab points upward on the windshield

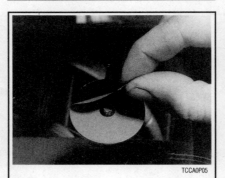

Fig. 56 Peel the backing off the exposed side of the adhesive disc . . .

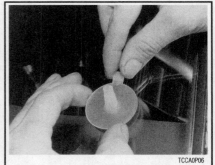

Fig. 57 . . . then, position the plastic pedestal on the adhesive disc, ensuring that the tabs are aligned

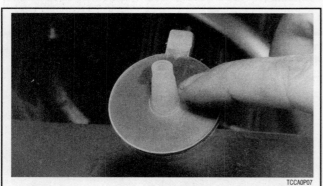

Fig. 58 Press the pedestal firmly on the adhesive disc to create an adequate seal . . .

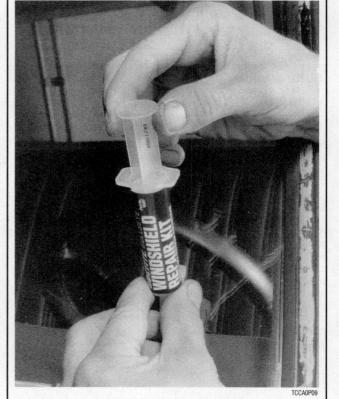

Fig. 60 Hold the syringe with one hand while pulling the plunger back with the other hand

Fig. 59 . . . then, install the applicator syringe nipple in the pedestal's hole

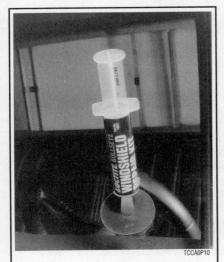

Fig. 61 After applying the solution, allow the entire assembly to sit until it has set completely

TCCA0P10

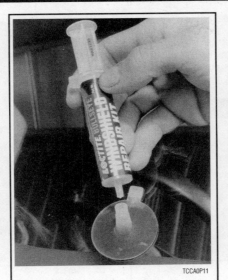

Fig. 62 After the solution has set, remove the syringe from the pedestal . . .

TCCA0P11

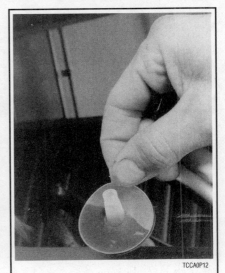

Fig. 63 . . . then, peel the pedestal off the adhesive disc . . .

TCCA0P12

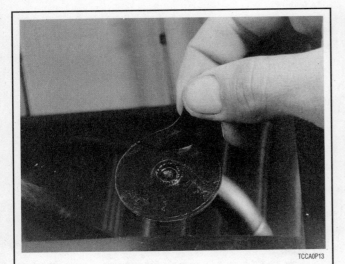

Fig. 64 . . . and peel the adhesive disc off of the windshield

TCCA0P13

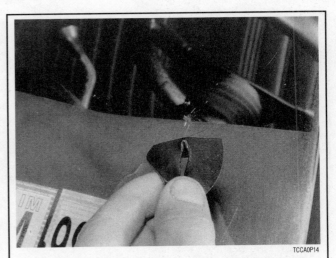

Fig. 65 The chip will still be slightly visible, but it should be filled with the hardened solution

TCCA0P14

is something that you can do to prolong or even prevent the need for replacement of a chipped windshield. There are many companies, which offer windshield chip repair products, such as Loctite's® Bullseye™ windshield repair kit. These kits usually consist of a syringe, pedestal and a sealing adhesive. The syringe is mounted on the pedestal and is used to create a vacuum which pulls the plastic layer against the glass. This helps make the chip transparent. The adhesive is then injected which seals the chip and helps to prevent further stress cracks from developing. Refer to the sequence of photos to get a general idea of what windshield chip repair involves.

➡Always follow the specific manufacturer's instructions.

Liftgate Glass

REMOVAL & INSTALLATION

1. Open the liftgate assembly.
2. Remove the right and left window garnish moldings.
3. Remove the two window bracket assemblies from the liftgate outer panel by drilling out the attaching rivets.
4. Lift the window from the weather-strip assembly.

5. Remove the four bolts and bushings from the window brackets, then carefully remove the window from the liftgate.
6. Installation is the reverse of the removal procedure.

Inside Rearview Mirror and Arm

REMOVAL & INSTALLATION

The rearview mirror is attached to a support with a retaining screw. The support is secured to the windshield glass. The glass supplier, using a plastic polyvinyl butyl adhesive, installs the support. To reinstall a mirror support arm to the windshield, follow the instructions included with an inside mirror installation kit, which may be purchased at most auto supply stores.

The basic steps of mirror and support replacement are as follows:
• Mark the outside of the windshield to where the mirror mounts.
• Separate the pedestal mount from the mirror.
• If glue was left on the windshield, scrape it off with a razor blade. Do the same to the pedestal mount.
• Clean the windshield thoroughly with alcohol, or window cleaner. Sand the windshield side of the pedestal mount lightly, then clean it very thoroughly.

• Wet a lint free cloth or paper towel and wipe the affected areas with water; allow to dry completely.

• Apply the accelerator to the windshield and pedestal, and following the directions on the mirror kit, apply the glue to the pedestal.

• Attach the pedestal to the windshield and hold it in position for 30 seconds. Reattach the mirror when the glue has set. Wait at least 30 minutes.

Seats

REMOVAL & INSTALLATION

Front Seat

▶ See Figures 66, 67 and 68

1. If removing the driver's seat, perform the following:
   a. Disconnect the negative battery cable.
   b. Detach the seat belt harness connector from the body wiring harness.

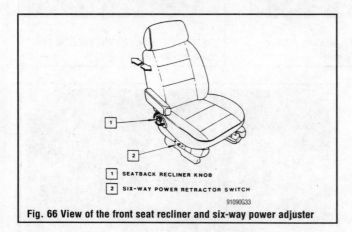

1	SEATBACK RECLINER KNOB		
2	SIX-WAY POWER RETRACTOR SWITCH		

91090G33

Fig. 66 View of the front seat recliner and six-way power adjuster

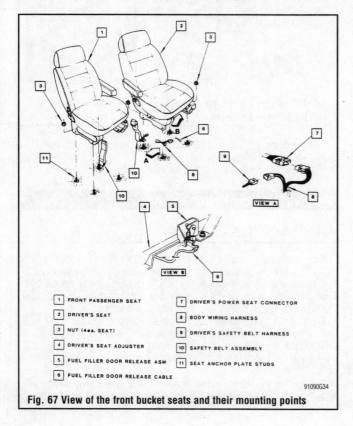

1	FRONT PASSENGER SEAT	7	DRIVER'S POWER SEAT CONNECTOR
2	DRIVER'S SEAT	8	BODY WIRING HARNESS
3	NUT (4 ea. SEAT)	9	DRIVER'S SAFETY BELT HARNESS
4	DRIVER'S SEAT ADJUSTER	10	SAFETY BELT ASSEMBLY
5	FUEL FILLER DOOR RELEASE ASM	11	SEAT ANCHOR PLATE STUDS
6	FUEL FILLER DOOR RELEASE CABLE		

91090G34

Fig. 67 View of the front bucket seats and their mounting points

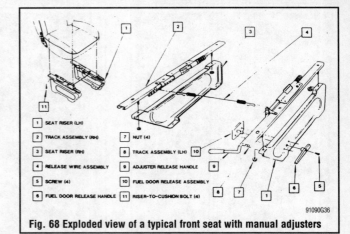

1	SEAT RISER (LH)	7	NUT (4)
2	TRACK ASSEMBLY (RH)	8	TRACK ASSEMBLY (LH)
3	SEAT RISER (RH)	9	ADJUSTER RELEASE HANDLE
4	RELEASE WIRE ASSEMBLY	10	FUEL DOOR RELEASE ASSEMBLY
5	SCREW (4)	11	RISER-TO-CUSHION BOLT (4)
6	FUEL DOOR RELEASE HANDLE		

91090G36

Fig. 68 Exploded view of a typical front seat with manual adjusters

c. If equipped, unplug the power seat connector from the body wiring harness.

d. Disconnect the fuel filler door release cable.

2. Remove the nuts attaching the seat frame to the seat anchor plate studs on the floor pan.

3. Disconnect the seat belt assembly, then remove the seat from the vehicle.

To install:

4. Install the seat belt assembly over the rear inboard seat stud on the right hand side of the driver's seat or on the left hand side of the passenger's seat.

5. Install the power seat connection, if so equipped.

6. If installing the driver's side seat, install the seat belt harness connector and the fuel filler door release cable.

7. Install the seal retaining nuts and tighten them to 20 ft. lbs. (27 Nm)

Rear Bucket Seat

▶ See Figures 69 and 70

1. Remove all plate hole plugs.

2. Pull up the seat back latch lever and fold the seat back forward onto the seat cushion.

3. Pull up on the rear latch release strap to release the latching bar clamping the rear of the seat assembly to the rear seat anchors.

4. Pivot the rear of the seat assembly upward and toward the front of the vehicle.

5. Pull upward on the front of the latching bar, disconnect the seat riser frame from the front seat anchors, and remove the seat from the vehicle.

To install:

6. Place the seat locks in the open position by pulling upward on the strap, at the rear of the seat cushion.

7. Install the seat assembly over either the second or third row anchor plates in the floor plan.

8. Install the front legs of the seat through the slots in the front anchor plates and onto the seat anchors.

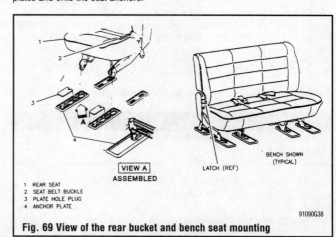

1	REAR SEAT
2	SEAT BELT BUCKLE
3	PLATE HOLE PLUG
4	ANCHOR PLATE

91090G38

Fig. 69 View of the rear bucket and bench seat mounting

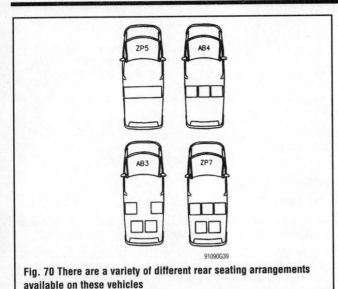

Fig. 70 There are a variety of different rear seating arrangements available on these vehicles

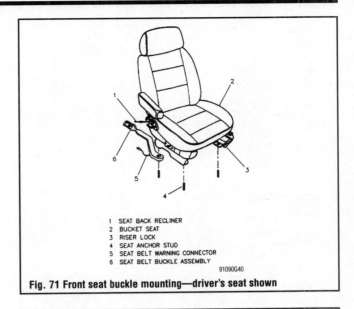

1   SEAT BACK RECLINER
2   BUCKET SEAT
3   RISER LOCK
4   SEAT ANCHOR STUD
5   SEAT BELT WARNING CONNECTOR
6   SEAT BELT BUCKLE ASSEMBLY

Fig. 71 Front seat buckle mounting—driver's seat shown

9. Close the seat locking levers to secure the seat.

10. Install the anchor plate hole plugs, over the open slots in the anchor plates, and snap them down securely into place.

11. Check that the seat is secured firmly to all 4 seat anchors.

Rear Bench Seat

▶ See Figures 69 and 70

1. Remove all plate hole plugs.

2. Fold the seat down onto the cushion of the seat.

3. Press the locking lever between the seat's rear legs to unlatch the seat assembly from the rear seat anchors.

4. Release the front seat legs from the seat anchors and remove the seat assembly.

To install:

5. Install the bench seat aligning the front of the seat over the second position in the anchor plates on the floor pan. Make sure the locks are in the open position.

6. Install the front legs of the seat through the slots in the front anchor.

7. Press the rear legs of the seat through the slots in the rear anchor plates and onto the seat anchors.

8. Unfold the seat back to an upright position.

9. Install the anchor plate hole plugs, over the open slots in the anchor plates, and snap them down securely into place.

10. Check that the bench seat is secured firmly to all 8 seat anchors.

Front Seat Belts

REMOVAL & INSTALLATION

▶ See Figures 71 and 72

➡The driver's and front passenger seat belt assemblies are attached to the body side frame locking B-pillars in a similar manner,

1. Remove the center B-pillar trim finish panel assembly from the body side frame.

2. Unsnap the plastic cover off the upper seat belt anchor bracket.

3. Remove the upper seat belt anchor bolt using a suitable Torx® driver.

4. Remove the lower seat belt anchor bolt using a ratchet with a Torx® driver.

5. Remove the seat belt retractor mechanism bolt using a ratchet with a Torx® driver.

6. Remove the seat belt retractor mechanism by feeding the assembly through one opening in the pillar trim finish panel and remove the seat belt retractor assembly.

7. Installation is the reverse of the removal procedure.

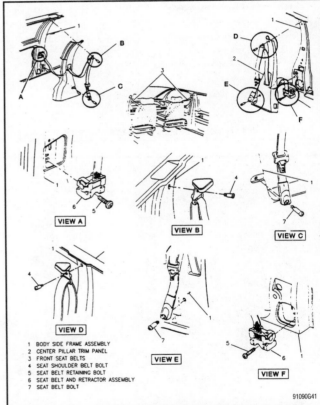

1   BODY SIDE FRAME ASSEMBLY
2   CENTER PILLAR TRIM PANEL
3   FRONT SEAT BELTS
4   SEAT SHOULDER BELT BOLT
5   SEAT BELT RETAINING BOLT
6   SEAT BELT AND RETRACTOR ASSEMBLY
7   SEAT BELT BOLT

Fig. 72 View of the different mountings for the front seat belt retention system

Shoulder Belt and Retractor Mechanism

REMOVAL & INSTALLATION

C-Pillar

▶ See Figures 73 and 74

➡The right and left side shoulder safety belts for second row bench or bucket seats are attached to the C-pillars in a similar manner.

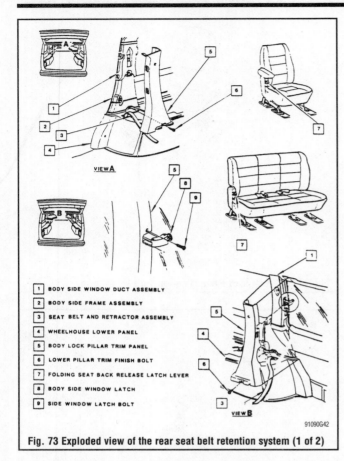

1 BODY SIDE WINDOW DUCT ASSEMBLY
2 BODY SIDE FRAME ASSEMBLY
3 SEAT BELT AND RETRACTOR ASSEMBLY
4 WHEELHOUSE LOWER PANEL
5 BODY LOCK PILLAR TRIM PANEL
6 LOWER PILLAR TRIM FINISH BOLT
7 FOLDING SEAT BACK RELEASE LATCH LEVER
8 BODY SIDE WINDOW LATCH
9 SIDE WINDOW LATCH BOLT

91090G42

Fig. 73 Exploded view of the rear seat belt retention system (1 of 2)

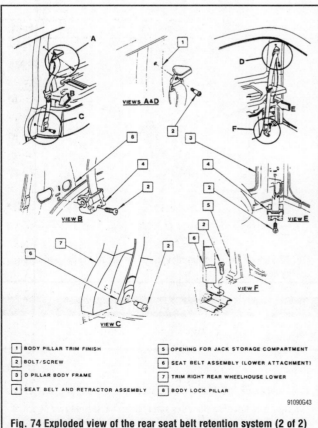

1 BODY PILLAR TRIM FINISH
2 BOLT/SCREW
3 D PILLAR BODY FRAME
4 SEAT BELT AND RETRACTOR ASSEMBLY
5 OPENING FOR JACK STORAGE COMPARTMENT
6 SEAT BELT ASSEMBLY (LOWER ATTACHMENT)
7 TRIM RIGHT REAR WHEELHOUSE LOWER
8 BODY LOCK PILLAR

91090G43

Fig. 74 Exploded view of the rear seat belt retention system (2 of 2)

1. Remove the center C-pillar trim finish panel assembly from the body side frame.
2. Unsnap the plastic cover off the upper seat belt anchor bracket.
3. Remove the upper seat belt anchor bolt using a suitable Torx® driver.
4. Remove the lower seat belt anchor bolt using a ratchet with a Torx® driver.
5. Remove the seat belt retractor mechanism bolt using a ratchet with a Torx® driver.
6. Remove the seat belt retractor mechanism by feeding assembly up through the opening in the pillar trim finish panel and remove the seat belt retractor assembly.
7. Installation is the reverse of the removal procedure.

D-Pillar

♦ **See Figures 73 and 74**

➡**The right and left side shoulder safety belts for third row bucket seats are attached to the D-pillars in a similar manner.**

1. Remove the jack storage compartment cover on the right side or the compressor/inflator rear shock absorber cover on the left side.
2. Use a suitable Torx® driver to remove the seat belt retractor anchor bolt.
3. Remove the anchor bolt securing the seat belt to the floor pan.
4. Unsnap the plastic cover from the upper belt anchor bracket at the roof end of the D-pillar.
5. Remove the upper seat belt anchor bolt using a suitable Torx® driver.
6. Remove the rear wheelhouse upper trim panel assembly.
7. Remove the shoulder belt retractor mechanism.
8. Installation is the reverse of the removal procedure.

Power Seat Adjuster and Motor Assembly

REMOVAL & INSTALLATION

♦ **See Figure 75**

1. Disconnect the negative battery cable.
2. Detach the 2-wire connector (power lead) from the floor.
3. Disconnect the fuel door latch cable from the fuel release mechanism.
4. Separate the seat adjuster from the floor pan by removing the four mounting stud nuts.
5. Remove the 4-mounting studs and separate the seat cushion from the seat adjuster.
6. Loosen the setscrew on the fuel release handle and remove the handle.
7. Drill out the two rivets from the fuel release assembly and remove the assembly.
8. Remove the inboard and outboard side shields by removing the two mounting screws from the top of the shields outward until detached from the seat adjuster.
9. Detach the 6 cable connector from the motor and remove the tie wrap from the inboard side shield.
10. Remove the switch module from the inboard side shield.
11. Spread the positive connection prongs, protruding from the rear at the wire harness connector, outward and separate the switch module from the wire harness connector.
12. Using an offset screwdriver, remove the four screws securing the motor to the transmission assembly.
13. Disconnect the drive cables from the motor.
    To install:
14. Install the 3 drive cables to the motor.
15. Align the drive cables in the motor with the bearing insert on the transmission assembly.
16. Using an offset screwdriver and four screws, install the motor to the transmission.
17. Snap the connector on the wire harnesses assembly into the switch module.
18. Align the switch module with the alignment slots in the inboard side shield and snap the switch module into place.

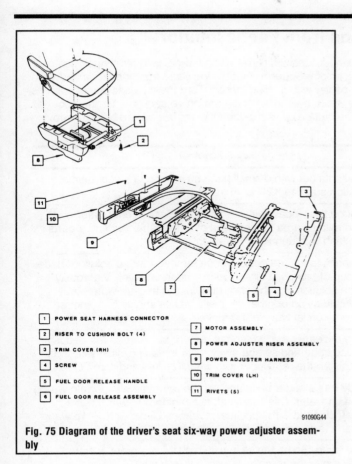

1	POWER SEAT HARNESS CONNECTOR
2	RISER TO CUSHION BOLT (4)
3	TRIM COVER (RH)
4	SCREW
5	FUEL DOOR RELEASE HANDLE
6	FUEL DOOR RELEASE ASSEMBLY
7	MOTOR ASSEMBLY
8	POWER ADJUSTER RISER ASSEMBLY
9	POWER ADJUSTER HARNESS
10	TRIM COVER (LH)
11	RIVETS (5)

91090G44

Fig. 75 Diagram of the driver's seat six-way power adjuster assembly

19. Route the wiring harness over the inboard upper support making certain the harness is situated in the cut out provided in the side shield. Secure the wiring harnesses to the motor with the tie wrap and reconnect the wiring harness to the motor.

20. Install the inboard and outboard side shields onto the upper supports and inserts the mounting screws.

21. Install the fuel release bracket to the inside left hand riser, using two rivets.

22. Install the fuel release handle.

23. Install the seat cushion to the adjuster.

24. Install the seat adjuster to the floor pan and tighten the bolts to 32 ft. lbs. (43 Nm).

25. Install the power lead to the connector.

26. Connect the fuel door release cable to the fuel door release lever mechanism.

27. Connect the negative battery cable.

TORQUE SPECIFICATIONS

Components	English	Metric
Air Inlet Grille Screw	18 inch lbs.	2 Nm
Door Jamb Switch Screw	53 inch lbs.	6 Nm
Hood Latch (Primary) support bolts	18 ft. lbs.	25 Nm
Secondary Latch to Hood Bolts	18 ft. lbs.	25 Nm
Front Door Lock Module Screws	89 inch lbs.	10 Nm
Door hinge-to-door bolts	16 ft. lbs.	22 Nm
Door hinge-to-pillar bolts	16 ft. lbs.	22 Nm
Door lock assembly retaining bolts	62 inch lbs.	7 Nm
Door striker bolts	18 ft. lbs.	25 Nm
Power Sliding Door Actuator Motor bolts	89 inch lbs.	10 Nm
Power Sliding Door Actuator Motor nuts	89 inch lbs.	10 Nm
Sliding Door Center Roller Bracket Bolts	18 ft. lbs.	25 Nm
Sliding Door Lower Roller Bracket Bolts	18 ft. lbs.	25 Nm
Front seat retaining nuts	30 ft. lbs.	40 Nm
Hood hinge bolts	18 ft. lbs.	25 Nm
Hood latch bolts	18 ft. lbs.	25 Nm
Outside mirror retaining bolts	89 inch lbs.	10 Nm
Power Rear Quarter Window Actuator Screws	89 inch lbs.	10 Nm
Front Impact Bar Bolts	18 ft. lbs.	25 Nm
Rear Impact Bar Bolts	18 ft. lbs.	25 Nm

91090C01

How to Remove Stains from Fabric Interior

For rest results, spots and stains should be removed as soon as possible. Never use gasoline, lacquer thinner, acetone, nail polish remover or bleach. Use a 3' x 3" piece of cheesecloth. Squeeze most of the liquid from the fabric and wipe the stained fabric from the outside of the stain toward the center with a lifting motion. Turn the cheesecloth as soon as one side becomes soiled. When using water to remove a stain, be sure to wash the entire section after the spot has been removed to avoid water stains. Encrusted spots can be broken up with a dull knife and vacuumed before removing the stain.

Type of Stain	How to Remove It
Surface spots	Brush the spots out with a small hand brush or use a commercial preparation such as K2R to lift the stain.
Mildew	Clean around the mildew with warm suds. Rinse in cold water and soak the mildew area in a solution of 1 part table salt and 2 parts water. Wash with upholstery cleaner.
Water stains	Water stains in fabric materials can be removed with a solution made from 1 cup of table salt dissolved in 1 quart of water. Vigorously scrub the solution into the stain and rinse with clear water. Water stains in nylon or other synthetic fabrics should be removed with a commercial type spot remover.
Chewing gum, tar, crayons, shoe polish (greasy stains)	Do not use a cleaner that will soften gum or tar. Harden the deposit with an ice cube and scrape away as much as possible with a dull knife. Moisten the remainder with cleaning fluid and scrub clean.
Ice cream, candy	Most candy has a sugar base and can be removed with a cloth wrung out in warm water. Oily candy, after cleaning with warm water, should be cleaned with upholstery cleaner. Rinse with warm water and clean the remainder with cleaning fluid.
Wine, alcohol, egg, milk, soft drink (non-greasy stains)	Do not use soap. Scrub the stain with a cloth wrung out in warm water. Remove the remainder with cleaning fluid.
Grease, oil, lipstick, butter and related stains	Use a spot remover to avoid leaving a ring. Work from the outisde of the stain to the center and dry with a clean cloth when the spot is gone.
Headliners (cloth)	Mix a solution of warm water and foam upholstery cleaner to give thick suds. Use only foam—liquid may streak or spot. Clean the entire headliner in one operation using a circular motion with a natural sponge.
Headliner (vinyl)	Use a vinyl cleaner with a sponge and wipe clean with a dry cloth.
Seats and door panels	Mix 1 pint upholstery cleaner in 1 gallon of water. Do not soak the fabric around the buttons.
Leather or vinyl fabric	Use a multi-purpose cleaner full strength and a stiff brush. Let stand 2 minutes and scrub thoroughly. Wipe with a clean, soft rag.
Nylon or synthetic fabrics	For normal stains, use the same procedures you would for washing cloth upholstery. If the fabric is extremely dirty, use a multi-purpose cleaner full strength with a stiff scrub brush. Scrub thoroughly in all directions and wipe with a cotton towel or soft rag.

TCCA0C01

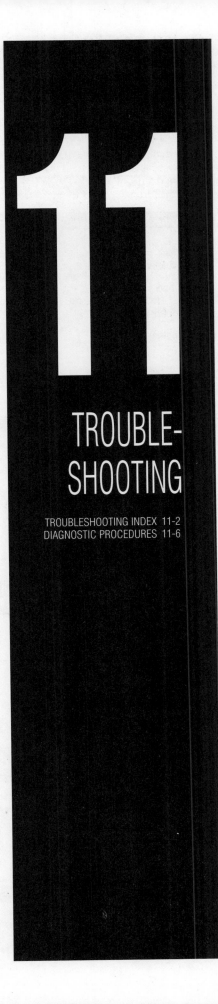

11

TROUBLE-SHOOTING

Condition   **Section/Item Number**

The following troubleshooting charts are divided into 7 sections covering engine, drive train, brakes, wheels/tires/steering/suspension, electrical accessories, instruments and gauges, and climate control. The first portion (or index) consists of a list of symptoms, along with section and item numbers. After selecting the appropriate condition, refer to the corresponding diagnostic procedure in the second portion's specified location.

INDEX

SECTION 1. ENGINE

A. Engine Starting Problems

Gasoline Engines

Engine turns over, but will not start	1-A, 1
Engine does not turn over when attempting to start	1-A, 2
Engine stalls immediately when started	1-A, 3
Starter motor spins, but does not engage	1-A, 4
Engine is difficult to start when cold	1-A, 5
Engine is difficult to start when hot	1-A, 6

Diesel Engines

Engine turns over but won't start	1-A, 1
Engine does not turn over when attempting to start	1-A, 2
Engine stalls after starting	1-A, 3
Starter motor spins, but does not engage	1-A, 4
Engine is difficult to start	1-A, 5

B. Engine Running Conditions

Gasoline Engines

Engine runs poorly, hesitates	1-B, 1
Engine lacks power	1-B, 2
Engine has poor fuel economy	1-B, 3
Engine runs on (diesels) when turned off	1-B, 4
Engine knocks and pings during heavy acceleration, and on steep hills	1-B, 5
Engine accelerates but vehicle does not gain speed	1-B, 6

Diesel Engines

Engine runs poorly	1-B, 1
Engine lacks power	1-B, 2

C. Engine Noises, Odors and Vibrations

Engine makes a knocking or pinging noise when accelerating	1-C, 1
Starter motor grinds when used	1-C, 2
Engine makes a screeching noise	1-C, 3
Engine makes a growling noise	1-C, 4
Engine makes a ticking or tapping noise	1-C, 5
Engine makes a heavy knocking noise	1-C, 6
Vehicle has a fuel odor when driven	1-C, 7
Vehicle has a rotten egg odor when driven	1-C, 8
Vehicle has a sweet odor when driven	1-C, 9
Engine vibrates when idling	1-C, 10
Engine vibrates during acceleration	1-C, 11

D. Engine Electrical System

Battery goes dead while driving	1-D, 1
Battery goes dead overnight	1-D, 2

E. Engine Cooling System

Engine overheats	1-E, 1
Engine loses coolant	1-E, 2
Engine temperature remains cold when driving	1-E, 3
Engine runs hot	1-E, 4

F. Engine Exhaust System

Exhaust rattles at idle speed	1-F, 1
Exhaust system vibrates when driving	1-F, 2
Exhaust system seems too low	1-F, 3
Exhaust seems loud	1-F, 4

Condition	Section/Item Number

SECTION 2. DRIVE TRAIN

A. Automatic Transmission

Transmission shifts erratically	2-A, 1
Transmission will not engage	2-A, 2
Transmission will not downshift during heavy acceleration	2-A, 3

B. Manual Transmission

Transmission grinds going into forward gears while driving	2-B, 1; 2-C, 2
Transmission jumps out of gear	2-B, 2
Transmission difficult to shift	2-B, 3; 2-C, 2
Transmission leaks fluid	2-B, 4

C. Clutch

Clutch slips on hills or during sudden acceleration	2-C, 1
Clutch will not disengage, difficult to shift	2-C, 2
Clutch is noisy when the clutch pedal is pressed	2-C, 3
Clutch pedal extremely difficult to press	2-C, 4
Clutch pedal remains down when pressed	2-C, 5
Clutch chatters when engaging	2-C, 6

D. Differential and Final Drive

Differential makes a low pitched rumbling noise	2-D, 1
Differential makes a howling noise	2-D, 2

E. Transfer Assembly

All Wheel and Four Wheel Drive Vehicles

Leaks fluid from seals or vent after being driven	2-E, 1
Makes excessive noise while driving	2-E, 2
Jumps out of gear	2-E, 3

F. Driveshaft

Rear Wheel, All Wheel and Four Wheel Drive Vehicles

Clunking noise from center of vehicle shifting from forward to reverse	2-F, 1
Excessive vibration from center of vehicle when accelerating	2-F, 2

G. Axles

All Wheel and Four Wheel Drive Vehicles

Front or rear wheel makes a clicking noise	2-G, 1
Front or Rear wheel vibrates with increased speed	2-G, 2

Front Wheel Drive Vehicles

Front wheel makes a clicking noise	2-G, 3
Rear wheel makes a clicking noise	2-G, 4

Rear Wheel Drive Vehicles

Front or rear wheel makes a clicking noise	2-G, 5
Rear wheel shudders or vibrates	2-G, 6

H. Other Drive Train Conditions

Burning odor from center of vehicle when accelerating	2-H, 1; 2-C, 1; 3-A, 9
Engine accelerates, but vehicle does not gain speed	2-H, 2; 2-C, 1; 3-A, 9

SECTION 3. BRAKE SYSTEM

Brakes pedal pulsates or shimmies when pressed	3-A, 1
Brakes make a squealing noise	3-A, 2
Brakes make a grinding noise	3-A, 3
Vehicle pulls to one side during braking	3-A, 4
Brake pedal feels spongy or has excessive brake pedal travel	3-A, 5
Brake pedal feel is firm, but brakes lack sufficient stopping power or fade	3-A, 6

Condition	Section/Item Number
Vehicle has excessive front end dive or locks rear brakes too easily	3-A, 7
Brake pedal goes to floor when pressed and will not pump up	3-A, 8
Brakes make a burning odor	3-A, 9

SECTION 4. WHEELS, TIRES, STEERING AND SUSPENSION

A. Wheels and Wheel Bearings

All Wheel and Four Wheel Drive Vehicles

Front wheel or wheel bearing loose	4-A, 1
Rear wheel or wheel bearing loose	4-A, 2

Front Wheel Drive Vehicles

Front wheel or wheel bearing loose	4-A, 1
Rear wheel or wheel bearing loose	4-A, 2

Rear Wheel Drive Vehicles

Front wheel or wheel bearing loose	4-A, 1
Rear wheel or wheel bearing loose	4-A, 2

B. Tires

Tires worn on inside tread	4-B, 1
Tires worn on outside tread	4-B, 2
Tires worn unevenly	4-B, 3

C. Steering

Excessive play in steering wheel	4-C, 1
Steering wheel shakes at cruising speeds	4-C, 2
Steering wheel shakes when braking	3-A, 1
Steering wheel becomes stiff when turned	4-C, 4

D. Suspension

Vehicle pulls to one side	4-D, 1
Vehicle is very bouncy over bumps	4-D, 2
Vehicle seems to lean excessively in turns	4-D, 3
Vehicle ride quality seems excessively harsh	4-D, 4
Vehicle seems low or leans to one side	4-D, 5

E. Driving Noises and Vibrations

Noises

Vehicle makes a clicking noise when driven	4-E, 1
Vehicle makes a clunking or knocking noise over bumps	4-E, 2
Vehicle makes a low pitched rumbling noise when driven	4-E, 3
Vehicle makes a squeaking noise over bumps	4-E, 4

Vibrations

Vehicle vibrates when driven	4-E, 5

SECTION 5. ELECTRICAL ACCESSORIES

A. Headlights

One headlight only works on high or low beam	5-A, 1
Headlight does not work on high or low beam	5-A, 2
Headlight(s) very dim	5-A, 3

B. Tail, Running and Side Marker Lights

Tail light, running light or side marker light inoperative	5-B, 1
Tail light, running light or side marker light works intermittently	5-B, 2
Tail light, running light or side marker light very dim	5-B, 3

C. Interior Lights

Interior light inoperative	5-C, 1
Interior light works intermittently	5-C, 2
Interior light very dim	5-C, 3

Condition	Section/Item Number

D. Brake Lights

One brake light inoperative	5-D, 1
Both brake lights inoperative	5-D, 2
One or both brake lights very dim	5-D, 3

E. Warning Lights

Ignition, Battery and Alternator Warning Lights, Check Engine Light, Anti-Lock Braking System (ABS) Light, Brake Warning Light, Oil Pressure Warning Light, and Parking Brake Warning Light

Warning light(s) remains on after the engine is started	5-E, 1
Warning light(s) flickers on and off when driving	5-E, 2
Warning light(s) inoperative with ignition on, and engine not started	5-E, 3

F. Turn Signal and 4-Way Hazard Lights

Turn signals or hazard lights come on, but do not flash	5-F, 1
Turn signals or hazard lights do not function on either side	5-F, 2
Turn signals or hazard lights only work on one side	5-F, 3
One signal light does not work	5-F, 4
Turn signals flash too slowly	5-F, 5
Turn signals flash too fast	5-F, 6
Four-way hazard flasher indicator light inoperative	5-F, 7
Turn signal indicator light(s) do not work in either direction	5-F, 8
One turn signal indicator light does not work	5-F, 9

G. Horn

Horn does not operate	5-G, 1
Horn has an unusual tone	5-G, 2

H. Windshield Wipers

Windshield wipers do not operate	5-H, 1
Windshield wiper motor makes a humming noise, gets hot or blows fuses	5-H, 2
Windshield wiper motor operates but one or both wipers fail to move	5-H, 3
Windshield wipers will not park	5-H, 4

SECTION 6. INSTRUMENTS AND GAUGES

A. Speedometer (Cable Operated)

Speedometer does not work	6-A, 1
Speedometer needle fluctuates when driving at steady speeds	6-A, 2
Speedometer works intermittently	6-A, 3

B. Speedometer (Electronically Operated)

Speedometer does not work	6-B, 1
Speedometer works intermittently	6-B, 2

C. Fuel, Temperature and Oil Pressure Gauges

Gauge does not register	6-C, 1
Gauge operates erratically	6-C, 2
Gauge operates fully pegged	6-C, 3

SECTION 7. CLIMATE CONTROL

A. Air Conditioner

No air coming from air conditioner vents	7-A, 1
Air conditioner blows warm air	7-A, 2
Water collects on the interior floor when the air conditioner is used	7-A, 3
Air conditioner has a moldy odor when used	7-A, 4

B. Heater

Blower motor does not operate	7-B, 1
Heater blows cool air	7-B, 2
Heater steams the windshield when used	7-B, 3

DIAGNOSTIC PROCEDURES

1. ENGINE

1-A. Engine Starting Problems

Gasoline Engines

1. Engine turns over, but will not start

a. Check fuel level in fuel tank, add fuel if empty.

b. Check battery condition and state of charge. If voltage and load test below specification, charge or replace battery.

c. Check battery terminal and cable condition and tightness. Clean terminals and replace damaged, worn or corroded cables.

d. Check fuel delivery system. If fuel is not reaching the fuel injectors, check for a loose electrical connector or defective fuse, relay or fuel pump and replace as necessary.

e. Engine may have excessive wear or mechanical damage such as low cylinder cranking pressure, a broken camshaft drive system, insufficient valve clearance or bent valves.

f. Check for fuel contamination such as water in the fuel. During winter months, the water may freeze and cause a fuel restriction. Adding a fuel additive may help, however the fuel system may require draining and purging with fresh fuel.

g. Check for ignition system failure. Check for loose or shorted wires or damaged ignition system components. Check the spark plugs for excessive wear or incorrect electrode gap. If the problem is worse in wet weather, check for shorts between the spark plugs and the ignition coils.

h. Check the engine management system for a failed sensor or control module.

2. Engine does not turn over when attempting to start

a. Check the battery state of charge and condition. If the dash lights are not visible or very dim when turning the ignition key on, the battery has either failed internally or discharged, the battery cables are loose, excessively corroded or damaged, or the alternator has failed or internally shorted, discharging the battery. Charge or replace the battery, clean or replace the battery cables, and check the alternator output.

b. Check the operation of the neutral safety switch. On automatic transmission vehicles, try starting the vehicle in both Park and Neutral. On manual transmission vehicles, depress the clutch pedal and attempt to start. On some vehicles, these switches can be adjusted. Make sure the switches or wire connectors are not loose or damaged. Replace or adjust the switches as necessary.

c. Check the starter motor, starter solenoid or relay, and starter motor cables and wires. Check the ground from the engine to the chassis. Make sure the wires are not loose, damaged, or corroded. If battery voltage is present at the starter relay, try using a remote starter to start the vehicle for test purposes only. Replace any damaged or corroded cables, in addition to replacing any failed components.

d. Check the engine for seizure. If the engine has not been started for a long period of time, internal parts such as the rings may have rusted to the cylinder walls. The engine may have suffered internal damage, or could be hydro-locked from ingesting water. Remove the spark plugs and carefully attempt to rotate the engine using a suitable breaker bar and socket on the crankshaft pulley. If the engine is resistant to moving, or moves slightly and then binds, do not force the engine any further before determining the problem.

3. Engine stalls immediately when started

a. Check the ignition switch condition and operation. The electrical contacts in the run position may be worn or damaged. Try restarting the engine with all electrical accessories in the off position. Sometimes turning the key on an off will help in emergency situations, however once the switch has shown signs of failure, it should be replaced as soon as possible.

b. Check for loose, corroded, damaged or shorted wires for the ignition system and repair or replace.

c. Check for manifold vacuum leaks or vacuum hose leakage and repair or replace parts as necessary.

d. Measure the fuel pump delivery volume and pressure. Low fuel pump pressure can also be noticed as a lack of power when accelerating. Make sure the fuel pump lines are not restricted. The fuel pump output is not adjustable and requires fuel pump replacement to repair.

e. Check the engine fuel and ignition management system. Inspect the sensor wiring and electrical connectors. A dirty, loose or damaged sensor or control module wire can simulate a failed component.

f. Check the exhaust system for internal restrictions.

4. Starter motor spins, but does not engage

a. Check the starter motor for a seized or binding pinion gear.

b. Remove the flywheel inspection plate and check for a damaged ring gear.

5. Engine is difficult to start when cold

a. Check the battery condition, battery state of charge and starter motor current draw.

Replace the battery if marginal and the starter motor if the current draw is beyond specification.

b. Check the battery cable condition. Clean the battery terminals and replace corroded or damaged cables.

c. Check the fuel system for proper operation. A fuel pump with insufficient fuel pressure or clogged injectors should be replaced.

d. Check the engine's tune-up status. Note the tune-up specifications and check for items such as severely worn spark plugs; adjust or replace as needed. On vehicles with manually adjusted valve clearances, check for tight valves and adjust to specification.

e. Check for a failed coolant temperature sensor, and replace if out of specification.

f. Check the operation of the engine management systems for fuel and ignition; repair or replace failed components as necessary.

6. Engine is difficult to start when hot

a. Check the air filter and air intake system. Replace the air filter if it is dirty or contaminated. Check the fresh air intake system for restrictions or blockage.

b. Check for loose or deteriorated engine grounds and clean, tighten or replace as needed.

c. Check for needed maintenance. Inspect tune-up and service related items such as spark plugs and engine oil condition, and check the operation of the engine fuel and ignition management system.

Diesel Engines

1. Engine turns over but won't start

a. Check engine starting procedure and restart engine.

b. Check the glow plug operation and repair or replace as necessary.

c. Check for air in the fuel system or fuel filter and bleed the air as necessary.

d. Check the fuel delivery system and repair or replace as necessary.

e. Check fuel level and add fuel as needed.

f. Check fuel quality. If the fuel is contaminated, drain and flush the fuel tank.

g. Check engine compression. If compression is below specification, the engine may need to be renewed or replaced.

h. Check the injection pump timing and set to specification.

i. Check the injection pump condition and replace as necessary.

j. Check the fuel nozzle operation and condition or replace as necessary.

2. Engine does not turn over when attempting to start

a. Check the battery state of charge and condition. If the dash lights are not visible or very dim when turning the ignition key on, the battery has either failed internally or discharged, the battery cables are loose, excessively corroded or damaged, or the alternator has failed or internally shorted, discharging the battery. Charge or replace the battery, clean or replace the battery cables, and check the alternator output.

b. Check the operation of the neutral safety switch. On automatic transmission vehicles, try starting the vehicle in both Park and Neutral. On manual transmission vehicles, depress the clutch pedal and attempt to start. On some vehicles, these switches can be adjusted. Make sure the switches or wire connectors are not loose or damaged. Replace or adjust the switches as necessary.

c. Check the starter motor, starter solenoid or relay, and starter motor cables and wires. Check the ground from the engine to the chassis. Make sure the wires are not loose, damaged, or corroded. If battery voltage is present at the starter relay, try using a remote starter to start the vehicle for test purposes only. Replace any damaged or corroded cables, in addition to replacing any failed components.

d. Check the engine for seizure. If the engine has not been started for a long period of time, internal parts such as the rings may have rusted to the cylinder walls. The engine may have suffered internal damage, or could be hydro-locked from ingesting water. Remove the injectors and carefully attempt to rotate the engine using a suitable breaker bar and socket on the crankshaft pulley. If the engine is resistant to moving, or moves slightly and then binds, do not force the engine any further before determining the cause of the problem.

3. Engine stalls after starting

a. Check for a restriction in the fuel return line or the return line check valve and repair as necessary.

b. Check the glow plug operation for turning the glow plugs off too soon and repair as necessary.

c. Check for incorrect injection pump timing and reset to specification.

d. Test the engine fuel pump and replace if the output is below specification.

e. Check for contaminated or incorrect fuel. Completely flush the fuel system and replace with fresh fuel.

f. Test the engine's compression for low compression. If below specification, mechanical repairs are necessary to repair.

g. Check for air in the fuel. Check fuel tank fuel and fill as needed.

h. Check for a failed injection pump. Replace the pump, making sure to properly set the pump timing.

4. Starter motor spins, but does not engage
a. Check the starter motor for a seized or binding pinion gear.
b. Remove the flywheel inspection plate and check for a damaged ring gear.

1-B. Engine Running Conditions

Gasoline Engines

1. Engine runs poorly, hesitates
a. Check the engine ignition system operation and adjust if possible, or replace defective parts.
b. Check for restricted fuel injectors and replace as necessary.
c. Check the fuel pump output and delivery. Inspect fuel lines for restrictions. If the fuel pump pressure is below specification, replace the fuel pump.
d. Check the operation of the engine management system and repair as necessary.

2. Engine lacks power
a. Check the engine's tune-up status. Note the tune-up specifications and check for items such as severely worn spark plugs; adjust or replace as needed. On vehicles with manually adjusted valve clearances, check for tight valves and adjust to specification.
b. Check the air filter and air intake system. Replace the air filter if it is dirty or contaminated. Check the fresh air intake system for restrictions or blockage.
c. Check the operation of the engine fuel and ignition management systems. Check the sensor operation and wiring. Check for low fuel pump pressure and repair or replace components as necessary.
d. Check the throttle linkage adjustments. Check to make sure the linkage is fully opening the throttle. Replace any worn or defective bushings or linkages.
e. Check for a restricted exhaust system. Check for bent or crimped exhaust pipes, or internally restricted mufflers or catalytic converters. Compare inlet and outlet temperatures for the converter or muffler. If the inlet is hot, but outlet cold, the component is restricted.
f. Check for a loose or defective knock sensor. A loose, improperly torqued or defective knock sensor will decrease spark advance and reduce power. Replace defective knock sensors and install using the recommended torque specification.
g. Check for engine mechanical conditions such as low compression, worn piston rings, worn valves, worn camshafts and related parts. An engine which has severe mechanical wear, or has suffered internal mechanical damage must be rebuilt or replaced to restore lost power.
h. Check the engine oil level for being overfilled. Adjust the engine's oil level, or change the engine oil and filter, and top off to the correct level.
i. Check for an intake manifold or vacuum hose leak. Replace leaking gaskets or worn vacuum hoses.
j. Check for dragging brakes and replace or repair as necessary.
k. Check tire air pressure and tire wear. Adjust the pressure to the recommended settings. Check the tire wear for possible alignment problems causing increased rolling resistance, decreased acceleration and increased fuel usage.
l. Check the octane rating of the fuel used during refilling, and use a higher octane rated fuel.

3. Poor fuel economy
a. Inspect the air filter and check for any air restrictions going into the air filter housing. Replace the air filter if it is dirty or contaminated.
b. Check the engine for tune-up and related adjustments. Replace worn ignition parts, check the engine ignition timing and fuel mixture, and set to specifications if possible.
c. Check the tire size, tire wear, alignment and tire pressure. Large tires create more rolling resistance, smaller tires require more engine speed to maintain a vehicle's road speed. Excessive tire wear can be caused by incorrect tire pressure, incorrect wheel alignment or a suspension problem. All of these conditions create increased rolling resistance, causing the engine to work harder to accelerate and maintain a vehicle's speed.
d. Inspect the brakes for binding or excessive drag. A sticking brake caliper, overly adjusted brake shoe, broken brake shoe return spring, or binding parking brake cable or linkage can create a significant drag, brake wear and loss of fuel economy. Check the brake system operation and repair as necessary.

4. Engine runs on (diesels) when turned off
a. Check for idle speed set too high and readjust to specification.
b. Check the operation of the idle control valve, and replace if defective.
c. Check the ignition timing and adjust to recommended settings. Check for defective sensors or related components and replace if defective.
d. Check for a vacuum leak at the intake manifold or vacuum hose and replace defective gaskets or hoses.
e. Check the engine for excessive carbon build-up in the combustion chamber. Use a recommended decarbonizing fuel additive or disassemble the cylinder head to remove the carbon.

f. Check the operation of the engine fuel management system and replace defective sensors or control units.
g. Check the engine operating temperature for overheating and repair as necessary.

5. Engine knocks and pings during heavy acceleration, and on steep hills
a. Check the octane rating of the fuel used during refilling, and use a higher octane rated fuel.
b. Check the ignition timing and adjust to recommended settings. Check for defective sensors or related components and replace if defective.
c. Check the engine for excessive carbon build-up in the combustion chamber. Use a recommended decarbonizing fuel additive or disassemble the cylinder head to remove the carbon.
d. Check the spark plugs for the correct type, electrode gap and heat range. Replace worn or damaged spark plugs. For severe or continuous high speed use, install a spark plug that is one heat range colder.
e. Check the operation of the engine fuel management system and replace defective sensors or control units.
f. Check for a restricted exhaust system. Check for bent or crimped exhaust pipes, or internally restricted mufflers or catalytic converters. Compare inlet and outlet temperatures for the converter or muffler. If the inlet is hot, but outlet cold, the component is restricted.

6. Engine accelerates, but vehicle does not gain speed
a. On manual transmission vehicles, check for causes of a slipping clutch. Refer to the clutch troubleshooting section for additional information.
b. On automatic transmission vehicles, check for a slipping transmission. Check the transmission fluid level and condition. If the fluid level is too high, adjust to the correct level. If the fluid level is low, top off using the recommended fluid type. If the fluid exhibits a burning odor, the transmission has been slipping internally. Changing the fluid and filter may help temporarily, however in this situation a transmission may require overhauling to ensure long-term reliability.

Diesel Engines

1. Engine runs poorly
a. Check the injection pump timing and adjust to specification.
b. Check for air in the fuel lines or leaks, and bleed the air from the fuel system.
c. Check the fuel filter, fuel feed and return lines for a restriction and repair as necessary.
d. Check the fuel for contamination, drain and flush the fuel tank and replenish with fresh fuel.

2. Engine lacks power
a. Inspect the air intake system and air filter for restrictions and, if necessary, replace the air filter.
b. Verify the injection pump timing and reset if out of specification.
c. Check the exhaust for an internal restriction and replace failed parts.
d. Check for a restricted fuel filter and, if restricted, replace the filter.
e. Inspect the fuel filler cap vent . When removing the filler cap, listen for excessive hissing noises indicating a blockage in the fuel filler cap vents. If the filler cap vents are blocked, replace the cap.
f. Check the fuel system for restrictions and repair as necessary.
g. Check for low engine compression and inspect for external leakage at the glow plugs or nozzles. If no external leakage is noted, repair or replace the engine.

ENGINE PERFORMANCE TROUBLESHOOTING HINTS

When troubleshooting an engine running or performance condition, the mechanical condition of the engine should be determined *before* lengthy troubleshooting procedures are performed.

The engine fuel management systems in fuel injected vehicles rely on electronic sensors to provide information to the engine control unit for precise fuel metering. Unlike carburetors, which use the incoming air speed to draw fuel through the fuel metering jets in order to provide a proper fuel-to-air ratio, a fuel injection system provides a specific amount of fuel which is introduced by the fuel injectors into the intake manifold or intake port, based on the information provided by electronic sensors.

The sensors monitor the engine's operating temperature, ambient temperature and the amount of air entering the engine, engine speed and throttle position to provide information to the engine control unit, which, in turn, operates the fuel injectors by electrical pulses. The sensors provide information to the engine control unit using low voltage electrical signals. As a result, an unplugged sensor or a poor electrical contact could cause a poor running condition similar to a failed sensor.

When troubleshooting a fuel related engine condition on fuel injected vehicles, carefully inspect the wiring and electrical connectors to the related components. Make sure the electrical connectors are fully connected, clean and not physically damaged. If necessary, clean the electrical contacts using electrical contact cleaner. The use of cleaning agents not specifically designed for electrical contacts should not be used, as they could leave a surface film or damage the insulation of the wiring.

The engine electrical system provides the necessary electrical power to operate the vehicle's electrical accessories, electronic control units and sensors. Because engine management systems are sensitive to voltage changes, an alternator which over or undercharges could cause engine running problems or component failure. Most alternators utilize internal voltage regulators which cannot be adjusted and must be replaced individually or as a unit with the alternator.

Ignition systems may be controlled by, or linked to, the engine fuel management system. Similar to the fuel injection system, these ignition systems rely on electronic sensors for information to determine the optimum ignition timing for a given engine speed and load. Some ignition systems no longer allow the ignition timing to be adjusted. Feedback from low voltage electrical sensors provide information to the control unit to determine the amount of ignition advance. On these systems, if a failure occurs the failed component must be replaced. Before replacing suspected failed electrical components, carefully inspect the wiring and electrical connectors to the related components. Make sure the electrical connectors are fully connected, clean and not physically damaged. If necessary, clean the electrical contacts using electrical contact cleaner. The use of cleaning agents not specifically designed for electrical contacts should be avoided, as they could leave a surface film or damage the insulation of the wiring.

1-C. Engine Noises, Odors and Vibrations

1. Engine makes a knocking or pinging noise when accelerating
a. Check the octane rating of the fuel being used. Depending on the type of driving or driving conditions, it may be necessary to use a higher octane fuel.
b. Verify the ignition system settings and operation. Improperly adjusted ignition timing or a failed component, such as a knock sensor, may cause the ignition timing to advance excessively or prematurely. Check the ignition system operation and adjust, or replace components as needed.
c. Check the spark plug gap, heat range and condition. If the vehicle is operated in severe operating conditions or at continuous high speeds, use a colder heat range spark plug. Adjust the spark plug gap to the manufacturer's recommended specification and replace worn or damaged spark plugs.

2. Starter motor grinds when used
a. Examine the starter pinion gear and the engine ring gear for damage, and replace damaged parts.
b. Check the starter mounting bolts and housing. If the housing is cracked or damaged replace the starter motor and check the mounting bolts for tightness.

3. Engine makes a screeching noise
a. Check the accessory drive belts for looseness and adjust as necessary.
b. Check the accessory drive belt tensioners for seizing or excessive bearing noises and replace if loose, binding, or excessively noisy.
c. Check for a seizing water pump. The pump may not be leaking; however, the bearing may be faulty or the impeller loose and jammed. Replace the water pump.

4. Engine makes a growling noise
a. Check for a loose or failing water pump. Replace the pump and engine coolant.
b. Check the accessory drive belt tensioners for excessive bearing noises and replace if loose or excessively noisy.

5. Engine makes a ticking or tapping noise
a. On vehicles with hydraulic lash adjusters, check for low or dirty engine oil and top off or replace the engine oil and filter.
b. On vehicles with hydraulic lash adjusters, check for collapsed lifters and replace failed components.
c. On vehicles with hydraulic lash adjusters, check for low oil pressure caused by a restricted oil filter, worn engine oil pump, or oil pressure relief valve.
d. On vehicles with manually adjusted valves, check for excessive valve clearance or worn valve train parts. Adjust the valves to specification or replace worn and defective parts.
e. Check for a loose or improperly tensioned timing belt or timing chain and adjust or replace parts as necessary.
f. Check for a bent or sticking exhaust or intake valve. Remove the engine cylinder head to access and replace.

6. Engine makes a heavy knocking noise
a. Check for a loose crankshaft pulley or flywheel; replace and torque the mounting bolt(s) to specification.
b. Check for a bent connecting rod caused by a hydro-lock condition. Engine disassembly is necessary to inspect for damaged and needed replacement parts.
c. Check for excessive engine rod bearing wear or damage. This condition is also associated with low engine oil pressure and will require engine disassembly to inspect for damaged and needed replacement parts.

7. Vehicle has a fuel odor when driven
a. Check the fuel gauge level. If the fuel gauge registers full, it is possible that the odor is caused by being filled beyond capacity, or some spillage occurred during refueling. The odor should clear after driving an hour, or twenty miles, allowing the vapor canister to purge.
b. Check the fuel filler cap for looseness or seepage. Check the cap tightness and, if loose, properly secure. If seepage is noted, replace the filler cap.
c. Check for loose hose clamps, cracked or damaged fuel delivery and return lines, or leaking components or seals, and replace or repair as necessary.
d. Check the vehicle's fuel economy. If fuel consumption has increased due to a failed component, or if the fuel is not properly ignited due to an ignition related failure, the catalytic converter may become contaminated. This condition may also trigger the check engine warning light. Check the spark plugs for a dark, rich condition or verify the condition by testing the vehicle's emissions. Replace fuel fouled spark plugs, and test and replace failed components as necessary.

8. Vehicle has a rotten egg odor when driven
a. Check for a leaking intake gasket or vacuum leak causing a lean running condition. A lean mixture may result in increased exhaust temperatures, causing the catalytic converter to run hotter than normal. This condition may also trigger the check engine warning light. Check and repair the vacuum leaks as necessary.
b. Check the vehicle's alternator and battery condition. If the alternator is overcharging, the battery electrolyte can be boiled from the battery, and the battery casing may begin to crack, swell or bulge, damaging or shorting the battery internally. If this has occurred, neutralize the battery mounting area with a suitable baking soda and water mixture or equivalent, and replace the alternator or voltage regulator. Inspect, service, and load test the battery, and replace if necessary.

9. Vehicle has a sweet odor when driven
a. Check for an engine coolant leak caused by a seeping radiator cap, loose hose clamp, weeping cooling system seal, gasket or cooling system hose and replace or repair as needed.
b. Check for a coolant leak from the radiator, coolant reservoir, heater control valve or under the dashboard from the heater core, and replace the failed part as necessary.
c. Check the engine's exhaust for white smoke in addition to a sweet odor. The presence of white, steamy smoke with a sweet odor indicates coolant leaking into the combustion chamber. Possible causes include a failed head gasket, cracked engine block or cylinder head. Other symptoms of this condition include a white paste build-up on the inside of the oil filler cap, and softened, deformed or bulging radiator hoses.

10. Engine vibrates when idling
a. Check for loose, collapsed, or damaged engine or transmission mounts and repair or replace as necessary.
b. Check for loose or damaged engine covers or shields and secure or replace as necessary.

11. Engine vibrates during acceleration
a. Check for missing, loose or damaged exhaust system hangers and mounts; replace or repair as necessary.
b. Check the exhaust system routing and fit for adequate clearance or potential rubbing; repair or adjust as necessary.

1-D. Engine Electrical System

1. Battery goes dead while driving
a. Check the battery condition. Replace the battery if the battery will not hold a charge or fails a battery load test. If the battery loses fluid while driving, check for an overcharging condition. If the alternator is overcharging, replace the alternator or voltage regulator. (A voltage regulator is typically built into the alternator, necessitating alternator replacement or overhaul.)
b. Check the battery cable condition. Clean or replace corroded cables and clean the battery terminals.
c. Check the alternator and voltage regulator operation. If the charging system is over or undercharging, replace the alternator or voltage regulator, or both.
d. Inspect the wiring and wire connectors at the alternator for looseness, a missing ground or defective terminal, and repair as necessary.
e. Inspect the alternator drive belt tension, tensioners and condition. Properly tension the drive belt, replace weak or broken tensioners, and replace the drive belt if worn or cracked.

2. Battery goes dead overnight
a. Check the battery condition. Replace the battery if the battery will not hold a charge or fails a battery load test.
b. Check for a voltage draw, such as a trunk light, interior light or glove box light staying on. Check light switch position and operation, and replace if defective.
c. Check the alternator for an internally failed diode, and replace the alternator if defective.

1-E. Engine Cooling System

1. Engine overheats

a. Check the coolant level. Set the heater temperature to full hot and check for internal air pockets, bleed the cooling system and inspect for leakage. Top off the cooling system with the correct coolant mixture.

b. Pressure test the cooling system and radiator cap for leaks. Check for seepage caused by loose hose clamps, failed coolant hoses, and cooling system components such as the heater control valve, heater core, radiator, radiator cap, and water pump. Replace defective parts and fill the cooling system with the recommended coolant mixture.

c. On vehicles with electrically controlled cooling fans, check the cooling fan operation. Check for blown fuses or defective fan motors, temperature sensors and relays, and replace failed components.

d. Check for a coolant leak caused by a failed head gasket, or a porous water jacket casting in the cylinder head or engine block. Replace defective parts as necessary.

e. Check for an internally restricted radiator. Flush the radiator or replace if the blockage is too severe for flushing.

f. Check for a damaged water pump. If coolant circulation is poor, check for a loose water pump impeller. If the impeller is loose, replace the water pump.

2. Engine loses coolant

a. Pressure test the cooling system and radiator cap for leaks. Check for seepage caused by loose hose clamps, failed coolant hoses, and cooling system components such as the heater control valve, heater core, radiator, radiator cap, and water pump. Replace defective parts and fill the cooling system with the recommended coolant mixture.

b. Check for a coolant leak caused by a failed head gasket, or a porous water jacket casting in the cylinder head or engine block. Replace defective parts as necessary.

3. Engine temperature remains cold when driving

a. Check the thermostat operation. Replace the thermostat if it sticks in the open position.

b. On vehicles with electrically controlled cooling fans, check the cooling fan operation. Check for defective temperature sensors and stuck relays, and replace failed components.

c. Check temperature gauge operation if equipped to verify proper operation of the gauge. Check the sensors and wiring for defects, and repair or replace defective components.

4. Engine runs hot

a. Check for an internally restricted radiator. Flush the radiator or replace if the blockage is too severe for flushing.

b. Check for a loose or slipping water pump drive belt. Inspect the drive belt condition. Replace the belt if brittle, cracked or damaged. Check the pulley condition and properly tension the belt.

c. Check the cooling fan operation. Replace defective fan motors, sensors or relays as necessary.

d. Check temperature gauge operation if equipped to verify proper operation of the gauge. Check the sensors and wiring for defects, and repair or replace defective components.

e. Check the coolant level. Set the heater temperature to full hot, check for internal air pockets, bleed the cooling system and inspect for leakage. Top off the cooling system with the correct coolant mixture. Once the engine is cool, recheck the fluid level and top off as needed.

NOTE: The engine cooling system can also be affected by an engine's mechanical condition. A failed head gasket or a porous casting in the engine block or cylinder head could cause a loss of coolant and result in engine overheating.

Some cooling systems rely on electrically driven cooling fans to cool the radiator and use electrical temperature sensors and relays to operate the cooling fan. When diagnosing these systems, check for blown fuses, damaged wires and verify that the electrical connections are fully connected, clean and not physically damaged. If necessary, clean the electrical contacts using electrical contact cleaner. The use of cleaning agents not specifically designed for electrical contacts could leave a film or damage the insulation of the wiring.

1-F. Engine Exhaust System

1. Exhaust rattles at idle speed

a. Check the engine and transmission mounts and replace mounts showing signs of damage or wear.

b. Check the exhaust hangers, brackets and mounts. Replace broken, missing or damaged mounts.

c. Check for internal damage to mufflers and catalytic converters. The broken pieces from the defective component may travel in the direction of the exhaust flow and collect and/or create a blockage in a component other than the one which failed, causing engine running and stalling problems. Another symptom of a restricted exhaust is low engine manifold vacuum. Remove the exhaust system and carefully remove any loose or broken pieces, then replace any failed or damaged parts as necessary.

d. Check the exhaust system clearance, routing and alignment. If the exhaust is making contact with the vehicle in any manner, loosen and reposition the exhaust system.

2. Exhaust system vibrates when driving

a. Check the exhaust hangers, brackets and mounts. Replace broken, missing or damaged mounts.

b. Check the exhaust system clearance, routing and alignment. If the exhaust is making contact with the vehicle in any manner, check for bent or damaged components and replace, then loosen and reposition the exhaust system.

c. Check for internal damage to mufflers and catalytic converters. The broken pieces from the defective component may travel in the direction of the exhaust flow and collect and/or create a blockage in a component other than the one which failed, causing engine running and stalling problems. Another symptom of a restricted exhaust is low engine manifold vacuum. Remove the exhaust system and carefully remove any loose or broken pieces, then replace any failed or damaged parts as necessary.

3. Exhaust system hangs too low

a. Check the exhaust hangers, brackets and mounts. Replace broken, missing or damaged mounts.

b. Check the exhaust routing and alignment. Check and replace bent or damaged components. If the exhaust is not routed properly, loosen and reposition the exhaust system.

4. Exhaust sounds loud

a. Check the system for looseness and leaks. Check the exhaust pipes, clamps, flange bolts and manifold fasteners for tightness. Check and replace any failed gaskets.

b. Check and replace exhaust silencers that have a loss of efficiency due to internally broken baffles or worn packing material.

c. Check for missing mufflers and silencers that have been replaced with straight pipes or with non-original equipment silencers.

NOTE: Exhaust system rattles, vibration and proper alignment should not be overlooked. Excessive vibration caused by collapsed engine mounts, damaged or missing exhaust hangers and misalignment may cause surface cracks and broken welds, creating exhaust leaks or internal damage to exhaust components such as the catalytic converter, creating a restriction to exhaust flow and loss of power.

2. DRIVE TRAIN

2-A. Automatic Transmission

1. Transmission shifts erratically

a. Check and if not within the recommended range, add or remove transmission fluid to obtain the correct fluid level. Always use the recommended fluid type when adding transmission fluid.

b. Check the fluid level condition. If the fluid has become contaminated, fatigued from excessive heat or exhibits a burning odor, change the transmission fluid and filter using the recommended type and amount of fluid. A fluid which exhibits a burning odor indicates that the transmission has been slipping internally and may cause future repairs.

c. Check for an improperly installed transmission filter, or missing filter gasket, and repair as necessary.

d. Check for loose or leaking gaskets, pressure lines and fittings, and repair or replace as necessary.

e. Check for loose or disconnected shift and throttle linkages or vacuum hoses, and repair as necessary.

2. Transmission will not engage

a. Check the shift linkage for looseness, wear and proper adjustment, and repair as necessary.

b. Check for a loss of transmission fluid and top off as needed with the recommended fluid.

c. If the transmission does not engage with the shift linkage correctly installed and the proper fluid level, internal damage has likely occurred, requiring transmission removal and disassembly.

3. Transmission will not downshift during heavy acceleration

a. On computer controlled transmissions, check for failed sensors or control units and repair or replace defective components.

b. On vehicles with kickdown linkages or vacuum servos, check for proper linkage adjustment or leaking vacuum hoses or servo units.

NOTE: Many automatic transmissions use an electronic control module, electrical sensors and solenoids to control transmission shifting. When troubleshooting a vehicle with this type of system, be sure the electrical connectors are fully connected, clean and not physically damaged. If necessary, clean the electrical contacts using electrical contact cleaner. The use of cleaning agents not specifically designed for electrical contacts could leave a film or damage the insulation of the wiring.

2-B. Manual Transmission

1. Transmission grinds going into forward gears while driving
a. Check the clutch release system. On clutches with a mechanical or cable linkage, check the adjustment. Adjust the clutch pedal to have 1 inch (25mm) of free-play at the pedal.
b. If the clutch release system is hydraulically operated, check the fluid level and, if low, top off using the recommended type and amount of fluid.
c. Synchronizers worn. Remove transmission and replace synchronizers.
d. Synchronizer sliding sleeve worn. Remove transmission and replace sliding sleeve.
e. Gear engagement dogs worn or damaged. Remove transmission and replace gear.

2. Transmission jumps out of gear
a. Shift shaft detent springs worn. Replace shift detent springs.
b. Synchronizer sliding sleeve worn. Remove transmission and replace sliding sleeve.
c. Gear engagement dogs worn or damaged. Remove transmission and replace gear.
d. Crankshaft thrust bearings worn. Remove engine and crankshaft, and repair as necessary.

3. Transmission difficult to shift
a. Verify the clutch adjustment and, if not properly adjusted, adjust to specification.
b. Synchronizers worn. Remove transmission and replace synchronizers.
c. Pilot bearing seized. Remove transmission and replace pilot bearing.
d. Shift linkage or bushing seized. Disassemble the shift linkage, replace worn or damaged bushings, lubricate and reinstall.

4. Transmission leaks fluid
a. Check the fluid level for an overfilled condition. Adjust the fluid level to specification.
b. Check for a restricted transmission vent or breather tube. Clear the blockage as necessary and check the fluid level. If necessary, top off with the recommended lubricant.
c. Check for a porous casting, leaking seal or gasket. Replace defective parts and top off the fluid level with the recommended lubricant.

2-C. Clutch

1. Clutch slips on hills or during sudden acceleration
a. Check for insufficient clutch pedal free-play. Adjust clutch linkage or cable to allow about 1 inch (25mm) of pedal free-play.
b. Clutch disc worn or severely damaged. Remove engine or transmission and replace clutch disc.
c. Clutch pressure plate is weak. Remove engine or transmission and replace the clutch pressure plate and clutch disc.
d. Clutch pressure plate and/or flywheel incorrectly machined. If the clutch system has been recently replaced and rebuilt, or refurbished parts have been used, it is possible that the machined surfaces decreased the clutch clamping force. Replace defective parts with new replacement parts.

2. Clutch will not disengage, difficult to shift
a. Check the clutch release mechanism. Check for stretched cables, worn linkages or failed clutch hydraulics and replace defective parts. On hydraulically operated clutch release mechanisms, check for air in the hydraulic system and bleed as necessary.
b. Check for a broken, cracked or fatigued clutch release arm or release arm pivot. Replace defective parts and properly lubricate upon assembly.
c. Check for a damaged clutch hub damper or damper spring. The broken parts tend to become lodged between the clutch disc and the pressure plate. Disassemble clutch system and replace failed parts.
d. Check for a seized clutch pilot bearing. Disassemble the clutch assembly and replace the defective parts.
e. Check for a defective clutch disc. Check for warpage or lining thicknesses larger than original equipment.

3. Clutch is noisy when the clutch pedal is pressed
a. Check the clutch pedal stop and pedal free-play adjustment for excessive movement and adjust as necessary.
b. Check for a worn or damaged release bearing. If the noise ceases when the pedal is released, the release bearing should be replaced.

c. Check the engine crankshaft axial play. If the crankshaft thrust bearings are worn or damaged, the crankshaft will move when pressing the clutch pedal. The engine must be disassembled to replace the crankshaft thrust bearings.

4. Clutch pedal extremely difficult to press
a. Check the clutch pedal pivots and linkages for binding. Clean and lubricate linkages.
b. On cable actuated clutch systems, check the cable routing and condition. Replace kinked, frayed, damaged or corroded cables and check cable routing to avoid sharp bends. Check the engine ground strap for poor conductivity. If the ground strap is marginal, the engine could try to ground itself via the clutch cable, causing premature failure.
c. On mechanical linkage clutches, check the linkage for binding or misalignment. Lubricate pivots or linkages and repair as necessary.
d. Check the release bearing guide tube and release fork for a lack of lubrication. Install a smooth coating of high temperature grease to allow smooth movement of the release bearing over the guide tube.

5. Clutch pedal remains down when pressed
a. On mechanical linkage or cable actuated clutches, check for a loose or disconnected link.
b. On hydraulically actuated clutches, check the fluid level and check for a hydraulic leak at the clutch slave or master cylinder, or hydraulic line. Replace failed parts and bleed clutch hydraulic system. If no leakage is noted, the clutch master cylinder may have failed internally. Replace the clutch master cylinder and bleed the clutch hydraulic system.

6. Clutch chatters when engaging
a. Check the engine flywheel for warpage or surface variations and replace or repair as necessary.
b. Check for a warped clutch disc or damaged clutch damper hub. Remove the clutch disc and replace.
c. Check for a loose or damaged clutch pressure plate and replace defective components.

NOTE: The clutch is actuated either by a mechanical linkage, cable or a clutch hydraulic system. The mechanical linkage and cable systems may require the clutch pedal free-play to be adjusted as the clutch disc wears. A hydraulic clutch system automatically adjusts as the clutch wears and, with the exception of the clutch pedal height, no adjustment is possible.

2-D. Differential and Final Drive

1. Differential makes a low pitched rumbling noise
a. Check fluid level type and amount. Replace the fluid with the recommended type and amount of lubricant.
b. Check the differential bearings for wear or damage. Remove the bearings, inspect the drive and driven gears for wear or damage, and replace components as necessary.

2. Differential makes a howling noise
a. Check fluid level type and amount. Replace the fluid with the recommended type and amount of lubricant.
b. Check the differential drive and driven gears for wear or damage, and replace components as necessary.

2-E. Transfer Assembly

All Wheel and Four Wheel Drive Vehicles

1. Leaks fluid from seals or vent after being driven
a. Fluid level overfilled. Check and adjust transfer case fluid level.
b. Check for a restricted breather or breather tube, clear and check the fluid level and top off as needed.
c. Check seal condition and replace worn, damaged, or defective seals. Check the fluid level and top off as necessary.

2. Makes excessive noise while driving
a. Check the fluid for the correct type of lubricant. Drain and refill using the recommended type and amount of lubricant.
b. Check the fluid level. Top off the fluid using the recommended type and amount of lubricant.
c. If the fluid level and type of lubricant meet specifications, check for internal wear or damage. Remove assembly and disassemble to inspect for worn, damaged, or defective components.

3. Jumps out of gear
a. Stop vehicle and make sure the unit is fully engaged.
b. Check for worn, loose or an improperly adjusted linkage. Replace and/or adjust linkage as necessary.
c. Check for internal wear or damage. Remove assembly and disassemble to inspect for worn, damaged, or defective components.

2-F. Driveshaft

Rear Wheel, All Wheel and Four Wheel Drive Vehicles

1. Clunking noise from center of vehicle shifting from forward to reverse
a. Worn universal joint. Remove driveshaft and replace universal joint.

2. Excessive vibration from center of vehicle when accelerating
a. Worn universal joint. Remove driveshaft and replace universal joint.
b. Driveshaft misaligned. Check for collapsed or damaged engine and transmission mounts, and replace as necessary.
c. Driveshaft bent or out of balance. Replace damaged components and reinstall.
d. Driveshaft out of balance. Remove the driveshaft and have it balanced by a competent professional, or replace the driveshaft assembly.

NOTE: Most driveshafts are linked together by universal joints; however, some manufacturers use Constant Velocity (CV) joints or rubber flex couplers.

2-G. Axles

All Wheel and Four Wheel Drive Vehicles

1. Front or rear wheel makes a clicking noise
a. Check for debris such as a pebble, nail or glass in the tire or tire tread. Carefully remove the debris. Small rocks and pebbles rarely cause a puncture; however, a sharp object should be removed carefully at a facility capable of performing tire repairs.
b. Check for a loose, damaged or worn Constant Velocity (CV) joint and replace if defective.

2. Front or rear wheel vibrates with increased speed
a. Check for a bent rim and replace, if damaged.
b. Check the tires for balance or internal damage and replace if defective.
c. Check for a loose, worn or damaged wheel bearing and replace if defective.
d. Check for a loose, damaged or worn Constant Velocity (CV) joint and replace if defective.

Front Wheel Drive Vehicles

3. Front wheel makes a clicking noise
a. Check for debris such as a pebble, nail or glass in the tire or tire tread. Carefully remove the debris. Small rocks and pebbles rarely cause a puncture; however, a sharp object should be removed carefully at a facility capable of performing tire repairs.

b. Check for a loose, damaged or worn Constant Velocity (CV) joint and replace if defective.

4. Rear wheel makes a clicking noise
a. Check for debris such as a pebble, nail or glass in the tire or tire tread. Carefully remove the debris. Small rocks and pebbles rarely cause a puncture; however, a sharp object should be removed carefully at a facility capable of performing tire repairs.

Rear Wheel Drive Vehicles

5. Front or rear wheel makes a clicking noise
a. Check for debris such as a pebble, nail or glass in the tire or tire tread. Carefully remove the debris. Small rocks and pebbles rarely cause a puncture; however, a sharp object should be removed carefully at a facility capable of performing tire repairs.

6. Rear wheel shudders or vibrates
a. Check for a bent rear wheel or axle assembly and replace defective components.
b. Check for a loose, damaged or worn rear wheel bearing and replace as necessary.

2-H. Other Drive Train Conditions

1. Burning odor from center of vehicle when accelerating
a. Check for a seizing brake hydraulic component such as a brake caliper. Check the caliper piston for surface damage such as rust, and measure for out-of-round wear and caliper-to-piston clearance. For additional information on brake related odors, refer to section 3-A, condition number 9.
b. On vehicles with a manual transmission, check for a slipping clutch. For possible causes and additional information, refer to section 2-C, condition number 1.
c. On vehicles with an automatic transmission, check the fluid level and condition. Top off or change the fluid and filter using the recommended replacement parts, lubricant type and amount. If the odor persists, transmission removal and disassembly will be necessary.

2. Engine accelerates, but vehicle does not gain speed
a. On vehicles with a manual transmission, check for a slipping or damaged clutch. For possible causes and additional information refer to section 2-C, condition number 1.
b. On vehicles with an automatic transmission, check the fluid level and condition. Top off or change the fluid and filter using the recommended replacement parts, lubricant type and amount. If the slipping continues, transmission removal and disassembly will be necessary.

3. BRAKE SYSTEM

3-A. Brake System Troubleshooting

1. Brake pedal pulsates or shimmies when pressed
a. Check wheel lug nut torque and tighten evenly to specification.
b. Check the brake rotor for trueness and thickness variations. Replace the rotor if it is too thin, warped, or if the thickness varies beyond specification. Some rotors can be machined; consult the manufacturer's specifications and recommendations before using a machined brake rotor.
c. Check the brake caliper or caliper bracket mounting bolt torque and inspect for looseness. Torque the mounting bolts and inspect for wear or any looseness, including worn mounting brackets, bushings and sliding pins.
d. Check the wheel bearing for looseness. If the bearing is loose, adjust if possible, otherwise replace the bearing.

2. Brakes make a squealing noise
a. Check the brake rotor for the presence of a ridge on the outer edge; if present, remove the ridge or replace the brake rotor and brake pads.
b. Check for debris in the brake lining material, clean and reinstall.
c. Check the brake linings for wear and replace the brake linings if wear is approaching the lining wear limit.
d. Check the brake linings for glazing. Inspect the brake drum or rotor surface and replace, along with the brake linings, if the surface is not smooth or even.
e. Check the brake pad or shoe mounting areas for a lack of lubricant or the presence of surface rust. Clean and lubricate with a recommended high temperature brake grease.

3. Brakes make a grinding noise
a. Check the brake linings and brake surface areas for severe wear or damage. Replace worn or damaged parts.
b. Check for a seized or partially seized brake causing premature or uneven brake wear, excessive heat and brake rotor or drum damage. Replace defective parts and inspect the wheel bearing condition, which could have been damaged due to excessive heat.

4. Vehicle pulls to one side during braking
a. Check for air in the brake hydraulic system. Inspect the brake hydraulic seals, fluid lines and related components for fluid leaks. Remove the air from the brake system by bleeding the brakes. Be sure to use fresh brake fluid that meets the manufacturer's recommended standards.
b. Check for an internally restricted flexible brake hydraulic hose. Replace the hose and flush the brake system.
c. Check for a seizing brake hydraulic component such as a brake caliper. Check the caliper piston for surface damage such as rust, and measure for out-of-round wear and caliper-to-piston clearance. Overhaul or replace failed parts and flush the brake system.
d. Check the vehicle's alignment and inspect for suspension wear. Replace worn bushings, ball joints and set alignment to the manufacturer's specifications.
e. If the brake system uses drum brakes front or rear, check the brake adjustment. Inspect for seized adjusters and clean or replace, then properly adjust.

5. Brake pedal feels spongy or has excessive travel
a. Check the brake fluid level and condition. If the fluid is contaminated or has not been flushed every two years, clean the master cylinder reservoir, and bleed and flush the brakes using fresh brake fluid that meets the manufacturer's recommended standards.
b. Check for a weak or damaged flexible brake hydraulic hose. Replace the hose and flush the brake system.
c. If the brake system uses drum brakes front or rear, check the brake adjustment. Inspect for seized adjusters and clean or replace, then properly adjust.

6. Brake pedal feel is firm, but brakes lack sufficient stopping power or fade
a. Check the operation of the brake booster and brake booster check valve. Replace worn or failed parts.
b. Check brake linings and brake surface areas for glazing and replace worn or damaged parts.
c. Check for seized hydraulic parts and linkages, and clean or replace as needed.

7. Vehicle has excessive front end dive or locks rear brakes too easily
a. Check for worn, failed or seized brake proportioning valve and replace the valve.
b. Check for a seized, disconnected or missing spring or linkage for the brake proportioning valve. Replace missing parts or repair as necessary.

8. Brake pedal goes to floor when pressed and will not pump up
a. Check the brake hydraulic fluid level and inspect the fluid lines and seals for leakage. Repair or replace leaking components, then bleed and flush the brake system using fresh brake fluid that meets the manufacturer's recommended standards.
b. Check the brake fluid level. Inspect the brake fluid level and brake hydraulic seals. If the fluid level is ok, and the brake hydraulic system is free of hydraulic leaks, replace the brake master cylinder, then bleed and flush the brake system using fresh brake fluid that meets the manufacturer's recommended standards.

9. Brakes produce a burning odor
a. Check for a seizing brake hydraulic component such as a brake caliper. Check the caliper piston for surface damage such as rust, and measure for out-of-round wear and caliper-to-piston clearance. Overhaul or replace failed parts and flush the brake system.
b. Check for an internally restricted flexible brake hydraulic hose. Replace the hose and flush the brake system.
c. Check the parking brake release mechanism, seized linkage or cable, and repair as necessary.

4. WHEELS, TIRES, STEERING AND SUSPENSION

4-A. Wheels and Wheel Bearings

1. Front wheel or wheel bearing loose

All Wheel and Four Wheel Drive Vehicles
a. Torque lug nuts and axle nuts to specification and recheck for looseness.
b. Wheel bearing worn or damaged. Replace wheel bearing.

Front Wheel Drive Vehicles
a. Torque lug nuts and axle nuts to specification and recheck for looseness.
b. Wheel bearing worn or damaged. Replace wheel bearing.
c. Wheel bearing out of adjustment. Adjust wheel bearing to specification; if still loose, replace.

Rear Wheel Drive Vehicles
a. Wheel bearing out of adjustment. Adjust wheel bearing to specification; if still loose, replace.
b. Torque lug nuts to specification and recheck for looseness.
c. Wheel bearing worn or damaged. Replace wheel bearing.

2. Rear wheel or wheel bearing loose

All Wheel and Four Wheel Drive Vehicles
a. Torque lug nuts and axle nuts to specification and recheck for looseness.
b. Wheel bearing worn or damaged. Replace wheel bearing.

Front Wheel Drive Vehicles
a. Wheel bearing out of adjustment. Adjust wheel bearing to specification; if still loose, replace.
b. Torque lug nuts to specification and recheck for looseness.
c. Wheel bearing worn or damaged. Replace wheel bearing.

Rear Wheel Drive Vehicles
a. Torque lug nuts to specification and recheck for looseness.
c. Wheel bearing worn or damaged. Replace wheel bearing.

4-B. Tires

1. Tires worn on inside tread
a. Check alignment for a toed-out condition. Check and set tire pressures and properly adjust the toe.
b. Check for worn, damaged or defective suspension components. Replace defective parts and adjust the alignment.

2. Tires worn on outside tread
a. Check alignment for a toed-in condition. Check and set tire pressures and properly adjust the toe.
b. Check for worn, damaged or defective suspension components. Replace defective parts and adjust the alignment.

3. Tires worn unevenly
a. Check the tire pressure and tire balance. Replace worn or defective tires and check the alignment; adjust if necessary.

BRAKE PERFORMANCE TROUBLESHOOTING HINTS

Brake vibrations or pulsation can often be diagnosed on a safe and careful test drive. A brake vibration which is felt through the brake pedal while braking, but not felt in the steering wheel, is most likely caused by brake surface variations in the rear brakes. If both the brake pedal and steering wheel vibrate during braking, a surface variation in the front brakes, or both front and rear brakes, is very likely.

A brake pedal that pumps up with repeated use can be caused by air in the brake hydraulic system or, if the vehicle is equipped with rear drum brakes, the brake adjusters may be seized or out of adjustment. A quick test for brake adjustment on vehicles with rear drum brakes is to pump the brake pedal several times with the vehicle's engine not running and the parking brake released. Pump the brake pedal several times and continue to apply pressure to the brake pedal. With pressure being applied to the brake pedal, engage the parking brake. Release the brake pedal and quickly press the brake pedal again. If the brake pedal pumped up, the rear brakes are in need of adjustment. Do not compensate for the rear brake adjustment by adjusting the parking brake, this will cause premature brake lining wear.

To test a vacuum brake booster, pump the brake pedal several times with the vehicle's engine off. Apply pressure to the brake pedal and then start the engine. The brake pedal should move downward about one inch (25mm).

b. Check for worn shock absorbers. Replaced failed components, worn or defective tires and check the alignment; adjust if necessary.
c. Check the alignment settings. Check and set tire pressures and properly adjust the alignment to specification.
d. Check for worn, damaged or defective suspension components. Replace defective parts and adjust the alignment to specification.

4-C. Steering

1. Excessive play in steering wheel
a. Check the steering gear free-play adjustment and properly adjust to remove excessive play.
b. Check the steering linkage for worn, damaged or defective parts. Replace failed components and perform a front end alignment.
c. Check for a worn, damaged, or defective steering box, replace the steering gear and check the front end alignment.

2. Steering wheel shakes at cruising speeds
a. Check for a bent front wheel. Replace a damaged wheel and check the tire for possible internal damage.
b. Check for an unevenly worn front tire. Replace the tire, adjust tire pressure and balance.
c. Check the front tires for hidden internal damage. Tires which have encountered large pot holes or suffered other hard blows may have sustained internal damage and should be replaced immediately.
d. Check the front tires for an out-of-balance condition. Remove, spin balance and reinstall. Torque all the wheel bolts or lug nuts to the recommended specification.
e. Check for a loose wheel bearing. If possible, adjust the bearing, or replace the bearing if it is a non-adjustable bearing.

3. Steering wheel shakes when braking
a. Refer to section 3-A, condition number 1.

4. Steering wheel becomes stiff when turned
a. Check the steering wheel free-play adjustment and reset as needed.
b. Check for a damaged steering gear assembly. Replace the steering gear and perform a front end alignment.
c. Check for damaged or seized suspension components. Replace defective components and perform a front end alignment.

4-D. Suspension

1. Vehicle pulls to one side
a. Tire pressure uneven. Adjust tire pressure to recommended settings.
b. Tires worn unevenly. Replace tires and check alignment settings.
c. Alignment out of specification. Align front end and check thrust angle.
d. Check for a dragging brake and repair or replace as necessary.

2. Vehicle is very bouncy over bumps
a. Check for worn or leaking shock absorbers or strut assemblies and replace as necessary.
b. Check for seized shock absorbers or strut assemblies and replace as necessary.

NOTE: When one shock fails, it is recommended to replace front or rear units as pairs.

3. Vehicle leans excessively in turns
a. Check for worn or leaking shock absorbers or strut assemblies and replace as necessary.
b. Check for missing, damaged, or worn stabilizer links or bushings, and replace or install as necessary.

4. Vehicle ride quality seems excessively harsh
a. Check for seized shock absorbers or strut assemblies and replace as necessary.
b. Check for excessively high tire pressures and adjust pressures to vehicle recommendations.

5. Vehicle seems low or leans to one side
a. Check for a damaged, broken or weak spring. Replace defective parts and check for a needed alignment.
b. Check for seized shock absorbers or strut assemblies and replace as necessary.
c. Check for worn or leaking shock absorbers or strut assemblies and replace as necessary.

4-E. Driving Noises and Vibrations

Noises

1. Vehicle makes a clicking noises when driven
a. Check the noise to see if it varies with road speed. Verify if the noise is present when coasting or with steering or throttle input. If the clicking noise frequency changes with road speed and is not affected by steering or throttle input, check the tire treads for a stone, piece of glass, nail or another hard object imbedded into the tire or tire tread. Stones rarely cause a tire puncture and are easily removed. Other objects may create an air leak when removed. Consider having these objects removed immediately at a facility equipped to repair tire punctures.
b. If the clicking noise varies with throttle input and steering, check for a worn Constant Velocity (CV-joint) joint, universal (U- joint) or flex joint.

2. Vehicle makes a clunking or knocking noise over bumps
a. A clunking noise over bumps is most often caused by excessive movement or clearance in a suspension component. Check the suspension for soft, cracked, damaged or worn bushings. Replace the bushings and check the vehicle's alignment.
b. Check for loose suspension mounting bolts. Check the tightness on subframe bolts, pivot bolts and suspension mounting bolts, and torque to specification.
c. Check the vehicle for a loose wheel bearing. Some wheel bearings can be adjusted for looseness, while others must be replaced if loose. Adjust or replace the bearings as recommended by the manufacturer.
d. Check the door latch adjustment. If the door is slightly loose, or the latch adjustment is not centered, the door assembly may create noises over bumps and rough surfaces. Properly adjust the door latches to secure the door.

3. Vehicle makes a low pitched rumbling noise when driven
a. A low pitched rumbling noise is usually caused by a drive train related bearing and is most often associated with a wheel bearing which has been damaged or worn. The damage can be caused by excessive brake temperatures or physical contact with a pot hole or curb. Sometimes the noise will vary when turning. Left hand turns increase the load on the vehicle's right side, and right turns load the left side. A failed front wheel bearing may also cause a slight steering wheel vibration when turning. A bearing which exhibits noise must be replaced.
b. Check the tire condition and balance. An internally damaged tire may cause failure symptoms similar to failed suspension parts. For diagnostic purposes, try a known good set of tires and replace defective tires.

4. Vehicle makes a squeaking noise over bumps
a. Check the vehicle's ball joints for wear, damaged or leaking boots. Replace a ball joint if it is loose, the boot is damaged and leaking, or the ball joint is binding. When replacing suspension parts, check the vehicle for alignment.
b. Check for seized or deteriorated bushings. Replace bushings that are worn or damaged and check the vehicle for alignment.
c. Check for the presence of sway bar or stabilizer bar bushings which wrap around the bar. Inspect the condition of the bushings and replace if worn or damaged. Remove the bushing bracket and apply a thin layer of suspension grease to the area where the bushings wrap around the bar and reinstall the bushing brackets.

Vibrations

5. Vehicle vibrates when driven
a. Check the road surface. Roads which have rough or uneven surfaces may cause unusual vibrations.
b. Check the tire condition and balance. An internally damaged tire may cause failure symptoms similar to failed suspension parts. For diagnostic purposes, try a known good set of tires and replace defective tires immediately.
c. Check for a worn Constant Velocity (CV-joint) joint, universal (U- joint) or flex joint and replace if loose, damaged or binding.
d. Check for a loose, bent, or out-of-balance axle or drive shaft. Replace damaged or failed components.

NOTE: Diagnosing failures related to wheels, tires, steering and the suspension system can often times be accomplished with a careful and thorough test drive. Bearing noises are isolated by noting whether the noises or symptoms vary when turning left or right, or occur while driving a straight line. During a left hand turn, the vehicle's weight shifts to the right, placing more force on the right side bearings, such that if a right side wheel bearing is worn or damaged, the noise or vibration should increase during light-to-heavy acceleration. Conversely, on right hand turns, the vehicle tends to lean to the left, loading the left side bearings.

Knocking noises in the suspension when the vehicle is driven over rough roads, railroad tracks and speed bumps indicate worn suspension components such as bushings, ball joints or tie rod ends, or a worn steering system.

5. ELECTRICAL ACCESSORIES

5-A. Headlights

1. One headlight only works on high or low beam
a. Check for battery voltage at headlight electrical connector. If battery voltage is present, replace the headlight assembly or bulb if available separately. If battery voltage is not present, refer to the headlight wiring diagram to troubleshoot.

2. Headlight does not work on high or low beam
a. Check for battery voltage and ground at headlight electrical connector. If battery voltage is present, check the headlight connector ground terminal for a proper ground. If battery voltage and ground are present at the headlight connector, replace the headlight assembly or bulb if available separately. If battery voltage or ground is not present, refer to the headlight wiring diagram to troubleshoot.
b. Check the headlight switch operation. Replace the switch if the switch is defective or operates intermittently.

3. Headlight(s) very dim
a. Check for battery voltage and ground at headlight electrical connector. If battery voltage is present, trace the ground circuit for the headlamp electrical connector, then clean and repair as necessary. If the voltage at the headlight electrical connector is significantly less than the voltage at the battery, refer to the headlight wiring diagram to troubleshoot and locate the voltage drop.

5-B. Tail, Running and Side Marker Lights

1. Tail light, running light or side marker light inoperative
a. Check for battery voltage and ground at light's electrical connector. If battery voltage is present, check the bulb socket and electrical connector ground terminal for a proper ground. If battery voltage and ground are present at the light connector, but not in the socket, clean the socket and the ground terminal connector. If battery voltage and ground are present in the bulb socket, replace the bulb. If battery voltage or ground is not present, refer to the wiring diagram to troubleshoot for an open circuit.
b. Check the light switch operation and replace if necessary.

2. Tail light, running light or side marker light works intermittently
a. Check the bulb for a damaged filament, and replace if damaged.
b Check the bulb and bulb socket for corrosion, and clean or replace the bulb and socket.
c. Check for loose, damaged or corroded wires and electrical terminals, and repair as necessary.
d. Check the light switch operation and replace if necessary.

3. Tail light, running light or side marker light very dim
a. Check the bulb and bulb socket for corrosion and clean or replace the bulb and socket.

b. Check for low voltage at the bulb socket positive terminal or a poor ground. If voltage is low, or the ground marginal, trace the wiring to, and check for loose, damaged or corroded wires and electrical terminals; repair as necessary.

c. Check the light switch operation and replace if necessary.

5-C. Interior Lights

1. Interior light inoperative

a. Verify the interior light switch location and position(s), and set the switch in the correct position.

b. Check for battery voltage and ground at the interior light bulb socket. If battery voltage and ground are present, replace the bulb. If voltage is not present, check the interior light fuse for battery voltage. If the fuse is missing, replace the fuse. If the fuse has blown, or if battery voltage is present, refer to the wiring diagram to troubleshoot the cause for an open or shorted circuit. If ground is not present, check the door switch contacts and clean or repair as necessary.

2. Interior light works intermittently

a. Check the bulb for a damaged filament, and replace if damaged.

b. Check the bulb and bulb socket for corrosion, and clean or replace the bulb and socket.

c. Check for loose, damaged or corroded wires and electrical terminals; repair as necessary.

d. Check the door and light switch operation, and replace if necessary.

3. Interior light very dim

a. Check the bulb and bulb socket for corrosion, and clean or replace the bulb and socket.

b. Check for low voltage at the bulb socket positive terminal or a poor ground. If voltage is low, or the ground marginal, trace the wiring to, and check for loose, damaged or corroded wires and electrical terminals; repair as necessary.

c. Check the door and light switch operation, and replace if necessary.

5-D. Brake Lights

1. One brake light inoperative

a. Press the brake pedal and check for battery voltage and ground at the brake light bulb socket. If present, replace the bulb. If either battery voltage or ground is not present, refer to the wiring diagram to troubleshoot.

2. Both brake lights inoperative

a. Press the brake pedal and check for battery voltage and ground at the brake light bulb socket. If present, replace both bulbs. If battery voltage is not present, check the brake light switch adjustment and adjust as necessary. If the brake light switch is properly adjusted, and battery voltage or the ground is not present at the bulb sockets, or at the bulb electrical connector with the brake pedal pressed, refer to the wiring diagram to troubleshoot the cause of an open circuit.

3. One or both brake lights very dim

a. Press the brake pedal and measure the voltage at the brake light bulb socket. If the measured voltage is close to the battery voltage, check for a poor ground caused by a loose, damaged, or corroded wire, terminal, bulb or bulb socket. If the ground is bolted to a painted surface, it may be necessary to remove the electrical connector and clean the mounting surface, so the connector mounts on bare metal. If battery voltage is low, check for a poor connection caused by either a faulty brake light switch, a loose, damaged, or corroded wire, terminal or electrical connector. Refer to the wiring diagram to troubleshoot the cause of a voltage drop.

5-E. Warning Lights

1. Warning light(s) stay on when the engine is started

Ignition, Battery or Alternator Warning Light

a. Check the alternator output and voltage regulator operation, and replace as necessary.

b. Check the warning light wiring for a shorted wire.

Check Engine Light

a. Check the engine for routine maintenance and tune-up status. Note the engine tune-up specifications and verify the spark plug, air filter and engine oil condition; replace and/or adjust items as necessary.

b. Check the fuel tank for low fuel level, causing an intermittent lean fuel mixture. Top off fuel tank and reset check engine light.

c. Check for a failed or disconnected engine fuel or ignition component, sensor or control unit and repair or replace as necessary.

d. Check the intake manifold and vacuum hoses for air leaks and repair as necessary.

e. Check the engine's mechanical condition for excessive oil consumption.

Anti-Lock Braking System (ABS) Light

a. Check the wheel sensors and sensor rings for debris, and clean as necessary.

b. Check the brake master cylinder for fluid leakage or seal failure and replace as necessary.

c. Check the ABS control unit, pump and proportioning valves for proper operation; replace as necessary.

d. Check the sensor wiring at the wheel sensors and the ABS control unit for a loose or shorted wire, and repair as necessary.

Brake Warning Light

a. Check the brake fluid level and check for possible leakage from the hydraulic lines and seals. Top off brake fluid and repair fluid leakage as necessary.

b. Check the brake linings for wear and replace as necessary.

c. Check for a loose or shorted brake warning light sensor or wire, and replace or repair as necessary.

Oil Pressure Warning Light

a. Stop the engine immediately. Check the engine oil level and oil filter condition, and top off or change the oil as necessary.

b. Check the oil pressure sensor wire for being shorted to ground. Disconnect the wire from the oil pressure sensor and with the ignition in the ON position, but not running, the oil pressure light should not be working. If the light works with the wire disconnected, check the sensor wire for being shorted to ground. Check the wire routing to make sure the wire is not pinched and check for insulation damage. Repair or replace the wire as necessary and recheck before starting the engine.

c. Remove the oil pan and check for a clogged oil pick-up tube screen.

d. Check the oil pressure sensor operation by substituting a known good sensor.

e. Check the oil filter for internal restrictions or leaks, and replace as necessary.

WARNING: If the engine is operated with oil pressure below the manufacturer's specification, severe (and costly) engine damage could occur. Low oil pressure can be caused by excessive internal wear or damage to the engine bearings, oil pressure relief valve, oil pump or oil pump drive mechanism.

Before starting the engine, check for possible causes of rapid oil loss, such as leaking oil lines or a loose, damaged, restricted, or leaking oil filter or oil pressure sensor. If the engine oil level and condition are acceptable, measure the engine's oil pressure using a pressure gauge, or determine the cause for the oil pressure warning light to function when the engine is running, before operating the engine for an extended period of time. Another symptom of operating an engine with low oil pressure is the presence of severe knocking and tapping noises.

Parking Brake Warning Light

a. Check the brake release mechanism and verify the parking brake has been fully released.

b. Check the parking brake light switch for looseness or misalignment.

c. Check for a damaged switch or a loose or shorted brake light switch wire, and replace or repair as necessary.

2. Warning light(s) flickers on and off when driving

Ignition, Battery or Alternator Warning Light

a. Check the alternator output and voltage regulator operation. An intermittent condition may indicate worn brushes, an internal short, or a defective voltage regulator. Replace the alternator or failed component.

b. Check the warning light wiring for a shorted, pinched or damaged wire and repair as necessary.

Check Engine Light

a. Check the engine for required maintenance and tune-up status. Verify engine tune-up specifications, as well as spark plug, air filter and engine oil condition; replace and/or adjust items as necessary.

b. Check the fuel tank for low fuel level causing an intermittent lean fuel mixture. Top off fuel tank and reset check engine light.

c. Check for an intermittent failure or partially disconnected engine fuel and ignition component, sensor or control unit; repair or replace as necessary.

d. Check the intake manifold and vacuum hoses for air leaks, and repair as necessary.

e. Check the warning light wiring for a shorted, pinched or damaged wire and repair as necessary.

Anti-Lock Braking System (ABS) Light

a. Check the wheel sensors and sensor rings for debris, and clean as necessary.

b. Check the brake master cylinder for fluid leakage or seal failure and replace as necessary.

c. Check the ABS control unit, pump and proportioning valves for proper operation, and replace as necessary.

d. Check the sensor wiring at the wheel sensors and the ABS control unit for a loose or shorted wire and repair as necessary.

Brake Warning Light

a. Check the brake fluid level and check for possible leakage from the hydraulic lines and seals. Top off brake fluid and repair leakage as necessary.

b. Check the brake linings for wear and replace as necessary.

c. Check for a loose or shorted brake warning light sensor or wire, and replace or repair as necessary.

Oil Pressure Warning Light

a. Stop the engine immediately. Check the engine oil level and check for a sudden and rapid oil loss, such as a leaking oil line or oil pressure sensor, and repair or replace as necessary.

b. Check the oil pressure sensor operation by substituting a known good sensor.

c. Check the oil pressure sensor wire for being shorted to ground. Disconnect the wire from the oil pressure sensor and with the ignition in the ON position, but not running, the oil pressure light should not be working. If the light works with the wire disconnected, check the sensor wire for being shorted to ground. Check the wire routing to make sure the wire is not pinched and check for insulation damage. Repair or replace the wire as necessary and recheck before starting the engine.

d. Remove the oil pan and check for a clogged oil pick-up tube screen.

Parking Brake Warning Light

a. Check the brake release mechanism and verify the parking brake has been fully released.

b. Check the parking brake light switch for looseness or misalignment.

c. Check for a damaged switch or a loose or shorted brake light switch wire, and replace or repair as necessary.

3. Warning light(s) inoperative with ignition on, and engine not started

a. Check for a defective bulb by installing a known good bulb.

b. Check for a defective wire using the appropriate wiring diagram(s).

c. Check for a defective sending unit by removing and then grounding the wire at the sending unit. If the light comes on with the ignition on when grounding the wire, replace the sending unit.

5-F. Turn Signal and 4-Way Hazard Lights

1. Turn signals or hazard lights come on, but do not flash

a. Check for a defective flasher unit and replace as necessary.

2. Turn signals or hazard lights do not function on either side

a. Check the fuse and replace, if defective.

b. Check the flasher unit by substituting a known good flasher unit.

c. Check the turn signal electrical system for a defective component, open circuit, short circuit or poor ground.

3. Turn signals or hazard lights only work on one side

a. Check for failed bulbs and replace as necessary.

b. Check for poor grounds in both housings and repair as necessary.

4. One signal light does not work

a. Check for a failed bulb and replace as necessary.

b. Check for corrosion in the bulb socket, and clean and repair as necessary.

c. Check for a poor ground at the bulb socket, and clean and repair as necessary.

5. Turn signals flash too slowly

a. Check signal bulb(s) wattage and replace with lower wattage bulb(s).

6. Turn signals flash too fast

a. Check signal bulb(s) wattage and replace with higher wattage bulb(s).

b. Check for installation of the correct flasher unit and replace if incorrect.

7. Four-way hazard flasher indicator light inoperative

a. Verify that the exterior lights are functioning and, if so, replace indicator bulb.

b. Check the operation of the warning flasher switch and replace if defective.

8. Turn signal indicator light(s) do not work in either direction

a. Verify that the exterior lights are functioning and, if so, replace indicator bulb(s).

b. Check for a defective flasher unit by substituting a known good unit.

9. One turn signal indicator light does not work

a. Check for a defective bulb and replace as necessary.

b. Check for a defective flasher unit by substituting a known good unit.

5-G. Horn

1. Horn does not operate

a. Check for a defective fuse and replace as necessary.

b. Check for battery voltage and ground at horn electrical connections when pressing the horn switch. If voltage is present, replace the horn assembly. If voltage or ground is not present, refer to Chassis Electrical coverage for additional troubleshooting techniques and circuit information.

2. Horn has an unusual tone

a. On single horn systems, replace the horn.

b. On dual horn systems, check the operation of the second horn. Dual horn systems have a high and low pitched horn. Unplug one horn at a time and recheck operation. Replace the horn which does not function.

c. Check for debris or condensation build-up in horn and verify the horn positioning. If the horn has a single opening, adjust the opening downward to allow for adequate drainage and to prevent debris build-up.

5-H. Windshield Wipers

1. Windshield wipers do not operate

a. Check fuse and replace as necessary.

b. Check switch operation and repair or replace as necessary.

c. Check for corroded, loose, disconnected or broken wires and clean or repair as necessary.

d. Check the ground circuit for the wiper switch or motor and repair as necessary.

2. Windshield wiper motor makes a humming noise, gets hot or blows fuses

a. Wiper motor damaged internally; replace the wiper motor.

b. Wiper linkage bent, damaged or seized. Repair or replace wiper linkage as necessary.

3. Windshield wiper motor operates, but one or both wipers fail to move

a. Windshield wiper motor linkage loose or disconnected. Repair or replace linkage as necessary.

b. Windshield wiper arms loose on wiper pivots. Secure wiper arm to pivot or replace both the wiper arm and pivot assembly.

4. Windshield wipers will not park

a. Check the wiper switch operation and verify that the switch properly interrupts the power supplied to the wiper motor.

b. If the wiper switch is functioning properly, the wiper motor parking circuit has failed. Replace the wiper motor assembly. Operate the wiper motor at least one time before installing the arms and blades to ensure correct positioning, then recheck using the highest wiper speed on a wet windshield to make sure the arms and blades do not contact the windshield trim.

6. INSTRUMENTS AND GAUGES

6-A. Speedometer (Cable Operated)

1. Speedometer does not work

a. Check and verify that the speedometer cable is properly seated into the speedometer assembly and the speedometer drive gear.

b. Check the speedometer cable for breakage or rounded-off cable ends where the cable seats into the speedometer drive gear and into the speedometer assembly. If damaged, broken or the cable ends are rounded off, replace the cable.

c. Check speedometer drive gear condition and replace as necessary.

d. Install a known good speedometer to test for proper operation. If the substituted speedometer functions properly, replace the speedometer assembly.

2. Speedometer needle fluctuates when driving at steady speeds.

a. Check speedometer cable routing or sheathing for sharp bends or kinks. Route cable to minimize sharp bends or kinks. If the sheathing has been damaged, replace the cable assembly.

b. Check the speedometer cable for adequate lubrication. Remove the cable, inspect for damage, clean, lubricate and reinstall. If the cable has been damaged, replace the cable.

3. Speedometer works intermittently

a. Check the cable and verify that the cable is fully installed and the fasteners are secure.

b. Check the cable ends for wear and rounding, and replace as necessary.

6-B. Speedometer (Electronically Operated)

1. Speedometer does not work
a. Check the speed sensor pickup and replace as necessary.
b. Check the wiring between the speed sensor and the speedometer for corroded terminals, loose connections or broken wires and clean or repair as necessary.
c. Install a known good speedometer to test for proper operation. If the substituted speedometer functions properly, replace the speedometer assembly.

2. Speedometer works intermittently
a. Check the wiring between the speed sensor and the speedometer for corroded terminals, loose connections or broken wires and clean or repair as necessary.
b. Check the speed sensor pickup and replace as necessary.

6-C. Fuel, Temperature and Oil Pressure Gauges

1. Gauge does not register
a. Check for a missing or blown fuse and replace as necessary.
b. Check for an open circuit in the gauge wiring. Repair wiring as necessary.

c. Gauge sending unit defective. Replace gauge sending unit.
d. Gauge or sending unit improperly installed. Verify installation and wiring, and repair as necessary.

2. Gauge operates erratically
a. Check for loose, shorted, damaged or corroded electrical connections or wiring and repair as necessary.
b. Check gauge sending units and replace as necessary.

3. Gauge operates fully pegged
a. Sending unit-to-gauge wire shorted to ground.
b. Sending unit defective; replace sending unit.
c. Gauge or sending unit not properly grounded.
d. Gauge or sending unit improperly installed. Verify installation and wiring, and repair as necessary.

7. CLIMATE CONTROL

7-A. Air Conditioner

1. No air coming from air conditioner vents
a. Check the air conditioner fuse and replace as necessary.
b. Air conditioner system discharged. Have the system evacuated, charged and leak tested by an MVAC certified technician, utilizing approved recovery/recycling equipment. Repair as necessary.
c. Air conditioner low pressure switch defective. Replace switch.
d. Air conditioner fan resistor pack defective. Replace resistor pack.
e. Loose connection, broken wiring or defective air conditioner relay in air conditioning electrical circuit. Repair wiring or replace relay as necessary.

2. Air conditioner blows warm air
a. Air conditioner system is discharged. Have the system evacuated, charged and leak tested by an MVAC certified technician, utilizing approved recovery/recycling equipment. Repair as necessary.
b. Air conditioner compressor clutch not engaging. Check compressor clutch wiring, electrical connections and compressor clutch, and repair or replace as necessary.

3. Water collects on the interior floor when the air conditioner is used
a. Air conditioner evaporator drain hose is blocked. Clear the drain hose where it exits the passenger compartment.
b. Air conditioner evaporator drain hose is disconnected. Secure the drain hose to the evaporator drainage tray under the dashboard.

4. Air conditioner has a moldy odor when used
a. The air conditioner evaporator drain hose is blocked or partially re-stricted, allowing condensation to build up around the evaporator and drainage tray. Clear the drain hose where it exits the passenger compartment.

7-B. Heater

1. Blower motor does not operate
a. Check blower motor fuse and replace as necessary.
b. Check blower motor wiring for loose, damaged or corroded contacts and repair as necessary.
c. Check blower motor switch and resistor pack for open circuits, and repair or replace as necessary.
d. Check blower motor for internal damage and repair or replace as necessary.

2. Heater blows cool air
a. Check the engine coolant level. If the coolant level is low, top off and bleed the air from the cooling system as necessary and check for coolant leaks.
b. Check engine coolant operating temperature. If coolant temperature is below specification, check for a damaged or stuck thermostat.
c. Check the heater control valve operation. Check the heater control valve cable or vacuum hose for proper installation. Move the heater temperature control from hot to cold several times and verify the operation of the heater control valve. With the engine at normal operating temperature and the heater temperature control in the full hot position, carefully feel the heater hose going into and exiting the control valve. If one heater hose is hot and the other is much cooler, replace the control valve.

3. Heater steams the windshield when used
a. Check for a loose cooling system hose clamp or leaking coolant hose near the engine firewall or under the dash area, and repair as necessary.
b. Check for the existence of a sweet odor and fluid dripping from the heater floor vents, indicating a failed or damaged heater core. Pressure test the cooling system with the heater set to the fully warm position and check for fluid leakage from the floor vents. If leakage is verified, remove and replace the heater core assembly.

NOTE: On some vehicles, the dashboard must be disassembled and removed to access the heater core.

GLOSSARY

AIR/FUEL RATIO: The ratio of air-to-gasoline by weight in the fuel mixture drawn into the engine.

AIR INJECTION: One method of reducing harmful exhaust emissions by injecting air into each of the exhaust ports of an engine. The fresh air entering the hot exhaust manifold causes any remaining fuel to be burned before it can exit the tailpipe.

ALTERNATOR: A device used for converting mechanical energy into electrical energy.

AMMETER: An instrument, calibrated in amperes, used to measure the flow of an electrical current in a circuit. Ammeters are always connected in series with the circuit being tested.

AMPERE: The rate of flow of electrical current present when one volt of electrical pressure is applied against one ohm of electrical resistance.

ANALOG COMPUTER: Any microprocessor that uses similar (analogous) electrical signals to make its calculations.

ARMATURE: A laminated, soft iron core wrapped by a wire that converts electrical energy to mechanical energy as in a motor or relay. When rotated in a magnetic field, it changes mechanical energy into electrical energy as in a generator.

ATMOSPHERIC PRESSURE: The pressure on the Earth's surface caused by the weight of the air in the atmosphere. At sea level, this pressure is 14.7 psi at 32°F (101 kPa at 0°C).

ATOMIZATION: The breaking down of a liquid into a fine mist that can be suspended in air.

AXIAL PLAY: Movement parallel to a shaft or bearing bore.

BACKFIRE: The sudden combustion of gases in the intake or exhaust system that results in a loud explosion.

BACKLASH: The clearance or play between two parts, such as meshed gears.

BACKPRESSURE: Restrictions in the exhaust system that slow the exit of exhaust gases from the combustion chamber.

BAKELITE: A heat resistant, plastic insulator material commonly used in printed circuit boards and transistorized components.

BALL BEARING: A bearing made up of hardened inner and outer races between which hardened steel balls roll.

BALLAST RESISTOR: A resistor in the primary ignition circuit that lowers voltage after the engine is started to reduce wear on ignition components.

BEARING: A friction reducing, supportive device usually located between a stationary part and a moving part.

BIMETAL TEMPERATURE SENSOR: Any sensor or switch made of two dissimilar types of metal that bend when heated or cooled due to the different expansion rates of the alloys. These types of sensors usually function as an on/off switch.

BLOWBY: Combustion gases, composed of water vapor and unburned fuel, that leak past the piston rings into the crankcase during normal engine operation. These gases are removed by the PCV system to prevent the buildup of harmful acids in the crankcase.

BRAKE PAD: A brake shoe and lining assembly used with disc brakes.

BRAKE SHOE: The backing for the brake lining. The term is, however, usually applied to the assembly of the brake backing and lining.

BUSHING: A liner, usually removable, for a bearing; an anti-friction liner used in place of a bearing.

CALIPER: A hydraulically activated device in a disc brake system, which is mounted straddling the brake rotor (disc). The caliper contains at least one piston and two brake pads. Hydraulic pressure on the piston(s) forces the pads against the rotor.

CAMSHAFT: A shaft in the engine on which are the lobes (cams) which operate the valves. The camshaft is driven by the crankshaft, via a belt, chain or gears, at one half the crankshaft speed.

CAPACITOR: A device which stores an electrical charge.

CARBON MONOXIDE (CO): A colorless, odorless gas given off as a normal byproduct of combustion. It is poisonous and extremely dangerous in confined areas, building up slowly to toxic levels without warning if adequate ventilation is not available.

CARBURETOR: A device, usually mounted on the intake manifold of an engine, which mixes the air and fuel in the proper proportion to allow even combustion.

CATALYTIC CONVERTER: A device installed in the exhaust system, like a muffler, that converts harmful byproducts of combustion into carbon dioxide and water vapor by means of a heat-producing chemical reaction.

CENTRIFUGAL ADVANCE: A mechanical method of advancing the spark timing by using flyweights in the distributor that react to centrifugal force generated by the distributor shaft rotation.

CHECK VALVE: Any one-way valve installed to permit the flow of air, fuel or vacuum in one direction only.

CHOKE: A device, usually a moveable valve, placed in the intake path of a carburetor to restrict the flow of air.

CIRCUIT: Any unbroken path through which an electrical current can flow. Also used to describe fuel flow in some instances.

CIRCUIT BREAKER: A switch which protects an electrical circuit from overload by opening the circuit when the current flow exceeds a predetermined level. Some circuit breakers must be reset manually, while most reset automatically.

COIL (IGNITION): A transformer in the ignition circuit which steps up the voltage provided to the spark plugs.

COMBINATION MANIFOLD: An assembly which includes both the intake and exhaust manifolds in one casting.

COMBINATION VALVE: A device used in some fuel systems that routes fuel vapors to a charcoal storage canister instead of venting them into the atmosphere. The valve relieves fuel tank pressure and allows fresh air into the tank as the fuel level drops to prevent a vapor lock situation.

COMPRESSION RATIO: The comparison of the total volume of the cylinder and combustion chamber with the piston at BDC and the piston at TDC.

CONDENSER: 1. An electrical device which acts to store an electrical charge, preventing voltage surges. 2. A radiator-like device in the air conditioning system in which refrigerant gas condenses into a liquid, giving off heat.

CONDUCTOR: Any material through which an electrical current can be transmitted easily.

CONTINUITY: Continuous or complete circuit. Can be checked with an ohmmeter.

COUNTERSHAFT: An intermediate shaft which is rotated by a mainshaft and transmits, in turn, that rotation to a working part.

CRANKCASE: The lower part of an engine in which the crankshaft and related parts operate.

CRANKSHAFT: The main driving shaft of an engine which receives reciprocating motion from the pistons and converts it to rotary motion.

CYLINDER: In an engine, the round hole in the engine block in which the piston(s) ride.

CYLINDER BLOCK: The main structural member of an engine in which is found the cylinders, crankshaft and other principal parts.

CYLINDER HEAD: The detachable portion of the engine, usually fastened to the top of the cylinder block and containing all or most of the combustion chambers. On overhead valve engines, it contains the valves and their operating parts. On overhead cam engines, it contains the camshaft as well.

DEAD CENTER: The extreme top or bottom of the piston stroke.

DETONATION: An unwanted explosion of the air/fuel mixture in the combustion chamber caused by excess heat and compression, advanced timing, or an overly lean mixture. Also referred to as "ping".

DIAPHRAGM: A thin, flexible wall separating two cavities, such as in a vacuum advance unit.

DIESELING: A condition in which hot spots in the combustion chamber cause the engine to run on after the key is turned off.

DIFFERENTIAL: A geared assembly which allows the transmission of motion between drive axles, giving one axle the ability to turn faster than the other.

DIODE: An electrical device that will allow current to flow in one direction only.

DISC BRAKE: A hydraulic braking assembly consisting of a brake disc, or rotor, mounted on an axle, and a caliper assembly containing, usually two brake pads which are activated by hydraulic pressure. The pads are forced against the sides of the disc, creating friction which slows the vehicle.

DISTRIBUTOR: A mechanically driven device on an engine which is responsible for electrically firing the spark plug at a predetermined point of the piston stroke.

DOWEL PIN: A pin, inserted in mating holes in two different parts allowing those parts to maintain a fixed relationship.

DRUM BRAKE: A braking system which consists of two brake shoes and one or two wheel cylinders, mounted on a fixed backing plate, and a brake drum, mounted on an axle, which revolves around the assembly.

DWELL: The rate, measured in degrees of shaft rotation, at which an electrical circuit cycles on and off.

ELECTRONIC CONTROL UNIT (ECU): Ignition module, module, amplifier or igniter. See Module for definition.

ELECTRONIC IGNITION: A system in which the timing and firing of the spark plugs is controlled by an electronic control unit, usually called a module. These systems have no points or condenser.

END-PLAY: The measured amount of axial movement in a shaft.

ENGINE: A device that converts heat into mechanical energy.

EXHAUST MANIFOLD: A set of cast passages or pipes which conduct exhaust gases from the engine.

FEELER GAUGE: A blade, usually metal, or precisely predetermined thickness, used to measure the clearance between two parts.

FIRING ORDER: The order in which combustion occurs in the cylinders of an engine. Also the order in which spark is distributed to the plugs by the distributor.

FLOODING: The presence of too much fuel in the intake manifold and combustion chamber which prevents the air/fuel mixture from firing, thereby causing a no-start situation.

FLYWHEEL: A disc shaped part bolted to the rear end of the crankshaft. Around the outer perimeter is affixed the ring gear. The starter drive engages the ring gear, turning the flywheel, which rotates the crankshaft, imparting the initial starting motion to the engine.

FOOT POUND (ft. lbs. or sometimes, ft.lb.): The amount of energy or work needed to raise an item weighing one pound, a distance of one foot.

FUSE: A protective device in a circuit which prevents circuit overload by breaking the circuit when a specific amperage is present. The device is constructed around a strip or wire of a lower amperage rating than the circuit it is designed to protect. When an amperage higher than that stamped on the fuse is present in the circuit, the strip or wire melts, opening the circuit.

GEAR RATIO: The ratio between the number of teeth on meshing gears.

GENERATOR: A device which converts mechanical energy into electrical energy.

HEAT RANGE: The measure of a spark plug's ability to dissipate heat from its firing end. The higher the heat range, the hotter the plug fires.

HUB: The center part of a wheel or gear.

HYDROCARBON (HC): Any chemical compound made up of hydrogen and carbon. A major pollutant formed by the engine as a byproduct of combustion.

HYDROMETER: An instrument used to measure the specific gravity of a solution.

INCH POUND (inch lbs.; sometimes in.lb. or in. lbs.): One twelfth of a foot pound.

INDUCTION: A means of transferring electrical energy in the form of a magnetic field. Principle used in the ignition coil to increase voltage.

INJECTOR: A device which receives metered fuel under relatively low pressure and is activated to inject the fuel into the engine under relatively high pressure at a predetermined time.

INPUT SHAFT: The shaft to which torque is applied, usually carrying the driving gear or gears.

INTAKE MANIFOLD: A casting of passages or pipes used to conduct air or a fuel/air mixture to the cylinders.

JOURNAL: The bearing surface within which a shaft operates.

KEY: A small block usually fitted in a notch between a shaft and a hub to prevent slippage of the two parts.

MANIFOLD: A casting of passages or set of pipes which connect the cylinders to an inlet or outlet source.

MANIFOLD VACUUM: Low pressure in an engine intake manifold formed just below the throttle plates. Manifold vacuum is highest at idle and drops under acceleration.

MASTER CYLINDER: The primary fluid pressurizing device in a hydraulic system. In automotive use, it is found in brake and hydraulic clutch systems and is pedal activated, either directly or, in a power brake system, through the power booster.

MODULE: Electronic control unit, amplifier or igniter of solid state or integrated design which controls the current flow in the ignition primary circuit based on input from the pick-up coil. When the module opens the primary circuit, high secondary voltage is induced in the coil.

NEEDLE BEARING: A bearing which consists of a number (usually a large number) of long, thin rollers.

OHM: (Ω) The unit used to measure the resistance of conductor-to-electrical flow. One ohm is the amount of resistance that limits current flow to one ampere in a circuit with one volt of pressure.

OHMMETER: An instrument used for measuring the resistance, in ohms, in an electrical circuit.

OUTPUT SHAFT: The shaft which transmits torque from a device, such as a transmission.

OVERDRIVE: A gear assembly which produces more shaft revolutions than that transmitted to it.

OVERHEAD CAMSHAFT (OHC): An engine configuration in which the camshaft is mounted on top of the cylinder head and operates the valve either directly or by means of rocker arms.

OVERHEAD VALVE (OHV): An engine configuration in which all of the valves are located in the cylinder head and the camshaft is located in the cylinder block. The camshaft operates the valves via lifters and pushrods.

OXIDES OF NITROGEN (NOx): Chemical compounds of nitrogen produced as a byproduct of combustion. They combine with hydrocarbons to produce smog.

OXYGEN SENSOR: Use with the feedback system to sense the presence of oxygen in the exhaust gas and signal the computer which can reference the voltage signal to an air/fuel ratio.

PINION: The smaller of two meshing gears.

PISTON RING: An open-ended ring with fits into a groove on the outer diameter of the piston. Its chief function is to form a seal between the piston and cylinder wall. Most automotive pistons have three rings: two for compression sealing; one for oil sealing.

PRELOAD: A predetermined load placed on a bearing during assembly or by adjustment.

PRIMARY CIRCUIT: the low voltage side of the ignition system which consists of the ignition switch, ballast resistor or resistance wire, bypass, coil, electronic control unit and pick-up coil as well as the connecting wires and harnesses.

PRESS FIT: The mating of two parts under pressure, due to the inner diameter of one being smaller than the outer diameter of the other, or vice versa; an interference fit.

RACE: The surface on the inner or outer ring of a bearing on which the balls, needles or rollers move.

REGULATOR: A device which maintains the amperage and/or voltage levels of a circuit at predetermined values.

RELAY: A switch which automatically opens and/or closes a circuit.

RESISTANCE: The opposition to the flow of current through a circuit or electrical device, and is measured in ohms. Resistance is equal to the voltage divided by the amperage.

RESISTOR: A device, usually made of wire, which offers a preset amount of resistance in an electrical circuit.

RING GEAR: The name given to a ring-shaped gear attached to a differential case, or affixed to a flywheel or as part of a planetary gear set.

ROLLER BEARING: A bearing made up of hardened inner and outer races between which hardened steel rollers move.

ROTOR: 1. The disc-shaped part of a disc brake assembly, upon which the brake pads bear; also called, brake disc. 2. The device mounted atop the distributor shaft, which passes current to the distributor cap tower contacts.

SECONDARY CIRCUIT: The high voltage side of the ignition system, usually above 20,000 volts. The secondary includes the ignition coil, coil wire, distributor cap and rotor, spark plug wires and spark plugs.

SENDING UNIT: A mechanical, electrical, hydraulic or electro-magnetic device which transmits information to a gauge.

SENSOR: Any device designed to measure engine operating conditions or ambient pressures and temperatures. Usually electronic in nature and designed to send a voltage signal to an on-board computer, some sensors may operate as a simple on/off switch or they may provide a variable voltage signal (like a potentiometer) as conditions or measured parameters change.

SHIM: Spacers of precise, predetermined thickness used between parts to establish a proper working relationship.

SLAVE CYLINDER: In automotive use, a device in the hydraulic clutch system which is activated by hydraulic force, disengaging the clutch.

SOLENOID: A coil used to produce a magnetic field, the effect of which is to produce work.

SPARK PLUG: A device screwed into the combustion chamber of a spark ignition engine. The basic construction is a conductive core inside of a ceramic insulator, mounted in an outer conductive base. An electrical charge from the spark plug wire travels along the conductive core and jumps a preset air gap to a grounding point or points at the end of the conductive base. The resultant spark ignites the fuel/air mixture in the combustion chamber.

SPLINES: Ridges machined or cast onto the outer diameter of a shaft or inner diameter of a bore to enable parts to mate without rotation.

TACHOMETER: A device used to measure the rotary speed of an engine, shaft, gear, etc., usually in rotations per minute.

THERMOSTAT: A valve, located in the cooling system of an engine, which is closed when cold and opens gradually in response to engine heating, controlling the temperature of the coolant and rate of coolant flow.

TOP DEAD CENTER (TDC): The point at which the piston reaches the top of its travel on the compression stroke.

TORQUE: The twisting force applied to an object.

TORQUE CONVERTER: A turbine used to transmit power from a driving member to a driven member via hydraulic action, providing changes in drive ratio and torque. In automotive use, it links the driveplate at the rear of the engine to the automatic transmission.

TRANSDUCER: A device used to change a force into an electrical signal.

TRANSISTOR: A semi-conductor component which can be actuated by a small voltage to perform an electrical switching function.

TUNE-UP: A regular maintenance function, usually associated with the replacement and adjustment of parts and components in the electrical and fuel systems of a vehicle for the purpose of attaining optimum performance.

TURBOCHARGER: An exhaust driven pump which compresses intake air and forces it into the combustion chambers at higher than atmospheric pressures. The increased air pressure allows more fuel to be burned and results in increased horsepower being produced.

VACUUM ADVANCE: A device which advances the ignition timing in response to increased engine vacuum.

VACUUM GAUGE: An instrument used to measure the presence of vacuum in a chamber.

VALVE: A device which control the pressure, direction of flow or rate of flow of a liquid or gas.

VALVE CLEARANCE: The measured gap between the end of the valve stem and the rocker arm, cam lobe or follower that activates the valve.

VISCOSITY: The rating of a liquid's internal resistance to flow.

VOLTMETER: An instrument used for measuring electrical force in units called volts. Voltmeters are always connected parallel with the circuit being tested.

WHEEL CYLINDER: Found in the automotive drum brake assembly, it is a device, actuated by hydraulic pressure, which, through internal pistons, pushes the brake shoes outward against the drums.

MASTER
INDEX

Total Car Care, continued

Eclipse 1990-98
PART NO. 8415/50400
Pick-Ups and Montero 1983-95
PART NO. 8666/50500
NISSAN
Datsun 210/1200 1973-81
PART NO. 52300
Datsun 200SX/510/610/710/
810/Maxima 1973-84
PART NO. 52302
Nissan Maxima 1985-92
PART NO. 8261/52450
Maxima 1993-98
PART NO. 52452
Pick-Ups and Pathfinder 1970-88
PART NO. 8585/52500
Pick-Ups and Pathfinder 1989-95
PART NO. 8145/52502
Sentra/Pulsar/NX 1982-96
PART NO. 8263/52700

Stanza/200SX/240SX 1982-92
PART NO. 8262/52750
240SX/Altima 1993-98
PART NO. 52752
Datsun/Nissan Z and ZX 1970-88
PART NO. 8846/52800
RENAULT
Coupes/Sedans/Wagons 1975-85
PART NO. 58300
SATURN
Coupes/Sedans/Wagons 1991-98
PART NO. 8419/62300
SUBARU
Coupes/Sedan/Wagons 1970-84
PART NO. 8790/64300
Coupes/Sedans/Wagons 1985-96
PART NO. 8259/64302
SUZUKI
Samurai/Sidekick/Tracker 1986-98
PART NO. 66500

TOYOTA
Camry 1983-96
PART NO. 8265/68200
Celica/Supra 1971-85
PART NO. 68250
Celica 1986-93
PART NO. 8413/68252
Celica 1994-98
PART NO. 68254
Corolla 1970-87
PART NO. 8586/68300
Corolla 1988-97
PART NO. 8414/68302
Cressida/Corona/Crown/MkII 1970-82
PART NO. 68350
Cressida/Van 1983-90
PART NO. 68352
Pick-ups/Land Cruiser/4Runner 1970-88
PART NO. 8578/68600
Pick-ups/Land Cruiser/4Runner 1989-98
PART NO. 8163/68602

Previa 1991-97
PART NO. 68640
Tercel 1984-94
PART NO. 8595/68700
VOLKSWAGEN
Air-Cooled 1949-69
PART NO. 70200
Air-Cooled 1970-81
PART NO. 70202
Front Wheel Drive 1974-89
PART NO. 8663/70400
Golf/Jetta/Cabriolet 1990-93
PART NO. 8429/70402
VOLVO
Coupes/Sedans/Wagons 1970-89
PART NO. 8786/72300
Coupes/Sedans/Wagons 1990-98
PART NO. 8428/72302

General Interest / Recreational Books

We offer specialty books on a variety of topics including Motorcycles, ATVs, Snowmobiles and automotive subjects like Detailing or Body Repair. Each book from our General Interest line offers a blend of our famous Do-It-Yourself procedures and photography with additional information on enjoying automotive, marine and recreational products. Learn more about the vehicles you use and enjoy while keeping them in top running shape.

ATV Handbook
PART NO. 9123
Auto Detailing
PART NO. 8394
Auto Body Repair
PART NO. 7898

Briggs & Stratton Vertical Crankshaft Engine
PART NO. 61-1-2
Briggs & Stratton Horizontal Crankshaft Engine
PART NO. 61-0-4
Briggs & Stratton Overhead Valve (OHV) Engine
PART NO. 61-2-0
Easy Car Care
PART NO. 8042

Motorcycle Handbook
PART NO. 9099
Snowmobile Handbook
PART NO. 9124
Small Engine Repair (Up to 20 Hp)
PART NO. 8325

Total Service Series

These innovative books offer repair, maintenance and service procedures for automotive related systems. They cover today's complex vehicles in a user-friendly format, which places even the most difficult automotive topic well within the reach of every Do-It-Yourselfer. Each title covers a specific subject from Brakes and Engine Rebuilding to Fuel Injection Systems, Automatic Transmissions and even Engine Trouble Codes.

Automatic Transmissions/Transaxles Diagnosis and Repair
PART NO. 8944
Brake System Diagnosis and Repair
PART NO. 8945
Chevrolet Engine Overhaul Manual
PART NO. 8794

Engine Code Manual
PART NO. 8851
Ford Engine Overhaul Manual
PART NO. 8793
Fuel Injection Diagnosis and Repair
PART NO. 8946

Collector's Hard-Cover Manuals

Chilton's Collector's Editions are perfect for enthusiasts of vintage or rare cars. These hard-cover manuals contain repair and maintenance information for all major systems that might not be available elsewhere. Included are repair and overhaul procedures using thousands of illustrations. These manuals offer a range of coverage from as far back as 1940 and as recent as 1997, so you don't need an antique car or truck to be a collector.

Auto Repair Manual 1993-97
PART NO. 7919
Auto Repair Manual 1988-92
PART NO. 7906
Auto Repair Manual 1980-87
PART NO. 7670
Auto Repair Manual 1972-79
PART NO. 6914
Auto Repair Manual 1964-71
PART NO. 5974

Auto Repair Manual 1954-63
PART NO. 5652
Auto Repair Manual 1940-53
PART NO. 5631
Import Car Repair Manual 1993-97
PART NO. 7920
Import Car Repair Manual 1988-92
PART NO.7907
Import Car Repair Manual 1980-87
PART NO. 7672

Truck and Van Repair Manual 1993-97
PART NO. 7921
Truck and Van Repair Manual 1991-95
PART NO. 7911
Truck and Van Repair Manual 1986-90
PART NO. 7902
Truck and Van Repair Manual 1979-86
PART NO. 7655
Truck and Van Repair Manual 1971-78
PART NO. 7012